"Composed in the style of the great medieval *catenae*, this new anthology of patristic commentary on Holy Scripture, conveniently arranged by chapter and verse, will be a valuable resource for prayer, study and proclamation. By calling attention to the rich Christian heritage preceding the separations between East and West and between Protestant and Catholic, this series will perform a major service to the cause of ecumenism."

AVERY CARDINAL DULLES, S.J.
Laurence J. McGinley Professor of Religion and Society
Fordham University

"The initial cry of the Reformation was *ad fontes*—back to the sources! The Ancient Christian Commentary on Scripture is a marvelous tool for the recovery of biblical wisdom in today's church. Not just another scholarly project, the ACCS is a major resource for the renewal of preaching, theology and Christian devotion."

TIMOTHY GEORGE
Dean, Beeson Divinity School, Samford University

"Modern church members often do not realize that they are participants in the vast company of the communion of saints that reaches far back into the past and that will continue into the future, until the kingdom comes. This Commentary should help them begin to see themselves as participants in that redeemed community."

ELIZABETH ACHTEMEIER
Union Professor Emerita of Bible and Homiletics
Union Theological Seminary in Virginia

"Contemporary pastors do not stand alone. We are not the first generation of preachers to wrestle with the challenges of communicating the gospel. The Ancient Christian Commentary on Scripture puts us in conversation with our colleagues from the past, that great cloud of witnesses who preceded us in this vocation. This Commentary enables us to receive their deep spiritual insights, their encouragement and guidance for present-day interpretation and preaching of the Word. What a wonderful addition to any pastor's library!"

WILLIAM H. WILLIMON
Dean of the Chapel and Professor of Christian Ministry
Duke University

"Here is a nonpareil series which reclaims the Bible as the book of the church by making accessible to earnest readers of the twenty-first century the classrooms of Clement of Alexandria and Didymus the Blind, the study and lecture hall of Origen, the cathedrae of Chrysostom and Augustine, the scriptorium of Jerome in his Bethlehem monastery."

GEORGE LAWLESS
Augustinian Patristic Institute and Gregorian University, Rome

"We are pleased to witness publication of the
Ancient Christian Commentary on Scripture. It is most beneficial for us to learn
how the ancient Christians, especially the saints of the church
who proved through their lives their devotion to God and his Word, interpreted
Scripture. Let us heed the witness of those who have gone before us in the faith."

METROPOLITAN THEODOSIUS
Primate, Orthodox Church in America

"Across Christendom there has emerged a widespread interest
in early Christianity, both at the popular and scholarly level. . . .
Christians of all traditions stand to benefit from this project, especially clergy
and those who study the Bible. Moreover, it will allow us to see how our traditions are
both rooted in the scriptural interpretations of the church fathers while at
the same time seeing how we have developed new perspectives."

ALBERTO FERREIRO
Professor of History, Seattle Pacific University

"The Ancient Christian Commentary on Scripture fills a long overdue need for scholars and
students of the church fathers. . . . Such information will be of immeasurable
worth to those of us who have felt inundated by contemporary interpreters and novel theories
of the biblical text. We welcome some 'new' insight from the
ancient authors in the early centuries of the church."

H. WAYNE HOUSE
Professor of Theology and Law
Trinity University School of Law

"Chronological snobbery—the assumption that our ancestors working without benefit of
computers have nothing to teach us—is exposed as nonsense by this magnificent
new series. Surfeited with knowledge but starved of wisdom, many of us are
more than ready to sit at table with our ancestors and listen to their holy
conversations on Scripture. I know I am."

EUGENE H. PETERSON
Professor Emeritus of Spiritual Theology
Regent College

"Few publishing projects have encouraged me as much as the recently announced Ancient Christian Commentary on Scripture with Dr. Thomas Oden serving as general editor. . . . How is it that so many of us who are dedicated to serve the Lord received seminary educations which omitted familiarity with such incredible students of the Scriptures as St. John Chrysostom, St. Athanasius the Great and St. John of Damascus? I am greatly anticipating the publication of this Commentary."

Fr. Peter E. Gillquist
Director, Department of Missions and Evangelism
Antiochian Orthodox Christian Archdiocese of North America

"The Scriptures have been read with love and attention for nearly two thousand years, and listening to the voice of believers from previous centuries opens us to unexpected insight and deepened faith. Those who studied Scripture in the centuries closest to its writing, the centuries during and following persecution and martyrdom, speak with particular authority. The Ancient Christian Commentary on Scripture will bring to life the truth that we are invisibly surrounded by a 'great cloud of witnesses.'"

Frederica Mathewes-Green
Commentator, National Public Radio

"For those who think that church history began around 1941 when their pastor was born, this Commentary will be a great surprise. Christians throughout the centuries have read the biblical text, nursed their spirits with it and then applied it to their lives. These commentaries reflect that the witness of the Holy Spirit was present in his church throughout the centuries. As a result, we can profit by allowing the ancient Christians to speak to us today."

Haddon Robinson
Harold John Ockenga Distinguished Professor of Preaching
Gordon-Conwell Theological Seminary

"All who are interested in the interpretation of the Bible will welcome the forthcoming multivolume series Ancient Christian Commentary on Scripture. Here the insights of scores of early church fathers will be assembled and made readily available for significant passages throughout the Bible and the Apocrypha. It is hard to think of a more worthy ecumenical project to be undertaken by the publisher."

Bruce M. Metzger
Professor of New Testament, Emeritus
Princeton Theological Seminary

ANCIENT CHRISTIAN
COMMENTARY on SCRIPTURE

OLD TESTAMENT
VIII

PSALMS 51-150

EDITED BY

QUENTIN F. WESSELSCHMIDT

GENERAL EDITOR
THOMAS C. ODEN

InterVarsity Press
Downers Grove, Illinois

InterVarsity Press
P.O. Box 1400, Downers Grove, IL 60515-1426
World Wide Web: www.ivpress.com
E-mail: mail@ivpress.com

©2007 by the Institute of Classical Christian Studies (ICCS), Thomas C. Oden and Quentin F. Wesselschmidt

InterVarsity Press® is the book-publishing division of InterVarsity Christian Fellowship/USA®, a student movement active on campus at hundreds of universities, colleges and schools of nursing in the United States of America, and a member movement of the International Fellowship of Evangelical Students. For information about local and regional activities, write Public Relations Dept., InterVarsity Christian Fellowship/USA, 6400 Schroeder Rd., P.O. Box 7895, Madison, WI 53707-7895, or visit the IVCF website at <www.intervarsity.org>.

Scripture quotations, unless otherwise noted, are from the Revised Standard Version of the Bible, copyright 1946, 1952, 1971 by the Division of Christian Education of the National Council of the Churches of Christ in the U.S.A., and are used by permission.

Selected excerpts from The Works of Saint Augustine: A Translation for the 21st Century, edited by John E. Rotelle, ©1990-. Used by permission of the Augustinian Heritage Institute.

Selected excerpts from Faith Gives Fullness to Reasoning: The Five Theological Orations of Gregory Nazianzen, by F. W. Norris, ©1991. Used by permission of E. J. Brill, Leiden, The Netherlands.

Selected excerpts from Fathers of the Church: A New Translation, ©1947-, used by permission of The Catholic University of America Press, Washington, D.C. Full bibliographic information on volumes of Fathers of the Church may be found in the Bibliography of works in English Translation.

Selected excerpts from The Syriac Fathers on Prayer and the Spiritual Life, translated by Sebastian Brock, Cistercian Studies 101, ©1987; St. Athanasius, Life of St. Antony, translated by Tim Vivian and Apostolos N. Athanassakis with Rowan A. Greer, Cistercian Studies 202, ©2003; Bede the Venerable, Commentary on the Acts of the Apostles, translated by Lawrence T. Martin, Cistercian Studies 117, ©1989; Bede the Venerable, Homilies on the Gospels, translated by Lawrence T. Martin and David Hurst, Cistercian Studies 110 and 111, ©1991; Evagrius of Pontus, Praktikos and the Chapters on Prayer, translated by John Eudes Bamberger, Cistercian Studies 4, ©1981; Pachomian Koinonia: The Lives, Rules, and Other Writings of Saint Pachomius, translated by Armand Veilleux, Cistercian Studies 46, ©1980-1982. Used by permission of Cistercian Publications, Kalamazoo, Michigan. All rights reserved.

Selected excerpts from Basil of Caesarea, On the Holy Spirit, translated and edited by D. Anderson, ©1980; Cyril of Alexandria, On the Unity of Christ, Translated by John A. McGuckin, ©1995; Gregory of Nyssa, On the Soul and the Resurrection, Translated by Catharine P. Roth, ©1993. Used by permission of St. Vladimir's Seminary Press.

Selected excerpts from John Cassian, The Conferences, translated and annotated by Boniface Ramsey, Ancient Christian Writers 57, ©1997; Cassiodorus, Explanation of the Psalms, translated by P. G. Walsh, Ancient Christian Writers 51, 52 and 53, ©1990, 1991; Origen, Origen: An Exhortation to Martyrdom, Prayer and Selected Writings, translated by Rowan A. Greer, The Classics of Western Spirituality, ©1979; Pseudo-Dionysius, Pseudo-Dionysius: The Complete Works, translated by Colm Luibheid, The Classics of Western Spirituality, ©1987. Reprinted by permission of Paulist Press, Inc. <www. paulistpress.com>.

Selected excerpts from The Ascetical Homilies of Saint Isaac the Syrian, ©1984. Used by permission of Holy Transfiguration Monastery, Boston, Massachusetts.

Selected excerpts from Augustine: Earlier Writings, translated by John H. S. Burleigh, The Library of Christian Classics 6, ©1953; Christology of the Later Fathers, translated by Archibald Robertson and edited by Edward Rochie Hardy, The Library of Christian Classics 3, ©1954; Confessions and Enchiridion, Translated by Albert C. Outler, The Library of Christian Classics 7, ©1955; Cyril of Jerusalem and Nemesius of Emesa, translated by William Telfer, The Library of Christian Classics 4, ©1955; Early Christian Fathers, translated by Cyril C. Richardson, The Library of Christian Classics 1, ©1953; Early Latin Theology, translated by S. L. Greenslade, The Library of Christian Classics 5, ©1956; Western Asceticism, edited and translated by Owen Chadwick, The Library of Christian Classics 12, ©1958. Used by permission of SCM and Westminster John Knox Presses, London, England, and Louisville, Kentucky.

Selected excerpts from Athanasius, The Resurrection Letters, paraphrased and introduced by Jack N. Sparks, ©1979. Used by permission of Thomas Nelson, Inc., Nashville, Tennessee.

Selected excerpts from Bede the Venerable, On the Tabernacle, translated by Arthur G. Holder, Translated Texts for Historians 18, ©1994. Used by permission of Liverpool University Press, Liverpool, England.

Selected excerpts from St. Augustine, Concerning the City of God Against the Pagans, translated by Henry Bettenson, ©1984. Used by permission of Penguin Press, London.

Selected excerpts from Ephrem the Syrian, Commentary on Tatian's Diatessaron, translated and edited by C. McCarthy, Journal of Semitic Studies Supplement 2, ©1993. Used by permission of Oxford University Press.

Selected excerpts from The Message of the Fathers of the Church, edited by Thomas Halton, ©1983-. Used by permission of The Liturgical Press, Collegeville, Minnesota. Full bibliographic information on volumes of The Message of Fathers of the Church may be found in the Bibliography of Works in English Translation.

Selected excerpts from Eusebius, the Church History: A New Translation with Commentary, translated by Paul L. Maier, ©1999. Used by permission of Kregel Publications, Grand Rapids, Michigan.

Selected excerpts from The Montanist Oracles and Testimonia, North American Patristic Society Monograph Series 14, ©1989. Used by permission of Mercer University Press, Macon, Georgia.

Selected excerpts from Ambrose, On Virginity, translated by Daniel Callam, ©1996. Used by permission of Peregrina Publishing Co., Toronto, Ontario.

Every effort has been made to trace and contact copyright holders for additional materials quoted in this book. The authors will be pleased to rectify any omissions in future editions if notified by copyright holders.

Cover photograph: Scala/Art Resource, New York. View of the apse. S. Vitale, Ravenna, Italy.

Spine photograph: Byzantine Collection, Dumbarton Oaks, Washington D.C. Pendant cross (gold and enamel). Constantinople, late sixth century.

ISBN 10 0-8308-1478-7

ISBN 13 978-0-8308-1478-7

Printed in the United States of America ∞

Library of Congress Cataloging-in-Publication Data

Psalms 51-150/edited by Quentin F. Wesselschmidt.
    p. cm.—(Ancient Christian commentary on Scripture. Old
    Testament; 8)
    Includes bibliographical references (p.) and indexes.
    ISBN-13: 978-0-8308-1478-7 (cloth: alk. paper)
    1. Bible. O.T. Psalms LI-CL—Commentaries. I. Wesselschmidt,
    Quentin F., 1937-
    BS1430.53.P73 2007
    223'.207709—dc22
          2007026759

P	27	26	25	24	23	22	21	20	19	18	17	16	15	14	13	12	11	10	9	8	7	6	5	4	3	2	1
Y	31	30	29	28	27	26	25	24	23	22	21	20	19	18	17	16	15	14	13	12	11	10	09	08	07

ANCIENT CHRISTIAN COMMENTARY
PROJECT RESEARCH TEAM

GENERAL EDITOR
Thomas C. Oden

ASSOCIATE EDITOR
Christopher A. Hall

OPERATIONS MANAGER AND
TRANSLATIONS PROJECT COORDINATOR
Joel Elowsky

RESEARCH AND ACQUISITIONS DIRECTOR
Michael Glerup

EDITORIAL SERVICES DIRECTOR
Warren Calhoun Robertson

ORIGINAL LANGUAGE VERSION DIRECTOR
Konstantin Gavrilkin

GRADUATE RESEARCH ASSISTANTS

Steve Finlan	*Vladimir Kharlamov*
Jill Comings	*Kevin M. Lowe*
Grant Gieseke	*Nebojsa Tumara*
	Jeffery Wittung

ADMINISTRATIVE ASSISTANT
Judy Cincotta

Contents

GENERAL INTRODUCTION

The Ancient Christian Commentary on Scripture has as its goal the revitalization of Christian teaching based on classical Christian exegesis, the intensified study of Scripture by lay persons who wish to think with the early church about the canonical text, and the stimulation of Christian historical, biblical, theological and pastoral scholars toward further inquiry into scriptural interpretation by ancient Christian writers.

The time frame of these documents spans seven centuries of exegesis, from Clement of Rome to John of Damascus, from the end of the New Testament era to A.D. 750, including the Venerable Bede.

Lay readers are asking how they might study sacred texts under the instruction of the great minds of the ancient church. This commentary has been intentionally prepared for a general lay audience of nonprofessionals who study the Bible regularly and who earnestly wish to have classic Christian observation on the text readily available to them. The series is targeted to anyone who wants to reflect and meditate with the early church about the plain sense, theological wisdom and moral meaning of particular Scripture texts.

A commentary dedicated to allowing ancient Christian exegetes to speak for themselves will refrain from the temptation to fixate endlessly upon contemporary criticism. Rather, it will stand ready to provide textual resources from a distinguished history of exegesis that has remained massively inaccessible and shockingly disregarded during the last century. We seek to make available to our present-day audiences the multicultural, multilingual, transgenerational resources of the early ecumenical Christian tradition.

Preaching at the end of the first millennium focused primarily on the text of Scripture as understood by the earlier esteemed tradition of comment, largely converging on those writers that best reflected classic Christian consensual thinking. Preaching at the end of the second millennium has reversed that pattern. It has so forgotten most of these classic comments that they are vexing to find anywhere, and even when located they are often available only in archaic editions and inadequate translations. The preached word in our time has remained largely bereft of previously influential patristic inspiration. Recent scholarship has so focused attention upon post-Enlightenment historical and literary methods that it has left this longing largely unattended and unserved.

This series provides the pastor, exegete, student and lay reader with convenient means to see what Athanasius or John Chrysostom or the desert fathers and mothers had to say about a particular text for preaching, for study and for meditation. There is an emerging awareness among Catholic, Protestant and Orthodox laity that vital biblical preaching and spiritual formation need deeper grounding beyond the scope of the historical-critical orientations that have governed biblical studies in our day.

Hence this work is directed toward a much broader audience than the highly technical and specialized scholarly field of patristic studies. The audience is not limited to the university scholar concentrating on the study of the history of the transmission of the text or to those with highly focused philological interests in textual morphology or historical-critical issues. Though these are crucial concerns for specialists, they are not the paramount interests of this series.

This work is a Christian Talmud. The Talmud is a Jewish collection of rabbinic arguments and comments on the Mishnah, which epitomized the laws of the Torah. The Talmud originated in approximately the same period that the patristic writers were commenting on texts of the Christian tradition. Christians from the late patristic age through the medieval period had documents analogous to the Jewish Talmud and Midrash (Jewish commentaries) available to them in the *glossa ordinaria* and catena traditions, two forms of compiling extracts of patristic exegesis. In Talmudic fashion the sacred text of Christian Scripture was thus clarified and interpreted by the classic commentators.

The Ancient Christian Commentary on Scripture has venerable antecedents in medieval exegesis of both eastern and western traditions, as well as in the Reformation tradition. It offers for the first time in this century the earliest Christian comments and reflections on the Old and New Testaments to a modern audience. Intrinsically an ecumenical project, this series is designed to serve Protestant, Catholic and Orthodox lay, pastoral and scholarly audiences.

In cases where Greek, Latin, Syriac and Coptic texts have remained untranslated into English, we provide new translations. Wherever current English translations are already well rendered, they will be utilized, but if necessary their language will be brought up to date. We seek to present fresh dynamic equivalency translations of long-neglected texts which historically have been regarded as authoritative models of biblical interpretation.

These foundational sources are finding their way into many public libraries and into the core book collections of many pastors and lay persons. It is our intent and the publisher's commitment to keep the whole series in print for many years to come.

Thomas C. Oden
General Editor

A GUIDE TO USING THIS COMMENTARY

Several features have been incorporated into the design of this commentary. The following comments are intended to assist readers in making full use of this volume.

Pericopes of Scripture

The scriptural text has been divided into pericopes, or passages, usually several verses in length. Each of these pericopes is given a heading, which appears at the beginning of the pericope. For example, the first pericope in the commentary on Psalms 51-150 is "51:1-9 A Prayer for Forgivenness and Spiritual Cleansing." This heading is followed by the Scripture passage quoted in the Revised Standard Version (RSV) across the full width of the page. The Scripture passage is provided for the convenience of readers, but it is also in keeping with medieval patristic commentaries, in which the citations of the Fathers were arranged around the text of Scripture.

Overviews

Following each pericope of text is an overview of the patristic comments on that pericope. The format of this overview varies within the volumes of this series, depending on the requirements of the specific book of Scripture. The function of the overview is to provide a brief summary of all the comments to follow. It tracks a reasonably cohesive thread of argument among patristic comments, even though they are derived from diverse sources and generations. Thus the summaries do not proceed chronologically or by verse sequence. Rather they seek to rehearse the overall course of the patristic comment on that pericope.

We do not assume that the commentators themselves anticipated or expressed a formally received cohesive argument but rather that the various arguments tend to flow in a plausible, recognizable pattern. Modern readers can thus glimpse aspects of continuity in the flow of diverse exegetical traditions representing various generations and geographical locations.

Topical Headings

An abundance of varied patristic comment is available for each pericope of these letters. For this reason we have broken the pericopes into two levels. First is the verse with its topical heading. The patristic comments are then focused on aspects of each verse, with topical headings summarizing the essence of the patristic comment by evoking a key phrase, metaphor or idea. This feature provides a bridge by which modern readers can enter into the heart of the patristic comment.

Identifying the Patristic Texts

Following the topical heading of each section of comment, the name of the patristic commentator is given. An English translation of the patristic comment is then provided. This is immediately followed by the title of the patristic work and the textual reference—either by book, section and subsection or by book-and-verse references.

The Footnotes

Readers who wish to pursue a deeper investigation of the patristic works cited in this commentary will find the footnotes especially valuable. A footnote number directs the reader to the notes at the bottom of the right-hand column, where in addition to other notations (clarifications or biblical cross references) one will find information on English translations (where available) and standard original-language editions of the work cited. An abbreviated citation (normally citing the book, volume and page number) of the work is provided. A key to the abbreviations is provided on page xv. Where there is any serious ambiguity or textual problem in the selection, we have tried to reflect the best available textual tradition.

Where original language texts have remained untranslated into English, we provide new translations. Wherever current English translations are already well rendered, they are utilized, but where necessary they are stylistically updated. A single asterisk (*) indicates that a previous English translation has been updated to modern English or amended for easier reading. The double asterisk (**) indicates either that a new translation has been provided or that some extant translation has been significantly amended. We have standardized spellings and made grammatical variables uniform so that our English references will not reflect the odd spelling variables of the older English translations. For ease of reading we have in some cases edited out superfluous conjunctions.

For the convenience of computer database users the digital database references are provided to either the Thesaurus Linguae Graecae (Greek texts) or to the Cetedoc (Latin texts) in the appendix found on pages 431-39 and in the bibliography found on pages 459-478.

Abbreviations

AC	Augustine. *Confessions*. Translated by R. S. Pine-Coffin. Harmondsworth, Middlesex, England: Penguin, 1961. Reprint, New York: Penguin, 1986.
ACW	Ancient Christian Writers: The Works of the Fathers in Translation. Mahwah, N.J.: Paulist Press, 1946–.
AF	J. B. Lightfoot and J. R. Harmer, trans. *The Apostolic Fathers*. Edited by M. W. Holmes. 2nd ed. Grand Rapids, Mich.: Baker, 1989.
AHSIS	Dana Miller, ed. *The Ascetical Homilies of Saint Isaac the Syrian*. Boston, Mass.: Holy Transfiguration Monastery, 1984.
ANCL	The Ante-Nicene Christian Library: Translations of the Writings of the Fathers down to A.D. 325. Alexander Roberts and James Donaldson, eds. Edinburgh: T & T Clark, 1867-1897.
ANF	A. Roberts and J. Donaldson, eds. Ante-Nicene Fathers. 10 vols. Buffalo, N.Y.: Christian Literature, 1885-1896. Reprint, Grand Rapids, Mich.: Eerdmans, 1951-1956. Reprint, Peabody, Mass.: Hendrickson, 1994.
AOV	Ambrose. *On Virginity*. Translated by Daniel Callam, CSB. Toronto: Peregrina Publishing Co., 1996.
ARL	St. Athanasius. *The Resurrection Letters*. Paraphrased and introduced by Jack N. Sparks. Nashville: Thomas Nelson, 1979.
CCL	Corpus Christianorum. Series Latina. Turnhout, Belgium: Brepols, 1953–.
CG	Augustine. *The City of God*. Translated by Henry S. Bettenson with an introduction by David Knowles. Harmondsworth, Middlesex, England: Penguin, 1972. Reprint, with an introduction by John O'Meara, 1984.
CS	Cistercian Studies. Kalamazoo, Mich.: Cistercian Publications, 1973–.
CSEL	Corpus Scriptorum Ecclesiasticorum Latinorum. Vienna, 1866–.
ECH	Paul L. Maier, trans. *Eusebius, the Church History: A New Translation with Commentary.* Grand Rapids, Mich.: Kregel Publications, 1999.
ECTD	C. McCarthy, trans. and ed. *Saint Ephrem's Commentary on Tatian's Diatessaron: An English Translation of Chester Beatty Syriac MS 709. Journal of Semitic Studies* Supplement 2. Oxford: Oxford University Press, 1993.
FC	Fathers of the Church: A New Translation. Washington, D.C.: Catholic University of America Press, 1947–.
FGFR	F. W. Norris. *Faith Gives Fullness to Reasoning: The Five Theological Orations of Gregory Nazianzen.* Leiden and New York: E. J. Brill, 1990.
GNSR	Gregory of Nyssa. *On the Soul and the Resurrection*. Translated by Catharine P. Roth. Crestwood, N.Y.: St. Vladimir's Seminary Press, 1993.
LCC	J. Baillie et al., eds. The Library of Christian Classics. 26 vols. Philadelphia: Westminster, 1953-1966.
LCL	Loeb Classical Library. Cambridge, Mass.: Harvard University Press; London: Heinemann, 1912–.
MFC	Message of the Fathers of the Church. Edited by Thomas Halton. Collegeville, Minn.: The Liturgical Press, 1983-.
MOT	R. E. Heine, ed. *The Montanist Oracles and Testimonia.* North American Patristic Society Monograph Series 14. Macon, Ga.: Mercer University Press, 1989.

NPNF	P. Schaff et al., eds. *A Select Library of the Nicene and Post-Nicene Fathers of the Christian Church.* 2 series (14 vols. each). Buffalo, N.Y.: Christian Literature, 1887-1894. Reprint, Grand Rapids, Mich.: Eerdmans, 1952-1956. Reprint, Peabody, Mass.: Hendrickson, 1994.
OHS	Basil of Caesarea. *On the Holy Spirit.* Translated by David Anderson. Crestwood, N.Y.: St. Vladimir's Seminary Press, 1980.
OSW	*Origen: An Exhortation to Martyrdom, Prayer and Selected Writings.* Translated by Rowan A. Greer with preface by Hans Urs von Balthasar. The Classics of Western Spirituality. New York: Paulist Press, 1979.
OUC	St. Cyril of Alexandria. *On the Unity of Christ.* Translated by John A. McGuckin. Crestwood, N.Y.: St. Vladimir's Seminary Press, 1995.
PDCW	*Pseudo-Dionysius: The Complete Works.* Translated by Colm Luibheid. The Classics of Western Spirituality. New York: Paulist Press, 1987.
PG	J.-P. Migne, ed. Patrologiae cursus completus. Series Graeca. 166 vols. Paris: Migne, 1857-1886.
PHF	A. Isho, comp., 7th century. *The Paradise, or Garden of the Holy Fathers, being histories of the anchorites, recluses, monks, coenobites and ascetic fathers of the deserts of Egypt between A.D. CCL and CCCC circiter.* 2 vols. London: Chatto & Windus, 1907.
PL	J.-P. Migne, ed. Patrologiae cursus completus. Series Latina. 221 vols. Paris: Migne, 1844-1864.
POG	Eusebius. *The Proof of the Gospel.* 2 vols. Translated by W. J. Ferrar. London: SPCK, 1920. Reprint, Grand Rapids, Mich.: Baker, 1981.
TTH	G. Clark, M. Gibson and M. Whitby, eds. Translated Texts for Historians. Liverpool: Liverpool University Press, 1985–.
WSA	J. E. Rotelle, ed. *Works of St. Augustine: A Translation for the Twenty-First Century.* Hyde Park, N.Y.: New City Press, 1995.

Introduction to Psalms 51-150

The Old Testament Book of Psalms has always played an important role in the life of the church, as it still does today. It is one of the best known and most often cited books of the Bible. Select psalms have provided the basis for some familiar and well-loved hymns, such as Martin Luther's "A Mighty Fortress," which is based on Psalm 46. The Psalms have pervaded much of the daily life of the church, providing the words of common, daily prayers, such as Psalm 118:1, "O give thanks to the Lord for he is good and his mercy endures forever." Psalms, such as Psalm 23 have provided words of comfort and hope for many Christians during times of distress, illness, and bereavement. The Psalms remain a prominent feature of church liturgies in the form of the psalmody or the words of Introits and Graduals in worship services. The universal appeal of the Psalms may be summarized succinctly in the words of Johanna Manley:

> Now the prophets teach one thing, historians another, the law something else, and the form of advice found in the proverbs something different still. But the Book of Psalms has taken over what is profitable for all. It foretells coming events; it recalls history; it frames laws for life; it suggests what must be done; and in general, it is the common treasury of good doctrine, carefully finding what is suitable for each one. The old wounds of souls it cures completely, and to the recently wounded it brings speedy improvements; the diseased it treats, the unharmed it preserves. On the whole it effaces, as far as possible, the passions, which subtly exercise dominion over souls during the lifetime of man, and it does this with a certain orderly persuasion and sweetness which produces sound thoughts.[1]

Horace D. Hummel writes, "It is almost redundant to underscore the importance of the Psalter, whether in contemporary life or in the history of the church ... whether in public worship or in private devotion."[2]

The popularity of psalms in Christianity goes back to Jesus Christ himself, who quoted them on a number of occasions in regard to important moments in his ministry. Lee M. McDonald has rightly observed, "in the life and teaching of Jesus in the Gospels, the Psalms are cited more times than any of the other books of the Old Testament."[3] In response to the second temptation in the wilderness in Matthew 4:6, Jesus quoted Psalm 91:11, 12. When Jesus cried out on the cross, "My God, my God, why

---

[1]Johanna Manley, ed. *Grace for Grace: The Psalter and the Holy Fathers* (Menlo Park, CA: Monastery Books, 1992 [repr. 1996]), p. 1.

[2]Horace D. Hummel, *The Word Becoming Flesh: An Introduction to the Origin, Purpose, and Meaning of the Old Testament* (St. Louis: Concordia Publishing House, 1979), p. 404.

[3]Lee M. McDonald, *The Formation of the Christian Biblical Canon*. Revised and Expanded Edition (Peabody, Mass., Hendrickson Publishers, 1995), p. 100.

have you forsaken me" (Mt 27:46 and Mk 15:34), he was quoting directly Psalm 22:1a.; and when he said, "Into your hands I commit my spirit" (Lk 23:46), he was quoting Psalm 31:5. The giving of sour wine to Jesus on the cross was a fulfillment of the prophecy given in Psalm 69:21. Psalm 69:9a was quoted in John's account of Jesus' cleansing the temple in 2:17.

E. Earle Ellis observes, "Jesus and the New Testament writers give a prominent place to the Old Testament in the formulation of their teachings. Like other Jewish groups, they concentrate their biblical quotations on certain portions of the Scriptures, especially the Pentateuch, Isaiah, and the Psalms, and they employ them more in some New Testament books than in others."[4] According to H. B. Swete, the psalms are quoted forty times in the New Testament.[5]

The psalms were very well known and abundantly quoted by the early church fathers.[6] Johanna Manley remarks, "The Church Fathers, full of wisdom, all show enormous respect and honour for the great Prophet David. Their writings, including those of the other prophets, such as Isaiah, are thoroughly laced with the Psalms."[7] Jerome advised Paula, a monastic-minded, noble Roman woman, to begin her study of Scripture by learning the Psalter first and then proceeding to the other books of the Bible.[8] When reading the church fathers and paying special attention to their citations of Scripture, one is struck by the abundance of and facility with which quotations occur, almost in a rapid-fire fashion.

The early church found the Psalms useful in a number of ways. They enriched the liturgical life of the church, serving both as hymns and as one of the Scripture readings. The prophetic nature of many psalms helped to substantiate the veracity of the church's teachings, especially regarding the essential nature of the Son of God and the messianic role of Jesus Christ as the Savior of the human race. The psalms, as well as the Old Testament generally, were often used to validate the teachings expressed in what eventually became the New Testament canon. Along with other books of the Old Testament they were used to defend orthodox Christian teachings over against heretical innovations. Since the early Christians lived in an often hostile world which advocated and lived an ungodly lifestyle, the Psalms were often used to support and encourage Christian morality. John F. Brug sees a twofold use of the Psalms when he says, "Psalms is the hymnbook of the Bible. . . . Psalms is also the prayer book of the Bible."[9] Along these lines, "[Martin] Luther suggested that the psalms could be divided into five main types: (1) messianic psalms which speak of Christ . . . (2) teaching psalms which emphasize doctrine . . . (3) comfort psalms . . . (4) psalms of prayer and petition . . . and (5) thanksgiving psalms."[10]

Regarding the liturgical use of the Psalms one can possibly go as far back as Pliny the Younger, who, as a

---

[4]E. Earle Ellis, *The Old Testament in Early Christianity: Canon and Interpretation in the Light of Modern Research* (Grand Rapids: Baker Book House, 1991), p. 77.

[5]See ibid., p. 53.

[6]Graham W. Woolfenden in "The Use of the Psalter by Early Monastic Communities" in *Studia Patristica*, ed. Elizabeth A. Livingstone, vol. 26 (Leuven: Peeters Press, 1993), p. 89, notes that use among the apostolic fathers was not consistent, with 1 Clement quoting the Psalms more frequently than Polycarp, Barnabas, or Ignatius. The Psalms are referred to more extensively in the apologists like Justin Martyr and Clement of Alexandria, and still more in Origen who wrote commentaries on the Psalms.

[7]Manley, *Grace for Grace*, p. iii.

[8]See Jerome *Ep.* 107.12.

[9]John F. Brug, *A Commentary on Psalms 1-72* (Milwaukee: Northwestern Publishing House, 2005), p. 12.

[10]Ibid., p. 16.

newly appointed Roman governor in Bithynia, wrote a letter to Emperor Trajan for instructions on how to handle the persecution of Christians in his province. In his letter, he gives a brief description of Christian worship. One liturgical feature he observed was that the Christians were accustomed to assemble on the first day of the week and *"carmen . . . dicere secum invicem"* (to sing a song antiphonally).[11] Given Pliny's limited understanding of Christianity, it is very possible that *carmen* could refer to a selection from the Psalms.

At the beginning of the third century Tertullian is another witness to the liturgical use of the Psalms. *The Oxford History of Christian Worship* cites the following testimony from this author: "[Tertullian] describes similar practices at the agape: 'After the washing of hands and the lighting of lamps, each is urged to come into the middle and sing to God, either from sacred scriptures or from his own invention (*de proprio ingenio*).' "[12] The liturgical use of the psalms increased with the growth of the church in the fourth century: "The Constantinian Settlement (313) provided the opportunity for much larger assemblies to meet, with consequent changes to the ordering and content of services, and the rise of desert and (especially) urban monasticism provided a renewed focus on the reciting and singing of biblical Psalms that became a regular feature of Eucharistic services."[13] However, later in the fourth and early fifty centuries there was some question as to whether or not the Eucharistic psalm was to be sung or read as one of the Scripture lessons. Athanasius forbade the new melodic style of singing a psalm while Ambrose encouraged it; Augustine was somewhat undecided but grudgingly accepted the singing of a psalm.[14]

At this same time there is clear evidence of the importance of psalms in the worship and vigils of the monastic communities. Near the end of the fourth century we have the following information about religious life and observances of the church year in the Middle East by a Western nun, Egeria: "From then [before cock-crow] until daybreak they [monks and virgins] join in singing the refrains to the hymns, psalms, and antiphons."[15] Then, in the early fifth century John Cassian gives the following description of the Desert Fathers in Egypt: "As they were going to celebrate their daily rites and prayers, one rose up in the midst to chant the Psalms to the Lord, and while they were all sitting (as is still the custom in Egypt), with their minds intently fixed on the words of the chanter when he had sung eleven Psalms, separated by prayers introduced between them, verse after verse being evenly enunciated, he finished the twelfth with a response of Alleluia, and then, by his sudden disappearance from the eyes of all, put an end at once to their discussion of their service."[16]

Of much greater importance was the use of the Psalms in support of the church's teachings. Lee M. McDonald notes: "The theology of the New Testament was without question firmly grounded in references to Old Testament texts that were believed to support the church's messianic claims about Jesus as

---

[11]*Epp.* 10 (ad Trajan 96).

[12]Geoffrey Wainwright and Karen B. Westerfield Tucker, eds. *The Oxford History of Christian Worship* (Oxford/New York: Oxford University Press, 2005), p. 770. Tertullian's quotation comes from his *Apologeticum* 39:17-18. The reference to singing "from sacred scriptures" surely refers to the Psalms.

[13]Wainwright and Tucker, *Oxford History of Christian Worship*, p. 770.

[14]Cf. ibid., p. 775.

[15]Egeria *Pilgrimage of Egeria* 24. Quoted from James F. White, *Documents of Christian Worship: Descriptive and Interpretative Sources* (Louisville: Westminster/John Knox Press, 1992), p. 85.

[16]*Institutes* 2, 3, 5-6 (NPNF 2 11:205, 207), quoted from White, *Documents of Christian Worship*, pp. 88-89.

well as their support for Christian conduct. That is beyond dispute."[17] Later he observes, "The Christian use of the Old Testament was highly selective and designed especially to clarify or confirm Christian belief. . . . The most common way the Old Testament was appealed to by the Christian community in their first hundred years was by using it primarily, though not exclusively, as a predictive book."[18] Psalms 22 and 69 describe most fully the suffering of Christ. His rejection by the leaders of Israel was predicted in Psalm 118:22, and his being mocked and jeered during his suffering was foretold in Psalm 22:8. Psalms 41:9 and 55:12-14 speak of his being betrayed by a friend (Judas). Jesus' being given vinegar to drink was prophesied in Psalm 69:21, and that his clothes would be divided by lot in Psalm 22:18. His resurrection from the dead was foretold in Psalm 16:10 and his everlasting reign as priest and king in Psalm 110.[19] Such Old Testament prophecies served to validate Jesus as the promised messiah: "The messianic psalms have great value as a testimony to Christ. Only the four gospels and perhaps Isaiah surpass the psalms as sources of information about the feelings, words, and deeds of Christ while he was on earth, carrying out his work as our Savior."[20]

On the basis of the patristic evidence there is no doubt that, within the Old Testament canon, the Psalms played a very prominent role in the church's confirmation of her teachings, which were initially transmitted orally in the apostolic and post-apostolic proclamation. The first written Scriptures for the church was the Old Testament. But as the New Testament books were written, disseminated, and acknowledged as canonically authoritative, the church went back to the Old Testament to confirm the teachings initially grounded in the apostolic tradition but increasingly based on the New Testament. This was essential since the development of doctrine and recognition of the New Testament canon were not consecutive but concurrent developments. The Psalms clearly played a crucial role in this process.

The early church also saw the need to emphasize the unity of the Old and the New Testament, especially in the second century when the Gnostics and Marcion denigrated the Old Testament as being written by an inferior, if not an evil, deity and that its message was not compatible with that of the New Testament.[21] Since Marcion designated his own New Testament canon (a shortened version of the Gospel of Luke and ten Pauline letters, not including the three pastoral letters), the early church saw the need to show a relation between the Old Testament and the New Testament in their entirety. Two ways of doing this were to point out the similarity of messages in the Old and the New Testament and to demonstrate that the New Testament authors quoted extensively from the Old Testament. This would also demonstrate that the author of both Testaments were not different deities but one and the same God.

Closely associated with this was the need for the church to counter the various Trinitarian, christological, and anthropological heresies. The Psalms played a prominent role in refuting these heresies. In response to the Gnostic belief that the visible, material world was created evil by the Demiurge, a defective god or aeon, the early fathers emphasized that the world was created good by the only true, triune God.

---

[17]McDonald, *Formation*, p. 101.

[18]Ibid., pp. 119-120.

[19]Brug, *Commentary*, pp. 20-21.

[20]Ibid., p. 20.

[21]See David S. Dockery, *Biblical Interpretation Then and Now: Contemporary Hermeneutics in the Light of the Early Church* (Grand Rapids: Baker, 1992), p. 45.

And in response to Gnostic and docetic views of the human nature of the incarnate Christ, which denied the reality of his human nature, they turned to quotations which clearly affirmed that his human nature was consubstantial with ours, with the exception of sin. Very helpful in this regard were the psalms which speak of a suffering Messiah, such as Psalms 22 and 69.

When the Trinitarian heresies arose, namely, subordinationism, modalism, Arianism, and Macedonianism or Pneumatomachianism, it was necessary to see testimonies of three persons in one Godhead in the Old Testament and certainly in the Psalms. Since the Psalms were considered prophecy and David was one of the great prophets of the Old Testament, they were greatly relied upon to prove the veracity of the New Testament teachings regarding Jesus Christ, especially the facts of his life and the truthfulness of his message. Bertrand de Margerie has made the following two comments regarding Hilary of Poitiers, " . . . he [Hilary], along with all other Fathers of the Church, held that the entire Old Testament—and most particularly the Psalms—is for the most part Christological,"[22] and "in scrutinizing the Psalms, for instance, Hilary constantly seeks their prophetic inner meaning, ceaselessly examines them in the light of Paul's Letters (cf. Rom 2:16), while discovering in the Psalms an adumbration of Christ's actions and passions."[23] Concerning Jerome he says, "For any serious reader of Jerome's commentaries on the Old Testament, and particularly the Psalms, knows full well that the exegetical approach reflected in these writings is essentially Christocentric."[24]

In order to refute the christological heresies, namely, Apollinarianism, Nestorianism, Eutychianism, and Monophysitism, they quoted Psalm verses which supported both his divine nature and his human nature, as well as the relation of the two natures in one person. Of course, these were controversies in regard to which the Psalms would seem to make less specific statements. But there are quotations which speak of the Son's equality with and eternal generation from the Father, his personal distinction from the Father, and his incarnation.

When Pelagianism arose at the beginning of the fifth century, the church fathers spent a considerable amount of ink proving the reality of original sin, that it originated with Adam and Eve in the Garden of Eden and was transmitted to every single one of their descendents in the human race. To counter this heresy, they found ample proof throughout the Psalms. The early fathers are firmly convinced that the Psalms, especially Psalm 51, very clearly attest to the reality of original sin and that it, along with actual sins, must be forgiven in order for believers to inherit eternal life. While there was a definite legal tendency in the early church, there are clear references to the Psalms in support of divine grace and that God is the source of salvation.

Prayer has always been an important part of the life of the church. As noted above, John F. Brug sees the Psalms as the prayer book of the Bible, and Martin Luther considered one division of the Psalms as prayers and petitions. Fittingly then, the early fathers find in the Psalms numerous examples of prayers and also guidelines for prayer, such as the best time to pray, frequency of prayer, the attitude with which one should pray, and the confidence that God will hear the prayers of his people.

---

[22]Bertrand de Margerie, SJ, *An Introduction to the History of Exegesis*, 3 vols. (Petersham, MA: Saint Bede's Publications, 1995), 2:54.
[23]Ibid., 2:54.
[24]Ibid, 2:125.

Another frequent use of the Psalms was as a source of moral directives. Christian morality had always been an important theme of early Christian literature, beginning with the hortatory genre, which preceded the apologetic and polemical genres. This may be due partially to the legalistic bent of much patristic writings, but also because of the difficulty of living a truly God-pleasing life in a world dominated by secularism and a plurality of religions. The Psalms are frequently quoted to encourage people to be merciful in imitation of their merciful God, to guard against pride and a desire for vengeance, to be patient in hardships, and to be generous in helping the poor. These early writers find in the Psalms the quandary of trying to answer the perennially imponderable question of why the wicked seem to prosper in this world while the righteous seem to suffer and often lack even basic temporal goods. In attempting to answer this puzzle, they strongly advise people against placing their trust in material possessions and remind their readers that the ungodly who seem to prosper now will eventually be punished for their wickedness and lack of faith. The Book of Psalms firmly asserts that God is a God of judgment who will not let sin go unpunished, if not always in this life, certainly on the day of judgment and in the next life.

In working through citations from the Psalms in early Christian literature, we are struck by the prominent place the Psalms had in the life of the early church, as a source of defense against false teachings, as a fountain of moral guidelines, as a source of comfort in affliction, and as a solid foundation for the Christian hope of eternal life. Readers of patristic literature are amazed with the way in which numerous passages from the Psalms and other Old Testament books are employed in support of a particular point of doctrine. With few books and without modern-day reference resources they had to depend on their memory, which was cultivated much more extensively in the ancient world than it is today. Graham W. Woolfenden asks why the Psalter became such a dominant source of meditational material, more so than any other book of the Bible in the monastic communities and then quotes Abba Philimon who said, when asked why he preferred the Psalms to other parts of Scripture: "God has impressed the power of the psalms on my poor soul as He did on the soul of the prophet David. I cannot be separated from the sweetness of the visions about which they speak: they embrace all Scriptures."[25] The idea that the Psalms were a kind of condensation of all Scripture may have led to the emphasis on memorization of the Psalms. We have already referred to Jerome's advise to Paula. Woolfenden adds to this,

> Pachomius required the learning of "at least the New Testament and the Psalter." The late fifth century *Regula Orientalis* expected praying and psalmody whilst at work or on a journey, which would imply memorization in a world of few books. The same work expected postulates to learn the Lord's Prayer and as many psalms as they are able, whilst waiting to be admitted. It is now thought that Benedict's concern for *Lectio Divina* was also to do with memorizing psalms and as late as 787, bishops were expected by Nicaea II to know the Psalter by heart.[26]

In commenting on Psalm 1 and comparing the benefit of the Psalms to the rest of the Bible, Basil the Great said, "the Book of Psalms encompasses the benefit of them all. It foretells what is to come and memorializes history; it legislates for life, gives advice on practical matters, and serves in general as a repository of

---

[25]Woolfenden, "Use of the Psalter," p. 91.
[26]Ibid., p. 92.

good teachings, carefully searching out what is suitable for each individual."[27]

Christians in the twenty-first century still find the Psalms a great source of inspiration, comfort, guidance, and a real wellspring of the doctrinal truths which lead to eternal salvation. It is hoped that in some small way readers of the excerpts in this volume will have their spiritual lives greatly enriched.

Quentin F. Wesselschmidt

---

[27]Quoted from ibid., p. 92.

51:1-9 A PRAYER FOR FORGIVENESS
AND SPIRITUAL CLEANSING

To the choirmaster. A Psalm of David,
when Nathan the prophet came to him,
after he had gone in to Bathsheba.

¹*Have mercy on me, O God, according to thy*
steadfast love;
according to thy abundant mercy blot out
my transgressions.
²*Wash me thoroughly from my iniquity,*
and cleanse me from my sin!

³*For I know my transgressions,*
and my sin is ever before me.
⁴*Against thee, thee only, have I sinned,*
and done that which is evil in thy sight,

so that thou art justified in thy sentence
and blameless in thy judgment.
⁵*Behold, I was brought forth in iniquity,*
and in sin did my mother conceive me.

⁶*Behold, thou desirest truth in the inward*
being;
therefore teach me wisdom in my secret
heart.
⁷*Purge me with hyssop, and I shall be clean;*
wash me, and I shall be whiter than snow.
⁸*Fill*ˣ *me with joy and gladness;*
let the bones which thou hast broken rejoice.
⁹*Hide thy face from my sins,*
and blot out all my iniquities.

x Syr: Heb *Make to hear*

OVERVIEW: Because penitent believers receive mercy from God, they should in turn be merciful to others; such mercy is a fundamental Christian virtue (CHRYSOSTOM). In monastic asceticism regular and frequent praying was a main feature of daily life, and no prayer was more important than the Kyrie, "Lord have mercy" (DESERT FATHERS). Repentance, which includes confession and contrition, must precede forgiveness (FULGENTIUS). King David progressed from the serious sin of adultery to an even greater sin of murder, and the greater the sin the greater the measure of divine mercy that is needed for forgiveness (JEROME). In the mind of the ascetics, strong consciousness of one's sinfulness is a necessary antidote to pride and self-glory, which are the root causes of sin (PACHOMIUS). People desire that God preserve their human nature but remedy its sinful flaw (AUGUSTINE). Although sin against God is a sin to death, as confessed by the prodigal son, it is forgivable to the penitent (AMBROSE).

Since the sin of Adam, with all its consequences, even death, is passed on to every member of the human race, even newborn infants need baptism in order to receive God's grace and the gift of immortality (AUGUSTINE). Scripture clearly states in various passages that infants are sinful from the beginning of their existence (ORIGEN). There always are attempts by heretics and philosophers to try to ameliorate human sinfulness and cast human nature in a more positive light, but the weight of biblical testimony is clearly in support of the complete depravity of human nature from conception and birth. It is clear from the propensity of sin that no one is without sins; the reason we all die is because we all continue in the transgression of Adam (JEROME). Through the remission of our sins God gives us the white robes of righteousness (AMBROSE). David testifies to the fact of original sin. We follow in God's footsteps when we hate sin as he does, and hostility to sin leads us to pray that God will overlook and pardon our sins (AUGUSTINE).

God no longer expects bloody sacrifices of animals; they have been replaced by the praise that issues from humble hearts (AUGUSTINE). Such contrition has its reward, namely, our eternal redemption (EPISTLE OF BARNABAS). Forgiveness produces a profound change in the heart; for example, the forgiven person no longer desires revenge. A profound change in the heart translates into a new level of communal life (CHRYSOSTOM). Sin, no matter how great, does not separate the individual from the church, once true sorrow over sin has been manifested (AUGUSTINE). The only sacrifice God demands of us is that we have a contrite heart and become a new creation in Christ (GREGORY OF NAZIANZUS).

51:1-4 Prayer for Divine Mercy and Forgiveness

EMULATING GOD'S MERCY. CHRYSOSTOM: Beloved,[1] let us praise her,[2] through whom we have been saved. Let us love her; let us prefer her to wealth. Let us have a merciful soul apart from wealth. Nothing is more characteristic of a Christian than mercy. There is nothing that unbelievers

and all people are so amazed at as when we are merciful. For we ourselves are often in need of this mercy and say to God, "Have mercy on us according to the greatness of your mercy." Let us begin first ourselves; yet we do not begin first. For he has already shown his mercy that he has toward us. But, beloved, let us follow second. For if people have mercy on one who was merciful, even if he has committed countless sins, God is much more merciful. ON THE EPISTLE TO THE HEBREWS 32.3.[3]

"LORD, HAVE MERCY" IS AN AUTHENTIC PRAYER. DESERT FATHERS: Some monks called Euchites,[4] or "men of prayer," once came to Abba Lucius in the ninth region of Alexandria. And the old man asked them, "What work do you do with your hands?" And they said, "We do not work with our hands. We obey St. Paul's command and pray without ceasing." The old man said to them, "Do you not eat?" They said, "Yes, we eat." And the old man said to them, "When you are eating, who prays for you?" Again, he asked them, "Do you not sleep?" They said, "We sleep." And the old man said, "Who prays for you while you are asleep?" They would not answer him. And he said to them, "Forgive me, brothers, but you do not practice what you say. I will show you how I pray without ceasing though I work with my hands. With God's help, I sit and collect a few palm leaves, and interweave them and say, 'Have mercy on me, O God, according to your great mercy: and according to the multitude of your mercies do away with my iniquity.'" And he said to them, "Is that prayer, or is it not?" They said, "It is prayer." SAYINGS OF THE FATHERS 12.9.[5]

GOD FORGIVES CONTRITE AND PENITENT SINNERS. FULGENTIUS OF RUSPE: Finally, holy David successfully gained divine mercy because, having been converted by the humility of a contrite heart, he condemned the evil he had done by

---

[1]The people to whom the homily is addressed. [2]Mercifulness or charity. [3]PG 63:224. [4]Members of a celebrated heretical sect, also known as Messalians. [5]LCC 12:142-43*.

acknowledging it and did not put off punishment by doing penance for the lust of the evil deed he had fallen into; because, if he had not punished the cause of the guilt in which he was held, without a doubt he would have been punished. Having been converted to penance, he acknowledged his crime, fearing lest he would have to acknowledge the penalty by being condemned. By doing penance, he punished himself by acknowledging what he wanted to be overlooked by the Lord in himself. Finally, since he said, "Have mercy on me, O God, according to your steadfast love; according to your abundant mercy blot out my transgressions. Wash me thoroughly from my iniquity, and cleanse me from my sin." Immediately following this he added, "For I know my transgressions, and my sin is ever before me." He acknowledged his sin, not that by sinning he might increase it the more, but that by repenting, he might wash it away; and so the domination of sin, which blameworthy enjoyment had brought in, true conversion removed. And because David, converted with all his heart, groaned, he was immediately saved and thus in him was fulfilled what is commanded through the prophet: "If you are converted and groan, you will be saved."[6] ON THE FORGIVENESS OF SINS 1.12.3.[7]

A GREAT SIN NEEDS GREAT MERCY. JEROME: Psalm 50 [51] shows the complete repentance of a sinner when David, who had gone into Bathsheba, the wife of Uriah the Hittite and was rebuked by the prophet Nathan, said, "I have sinned." Immediately he deserved to hear "The Lord has removed your sin from you."[8] For he, who had added homicide to adultery and was moved to tears, said, "God, have compassion on me according to your great pity, and according to the multitude of your mercies take away my iniquity." Since a great sin needed great mercy, he added, "Wash me completely from my iniquity, and my offense is always before me. I have sinned against you only"—for a king did not fear anyone else—"and I have done evil in your sight so that you will be justified in your speaking and you

overcome when you judge." "For God has included all things under sin so that he may be merciful to all."[9] He made so much progress that he who a little earlier had been a penitent sinner became a master and was able to say, "I will teach the unjust your ways, and sinners will be converted to you."[10] Since confession and beauty are before God,[11] the one who confesses his sins and says, "My wounds have been destroyed and become putrefied,"[12] changes the foulness of his wounds into a healthy state. But "he who hides his sins will not prosper."[13] LETTER 122.3.[14]

KNOWLEDGE OF SIN IS AN ANTIDOTE TO VAINGLORY. PACHOMIUS: As the holy old man Pachomius was journeying to his own monastery and had come near the desert called Amnon, legions of demons rose both on his right hand and on his left, some following him and others running in front of him, saying, "Behold the blessed man of God." They were doing this, wishing to sow vainglory in him. But he knew their cunning, and the more they shouted, the more he cried out to God, confessing his sins. And undoing the demons' cunning, he spoke out to them, saying, "O wicked ones! You cannot carry me away with you into vainglory, for I know my failures, for which I ought to weep constantly over eternal punishment. I have therefore no need of your false speech and guileful deceit, for your work is the destruction of the soul. And I am not carried away by your praises, for I know the cunning of your unholy minds." And although holy Pachomius said these things to them, they did not stop their shamelessness; they followed alongside the blessed man until he drew near his monastery. PARALIPOMENA 8.14.[15]

SAVE HUMAN NATURE BUT REMEDY THE FLAW OF SIN. AUGUSTINE: As we were singing

---

[6]Is 30:15. [7]FC 95:125. [8]2 Sam 12:13. [9]Rom 11:32. [10]Ps 51:13 (50:15 LXX, Vg.). [11]Ps 96:6 (95:6 LXX, Vg.). [12]Ps 38:5 (37:6 LXX, Vg.). [13]Prov 28:13. [14]CSEL 56.1:63-64. [15]CS 46:35-36.

of the Lord, we asked him to turn his face away from our sins and to blot out all our misdeeds. But you can also take note, brothers, of what we heard in the same psalm: "Since I myself acknowledge my misdeed, and my sin is always before me." Now somewhere else he says to God, "Do not turn your face away from me,"[16] while here we have just said to him, "Turn your face away from my sins." So since man[17] and sinner are one person, the man says, "Do not turn your face away from me," while the sinner says, "Turn your face away from my sins." So what it amounts to is: "Do not turn your face away from what you have done; turn your face away from what I have done. Let your eye," he says, "distinguish between them, or else the nature may perish because of the flaw. You have done something, I too have done something. What you have done is called nature; what I have done is called a flaw. May the flaw be remedied and thus the nature preserved." SERMON 19.1.[18]

SINS OF WHICH WE ARE UNAWARE. CASSIODORUS: Who can understand sins? From my secret ones, cleanse me, O Lord. See how the gate of the third section swings open,[19] in which the prophet begs that all his sins may be wiped clean, so that his mouth's utterance may be made acceptable in the eyes of the Lord. But whereas human errors transgress in three ways, by thought, word and deed, he confines this boundless sea of sins to brief compass and attests that it springs forth from two sources. Secret sins are those termed "original," in which we are conceived and born and by which we sin with secret longing, as when we desire our neighbor's property, or long for vengeance on our enemies, or wish to become more eminent than the rest, or seek more succulent food or commit similar sins that sprout in and steal on us in such a way that they seem hidden from many before they take effect. If they do become obvious to anyone—and Solomon warns, Do not yield to your lustful desires[20]—we must yet realize that there are many sins of which we are wholly ignorant,

whose sources and deceptions we cannot realize. So in the phrase "who can understand sins?" we must additionally interpret this [as we do] all sins. Since the psalmist will say in Psalm 51: "My sin is always before me," and in another place: "I have acknowledged my sin to you,"[21] how can the sinner fail to understand the sins that he is constrained to confess? But if one adds "all," then this objection clearly falls. EXPOSITIONS OF THE PSALMS 18.13.[22]

SIN IS AN OFFENSE AGAINST GOD. AMBROSE: "I [the prodigal son] have sinned," he says, "against heaven and before you."[23] He confesses what is clearly a sin to death,[24] that you may not think that any one doing penance is rightly shut out from pardon. For one who has sinned against heaven has sinned either against the kingdom of heaven or against his own soul, which is a sin to death, and against God, to whom alone is said: "Against you only have I sinned and done evil before you." CONCERNING REPENTANCE 2.3.17.[25]

51:5-9 Acknowledgment of Original Sin

HUMAN BEINGS ARE SINFUL FROM CONCEPTION. AUGUSTINE: So it is because of this quite unique innocence[26] that the psalm says, "Against you alone have I sinned and done what is evil in your presence, that you may be justified in your words and may overcome when you are judged," because he could find not a hint of evil in you [Jesus Christ]. Why could he find it in you,

---

[16]Ps 27:9 (26:9 LXX, Vg.). [17]Here Augustine distinguishes between "man" as a righteous, justified believer and the person who continues to sin, much like Martin Luther's characterization of a Christian individual as being "saint and sinner" at the same time. [18]*WSA* 3 1:378. [19]Cassiodorus is referring to Psalm 19:12 (18:12 LXX), which is the beginning of the third section into which he divided the psalm. [20]See Prov 4:14. [21]Ps 32:5 (31:5 LXX, Vg.). [22]*ACW* 51:201-2*. [23]Lk 15:18. [24]A sin against God committed by a person who rejects God's offer of forgiveness and thereby does not receive the sacraments of the church as a means of receiving God's grace. [25]NPNF 2 10:347*. [26]Augustine is speaking about the sinlessness of Jesus Christ, which was unique since he was the only person with a human nature to be without sin after the fall of Adam and Eve.

though, O human race? Because it goes on to say, "For I myself was conceived in iniquity, and in sins did my mother conceive me." It is David saying this. Inquire how David was born; you will discover that it was of a lawful wife, not of adultery. So in terms of what sort of propagation does he say "I was conceived in iniquity"? It can only be that there is here a kind of propagation or transmission of death, which every person contracts who is born of the union of man and woman. SERMON 170.4.[27]

EVEN INFANTS NEED A SACRIFICE FOR THEIR SIN. ORIGEN: Celsus[28] has not explained how error accompanies the "becoming," or product of generation; nor has he expressed himself with sufficient clearness to enable us to compare his ideas with ours and to pass judgment on them. But the prophets, who have given some wise suggestions on the subject of things produced by generation, tell us that a sacrifice for sin was offered even for newborn infants, as not being free from sin. They say, "I was shaped in iniquity, and in sin did my mother conceive me"; also, "They are estranged from the womb"; which is followed by the singular expression, "They go astray as soon as they are born, speaking lies."[29] AGAINST CELSUS 7.50.[30]

EVEN A DAY-OLD INFANT IS SINFUL. JEROME: But we, according to the epistle of James, "all stumble in many things,"[31] and "no one is pure from sin, no not if his life is but a day long."[32] For who will boast "that he has a clean heart? or who will be sure that he is pure from sin?" And we are held guilty after the likeness of Adam's transgression. Hence David says, "Behold, I was shaped in iniquity, and in sin did my mother conceive me." And the blessed Job, "Even if I were righteous, my mouth will speak wickedness; even if I were perfect, I will be found guilty. If I wash myself with soap and make my hands ever so clean, yet you will plunge me in the ditch, and even my own clothes will abhor me."[33] AGAINST JOVINIANUS 2.2.[34]

NO ONE IS WITHOUT SIN. JEROME: I need not go through the lives of the saints or call attention to the moles and blemishes that mark the fairest skins. Many of our writers, it is true, unwisely take this course; however, a few sentences of Scripture will dispose alike of the heretics and the philosophers. What does Paul say? "For God has imprisoned all in disobedience so that he may be merciful to all";[35] and in another place, "All have sinned and come short of the glory of God."[36] The preacher also who is the mouthpiece of the divine Wisdom freely protests and says, "There is not a just person on earth, that does good and sins not,"[37] and again, "When your people sin against you—for there is no one who does not sin,"[38] and "who can say, I have made my heart clean?"[39] and "none is clean from stain, not even if his life on earth has been but for one day." David insists on the same thing when he says, "Behold, I was shaped in iniquity, and in sin did my mother conceive me"; and in another psalm, "in your sight shall no man living be justified."[40] This last passage they try to explain away from motives of reverence, arguing that the meaning is that no human being is perfect in comparison with God. Yet the Scripture does not say, "in comparison with you no one living shall be justified" but "in your sight no one living shall be justified." And when it says "in your sight" it means that those who seem holy to people are by no means holy to God in his fuller knowledge. For "man looks on the outward appearance, but the Lord looks on the heart."[41] But if in the sight of God who sees all things and to whom the secrets of the heart lie open[42] no one is just; then these heretics,[43] instead of adding to human dignity,

---

[27]WSA 3 5:241. [28]Celsus was a pagan Platonist who wrote what is considered one of the most competent literary attacks on Christianity (c. 180). It was not answered until Origen wrote his response, *Against Celsus*, about fifty years later. [29]Ps 58:3 (57:4 LXX). [30]ANCL 23:472. [31]Jas 3:2. [32]Job 14:4-5 (LXX). [33]Job 9:20, 30-31 (LXX). [34]NPNF 2 6:388. [35]Rom 11:32. [36]Rom 3:23. [37]Eccles 7:20. [38]1 Kings 8:46. [39]Prov 20:9. [40]Ps 143:2 (142:2 LXX, Vg.). [41]1 Sam 16:7. [42]Ps 44:21 (43:22 LXX, Vg.); Heb 4:13. [43]The Pelagians, who denied original sin and believed that people are capable of earning their own salvation by doing good.

clearly take away from God's power. I might bring together many other passages of Scripture of the same import; but were I to do so, I should exceed the limits not of a letter but of a volume. LETTER 133.2.[44]

CLOTHED IN WHITE ROBES. AMBROSE: After this white robes[45] were given to you as a sign that you were putting off the covering of sins and putting on the chaste veil of innocence, of which the prophet said, "Purge me with hyssop, and I shall be cleansed; wash me, and I shall be made whiter than snow."[46] For one who is baptized is seen to be purified according to the law and according to the gospel: according to the law, because Moses sprinkled the blood of the lamb with a bunch of hyssop;[47] according to the gospel, because Christ's garments were white as snow, when in the Gospel he showed forth the glory of his resurrection. One, then, whose guilt is forgiven is made whiter than snow. Thus God said through Isaiah: "Though your sins are as scarlet, I will make them white as snow."[48] ON THE MYSTERIES 7.34.[49]

CONTRITION LEADS TO FORGIVENESS. AUGUSTINE: So all past sins are forgiven people on conversion; but for the rest of this life there are certain grave and deadly sins, from which one can be released only by the most vehement and distressing humbling of the heart and contrition of spirit[50] and the pain of repentance. These are forgiven through the keys of the church.[51] If you start judging yourself, you see, if you start being displeased with yourself, God will come along to show you mercy. If you are willing to punish yourself, he will spare you. In fact, all who repent and do penance well are punishing themselves. They have to be severe with themselves, so that God may be lenient with them. As David says, "Turn your face away from my sins, and blot out all my iniquities." But on what terms? He says in the same psalm, "Since I acknowledge my iniquity, and my sin is always before me."[52] So if you acknowledge it, God overlooks it. SERMON 278.12.[53]

IT IS GODLY TO HATE SIN. AUGUSTINE: God does not listen to sinners. When he[54] was beating his breast, he was punishing his sins; when he was punishing his sins, he was associating himself with God as judge. God, you see, hates sins; if you too hate them, you are beginning to join God, so that you can say to him, "Turn your face away from my sins." Turn your face away—but from what? From my sins. "Do not turn your face away from me."[55] What's the meaning of "your face from my sins"? Don't see them, don't look at them; overlook them instead, so that you can pardon me. SERMON 136A.2.[56]

---

[44]NPNF 2 6:273*. [45]It was the custom in the early church to give catechumens a white robe after they had been baptized. [46]Ps 51:7 (50:9 LXX, Vg.). [47]Ex 12:22. [48]Is 1:18. [49]NPNF 2 10:321*. [50]Ps 51:17 (50:19 LXX, Vg.). [51]See Mt 16:19; 18:18. [52]Ps 51:3 (50:5 LXX, Vg.). [53]WSA 3 8:56. [54]The tax collector (Lk 18:13-14). [55]Ps 27:9 (26:9 LXX, Vg.). [56]WSA 3 4:360.

51:10-19 A CLEAN HEART

[10]Create in me a clean heart, O God,
  and put a new and right[y] spirit within me.
[11]Cast me not away from thy presence,
  and take not thy holy Spirit from me.
[12]Restore to me the joy of thy salvation,
  and uphold me with a willing spirit.

¹³*Then I will teach transgressors thy ways,*
    and sinners will return to thee.
¹⁴*Deliver me from bloodguiltiness,ᶻ O God,*
    thou God of my salvation,
    and my tongue will sing aloud of thy
    deliverance.

¹⁵*O Lord, open thou my lips,*
    and my mouth shall show forth thy praise.
¹⁶*For thou hast no delight in sacrifice;*
    were I to give a burnt offering, thou wouldst
    not be pleased.
¹⁷*The sacrifice acceptable to Godᵃ is a broken*
    spirit;
    a broken and contrite heart, O God, thou
    wilt not despise.

¹⁸*Do good to Zion in thy good pleasure;*
    rebuild the walls of Jerusalem,
¹⁹*then wilt thou delight in right sacrifices,*
    in burnt offerings and whole burnt offerings;
    then bulls will be offered on thy altar.

y *Or* steadfast   z *Or* death   a *Or* My sacrifice, O God

OVERVIEW: The spiritual cleansing of the penitent sinner is a divine work attributed to the Holy Spirit in his work of sanctification (HIPPOLYTUS). So thoroughly is a person tainted by the corruption of sin that the cleansing of the stain is extremely difficult (GREGORY OF NAZIANZUS, CHRYSOSTOM). Since sin incapacitates human nature's ability to do good, whatever good we do, once redemption and sanctification occur, is by participation in the divine goodness and is a gift of the Holy Spirit (AUGUSTINE, BEDE). The right spirit that David prays for is to be understood as the Holy Spirit (BASIL). When God gazes on a human being, he either pardons the person's sins or punishes him because of them (CASSIODORUS). Within the cleansed heart and life of the believer, there is room and a place only for Christ, not for Christ and Satan (JEROME). David as a public figure and leader of Israel promised to be an example and teacher of the meaning of true repentance to others (CALLISTUS). The apostles became exemplars of spiritual virtues already mandated by David in the Psalms (AUGUSTINE). The doing of good by the power of the Holy Spirit necessitates having a clean heart (BEDE).

51:10-14 The Stain of Sin Can Be Removed by God Alone

THE HOLY SPIRIT'S ROLE IN REGENERATION. HIPPOLYTUS: This is the Spirit who at the beginning "moved on the face of the waters";[1] by whom the world moves; by whom creation consists and all things have life; who also worked mightily in the prophets[2] and descended in flight on Christ.[3] This is the Spirit who was given to the apostles in the form of fiery tongues.[4] This is the Spirit who David sought when he said, "Create in me a clean heart, O God, and renew a right spirit within me." Of this Spirit Gabriel also spoke to the Virgin, "The Holy Spirit shall come upon you, and the power of the Highest shall overshadow you."[5] By this Spirit Peter spoke that blessed word, "You are the Christ, the Son of the living God."[6] By this Spirit the rock of the church was established.[7] This is the Spirit, the Comforter, who is sent because of you, that he may show you[8] to be the Son of God. ON THE THEOPHANY 9.[9]

THE ENTIRE BODY NEEDS CLEANSING. GREGORY OF NAZIANZUS: In addition to what has already been said, those who cleanse the head, which is the seat of knowledge, would do well to hold fast to Christ as their head. It is from him that the entire body is joined together[10] and rec-

---

[1]Gen 1:2. [2]Acts 28:25. [3]Mt 3:16. [4]Acts 2:3. [5]Lk 1:35. [6]Mt 16:16. [7]Mt 16:18. [8]Jn 16:26. [9]ANF 5:237*. [10]Col 2:19.

onciled. And to cast aside our sin which arises and to seek to surpass the better part. It is also good that they should cleanse the shoulder so that it will be able to bear the cross of Christ, which is not borne easily by everyone. It is also good to consecrate the hands and the feet—the hands so that they may be lifted up in every holy place and grasp the teachings of Christ lest the Lord be angered at any time[11] and to believe the Word by living it as when it was given into the hand of the prophet; the feet so that they will not be quick to shed blood or rush into evil but that they may be ready to hurry to the gospel and to their high calling and to receive Christ, who washes and purifies them. If anyone is clean in his stomach, which is able to hold and digest the food of the Word, he should not make a god of nourishment and meat that perishes; rather he should especially reduce its size so that he may receive the Word of the Lord in its very midst and to grieve deeply over the failing of Israel. I also find the heart and the inward parts worthy of honor. David convinced me of this when he asked that a clean heart be created within him and a right spirit be consecrated in his innermost being—by this I think he clearly means his mind and its emotions or thoughts. ON HOLY BAPTISM, ORATION 40.39.[12]

SIN IS A DIFFICULT STAIN TO REMOVE. CHRYSOSTOM: It would be better to be defiled with unclean mud than with sins. A person who is defiled with mud can wash it off in a short time and become like one who had never fallen into that mire at all. But one who has fallen into the deep pit of sin has contracted a defilement that is not cleansed by water but needs a long period of time, strict repentance, tears and lamentations and more wailing—and that more fervent than we show at the loss of one of our dearest friends. For this defilement attaches to us from without, wherefore we also quickly put it away, but the other is generated from within, where it is more difficult to wash it off and to cleanse ourselves from it. "For from the heart" (it is said) "proceed evil thoughts, fornications, adulteries, thefts, false witnesses."[13] Thus, the prophet also said, "Create in me a clean heart, O God." And another prophet said, "Wash your heart from wickedness, O Jerusalem."[14] (You see that it is both our [work] and God's.) And again, "Blessed are the pure in heart, for they shall see God."[15] ON THE EPISTLE TO THE HEBREWS 12.7.[16]

MADE GOOD BY GOD'S GRACE. AUGUSTINE: We are then truly free when God ordered our lives, that is, formed and created us not as individuals—this he has already done—but also as good people, which he is now doing by his grace, that we may indeed be new creatures in Christ Jesus.[17] Accordingly, the prayer "Create in me a clean heart, O God." This does not mean, as far as the natural human heart is concerned, that God has not already created this. ENCHIRIDION 9.31.[18]

THE GUEST ROOM OF THE HEART. BEDE: Let us call to mind that he promised that [Jesus] would send the grace of the Spirit to his disciples, and he did send it. And let us take care with all watchfulness, lest by our seductive thoughts we grieve the Holy Spirit of God, in whom we have been sealed for the day of redemption.[19] For so it is written, "The Holy Spirit will flee the pretense of discipline, and will remove himself from thoughts that are without understanding."[20] When the psalmist was burning with the desire to receive this Spirit, he providently sought first [to have] the guest chamber of a clean heart in which he could receive him, and so at length [he] sought the entry of so great a guest. "Create a clean heart in me, O God," he said, "renew an upright spirit in my inmost parts." He entreated that first a clean heart be created in him and then that an upright spirit be renewed in his inmost parts, because he knew that an upright spirit

---

[11]Ps 2:12. [12]PG 36:413-16. [13]Mt 15:19. [14]Jer 4:14. [15]Mt 5:8. [16]NPNF 1 14:426*. [17]See Gal 6:15; 2 Cor 5:17. [18]LCC 7:357*. [19]Eph 4:30. [20]Wis 1:5.

could have no place in a defiled heart. HOMILIES ON THE GOSPELS 2.11.[21]

ALL GOOD IS A GIFT OF THE SPIRIT. BEDE: It is only by participation in the divine goodness that a rational creature is recognized as being capable of becoming good. Hence the Lord also bears witness by a benevolent promise that "your Father from heaven will give his good Spirit to those who ask him."[22] This is to point out that those who of themselves are evil can become good through receiving the gift of the Spirit. He pledged that his good Spirit would be given by the Father to those asking for him, because whether we desire to secure faith, hope and charity, or any other heavenly goods at all, they are not bestowed on us in any other way than by the gift of the Holy Spirit. So it is that the same Spirit, in Isaiah, is named the Spirit of wisdom and understanding, the Spirit of counsel and fortitude, the Spirit of knowledge and piety, the Spirit of the fear of the Lord;[23] and in another place, the Spirit of love and peace[24] [and] the Spirit of grace and prayers.[25] Undoubtedly whatever good we truly have, whatever we do well, this we receive from the lavishness of the same Spirit. When a prophet who understood this was seeking purity of heart, saying, "Create a pure heart in me, O Lord," he immediately added, "Renew a steadfast spirit within me." If the steadfast Spirit of the Lord does not fill our innermost being, we have no pure heart where he may abide. When in his eager longing for an advance in good for his work he had said, "Lord, I have had recourse to you, teach me to do your will,"[26] he at once showed in what way he had to secure this when he went on, "Let your good Spirit lead me into the right way."[27] HOMILIES ON THE GOSPELS 2.14.[28]

TITLES OF THE HOLY SPIRIT. BASIL THE GREAT: We shall now examine what kinds of ideas about the Spirit we hold in common, as well as those that we have gathered from the Scriptures or received from the unwritten tradition of the Fathers. First of all, who can listen to the Spirit's titles and not be lifted up in his soul? Whose thoughts would not be raised to contemplate the supreme nature? He is called the Spirit of God,[29] the Spirit of truth who proceeds from the Father,[30] right Spirit, willing Spirit. His first and most proper title is Holy Spirit, a name most especially appropriate to everything that is incorporeal, purely immaterial and indivisible. ON THE HOLY SPIRIT 9.22.[31]

THE FORGIVING GAZE OF GOD. CASSIODORUS: The words "and has looked on"[32] denote the grace of the pitying Lord, for we say that we look on those to whom we claim something has been granted. Notice that he does not mention the sins that he looked on, but "the sons of men."[33] When he looks on faults, he punishes, but when he gazes on a person he pardons. As the psalmist says in Psalm 51: "Turn your face away from my sins,"[34] and elsewhere: "Do not turn your face away from me." So we must realize and remember this difference. EXPOSITIONS OF THE PSALMS 32.13.[35]

CHRIST AND THE DEVIL CANNOT COEXIST IN THE HUMAN HEART. JEROME: "The one who says, I know him, and does not keep his commandments is a liar, and the truth is not in him. But whoever keeps his word, in him the love of God has been truly perfected. By this we know that we are in him; he who says that he abides in him ought himself also to walk as he walked."[36] My reason for telling you, little children, that everyone who is born of God does not sin, is that you should not sin and that you should know that as long as you do not sin you abide in the birth[37] that God has given you. Truly, they who abide in that birth cannot sin. "For what does light have

---

[21]CS 111:106. [22]Lk 11:13. [23]Is 11:2-3. [24]2 Cor 13:11. [25]Zech 12:10. [26]Ps 143:9-10 (142:9-10 LXX, Vg.). [27]Ps 143:10 (142:10 LXX, Vg.). [28]CS 111:132-33*. [29]Mt 12:28, etc. [30]Jn 15:26. [31]OHS 42*. [32]Ps 33:13 (32:13 LXX, Vg.). [33]Ps 33:13 (32:13 LXX, Vg.). [34]Ps 51:9 (50:11 LXX, Vg.). [35]ACW 51:320*. [36]1 Jn 2:4-6. [37]Jerome is no doubt referring here to the new birth of the Spirit that Jesus mentions in John 3:3.

in common with darkness? Or Christ with Belial?"[38] As day is distinct from night, so righteousness and unrighteousness, sin and good works, Christ and Antichrist cannot blend. If we give Christ a lodging place in our hearts, we banish the devil therefrom. If we sin and the devil enters through the gate of sin, Christ will immediately withdraw. Hence David after sinning says, "Restore to me the joy of your salvation," that is, the joy that he had lost by sinning. AGAINST JOVINIANUS 2.2.[39]

RESTORED THROUGH REPENTANCE. CALLISTUS OF ROME: People are in error who think that the priests of the Lord, after a lapse, although they may have exhibited true repentance, are not capable of ministering to the Lord and engaging their honorable offices, even though they may lead a good life thereafter and perform their priesthood correctly. Individuals who hold this opinion are not only in error but also seem to argue and act in opposition to the power of the keys committed to the church, of which it is said, "Whatever you shall loose on earth shall be loosed in heaven."[40] In short, this opinion either is not the Lord's or it is true. Be that as it may, we believe without hesitation that both the priests of the Lord and other believers may return to their place of honor after a proper satisfaction for their error, as the Lord testifies through his prophet: "Shall he who falls not also rise again? and shall he who turns away not return?"[41] In another passage the Lord says, "I desire not the death of the sinner, but that he may turn and live."[42] The prophet David, on his repentance, said, "Restore to me the joy of your salvation, and uphold me with your free Spirit." And he indeed, after his repentance, taught others also and offered sacrifice to God, giving thereby an example to the teachers of the holy church, that if they have fallen and thereafter have exhibited a right repentance to God, they may do both things in like manner. For he taught when he said, "I will teach transgressors your ways, and sinners will be converted to you." And he offered sacrifice for himself when he said, "The sacrifice for God is a broken spirit."[43] For the prophet, seeing his own transgressions purged by repentance, had no doubt as to healing those of others by preaching and by making offering to God. Thus the shedding of tears moves the mind's feeling (*passionem*). And when the satisfaction is made good, the mind is turned aside from anger. For how does that person think that mercy will be shown to himself, who does not forgive his neighbor? If offences abound, then, let mercy also abound; for with the Lord there is mercy, and with him is plentiful redemption.[44] EPISTLE 2.6.[45]

LESSONS FROM APOSTOLIC EXAMPLE. AUGUSTINE: So then Rome, the head of the nations, has these two lights of the nations[46] lit by the one who enlightens every person who comes into this world[47]—one light in which God has exalted the most abject lowliness, the other in which he cured the wickedness that deserved to be condemned. With the former let us learn not to be proud, with the latter not to despair. How simply these great examples have been set before us, and how salutary they are! Let us always commemorate them and in praising them glorify that true light.[48] So none of us should get a swollen head about having a high position in the world; Peter was a fisherman. None of us, reflecting on our own iniquity, should run away from God's mercy; Paul was a persecutor. The former says, "The Lord has become the refuge of the poor";[49] the latter says, "Let me teach the wicked your ways, and the godless will be converted to you." SERMON 381.1.[50]

51:15-19 True Worship That Pleases God Follows Absolution and Forgiveness

---

[38]2 Cor 6:14-15. [39]NPNF 2 6:387-88**. [40]Mt 18:18. [41]Jer 8:4. [42]Ezek 18:32; 33:11. [43]Ps 51:17 (50:19 LXX, Vg.). [44]Ps 130:7 (129:6 LXX, Vg.). [45]ANF 8:617-18*. [46]Augustine is referring to Peter and Paul, whom he believed were both martyred in Rome. The reference to their being lights is based on John 1:9, where John refers to Jesus Christ as the true Light who enlightens people, especially those who bear witness to him as did these two apostles. [47]Jn 1:9. [48]Jn 1:9. [49]Ps 9:9 (9:10 LXX, Vg.). [50]WSA 3 10:373.

THE SACRIFICE OF A CONTRITE HEART.
AUGUSTINE: At the time David spoke in this
way: "Since if you had wanted a sacrifice I
would certainly have given one; in burnt offerings you will not delight." [However,] those sacrifices that were still offered to God are no
longer offered now. He was prophesying, therefore, when he said this: he was rejecting current
customs and foreseeing future ones. "In burnt
offerings," he says, "you will not delight. When
you [the congregation] stop delighting in burnt
offerings, will you be left without any sacrifice?
Certainly not." "A sacrifice to God is a contrite
spirit: a contrite and humbled heart God does
not despise." Therefore you do have something
to offer. Don't look around the flock, don't fit
out ships and travel to far distant regions to
bring back incense. Look in your own heart for
what may be acceptable to God. The heart has
to be crushed. Why be afraid it will be destroyed
if you crush it? There you have the answer:
"Create a clean heart in me, O God."[51] For a
clean heart to be created, let the unclean heart
be crushed. SERMON 19.3.[52]

CAREFUL FOR SALVATION. EPISTLE OF BARNA-
BAS: To us, therefore, David says, "A sacrifice to
God is a broken heart"; "an aroma pleasing to the
Lord is a heart that glorifies its Maker."[53] So,
brothers, we ought to give very careful attention to
our salvation, lest the evil one should cause some
error to slip into our midst and thereby hurl us
away from our life. EPISTLE OF BARNABAS 2.10.[54]

**THERE IS NO VENGEANCE IN A CONTRITE
HEART.** CHRYSOSTOM: Other things too must be
added to humbleness of mind if it is such as the
blessed David knew, when he said, "A broken and
a contrite heart God will not despise." For that
which is broken does not rise up, does not strike,
but is ready to be ill-treated and itself does not
rise up. Such is contrition of heart: though it is
insulted, though it is enticed by evil, it is quiet
and is not eager for vengeance. ON THE EPISTLE
TO THE HEBREWS 9.8.[55]

HUMILITY IS LOVELY TO GOD. CHRYSOSTOM:
But how shall a person find grace with God?
How else, except by lowliness of mind? For
"God," James says, "resists the proud but gives
grace to the humble";[56] and "the sacrifice of
God is a broken spirit, and a heart that is
brought low God will not despise." For if humility is so lovely to human beings, it is much more
so with God. Thus both the Gentiles found
grace and the Jews did not fall from grace in any
other way, "for they were not subject to the
righteousness of God."[57] The lowly person of
whom I am speaking is pleasing and delightful
to all people, and dwells in continual peace
and has in him no ground for contentions. For
even if you insult him, even if you abuse him,
whatever you say, he will be silent and will bear
it meekly; he will have so great a peace toward
all people that one cannot even describe it. Yes,
and with God also. For the commandments of
God are to be at peace with human beings: and
thus our whole life is made prosperous, through
peace one with another. HOMILIES ON 1 CORIN-
THIANS 1.4.[58]

AN APPROPRIATE ANGER TOWARD ONESELF.
AUGUSTINE: So this lad[59] had already crushed his
heart in a region afflicted with famine; I mean, he
had returned to his heart to pound his heart; he
had previously left his heart in pride; he had now
returned to his heart in anger. He was angry with
himself, ready to punish not himself but his
wrongdoing; he had returned, ready to earn his
father's right response. He spoke in anger, according to the text, "Be angry, and do not sin."[60] Repentance, you see, always means being angry with
yourself, seeing that because you are angry, you
punish yourself. That is the source of all those
gestures in penitents who are truly repentant,
truly sorry; the source of tearing the hair, of

[51]Ps 51:10 (50:12 LXX, Vg.). [52]WSA 3 1:380*. [53]Source is unknown;
according to a note in Codex Hierosolymitanus, it is from the no
longer extant *Apocalypse of Adam*. [54]AF 277-79*. [55]NPNF 1 14:412*.
[56]Jas 4:6. [57]Rom 10:3. [58]NPNF 1 12:4**. [59]The prodigal son (Lk
15:11-32). [60]Ps 4:4 (4:5 LXX, Vg.).

wrapping oneself in sackcloth, of beating the breast. Surely these are all indications of being savage with oneself, being angry with oneself. What the hand does outwardly, the conscience does inwardly; it lashes itself in its thoughts, it beats itself, indeed, to speak more truly, it slays itself. It is by slaying itself, you see, that it offers itself "a sacrifice to God, a crushed spirit; a contrite and humbled heart God does not reject." Just so, then, this lad by pounding, humbling, beating his heart, slew his heart. SERMON 112A.5.[61]

SORROW OVER SINS IS A MEASURE OF REPENTANCE. AUGUSTINE: No matter how great our crimes, forgiveness of them should never be despised in the holy church for those who truly repent, each according to the measure of his sin. And, in the act of repentance, where a crime has been committed of such gravity as also to cut off the sinner from the body of Christ, we should not consider the amount of time as much as the degree of sorrow. For "a contrite and humbled heart God will not despise." ENCHIRIDION 17.65.[62]

A CONTRITE HEART AND THE SACRIFICE OF PRAISE. GREGORY OF NAZIANZUS: I have not yet alluded to the true and first wisdom, for which our wonderful husbandman and shepherd[63] is conspicuous. The first wisdom is a life worthy of praise, in which a person keeps himself pure for God or is purified for him who is all-pure and all-luminous. God demands of us, as his only sacrifice, purification—that is, a contrite heart, the sacrifice of praise,[64] a new creation in Christ,[65] the new man,[66] and the like, as the Scripture loves to call it. ON HIS FATHER'S SILENCE, ORATION 16.2.[67]

---

[61]WSA 3 4:156*. [62]LCC 7:377*. [63]The reference is to Gregory's father, who was too overwhelmed by the calamities that had befallen the people of Nazianzus to be able to address the people who had flocked to the church. [64]Ps 50:23 (49:23 LXX); 51:19 (50:19 LXX). [65]2 Cor 5:17. [66]Eph 4:24. [67]NPNF 2 7:247*.

52:1-9 FEARLESS CONFIDENCE IN GOD

To the choirmaster. A Maskil of David, when Doeg, the Edomite, came and told Saul, "David has come to the house of Ahimelech."

[1]*Why do you boast, O mighty man, of mischief done against the godly?*[b]
   All the day [2]*you are plotting destruction.*
Your tongue is like a sharp razor, you worker of treachery.
[3]*You love evil more than good,*

   and lying more than speaking the truth.   Selah
[4]*You love all words that devour, O deceitful tongue.*

[5]*But God will break you down for ever; he will snatch and tear you from your tent; he will uproot you from the land of the living.*   Selah
[6]*The righteous shall see, and fear, and shall laugh at him, saying,*

⁷"See the man who would not make God his
    refuge,
but trusted in the abundance of his riches,
    and sought refuge in his wealth!"ᶜ

⁸But I am like a green olive tree
    in the house of God.

I trust in the steadfast love of God
    for ever and ever.
⁹I will thank thee for ever,
    because thou hast done it.
I will proclaimᵈ thy name, for it is good,
    in the presence of the godly.

b Cn Compare Syr: Heb *the kindness of God*   c Syr Tg: Heb *his destruction*   d Cn: Heb *wait for*

OVERVIEW: The confusion of languages at the tower of Babel ended humanity's united effort in doing evil, but on Pentecost the Holy Spirit began to restore that lingual unity and harmony among people (GREGORY OF NAZIANZUS). When David compares himself with an olive tree, he is designating himself as a just and holy person, since various species of trees and types of wood symbolize various virtues, such as prudence, knowledge and justice (ORIGEN). The grafting of branches or sprigs from wild olive trees to good, cultivated ones represents a catechumen's transition from a life of sin and defilement to a life of righteousness and purity (CYRIL OF JERUSALEM).

52:4 The Dangers of a Deceitful Tongue

A NEW HARMONY OF LANGUAGES AT PENTECOST. GREGORY OF NAZIANZUS: The old confusion of tongues was beneficial when people, who were of one language in wickedness and impiety, just as some still are, were building the tower.[1] But by the confusion of their language, the unity of their intention was broken up and their undertaking destroyed. Much more worthy of praise is the present miraculous unity of language [at Pentecost]. Being poured from one Spirit on many people, it brings them again into harmony. And there is a diversity of gifts, which stands in need of yet another gift to discern which is the best, where all are praiseworthy. That division also might be called noble of which David says, "Confuse the wicked, O Lord, confound their speech."[2] Why? Because "you love every harmful word, O you deceitful tongue!" Here he very expressly indicts the tongues of the present day[3] that sever the Godhead. ON PENTECOST, ORATION 41.16.[4]

52:8 Like a Green Olive Tree

THE OLIVE TREE SYMBOLIZES A JUST AND HOLY PERSON. ORIGEN: But do you want me to show you from the Scriptures that trees or wood are given the name of individual virtues, which we mentioned above? I turn to the most wise Solomon as a witness when he said about wisdom, "The tree of life is for all who embrace it."[5] Therefore, if "wisdom is the tree of life," without a doubt, there is another tree of prudence, another of knowledge and another of justice. For logically it is not said that only wisdom, of all the virtues, was worthy to be called "the tree of life" but that the other virtues did not receive names of similar sort. Therefore, "the trees of the field will give their fruit."[6] This is what I believe the blessed David also understood about himself when he said, "But I am as a fruitful olive tree in the house of God." From this he clearly shows that the olive tree designates a just and holy person. HOMILIES ON LEVITICUS 16.4.3.[7]

BEAR WORTHY FRUIT. CYRIL OF JERUSALEM: You are being armed not with perishable but with spiritual weapons. The paradise in which you are

---

[1]Gen 11:7. [2]Ps 55:9 (54:10 LXX). [3]Arians, Macedonians, and similar heretical sects. [4]NPNF 2 7:384-85**. [5]Prov 3:18. [6]Lev 26:4. [7]FC 83:268-69*. [8]See Gen 2:19.

being planted is the soul's paradise, wherein you will be named[8] with a name you did not have before. You were a catechumen till now, but now you are to be called believer. Henceforth you are transplanted among the olives of that paradise or are being grafted on a good olive tree being taken from a wild olive.[9] You pass from sins to righteousness, from defilements to purity. You are becoming part of the holy Vine. If, then, you abide in the Vine,[10] you grow into a fruitful branch; but if you do not so abide, you will be burned up in the fire. Let us therefore bring forth worthy fruit. For let not that come about, that there should happen to us what happened to the barren fig tree in the Gospel.[11] Let not Jesus come in these days and utter the curse on the fruitless; instead may all of you say, "I am like a green olive tree in the house of God; my trust is in the tender mercy of God, forever and ever"; not a material olive tree but a spiritual and glorious one. It is God who plants and waters, but it is yours to bear fruit; God's to bestow the gift, and yours to receive it and keep it forever. But do not esteem the gift lightly because it is given freely. Rather, receive it reverently and guard it with care. CATECHETICAL LECTURES 1.4.[12]

---

[9]Rom 11:17-24. [10]Jn 15:1-8. [11]Mk 11:13-14, 20-21. [12]LCC 4:80*.

53:1-6 THE FOLLY OF EVIL PEOPLE

*To the choirmaster: according to
Mahalath.
A Maskil of David.*

[1]*The fool says in his heart,
   "There is no God."
They are corrupt, doing abominable iniquity;
   there is none that does good.*

[2]*God looks down from heaven
   upon the sons of men
to see if there are any that are wise,
   that seek after God.*

[3]*They have all fallen away;
   they are all alike depraved;
there is none that does good,
   no, not one.*

[4]*Have those who work evil no understanding,
   who eat up my people as they eat bread,
   and do not call upon God?*

[5]*There they are, in great terror,
   in terror such as has not been!
For God will scatter the bones of the ungodly;[e]
   they will be put to shame,[f] for God has rejected them.*

[6]*O that deliverance for Israel would come from Zion!
   When God restores the fortunes of his people,
   Jacob will rejoice and Israel be glad.*

e Cn Compare Gk Syr: Heb *him who encamps against you*   f Gk: Heb *you will put to shame*

OVERVIEW: There is no sin that is more irrational or senseless than the sin of disbelief (SALVIAN). Pride, which has examples in both Testaments, attempts to make a person pleasing to himself but results in his becoming displeasing to God (PAULINUS). The root cause of atheism is human pride, which tries to elevate humanity above God but ends in removing all chances of its receiving rewards for virtues (MARTIN).

53:1 Only Fools Deny the Existence of God

THE SIN OF DISBELIEF. SALVIAN THE PRESBYTER: To such people[1] the word of the prophet can be applied most fittingly: "The fool says in his heart, there is no God." They who say that nothing is seen by God almost deprive him of eyes and even take away substance from him. For when they say he sees nothing, they say he does not exist at all. Although no evil deed is based on reason, because crime cannot be joined with reason, there is no sin, I believe, more irrational or senseless. What is more insane than for anybody, who does not deny that God is the creator of the universe, to deny his governance? How does he admit that God created the world and neglects what he created? As if, indeed, he took pains in creating all things so that he would neglect what he had made! THE GOVERNANCE OF GOD 4.9.[2]

53:5 The Disease of Pride

THE PROUD ARE CONFOUNDED. PAULINUS OF NOLA: Perhaps he calls them saints in this psalm in the same way that he calls them just in the Gospel when he says, "I am not come to call the just but sinners,"[3] that is, those just who boast of the holiness of their race and the letter of the Law,[4] to whom it is said, "Do not boast of your father Abraham, for God is able of these stones to raise up children to Abraham."[5] This type is exemplified in the Pharisee[6] who recited his good works in the temple, as if recalling them to

an ignorant Lord, not praying to be heard but demanding the reward due to his good conduct. Yet, this was displeasing to God because he tore down by his pride what he had built up by his justice; he did not do this silently but at the top of his voice; and it is evident that he did not speak to divine ears, because he wished to be heard by people. Hence, he was not pleasing to God because he was pleasing to himself. "For God has scattered the bones of people pleasing to themselves; they have been confounded," he says, "because he has despised them," who "does not despise a contrite and humbled heart."[7] LETTER 121.[8]

THE DISEASE OF PRIDE. MARTIN OF BRAGA: Such a person[9] not only cuts himself off from the rewards of his virtues but even lays himself open to being condemned to eternal punishment, because the good action, which ought to be performed in consideration of a merciful God, has been performed in order to gain praise. Take away the favors, take away people's admiration, and you will find few who do something good either for the love of God, or barring that, for fear of God; yet no less is the blame with which we are tainted, because we place people before God and human glory before heavenly glory. This disease of pride is acute; it poisons from either side, and it wounds when least expected.[10] For some boast of themselves because they are good, others because they are bad. Of the good who boast, it is said, "For God has scattered the bones of those who are pleased with themselves."[11] Of the evil who boast it is said, "For the wicked person is praised in the desires of his soul, and the worker

---

[1]People who claim that no one deserves the kind of judgment God decreed on the people of Gomorrah because no one has sinned so severely. Yet Christ says that those who reject the gospel will deserve a worse punishment (see Mt 11:23-24). [2]FC 3:105*. [3]Mt 9:13. [4]Rom 2:23. [5]Mt 3:9; Lk 3:8. [6]Lk 18:10-14. [7]Ps 51:17 (50:19 LXX, Vg.). [8]FC 18:318-19**. [9]People who seek glory for themselves, such as, the hypocrites mentioned in Mt 6:2. [10]Cf. Cassian *Institutes* 11.10.3 (CSEL 17:199). [11]Cf. Ps 53:5 in Cassian *Institutes* 11.12 (CSEL 17:200).

of injustice shall be blessed."[12] There are also the words of the apostle: "Their god is the belly, their glory is in their shame."[13] DRIVING AWAY VANITY 4.[14]

[12]Ps 9B.3. In the Septuagint, Psalms 9 and 10 were treated as one Psalm and arranged acrostically, in which each verse or group of verses began with a different letter of the Hebrew alphabet. Here B is the equivalent to the Hebrew *beth*. [13]Phil 3:19. [14]FC 62:38-39*.

54:1-7 A PRAYER FOR DELIVERANCE FROM OUR ENEMIES

*To the choirmaster: with stringed
instruments. A Maskil of David, when
the Ziphites went and told Saul,
"David is in hiding among us."*

[1]*Save me, O God, by thy name,
    and vindicate me by thy might.*
[2]*Hear my prayer, O God;
    give ear to the words of my mouth.*

[3]*For insolent men[g] have risen against me,
    ruthless men seek my life;*

*   they do not set God before them.*   Selah
[4]*Behold, God is my helper;
    the Lord is the upholder[h] of my life.*
[5]*He will requite my enemies with evil;
    in thy faithfulness put an end to them.*

[6]*With a freewill offering I will sacrifice to thee;
    I will give thanks to thy name, O LORD,
        for it is good.*
[7]*For thou hast delivered me from every trouble,
    and my eye has looked in triumph on
        my enemies.*

g Another reading is *strangers*   h Gk Syr Jerome: Heb *of* or *with those who uphold*

OVERVIEW: David, praying for deliverance from his suffering and the attacks of his enemies, is seen as a type of the suppliant Savior in the Garden of Gethsemane and as a model of Christ who is the exemplar of perfect prayer (HILARY). In this life God judges the righteous and the unrighteous, but the righteous will be spared the fate of the wicked in the final judgment (AUGUSTINE). David, who spoke as the mouthpiece of Christ, assures us that God will hear our prayers (HILARY). Prayer is also seen as a sacrifice that must be voluntary and continuous (CASSIAN). Through baptismal regeneration and the gift of the Holy Spirit God has given his faithful people the free-

dom to serve him willingly, instead of by compulsion (VALERIAN).

54:1-2 The Example and Meaning of Prayer for Salvation and Judgment

DAVID IS A TYPE OF CHRIST IN GETHSEMANE.
HILARY OF POITIERS: The suffering of the prophet David is . . . a type of the passion of our God and Lord Jesus Christ. This is why David's prayer also corresponds in sense with the prayer of Christ, who being the Word, was made flesh. As man, Christ suffered all things in a human fashion and spoke in a human fashion in every-

thing he said. He, who bore human infirmities and took on himself the sins of people, approached God in prayer with the humility proper to human beings. This interpretation, even though we are unwilling and slow to receive it, is required by the meaning and force of the words, so that there can be no doubt that everything in the psalm is uttered by David as Christ's mouthpiece. For he says, "Save me, O God, by your name." Thus he prays in bodily humiliation, using the words of his own prophet, the only-begotten Son of God, who at the same time was claiming again the glory that he had possessed from eternity. David asks to be saved by the name of God whereby he was called and wherein he was begotten, in order that the name of God, which rightly belonged to his former nature and kind, might be able to save him in that body wherein he had been born. HOMILY ON PSALM 54.4.[1]

THE MEANING OF DIVINE JUDGMENT. AUGUSTINE: There are two ways to interpret the affirmation that he "shall judge the living and the dead." On the one hand, we may understand by "the living" those who are not yet dead but who will be found living in the flesh when he comes; and we may understand by "the dead" those who have left the body or who shall have left it before his coming. Or, on the other hand, "the living" may signify "the righteous," and "the dead" may signify "the unrighteous"—since the righteous are to be judged as well as the unrighteous. For sometimes the judgment of God is passed on the evil people, as in the word, "But they who have done evil [shall come forth] to the resurrection of judgment."[2] And sometimes it is passed on the good, as in the word, "Save me, O God, by your name, and judge me in your strength." Indeed, it is by the judgment of God that the distinction between good and evil is made, to the end that, being freed from evil and not destroyed with the evildoers, the good may be set apart at his right hand.[3] This is why the psalmist cried, "Judge me, O God," and, as if to explain what he had said,

"and defend my cause against an unholy nation."[4] ENCHIRIDION 14.55.[5]

DAVID EXEMPLIFIES THE PERFECT PRAYERS OF CHRIST. HILARY OF POITIERS: "Hear my prayer, O God, give ear to the words of my mouth." The obvious thing for the prophet to say was, "O God, hear me." But because he is speaking as the mouthpiece of him who alone knew how to pray, we are constantly and repeatedly assured that God will hear our prayer. The words of Paul teach us that no one knows how he ought to pray: "For we know not how to pray as we ought."[6] A human being in his weakness, therefore, has no right to demand that his prayer should be heard; for even the teacher of the Gentiles does not know the true purpose and intention of prayer, even after the Lord had provided a model. What we are shown here is the perfect confidence of Jesus, who alone sees the Father, who alone knows the Father, who alone can pray all night long—the Gospel tells us that the Lord continued all night in prayer[7]—who in the mirror of words has shown us the true image of the deepest of all mysteries in the simple words we use in prayer. And so, in demanding that his prayer be heard and in order to teach us that this was the prerogative of his perfect confidence, David added, "Give ear to the words of my mouth." Now can any person have such confidence that he can desire that the words of his mouth should be heard? It is with words, for instance, that we express emotions and mental instincts, when inflamed by anger, moved by hatred to slander, by flattery to fawn, motivated by hope of gain or fear of shame to lie or by resentment at injury to insult someone? Was there ever a person who was pure and patient throughout his life who was not subject to these human shortcomings? The only person who could have confidently desired this is one who has not sinned, in whose mouth there has been

[1]NPNF 2 9:244**. [2]Jn 5:29. [3]See Mt 25:32-33. [4]Ps 43:1 (42:1 LXX, Vg.). [5]LCC 7:371*. [6]Rom 8:26. [7]Lk 6:12.

no deceit, who gave his back to the smiters, who did not turn his cheek away from the blow, who did not avoid scorn and spitting, who never resisted the will of him who ordered it all but was always gladly obedient. HOMILY ON PSALM 54.6.[8]

54:6 Prayer as Voluntary Sacrifice to God

PRAISE OF GOD SHOULD BE VOLUNTARY AND CONTINUOUS. JOHN CASSIAN: For, among these latter [Egyptians monks], the offices[9] that we are obliged to render to the Lord at different hours and at intervals of time, at the call of the summoner, are celebrated continuously and spontaneously throughout the course of the whole day, in tandem with their work. For they are constantly doing manual labor alone in their cells in such a way that they almost never omit meditation on the psalms and on other parts of Scripture, and to this they add entreaties and prayers at every moment, taking up the whole day in offices that we celebrate at fixed times. Hence apart from the evening and nighttime gatherings, they celebrate no public service during the day except on Saturday and Sunday, when they gather at the third hour for holy Communion. For what is unceasingly offered is greater than what is rendered at particular moments, and a voluntary service is more pleasing than functions that are carried out by canonical obligation. This is why David him-

self rejoices somewhat boastfully when he says, "Willingly shall I sacrifice to you." And, "May the free offerings of my mouth be pleasing to you, Lord."[10] INSTITUTES 3.2.[11]

SERVICE TO GOD SHOULD BE WILLING, NOT COMPULSORY. VALERIAN OF CIMIEZ: Listen to the prophet's voice: "I will freely sacrifice to you, O Lord." Learn how different an imposed servitude is from a voluntary one. A person who finds his own negligence accusing himself of suffering self-imposed servitude can never pass a day without regret. A person who obeys his Lord because of some solemn promise and thus reluctantly gains grace has stored up an injury for himself, since the prophet says, "Cursed is he who does the works of the Lord negligently."[12] If each one of you reflects on the wonderful gift of the acquired liberty that our Christ has granted to his faithful people through the regeneration of the life-giving bath [baptism] and through the pouring out of the Holy Spirit, he understands that God should not be served halfheartedly. Even though we daily give God whatever honor or gift we can, we never pay him all we owe. HOMILY 3.3.[13]

---

[8]NPNF 2 9:244-45**. [9]Minor worship services such as matins and vespers. [10]Ps 119:108 (118:108 LXX). [11]ACW 58:59. [12]Jer 48:10. [13]FC 17:318-19*.

55:1-23 PRAYER FOR HELP AGAINST CONSPIRACY

To the choirmaster: with stringed instruments. A Maskil of David.

[1]Give ear to my prayer, O God;
 and hide not thyself from my supplication!
[2]Attend to me, and answer me;

I am overcome by my trouble.
I am distraught [3]by the noise of the enemy,
 because of the oppression of the wicked.
For they bring[i] trouble upon me,
 and in anger they cherish enmity against me.

⁴My heart is in anguish within me,
　the terrors of death have fallen upon me.
⁵Fear and trembling come upon me,
　and horror overwhelms me.
⁶And I say, "O that I had wings like a dove!
　I would fly away and be at rest;
⁷yea, I would wander afar,
　I would lodge in the wilderness.　　　Selah

⁸I would haste to find me a shelter
　from the raging wind and tempest."

⁹Destroy their plans,ʲ O Lord, confuse their
　　　tongues;
　for I see violence and strife in the city.
¹⁰Day and night they go around it
　on its walls;
and mischief and trouble are within it,
　¹¹ruin is in its midst;
oppression and fraud
　do not depart from its market place.

¹²It is not an enemy who taunts me—
　then I could bear it;
it is not an adversary who deals insolently
　　　with me—
　then I could hide from him.
¹³But it is you, my equal,
　my companion, my familiar friend.
¹⁴We used to hold sweet converse together;
　within God's house we walked in fellowship.
¹⁵Let deathᵏ come upon them;
　let them go down to Sheol alive;

let them go away in terror into their graves.ˡ

¹⁶But I call upon God;
　and the LORD will save me.
¹⁷Evening and morning and at noon
　I utter my complaint and moan,
　and he will hear my voice.
¹⁸He will deliver my soul in safety
　from the battle that I wage,
　for many are arrayed against me.
¹⁹God will give ear, and humble them,
　he who is enthroned from of old;
because they keep no law,ᵐ
　and do not fear God.　　　Selah

²⁰My companion stretched out his hand against
　　　his friends,
　he violated his covenant.
²¹His speech was smoother than butter,
　yet war was in his heart;
his words were softer than oil,
　yet they were drawn swords.

²²Cast your burdenⁿ on the LORD,
　and he will sustain you;
he will never permit
　the righteous to be moved.

²³But thou, O God, wilt cast them down
　into the lowest pit;
men of blood and treachery
　shall not live out half their days.
But I will trust in thee.

---

i Cn Compare Gk: Heb *they cause to totter*　j Tg: Heb lacks *their plans*　k Or *desolations*　l Cn: Heb *evils are in their habitation, in their midst*　m Or *do not change*　n Or *what he has given you*

OVERVIEW: Christians become weary and fearful in this life because of persecution and tribulations and long to be with Christ, in whose bosom there will be everlasting relief (AUGUSTINE). Escape from the world might be aided by solitude of mind and place but is secured only in Christ, by the grace of God (AMBROSE, BEDE). It is possible to endure suffering from a recognized enemy, but it is difficult to experience injury from a friend, especially when it involves a perversion of true doctrine (BASIL, AMBROSE). In this world people can live virtuous or immoral lives and be rewarded accordingly at death, but the greatest life is life in eternity, and the best death is that which is the transition between this world and eternal life (AMBROSE).

Refusal to repent of wickedness is punished with continuation in wickedness and culminates in eternal condemnation (FULGENTIUS). To know that New Testament events, such as Judas's betrayal of Jesus, had been prophesied in the Old Testament should strengthen the faith of catechumens (RUFINUS). Heretics motivate the church to define and better understand its teachings (GREGORY THE GREAT). God's promise of help in times of adversity enables a person to bear his burdens patiently (BASIL). No one should be discouraged if he is less fortunate in this life than others because God offers his true support to everyone (BASIL, CHRYSOSTOM). No one should be so proud or foolish as to think they do not need the grace and help of God in a world full of dangers (LEO, FULGENTIUS). Only the most foolish rely on themselves, instead of on God, for the provisions of this life (ISAAC).

55:5-8 Escape from the Problems of Life

WEARINESS BELONGS TO TEMPORAL LIFE.
AUGUSTINE: And yet, persecution and tribulation had become so great that he [Paul] was weary of life itself. Fear and trembling had come on him, and darkness had enveloped him, as you have heard when it was read in the psalm. That is the voice of the body of Christ, the voice of the members of Christ. Would you like to recognize it as your own voice? Then, be one of Christ's members, and hear what the psalm says: "Fear and trembling are come on me, and darkness has covered me. And I said, Who will give me wings like a dove, and I will fly and be at rest." Is not this

similar to the cry of the apostle when he says, "so that we were weary even of life"? It is as though he were suffering weariness from the slime of the body, for he was longing to fly to Christ while the abundance of tribulations was impeding his flight without rendering it impossible. Yes, he was weary of life, weary of this life; for weariness is not to be found in the everlasting life, to which he refers when he says, "For to me to live is Christ and to die is gain."[1] SERMON 13.5.[2]

FLEE FROM THE EVILS OF THE WORLD.
AMBROSE: As for the person who wishes to be lifted up by the hand of Christ, let him first fly away himself, let him have his own wings, for one who flees from the world has wings. And if he does not have wings of his own—and perhaps only the individual who is able to fly has them—if then he does not have his own, let him get them from the one who has them. Thus a person who flees from the world does fly. "Behold, I have gone far off flying away, and I remained in the wilderness." Thus, David flew away like the night raven in the dwelling, like the lone sparrow in the house.[3] Now if you apply this to Christ, he flew away in the passion of his body, so that he could protect the peoples of the nations under the shadow of his wings.[4] He flew away from the Godhead; he remained in the body and dwelled in the desert, so that the children of the deserted wife might be more than those of her who had a husband.[5] Therefore let us seek after Christ's body that we also may rise again; for where the body is, there also will the eagles be.[6] FLIGHT FROM THE WORLD 5.30.[7]

SOLITUDE OF MIND PROVIDES ESCAPE FROM EARTHLY DESIRES. BEDE: Typologically, however, the desert where John [the Baptist] remained separated from the allurements of the world designates the lives of the saints, who, whether they live as solitaries or mingled with

---

[1]Phil 1:21. [2]FC 11:346-47. [3]Ps 102:7-8 (101:8-9 LXX, Vg.). [4]Ps 17:8 (16:8 LXX, Vg.). [5]Is 54:1; Gal 4:27. [6]Mt 24:28. [7]FC 65:304-5*.

the crowds, always reject the desires of the present world with the whole intention of their minds. They take delight in clinging only to God in the secrecy of their heart and in placing their hope in him. This solitude of mind, most dear to God, is what the prophet desired to attain with the help of the grace of the Holy Spirit when he said, "Who will give me wings as of a dove, and I will fly away and rest?" And as soon as he had secured this [solitude] by the Lord's help, he gave thanks, and as though reviling the entanglements of ordinary earthly desires, he continued, "Behold, I have withdrawn afar in flight, and I have remained in solitude."[8] HOMILIES ON THE GOSPELS 1.1.[9]

55:12-15 We Are Beset by Many Kinds of Enemies

WHO CAN BEAR TO BE REVILED BY A FRIEND? BASIL THE GREAT: But what especially strengthens us in our desire for union with you is the account of your reverences'[10] zeal for orthodoxy—the fact that neither by a vast number of treatises nor by subtlety of sophisms was your firmness of heart overcome, but that you recognized those who were making innovations contrary to the teachings of the apostles and did not consent to cover over in silence the harm done by them. Truly, we have found great grief among all those who are clinging to the peace of the Lord because of the manifold innovations of Apollinaris of Laodicea,[11] who has grieved us so much more in that he seemed to belong to our party in the beginning. In fact, any suffering from an evident enemy, even if the pain is excessive, can somehow be borne by the one afflicted, as it is written: "For if my enemy had reviled me, I would verily have borne with it." But, to experience some hurt from one who is of like spirit and an intimate friend, this is most certainly hard to bear and holds no consolation. For, him whom we had expected to have as a fellow defender of the truth, him, I say, we have now found hindering in many places those who are being saved by per-

verting their minds and drawing them away from the right doctrine. LETTER 265.[12]

NOTHING IS WORSE THAN A TREACHEROUS FRIEND. AMBROSE: So one who does the will of God is his friend and is honored with this name. He who is of one mind with him, he too is his friend. For there is unity of mind in friends, and no one is more hateful than the person who injures friendship. Hence in the traitor the Lord found this the worst point on which to condemn his treachery, namely, that Judas gave no sign of gratitude and had mingled the poison of malice at the table of friendship. So he says, "It was you, a man of like mind, my guide and my acquaintance, who ever did take pleasant meals with me." That is: it could not be endured, for you did fall on him who granted grace to you. "For if my enemy had reproached me I could have borne it, and I would have hid myself from him who hated me." An enemy can be avoided; a friend cannot, if he desires to lay a plot. Let us guard against him to whom we do not entrust our plans; we cannot guard against him to whom we have already entrusted them. And so to demonstrate all the hatefulness of the sin he did not say, You, my servant, my apostle; but you, a man of like mind with me; that is, you are not my betrayer but your own, for you did betray a man of like mind with yourself. DUTIES OF THE CLERGY 3.136.[13]

DIFFERENT WAYS TO UNDERSTAND LIVING AND DYING. AMBROSE: Putting aside, therefore, conceptions due to common usage, let us reflect on the meaning of "to live in life" and "to die in death" and also "to live in death" and "to die in life." I believe that, in accord with the Scriptures,

---

[8]Ps 55:7 (54:8 LXX, Vg.). [9]CS 110:2-3. [10]The reference is to three Egyptian bishops who had been exiled to Palestine during the Apollinarian controversy, namely, Eulogius, Alexander and Harpocration. [11]He introduced the first of the christological heresies. He denied that Christ's human nature possessed a rational human soul. He was condemned for his views at the second ecumenical council (Constantinople I) in 381. [12]FC 28:245-46. [13]NPNF 2 10:89*.

"to live in life" signifies a wonderful life of happiness and that it seems to point toward an experience of life's natural functions joined and, by participation, mingled with the grace of a blessed life. This concept, "to live in life," means "to live in virtue," to bring about in the life of this body of ours a participation in the life of blessedness. On the other hand, what does "to die in death" mean if not the disintegration of the body at the time of death, when the flesh is devoid of its customary function of carrying on life and the soul is unable to partake in life eternal? There is also the person who "dies in life," that is to say, one who is alive in body but, because of his acts, is dead. These are the people who, as the prophet says, "go down alive into hell," and she of whom the apostle speaks: "For she is dead while she is still alive."[14] There remains the fourth category, for there are those who "live in death" like the holy martyrs who give up their lives so that they may live. The flesh dies, but what is good does survive. Far from us, therefore, be the thought of living as participants in death. On the contrary, we should face death and thus become sharers in life. The saint does not desire to be a participant in this life of ours when he states, "To depart [this life] and be with Christ."[15] This has been much better stated by another: "Woe to me that my sojourning has been prolonged."[16] The psalmist was grieving because he had certain limitations due to the frailty of this life, since he hopes for a share in life eternal. Therefore I can ... state that, although "to live in life" is a good thing, "to live for life" would be of doubtful benefit. One can speak of "living for life," that is, for the life of eternity with its struggle with the life of the body. One can also speak of "living for life" in another sense. Anyone, even a pious person, can have a desire for this corporeal life of ours. We can take the example of one who thinks that he ought to live so virtuously as to arrive by his good actions at a ripe old age. Many people who are in weak health, but who still find life a pleasurable thing, are in this category. ON PARADISE 9.44.[17]

55:19-23 Cast Your Care on the Lord

PUNISHMENT IS THE REWARD OF IMPENITENCE. FULGENTIUS OF RUSPE: Just as the most holy David blames the stubbornness of miserable and unhappy people who decline to be changed from evil to good during the course of this life, so he announces the coming punishment of divine retribution, saying, "For them there is no change, and they have not feared God." And lest they who were not willing to be changed vainly promise themselves that they will receive the forgiveness of sins at the end of their earthly life, he then added, "He extended his hand in retribution." The beginning of this retribution starts when the wicked person, receiving the reward that his error demanded, by a just judgment is allowed to remain in his wickedness. The completion comes when, for these same iniquities, he will be tortured by eternal fire. Nor should this retribution be considered small by which the wicked person, deprived of the light of justice, is permitted to wander in his darkness, prejudged not by blindness of the flesh but of the heart. This also is relevant to the accumulation of retribution, if the blind person not only is unable to perceive the light but also with pleasure seeks to increase the darkness of his blindness. ON THE FORGIVENESS OF SINS 2.13.1.[18]

THE FULFILLMENT OF PROPHECIES. RUFINUS OF AQUILEIA: If it does not make you weary, let me point out, as briefly as possible, specific references to prophecy in the Gospels, so that those who are being instructed in the basic elements of the faith may have these testimonies written on their hearts, lest they should be surprised by any doubt they may entertain concerning the things that they believe. We are told in the Gospel that Judas, one of Christ's friends and associates at their last meal together, betrayed him. Let me show you how this is foretold in the Psalms: "He

---

[14]1 Tim 5:6. [15]Phil 1:23. [16]Ps 119:5 (118:5 LXX, Vg.). [17]FC 42:322-23*. [18]FC 95:167**.

who has eaten my bread has lifted up his heel against me";[19] and in another place, "My friends and my neighbors drew near and set themselves against me";[20] and again, "His words were smoother than oil, and yet they are real darts." What then is meant when it says that his words were smooth? "Judas came to Jesus and said to him, Hail, Master, and kissed him."[21] Thus through the soft blandishment of a kiss he implanted the execrable dart of betrayal. In response the Lord said to him, "Judas, do you betray the Son of Man with a kiss?"[22] You observe that he was appraised by the traitor's covetousness at thirty pieces of silver. COMMENTARY ON THE APOSTLES' CREED 20.[23]

THE CHURCH IS STRENGTHENED BY COUNTERING HERESY. GREGORY THE GREAT: Moreover there is this by the great favor of almighty God; that among those who are divided from the doctrines of the holy church there is no unity, since every kingdom divided against itself shall not stand.[24] And holy church is always more thoroughly equipped in its teaching when assaulted by the questionings of heretics; so that what was said by the psalmist concerning God against heretics is fulfilled, "They are divided from the wrath of his countenance, and his heart has drawn near." For while they are divided in their wicked error, God brings his heart near to us, because, being taught by contradictions, we more thoroughly learn to understand him. LETTER 8.2.[25]

GOD'S PROMISE OF HELP IN TIMES OF ADVERSITY. BASIL THE GREAT: All of them will stand about Job when the Judge of human life will gather together the universal church, when the trumpet that is to announce the coming of the King calls loudly to the tombs and demands the bodies that have been entrusted to their charge. Then, they who now appear to be dead will take their place before the Maker of the whole world more quickly than will the living. For this reason, I think, the Lord allotted to Job a double portion of his other wealth but judged that he would be

satisfied with the same number of children as before. Do you see how many blessings the just Job reaped from his patience? You, also, should therefore bear patiently any harm that may have come to you from yesterday's fire enkindled by a demon's treachery, and alleviate your feelings of distress over your misfortune with more courageous thoughts, in accordance with the words of the Scripture: "Cast your care on the Lord, and he will sustain you." HOMILY ON DETACHMENT 21.[26]

DO NOT BE DISCOURAGED BY EXCESSIVE BURDENS. BASIL THE GREAT: But do not lament a burden that surpasses your[27] strength. For if you were the one destined to bear this responsibility alone, it would not be merely heavy but utterly unendurable. But, if the Lord is the one who helps you bear it, "Cast your care on the Lord," and he himself will bear it. Only, let me urge you in all things to guard against this—that you be not carried along with others by wicked customs, but that through the wisdom given to you by God you change the formerly adopted evil practices into something good. For Christ has sent you, not to follow others but that you yourself may guide those who are being saved. LETTER 161.[28]

GOD OFFERS TO HELP EVERYONE. CHRYSOSTOM: With this in mind, then, let each of us apply the remedies from Scripture appropriate to ourselves. This, you see, is the reason these matters are freely proposed to everyone: people of good will are able to apply the fitting remedy to the ailment that is threatening them and secure a rapid return to health—provided someone does not resist the healing processes of the treatment but rather gives evidence of personal gratitude. There is, after all, no ailment of soul or body besetting the human race that cannot come to healing from

---

[19]Ps 41:9 (40:10 LXX, Vg.). [20]Ps 35:15 (34:15 LXX, Vg.). [21]Mt 26:49. [22]Lk 22:48. [23]NPNF 2 3:551**. [24]Lk 11:17. [25]NPNF 2 12:232. [26]FC 9:505*. [27]Amphilochius, a retired lawyer, to whom this letter was written on his consecration as bishop of Iconium. [28]FC 13:320-21*.

this source. Why is that, tell me? A person comes to this source burdened with care and the pressure of affairs and on that account is overwhelmed with despair on entering—only to hear at once the words of the inspired author, "Why are you grief-stricken, my soul, and why do you trouble me? Hope in God, for I shall praise him, my God, the help of my countenance."[29] Receiving sufficient encouragement from this, he goes away throwing off all that faintheartedness. Likewise another person is oppressed by poverty and at his last gasp, depressed at seeing others flush with money, full of their own importance and putting on airs; this person in turn hears the words of the same inspired author, "Cast your care on the Lord, and he will sustain you"; and again, "Do not worry when someone becomes rich and the luxury of his house increases, because at his death he will not take any of it with him."[30] Another person, too, is in dire straits through being subjected to scheming and calumnies and finds life insupportable, unable to find human help from any quarter; but this person too is instructed by this blessed author in the midst of such terrible difficulties not to take refuge in human resource—listen, after all, to his words, "While I remembered them in prayer, they spoke calumnies against me."[31] Do you see from what source he looks for assistance? Other people, he is saying, concoct schemes and calumnies and plots, whereas I take refuge in the unassailable rampart, in the firm anchor, in the haven waves cannot threaten—that is, in prayer, by means of which all difficulties are made light and easy for me. HOMILIES ON GENESIS 29.2.[32]

EVERYONE NEEDS GOD'S HELP. LEO THE GREAT: May human obedience never withdraw itself from the grace of God, nor may it fall from that good without which it cannot be good. If it feels anything impossible for itself or arduous in the performance of the commandments, let it not abide in itself but return to the one who commanded it, for he gives an order to excite desire and afford help, as the prophet says: "Cast your care on the Lord, and he himself will support you." Are there any so immoderately proud that they assume themselves to be so perfectly untouched and unstained that they need no renewal? Such an opinion is thoroughly mistaken, and they grow old in excessive vanity if, among the temptations of this life, they believe themselves immune from every wound. Everything is full of danger, everything full of pitfalls. Desires drive us, enticements lure us, money attracts us, loss hinders us, and the tongues of slanderers are bitter. The mouths of those who praise us are not always trustworthy; here hate rages, there a lying service deceives, so that it is easier to avoid discord than to escape falsehood. SERMON 43.1.[33]

GOD'S FREE GIFT OF GRACE. FULGENTIUS OF RUSPE: In your zeal for good works and your contempt of human praise, be careful lest you wish to assign the good that you do, not to the grace of God but to your own strength. Hold firmly that there can be no ability in you for good will or good works unless you received it by the free gift of divine mercy. Know, therefore, that it is God working in you both to will and to do, for a good will. Accordingly, work out your salvation in fear and trembling. Humble yourself in the sight of God that he may exalt you. Ask from him the beginning of a good will. Ask from him the effects of good works. Seek from him the gift of perseverance. Do not think at any time that you can either will or do anything good, once his assistance has ceased. Ask him to turn away your eyes lest they see vanity; ask him to show you the way in which you should walk; petition him to direct your steps according to his word, and let no wickedness rule over you. Pray to him that he direct the works of your hands for you. "Be strong and let your heart take courage; wait for the Lord."[34] LETTER 2.36.[35]

---

[29]Ps 42:5-6 (41:6-7 LXX). [30]Ps 49:16-17 (48:17-18 LXX). [31]Ps 109:4 (108:4 LXX). [32]FC 82:199-200. [33]FC 93:186. [34]Ps 27:14 (26:14 LXX, Vg.); Ps 55:22 (54:23 LXX, Vg.). [35]FC 95:309.

RELY ON GOD FOR THE NECESSITIES OF LIFE.
ISAAC OF NINEVEH: If you believe that God
makes provision for you, why be anxious and concerned about temporal affairs and the needs of
your flesh? But if you do not believe that God
makes provision for you, and for this reason you
take pains to provide for your need separately
from Him, then you are the most wretched of all
men. Why even be alive or go on living in such a
case? "Cast thy care upon the Lord, and He will
nourish thee," and you shall never be dismayed at
any terror that overtakes you.[36] ASCETICAL HOM-
ILIES 5.[37]

---

[36]See Prov 3:25. [37]AHSIS 45.

56:1-13 TRUST THE MERCY OF GOD
IN THE MIDST OF FEAR

*To the choirmaster: according to
The Dove on Far-off Terebinths. A
Miktam of David, when the Philistines
seized him in Gath.*

*¹Be gracious to me, O God, for men trample
    upon me;
  all day long foemen oppress me;
²my enemies trample upon me all day long,
  for many fight against me proudly.
³When I am afraid,
  I put my trust in thee.
⁴In God, whose word I praise,
  in God I trust without a fear.
  What can flesh do to me?*

*⁵All day long they seek to injure my cause;
  all their thoughts are against me for evil.
⁶They band themselves together, they lurk,
  they watch my steps.
As they have waited for my life,*

*⁷so recompense[o] them for their crime;
  in wrath cast down the peoples, O God!*

*⁸Thou hast kept count of my tossings;
  put thou my tears in thy bottle!
  Are they not in thy book?
⁹Then my enemies will be turned back
  in the day when I call.
  This I know, that[p] God is for me.
¹⁰In God, whose word I praise,
  in the LORD, whose word I praise,
¹¹in God I trust without a fear.
  What can man do to me?*

*¹²My vows to thee I must perform, O God;
  I will render thank offerings to thee.
¹³For thou hast delivered my soul from death,
  yea, my feet from falling,
that I may walk before God
  in the light of life.*

o Cn: Heb *deliver* p Or *because*

Overview: There is a marked difference between
people who live by God's standards and those
who live by human standards (AUGUSTINE). The
church is constantly assailed by the devil, who

never wearies in his wiley efforts to destroy it (CASSIODORUS). In this life of vanity, uncertainty and stormy conditions, we know that God saves us by his mercy in Jesus Christ (JEROME). When God saves a person from his enemies, he does so not because of human merits but because of the justification won by Christ and given through grace (AUGUSTINE). We praise God for what he accomplishes in our hearts and minds through those who proclaim his Word (AUGUSTINE).

56:1-2 The Enemies of God's People

TRAMPLED BY THOSE WHO LIVE BY HUMAN STANDARDS. AUGUSTINE: And what is the drift of what we have just been singing to the Lord in the psalm? "Have mercy on me, Lord, because man has trampled on me." "Man" means whoever lives according to merely human criteria. Well, anyway, those who live according to God's standards are told, "You are gods, and all of you sons of the Most High."[1] But to the reprobate, who were called to be children of God but preferred rather merely to be human, that is, to live only according to human standards, "you," it says, "shall die like people and fall like one of the princes."[2] Surely the fact that we human beings are mortal should serve to teach us our place, not to make us boastful. What does a worm, which is due to die tomorrow, have to boast about? SERMON 97.2.[3]

SATAN IS THE CHURCH'S UNRELENTING ENEMY. CASSIODORUS: "Have mercy on me, O Lord, for man has trodden me underfoot: All day long he has afflicted me by warring against me." Virgin mother church, who begets the faithful without losing her virginity, begs her heavenly Bridegroom with devoted tears not to allow her to be afflicted by the enemy, for she is known to be still surrounded by the calamity of this world. "Has trodden" renews the metaphor of the winepress in the heading,[4] for the harder the grapes are trodden, the more wine is squeezed out. "Man" here simply signifies the devil; as the Lord

says of him in the Gospel, "The hostile man who sowed the weeds is the devil."[5] Next comes "All day long he has afflicted me by warring against me." The holy church is describing what she suffers in this world, for we know that she endures struggles with the devil without any relief. As Paul says, "Our wrestling is not against flesh and blood but against the principalities and powers of this darkness."[6] This is an oppressive war because it is secret; the fighting is difficult because the struggle is with one who is stronger. How difficult it is to wrestle with an enemy whose nets we do not see! Morever, our enemy does not weary of toil, nor does he at any time depart when overcome. He returns all the more oppressively if by divine grace we have been able to conquer him. We speak of war figuratively by *antiphrasis*,[7] just as we speak of the grove without light[8] and of the fishpond without fish. So let none of the faithful complain that he is troubled by the incessant wiles of the devil, for if we wish to belong to Christ we must always endure the enmity of the devil in this life. EXPOSITIONS OF THE PSALMS 55.2.[9]

56:7 Divine Grace Precedes Human Merit

REFUGE FROM THE TEMPEST IS FOUND IN THE POWER OF GOD. JEROME: For God has made our days short, and our substance is as nothing in his sight. "All things are vanity, everyone living,"[10] whether living in the body or living in virtues, and yet all things are vanity. His condition is one of fluctuation and uncertainty, and, while he does not fear, he suffers a storm in fair weather. For when he was in honor, he did not understand; he

---

[1]Ps 82:6 (81:6 LXX, Vg.). [2]Ps 82:7 (81:7 LXX, Vg.). [3]WSA 3 4:36-37**. [4]The heading of the psalm reads, "Unto the end, for a people that is removed at a distance from the saints, David, in the inscription of the title, when the Philistines held him in Gath." Gath (a city) denotes "winepress" (ACW 52:30). [5]Mt 13:39. [6]Eph 6:12. [7]A figure of speech in which the meaning of the words is the opposite of their generally accepted meaning. [8]Antiphrasis is a figure of speech that was often exemplified by ancient authorities with the expression *lucus quid non lucet*. Compare references to Diomedes and Charisius in Lewis and Short, *Latin Dictionary*. [9]ACW 52:31*. [10]Ps 39:6 (38:6 LXX, Vg.).

has been compared with senseless beasts and is created similar to them.[11] "For nothing," he says, "shall he save them" (a reference, undoubtedly, to the just who are saved not through their own merit but through the mercy of God), "and my offenses are not hidden from you."[12] These words are spoken in the person of Christ. If he, who did not sin nor was guile found in his mouth, suffered for us and bore our sins, how much more ought we to confess our faults? "My soul," he says, "refused to be comforted,"[13] considering the sins that I had committed. "I remembered God and was delighted,"[14] knowing that I was to be saved by his mercy. "I meditated in the night with my own heart, and I swept my soul. And I said, 'Now I have begun, this is the change of the right hand of the Most High.'"[15] These are the words of a just person who, after meditating in his sleep and feeling pangs of conscience, says in the end, "Now I have begun," either to do penance[16] or to enter the threshold of knowledge; and this very change from good to better is a change not of my own strength but of the right hand and power of God. AGAINST THE PELAGIANS 2.19.[17]

WE ARE SAVED ON THE BASIS OF GRACE, NOT MERIT. AUGUSTINE: You see, "he was handed over on account of our sins, and rose again on account of our justification."[18] Your justification, your circumcision, does not come from you. "It is by grace that you have been saved through faith; and this not from yourselves, but it is God's gift; not from works."[19] In case by any chance you should say, "I deserved it, that is why I received it." Do not think you received it by deserving it, because you would not deserve it unless you had received it. Grace came before your deserving or merit; it is not grace coming from merit but merit from grace. Because if grace comes from merit, it

means you have bought it, not received it free, *gratis*, for nothing. "For nothing," it says, "you will save them." What is the meaning of "for nothing you will save them"? You can find no reason in them to save them, and yet you save them. You give for nothing, you save for nothing. You precede all merits, so that my merits follow your gifts. Of course, you give for nothing, save for nothing, since you can find no reason for saving and many reasons for condemning. SERMON 169.3.[20]

56:10 *Praise the Word of God*

WE PRAISE THE LORD FOR WHAT HE DOES. AUGUSTINE: We heard the readings of the Scriptures while they were being recited. That is the material that has been given me to talk about. That is what I have to understand, that is from what I have to sow what wisdom I have gotten, with the help of him in whose hand, as it is written, are both "we and our words."[21] Nor is it simply pointless, what is written somewhere else: "I will praise the word, in the Lord I will praise the word." What is praised in the Lord is what the Lord gives. So although I am fairly feeble, I am for all that his instrument. I grasp what I can; I share without grudging what I grasp. May he make good in your minds whatever I have done less well, because even what I do manage to convey to your ears is not worth anything, is it, unless he does the whole work in your minds? SERMON 48.1.[22]

---

[11]See Ps 49:20 (48:21 LXX, Vg.). [12]Ps 69:5 (68:6 LXX, Vg.). [13]Ps 77:2 (76:3 LXX, Vg.). [14]Ps 77:3 (76:4 LXX, Vg.). [15]Ps 77:6, 10 (76:7, 11 LXX, Vg.). [16]Penance in the early church involved confession of sins, performing some good works or spiritual discipline and then receiving absolution. [17]FC 53:325-26*. [18]Rom 4:25 [19]Eph 2:8-9. [20]WSA 3 5:223-24. [21]Wis 7:16. [22]WSA 3 2:327*.

57:1-11 A Prayer for Deliverance

To the choirmaster: according to Do
Not Destroy. A Miktam of David, when
he fled from Saul, in the cave.

1*Be merciful to me, O God, be merciful to me,*
for in thee my soul takes refuge;
in the shadow of thy wings I will take refuge,
till the storms of destruction pass by.
2*I cry to God Most High,*
to God who fulfils his purpose for me.
3*He will send from heaven and save me,*
he will put to shame those who trample
upon me. Selah
God will send forth his steadfast love and his
faithfulness!

4*I lie in the midst of lions*
that greedily devour[q] *the sons of men;*
their teeth are spears and arrows,
their tongues sharp swords.
5*Be exalted, O God, above the heavens!*
Let thy glory be over all the earth!

6*They set a net for my steps;*
my soul was bowed down.
They dug a pit in my way,
but they have fallen into it themselves
Selah
7*My heart is steadfast, O God,*
my heart is steadfast!
I will sing and make melody!
8*Awake, my soul!*
Awake, O harp and lyre!
I will awake the dawn!
9*I will give thanks to thee, O Lord, among the*
peoples;
I will sing praises to thee among the nations.
10*For thy steadfast love is great to the heavens,*
thy faithfulness to the clouds.

11*Be exalted, O God, above the heavens!*
Let thy glory be over all the earth!

q Cn: Heb *are aflame*

Overview: Because of sin we live in constant need of forgiveness and must daily pray for God's mercy. In heaven we will have protection even though we will need no shelter. Sins committed by the tongue are equal to those committed by the hands (Augustine). The tongue can be used for evil, and its wrongful use can contribute to our doom (Athanasius). Members of the body, such as the tongue, can be used for good or evil (Chrysostom). God protects us from the assaults of our spiritual enemies by the assurance that he will judge us righteous (Rufinus). If we urge others to do evil, we are as guilty as they (Augustine).

We cannot know the truth of God's Word unless God opens our eyes. In our worship it is the Son, not the Father, who is exalted (Augustine). The psalmist foresaw the fulfillment of God's promise to send his Son into the world (Bede). Satan leads people astray by directing their attention to temporal, earthly things (Augustine). God strengthens the will of those whose faith is tested by evil, even martyrdom (Caesarius).

57:1-4 *Need for God's Mercy and Right Conduct*

Everyone, Even the Most Saintly, Needs to Pray. Augustine: So let us call out to him what we have just been singing: "Have mercy on me, God, have mercy on me because in you my soul has put its trust." "Have mercy on me, God," he says. Why? "Because in you my soul has put its trust." This, he says, is the sacrifice I offer you, so that you may hear me: "because in you my soul has put its trust. Whoever hoped in the Lord and was left in the lurch?"[1] Even great saints are subject to temptation, and however much progress we make in God, we live in need of pardon. Was it little lambs and not the rams of the flock that the Lord Jesus taught how to pray? It was his disciples, our apostles, the very leaders of the flock, whose children we are, of whom it is said, "Bring to the Lord the children of rams";[2] yes, it was these rams he was teaching to pray, when he told them to say, "Forgive us our debts."[3] If this is a daily prayer, then we live in need of pardon. All our sins were forgiven us in baptism, and we live in need of pardon. We make progress if our hope is nourished in God and strengthened by his aid to enable us to put a brake on all covetousness. Let us keep on fighting; our struggles are known to him, and he knows how to be both a spectator and a helper. SERMON 77A.1.[4]

BE CHARITABLE IN THIS WORLD. AUGUSTINE: You will not be able to move to the good place from the bad place unless you do good in the bad place. What sort of place is that other? One where nobody goes hungry. So if you want to live in the good place where nobody goes hungry, in this world "share your food with the hungry."[5] Because in that blessed place nobody is a foreigner, and all are living in their own native land; so if you wish to be in the good place, whenever in this bad place you find a foreigner who has nowhere to go, welcome him into your home. Show hospitality in the bad place, in order to get to the place where you cannot be a "guest worker." In the good place nobody is in need of clothes; there is no cold weather there, nor hot weather. What need of shelter, what need of clothing? There will be no shelters there, but there will be protection; so in fact even there we

find shelter: "under the shadow of your wings will I hope." So in this bad place provide shelter for the person who has none, so that you may find yourself in the good place, where you can enjoy such shelter that you need never want to patch your thatched roof. After all, there are no showers of rain there but instead a perennial fountain of truth. But the shower from this [fountain] makes you glad, not wet; this shower is the fountain of life itself. What is the meaning of "Lord, with you is the fountain of life"?[6] It means, "And the Word was with God."[7] SERMON 217.5.[8]

EVIL IS SHARPER THAN A TWO-EDGED SWORD. ATHANASIUS: One thing you can count on: Corruption does not save those who get into it. On the contrary, it sets itself up against them, tears them down and brings about their doom. Woe to those people against whom this prophecy is written! For the evil they pursue is sharper than a two-edged sword, and it will first slay those who lay hold of it. Even their own tongue, as the psalmist points out, "is a sharp sword, and their teeth are spears and arrows." FESTAL LETTERS 9.[9]

THE TONGUE CAN BE A WEAPON FOR SIN OR JUSTICE. CHRYSOSTOM: Casting away therefore all anxiety and superfluous care, let us return to ourselves; and let us adorn the body and the soul with the ornament of virtue; converting our bodily members into instruments of righteousness and not instruments of sin.

And first of all, let us discipline our tongue to be the minister of the grace of the Spirit, expelling from the mouth all bitterness and malice and the practice of using disgraceful words. For it is in our power to make each one of our members an instrument of wickedness or of righteousness. Hear then how people make the tongue an instrument, some of sin, others of righteousness!

[1]Sir 2:10. [2]Ps 29:1 (28:1 LXX, Vg.). [3]Mt 6:12. [4]WSA 3 3:327. [5]Is 58:7. [6]Ps 36:9 (35:10 LXX, Vg.). [7]Jn 1:1. [8]WSA 3 6:180*. [9]ARL 151-52.

"Their tongue is a sharp sword." But another speaks thus of his own tongue: "My tongue is the pen of a ready writer."[10] The former worked destruction; the latter wrote the divine law. So one was a sword, the other a pen, not according to its own nature but according to the choice of those who employed it. For the nature of this tongue and of that was the same, but the operation was not the same. HOMILIES CONCERNING THE STATUES 4.10-11.[11]

HOW TO ENDURE FALSE CHARGES. RUFINUS OF AQUILEIA: I have read the document[12] sent from the East by our friend and good brother to a distinguished member of the Senate, Pammachius, which you have copied and forwarded to me. It brought to my mind the words of the prophet: "The sons of men whose teeth are spears and arrows and their tongue a sharp sword." But for these wounds that people inflict on one another with the tongue we can hardly find a physician; so I have turned to Jesus, the heavenly physician, and he has brought out for me from the medicine chest of the gospel an antidote of sovereign power; he has assuaged the violence of my grief with the assurance of the righteous judgment that I shall have at his hands. The potion that our Lord dispensed to me was nothing else than these words: "Blessed are you when people persecute you and say all manner of evil against you falsely. Rejoice and leap for joy, for great is your reward in heaven, for so persecuted they the prophets who were before you."[13] With this medicine I was content, and, as far as the matter concerned me, I had determined for the future to keep silence; for I said to myself, "If they have called the master of the house Beelzebub, how much more them of his household?" (that is, you and me, unworthy though we are). And, if it was said of him, "He is a deceiver, he deceives the people," I must not be indignant if I hear that I am called a heretic and that the name of mole is applied to me because of the slowness of my mind or indeed my blindness. Christ who is my Lord, yes, and who is God over all, was called "a gluttonous man and a drunkard,

a friend of publicans and sinners." How can I, then, be angry when I am called a carnal man who lives in luxury? APOLOGY 1.1.[14]

UNGODLY VOICES SHOUTED, "CRUCIFY HIM." AUGUSTINE: But if, after all these preceding actions of yours,[15] you also shouted, "Crucify, crucify," hear what the prophet also shouts against you, "The sons of men, their teeth are weapons and arrows, their tongue a sharpened sword." See with what weapons, with what arrows, with what sword you have put to death a just man when you said that it was not lawful for you to put anyone to death. So it is that, although the chief priests had not come themselves but had sent others to arrest Jesus, the Evangelist Luke in the same place in his narrative said, "But Jesus said to those who had come to him," namely, "the chief priests and the magistrates of the temple and the elders, 'Have you come out, as it were, against a thief?'" and so on. Since, therefore, the chief priests [came] not themselves but in those whom they have sent for arresting Jesus, what else does it mean than that they themselves came in their power of giving the order? So all who shouted with ungodly voices for him to be crucified, they themselves killed him, not indeed by themselves but yet by him who was driven to this sacrilegious crime by their shouting. TRACTATES ON THE GOSPEL OF JOHN 114.4.[16]

WE SIN BY ENCOURAGING OTHERS TO SIN. AUGUSTINE: See the kind of murder, brothers.[17]

---

[10]Ps 45:1 (44:2 LXX). [11]NPNF 1 9:369. [12]This letter was written to Apronianus, a friend of Rufinus's and a convert to the Christian faith, in reply to Jerome's letter to Pammachius (*Epistle* 84)—the document referred to here. The context of Jerome's letter and Rufinus's response is the Origenistic controversy of the fourth century—specifically Rufinus's translation of Origen's *On First Principles.* Jerome accused Rufinus of altering Origen's writing so that it would be more orthodox. [13]Mt 5:10-12. [14]NPNF 2 3:435*. [15]Jews who demanded Pontius Pilate to sentence Jesus to death. [16]FC 92:18-19**. [17]In reference to John 8:44 in the preceding section, Augustine is speaking of Satan as the one who motivated the religious leaders to plot Jesus' death and the one who was responsible for the death of Adam and Eve by tempting them to sin.

The devil is called a murderer, not armed with a sword, not girded with a weapon; he came to humankind, he planted an evil word, and he killed him. Do not, then, think that you are not a murderer when you persuade your brother to do evils; if you persuade your brother to do evils, you kill him. And, that you may know that you kill him, hear the psalm: "The sons of men, their teeth are weapons and arrows, their tongue a sharp sword." TRACTATES ON THE GOSPEL OF JOHN 42.11.2.[18]

57:5 God Is to Be Exalted

GOD OPENS OUR EYES TO THE TRUTH OF HIS WORD. AUGUSTINE: In the same way I too was having the truth about the catholic church, as it is spread throughout the whole world, dinned into me from every side by the words of the divine Scriptures; and the false accusations about the betrayers leveled against it by my relatives made me deaf.[19] I am not comparing myself with Paul's merits but with his sins. Even if I have not been found worthy to be as good as he was, still, before receiving the remedy of correction, I was not as bad. He failed to recognize the bridegroom in the books he read, and I failed to recognize the bride. The one who revealed to him what is written about Christ's glorification, "Be exalted over the heavens, God," also revealed to me what follows about the spread of the church: "over the whole earth your glory."[20] The evidence of both texts is plain to those who can see but hidden from the blind. It was the baptism of Christ that opened his eyes, the peace of Christ that opened mine. He was made new by the washing of the holy water; whereas it was charity that covered the multitude of my sins. SERMON 360.[21]

CHRIST IS EXALTED ABOVE THE HEAVENS. AUGUSTINE: Call to mind the psalm.[22] To whom was it said, "Be exalted above the heavens, O God"?[23] Who was being spoken to? It would not be said to God the Father, would it, "be exalted," seeing that he has never been brought low? No,

you are exalted, you who were enclosed in your mother's womb; you who were made in her whom you had made; you who lay in the manger; you, suckled at the breast as a baby, according to the very nature of flesh; you, holding up the world and being held by your mother; you, the baby acknowledged by Simeon the old man and praised as great; you, seen by the widow Anna being suckled and acknowledged as almighty; you, who were hungry for our sakes, thirsty for our sakes, tired along the road for our sakes—did you ever hear of bread being hungry, a fountain being thirsty, a road being tired?—you who endured all these things on our account; you who went to sleep, and yet you "slumber not, watching over Israel";[24] you, finally, whom Judas sold, whom the Jews bought and did not gain possession of; you, arrested, bound, scourged, crowned with thorns, hung on the tree, pierced with the lance, you dead, you buried: "be exalted above the heavens, O God." SERMON 262.4.[25]

WE RESPOND IN PRAYER. BEDE: Amos too speaks of the glory of the humanity [Christ] had assumed: "He who builds a means of ascent in heaven and founds his promise on earth."[26] He built a means of ascent in heaven when he created for himself a human body and soul in which he would be able to mount up to heaven. He founded his promise on earth when by sending the Spirit from above he filled all the ends of the earth with the gift of his faith, as he had promised. The psalmist, foreseeing in his spirit that the gift of this promise would come and desiring that it come quickly, said, "Be exalted, O God, above the heavens, and let your glory be over all the earth!" Here he clearly means that before our

---

[18]FC 88:157. [19]In this brief sermon regarding a Donatist heretic who returned to the true faith, Augustine contrasts his life before and after his conversion and notes that before his conversion he was influenced by the anti-Christian views and accusations of his pagan relatives. [20]Ps 57:5, 11 (56:6, 12 LXX, Vg.). [21]WSA 3 10:222-23. [22]The responsorial psalm that had just been sung. The verse he quotes is the refrain of the psalm. [23]Ps 57:5, 11 (56:6, 12 LXX, Vg.). [24]Ps 121:4 (120:4 LXX, Vg.). [25]WSA 3 7:217. [26]Amos 9:6.

Redeemer assumed a mortal body and demolished the kingdom of death, "God was known only in Judah, and in Israel was his name great."[27] But when the God-man arose from the dead and penetrated the heights of heaven, then the glory of his name was proclaimed and believed throughout the whole wide world. HOMILIES ON THE GOSPELS 2.15.[28]

57:6-8 Faithful in the Midst of Dangers

THE HOSTS OF SATAN SEEK TO DESTROY OUR SOULS. AUGUSTINE: We heard the apostle telling us, "We are ambassadors for Christ, exhorting you to be reconciled with God."[29] He would not be exhorting us to be reconciled unless we had been enemies. So the whole world was the Savior's enemy, the captor's friend; that is, God's enemy, the devil's friend. And the whole human race, like this woman,[30] was bent over and bowed down to the ground. There is someone who already understands these enemies, and he cries out against them and says to God, "They have bowed my soul down." The devil and his angels have bowed the souls of men and women down to the ground; that is, have bent them forward to be intent on temporal and earthly things and stop them from seeking the things that are above.[31] SERMON 162B.[32]

A STEADFAST HEART EQUALS A STRONG WILL. CAESARIUS OF ARLES: Our Lord Jesus Christ gave great assurance to his witnesses, that is, to the martyrs who, on account of their human weakness, were worried that perhaps they would perish after death if they died while confessing him. He did this by telling them, "Not a hair of your head will be harmed."[33] Are you, whose hair will not be harmed, afraid of perishing? If inconsequential things in your life are protected in this way, under how much protection is your soul? A hair, which you do not feel when it is cut, does not perish; does the soul, through which you feel, perish? To be sure, he foretold that they were going to suffer many difficult circumstances, in order that by his prediction he might make them stronger. They said, then, to him, "My heart is steadfast." What does this mean, "My heart is steadfast," except that my will is strong? In their martyrdom the martyrs had their will steadfast, but "their will was made steadfast by the Lord."[34] As they thought about the future harsh and difficult evils, he added, "By patient endurance you will save your lives."[35] By patient endurance, he said, for patient endurance would not be there if your will were not in it. "In patient endurance," but where does ours come from? Both what we possess and what is given to us are ours, for if it were not ours, it would not be given to us. How do you give something to another, unless it comes to belong to the one to whom you are giving it? That confession is revealed: "Will not my soul be subject to God? For from him comes my patience."[36] He himself tells us, "In patient endurance." Let us also say to him, "From him comes my hope." He made it yours by giving it to you; do not be ungrateful by attributing it to yourself. SERMON 226.1.[37]

---

[27]Ps 76:1 (75:2 LXX, Vg.). [28]CS 111:143-44. [29]2 Cor 5:20. [30]The woman who could not stand up straight (Lk 13:11-17) but was healed by Jesus. [31]See Col 3:1. [32]*WSA* 3 5:167. [33]Lk 21:18. [34]See Prov 8:35. [35]Lk 21:19. [36]See Ps 62:1 (61:2 LXX, Vg.). [37]FC 66:156-57*.

58:1-11 A PRAYER FOR JUSTICE

*To the choirmaster: according to Do Not
Destroy. A Miktam of David.*

¹*Do you indeed decree what is right, you gods?*ˢ
  Do you judge the sons of men uprightly?
²*Nay, in your hearts you devise wrongs;*
  your hands deal out violence on earth.

³*The wicked go astray from the womb,*
  they err from their birth, speaking lies.
⁴*They have venom like the venom of a serpent,*
  like the deaf adder that stops its ear,
⁵*so that it does not hear the voice of charmers*
  or of the cunning enchanter.

⁶*O God, break the teeth in their mouths;*
  tear out the fangs of the young lions, O LORD!
⁷*Let them vanish like water that runs away;*

like grass let them be trodden down
  *and wither.*ᵗ
⁸*Let them be like the snail which dissolves into
  slime,*
  *like the untimely birth that never sees
  the sun.*
⁹*Sooner than your pots can feel the heat of
  thorns,*
  *whether green or ablaze, may he sweep
  them away!*

¹⁰*The righteous will rejoice when he sees the
  vengeance;*
  *he will bathe his feet in the blood of
  the wicked.*
¹¹*Men will say, "Surely there is a reward for
  the righteous;*
  surely there is a God who judges on earth."

s Or *mighty lords*   **t** Cn: Heb *uncertain*

OVERVIEW: A distinction must be made between judging and condemning, with Christians having the right to judge people, if done fairly and within certain boundaries; but only God has the right of eternal condemnation (AUGUSTINE). Human beings, who are sinful from conception, need a circumcision in spirit, not in the flesh. God will defeat the forces of evil (JEROME). The enemies of Christ reject testimonies about his divine majesty (AUGUSTINE). Sin, which affects all humanity, resulted from the cunningness and deception of Satan (AMBROSE). Sin has affected the depth of the soul and has become a malignant disease, which we try either to hide or excuse (GREGORY NAZIANZUS). When God follows through on his threats to punish evil, he motivates others to fear him and to live more God-pleasing lives (CHRYSOSTOM). God vents his wrath on the wicked so that others may be led to repentance and give thanks to him for his great mercy toward them (AUGUSTINE).

58:1 *Judge Other People Justly*

BE CAREFUL IN JUDGING OTHERS. AUGUSTINE: How, then, did Christ say, "All things that I have heard from the Father I have made known to you,"[1] except in this way, that what he was certainly going to accomplish through the Holy Spirit, he spoke to us as if he had already accomplished it? Therefore, whenever we hear that one who believes in Christ will not be judged, we are to understand that he will not be condemned. The word *judged* is used in place of "condemned,"

---

[1]Jn 15:15.

as where the apostle says, "Let not him who does not eat condemn him who eats,"[2] that is, let him not think evil of him. And the Lord says, "Do not judge that you may not be judged."[3] He does not take from us the power to judge, since the prophet also declares, "If you truly love justice, judge right things, O sons of men." And the Lord says, "Judge not according to personal considerations, but render a just judgment."[4] But, in that passage where he forbids judging, he admonishes us not to condemn a person whose purpose is hidden from us, or when we do not know how a person will turn out later on. Accordingly, when he said, "He shall not come to judgment,"[5] he meant that he will not come to damnation. And in saying "but he who does not believe is already judged," he meant that such a person stands already condemned in the foreknowledge of God, who knows what is in store for nonbelievers. Christian Combat 27.29.[6]

58:3-9 Original Sin

Everyone Is a Sinner and Needs God's Mercy. Jerome: Atticus:[7] I grant you that they are just men, but I cannot agree with you at all that they are without sin. For I say that humanity can be without fault, which in Greek is called *kakia* ["wickedness"], but I deny that it is *anamartētos* ["faultless"], that is to say *sine peccato* ["without sin"]. For this is a virtue that befits God alone; and every creature is subject to sin and stands in need of the mercy of God, as Scripture says: "The earth is full of the mercy of the Lord."[8] And lest I seem to be discussing certain little faults, so to speak, of the saints, into which they slipped through error, I shall produce a few testimonies that refer not to individuals but rather to all people in general. In the thirty-first psalm, it is written, "I said I will confess against myself my injustice to the Lord, and you have forgiven the wickedness of my heart."[9] And it continues immediately, "For this" (that is to say, for this impiety or iniquity, for both words can be understood in this passage) "shall everyone that

is holy pray to you in a seasonable time."[10] If one is holy, what is his reason for praying for forgiveness of his iniquity? If one has iniquity, in what sense is he called holy? In the sense, to be sure, that it is also written in another place: "A just person shall fall seven times and shall rise again."[11] And, "The just is accuser of himself in the beginning of his speech."[12] And in another place: "The wicked are alienated from the womb, they have gone astray from the womb, they have spoken false things." They became sinful at the very moment they were born in the likeness of Adam's sin, who was a figure of the one who was to come, or at the moment when Christ was born of a virgin. It has been written about him: "Every one who opens the womb shall be called holy to the Lord."[13] Against the Pelagians 2.4.[14]

God Will Defeat the Forces of Evil. Jerome: Therefore, having been taught by these examples,[15] I did not want to bite back at him who bites back at me or to retaliate in kind; and I chose rather to charm out the fury of a madman[16] by incantation and to pour the antidote of a single look into a poisoned heart. But I am afraid that my efforts are in vain and that I shall be forced to sing the well-known song of David and console myself with these words: "The sinners are alienated from the assembly; they have gone astray from the womb; they have spoken false things. Their madness is according to the likeness of a serpent, like the deaf asp that stops its ears, which will not hear the voice of the charmers nor of the wizard that charms wisely. God shall break in pieces their teeth in their mouths; the Lord shall break the teeth of the lions. They shall come to nothing, like water running down; he has bent his bow until they are weakened. Like wax that melts, they shall be taken

[2]Rom 14:3. [3]Mt 7:1. [4]Jn 7:24. [5]Jn 5:24. [6]FC 2:344*. [7]This book is in the form of a dialogue between Atticus, a true believer and supporter of Augustine's theology, and Critobulus, a Pelagian heretic. [8]Ps 33:5 (32:5 LXX, Vg.). [9]Ps 32:5 (31:5 LXX, Vg.). [10]Ps 32:6 (31:6 LXX, Vg.). [11]Prov 24:16. [12]Prov 18:17. [13]Lk 2:23; Ex 13:2; 34:19. [14]FC 53:298-99. [15]Jerome is referring to passages previously cited from Proverbs 25-30, such as Proverbs 25:18, 26:2; 4:5; etc. [16]Rufinus.

away: fire has fallen on them, and they have not seen the sun." And again: "The just shall rejoice when he shall see the revenge of the wicked; he shall wash his hands in the blood of the sinner."[17] And people shall say, "If, indeed, there is a reward to the just, there is, indeed, a God who judges them on the earth."[18] AGAINST RUFINUS 3.43.[19]

LIKE DEAF SNAKES WHO BLOCK THEIR EARS. AUGUSTINE: The heavens were opened, and Stephen saw the chief of martyrs; he saw Jesus standing at the Father's right hand; he saw, so that he would not keep quiet. As for his persecutors, they could not see, but they could be envious; and the reason they did not see was that they were envious.[20] As for Stephen, he did not keep quiet about what he saw, in order to reach the one whom he saw. "Behold," he said, "I can see the heavens opened, and the Son of man standing at the right hand of majesty."[21] Immediately they covered their ears, as against a blasphemy. You can recognize them in the psalm: "Like the deaf cobra," it says, "that blocks its ears, in order not to hear the voice of the charmer and the spell cast by the wise one."[22] Just as snakes, you see, in order to avoid bursting out and leaving their dens when they are being charmed, are said to press one ear to the ground and block the other with their tails—and yet the charmer brings them out. So also Stephen's persecutors were still hissing in their dens, while seething in their hearts. They were not yet bursting out; they blocked their ears. Let them burst out now, let them show what they really are; let them rush for the stones. They rushed, they stoned him. SERMON 316.2.[23]

THE WILINESS OF SATAN. AMBROSE: Though it appears that the serpent's nature is being delineated in the foregoing,[24] rather, every vessel of evil is being delineated, and every serpent of depravity who casts himself down on the belly and hides his poison inside himself and ponders it inwardly in his breast. He[25] is slippery in his thoughts, he advances in his deceits and wraps himself in his deceptions; he is always moving

and stirring his poisons by thought and treading on his belly as well, that is, the seedbed of his heart. For this reason, David fittingly says, "Sinners are alienated from the womb; they have gone astray from the womb; they have spoken false things. Their madness is according to the likeness of a serpent, like the deaf asp that stops its ears, that will not hear the voice of the charmers or of the wizard that are invoked by the wise person."[26] For this reason, the statement that we read in the prophetic book also seems fitting, "My heart, my heart is in pain!"[27] For wickedness exists there, where there ought to be guiltlessness; what should be more calm in us experiences the greater suffering. It is trodden down by the footsteps of evil, pricked by its claws and agitated by a kind of advance and increase of depravity where there exists the procreative seed of an everlasting posterity. FLIGHT FROM THE WORLD 7.42.[28]

THE VOICE OF THE CHARMER. GREGORY OF NAZIANZUS: We hide away our sin, cloaking it over in the depth of our soul, like some festering and malignant disease, as if by escaping human notice we could escape the mighty eye of God and justice. Or else we make excuses for our sins[29] by devising pleas in defense of our falls or by tightly closing our ears. Like the snake that stops its ears, we are obstinate in refusing to hear the voice of the charmer and be treated with the medicines of wisdom, by which spiritual sickness is healed. IN DEFENSE OF HIS FLIGHT TO PONTUS, ORATION 2.20.[30]

58:10-11 *The Judgment and Mercy of God*

GOD'S THREATS OF PUNISHMENT ARE NOT

---

[17]Ps 58:10 (57:11 LXX, Vg.). [18]Ps 58:11 (57:12 LXX, Vg.). [19]FC 53:219-20**. [20]An untranslatable play on words: *Non illi videbant, sed invidebant; et ideo non videbant, quia invidebant.* [21]Acts 7:55. [22]Ps 58:4-5 (57:5-6 LXX, Vg.). [23]WSA 3 9:138*. [24]See Gen 3:14 (LXX). [25]The serpent, who represents Satan. [26]The last part of the quotation is Ambrose's translation of the words *para sophou* ("from a wise man"), which occur in the Septuagint. [27]Jer 4:19. [28]FC 65:312-13*. [29]Ps 141:4 (140:4 LXX). [30]NPNF 2 7:209*.

VAIN THREATS. CHRYSOSTOM: And do you wish that I should speak of another instance of God's goodness? It is not only this,[31] but that he does not allow the good to become bad. For if they were destined to meet with the same things, they would all be bad. But now this also greatly consoles the good. For hear the prophet, saying, "The righteous shall rejoice when he sees the vengeance on the ungodly; he shall wash his hands in the blood of the sinner." Not rejoicing on account of it, God forbid, but fearing that he might suffer the same things, he will render his own life more pure. This then is a mark of God's great care. Yes, you say, but he ought only to threaten and not to punish also. But if he does punish, and still you say it is a matter of threat, and on that account become more slothful, if it were really just a threat, would you not become more lazy? If the Ninevites had known it was a matter of threat, they would not have repented. But because they repented, they caused the threat to stop at words only. Do you wish it to be a threat only? You have the disposal of that matter. Become a better person, and it stops only at the threat. But if, which be far from you, you despise the threat, you will come to the experience of it. Those who lived before the flood, if they had feared the threat, would not have experienced the execution of it. And we, if we fear the threat, shall not expose ourselves to experience the reality. God forbid we should. And may the merciful God grant that we all henceforth, having been brought to sound mind, may obtain those unspeakable blessings. HOMILIES ON PHILEMON 3.[32]

LESSONS FROM GOD'S PUNISHMENT OF THE WICKED. AUGUSTINE: There is no advantage for vessels fitted for destruction that God patiently endures them, to destroy them in due order and to use them as a means of salvation for those on whom he has mercy. But there is advantage for those for whose salvation God uses this means. As it is written, "The just shall wash his hands in the blood of the wicked," that is, he shall be cleansed from evil works by the fear of God when he sees the punishment of sinners. That God shows his wrath in bearing with vessels of wrath avails to set a useful example to others but also to "make known the riches of his glory on vessels of mercy that he prepared for glory."[33] The hardening of the ungodly demonstrates two things—that a person should fear and turn to God in piety and that thanks should be given for his mercy to God who shows by the penalty inflicted on some the greatness of his gift to others. If the penalty he exacts from the former is not just, he makes no gift to those from whom he does not exact it. But because it is just, and there is no unrighteousness with God who punishes, who is sufficient to give thanks to him? For he remits a debt which, if God wanted to exact it, no person could deny was justly due. ON VARIOUS QUESTIONS TO SIMPLICIAN 2.18.[34]

---

[31]Chrysostom had just been saying that to punish people for evildoing is a mark of goodness, but to leave them unpunished is a cruelty. [32]NPNF 1 13:557*. [33]Rom 9:23 [34]LCC 6:401.

59:1-17 A PRAYER FOR DELIVERANCE FROM ENEMIES

To the choirmaster: according to Do Not Destroy. A Miktam of David, when Saul sent men to watch his house in order to kill him.

---

¹Deliver me from my enemies, O my God,
  protect me from those who rise up against
    me,
²deliver me from those who work evil,
  and save me from bloodthirsty men.

³For lo, they lie in wait for my life;
  fierce men band themselves against me.
For no transgression or sin of mine, O LORD,
  ⁴for no fault of mine, they run and make
    ready.

Rouse thyself, come to my help, and see!
  ⁵Thou, LORD God of hosts, art God of Israel.
Awake to punish all the nations;
  spare none of those who treacherously plot
    evil.   Selah

⁶Each evening they come back,
  howling like dogs
  and prowling about the city.
⁷There they are, bellowing with their mouths,
  and snarling withᵘ their lips—
  for "Who," they think, "will hear us?"

⁸But thou, O LORD, dost laugh at them;
  thou dost hold all the nations in derision.
⁹O my Strength, I will sing praises to thee;ᵛ
  for thou, O God, art my fortress.
¹⁰My God in his steadfast love will meet me;

my God will let me look in triumph on my
  enemies.

¹¹Slay them not, lest my people forget;
  make them totter by thy power, and bring
    them down,
  O Lord, our shield!
¹²For the sin of their mouths, the words of their
    lips,
  let them be trapped in their pride.
For the cursing and lies which they utter,
  ¹³consume them in wrath,
  consume them till they are no more,
that men may know that God rules over Jacob
  to the ends of the earth.   Selah

¹⁴Each evening they come back,
  howling like dogs
  and prowling about the city.
¹⁵They roam about for food,
  and growl if they do not get their fill.

¹⁶But I will sing of thy might;
  I will sing aloud of thy steadfast love in
    the morning.
For thou hast been to me a fortress
  and a refuge in the day of my distress.
¹⁷O my Strength, I will sing praises to thee,
  for thou, O God, art my fortress,
  the God who shows me steadfast love.

u Cn: Heb *swords in*   v Syr: Heb *I will watch for thee*

OVERVIEW: References to the sword or other weapons symbolize the tribulation and suffering experienced by Joseph in the Old Testament, Mary, the disciples and martyrs.

As the psalmist declares and the New Testament affirms, human beings must rely on the strength of God in all that they think and do. Almsgiving does not earn forgiveness for the wicked; only God can enable us to be true almoners. We are predisposed and motivated to will what is good by the mercy of God. Because of his mercy God has foreknown and predestined the salvation of those who will be saved (AUGUSTINE). In spite of our self-deception, we can neither will nor do good on our own (CASSIODORUS). Faith and all our good works have their origin in

God; consequently, heaven itself is a gift based on what God, not we, has done (Bede).

God has threatened with eternal punishment those who believe in a false Christ (Tertullian). God spared the Jews even when apostate so that their preservation of the Law and the Scriptures might provide the seed of the church (Augustine).

59:7 The Tribulation of God's People

The Piercing Sword of the Persecutors. Augustine: Concerning the words of Simeon, where he says to the virgin mother of the Lord, "And a sword shall pierce your soul,"[1] I have set forth in another letter what I think, and I sent you a copy some time ago, which you[2] saw among other things. As to his adding, "that out of many hearts thoughts may be revealed," I think it is to be taken in the sense that by the passion of the Lord both the plots of the Jews and the weakness of the disciples were made manifest. It is possible to believe that tribulation is signified by the word *sword*, that tribulation through which Mary's mother's heart was wounded by the feeling of grief. That sword was in the lips of the persecutors, of which it says in the psalm, "And a sword is in their lips."[3] They were the "sons of men whose teeth are weapons and arrows and their tongue a sharp sword."[4] The iron that pierced the soul of Joseph[5] seems to me to be an expression of bitter tribulation; thus, it is plainly said, "The iron pierced his soul until his word came," that is, he remained that long in bitter tribulation until his prediction was fulfilled. From then on he was held in great esteem and was free from tribulation. But, lest human wisdom should receive the credit because his word came, that is, what he foretold came to pass, in its own way the holy Scripture gives the glory of it to God, and adds at once, "The word of the Lord inflamed him."[6] Letter 149.[7]

59:9-10 The Necessity of God's Grace

We Are Insufficient of Ourselves. Augustine: Therefore, it is good for a person to say truthfully and with the full strength of his free will, "I will provide you with my strength," because the man who thought he could keep it without the help of him who gave it went abroad into a far country and wasted his substance, living riotously. But, worn down by the wretchedness of a harsh slavery, he returned to himself and said, "I will arise and go to my father."[8] But how could he have had this good thought if the most merciful Father had not whispered it to him in secret? It was because he understood this that the minister of the New Testament[9] said, "Not that we are sufficient to think anything of ourselves as of ourselves, but our sufficiency is from God."[10] Consequently, when the psalmist also had said, "I will provide you with my strength," lest he should attribute to himself the fact that he was keeping it, and as if he recalled to mind that "except the Lord keep the city, they watch in vain that keep it,"[11] and that "he shall neither slumber nor sleep that keeps Israel,"[12] he added the reason of his being able to keep it, or, rather, the guard by whom it is kept and said, "For you, O God, are my protector." Letter 186.[13]

Alms Cannot Compensate for Evil. Augustine: There is no need of such self-deception on the part of those who, through giving, however profusely, alms of their fruits or of money of whatever kind, believe that they are purchasing the right to persist with impunity in the enormity and wickedness of their misdeeds and vices. Not only do they perform such wickedness, but they so love it as to desire to persist in it forever, provided they can do so with impunity. "But one who loves iniquity hates his own soul";[14] and whoever hates his

---

[1]Lk 2:35. [2]Paulinus of Nola, an acquaintance to whom Augustine addresses this letter. [3]Augustine is importing into this verse the imagery of Psalm 57:4, in which the tongue is understood as a sword. [4]Ps 57:4 (56:5 LXX, Vg.). [5]Gen 40; 41. [6]Ps 105:19 (104:19 LXX, Vg.). [7]FC 20:264-65**. [8]Lk 15:18. [9]See Eph 3:7. [10]2 Cor 3:5. [11]Ps 127:1 (126:1 LXX, Vg.). [12]Ps 121:4 (120:4 LXX, Vg.). [13]FC 30:194-95*. [14]Ps 11:5 (10:6 LXX, Vg.).

own soul does not show mercy but cruelty toward it. For in loving it according to the world, he hates it according to God. If, then, he wished to give to it those alms by which all things would be clean to him,[15] he would hate his soul according to the world and love it according to God. Now no one gives alms at all unless he has the means of giving from One who has no need of it; and therefore it has been said, "His mercy shall go before me." ENCHIRIDION 20.77.[16]

GOD'S MERCY PRECEDES HUMAN GOOD WILL. AUGUSTINE: For a person's good will comes before many other gifts from God, but not all of them. One of the gifts it does not antedate is—just itself! Thus in the sacred Writings we read "his mercy goes before me" and "his mercy shall follow me."[17] It predisposes a person before he wills, to prompt his willing. It follows the act of willing, lest one's will be frustrated. Otherwise, why are we admonished to pray for our enemies,[18] who are plainly not now willing to live piously, unless it is that God is even now at work in them and in their will? Or again, why are we admonished to ask in order to receive, unless it is that he who grants us what we will is he through whom it comes to pass that we will? We pray for enemies, therefore, that the mercy of God should go before them, as it goes before us; we pray for ourselves that his mercy shall follow us. ENCHIRIDION 9.32.[19]

GOD'S MERCY IS MANIFESTED BY THE CONDEMNATION OF THE WICKED. AUGUSTINE: But far be it from us to say that those who "according to his purpose are called . . . , whom he foreknew" and "predestined to be conformable to the image of his Son"[20] should be abandoned to their own desire, so that they perish. For this is suffered by the "vessels of wrath, fitted for destruction,"[21] and by their very perdition God makes known "the riches of his glory on the vessels of his mercy."[22] It is for this reason that after saying, "My God, his mercy shall come before me," the

psalmist at once adds, "God shall let me see over my enemies." Therefore it happens to them as is written, "Wherefore God gave them up to the desires of their heart."[23] But this does not happen to the predestined, whom the Spirit of God rules, for their cry is not in vain, "Give me not up, O Lord, from my desire, to the wicked,"[24] since it is also against these same desires that they have prayed, as is written, "Take away from me the greediness of the belly, and let not the lusts of the flesh take hold of me."[25] God grants this favor to those over whom he rules but not to those who think they are fit to rule themselves and who, in the stiff-necked presumptuousness of their own will, disdain to have him as their guide. PROCEEDINGS OF PELAGIANS 7.[26]

WE CAN DO NO GOOD WITHOUT GOD'S GRACE. CASSIODORUS: There is also the Pelagians'[27] second wickedness, for they so attribute free will to their human powers that they believe that they can devise or do some good of their own accord without God's grace. If this were possible, why should the prophet say, "My God, his mercy shall precede me"? When you hear that you have been anticipated by the Lord's mercy, you are given to understand that nothing of your own devising occurred first. In another psalm too he says, "Unless the Lord build the house, they labor in vain who build."[28] He also says, "The steps of a person are directed by the Lord, and he will delight in his way."[29] In another place too the psalmist attests, "The Lord lifts up them who are cast down: the Lord loosens them who are fettered: the Lord enlightens the blind."[30] Since you hear that the Lord precedes, builds, directs, lifts up, loosens and enlightens when no merits anticipate him, what do you see has been initiated as your own except that by which you can be justly

---

[15]Lk 11:41. [16]FC 2:435*. [17]Ps 23:6 (22:6 LXX, Vg.). [18]Mt 5:44. [19]LCC 7:359*. [20]Rom 8:28-29. [21]Rom 9:22. [22]Rom 9:23. [23]Rom 1:24. [24]Ps 140:8 (139:9 LXX, Vg.). [25]Sir 23:6. [26]FC 86:117-18*. [27]The Pelagian heresy denied original sin and maintained that Adam and Eve were created mortal. [28]Ps 127:1 (126:1 LXX, Vg.). [29]Ps 37:23 (36:23 LXX, Vg.). [30]Ps 146:7-8 (145:7-8 LXX, Vg.).

condemned by reason of your pride? . . . But you interpret these and similar passages most perversely, believing that people take the first step of their good intentions of their own accord and subsequently obtain the help of the Godhead, so that (to express the matter sacrilegiously) we are the cause of his kindness and he is not the cause of his own. Expositions of the Psalms 50.7.[31]

God Is Responsible for Faith and Good Works. Bede: In order not to falter in good works, we ought always to rely for support on the help of the one who says, "For without me you can do nothing."[32] Hence in order to express the fact that the start of faith and good action is given to us by the Lord, the psalmist properly says, "My God, his mercy goes before me." Again, in order to teach that the good things we do must be accomplished with his assistance, he says, "And your mercy follows after me all the days of my life."[33] In order to show that the prize of eternal life rendered for good works is bestowed on us freely, he says, "Who crowns you in compassion and mercy." He crowns us indeed in mercy and compassion when he repays us with the reward of heavenly blessedness for the good works that he himself has mercifully granted us to carry out. Homilies on the Gospels 1.2.[34]

59:11 Reasons for Divine Mercy and Judgment

God's Retribution Against Those Who Reject Christ. Tertullian: So likewise that conditional threat of the sword, "If you refuse and do not listen to me, the sword shall devour you,"[35] has proved that the sword was Christ, for rebellion against whom they have perished. In the fifty-ninth psalm he demands of the Father their dispersion: "Scatter them in your power." By Isaiah he also says, as he finishes a prophecy of their consumption by fire: "Because of me this has happened to you; you shall lie down in sorrow."[36] But all this would be meaningless enough, if they suffered this retribution not on account of him who

had in prophecy assigned their suffering to his own cause but for the sake of the Christ of the other god.[37] Well, then, although you affirm that it is the Christ of the other god[38] who was driven to the cross by the powers and authorities of the Creator, as it were by hostile beings, still I have to say, see how manifestly he was defended by the Creator: there were given to him both "the wicked for his burial," even those who had strenuously maintained that his corpse had been stolen, "and the rich for his death,"[39] even those who had redeemed him from the treachery of Judas, as well as from the lying report of the soldiers that his body had been taken away. Against Marcion 3.23.[40]

A Prophecy of the Christian Church. Augustine: Like Cain, who in envy and pride killed his just brother, they[41] have been marked with a sign so that no one may kill them. Indeed, this fact can be quite definitely noted in Psalm 59, where Christ, speaking according to his human nature, says, "My God has made revelation to me concerning my enemies: do not kill them lest they forget your law." Strangely enough, by means of this people, enemies of the Christian faith, proof has been furnished to the Gentiles as to how Christ was foretold, lest, perhaps, when the Gentiles had seen how manifestly the prophecies were fulfilled, they should think that the Scriptures were made up by the Christians, since things that they perceived as accomplished facts were read aloud as foretold about Christ. Therefore, the sacred books are handed down by the Jews, and thus God, in regard to our enemies, makes clear to us that he did not kill them, that is, he did not annihilate them from the face of the earth so that they might not forget his law, for by reading it and by observing it, though only outwardly, they keep it in mind and thus bring judgment on themselves and furnish testimony to us. Sermon 201.3.[42]

---

[31]ACW 51:499*. [32]Jn 15:5. [33]Ps 23:6 (22:6 LXX, Vg.). [34]CS 110:12*. [35]Is 1:20. [36]Is 50:11. [37]The God of the Old Testament. Marcion believed that the God revealed in the Old Testament was not the same as the God revealed in the New Testament. [38]Ibid. [39]See Is 53:9. [40]ANF 3:341-42*. [41]The Jews. [42]FC 38:70-71**.

60:1-12 A NATIONAL PRAYER FOR GOD'S HELP

*To the choirmaster: according to Shushan
Eduth. A Miktam of David; for instruction; when he strove with Aram-naha-
raim and with Aram-zobah, and when
Joab on his return killed twelve thousand
of Edom in the Valley of Salt.*

¹*O God, thou hast rejected us, broken our
     defenses;*
   thou hast been angry; oh, restore us.
²*Thou hast made the land to quake, thou
     hast rent it open;*
   repair its breaches, for it totters.
³*Thou hast made thy people suffer hard things;*
   *thou hast given us wine to drink that made
     us reel.*

⁴*Thou hast set up a banner for those who fear
     thee,*
   *to rally to it from the bow.*ʷ   Selah
⁵*That thy beloved may be delivered,*
   give victory by thy right hand and answer us!

⁶*God has spoken in his sanctuary:*ˣ
   *"With exultation I will divide up
     Shechem*
   and portion out the Vale of Succoth.
⁷*Gilead is mine; Manasseh is mine;*
   Ephraim is my helmet;
   Judah is my scepter.
⁸*Moab is my washbasin;*
   upon Edom I cast my shoe;
   over Philistia I shout in triumph."

⁹*Who will bring me to the fortified city?*
   Who will lead me to Edom?
¹⁰*Hast thou not rejected us, O God?*
   *Thou dost not go forth, O God, with our
     armies.*
¹¹*O grant us help against the foe,*
   for vain is the help of man!
¹²*With God we shall do valiantly;*
   it is he who will tread down our foes.

w Gk Syr Jerome: Heb *truth*   x Or *by his holiness*

OVERVIEW: Once we taste the love of God, we
only thirst for more, especially as we long for our
heavenly reward (CAESARIUS). We can recognize
God's blessings only through the hardships that
God makes us endure. Christ, descended in the
flesh from the patriarchs, offers forgiveness of
sins through baptismal cleansing and thereby
grants security to the penitent. God casts us off
because of our great wickedness, but then, out of
mercy, redeems us through the sacrifice of his
Son (BASIL). God brings everyone into subjection
to Christ (THEODORET).

God rejects humans because of their sin, but
then accepts them again because of his mercy
(BASIL). Since one cannot save himself, he
needs the salvation of God, which comes
through baptism. God trains us for eternity by
denying us certain things in this life; what may
seem good here is, in reality, vain and fleeting
(AUGUSTINE). Christ, who is the source of our
salvation, must be God since salvation cannot
come from human beings (VICTORINUS). The
God who enables the faithful to do good is the
triune God, even though we may attribute certain activities to one person of the Trinity (FUL-
GENTIUS).

60:3-8 Joy and Security of Salvation

ALWAYS EAGER FOR SALVATION. CAESARIUS OF ARLES: When a person lays aside his past sinfulness, he is suddenly endowed with new dignity, with that cup of divine love of which it is said, "And your cup which inebriated me, how it overflows!"[1] Inebriated with that cup, I repeat, hearts taste the sweetness of heavenly things through the strength of spiritual wisdom. Then they may merit to hear, "Taste and see how good the Lord is."[2] Now he said "taste," because love of God can refresh the soul but cannot satisfy the desire, regardless of the amount of faith or longing with which it is sought. More and more, it arouses thirst when it is, as it were, tasted beforehand with the edge of the lips, and for this reason he says of himself, "He who eats of me will hunger still, he who drinks of me will thirst for more."[3] Because of its sweetness, it arouses an appetite for itself, but it does not cause disgust from satiety. Just as people who are experienced in drinking wine are likely to thirst all the more when they have become drunk, so it is with the devout and chaste soul that is prudent and contrite and that can, therefore, say with the psalmist, "You have given us stupefying wine," when it has begun to think about hope in a future life and to imbibe a thirst for heavenly goods. It knows how to be filled but not how to be satisfied, so that the more it consumes according to its capacity, the more it lacks in its eagerness, and it can join with the prophet in that word of longing: "My soul pines for your salvation";[4] and again: "My flesh and my heart waste away, O God of my heart";[5] moreover, "My soul yearns and pines for the courts of the Lord."[6] SERMON 167.1.[7]

THE WINE OF SORROW. BASIL THE GREAT: Therefore, "O God, you have cast us off." You have cast off those who in proportion to their sins removed themselves a distance from you. You have destroyed the accumulations of our wickedness, doing good to us because of our weakness. You were angry, since "we were by nature children of wrath,"[8] having no hope and being without God in the world. You had mercy on us when "you sent forth your only-begotten Son as a propitiation for our sins,"[9] in order that in his blood we might find redemption. We would not know that we were having these kindnesses done to us, unless "you have made us drink the wine of sorrow." By wine he means the words that lead the hardened heart to conscious perception. HOMILIES ON THE PSALMS 20.3.[10]

SECURITY COMES THROUGH BAPTISM AND LOVE FOR GOD. BASIL THE GREAT: "Gilead is mine, and Manasseh is mine." Gilead is a grandson of Manasseh; this is said in order that he may show that the succession of the patriarchs, from whom is descended Christ according to the flesh, comes down from God. "And Ephraim is the support of my head. Judah is my king." He will join together by agreement the parts that are severed. "Moab is the washbasin of my hope." Or "a pot for washing," another of the interpreters says; or "a pot of security"; that is to say, the excommunicated person, who has been forbidden with threats to enter the church of the Lord. For the Moabite and the Ammonite will not enter until the third and until the tenth generation and until everlasting time.[11] Nevertheless, since baptism possesses remission for sins and produces security for the debtors, he, showing the deliverance through baptism and the affection for God, says, "Moab is a pot for washing" or "a pot of security." Therefore, all "foreigners are made subject,"[12] bowing down under the yoke of Christ; for this reason he will set his shoe in Edom. The shoe of the divinity is the God-bearing flesh, through which he approaches humans. In this hope, pronouncing blessed the time of the coming of the Lord, the prophet says, "Who will bring me into the fortified city."[13] Perhaps he means the church,

---

[1]See Ps 23:5 (22:5 LXX, Vg.). [2]Ps 34:8 (33:9 LXX, Vg.). [3]Sir 24:20. [4]Ps 119:81 (118:8 LXX, Vg.). [5]Ps 73:26 (72:26 LXX, Vg.). [6]Ps 84:2 (83:3 LXX, Vg.). [7]FC 47:403-4*. [8]Eph 2:3. [9]Rom 3:25; 1 Jn 4:10. [10]FC 46:337*. [11]See 2 Esdr 13:1. [12]Ps 60:12 (59:14 LXX). [13]Ps 60:9 (59:11 LXX).

a city, indeed, because it is a community governed conformably to laws; and fortified, because of the faith encompassing it. Whence one of the interpreters produced a very clear translation: "Into a city fortified all around." Who, then, will permit me to see this great spectacle, God living among people? These are the words of the Lord: "Many prophets and just people have longed to see what you see, and they have not seen it."[14] HOMILIES ON THE PSALMS 20.4.[15]

THE SHOE OF GOD IS THE FLESH OF CHRIST.
THEODORET OF CYR: All strangers have stooped and been put under the yoke of Christ, wherefore also "over Edom" does he "cast out" his "shoe." Now the shoe of the Godhead is the flesh that bore God whereby he came among humankind. DIALOGUE 1.[16]

60:11-12 Help and Salvation Come from God

DIVINE HELP. BASIL THE GREAT: Therefore, let the church of God be saluted and let it be taught to say what we were just saying: "Give us help from trouble; for the help of people is worthless." So, perhaps, the meaning of the psalm does not at all permit us to allege weakness, if indeed affliction is a patron of help and not an occasion of infirmity. To those, then, who were rejected through sin but then received again through the kindness of God, it is appropriate to say, "O God, you have cast us off and have destroyed us; you have been angry and have had mercy on us." HOMILIES ON THE PSALMS 20.1.[17]

GOD IS THE SOURCE OF SALVATION. AUGUSTINE: So, as I said, the creature baptized the Creator, the lamp the sun, and by doing so John the Baptist did not push himself forward but submitted himself. I mean, he said to the one who came to him, "Are you coming to me to be baptized? It is I who ought to be baptized by you."[18] A great confession, and a sound profession of humility by the lamp. If this had pushed itself forward against

the sun, the wind of pride would very soon have blown it out. So this is what the Lord foresaw, what the Lord taught by his baptism. Such a great one wished to be baptized by such a small one; to explain it in a word, the Savior by one needing to be saved. John, I mean, had perhaps remembered, great though he was, some sickness or other of his. Why else, after all did he say, "It is I who ought to be baptized by you"? Certainly the Lord's baptism means salvation, because "salvation is from the Lord."[19] "For vain is the salvation coming from people." So why, "It is I who ought to be baptized by you," if he had no need of any sort of cure? But in the Lord's own very humility there is a marvelous medicine; one was baptizing, the other healing. SERMON 292.4.[20]

PREPARATION FOR ETERNITY. AUGUSTINE: The first thing they must do is examine their own hearts, to see whether they are asking in faith. Any who ask in faith receive for their own good, and sometimes do not receive for their own good. When he does not cure the body, he wants to cure the soul. So trust him, and believe that since he has called you to an eternal kingdom, whatever he wishes is to your advantage. After all, what is this thing that you long for as though it mattered so enormously? Eternal life is what he has promised you, to reign with the angels is what he has promised you, rest without end is what he has promised you. And what, in comparison, is it that he does not give here and now? Isn't it true that "the health of human beings is vain"? Isn't it absolutely certain that all those who do get cured will eventually die? And when death comes, all those past events vanish like smoke. But when that other life that he has promised us comes, it will of course have no end. By denying you something here and now, he is equipping you for that life, he is preparing you for it, he is training you for it. SERMON 61A.5.[21]

---

[14]Mt 13:17. [15]FC 46:338-39*. [16]NPNF 2 3:179**. [17]FC 46:333-34*. [18]Mt 3:14. [19]Ps 3:8 (3:9 LXX, Vg.). [20]WSA 3 8:140*. [21]WSA 3 3:152.

CHRIST IS GOD. MARIUS VICTORINUS: Would a man who was only a man say this of himself?[22] For if a person says this, he blasphemes, and "God does not hear sinners."[23] But indeed Christ says that God hears him. He is therefore neither sinner nor mere man. It has also been said, "Vain is the hope in man." And it is said, "As for us we hope in our God."[24]

Christ is therefore God, not coming from any other substance; "the Father is living, and I live because of the Father,"[25] and, "I am the bread of life; the one who eats this will live for all time."[26] All the statements signify one substance. And that is why Jesus says that he is from above who says this: "If therefore you will see the Son of man ascending, where was he before?"[27] AGAINST ARIUS IA 2.1.B.7.[28]

WHATEVER WE ACCOMPLISH. FULGENTIUS OF RUSPE: For the Spirit of the Lord did not say, he who does the truth, that his works be clearly seen as done in the Holy Spirit but "as done in God,"[29] which we say are done not in the Father alone, or in the Son alone or in the Holy Spirit alone. But we confess that the truth is done by a human being in the holy Trinity itself, which is one God, in whom the blessed David indicates is the power of what is done by the faithful, saying, "With God we shall do valiantly; it is he who will tread down our foes." For he is the one God concerning whom the blessed apostle says, "For from him and through him and for him are all things. To him be glory forever."[30] BOOK TO VICTOR AGAINST THE SERMON OF FASTIDIOS THE ARIAN 3.3.[31]

---

[22]See Jn 6:57-58. [23]Jn 9:31. [24]Ps 20:7 (19:8 LXX, Vg.). [25]Jn 6:57. [26]Jn 6:35; 6:58. [27]Jn 6:62. [28]FC 69:98. [29]Jn 3:21. [30]Rom 11:36. [31]FC 95:396.

61:1-8 A PRAYER FOR RESTORATION TO GOD'S PRESENCE

To the choirmaster: with stringed instruments. A Psalm of David.

*¹Hear my cry, O God,
     listen to my prayer;
²from the end of the earth I call to thee,
     when my heart is faint.*

*Lead thou me
     to the rock that is higher than I;
³for thou art my refuge,
     a strong tower against the enemy.*

⁴Let me dwell in thy tent for ever!

Oh to be safe under the shelter of thy wings!
                                        Selah
*⁵For thou, O God, hast heard my vows,
     thou hast given me the heritage of those who
     fear thy name.*

*⁶Prolong the life of the king;
     may his years endure to all generations!
⁷May he be enthroned for ever before God;
     bid steadfast love and faithfulness watch
          over him!*

*⁸So will I ever sing praises to thy name,
     as I pay my vows day after day.*

OVERVIEW: The church, assailed by the gates of hell, temptation and heresies, will always prevail (BEDE). Although the church is built on a rock, it is not localized in one place but is present everywhere so that God hears cries for help no matter where they are uttered. A true Christian trusts in the living God and is willing to renounce the world and divest himself of worldly possessions if that becomes necessary in order for him to hold on to faith in Christ (AUGUSTINE).

61:2-3 Steadfastness of Faith

THE CHURCH STANDS FIRM AS A ROCK. BEDE: We should note that this flood of temptations assails the church in three ways: "one is tempted, drawn on and lured by one's own desire,"[1] or is worn down by the depravity of false brothers or is assaulted by the more open snares of those outside [the church]. In another place the Lord calls these temptations "the gates of the lower world," and rightly so, for if victorious they drag us down to eternal destruction. He says, "I shall build my church on this rock, and the gates of the lower world shall not prevail against it."[2] Although the gates of the devil strike against it, yet they do not overthrow Christ's church; although the flood of faithlessness inundates it, it does not undermine the house of faith. For [the church] is able to say truthfully to its helper, "When my heart was disquieted, you raised me up on a rock." It is not vanquished by external forces because, by suffering and acquiring the crown of martyrdom, it triumphs over the ferocity of the unbelievers who persecute it. It is not corrupted by false brothers because it refutes the dogmas of heretics by believing properly, and it avoids the vicious example of some Catholics by living soberly and justly and piously.[3] It is not blinded by the smoke of private greed because it is inwardly aflame with the ardor of the Lord's charity alone. HOMILIES ON THE GOSPELS 2.25.[4]

THE CHURCH CRIES OUT IN DISTRESS.

AUGUSTINE: For that church[5] is founded on a rock, as the Lord says: "On this rock I will build my church."[6] But they[7] build on the sand, as the same Lord says: "Every one who hears these sayings of mine and does not do them is like a foolish man who built his house on the sand."[8] But that you may not suppose that the church that is on a rock is in only one part of the earth and does not extend even to its furthest boundaries, hear its voice groaning from the psalm, amid the evils of it pilgrimage. For it says, "From the end of the earth have I cried to you; when my heart was distressed you did lift me up on the rock; you have led me, you, my hope, have become a tower of courage from the face of the enemy."[9] See how it cries from the end of the earth. . . . See how it is exalted on a rock. LETTERS OF PETILIAN THE DONATIST 2.109-246.[10]

HOLD TO CHRIST AT ALL COST. AUGUSTINE: It is clear that this obligation and condition of life[11] includes not only those who have responded so well to sound advice that they have sold their goods and distributed them to the poor, and, with their shoulders freed of every worldly burden, bear the light yoke of Christ.[12] They also include the weaker soul, who is less capable of such glorious perfection but who nevertheless remembers that he is a Christian when he hears that he must give up Christ or lose all his possessions. He will rather lay hold on the "tower of strength against the face of the enemy"[13] because, when he was building it by his faith, he took into account the charges with which it could be completed.[14] He embraced the faith with the intention of

---

[1]Jas 1:14. [2]Mt 16:18. [3]Tit 2:12. [4]CS 111:261. [5]The true, orthodox church. [6]Mt 16:18. [7]The Donatists, who were a schismatic group that originated in North Africa after the Diocletian persecution (303-311) and insisted that anyone who had denied the faith during the persecution could not be readmitted to the church. [8]Mt 7:26. [9]Ps 61:2-3 (60:3-4 LXX, Vg.). [10]NPNF 1 4:595*. [11]The reference is to people who have chosen to remain faithful and forfeit their worldly possessions rather than apostatize in order to keep their earthly goods during time of persecution. [12]Mt 11:30. [13]Ps 61:3 (60:4 LXX, Vg.). [14]Lk 14:28.

renouncing this world, not in word only, because, if he bought something he was as one not possessing it, and if he used this world he was as one not using it,[15] not placing his hope in the uncertainty of riches but in the living God.[16] LETTER 157.[17]

---

[15]1 Cor 7:30-31. [16]1 Tim 6:17. [17]FC 20:347**.

62:1-12 SIMPLE TRUST IN GOD

To the choirmaster: according to Jeduthun. A Psalm of David.

[1]*For God alone my soul waits in silence; from him comes my salvation.*
[2]*He only is my rock and my salvation, my fortress; I shall not be greatly moved.*

[3]*How long will you set upon a man to shatter him, all of you, like a leaning wall, a tottering fence?*
[4]*They only plan to thrust him down from his eminence.*
They take pleasure in falsehood.
They bless with their mouths, but inwardly they curse. Selah

[5]*For God alone my soul waits in silence, for my hope is from him.*
[6]*He only is my rock and my salvation, my fortress; I shall not be shaken.*
[7]*On God rests my deliverance and my honor; my mighty rock, my refuge is God.*

[8]*Trust in him at all times, O people; pour out your heart before him; God is a refuge for us.* Selah

[9]*Men of low estate are but a breath,* *men of high estate are a delusion;†*
in the balances they go up; they are together lighter than a breath.
[10]*Put no confidence in extortion, set no vain hopes on robbery; if riches increase, set not your heart on them.*

[11]*Once God has spoken; twice have I heard this:*
that power belongs to God;
[12]*and that to thee, O Lord, belongs steadfast love.*
For thou dost requite a man according to his work.

*LXX *But vain are the sons of people* †LXX *the sons of people are liars*

OVERVIEW: God alone can endow us with patience; it is arrogance to think we can acquire it on our own (AUGUSTINE). The Son of God calms our souls when disturbed by sins, both small and great. The soul corrupted by sin is like a leaning fence destined to fall, but God grants immortality so that the soul cannot fall a second time. People who interpret and understand evil deeds as virtuous acts invite eternal condemnation on themselves (Basil).

People, such as martyrs, who cultivate virtue (especially patience), must praise God and his grace, not themselves. In order to receive gifts from God, we must acknowledge him as the source of the gifts; if we do not, he will take back what he has given (Augustine). Since all glory belongs to God, God forbids us to glorify ourselves for whatever accomplishments we seem to achieve in this life (Basil). God gives us gifts for life's various needs; therefore, we should trust in him, not in ourselves (Augustine). God will aid us in all times of anguish and spiritual struggles (Pachomius). The reception of divine grace necessitates the expulsion of evil passions.

By nature we lie and cheat, but God has granted us an inner scale whereby we can weigh life and death, good and evil against each other and know which is best. Avoid the temptations of Satan, who, in his crafty ways, uses the appeal of earthly pleasures and vanities to lead people away from God (Basil). Worldly wealth and success are deceptive and unreal; it is Christians who possess true wealth. It is foolish and pointless to amass earthly treasures—we cannot take them into the next life, and our children may squander them. Since riches and pleasure corrupt, especially those gained wrongfully, we should seek only enough worldly possessions to sustain ourselves physically (Augustine). The joys of earthly wealth are fleeting, and people who gain wealth at the expense of others will be punished (Fulgentius). When God judges people, he rewards them according to their deeds, but fortunately for sinful humankind, God is merciful in his judgment (Basil).

62:1-4 God Is Our Source of Strength and Protection

Our Confidence Must Be in God. Augustine: Who endowed him[1] with such patience? Who? Let the psalm tell us. There, after all, we

can read, there we can sing, "Shall my soul not be subject to God? For it is from him that my patience comes." Whoever imagines that Saint Vincent was capable of these things by his own powers is making a very big mistake. Those, you see, who are confident they are capable of this by their own powers may seem to overcome by patience but are in fact being overcome by pride. Sermon 274.[2]

Help for People Disturbed by Their Sins: Basil the Great: "For he is my God and my savior; he is my protector, I shall be moved no more." The Son, who is from God, is our God. He is also Savior of the human race, who supports our weakness, who corrects the disturbance that springs up in our souls from temptations. "I shall be moved no more." Humanly he confesses his disturbance. "More." For it is impossible that there should not be some disturbance from temptations in the human soul. While we are committing small and few sins, we are in a way mildly disturbed, being tossed about like the leaves by a gentle breeze; but, when our vices are more and greater, in proportion to the increase of our sins the disturbance is apt to be intensified. Homilies on the Psalms 21.2.[3]

The Relentless Assaults of Satan. Basil the Great: "How long do you rush in upon a person? You all kill, as if you were tearing down a leaning wall and a tottering fence."[4] Again the homily speaks out against the depraved ministers of the devil, charging them with a lack of moderation in the snares they lay. Certainly, people are weak animals; but you rush on, not content with the first attack, but you attack a second and a third time, until you subdue the soul that has fallen beside you to such an extent that it is very similar to a leaning wall and a tottering fence.

---

[1]Augustine preached this sermon on the birthday of Vincent, a deacon in Saragossa, Spain, who was martyred in Valencia in 303, during the Diocletian persecution. [2]WSA 3 8:23-24. [3]FC 46:343. [4]Ps 62:3 (61:4 LXX).

Now, a wall, as long as it maintains an upright position, remains steadfast; but, when it leans, since it has been weakened, it is destined to fall. For if heavy bodies are joined together, they stand erect after leaning, but those which are composed of several parts no longer stand erect when pressure has been put on one part of them. The homily shows, therefore, that the nature of humankind, which is composite, was not susceptible to plots for a second fall. "You are God's tillage, God's building,"[5] it is said. The enemy has shattered this building; the Craftsman has repaired the rents made in it. Thus the fall was necessary because of sin, but the resurrection was great because it brings immortality. HOMILIES ON THE PSALMS 21.3.[6]

THE DANGER OF MISCONSTRUING EVIL FOR GOOD. BASIL THE GREAT: "But they have thought to cast away my price; they ran in thirst: they blessed with their mouth but cursed with their heart."[7] The price of [humanity's redemption] is the blood of Christ: "You have been bought," it is said, "with a price; do not become the slaves of people." The soldiers of Satan planned, therefore, to make this price useless to us, leading again into slavery those who had once been freed. "They ran in thirst." He is speaking of the eager plots of the demons, because they run against us, thirsting for our destruction. "They blessed with their mouth but cursed with their heart." There are many who approve evil deeds and say that the witty person is charming; the foulmouthed, statesmanlike; the bitter and irascible they name as one not to be despised; the miserly and selfish they praise as thrifty; the spendthrift, as bountiful; the fornicator and lewd, as one devoted to enjoyment and ease; and, in general, they gloss over every evil with the name of the proximate virtue. Such people bless with their mouth but curse with their heart. For by the auspiciousness of the words, they bring every curse on their life, making themselves liable to condemnation on the day of judgment because

of those things that they approved. HOMILIES ON THE PSALMS 21.3.[8]

62:5-8 God Is Our Refuge and Worthy of All Glory

PRAISE GOD FOR THE VIRTUE OF PATIENCE. AUGUSTINE: Let us by all means admire the courage of the holy martyrs in their sufferings; but in such a way that we proclaim the grace of God. They themselves, after all, certainly did not wish to be praised in themselves but in the one to whom it is said, "In the Lord shall my soul be praised."[9] Those who understand this are not proud; they ask shyly, they receive joyfully; they persevere, they do not lose any more what they have received. Because they are not proud, they are gentle; and that is why, after saying "In the Lord shall my soul be praised," he added, "Let the gentle hear and be glad."[10] Where would feeble flesh be, where would maggots and rottenness be, unless what we have been singing were true: "My soul will submit itself to God, since it is from him that my patience comes"? Now the virtue the martyrs had, in order to endure all the ills inflicted on them, is called patience. SERMON 283.1.[11]

GOD IS THE GIVER OF GIFTS. AUGUSTINE: Let the martyr turn his back on the unbelieving and ungrateful flatterer; let him turn his face toward the most generous of bountiful givers and impute his very martyrdom to God, not treating it as something he has offered to God from what is his own. Let him say instead, "In the Lord shall my soul be praised; let the gentle hear and be glad."[12] And when you say to him, "What do you mean, 'In the Lord shall my soul be praised?' So is it not being praised in yourself?"—he responds with, "Shall not my soul subject itself to God? For it is from him that my patience comes." So why is it[13]

---

[5]1 Cor 3:9. [6]FC 46:344**. [7]Ps 62:4 (61:5 LXX). [8]FC 46:344-45**. [9]Ps 34:2 (33:3 LXX, Vg.). [10]Ps 34:2 (33:3 LXX, Vg.). [11]WSA 3 8:83. [12]Ps 34:2 (33:3 LXX, Vg.). [13]Martyrdom considered as a gift from God.

mine? Because I opened my lap and was happy to receive it; it is from him, and it is mine. Both from him, and also mine; and because it is from him, it is mine all the more safely. It is mine, but it does not come to me from myself. In order really to possess my gift, I acknowledge God as the giver. Because if I do not acknowledge God as the giver, God takes away his good thing, and there only remains my bad thing, through my choice, through my free will. SERMON 284.3.[14]

HOPE IN GOD, OUR HELPER. AUGUSTINE: So: "Nobody is able to refrain from sexual intercourse, unless God grants it." You have a gift to protect you from such pleasures; since "this was itself a matter of wisdom, to know whose gift this was; nobody is continent unless God grants it."[15] You have a gift to help you endure pains; since "it is from him," he says, "my patience comes." "So hope in him, every assembly of the people." Hope in him; do not trust in your own powers. Confess your bad things to him; hope for your good things from him. Without his help you will be nothing, however proud you may be. So in order that you may be enabled to be humble, "pour out your hearts before him"; and to avoid remaining wrongly stuck on yourselves, say what comes next: "God is our helper."
SERMON 283.3.[16]

GIVE ALL GLORY TO GOD. BASIL THE GREAT: "In God is my salvation and my glory; he is the God of my help, and my hope is in God." Blessed is one who exults in none of the lofty things of life but regards God as his glory: who holds Christ as his boast; who is able to say, according to the apostle, "But as for me, God forbid that I should glory except in the cross of Christ."[17] Many are glorified in body, who devote their time to gymnastic contests, or, on the whole, who are vigorous in the flower of their age; and many, because of their valor in the wars, who consider the murdering of those of the same race bravery. In fact, rewards in wars and the trophies raised by a general and by cities, are according to the magnitude

of the slaughter. Others are glorified because they put walls around cities; and others, because of the structures of the aquaducts and the buildings of the great gymnasia. That person who has spent his wealth in fighting wild beasts and who exults in vain words of the people is puffed up with the praises and thinks himself something great, having his glory in his shame.[18] He even shows his sin inscribed on tablets in conspicuous places of the city. Another is extolled for his wealth; another, because he is a skillful and invincible orator, or he is acquainted with the wisdom of the world. It is proper to pity the glory of all these and to deem happy those who make God their glory. For if a certain one thinks he is something great because he is the servant of a king and is held in great honor by him, how much ought you to exalt yourself, because you are a servant of the great King and are called by him to the closest intimacy, having received the Spirit of the promise, so that, sealed with his approval, you are shown to be a child of God? HOMILIES ON THE PSALMS 21.4.[19]

TRUST COMPLETELY IN GOD. PACHOMIUS: And now, my child, if you take God as your hope, he will be your help in the time of your anguish; "for anyone who comes to God must believe that he exists and that he rewards those who search for him."[20] These words were written for us, that we may believe in God and do battle, great and little, by fastings, prayers and other religious practices. God will not forget even the saliva that has dried in your mouth as a result of fasting. On the contrary, everything will be returned to you at the moment of your anguish. Only humble yourself in all things, hold back your word even if you understand the whole affair. Do not quietly acquire the habit of abusing; on the contrary, joyfully put up with every trial. For if you knew the honor that results from trials you would not pray to be delivered from them, because it is preferable

---

[14]*WSA* 3 8:89*. [15]Wis 8:21. [16]*WSA* 3 8:84-85*. [17]Gal 6:14. [18]See Phil 3:19. [19]FC 46:345-46. [20]Heb 11:6.

for you to pray, to weep and to sigh until you are saved, rather than to relax and be led off a captive. O man, what are you doing in Babylon?[21] "You have grown old in an alien land"[22] because you did not submit to the test and because your relations with God are not proper. Therefore, brother, you must not relax. INSTRUCTIONS 16.[23]

DIVINE GRACE AND EVIL PASSIONS CANNOT COEXIST. BASIL THE GREAT: Since the psalmist is conscious of the use of sincere hope in God, he invites the people to a zeal equal to his own, saying, "Trust in him, all you people; pour out your hearts before him." It is impossible for us to become capable of divine grace unless we have driven out the evil passions that have preoccupied our souls. I know doctors who do not give the salutary medicines before they have drained out by means of an emetic the matter that was causing the sickness, which the intemperate had stored up in themselves through a bad diet. Perfume should not be poured into a vessel that had previously been filled with some foul-smelling liquid, unless it is washed out first. Therefore, it is necessary that its initial contents be poured out, in order that it may be able to contain that which is being brought in. HOMILIES ON THE PSALMS 21.4.[24]

62:9-10 The Deception of Worldly Wealth

TRUST NOT IN RICHES. BASIL THE GREAT: "But foolish are the sons of people." The psalmist knew that not all follow his instruction or permit themselves to hope in God, but that they have their hope in the follies of life. Therefore, he says, "But vain are the sons of people, the sons of people are liars."[25] Why vain? Because they are liars. Where, especially, is their deceit proved? "In the balances used for defrauding," he says. In what sort of balances does he mean? All people do not weigh in the balance, do they? All people are not wool sellers or butchers, are they? Or do not handle gold or silver, or in general themselves deal with these materials that the merchants are

accustomed to exchange by means of scales and weights, do they? But there is a large class of artisans, which does not need scales at all for its work; and there are many sailors and many who are always engaged about courts of justice and the duty of ruling, among whom there is deceit, but the deceit is not practiced through scales. What, then, does he mean? That there is a certain balance constructed in the interior of each of us by our Creator, on which it is possible to judge the nature of things. "I have set before you life and death, good and evil,"[26] two natures contrary to each other; balance them against each other in your own tribunal; weigh accurately which is more profitable to you: to choose a temporary pleasure and through it to receive eternal death, or having chosen suffering in the practice of virtue, to use it to attain everlasting delights. HOMILIES ON THE PSALMS 21.4.[27]

WEALTH IS A TRAP. BASIL THE GREAT: Thus, no one is able to see the perilous traps before he falls into them. In the same way, Satan, hostile to us from the beginning, sneaks into the shadows of worldly pleasures that grow thickly enough about the road of life to hide the brigand while he plots against us. There he lurks in secret and spreads his nets for our destruction. If, then, we would safely traverse the road of life lying before us, and offer to Christ our body and soul alike free from the shame of wounds and receive the crown for this victory, we must always and everywhere keep the eyes of our soul wide open, holding in suspicion everything that gives pleasure. We must unhesitatingly pass by such things, without allowing our thoughts to rest in them, even if we think that we see gold lying before us in heaps, ready to be picked up by any who so desire. "If riches abound," says the Scripture, "set not your heart on them." We must pay no heed,

---

[21]Babylon is understood here as a place of exile, captivity and testing of one's trust in God. [22]Bar 3:10. [23]CS 47:18-19. [24]FC 46:346-47. [25]FC 46:346-47. Basil is following the Septuagint here. [26]Deut 30:15 (LXX). [27]FC 46:347*.

even if the earth buds forth every kind of delicacy and offers luxurious dwellings to our gaze, for "our citizenship is in heaven; from whence also we look for the Savior, our Lord Jesus Christ."[28] Nor should we take notice when dancing and merrymaking and reveling and banquets ringing with the sound of the flute are offered for our enjoyment, for the Scripture says, "Vanity of vanities, and all is vanity."[29] HOMILY ON DETACHMENT 21.[30]

DO NOT SET YOUR HEART ON WORLDLY SUCCESS. AUGUSTINE: So, with your indulgence, what I have to say to you is this: do not love the success of this world, and those of you who may have it, do not set your hopes on it. It is false, it is deceptive, it is not really to be had. Well, even if you do have it, do not love it, do not rely on it, and it will not be a pit. "Command the rich of this world," says the apostle, "command them to be rich [in good works]."[31] But the rich of this world are Christians, they are believers. Command them. To do what? "Not to think highly of themselves or to have their hopes set on the uncertainty of riches." As the psalm also says, "If riches pour down," as from a spring where you can draw as much as you want without effort and what you draw will immediately vanish—if they flow, "do not set your heart on them," where it is flowing. If it is flowing, it is making a flood; you set your heart there, it carries it off. SERMON 25A.2.[32]

DO NOT DELIGHT IN RICHES. AUGUSTINE: So, then, that you may continue in prayers night and day, until that consolation comes to you, remember that you are desolate, however much you may abound in the good fortune of worldly wealth. The apostle did not attribute this gift[33] to just any widow, but he says, "She that is a widow indeed and desolate has trusted in the Lord and continues in prayers night and day."[34] But, note carefully what follows: "But she that lives in pleasures is dead while she is living,"[35] for one lives in the things that he loves, that he chiefly seeks after, by which he believes himself happy. There-

fore, what the Scripture says about riches, "If riches abound, do not set your heart on them," I say to you about pleasures: if pleasures abound, do not set your heart on them. Do not rely too strongly on the fact that they are not lacking to you, that they minister to your satisfaction abundantly, that they flow, so to speak, from a plentiful source of earthly happiness. All these things you must inwardly despise and reject; you must seek after no more of them than is needed to support your bodily health. Because of the necessary activities of this life, health is not to be despised until "this mortal shall put on immortality,"[36] and that is the true and perfect and unending health that is not refreshed by corruptible pleasure when it fails through earthly weakness but is maintained by heavenly strength and made young by eternal incorruptibility. The apostle says, "Do not make provision for the flesh in its desires,"[37] because our care of the flesh must be in view of the exigencies of salvation. "For no one ever hated his own flesh,"[38] as he also says. This seems to be the reason why he rebukes Timothy for too great chastisement of the body and advises him to "use a little wine for his stomach's sake and his frequent infirmities."[39] LETTER 130.[40]

THE VANITY OF TEMPORAL WEALTH. FULGENTIUS OF RUSPE: Thus to those who wish to have happiness in the goods of present things, the psalm says, "How long, you people, shall my honor suffer shame? How long will you love vain words and seek after lies?"[41] And in another text, "Put no confidence in extortion, and set no vain hopes on robbery; if riches increase, do not set your heart on them." The blessed James does not cease to reprove such people, saying, "Come now, you rich, weep and wail over your impending miseries. Your wealth has rotted away, your clothes have become moth-eaten, your gold and silver

---

[28]Phil 3:20. [29]Eccles 1:2. [30]FC 9:488*. [31]1 Tim 6:17-18. [32]WSA 3 2:90*. [33]A sense of desolation and need that led Proba, the wealthy widow to whom Augustine addressed this letter, to seek instruction in prayer. [34]1 Tim 5:5. [35]1 Tim 5:6. [36]1 Cor 15:54. [37]Rom 13:14. [38]Eph 5:29. [39]1 Tim 5:23. [40]FC 18:381-82*. [41]Ps 4:2 (4:3 LXX, Vg.).

have corroded, and that corrosion will be a testimony against you; it will devour your flesh like a fire. You have stored up treasure for the last days. Behold, the wages you withheld from the workers who harvested your fields are crying aloud, and the cries of the harvesters have reached the ears of the Lord of hosts. You have lived on earth in luxury and pleasure; you have fattened your hearts for the day of slaughter."[42] He commanded that the laughter and the joy of such people be turned to mourning and dejection, saying, "Cleanse your hands, you sinners, and purify your hearts, you of two minds. Begin to lament, to mourn, to weep. Let your laughter be turned into mourning and your joy into dejection. Humble yourselves before the Lord, and he will exalt you."[43] LETTER 7.19.[44]

GOD IS POWERFUL IN JUDGMENT AND MERCY. BASIL THE GREAT: Then he brings up a decision for all that was said, not now from his own words but one that he heard from God. "God has spoken once, these two things have I heard,"[45] he says. And let it not disturb anyone that what was said is, as it were, incredible, namely, that God spoke once and the prophet heard two things. For it is possible for someone to speak once but for the things spoken on the one occasion to be many. In fact, when a certain person met someone once, he discussed many things. The one who heard his words is able to say, "He talked with me once, but he spoke about many things." This is what was meant on the present occasion, the manifestation of God occurred to me once, but there are two matters about which he talked. He did not say, "God spoke of one thing, but I heard these two." If he had, the statement would seem to have some discrepancy in it. What were the two things that he heard? "That power belongs to God, and mercy to you, O Lord."[46] God is powerful, he says, in judgment, and likewise merciful. Therefore do not trust in iniquity, and do not hand yourself over to riches. Do not choose vanity; do not carry around the corrupt lawcourt of your soul. Knowing that our Lord is mighty, fear his

strength and do not despair of his kindness. Now, in order that we may not do wrong, fear is good; and in order that he who has once slipped into sin may not throw himself away through despair, the hope of mercy is good. For power belongs to God, and mercy is from him. HOMILIES ON THE PSALMS 21.5.[47]

THE FOLLY OF AMASSING WEALTH. AUGUSTINE: I am aware of that,[48] and I am saddened by it. You are disturbed, and—as he who is infallible tells us—you are troubled in vain. Yes, you are storing up treasures. Even though we grant that you are successful in every transaction, even though we say nothing about your losses, even though we make no mention of the great risks and the deaths that accompany every profitable transaction (I do not mean corporeal deaths; I mean the deaths that are occasioned by evil designs—for veracity dies so that profits may increase), yet, you are being inwardly stripped bare so that you may be outwardly adorned. Yes, suppose that we ignore those facts and make no reference to certain other facts; suppose that we disregard your reverses and consider only your successes. In that case, you are storing up treasures, profits are pouring in from all sides, money is flowing into your coffers as if in a fountain, and whenever a need arises it is engulfed by abundance. Nevertheless, have you not heard: "If riches abound, do not set your heart on them"? Yes, you are growing rich; so you are not disturbed unprofitably. Nevertheless, you are disturbed in vain. But you ask me, "Why am I disturbed in vain? See, I am filling my coffers, and my storehouses can hardly contain the treasures I am acquiring. How, then, am I disquieted in vain?" Because you are storing up treasures, and you do not know for whom you are gathering them. Or, if you know it, I beseech

---

[42]Jas 5:1-5. [43]Jas 4:8-10. [44]FC 95:363-64. [45]Ps 62:11 (61:12 LXX, Vg.). [46]Ps 62:11 (61:12 LXX, Vg.). [47]FC 46:349-50*. [48]The reference is to the troubles and anxieties of daily life being experienced by the people listening to Augustine's sermon.

you to tell me. I would hear you tell me that. So, if you are not disturbed in vain, tell me for whom you are gathering treasures. "For myself," you reply. Do you dare to say that, although you must die? "For my children," you reply. Do you dare to say that, since they, too, must die? "It is a pious duty for a parent to store up treasures for his children!" Rather, since a person must die, it is a great vanity for him to store up treasures for those who must die. If it is for yourself, why are you gathering treasures that you must leave behind when you die? This is also the case with regard to your children; they are to succeed you, but they are not to abide forever. I refrain from asking, "For what kind of children?" Perhaps debauchery may squander what avarice has amassed. By loose living, someone else squanders what you have amassed by your labors. But I leave this out of account. Perhaps your children will be upright, not dissolute. Perhaps they will preserve what you will have left and increase what you have saved, not dissipate what you have gathered. If your children do this, if in this regard they imitate you, their father, then they are just as vain as you are. What I was saying to you, I say to them. To your son I put this question: "For whom are you gathering?" To him also I say, "You are storing up treasures, and you do not know for whom you are gathering them." For just as you do not know, so neither does he. Even if vanity has remained in him, has truth therefore lost its force for him? SERMON 60.3.[49]

---

[49]FC 11:261-63*.

63:1-11 A PSALM OF LONGING FOR GOD

A Psalm of David, when he was in the Wilderness of Judah.

[1]*O God, thou art my God, I seek thee,*
my soul thirsts for thee;
my flesh faints for thee,
as in a dry and weary land where no water is.
[2]*So I have looked upon thee in the sanctuary,*
beholding thy power and glory.
[3]*Because thy steadfast love is better than life,*
my lips will praise thee.
[4]*So I will bless thee as long as I live;*
I will lift up my hands and call on thy name.

[5]*My soul is feasted as with marrow and fat,*
and my mouth praises thee with joyful lips,
[6]*when I think of thee upon my bed,*
and meditate on thee in the watches of the night;
[7]*for thou hast been my help,*
and in the shadow of thy wings I sing for joy.
[8]*My soul clings to thee;*
thy right hand upholds me.

[9]*But those who seek to destroy my life*
shall go down into the depths of the earth;
[10]*they shall be given over to the power of the sword,*

they shall be prey for jackals.
[11]*But the king shall rejoice in God;*

all who swear by him shall glory;
for the mouths of liars will be stopped.

OVERVIEW: Christ will dwell in bodies that are made an arid wasteland by self-denial and in lives devoid of worldly pleasures (MAXIMUS). The sacrifices and worship we offer to God must be the finest and best we can give him (AMBROSE). We can remember God and meditate on him best at night when we are quiet, restful and relieved of the distracting cares of the day (CHRYSOSTOM). We pray worthily when we are oblivious to place and self and entirely engaged in our thoughts of God (PHILOXENUS).

63:1-4 A Close Relationship with God

PREPARATION FOR THE INDWELLING OF CHRIST. MAXIMUS OF TURIN: In having done this,[1] then, God gave us the form of fasting, in order that dwelling in the desert, so to speak, during the time of the fasts we might abstain from rich foods, from pleasure and from women, so that Eve might not be united with us, lest by her charming persuasiveness she subvert us from our chaste observance. For a person who fasts and is chaste seems to dwell in the desert in a certain way at the time of Quadragesima.[2] The very body of the Christian is in a sense a desert when it is not filled with food and cheered with drink but is neglected in the desolation of parched fasting. Our body, I say, is a desert when the flesh pines away with abstinence, paleness is induced by thirst and the unadorned appearance of the whole person grows filthy through the contempt of material goods. Then Christ the Lord inhabits the desert of our body when he has found that our land is desolate because of hunger and parched because of thirst, according to what the prophet David says: "I have appeared to you in the holy place as in a land that is desolate, impenetrable and waterless." For we are unable to appear to him in the holy place unless the land of our body is desolate of worldly pleasures, impene-

trable to diabolical lusts and unmoistened by wanton desires. Then the Savior dwelling in this desert of our body overcomes there all the factions of the devil, and safe and secure from the thoughts of this world he takes it for his habitation, so that from then on we might see heaven and earth within ourselves as in a solitude; that is to say, we might think of nothing other than the Lord of the heavenly kingdom and the author of earthly resurrection. SERMON 50A.4.[3]

63:5-9 A Worthy Relationship with God

GIVE GOD YOUR BEST. AMBROSE: Now let us turn our attention to the characteristic of fatness or richness of which David speaks intelligibly when he says, "Let my soul be filled as with marrow and fatness." Before that he had said, "And may your whole burnt offering be made fat."[4] By this he means that the requirements for a sacrifice are that it be fat or rich, that it be glistening and that it be weighted with the sustenance inspired by faith and devotion and by the rich nourishment of the Word of God. Frequently we use the word *fat* or *rich* when we refer to something that is heavily and elaborately adorned, and to the finest victim as one that is not thin and scrawny. Wherefore we designate as "rich" a sacrifice that we desire to be regarded as the "finest." We also have proof of this when we consult the prophetic passage in the Scriptures where fine cows are compared with years of fertility![5] CAIN AND ABEL 2.5.17.[6]

ALWAYS REMEMBER GOD. CHRYSOSTOM: Why do we forget about wickedness? It is due to our remembrance of good things, due to our remem-

---

[1]The reference is to Christ's forty-day fast in the wilderness (Mt 4:1-2). [2]The forty days of the Lenten season. [3]ACW 50:123*. [4]Ps 20:3 (19:4 LXX, Vg.). [5]Gen 41:26. [6]FC 42:418-19.

brance of God. If we continually remember God, we cannot remember those things also. For [he says], "When I remembered you on my bed, I thought on you in the morning dawn." We ought then to have God always in remembrance, but then especially, when thought is undisturbed, when by means of that remembrance [one] is able to condemn himself, when he can retain [things] in memory. For in the daytime indeed, if we do remember, other cares and troubles entering in, drive the thought out again; but in the night it is possible to remember continually, when the soul is calm and at rest; when it is in the heaven, and under a serene sky. "The things that you say in your hearts you should grieve over on your beds,"[7] he says. For it was indeed right to remember this throughout the day also. But inasmuch as you are always full of cares and distracted amid the things of this life, at least then remember God on your bed; at the morning dawn meditate on him. ON THE EPISTLE TO THE HEBREWS 14.9.[8]

ELEMENTS OF WORTHY PRAYER. PHILOXENUS OF MABBUG: Pure prayer such as is worthy of God, O disciple of God, is not uttered by means of compound words. Prayer that is worthy of God consists in this: that one gather in one's mind from the entire world and not let it be secretly bound to anything; that one place it entirely at God's disposal and forget, during the time of prayer, everything that is material, including one's own self and the place where one is standing. One should be secretly swallowed up in the spirit of God, and one should clothe oneself in God at the time of prayer both outwardly and inwardly, set on fire with ardent love for him and entirely engulfed in his thoughts of God, entirely commingled in all of him, with the movements of one's thoughts suffused with wondrous recollection of God, while the soul has gone out in love to seek him whom it loves, just as David said, "My soul has gone out after you." EXCERPT ON PRAYER.[9]

---

[7]Ps 4:4 (4:5 LXX).   [8]NPNF 1 14:437.   [9]CS 101:129.

64:1-10 A PRAYER FOR PROTECTION

To the choirmaster. A Psalm of David.

[1]*Hear my voice, O God, in my complaint;*
   preserve my life from dread of the enemy,
[2]*hide me from the secret plots of the wicked,*
   from the scheming of evildoers,
[3]*who whet their tongues like swords,*
   who aim bitter words like arrows,
[4]*shooting from ambush at the blameless,*
   shooting at him suddenly and without fear.
[5]*They hold fast to their evil purpose;*
   they talk of laying snares secretly,

thinking, "Who can see us?[y]
   [6]*Who can search out our crimes?[z]*
We have thought out a cunningly conceived
      plot."
   For the inward mind and heart of a man are
      deep!

[7]*But God will shoot his arrow at them;*
   they will be wounded suddenly.
[8]*Because of their tongue he will bring them to*
      ruin;[a]
   all who see them will wag their heads.

⁹Then all men will fear;
   they will tell what God has wrought,
   and ponder what he has done.

¹⁰Let the righteous rejoice in the LORD,
   and take refuge in him!
Let all the upright in heart glory!

y Syr: Heb *them*   z Cn: Heb *they search out crimes*   a Cn: Heb *They will bring him to ruin, their tongue being against them*

OVERVIEW: There are good and bad kinds of fear, but fear of the Lord is a divine and good fear that sustains us against our spiritual enemies (BASIL). In this life we delight in God by faith; eventually our joy will be fully realized when we see God as he truly is (AUGUSTINE).

64:2 Fear of the Enemy

TRUST IN GOD DRIVES OUT FEAR. BASIL THE GREAT: What, really, does our spiritual father intend to teach? "I will teach you the fear of the Lord." When he ordered us above to fear the Lord, he also showed the profit that comes from fear, saying, "Those who fear him do not lack anything."[1] At present also, they hand down to us a certain teaching of divine fear. Now it is in the power of every one, even of the private individual, to say that it is necessary to be healthy; but, to say how health must be obtained, that certainly belongs to him who understands the art of medicine. Every fear is not a good and saving feeling, but there is also a hostile fear, which the prophet prays may not spring up in his soul, when he says, "Deliver my soul from the fear of the enemy." Fear of the enemy is that which produces in us a cowardliness with regard to death and misleads us to cower before distinguished persons. How, in fact, will he who fears these things be able in time of martyrdom to resist sin even to death and to pay his debt to the Lord, who died and rose again for us? He also, who is easily scared by the demons, has the fear of the enemy in him. On the whole, such a fear seems to be a passion born of unbelief. For no one who believes that he has at hand a strong helper is frightened by any of those who attempt to throw him into confusion. HOMILIES

ON THE PSALMS 16.8.[2]

64:10 Rejoice in the Lord

THE JUST PERSON DELIGHTS IN THE LORD. AUGUSTINE: "The just person will take delight in the Lord and hope in him, and all the upright of heart shall be praised." We have certainly sung this with voice and heart. Christian consciences and tongues have spoken these words to God: The just one will take delight not in the world but in the Lord. "Light has dawned for the just," it says somewhere else, "and delight for the upright of heart."[3] You may ask where delight is to be found. Here you have it: "The just one will take delight in the Lord." And somewhere else: "Delight in the Lord, and he will give you the aims of your heart."[4] What are we being shown? What is being granted us? What are we being told? To take delight in the Lord. But can you take delight in what you do not see? Or perhaps we do see the Lord? We have that safely promised us; but now "we walk by faith, as long as we are in the body we are away from the Lord."[5] By faith, not by sight. When will it be by sight? When another thing John says is fulfilled: "Beloved, we are children of God, and it has not yet appeared what we shall be. But we know that when he appears we shall be like him, because we shall see him as he is."[6] Then there will be great and perfect delight, then joy will be full, when it is no longer hope suckling us with milk but the real thing providing us with solid food. SERMON 21.1.[7]

---

[1]Ps 34:9 (33:10 LXX).   [2]FC 46:262.   [3]Ps 97:11 (96:11 LXX, Vg.).   [4]Ps 37:4 (36:4 LXX, Vg.).   [5]2 Cor 5:6-7.   [6]1 Jn 3:2.   [7]WSA 3 2:29.

65:1-13 PRAISE FOR GOD'S GREAT GOODNESS

To the choirmaster.
A Psalm of David. A Song.

¹Praise is due to thee,
　O God, in Zion;
and to thee shall vows be performed,
　² O Thou who hearest prayer!
To thee shall all flesh come
　³on account of sins.
When our transgressions prevail over us,^b
　thou dost forgive them.
⁴Blessed is he whom thou dost choose and bring
　　near,
　to dwell in thy courts!
We shall be satisfied with the goodness of thy
　　house,
　thy holy temple!

⁵By dread deeds thou dost answer us with
　　deliverance,
　O God of our salvation,
who art the hope of all the ends of the earth,
　and of the farthest seas;
⁶who by thy strength hast established the
　　mountains,
　being girded with might;

⁷who dost still the roaring of the seas,
　the roaring of their waves,
　the tumult of the peoples;
⁸so that those who dwell at earth's farthest
　　bounds
　are afraid at thy signs;
thou makest the outgoings of the morning and
　　the evening
　to shout for joy.

⁹Thou visitest the earth and waterest it,
　thou greatly enrichest it;
the river of God is full of water;
　thou providest their grain,
　for so thou hast prepared it.
¹⁰Thou waterest its furrows abundantly,
　settling its ridges,
softening it with showers,
　and blessing its growth.
¹¹Thou crownest the year with thy bounty;
　the tracks of thy chariot drip with fatness.
¹²The pastures of the wilderness drip,
　the hills gird themselves with joy,
¹³the meadows clothe themselves with flocks,
　the valleys deck themselves with grain,
　they shout and sing together for joy.

b Gk: Heb *me*

OVERVIEW: God gathers his faithful believers to himself in heaven, where they will sing praises to him in a new life free from the hardships and defilements of this world. The individual who possesses the goodness of God and godly virtue is happy and content in all the circumstances of life (AMBROSE).

We experience the evils of drought and short-age of food because God visits the earth in judgment on account of our sin (GREGORY OF NAZIANZUS). God blesses his people both now in the annual cycle of years and eternally in heaven (BEDE).

65:1-4 *The Great Blessing of Being Chosen by God*

GOD WILL GATHER HIS PEOPLE TO HIMSELF.
AMBROSE: The soul has to depart from the tortuousness of this life and the defilements of the earthly body. It must hasten to those heavenly gatherings, although it is granted to the saints alone to reach them. There it shall sing praise to God. For in the lesson taken from the prophet[1] we hear of those singing praise to God to the accompaniment of their harps,[2] "Great and marvelous are your works, O Lord God almighty, just and true are your ways, O King of the ages. Who will not fear you, O Lord, and magnify your name? For you only are holy: for all nations will come and worship before you."[3] And it shall see your marriage feast, O Lord Jesus, wherein the bride is led from earthly to heavenly dwellings, as all sing in joyous accord, "All flesh shall come to you," now no longer subject to the world but espoused to the Spirit, and shall look on bridal chambers adorned with linen, roses, lilies and garlands. For whom else are the nuptials so adorned? For they are adorned with the purple stripes of confessors, the blood of martyrs, the lilies of virgins and the crowns of priests. ON HIS BROTHER SATYRUS 2.132.[4]

GOD'S BLESSINGS ARE ALWAYS WITH US.
AMBROSE: What indeed is lacking to the one who possesses the good and has virtue always as his companion and ally? In what role of life is he not most powerful? In what poverty is he not rich? In what lowly status is he not noble? In what leisure not industrious? In what weakness not vigorous? In what infirmity not strong? In what quiet of sleep not active? Even when he is asleep, his own virtue does not forsake him. In what solitude is he not in a crowd? The happy life surrounds him, grace clothes him, the garment of glory makes him radiant. He is no less happy when at leisure than when he works, no less filled with glory when he sleeps than when he is awake, because he is no less safe and sound when sleeping than when he is awake. Now when can he appear to be on holiday? His mind is always at work. When can he appear to be alone? He is always with that

good of which the psalmist says, "We shall be filled with the good things of your house." When can he appear to be downcast? "His citizenship is in heaven."[5] When can he appear not to be handsome? He conforms himself to the likeness of the beautiful and only good; although weak in his members, he is strong in his spirit. JACOB AND THE HAPPY LIFE 8.39.[6]

65:9-11 God's Abundant Blessings

THE PURPOSE OF EVIL. GREGORY OF NAZIANZUS: Only let us recognize the purpose of the evil. Why have the crops withered, our storehouses been emptied, the pastures of our flocks failed, the fruits of the earth been withheld and the plains been filled with shame instead of such fatness? Why have valleys lamented and not abounded in corn, the mountains not dropped sweetness, as they shall do hereafter to the righteous, but been stripped and dishonored and received on the contrary the curse of Gilboa?[7] The whole earth has become as it was in the beginning, before it was adorned with its beauties. "You visited the earth and made it to drink," but the visitation has been for evil and the draught destructive. ON HIS FATHER'S SILENCE, ORATION 16.17.[8]

GOD BLESSES US WITH GOODNESS YEAR ROUND. BEDE: For the fact that each of the four rows worn on the chest contains three stones[9] corresponds to the sequence of the yearly cycle, which is divided into four seasons of three months each. Now in the Scriptures the entire year is designated as the time of our salvation, in which we strive for an eternal reward. As the Sav-

---

[1]John. [2]See Rev 14:2. [3]Rev 15:3-4. [4]FC 22:258. [5]Phil 3:20. [6]FC 65:144-45. [7]2 Sam 1:21. Gilboa was the place where Israel was defeated by the Philistines, resulting in the deaths of Saul and his three sons. [8]NPNF 2 7:253*. [9]Aaron bore twelve precious stones on his breast in order to signify that there would come a time in which the faith of the holy Trinity would be preached to the human race in all four parts of the world; thus twelve stones were arranged in three groups of four.

ior bears witness, he was sent in accordance with the saying of Isaiah to preach the acceptable year of the Lord and the day of recompense.[10] The psalmist also sings to him concerning the same year, saying, "You bless the crown of the year with your goodness." For in the present time he gives them the goodness of right faith and works, and on the day of recompense he will give the crown of everlasting blessing. ON THE TABERNACLE 3.6.[11]

---

[10]Is 61:2; Lk 4:19. [11]TTH 18:129-30*.

66:1-20 A PSALM OF PRAISE FOR GOD'S ANSWER TO PRAYER

To the choirmaster. A Song. A Psalm.

[1]*Make a joyful noise to God, all the earth;*
 [2]*sing the glory of his name;*
  give to him glorious praise!
[3]*Say to God, "How terrible are thy deeds!*
  So great is thy power that thy enemies
   cringe before thee.
[4]*All the earth worships thee;*
  they sing praises to thee,
  sing praises to thy name." Selah

[5]*Come and see what God has done:*
  he is terrible in his deeds among men.
[6]*He turned the sea into dry land;*
  men passed through the river on foot.
There did we rejoice in him,
 [7]*who rules by his might for ever,*
whose eyes keep watch on the nations—
  let not the rebellious exalt
   themselves Selah

[8]*Bless our God, O peoples,*
  let the sound of his praise be heard,
[9]*who has kept us among the living,*

and has not let our feet slip.
[10]*For thou, O God, hast tested us;*
  thou hast tried us as silver is tried.
[11]*Thou didst bring us into the net;*
  thou didst lay affliction on our loins;
[12]*thou didst let men ride over our heads;*
  we went through fire and through water;
yet thou hast brought us forth to a spacious
   place.[c]

[13]*I will come into thy house with burnt*
   offerings;
  I will pay thee my vows,
[14]*that which my lips uttered*
  and my mouth promised when I was in
   trouble.
[15]*I will offer to thee burnt offerings of fatlings,*
  with the smoke of the sacrifice of rams;
I will make an offering of bulls and goats.
   Selah
[16]*Come and hear, all you who fear God,*
  and I will tell what he has done for me.
[17]*I cried aloud to him,*
  and he was extolled with my tongue.
[18]*If I had cherished iniquity in my heart,*

the Lord would not have listened.
¹⁹But truly God has listened;
  he has given heed to the voice of my prayer.

²⁰Blessed be God,
  because he has not rejected my prayer
  or removed his steadfast love from me!

---

c Cn Compare Gk Syr Jerome Tg: Heb *saturation*

OVERVIEW: In order to understand the Word of God properly, it is necessary to understand the figures of speech and how they are used (AUGUSTINE). Just as God saved the Israelites by parting the Red Sea and destroying Pharaoh and his army, so he saves people who believe in Christ and destroys Satan (THEODORET). Temptations overwhelm and destroy some people, but they temper others spiritually to whom God grants deliverance (CYRIL OF JERUSALEM). God allows us to experience temptation but then delivers us from them (ATHANASIUS). Great care must be taken in keeping God's laws, because if we fail to obey them, we not only lose a great reward but also incur punishment (BASIL). All vows made to God, even those made in times of duress, must be kept and kept in a timely manner (FULGENTIUS).

66:4-6 Understanding Language and Symbolism

FIGURES OF SPEECH. AUGUSTINE: Also in this place (which we have been quoting),[1] the apostle to the Gentiles said that the wrath of God comes on the children of infidelity because of these evils.[2] When, however, he says, "And you yourselves once walked in them when they were your life,"[3] he shows well enough that they were not their life then. To them, indeed, they were dead, since their life was hidden with Christ in God. For the evils, in truth, were living in those who were not living in the evils, as I indicated a little while ago. Likewise, the vices, indeed, that were dwelling in the members of certain people were said to be their members, by a figure of speech in which the name of a place is given to the things contained within it, just as it is said that the whole forum speaks when what is meant is that the people who are in the forum are speaking. By this same figure of speech, there is sung in the psalm, "Let all the earth adore you," that is, all people who are on the earth. ON CONTINENCE 14.30.[4]

SALVATION THROUGH WATER. THEODORET OF CYR: Then [Symmachus][5] outlines what was done of old. "He turns the sea into dry land; they will cross the river on foot." The tense has been changed here: he spoke of the past as future, whereas the others retained the tense, Symmachus saying, "He turned the sea into dry land, they crossed the river on foot." This is the God, he is saying, who will grant us salvation as well, who of old divided sea and river, and bade our forebears cross without risk and accords the nations the crossing that they make when through the washing of regeneration they are reformed. In other words, just as at that time through the hand of the mighty Moses he divided the Red Sea at this point, . . . so now as well through the hand of the priests he renews the people who believe in Christ, while submerging in figure Pharaoh with his chariots—that is, the devil with his desires (the initiated know what I mean). COMMENTARY ON THE PSALMS 66.4.[6]

66:10-12 Deliverance from Temptation

GRATEFUL FOR DELIVERANCE. CYRIL OF JERUSALEM: "And lead us not into temptation, O Lord." Is it this then what the Lord teaches us

---

[1]He is referring to quotations from Colossians (e.g., Col 3:1-2, 6). [2]Unclean living, lust and greed. [3]Col 3:7. [4]FC 16:229*. [5]A third-century translator of a Greek version of the Old Testament. [6]FC 101:372-73.

to pray, that we may not to be tempted at all? How, then, is it said elsewhere, "an untempted person is a person unproved";[7] and again, "My brothers, count it all joy when you fall into various temptations"?[8] But does perchance the entering into temptation mean being overwhelmed by the temptation? For temptation is like a winter torrent difficult to cross. Those, therefore, who are not overwhelmed in temptations, pass through, showing themselves excellent swimmers and not being swept away by them at all; while those who are not such, enter into them and are overwhelmed. As for example, Judas having entered into the temptation of the love of money, did not swim through it but was overwhelmed and was strangled both in body and spirit. Peter entered into the temptation of the denial; but having entered, he was not overwhelmed by it but courageously swam through it and was delivered from the temptation. Listen again, in another place, to a company of unscathed saints, giving thanks for deliverance from temptation: "You, O God, have proved us; you have tried us by fire like silver is tried. You brought us into the net; you laid afflictions on our loins. You have caused people to ride over our heads; we went through fire and water; and you brought us out into a place of rest." You see them speaking boldly in regard to their having passed through and not been pierced. "But you brought us out into a place of rest"; now their coming into a place of rest is their being delivered from temptation. MYSTAGOGICAL LECTURES 23.17.[9]

GOD HELPS IN TIME OF DISTRESS. ATHANASIUS: And although the entrance is "straight and narrow," once inside we see a vast and limitless space, greater than any other anywhere. We have been told of these things by eyewitnesses and heirs. They speak of their trials and distresses: "You have placed afflictions before us," but then they add, "You brought us out into a spacious place"—and, "You gave us space in our distress."[10] FESTAL LETTERS 9.[11]

66:13-14 Keeping Our Obligations to God

CONSEQUENCES OF BREAKING GOD'S LAW. BASIL THE GREAT: If you require evidence from the Old Testament also in order for me to convince you that the judgment of God occurs in this way [as I have presented it[12]], Moses says, "You shall love the Lord your God with all your heart and with all your mind and with all your strength,"[13] and "You shall love your neighbor as yourself."[14] To this the Lord adds, "On these two commandments depend the whole law and the prophets."[15] The apostle also bears witness in the words: "Love, therefore, is the fulfilling of the law."[16] Moreover, they who do not observe these commands and do not perform the acts of justification that derive from them are liable to punishment, as Moses declares in the words "Cursed is every one who does not abide in all that is written in this book."[17] And David says, "If I have contemplated iniquity in my heart, the Lord will not hear me." In another place, also, he says, "There have they trembled for fear where there was no fear; for God has scattered the bones of those who attacked you."[18] There is need, then, of great diligence and of ceaseless care, lest, perhaps, in carrying out the commandment improperly as regards any of the details we have discussed, we may not only lose a reward so great and so blessed but also become the objects of threats so terrible. CONCERNING BAPTISM 2.8.[19]

VOWS TO GOD MUST BE KEPT. FULGENTIUS OF RUSPE: Therefore, because we have been speaking of the nature of marriage as the Lord has given it, consequently, this must be examined with the greatest care, namely, what you devoutly willed

---

[7]Tertullian On Baptism 20. [8]Jas 1:2. [9]NPNF 2 7:155-56*. [10]Ps 4:1 (4:2 LXX). [11]ARL 147. [12]Basil was addressing 1 Corinthians 13:1-3, which speaks about the necessity of love as the motive for all Christian conduct. Question 8 asks whether the work enjoined by a command is acceptable to God if the manner of performing it is not in conformity with the divine ordinance. [13]Deut 6:5. [14]Lev 19:18; Mt 19:19. [15]Mt 22:40. [16]Rom 13:10. [17]Deut 27:26. [18]Ps 53:5 (52:6 LXX). [19]FC 9:416-17**.

beforehand (if there could have been anything). Because the use of things conceded by God is not forbidden to human beings, one should not conclude that therefore one need not render to God what he has vowed. It is written: "I will pay you my vows, those that my lips uttered." And lest anyone seek to use tribulation as a reason for excusing himself, in order to gain the freedom to evade a promise or to think of himself as free from what he has vowed, by saying that he was forced to vow something not by his own will but because of tribulation, the blessed David teaches that everything that was legitimately promised, even in tribulation, must be given back to God, when he says to God, "I will pay you my vows, those that my lips uttered." And he added immediately, "my mouth promised when I was in trouble."[20] But in Deuteronomy, it is also written, "If you make a vow to the Lord your God, do not postpone fulfilling it; for the Lord your God will surely require it of you, and you would incur guilt. But if you refrain from vowing, you will not incur guilt. Whatever your lips utter, you must diligently perform, just as you have freely vowed to the Lord your God with your own mouth."[21] And Solomon says, "When you make a vow to God, do not delay fulfilling it; . . . Fulfill what you vow. It is better that you should not vow than that you should vow and not fulfill it."[22] LETTER 1.11.[23]

---

[20]Ps 66:14 (65:14 LXX, Vg.). [21]Deut 23:21-23. [22]Eccles 5:4-5. [23]FC 95:284-85.

67:1-7 A COMMUNAL PRAYER FOR GOD'S BLESSINGS

*To the choirmaster: with stringed instruments.
A Psalm. A Song.*

[1]*May God be gracious to us and bless us
  and make his face to shine upon us,* Selah
[2]*that thy way may be known upon earth,
  thy saving power among all nations.*
[3]*Let the peoples praise thee, O God;
  let all the peoples praise thee!*

[4]*Let the nations be glad and sing for joy,*

*for thou dost judge the peoples with equity
  and guide the nations upon earth.* Selah

[5]*Let the peoples praise thee, O God;
  let all the peoples praise thee!*

[6]*The earth has yielded its increase;
  God, our God, has blessed us.*
[7]*God has blessed us;
  let all the ends of the earth fear him!*

OVERVIEW: The pre-incarnate Christ declares himself as the only way to eternal salvation (AUGUSTINE). A sown kernel of wheat is analogous to the redeeming work of Christ, who died and rose to produce a bountiful harvest of redeemed souls (JEROME).

67:1-2 *The Way to Eternal Salvation*

CHRIST IS THE ONLY WAY TO SALVATION.
AUGUSTINE: This is, I repeat, the universal way
for the liberation of believers. The faithful Abraham received this divine message about it: "In
your seed all nations will be blessed."[1] Now Abraham was by birth a Chaldean, but he was bidden
to leave his country, his family and his father's
house, so that he might receive this promise and
that from him might issue the "seed prepared for
by the ministry of angels, the mediator offering
his hand";[2] so that in this mediator should be
found that universal way for the soul's liberation,
the way made available for all nations. Then
when he had first been liberated from the superstitions of the Chaldeans, Abraham worshiped
and followed the one true God and believed with
complete trust in his promises. This is the universal way of which the holy prophet speaks, when
he says, "May God have mercy on us and give us
his blessing. May he make his face to shine on us;
that we may know your way on the earth and
your salvation in all nations." Hence, so long
afterwards, the Savior, who took flesh from "the
seed of Abraham," said of himself, "I am the way,
the truth and the life."[3] CITY OF GOD 10.32.[4]

67:6 *God Has Blessed the Earth and Its Inhabitants*

A FRUITFUL HARVEST. JEROME: "The earth has
yielded its fruit," earth, holy Mary who is from
our earth, from our seed, from this clay, from
this slime, from Adam. "Dust you are, and to
dust you shall return."[5] This earth has yielded
its fruit; what it lost in the Garden of Eden, it
has found in the Son. "The earth has yielded its
fruit." First, it brought forth a flower. It says in
the Song of Songs, "I am the flower of the field
and the lily of the valleys."[6] This flower has
become fruit that we might eat it, that we might
consume its flesh. Would you like to know what
this fruit is? A Virgin from a virgin, the Lord
from the handmaid, God from man, Son from
mother, fruit from earth. Listen to what the
fruit itself says: "Unless the grain of wheat fall
into the ground and die, it cannot bring forth
much fruit."[7] "The earth has yielded its fruit"; it
has yielded a grain of wheat. Because the grain
of wheat has fallen into the ground and died, it
produces many fruits. The fruit is multiplied in
the head of grain. Because one had fallen, it rose
again with many; one grain of wheat has fallen
into the ground and a fruitful harvest came of it.
HOMILIES ON THE PSALMS 6.[8]

---

[1]Gen 22:18. [2]See Gal 3:19. [3]Jn 14:6. [4]CG 422-23. [5]Gen 3:19. [6]Song 2:1. [7]Jn 12:24. [8]FC 48:47*.

68:1-16 A PROCESSIONAL LITURGY

To the choirmaster.
A Psalm of David. A Song.

[1]*Let God arise, let his enemies be scattered;*
 let those who hate him flee before him!

[2]*As smoke is driven away, so drive them away;*
 as wax melts before fire,
  let the wicked perish before God!
[3]*But let the righteous be joyful;*
 let them exult before God;

let them be jubilant with joy!

⁴Sing to God, sing praises to his name;
  lift up a song to him who rides upon
    the clouds;ᵈ
  his name is the LORD, exult before him!

⁵Father of the fatherless and protector of
    widows
  is God in his holy habitation.
⁶God gives the desolate a home to dwell in;
  he leads out the prisoners to prosperity;
  but the rebellious dwell in a parched
    land.

⁷O God, when thou didst go forth before thy
    people,
  when thou didst march through the
    wilderness,   Selah
⁸the earth quaked, the heavens poured down
    rain,
  at the presence of God;
yon Sinai quaked at the presence of God,
  the God of Israel.
⁹Rain in abundance, O God, thou didst shed
    abroad;

thou didst restore thy heritage as it
    languished;
¹⁰thy flock found a dwelling in it;
  in thy goodness, O God, thou didst provide
    for the needy.

¹¹The Lord gives the command;
  great is the host of those who bore the
    tidings:
  ¹²"The kings of the armies, they flee,
    they flee!"
The women at home divide the spoil,
  ¹³though they stay among the sheepfolds—
the wings of a dove covered with silver,
  its pinions with green gold.
¹⁴When the Almighty scattered kings there,
  snow fell on Zalmon.

¹⁵O mighty mountain, mountain of Bashan;
  O many-peaked mountain, mountain
    of Bashan!
¹⁶Why look you with envy, O many-peaked
    mountain,
  at the mount which God desired for
    his abode,
  yea, where the LORD will dwell for ever?

d Or cast up a highway for him who rides through the deserts

OVERVIEW: Sinners will perish in the presence of God just as smoke dissipates in thin air and wax melts from heat (CASSIODORUS). As God promised in the Psalms, enemies of the gospel will fail and those who proclaim the truth will be admired by people of sound mind (JOHN). If one assists orphans, widows and the needy, he will be rewarded; his love of true wisdom will deepen, and he will glorify God (CHRYSOSTOM). Already in the Psalms the Holy Spirit announces that God will cause members of the church to be of one mind (CYPRIAN). The conduct of creatures in

the animal kingdom provides an example of how God desires people to live in harmony and with respect for one another (BASIL). Private prayer is allowed, but corporate prayer is better and is enhanced by hearing the reading of God's Word in public worship services (NICETAS).

The shaking of the earth and drops of dew from heaven at the presence of God are foreshadows of the earthquake at the time of Christ's crucifixion and the raining down of God's grace on the earth (THEODORET). In their literature, Greek pagan authors echo the truth about the power of

God as witnessed to in Holy Scripture (CLEMENT OF ALEXANDRIA). The Holy Spirit is the gracious rain that God sends down on his people to cleanse them and enable them to prophesy (AMBROSE). As God rained down manna in the wilderness, so he rained down the law of Moses at Sinai (JEROME). Like abundant rain God bestows his grace on us; it is the free gift of a loving God and is not given on the basis of human merit (AUGUSTINE). The preaching of the gospel receives its power from God, not from the nicety of language or the beauty of speech. If Christians and pagans proclaimed the same truth about God, only the preaching of Scripture would be effectual since Christian preaching is empowered by God (ORIGEN).

68:2-6 How God's People Should Live

SINNERS ARE COMPARED WITH SMOKE AND WAX. CASSIODORUS: "As smoke vanishes, so let them vanish away; as wax melts before the fire, so let sinners perish before the presence of God." In these two verses the punishment of sinners is foretold by two images. Smoke is a dark, thick mass that rises from the flames of this world that perish; the further it rises, the thinner it becomes through the empty air. Sinners are appropriately compared with it, for they produce from the fire of their wickedness smoke-bearing activities that through the action of pride rise to higher levels but inevitably like smoke vanish through their own self-exaltation. The second comparison that describes them follows. Wax is a soft, pliant substance gathered from honeycombs that melts under the fire's heat so that its substance is utterly dissipated. This image is appropriate for the wicked, for at God's judgment sinners disappear before his presence as the frail wax is consumed by the proximity of fire. Observe that the psalmist does not say that those to be tortured by enduring fire can be destroyed here and now in their substance. Rather, he says that they will perish before the presence of God, because they will never attain his grace and benefits, though

some misguided people[1] have sought to claim that they will. Note that in these verses the figure "parable" appears,[2] a comparison between things differing in kind; for smoke and wax are seen to be compared with sinners. EXPOSITIONS OF THE PSALMS 67.3.[3]

THE GOSPEL WILL NOT PASS AWAY. JOHN OF DAMASCUS: Concerning you,[4] the defenders of idolatry, were these words spoken by the prophet. For a very, very little while and your place shall not be found, but "just as the smoke vanishes, and just as wax melts near a fire, so you will fail." But, as touching the divine wisdom of the gospel, the Lord says, "Heaven and earth will pass away, but my words will not pass away."[5] And again the psalmist says, "You, Lord, in the beginning laid the foundation of the earth; and the heavens are the work of your hands. They shall perish, but you endure; and they all will wax old as does a garment, and you will fold them up as a vestment, and they shall be changed, but you are the same, and your years will not fail!"[6] And those divine preachers of the coming of Christ, those wise fishers of the world, whose nets drew all people from the depths of deceit, whom you, in your wickedness and bondage to sin, do vilify, did by signs and wonders and manifold powers shine as the sun in the world, giving sight to the blind, hearing to the deaf, motion to the lame and life to the dead. Their shadows alone healed all the ailments of humankind. The devils, whom you dread as gods, they not only cast forth from people's bodies but even drove out of the world itself by the sign of the cross, whereby they destroyed all sorcery and rendered witchcraft powerless. And these men, by curing every human disease by the power of Christ, and renewing all creation, are rightly admired as preachers of truth by all

---

[1]Cassiodorus probably has in mind the view of Origen that fallen angels and people condemned at the judgment (cf. *Princ.* 1.6 = PL 11:169; *Hom. I on Joshua* = PG 21:334) will ultimately be saved. [2]See Pss 1:3; 5:11; 17:8 (16:8 LXX). [3]ACW 52:122-23. [4]Theudas, a magician. [5]Mt 24:35. [6]Ps 102:25-27 (101:26-28 LXX).

persons of sound mind. Barlaam and Joseph 32.295-96.[7]

Love for the Downtrodden. Chrysostom: What do I mean? If you ever wish to associate with someone, make sure that you do not give your attention to those who enjoy health and wealth and fame as the world sees it, but take care of those in affliction, those in critical circumstances, those in prison, those who are utterly deserted and enjoy no consolation. Put a high value on associating with these; for from them you shall receive much profit, you will be a better lover of the true wisdom, and you will do all for the glory of God. And if you must visit someone, prefer to pay this honor to orphans, widows and those in want rather than to those who enjoy reputation and fame. God has said, "I am the father of orphans and the protector of widows."[8] And again, "Judge for the fatherless, defend the widow. Then come and let us talk, says the Lord."[9] Baptismal Instructions 6.12.[10]

Unity in the Church. Cyprian: Who then is so profane and lacking in faith, who so insane by the fury of discord as either to believe that the unity of God, the garment of the Lord, the church of Christ can be torn asunder or to dare to do so? He warns us in the Gospel, and teaches, saying, "And there shall be one flock and one shepherd."[11] And does anyone think that there can be either many shepherds or many flocks in one place? Likewise the apostle Paul introducing this same unity to us beseeches and urges us in these words: "I beseech you, brothers," he says, "by the name of our Lord Jesus Christ, that you all say the same thing, and that there be no dissensions among you but that you be perfectly united in the same mind and in the same judgment."[12] And again he says, "Bearing with one another in love, careful to preserve the unity of the Spirit, in the bond of peace."[13] Do you think that you can stand and live, withdrawing from the church and building for yourself other abodes and different dwellings, when

it was said to Rahab, in whom the church was prefigured: "You shall gather your father and your mother and your brethren and the entire house of your father to your own self in your house, and it will be that everyone who goes out of the door of your house shall be his own accuser";[14] likewise, when the sacrament of the Passover contains nothing else in the law of the exodus than that the lamb that is slain in the figure of Christ be eaten in one house? God speaks, saying, "In one house it shall be eaten; you shall not carry the flesh outside of the house."[15] The flesh of Christ and what is holy to the Lord cannot be carried outside, and there is no other house for believers except the one church. This house, this hospice of unanimity, the Holy Spirit designates and proclaims, when he says, "God who makes those of one mind to dwell in his house." In the house of God, in the church of Christ, those of one mind dwell; they persevere in concord and simplicity. The Unity of the Church 8.[16]

Unity and Mutual Respect. Basil the Great: Such characters the Lord calls ravenous wolves that show themselves in sheep's clothing.[17] Avoid inconstancy and fickleness, pursue truth, sincerity, simplicity. The serpent is subtle and for that reason has been condemned to crawl. The just person is without pretense, such as was Jacob.[18] Therefore, "the Lord makes the solitary to dwell in a house."[19] So in this great sea,[20] which stretches wide its arms, "there are creeping things without number, creatures little and great."[21] Nevertheless, there is a certain wisdom among them and an orderly arrangement. Not only are we able to find fault with the fish, but there is also something worthy of imitation in them. How is it that all of the different species of fishes,

---

[7]LCL 34:493, 495*. [8]Ps 68:5 (67:6 LXX). [9]Is 1:17-18. [10]ACW 31:97-98*. [11]Jn 10:16. [12]1 Cor 1:10. [13]Eph 4:2. [14]Josh 2:18-19. [15]Ex 12:46. [16]FC 36:102-3*. [17]See Mt 7:15. [18]See Gen 25:27. [19]Basil is following the Septuagint, which reads, *ho theos katoikizei monotropous en oikō*. [20]See Gen 1:20-21. Although Basil is not specific, he is referring most likely to the Mediterranean Sea. [21]Ps 104:25 (103:25 LXX).

having been allotted a place suitable for them, do not intrude on one another but stay within their own bounds? No surveyor apportioned the dwellings among them; they were not surrounded with walls or divided by boundaries; but what was useful for each was definitely and spontaneously settled. This bay gives sustenance to certain kinds of fish, and that one, to other kinds; and those that teem here are scarce elsewhere. No mountain extending upward with sharp peaks separates them; no river cuts off the means of crossing; but there is a certain law of nature that allots the habitat to each kind equally and justly according to its need. HOMILIES ON THE HEXAEMERON 7.3.[22]

THOSE WHO DWELL IN GOD'S HOUSE ARE BLESSED. NICETAS OF REMESIANA: Obviously, the time to pray is when we are all praying. Of course, you may pray privately whenever and as often as you choose. But do not, under the pretext of prayer, miss the lesson. You can always pray whenever you will, but you cannot always have a lesson at hand. Do not imagine that there is little to be gained by listening to the sacred lesson. The fact is that prayer is improved if our mind has been recently fed on reading and is able to roam among the thoughts of divine things that it has recently heard. The word of the Lord assures us that Mary, the sister of Martha, chose the better part when she sat at the feet of Jesus, listening intently to the word of God without a thought of her sister.[23] We need not wonder, then, if the deacon in a clear voice like a herald warns all that, whether they are praying or bowing the knees, singing hymns or listening to the lessons, they should all act together. God loves "people of one manner"[24] and, as was said before, "makes them to dwell in his house." And those who dwell in this house are proclaimed by the psalm to be blessed, because they will praise God forever and ever. Amen. LITURGICAL SINGING 14.[25]

68:7-13 The Power of God and His Word

EARTH'S TREMORS AND HEAVEN'S DEW. THE-ODORET OF CYR: "When you ventured forth in the midst of your people, O God, when you passed through the wilderness, earth shook and the heavens sent down drops." Symmachus[26] rendered it thus, "O God, when you went before your people, moving through the uninhabited land, earth shook and heaven sent down drops." On the point of passing through that barren and uninhabited land, which had not yet felt the light's ray, you disturbed the earth and shook it, and from heaven you sent down the shower of grace. Now, in the one case, this happened at the crucifixion. At that time the earth shook and the rocks broke open,[27] and all the earth was disturbed on gaining the impression that the Creator of all was hung up on the cross; in the other case, after the return to heaven. At that time the grace of the Spirit came on the apostles, like drops of dew. Then, to teach Jews more clearly who was doing all this, he added, "at the presence of the God of Sinai, at the presence of the God of Israel." The one who appeared to our forebears on Mount Sinai, he is saying, is the one who also shook the earth at the time of the passion to refute our folly and who made the gift of the Spirit. COMMENTARY ON THE PSALMS 68.6.[28]

EVEN THE HEATHEN ACKNOWLEDGE THE POWER OF GOD. CLEMENT OF ALEXANDRIA: Again, Aeschylus[29] the tragedian, setting forth the power of God, does not shrink from calling him the Highest, in these words:

> Place God apart from mortals; and think not
> That he is, like yourself, corporeal.
> You know him not. Now he appears as fire,
> Dread force; as water now; and now as gloom;
> And in the beasts is dimly shadowed forth,
> In wind, and cloud, in lightning, thunder, rain;
> And minister to him the seas and rocks,

---

[22]FC 46:110-11*. [23]See Lk 10:42. [24]See footnote on Psalm 68:6 (67:7 LXX) in previous entry. [25]FC 7:76. [26]A third-century translator of a Greek version of the Old Testament. [27]Mt 27:51. [28]FC 101:382-83. [29]One of the great Greek tragedians (525/4-456 B.C.).

Each fountain and the water's floods and
   streams.
The mountains tremble, and the earth, the vast
   Abyss of sea, and towering height of hills,
When on them looks the Sovereign's awful eye:
Almighty is the glory of the Most High God.[30]

Does he not seem to you to paraphrase that text,
"At the presence of the Lord the earth trembles"?
STROMATEIS 5.14.[31]

**THE CLEANSING AND RENEWING POWER OF
GOD'S SPIRIT.** AMBROSE: Damasus cleansed
not, Peter cleansed not, Ambrose cleansed not,
Gregory cleansed not; for ours is the ministry,
but the sacraments are yours. For human power
cannot confer what is divine, but it is, O Lord,
your gift and that of the Father, as you have spoken by the prophets, saying, "I will pour out of
my Spirit on all flesh, and their sons and their
daughters shall prophesy."[32] This is that typical
dew from heaven, this is that gracious rain, as we
read: "A gracious rain, dividing for his inheritance." For the Holy Spirit is not subject to any
foreign power or law but is the arbiter of his own
freedom, dividing all things according to the decision of his own will, to each, as we read, individually as he wills. ON THE HOLY SPIRIT 1.18.[33]

**THE LAW OF MOSES IS PICTURED AS A BOUN-
TIFUL RAIN.** JEROME: "O God, when you went
forth at the head of your people." This accords
with history, when God preceded his people as
they marched out of Egypt.[34] "When you
marched through the wilderness." God did not
delay in the desert but passed through it. "The
earth quaked; it rained from heaven at the presence of the God of Sinai." "It rained from heaven":
that is, it rained manna. Sinai signifies temptation. God dwells, therefore, in those who are
tempted and overcome temptation; in those who
seek sensual gratification, however, he does not
dwell. "A bountiful rain you showered down, O
God, on your inheritance." This refers to the law
that was given through Moses. "You restored the

land when it languished." The law languished
because no one was able to fulfill it except the
Lord, who said, "I have not come to destroy the
law but to fulfill."[35] HOMILIES ON THE PSALMS 7.[36]

GOD FREELY SHOWERS HIS GRACE ON US.
AUGUSTINE: First we had to be persuaded how
much God loved us, in case out of sheer despair we
lacked the courage to reach up to him. Also we had
to be shown what sort of people we are that he
loves, in case we should take pride in our own
worth and so bounce even further away from him
and sink ever more under our own strength. So he
dealt with us in such a way that we could progress
rather in his strength; he arranged it so that the
power of love should be brought to perfection in
the weakness of humility. This is the meaning of
the psalm where it says, "O God, you are setting
apart a voluntary rain for your inheritance, and it
has been weakened; but you have perfected it."
What he means by voluntary rain is nothing other
than grace, which is not paid out as earned but
given gratis; that is why it is called grace. He was
not obliged to give it because we deserved it; he
gave it voluntarily because he wished to. Knowing
this, we will put no trust in ourselves, and that is
what to be weakened means. He however perfects
us—as he said to the apostle Paul, "my grace is
enough for you; strength is made perfect in weakness."[37] So we needed to be persuaded how much
God loves us, and what sort of people he loves;
how much case we despaired, what sort in case we
grew proud. ON THE TRINITY 4.1.2.[38]

**PROCLAIMING THE WORD OF GOD WITH
POWER.** ORIGEN: And the divine Scriptures bear
witness both to the preaching of the gospel by the
apostles and to that by our Savior. David, on the
one hand, says of the apostles, and perhaps also of
the Evangelists, "The Lord shall give the word to
them that preach good tidings with great power;

---

[30]Fragment 239(464) spurious; LCL 14b 506-7. [31]ANF 2:474. [32]Joel
2:28. [33]NPN3 2 10:96*. [34]Ex 13:21. [35]Mt 5:17. [36]FC 48:52*.
[37]2 Cor 12:9. [38]WSA 1 5:153-54.

the king of powers[39] is of the beloved." At the same time he also teaches that it is not the composition of a speech and the utterance of sounds and the practiced beauty of speech that produce persuasion, but the provision of divine power. . . . Simon and Cleopas testify to this power and say, "Was not our heart burning on the road as he opened the Scripture to us?"[40] And since the quantity of power God supplies to those who speak also differs, the apostles had great power in accordance with David's statement: "The Lord shall give the word to them that preach good tidings with great power." COMMENTARY ON THE GOSPEL OF JOHN 1.48, 50.[41]

DIVINELY EMPOWERED PREACHING. ORIGEN: For the word of God declares that the preaching (although in itself true and most worthy of belief) is not enough to touch the human heart, unless God gives to the speaker a certain power and his words have a certain grace. It is only by

divine agency that this takes place in those who speak effectively. The prophet says in Psalm 67 [LXX] that "the Lord will give a word with great power to them who preach." Then, if it should be granted with respect to certain points, that the same doctrines are found among the Greeks as in our own Scriptures, yet they do not possess the same power of attracting and influencing the souls of people to follow them. Therefore the disciples of Jesus, men ignorant so far as Greek philosophy is concerned, traveled through many countries of the world and impressed, agreeably to the desire of the Logos, each one of their hearers according to his desires, so that they received a moral improvement in proportion to their willingness to accept of that which is good. AGAINST CELSUS 6.2.[42]

---

[39]Origen is here following the Septuagint, which has *ho Basileus tēn dynameōn*. [40]Lk 24:32. [41]FC 80:44. [42]ANF 4:573-74.**

68:17-35 FROM SINAI TO ZION

[17]With mighty chariotry, twice ten thousand,
    thousands upon thousands,
    the Lord came from Sinai into the
        holy place.[e]
[18]Thou didst ascend the high mount,
    leading captives in thy train,
    and receiving gifts among men,
even among the rebellious, that the LORD
        God may dwell there.

[19]Blessed be the Lord,
    who daily bears us up;
    God is our salvation.   Selah

[20]Our God is a God of salvation;
    and to God, the Lord, belongs escape
        from death.

[21]But God will shatter the heads of his
        enemies,
    the hairy crown of him who walks in
        his guilty ways.
[22]The Lord said,
    "I will bring them back from Bashan,
    I will bring them back from the
        depths of the sea,
[23]that you may bathe[f] your feet in blood,

69

that the tongues of your dogs may
    have their portion from the foe."

²⁴Thy solemn processions are seen,^g O God,
    the processions of my God, my King,
    into the sanctuary—
²⁵the singers in front, the minstrels last,
    between them maidens playing timbrels:
²⁶"Bless God in the great congregation,
    the LORD, O you who are of Israel's
    fountain!"
²⁷There is Benjamin, the least of them, in the
    lead,
    the princes of Judah in their throng,
    the princes of Zebulun, the princes of
    Naphtali.

²⁸Summon thy might, O God;
    show thy strength, O God, thou who
    hast wrought for us.
²⁹Because of thy temple at Jerusalem
    kings bear gifts to thee.
³⁰Rebuke the beasts that dwell among the

reeds,
    the herd of bulls with the calves of the
    peoples.
Trample^b under foot those who lust after
    tribute;
    scatter the peoples who delight in war.ⁱ
³¹Let bronze be brought from Egypt;
    let Ethiopia hasten to stretch out her hands
    to God.

³²Sing to God, O kingdoms of the earth;
    sing praises to the Lord,   Selah
³³to him who rides in the heavens, the ancient
    heavens;
    lo, he sends forth his voice, his mighty voice.
³⁴Ascribe power to God,
    whose majesty is over Israel,
    and his power is in the skies.
³⁵Terrible is God in his^j sanctuary,
    the God of Israel,
    he gives power and strength to his people.

Blessed be God!

e Cn: Heb *The Lord among them Sinai in the holy place* f Gk Syr Tg: Heb *shatter* g Or *have been seen* h Cn: Heb *trampling* i The Hebrew of verse 30 is obscure j Gk: Heb *from thy*

OVERVIEW: The world, as God's chariot, is controlled and guided by the reins of natural, fixed laws that God established for it (NOVATIAN). God first gives us the Holy Spirit so that through him we may receive divine grace (AMBROSE). The author of the psalm and the apostle Paul agree that God gives multiple gifts to humanity, the Holy Spirit being one of them. True happiness cannot be found on earth in this life, as even the incarnate Christ learned; instead it begins at death and is experienced only in heaven (AUGUSTINE). Christ is like the eagle, which often steals its prey from another, in that he has rescued us from the captivity of Satan and slavery to him and makes us captive to freedom (MAXIMUS).

Perpetrators of evil will not escape divine judgment; this is especially true of heretics, who will receive a due reward for their sacrilege (CASSIODORUS). God will overthrow those who become his enemies by their overweening pride. By his mercy and grace God will make our enemies like good dogs who serve their master (AUGUSTINE). The incarnation of Christ was heralded by Old Testament prophets; and Old Testament Israel, which lived by the law of Moses, were like people whose understanding was not fully developed and whose worship was only external (EUSEBIUS). The apostles are called springs because they water the whole earth with the sweet message of the gospel and the cup of the sacrament of the altar (MAXIMUS).

We are unable to do good unless God enables us to do so (FULGENTIUS). The conversion of the Ethiopian eunuch is seen as a direct fulfillment of the psalmist's prophecy (BEDE). Christians are accustomed to worship toward the east because, as the psalmist says, Christ ascended to the east and the Garden of Eden was located in the east (JOHN OF DAMASCUS).

68:17-20 *The Manifold Gifts of God*

THE REINS OF NATURAL LAW. NOVATIAN: This,[1] according to David, is God's chariot. "The chariot of God," he says, "is multiplied ten times a thousand times"; that is, it is incalculable, infinite, immeasurable. Under the yoke of the natural law that was given to all, some things are checked, as though they were drawn back by reins; whereas others are driven forward, as though they were urged on by slackened reins. "The world, this chariot of God and all that is therein, is guided by the angels"[2] and the stars. Although their movements are varied—bound, nevertheless, by fixed laws—we see them guided to their goals according to the time measured out to them. So may we deservedly cry out with the apostle as we admire the Maker and his works: "Oh, the depth of the riches of the wisdom and the knowledge of God; how inscrutable are his judgments and how unsearchable his ways,"[3] and the rest of the passage. ON THE TRINITY 8.10-11.[4]

THE HOLY SPIRIT IS ONE OF GOD'S MANY GIFTS. AMBROSE: It does not escape our notice that some copies[5] have likewise, according to Luke: "How much more shall your heavenly Father give a good gift to them that ask him." This good gift is the grace of the Spirit, which the Lord Jesus shed forth from heaven, after having been fixed to the gibbet of the cross, returning with the triumphal spoils of death deprived of its power, as you find it written: "Ascending up on high he led captivity captive, and gave good gifts to people." And well does he say "gifts," for as the

Son was given, of whom it is written: "Unto us a Child is born, unto us a Son is given,"[6] so, too, is the grace of the Spirit given. But why should I hesitate to say that the Holy Spirit also is given to us, since it is written: "The love of God is shed forth in our hearts by the Holy Spirit, who is given to us."[7] And since captive hearts certainly could not receive him, the Lord Jesus first led captivity captive, that our affections being set free, he might pour forth the gift of divine grace. ON THE HOLY SPIRIT 1.5.66.[8]

GOD GIVES HIS PEOPLE MANY GIFTS. AUGUSTINE: Then there is the apostle Paul: "To each one of us," he says, "is given grace according to the measure of the gift of Christ," and to show that the gift of Christ is the Holy Spirit he went on to add, "That is why it says, he ascended on high, he took captivity captive, he gave gifts to people." But it is public knowledge that when the Lord Jesus had ascended to heaven after his resurrection from the dead he gave the Holy Spirit; and being filled with it those who believed began to speak with the tongues of all people.[9] And do not let it worry you that he says "gifts," not "gift." He was quoting the text from a psalm, and what we read in the psalm is, "you have ascended on high, you have taken captivity captive, you have received gifts among people." This is the reading of most codices, especially the Greek ones, and we have it translated like this from the Hebrew. So the apostle said "gifts" just as the prophet did, not "gift"; but while the prophet said "you have received them among people," the apostle preferred to say "he has given them to people," in order that we might get the fullest meaning from both statements, the one prophetic, the other apostolic, since each has the authority of the divine utterance behind it. ON THE TRINITY 15.5.34.[10]

---

[1]Cf. the chariot imagery in Ezek 1:15ff.; 10:9. [2]See Ps 104:2-4 (103:2-4 LXX, Vg.). [3]Rom 11:33. [4]FC 67:41. [5]Other Gospel accounts (e.g., Mt 7:11). [6]Is 9:6. [7]Rom 5:5. [8]NPNF 2 10:102*. [9]See Acts 2:1-4. [10]WSA 1 5:422*.

True Happiness Begins at Death. Augustine: [David] had expectations from God in line with the old covenant, not realizing that it contains signs of things to come—so he was expecting to receive good fortune in this life from God, and he was looking on this earth for what God is keeping for his people in heaven. He wanted to be happy here, though happiness is not to be found here. Happiness, you see, is of course something great and good, but it has its own proper region. It was from the region of happiness that Christ came, and not even he found it here. He was jeered at, he was reviled, he was arrested, he was scourged, he was bound, he was knocked about, insulted with spittle, he was crowned with thorns, hanged on a tree. And finally—"even for the Lord is the departure of death." It is written in a psalm (those who caught the allusion applauded): "Even for the Lord is the departure of death." So why, slave, do you seek happiness here, where even for the Lord is the departure of death? Sermon 19.4.[11]

The Captive of Satan Becomes the Captive of Christ. Maximus of Turin: But how shall we handle the fact that an eagle frequently snatches prey and often seizes what belongs to others? Yet neither in this is the Savior dissimilar, for in a manner of speaking he made off with prey when he took the human being that had been held captive in the jaws of the underworld and carried him to heaven, leading the slave who had been rescued from the captivity of another's domination that is, diabolical power—as a captive to the heights, as it is written in the prophet: "Ascending on high he led captivity captive, he gave gifts to people." This phrase is to be understood in this way—that the captivity of the human being, whom the devil had captured for himself, the Lord captured for himself by rescuing him, and this very captive, as it says, he took to the heights of the heavens. Both captivities are called by the same name, then, but both are not equal, for the devil's captivity subjects a person to slavery, whereas Christ's captivity restores a per-

son to liberty. Sermon 56.2.[12]

68:21-27 The Power of God and His Word

Heretics Will Not Go Unpunished. Cassiodorus: "But God has shattered the heads of his enemies, of those who traverse heads of hairs in their sins."[13] To counter the belief that evil deeds of stubborn people would go unavenged, he says, "But God has shattered the heads of his enemies," that you might be aware that vengeance is visited also on the unfaithful and stubborn. "The heads of his enemies" are the sponsors of the Jewish secession, but doubtless also the teachers of heretics. The Jews persecuted Christ in the flesh, but the teachers of heretics rage more cruelly against him in his Godhead, if that is not a sacrilegious statement. Next comes "those who traverse heads of hair," in other words, those who seek out petty details of lying allegations, so that they seem to be traversing and scrutinizing even people's very heads of hair. This indicates the sophistry of their foolish questions, which ignore what will be profitable and in execrable argumentation seek out what is inessential. Then to prove that their researches are empty, he added, "in their sins." In their case the meditation that led to sinning was foolish; in their camp are Manichees, Priscillianists, Donatists, Montanists[14] and the rest who involved themselves in the foul odors of their muddy doctrines. Expositions of the Psalms 67.22.[15]

The Proud Will Be Defeated. Augustine: You ask what is meant by these words in Psalm 67 [LXX]: "But God shall break the heads of his

---

[11]WSA 3 1:381. [12]ACW 50:136*. [13]Cassiodorus is here following the Septuagint. [14]Manichaeism was a Gnostic-type, extremely dualistic religion that originated in Persia. Priscillianism was a Gnostic-Manichaean sect that arose in Spain and France and supposedly engaged in impure orgies. Donatism was a schism that developed as a result of the Diocletian persecution and that opposed apostasy and favored voluntary martyrdom. Montanism was a second-century heresy that insisted on strict moral conduct and readiness for the end of the world; it has sometimes been called the neo-pentecostal movement in the early church. [15]ACW 52:132-33.

enemies: the hairy crown of them that walk on in their sins." It seems to me it means simply that God will break the heads of his enemies who are too overwhelming, who rise too high in their sins. By a certain hyperbole he describes pride as rising so high and rushing along with such eagerness that it is like striding and running over the hair of the head. LETTER 149.[16]

THE TONGUE OF DOGS. AUGUSTINE: Likewise, in the same psalm, where it says, "the tongue of your dogs from the enemies by the same,"[17] dogs should not always be taken in an evil sense, otherwise the prophet would not blame "dogs not able to bark and loving to dream":[18] doubtless they would be praiseworthy dogs if they both knew how to bark and loved to watch. And certainly those three hundred men[19]—a most sacred number according to the letter of the cross[20]—would not have been chosen to win the victory because they lapped water as dogs do, unless some great mystery were signified. Good dogs watch and bark to protect their house and their master, their flock and their shepherd. Finally, even here in the praises offered by the church, when a selection is made from this prophecy, it is the tongue of dogs that is mentioned, not their teeth. "The tongue of your dogs," it says, "from the enemies," that is, that those who used to be your enemies and raged against you may become your dogs and may bark for you. It added "from the same" to make them understand that this is not effected by themselves, but "by the same," that is, by his mercy and grace. LETTER 149.[21]

PROPHECY OF THE INCARNATION. EUSEBIUS OF CAESAREA: I think that here none but the apostles can be meant by the rulers of Naphtali. For thence our Lord and Savior called them according to the quotation from Matthew. The Scripture is prophesying the coming of the Word of God to human beings and his incarnate sojourn here, when it says, "Your goings [solemn processions], O God, have been seen," and that which follows. And the prophets of old were like heralds of his

epiphany and arrived before him with proclamation and chant, with music of psaltery and choir and all kinds of spiritual instruments, in the midst of maidens playing on timbrels. For the inspired prophets going in every way into the midst of the Jewish synagogues heralded the coming of the Christ, and by the Holy Spirit they addressed the apostles of our Savior, saying, "Praise the Lord God in the congregations from the fountains of Israel." And the "fountains of Israel" must be the words delivered to Israel. "For they [the inspired prophets] first trusted the oracles of God," whence it will be necessary for us to draw and water the churches of Christ. By "maidens playing on timbrels" he suggested the souls that lived in the past by the more external law of Moses, calling them "maidens" because of their youth and imperfectly developed minds and "timbrel players" because of their devotion to external worship. PROOF OF THE GOSPEL 9.9.[22]

THE APOSTLES ARE THE SPRINGS OF ISRAEL. MAXIMUS OF TURIN: After Marah, then, the people of Israel come to the twelve springs.[23] We read in the prophet, "Bless the Lord from the springs of Israel." This is the Lord Christ, who is not blessed except by the mouths of the apostles and the teaching of the disciples. The apostles are to be called springs: like very pure springs they abound in the grace of preaching and, after the bitterness of the law, from the bountiful wisdom within themselves they distill the sweet cup of the sacrament. Nor is it to be wondered at if the drink of the springs is sweet when, in their midst, the food of the palms is sweeter. The apostles, then, are springs that water the face of the whole earth with the streams of their teaching and set before the wearied peoples of the nations the drink of the divine mystery. But the seventy palms growing near the apostolic springs I would

---

[16]FC 20:246-47*. [17]Augustine is here giving a literal translation of the Septuagint. [18]Is 56:10. [19]Judg 7:5-7 (the three hundred men who went with Gideon to defeat the Midianites). [20]C is the symbol for 100; it is the initial letter of *crux* (cross); this would make CCC most sacred. [21]FC 20:247*. [22]POG 2:172. [23]Num 33:9.

call those seventy disciples who, in the next grade after the apostles, are sent out by the Lord for the salvation of humankind, who the Evangelist Luke in his writing asserts were appointed in groups of two,[24] who, like palm trees, return with rejoicing after having cured people and boast to the Lord that even the demons are subject to them.[25] Rightly, then, are they compared with palm trees who have been rewarded with palms and who have shown themselves victorious over the devil. SERMON 68.4.[26]

68:28-33 Virtue and Praise

GOD ENABLES US TO WILL AND TO DO GOOD. FULGENTIUS OF RUSPE: Therefore we know both the will to do good and the ability to do good come from God. David agrees completely with this, showing that by the command of divine generosity the grace of a good will is granted: "Our steps are made firm by the Lord when he delights in our way."[27] We have no good works in us unless they come from God, and we bear witness that it is done in God, saying, "Show your strength, O God, as you have done for us before." And in another place: "With God we shall do valiantly,"[28] that is, the work of virtue. So here in the place of the work of virtue, he said "virtue" just as John, for the work of justice, spoke of doing justice. For he says, "The person who acts in righteousness is righteous."[29] Paul also wants us to do the will of God, saying, "May the God of peace, who brought up from the dead the great shepherd of the sheep by the blood of the eternal covenant, Jesus our Lord, furnish you with all that is good, that you may do his will."[30] LETTER TO MONIMUS 1.9.1.[31]

THE GOSPEL IS PROCLAIMED TO THE GENTILES. BEDE: "Arise and go to the south."[32] It is well that it was in the south that this man[33] was sought, found and washed clean. Burning with devotion in his breast, he deserved to be consecrated to God as, so to speak, the firstfruits of the Gentiles. In him especially was fulfilled that saying of the psalmist, "Ethiopia will stretch out its hands to God." COMMENTARY ON THE ACTS OF THE APOSTLES 8.26A.[34]

PRAISE GOD FOR HIS GOODNESS. JOHN OF DAMASCUS: And so, since God is spiritual light[35] and Christ in sacred Scripture is called "Sun of Justice" and "orient,"[36] the east should be dedicated to his worship. For everything beautiful should be dedicated to God from whom everything that is good receives its goodness. Also, the divine David says, "Sing to God, all you kingdoms of the earth: sing to the Lord; who mounts above the heaven of heavens, to the east." And still again, Scripture says, "And the Lord had planted a paradise in Eden to the east; wherein he placed man whom he had formed," and whom he cast out, when he had transgressed, "and made him to live over against the paradise of pleasure,"[37] or in the west. Thus it is that, when we worship God, we long for our ancient fatherland and gaze toward it. The tabernacle of Moses had the veil and the propitiatory[38] to the east; and the tribe of Judah, as being the more honorable, pitched their tents on the east;[39] and in the celebrated temple of Solomon the gate of the Lord was set to the east. As a matter of fact, when the Lord was crucified, he looked toward the west, and so we worship gazing toward him. And when he was taken up, he ascended to the east, and thus the apostles worshiped him, and thus he shall come in the same way as they had seen him going into heaven,[40] as the Lord said: "As lightning comes out of the east and appears even into the west, so shall also the coming of the Son of man be."[41] And so, while we are awaiting him, we worship toward the east. This is, moreover, the unwritten tradition of the apostles, for they have handed many things down to us unwritten. ORTHODOX FAITH 4.12.[42]

---

[24]See Lk 10:1. [25]See Lk 10:17. [26]ACW 50:167-68. [27]Ps 37:23 (36:23 LXX, Vg.). [28]Ps 60:12 (59:14 LXX, Vg.). [29]1 Jn 3:7. [30]Heb 13:20-21. [31]FC 95:198-99*. [32]Acts 8:26. [33]The Ethiopian eunuch (Acts 8:27). [34]CS 117:81. [35]See 1 Jn 1:5. [36]See Lk 1:78. [37]Gen 2:8; 3:24 (LXX). [38]See Lev 16:14. The Greek word is *hilastērion*. [39]See Num 2:3; Ezek 44:1-2. [40]See Acts 1:11. [41]Mt 24:27. [42]FC 37:353-54.

69:1-19 A PLEA FOR MERCY

To the choirmaster: according to Lilies.
A Psalm of David.

¹*Save me, O God!*
  For the waters have come up to my neck.
²*I sink in deep mire,*
  where there is no foothold;
I have come into deep waters,
  and the flood sweeps over me.
³*I am weary with my crying;*
  my throat is parched.
My eyes grow dim
  with waiting for my God.

⁴*More in number than the hairs of my head*
  are those who hate me without cause;
mighty are those who would destroy me,
  those who attack me with lies.
What I did not steal
  must I now restore?
⁵*O God, thou knowest my folly;*
  the wrongs I have done are not hidden from
    thee.

⁶*Let not those who hope in thee be put to*
    shame through me,
  O Lord GOD of hosts;
let not those who seek thee be brought to
    dishonor through me,
  O God of Israel.
⁷*For it is for thy sake that I have borne*
    reproach,
  that shame has covered my face.
⁸*I have become a stranger to my brethren,*
  an alien to my mother's sons.

⁹*For zeal for thy house has consumed me,*
  and the insults of those who insult thee
    have fallen on me.
¹⁰*When I humbled^k my soul with fasting,*
  it became my reproach.
¹¹*When I made sackcloth my clothing,*
  I became a byword to them.
¹²*I am the talk of those who sit in the gate,*
  and the drunkards make songs about me.

¹³*But as for me, my prayer is to thee, O LORD.*
  At an acceptable time, O God,
  in the abundance of thy steadfast love
    answer me.
With thy faithful help ¹⁴*rescue me*
  from sinking in the mire;
let me be delivered from my enemies
  and from the deep waters.
¹⁵*Let not the flood sweep over me,*
  or the deep swallow me up,
  or the pit close its mouth over me.

¹⁶*Answer me, O LORD for thy steadfast love is*
    good;
  according to thy abundant mercy, turn
    to me.
¹⁷*Hide not thy face from thy servant;*
  for I am in distress, make haste to answer
    me.
¹⁸*Draw near to me, redeem me,*
  set me free because of my enemies!

¹⁹*Thou knowest my reproach,*
  and my shame and my dishonor;
  my foes are all known to thee.

k Gk Syr: Heb *I wept with fasting my soul* or *I made my soul mourn with fasting*

OVERVIEW: Often we think of God's divine protection in a general way, but God comes to our aid in the specific needs of everyday life and circumstances (JEROME). Christ yielded voluntarily to the indignities of his passion and became obedient to death (AUGUSTINE). Christ, who did not deserve death, died because it was the will of his Father and to fulfill the prophecies regarding him (TERTULLIAN, AUGUSTINE). The psalmist foretold the passion of Christ, who died also for our offenses, which are known to God (AUGUSTINE). The passion of Christ is a good example of the fact that wicked people heap reproach and abuse on good and godly people (CASSIODORUS).

Christ's quotations from the Psalms are proof that he is the real author of both Testaments (ORIGEN). Faith is not a matter of external performance but of devout trust in Christ in whom we have an advocate with the Father (AMBROSE). All Christians should have such a zeal for God's house that they work to correct wickedness and consider God's house preferable to their own houses since God's house is where they receive eternal salvation (AUGUSTINE). The bottomless, fiery abyss of hell is the eternal punishment of those who refused to know God and were without faith and unrepentant (CAESARIUS).

69:1-3 Suffering and Deliverance

A PRAYER FOR RESCUE. JEROME: On the first occasion[1] we nearly perished of hunger and thirst while we were wandering about in the desert [without food] for five days and five nights. On the second occasion we traveled over savage, rugged mountains until our feet were pierced by the stones, and we suffered very great pain and very nearly had to yield up our souls. On the third occasion we sank in the mud several times more than waist deep, and there was none to help [us], and we cried out the words of the blessed David, "Save me, O God, for the waters have come even to my soul. I have sunk into a dark abyss, wherein is no place on which to stand. Save me from the mire so that I do not sink." On the fourth occasion a great flood burst on us at the time when the Nile floods, and we walked about in the water, and we sank down very nearly to the nostrils [of the animal that we rode], and we cried out and said, "Drown us not, O Lord, in a whirlpool of waters, and let not the abyss swallow us up, and let not the pit close its mouth over us."[2] THE HISTORIES OF THE MONKS 20.[3]

A PROPHECY OF CHRIST'S VOLUNTARY DEATH. AUGUSTINE: Previously, you see, when [Christ] was showing us an example of humility in the flesh, it was said with reference to his passion that the waves of the sea rose mightily against him, to which he yielded voluntarily for our sakes, so fulfilling the prophecy, "I came into the depth of the sea, and the tempest overwhelmed me." Thus he did not rebut the false witnesses or the savage roar of the crowd, "Have him crucified!"[4] He did not use his power to quell the raging hearts and stop the mouths of the furious mob, but he bore it all with patience. They did to him whatever they wanted, because "he became obedient unto death, even death on a cross."[5] SERMON 75.7.[6]

69:4-7 Christ's Suffering and Death Are Foretold

A PROPHECY OF CHRIST'S SUFFERING ON THE CROSS. TERTULLIAN: Christ did not speak deceitfully but displayed all justice and humility. He did not suffer that kind of death [crucifixion] for anything he had done but so that those things that the prophets had predicted would happen to him through you as the very Spirit of Christ already foretold in the Psalms, saying,

---

[1]This section contains a number of dangers and difficulties that Jerome and his associates encountered in visiting the monastic communities in Egypt. [2]Ps 69:14-15 (68:15-16 LXX, Vg.). [3]PHF 1:375**. [4]Mt 27:22. [5]Phil 2:8. [6]WSA 3 3:306-7.

"They repaid me evil instead of good";[7] "What I had not taken, I repaid";[8] "They pierced my hands and feet";[9] "They put gall in my drink, and they satisfied my thirst with vinegar";[10] and "They cast lots for my clothing."[11] The other things that you would commit against him have also been foretold. He patiently endured and suffered all those things not for anything he had done but so that the Scriptures might be fulfilled that were spoken by the prophets.[12] An Answer to the Jews 10.[13]

Christ's Death Was Payment for Adam's Sin. Augustine: Just as it was said to Jesus, "Why, then, will you die if you have not committed a sin that deserves the death penalty?" Immediately he answered, "I do what the Father has commanded me so that the world may know that I love the Father. Arise, let us go."[14] Where? To the place where he, who had done nothing deserving of death, would be handed over to death. The Father had commanded that he should die—he about whom it had been prophesied, "I must repay what I did not take." He was the one who was about to suffer death without deserving it and [thereby] redeem us from the penalty of death. Adam, however, had committed sin when he reached out his hand to the tree [to pick the forbidden fruit]; he presumptuously deceived himself that he could seize the name of divinity that cannot be shared with or given to anyone [except one who is God]; divinity was conferred on the Son of God by nature, not by robbery.[15] Tractates on the Gospel of John 79.2.[16]

Our Sins Are Known to God. Augustine: Psalm 68 [LXX] also includes in its title the words "for the things that will be entirely changed." This psalm sings of the passion of our Lord Jesus Christ, assuming to himself even certain words of his members, that is, of his faithful. For he himself did not have any sin, but he carried our sins; thus the psalm says "and my offenses are not hidden from you." Here is written and foretold what we read in the Gospel as having happened: "And

they gave me gall for my food, and in my thirst they gave me vinegar to drink."[17] In him, therefore, the old events have been changed that the title of the psalm predicted were to be changed. In Answer to the Jews 5.6.[18]

Abused at the Hands of the Wicked. Cassiodorus: Next comes: "And it was made a reproach to me." Good people are always a reproach to the wicked, because they are quite unwilling to sanction their crimes. They carefully withdraw from them, join in no compact with them. These reproaches bear witness to the slaps, scourgings and spitting that the Lord Savior endured from the mad crowd. Expositions of the Psalms 68.11.[19]

69:9-15 Faith and Zeal for God and Eternal Condemnation

Christ Quotes the Psalms. Origen: However, we must know that Psalm 68 [LXX], which contains the statement, "The zeal of your house has devoured me," and a little later "They gave me gall for my food, and in my thirst they gave me vinegar to drink,"[20] both having been recorded in the Gospels, is placed in the mouth of Christ, indicating no change in the person of the speaker. Commentary on the Gospel of John 10.222.[21]

Entreating God. Ambrose: "Not every one who says to me Lord, Lord, shall enter into the kingdom of heaven,"[22] says the Scripture. Faith, therefore, august sovereign,[23] must not be a mere matter of performance, for it is written, "The zeal of your house has devoured me." Let us then with faithful spirit and devout mind call on Jesus our Lord, let us believe that he is God, to the end that

---

[7]Ps 35:12 (34:12 LXX, Vg.). [8]Ps 69:4 (68:5 LXX, Vg.). [9]Ps 22:16 (21:17 LXX, Vg.). [10]Ps 69:21 (68:22 LXX, Vg.). [11]Ps 22:18 (21:19 LXX, Vg.). [12]See Mt 26:56, 27:34-35; Jn 19:23, 24, 28, 32-37. [13]CSEL 70:301-2. [14]Jn 14:31. [15]See Phil 2:6. [16]PL 35:1838-39. [17]Mt 27:34, 48; Mk 15:23; Jn 19:29. [18]FC 27:397*. [19]ACW 52:148*. [20]Ps 69:21 (68:22 LXX). [21]FC 80:304. [22]Mt 7:21. [23]The Roman emperor Gratian.

whatever we ask of the Father, we may obtain in his name.[24] For the Father's will is that he be entreated through the Son, the Son's that the Father be entreated.[25] ON THE CHRISTIAN FAITH 1.2.12.[26]

ZEAL FOR GOD'S HOUSE. AUGUSTINE: "And the disciples remembered that it was written, 'The zeal for your house has eaten me up.'"[27] For by zeal for the house of God the Lord cast those men out of the temple. Brothers, let each and every Christian in the members of Christ be consumed with zeal for God's house. Who is consumed with zeal for God's house? One who strives that all things that he, perhaps, sees are wicked there be corrected, [who] desires that they be improved, [who] does not keep quiet. If he cannot improve it, he suffers, he moans. The grain is not shaken out elsewhere than on the threshing floor; it puts up with the chaff that it may enter the storehouse when the chaff has been separated. You, if you are grain, do not be shaken out elsewhere than on the threshing floor in front of the storehouse, that you may not be picked up by birds before you are gathered into the storehouse. For the birds of the sky, the powers on high, are on the watch to snatch something from the threshing floor, and they snatch only what has been shaken out from there. Therefore let zeal for God's house consume you; let zeal for God's house, in which house of God he is a member, consume each and every Christian. TRACTATES ON THE GOSPEL OF JOHN 10.9.1.[28]

THE ETERNAL DESTINY OF FAITHLESS SOULS. CAESARIUS OF ARLES: For this reason, the unquenchable fire there will have to burn whatever healing penance and a salutary conversion of life here has failed to cure. The burning pit of hell will be open, and to it there will be a descent but no means of return. Souls that have been stripped of the garment of faith and are mortally dead will be buried there forever, destined to be cast into the darkness outside where they will not be visited for all eternity. They will be unhappily shut out in exterior darkness, I repeat, or rather they will still more unhappily be enclosed in it. Concerning this pit the prophet relates, "Let not the abyss swallow me up, nor the pit close its mouth over me." He said, "Let not the pit close its mouth over me" for this reason, because when it admits the guilty, it will be closed above and opened below, extending to the depths. No breathing space will be left, no breath of air will be available when the doors press down from above. Those who say farewell to the things of nature will be cast down there; since they have refused to know God, they will no longer be recognized by him, and dying to life they will live for endless death. The happy souls who now use their wealth wisely, content with bodily necessities and generous with their possessions, pure in themselves and not cruel toward others, free themselves from the fiery night of this infernal region. This punishment will detain those who will perish for all eternity, since they have lost the grace of baptism and have not restored it through repentance. To them it is said, "The chaff he will burn up with unquenchable fire."[29] SERMON 167.5.[30]

---

[24]See Jn 15:16; Lk 11:9-10; Mt 7:7-8; Mk 11:24. [25]Jn 16:23-24; 14:13. [26]NPNF 2 10:203*. [27]Jn 2:17, quoting Ps 69:9 (68:10 LXX). [28]FC 78:220. [29]Mt 3:12. [30]FC 47:406-7.

69:20-36 A PREFIGURING OF CALVARY

²⁰*Insults have broken my heart,*
so that I am in despair.
I looked for pity, but there was none;
and for comforters, but I found none.
²¹*They gave me poison for food,*
and for my thirst they gave me vinegar
to drink.

²²*Let their own table before them become a*
snare;
let their sacrificial feasts^l be a trap.
²³*Let their eyes be darkened, so that they*
cannot see;
and make their loins tremble continually.
²⁴*Pour out thy indignation upon them,*
and let thy burning anger overtake them.
²⁵*May their camp be a desolation,*
let no one dwell in their tents.
²⁶*For they persecute him whom thou hast*
smitten,
and him^m whom thou hast wounded,
they afflict still more.ⁿ
²⁷*Add to them punishment upon punishment;*
may they have no acquittal from thee.
²⁸*Let them be blotted out of the book of the*

living;
let them not be enrolled among the
righteous.

²⁹*But I am afflicted and in pain;*
let thy salvation, O God, set me on high!

³⁰*I will praise the name of God with a song;*
I will magnify him with thanksgiving.
³¹*This will please the* LORD *more than an ox*
or a bull with horns and hoofs.
³²*Let the oppressed see it and be glad;*
you who seek God, let your hearts revive.
³³*For the* LORD *hears the needy,*
and does not despise his own that are in
bonds.

³⁴*Let heaven and earth praise him,*
the seas and everything that moves therein.
³⁵*For God will save Zion*
and rebuild the cities of Judah;
and his servants shall dwell^o there and
possess it;
³⁶*the children of his servants shall inherit it,*
and those who love his name shall dwell in it.

l Tg: Heb *for security*   m One Ms Tg Compare Syr: Heb *those*   n Gk Syr: Heb *recount the pain of*   o Syr: Heb *and they shall dwell*

OVERVIEW: No matter how much evil we confront in this life or to what extent our hope is tested, we receive help from God (BASIL). Since no one is free of misery and suffering in this world, everyone should be sensitive and sympathetic to other people in their hardships (AUGUSTINE). When David speaks of suffering thirst, he was not speaking of himself but of Christ, thereby predicting one of Christ's state-ments on the cross. Biblical writers used allegory and various figures of speech, but much of Scripture must be interpreted literally, including David's prophecy of Christ's sixth word on the cross (TERTULLIAN). People who interpret Old Testament prophecies of Christ in light of his suffering, death and resurrection recognize his true identity (AUGUSTINE). David said that Christ suffered more afflictions during his passion than have been recorded in Scripture (APHRAHAT). Old Testament prophets foretold Christ's words on the cross; this is proof of his identity as the promised Messiah. Many Jews in refusing to believe in Christ are only fulfilling the prophecies of their apostasy by their own prophets. Only the true Israel, those who believe God's promises and trust in Christ, regardless of ethnic background, will receive from God a heavenly inheritance (AUGUSTINE). The many sufferings Christ experienced on the cross were endured voluntarily (LEO). By grace God has elected some people to salvation; others have come under his judgment because they rejected faith (AUGUSTINE). The cluster of grapes and the two men who carried them from the land of Canaan prefigured the wine of communion and the Jews and Gentiles who rejected and accepted Christ, respectively (CAESARIUS). The consignment of Judas to hell for his betrayal of Jesus and the election of Matthias as his replacement had been foretold already in the Psalms (BEDE). When members of the clergy are found guilty of public sins, they scandalize the church and taint the reputation of many others who are innocent of the offenses (AUGUSTINE). Just as the canonical books of Scripture constitute one book, so there is only one book of life, which contains the names of the redeemed (ORIGEN). The poor and sorrowful state of the human race is that it has been totally corrupted by the fall of Adam, cannot resist sinning and must hope in another, namely, Jesus Christ for its salvation (AUGUSTINE).

Since God needs nothing, the only thing he requires of his people is confession and contrition (CLEMENT OF ROME). Christ could not have died on the cross unless it was the will of the Father who delivered his Son up for our salvation (PETER CHRYSOLOGUS). God, though hidden to humanity by nature, has made it possible that those who seek him can find him (AUGUSTINE). The marvelous beauty of nature not only teaches us about God but also demands a grateful response (LEO).

69:20-29 Prophecies of Sufferings

WE DO NOT GIVE UP OUR HOPE IN THE LORD. BASIL THE GREAT: Since the holy God has promised those who hope in him a means of escape from every affliction, we, even if we have been cut off in the midst of a sea of evils and are racked by the mighty waves stirred up against us by the spirits of wickedness, nevertheless endure in Christ who strengthens us, and we have not slackened the intensity of our zeal for the churches, nor do we, as in a storm when the waves rise high, expect destruction. We still hold fast to our earnest endeavors as much as is possible, sensible of the fact that he who was swallowed by the whale was considered deserving of safety because he did not despair of his life but cried out to the Lord.[1] So, then, when we have reached the uttermost limit of evils, we do not stop hoping in the Lord, but we watch and see his help on all sides. Therefore, we have now turned also to you, our most honored brothers, whom we frequently expected to come to our aid in the time of tribulations.[2] When we were disappointed in our hope, we also said to ourselves, "I looked for one that would pity me, but there was none, and for those that would comfort me, but I found none." Our sufferings are such as to have reached even to the limits of our inhabited world; if, when one member suffers, all the members suffer along with it,[3] surely it was proper for you in your mercy also to be compassionate toward us who have been suffering for a long time. Not the nearness of the places, but the union of spirit, is apt to engender the friendship that we believe is entertained for us by your charity. LETTER 242.[4]

DETESTATION OF AFFECTIONLESS PEOPLE. AUGUSTINE: For the apostle censured and denounced certain people who, he said, were even

---

[1]See John 2. [2]This letter was written to the Western church in 376 asking for help during persecution of the orthodox Christians in the East by the Arian heretics during the reign of emperor Valens. [3]See 1 Cor 12:26. [4]FC 28:182**.

devoid of natural feelings.[5] One of the sacred psalms also blames those about whom it says, "I waited for someone to share my grief; but there was no one." In fact, complete exemption from pain, while we are in this place of misery, is certainly as one of the literary men of this world expressed it, "a piece of luck that one has to pay a high price for; the price of inhumanity of mind and insensitivity of body."[6] CITY OF GOD 14.9.[7]

PROPHECIES OF CHRIST'S SUFFERING AND CRUCIFIXION. TERTULLIAN:

A second time, in fact, let us show that Christ has already come, [as foretold] through the prophets, and has suffered, and has already been received back in the heavens and will come from there according to the predictions prophesied. For, after his advent, we read, according to Daniel, that the city itself had to be destroyed; and we recognize that it has indeed happened. For the Scripture says that "the city and the holy place are simultaneously destroyed together with the leader"[8]—undoubtedly [that Leader] who was to come "from Bethlehem" and from the tribe of "Judah." Whence, again, it is manifest that "the city must simultaneously be destroyed" at the time when its "Leader" had to suffer in it, [as foretold] through the Scriptures of the prophets, who say, "I have outstretched my hands the whole day to a rebellious people who contradict me, who walk in a way that is not good, but after their own sins."[9] And in the Psalms, David says, "They pierced my hands and feet: they counted all my bones; they themselves, moreover, stare and gloat over me, and for my thirst they gave me vinegar to drink."[10] David did not suffer these things so as to seem to have spoken properly of himself but of Christ who was crucified. AN ANSWER TO THE JEWS 12.[11]

CHRIST'S THIRST ON THE CROSS WAS REAL. TERTULLIAN:

Now, to counter all opinions[12] of this kind, let me dispel at once the preliminary idea on which they[13] rest their assertion that the prophets make all their announcements in figures of speech. Now, if this were true, the figures [of speech] themselves could not possibly have been distinguished, inasmuch as the truths would not have been declared, from which the figurative language is derived. And, indeed, if all are figures, where will that be of which they are the figures? How can you hold up a mirror to your face, if your face did not exist? But, in truth, all are not figures, but there are also literal statements; nor are all shadows, but there are bodies too, so that we even have prophecies about the Lord himself, which are clearer than daylight. For it was not figuratively that the Virgin conceived in her womb; nor in a trope did she bear Emmanuel, that is, Jesus, God with us.[14] Even granting that he was figuratively to take the power of Damascus and the spoils of Samaria,[15] still it was literally that he was to "enter into judgment with the elders and princes of the people."[16] For in the person of Pilate "the heathen raged," and in the person of Israel "the people imagined vain things"; "the kings of the earth" in Herod, and the rulers in Annas and Caiaphas, were gathered together against the Lord and "against his anointed."[17] He, again, was "led as a sheep to the slaughter, and as a sheep before the shearer," that is, Herod, "is dumb, so he opened not his mouth."[18] "He gave his back to scourges, and his cheek to blows, not turning his face even from the shame of spitting."[19] "He was numbered with the transgressors."[20] "He was pierced in his hands and his feet."[21] "They cast lots for his raiment";[22] "they gave him gall and made him drink vinegar"; "they shook their heads and mocked him."[23] "He was appraised by the traitor for thirty pieces of silver."[24] What figures of speech does Isaiah here give us? What tropes does David? What allegories does Jeremiah? Not even of his mighty works

---

[5]See Rom 1:31. [6]Cicero *Tusc. Disp.* 3.6.12. [7]CG 564*. [8]Dan 9:26. [9]Is 65:2; Rom 10:21. [10]Ps 22:16-17 (21:17-18 LXX, Vg.); Ps 69:21 (68:22 LXX, Vg.). [11]ANF 3:169**. [12]The heretical view that the soul is resurrected when it leaves the physical or material world. [13]Gnostic heretics who denied the resurrection of the flesh. [14]Is 7:14; Mt 1:23. [15]Is 8:4. [16]Is 3:13. [17]Ps 2:1-2. [18]Is 53:7. [19]Is 50:6 LXX. [20]Is 53:12. [21]Ps 22:16 (21:17 LXX, Vg.). [22]Ps 22:18 (21:19 LXX, Vg.). [23]Ps 22:7 (21:8 LXX, Vg.). [24]Zech 11:12.

have they used parabolic language. Or else, were not the eyes of the blind opened? Did not the tongue of the dumb recover speech?[25] Did not the relaxed hands and palsied knees become strong, and the lame leap as a hart?[26] No doubt we are accustomed also to give a spiritual significance to these statements of prophecy, according to the analogy of the physical diseases that were healed by the Lord; but still they were all fulfilled literally, thus showing that the prophets foretold both senses, except that very many of their words can only be taken in a pure and simple signification and free from all allegorical obscurity, as when we hear of the downfall of nations and cities of Tyre. . . . Who would prefer affixing a metaphorical interpretation to all these events, instead of accepting their literal truth? The realities are involved in the words, just as the words are read in the realities. Thus, we find that the allegorical style is not used in all parts of the prophetic record, although it occasionally occurs in certain portions of it. ON THE RESURRECTION OF THE FLESH 20.[27]

ON THE CROSS JESUS FULFILLED THE PROPHECY OF HIS THIRST. AUGUSTINE: Then [the Evangelist] continues: "Afterwards Jesus, knowing that all things were accomplished, that Scripture might be accomplished, says, 'I thirst.' Now there was a vessel set here full of vinegar, and putting a sponge full of vinegar around [a stalk of] hyssop, they raised it to his lips. When therefore Jesus had taken the vinegar, he said, 'It is finished.' And, bowing his head, he delivered over his spirit."[28] Who can so organize what he does as this man organized what he suffered? But the man, the Mediator of God and man,[29] the man about whom one reads that it was foretold: "And he is a man and who can know him?"[30] For the men through whom these things happened did know the man [to be] God. For he who was hidden as God was apparent as man; he who was apparent suffered these things and he who was hidden, the very same One, organized all these things. Therefore he saw that all the things were

finished that were necessary to be done before he took the vinegar and delivered over his spirit; and that this too might be accomplished that Scripture had foretold, "And in my thirst they gave me vinegar to drink," he said, "I thirst," as though he were to say, "In doing this you have fallen short; give what you are." For indeed the Jews themselves were the vinegar, deteriorating from the wine of the patriarchs and prophets, and, as it were, filled from a full vessel, from the iniquity of this world, having their heart like a sponge, deceitful, so to speak, in its cavernous and tortuous hiding places. But the hyssop around which they put the sponge full of vinegar, because it is a lowly herb and cleanses the breast, we take appropriately as the lowliness of Christ that they surrounded and thought they had come round to thwarting. And in regard to this is also that [place] in the psalm, "You will sprinkle me with hyssop, and I shall be cleansed."[31] For we are cleansed by the lowliness of Christ, because unless "he had humbled himself, made obedient even to the death of the cross,"[32] his blood assuredly would not have been poured out for the remission of sins, that is, for our cleansing. TRACTATES ON THE GOSPEL OF JOHN 119.4.[33]

CHRIST SUFFERED MORE AFFLICTIONS THAN ARE RECORDED IN SCRIPTURE. APHRAHAT: And furthermore David said concerning his passion, "For my food they gave gall, and for my thirst they did give me vinegar to drink." Again he said in that passage, "They have persecuted him whom you have struck and have added to the affliction of him that was slain." For they added many [afflictions] to him, much that was not written concerning him, cursings and revilings, such as the Scripture could not reveal, for their revilings were hateful. But, however, "the Lord was pleased to humiliate him and afflict him."[34] And "he was slain for our iniquity,"[35] and "was

---

[25]Is 35:5-6. [26]Is 35:3. [27]ANF 3:559-60**. [28]Jn 19:28-30. [29]1 Tim 2:5. [30]Jer 17:9 (LXX). [31]Ps 51:7 (50:9 LXX, Vg.). [32]Phil 2:8. [33]FC 92:47-48*. [34]Is 53:10. [35]Is 53:5.

humiliated for our sins and was made sin in his own person."[36] DEMONSTRATIONS 17.10.[37]

PROPHECY OF CHRIST'S WORDS ON THE CROSS. AUGUSTINE: For it was proclaimed beforehand by the very same prophets that they [Jews] would not understand, because it was necessary for other things to be fulfilled, and by a hidden and just decree of God, for due punishment to be paid in accordance with their merits. For, indeed, he whom they crucified, he to whom they gave gall and vinegar—although he was hanging on the cross—he said to the Father, for the sake of those whom he would have led from the darkness into the light, "Father, forgive them, for they know not what they do."[38] But, for the sake of the others whom he was to abandon for more hidden causes, he said long before through the prophet, "And they gave me gall for my food, and in my thirst they gave me vinegar to drink. Let their table become as a snare before them, and a recompense and a stumbling block. Let their eyes be darkened that they see not; and their back you always bend down." Therefore, they roam about anywhere and everywhere, their darkened eyes a most remarkable proof for our cause, so that through them our arguments are upheld at the very time that this same people is rejected. ON FAITH IN THINGS UNSEEN 6.9.[39]

MANY IN ISRAEL REFUSED TO ACCEPT CHRIST. AUGUSTINE: But the Jews who killed him and refused to believe in him, to believe that he had to die and rise again, suffered a more wretched devastation at the hands of the Romans and were utterly uprooted from their kingdom,[40] where they had already been under the dominion of foreigners. They were dispersed all over the world—for indeed there is no part of the earth where they are not to be found—and thus by evidence of their own scriptures they bear witness for us that we have not fabricated the prophecies about Christ. In fact, very many of the Jews, thinking over those prophecies both before his passion and more particularly after his resurrec-

tion, have come to believe in him. About them this prediction was made: "Even if the number of the children of Israel shall be like the sand of the sea, it is only a remnant that will be saved."[41] But the rest of them were blinded, and of them it was predicted, "Let their own table prove a snare in their presence, and a retribution and a stumbling block. Let their eyes be darkened, so that they may not see. Bend down their backs always." It follows that when the Jews do not believe in our Scriptures, their own scriptures are fulfilled in them, while they read them with blind eyes. CITY OF GOD 18.46.[42]

THE TRUE ISRAEL. AUGUSTINE: They themselves have become full of gall and bitterness in serving food of gall and vinegar to the living Bread. How else do they look on these prophecies in the psalm: "Let their eyes be darkened so that they do not see," and how are they to be upright in order to lift up their heart, they about whom it has been foretold, "and they always bend down their back together"?[43] These prophecies have not been made, however, about all the Jews; only about those to whom the predictions apply. These indictments do not concern those who believed in Christ at that time because of these very prophecies or those who have believed in Christ up to the present or who, henceforth, up to the end of the world, will believe in Christ, that is, the true Israel who will see the Lord face to face. "For they are not all Israelites who are sprung from Israel; nor because they are the descendants of Abraham, are they all his children; but through Isaac shall your posterity bear your name. This is to say, they are not the children of God who are the children of the flesh, but it is the children of promise who are reckoned as a posterity."[44] They belong to the spiritual Zion and the cities of Judah, that is, to the churches

---

[36]2 Cor 5:21. [37]NPNF 2 13:391*. [38]Lk 23:34. [39]FC 4:465-66*. [40]In A.D. 70. [41]Is 10:22. [42]CG 827-28. [43]Augustine is here following the LXX (68:24), which reads *kai ton nōton autōn dia pantos synkampson.* [44]Rom 9:6-8.

about whom the apostle says, "And I was unknown by sight to the churches of Judah, which were in Christ,"[45] since a little later in the same psalm appears, "For God will save Zion, and the cities of Judah shall be built up. And they shall dwell there and acquire it by inheritance. And the seed of his servants shall possess it; and they that love his name shall dwell therein."[46] When the Jews hear these words, they take them in their natural meaning and imagine an earthly Jerusalem that is in slavery with its children, not our eternal mother who is in heaven. IN ANSWER TO THE JEWS 5.6.[47]

THE VOLUNTARY SUFFERING OF CHRIST. LEO THE GREAT: You have truly and in very many places read something that pertains to the detestable wickedness of your crime and to the voluntary suffering of the Lord. He himself speaks through Isaiah: "I gave my back to the scourges, my cheeks to striking hands; my face I did not shield from the insult of spittle."[48] He says through David, "They put gall in my food, and in my thirst they gave me vinegar to drink." On yet another occasion, he says through David, "Many dogs surround me, a pack of evildoers closes in on me. They have pierced my hands and my feet, they have numbered all my bones. They watched me carefully and examined me. They divided my garments among them and cast lots for my clothes."[49] Lest only the kind of your crime might seem to be predicted and the power of the crucified one not foretold, you certainly did not read that the Lord descended from the cross. You did, however, read, "The Lord has reigned from the cross."[50] SERMON 55.2.[51]

PREDESTINED TO SALVATION BY THE GRACE OF GOD. AUGUSTINE: "Many hear the word of truth, but some believe and others speak against it. Therefore the former will to believe, but the latter do not will." Who would not know this? Who would deny it? But since in some persons the will is prepared by God and in others it is not, we must indeed distinguish what comes from his mercy and what comes from his judgment. "That which Israel sought," says the apostle, "he has not obtained, but the elect have obtained it, and the rest have been blinded. As it is written, 'God has given them the spirit of insensibility: eyes that they should not see, and ears that they should not hear, until this present day.' And David says, 'Let their table be made a snare, and a recompense and a stumbling block to them. Let their eyes be darkened, that they may not see; and bow down their back always.' "[52] Behold mercy and judgment: mercy on the elect, who have obtained the justice of God, but judgment on the others who have been blinded. And yet the former have believed, because they have willed, while the latter have not believed, because they have not willed. Hence, mercy and judgment were brought about in their own wills. Clearly, this election is through grace, not at all through merits. As the apostle had earlier said, "Even so then at this present time also, there is a remnant saved according to the election of grace. And if by grace, it is not now by works; otherwise grace is no more grace."[53] Therefore, it is by grace that the elect have obtained what they have obtained; there preceded nothing that they might first give so that it might be given to them in recompense. God saved them for nothing. As to those others who were blinded, as it clearly stated here, it was done in retribution. "All the ways of the Lord are mercy and truth."[54] But "his ways" are "unsearchable."[55] Hence, the mercy by which he freely liberates and the truth by which he justly judges are both unsearchable. PREDESTINATION OF THE SAINTS 6.11.[56]

A PREFIGUREMENT. CAESARIUS OF ARLES: That cluster of grapes that was brought from the land of promise on a lever across the shoulders of two men further prefigured Christ. Just as it was hung

---

[45]Gal 1:22. [46]Ps 69:35-36 (68:36-37 LXX, Vg.). [47]FC 27:397-98**. [48]Is 50:6. [49]Ps 22:16-18 (21:17-19 LXX, Vg.). [50]See Ps 96:10 (95:10 LXX, Vg.). [51]FC 93:238. [52]Rom 11:7-10, citing Is 6:9-10; Ps 69:22-23 (68:23-24 LXX, Vg.). [53]Rom 11:5-6. [54]Ps 25:10 (24:10 LXX, Vg.). [55]Rom 11:33. [56]FC 86:231-32.

on the wood and brought by the services of those two men, so Christ, who came from the flesh of a virgin as from the promised land, was between both Testaments, between the two peoples of the Jews and Gentiles, and was hung on the wood of the cross. Now of the two men who walked beneath the burden of that cluster of grapes, the first one signified the Jewish people of whom it is said, "Let their eyes grow dim so that they cannot see, and keep their backs always feeble." However, the man who came after prefigured our people, that is, the Gentiles who believe and keep Christ before their eyes. They intend always to follow him as a servant does his master or a disciple his teacher, as the Lord says in the Gospel: "If anyone wishes to come after me, let him deny himself, and take up his cross and follow me."[57] Moreover, this cluster of grapes poured forth the wine of his blood that was pressed out under the weight of the cross for our salvation and gave the church that chalice of his passion to drink. For this reason it was said to the apostles at the time of the birth of the church, "They are full of new wine."[58] SERMON 106.3.[59]

PROPHECIES OF JUDAS AND MATTHIAS. BEDE: "May his habitation become desolate, and may there be none to dwell in it, and may another take his office."[60] Indeed these verses are clear and plainly set forth by the blessed Peter's interpretation. On the one hand Judas received a deserved penalty for his double-dealing, and as he went to his own proper place (namely, infernal hell), by his untimely and impious death he forsook the common dwelling place of the human way of life. On the other hand, however, by Matthias's acceptance of the place of his [Judas's] ministry and apostolate, the most sacred fullness of apostolic perfection was restored.[61] COMMENTARY ON THE ACTS OF THE APOSTLES 1.20.[62]

DO NOT GRIEVE THE CHURCH BY FALLING INTO INIQUITY. AUGUSTINE: It is evident that those things[63] do not happen in the church without causing great sadness to the saints and the faithful; may he console us who foretold all these things and who warned us not to grow cold because of the prevalence of iniquity but to persevere to the end that we may be saved. As far as I am concerned, if there is in me the smallest spark of the charity of Christ, "Who of you is weak, and I am not weak; who is scandalized and I am not on fire?"[64] Do not increase my sufferings, therefore, by falling either into false suspicions or into the sins of others; do not, I beg of you, make me say of you, "And they have added to the grief of my wounds." For those who take pleasure in these sorrows of ours, of whom it was long ago foretold in the person of the body of Christ, "They that sat in the gate, spoke against me; and they that drank wine made me their song,"[65] are much more readily borne with; indeed, we have learned to pray for them and to wish them well. But, for what other purpose do they sit there, and what else do they aim at, except, when some bishop or cleric or monk or nun has fallen, that they may believe, assert and contend that all are like that—although it cannot be proved of all? Yet, when some married woman has been found to be an adulteress, they do not cast off their wives or accuse their mothers; but, when it is a case of those who profess a sacred calling, if some false charge has been rumored about or some true one has been published, they take it up, go to work on it, toss it about, so as to have it universally believed. Therefore, of those who take sweetness for their evil tongues from our sorrows, it is easy to compare them with those dogs, if, perchance, we are to take in an adverse sense, those who licked the sores of the beggar who lay before the rich man's gate and who bore hard and humiliating things until he came to rest in Abraham's bosom.[66] LETTER 78.[67]

THE UNITY OF SCRIPTURE. ORIGEN: If it is

---

[57]Mt 16:24. [58]Acts 2:13. [59]FC 47:127. [60]See also Ps 109:8 (108:8 LXX, Vg.). [61]Acts 1:26. [62]CS 117:19. [63]To slander or ruin the reputation of an innocent person. [64]2 Cor 11:29. [65]Ps 69:12 (68:13 LXX, Vg.). [66]Lk 16:20-22. [67]FC 12:380-81.

possible to prove that the sacred works are one book, but the non-sacred many, we must observe in addition that there is one book in the case of the living, from which those who deserve it are blotted out, as it is written, "Let them be blotted out of the book of the living." [By contrast], a plurality of books is brought in the case of those who are reserved for judgment, for Daniel says, "The court convened, and the books were opened."[68] Moses also testifies to the singleness of the divine book, saying, "If you forgive the people's sin, forgive; otherwise strike me out of the book that you have written."[69] COMMENTARY ON THE GOSPEL OF JOHN 5.7.[70]

THE FALL OF ADAM CORRUPTED THE HUMAN RACE. AUGUSTINE: For what is more fruitful or more filled with the truest confession than that passage in one of your letters in which you[71] humbly bewail the fact that our nature did not remain as it was created but was debased by the father of the human race? In your letter you said, "But I am poor and sorrowful," I, that am still hardened in the filth of an earthly image, having in me more of the first Adam than of the second, still give my attention to the senses of the flesh and to earthly acts. How shall I dare to depict myself when earthly corruption proves that I deny my heavenly image? I blush to paint what I am, I do not dare to paint what I am not. But what good will it do me, wretched as I am, "to hate iniquity and to love virtue,"[72] when I do rather what I hate and am too sluggish to strive to do what I love? I am torn apart, fighting with myself in an interior warfare, while "the spirit lusts against the flesh and the flesh against the spirit,"[73] and "the law of my body under the law of sin fights against the law of my mind."[74] Unhappy am I who have absorbed the poisonous taste of that hateful tree, not the wood of the cross! The ancestral poison hardens in me, from Adam the father, who by his fall has undone the whole race.[75] These and many other things you said, groaning over your misery and expecting the redemption of your body, knowing yourself saved by hope, if not yet in fact.[76] LETTER 186.[77]

69:30-32 People Encounter God and Respond Appropriately

CONTRITION: A SACRIFICE TO GOD. CLEMENT OF ROME: Brothers, the Lord of the universe has need of nothing; he requires nothing of anyone, except that confession be made to him. For David, the chosen one, says, "I will confess to the Lord, and it shall please him more than a young bullock with horns and hoofs. Let the poor see it and be glad." And again he says, "Sacrifice to God a sacrifice of praise, and render to the All-High your vows; and call on me in the day of affliction, and I will deliver you, and you shall glorify me."[78] "For a contrite spirit is a sacrifice to God."[79] 1 CLEMENT 52.[80]

CHRIST'S DEATH WAS THE WILL OF THE FATHER. PETER CHRYSOLOGUS: "And he killed for him the fattened calf."[81] About that David sang, "And it shall please God better than a young calf that has horns and hoofs." The calf was slain at this command of the Father, because the Christ, God as the Son of God, could not be slain without the command of his Father. Listen to the apostle: "He who has not spared even his own son but has delivered him for us all."[82] He is the calf who is daily and continually immolated for our food. SERMON 5.[83]

SEEK GOD CONTINUALLY. AUGUSTINE: Let us direct the mind's gaze and, with the Lord's help, let us search out God. The word of the divine canticle is "Seek God and your soul will live." Let us seek him who is to be found, let us seek him who has been found. He has been hidden so that he may be sought for and found; he is immeasurable so that, even though he has been found, he may be sought for. For this reason it is said else-

---

[68]Dan 7:10. [69]Ex 32:32. [70]FC 80:164-65. [71]Paulinus of Nola, to whom the letter is addressed. [72]Ps 45:7 (44:8 LXX, Vg.). [73]Gal 5:17. [74]Rom 7:23. [75]Paulinus of Nola *Epistle* 30.2. [76]Rom 8:23-24. [77]FC 30:219-20. [78]Ps 50:14-15 (49:14-15 LXX). [79]Ps 51:17 (50:19 LXX). [80]FC 1:49*. [81]Lk 15:30. [82]Rom 8:32. [83]FC 17:50*.

where, "Seek his face always."[84] For he fills the seeker as far as he has capacity, and he makes the finder more capacious, that he may seek again to be filled when he has begun to increase his capacity. TRACTATES ON THE GOSPEL OF JOHN 63.1.1.[85]

NATURE TESTIFIES TO GOD'S EXISTENCE. LEO THE GREAT: Always indeed, dearly beloved, "the earth is full of the Lord's kindness,"[86] and the nature of things itself is the teacher to each one of the faithful in the worship of God, while "heaven and earth, the sea and all things that are in them"[87] proclaim the goodness and power of their Creator. The wonderful beauty of the elements that serve him demands a due thanksgiving from the understanding creature.[88] SERMON 44.1.[89]

---

[84]Ps 105:4 (104:4 LXX, Vg.). [85]FC 90:42. [86]Ps 33:5 (32:5 LXX, Vg.). [87]See Ps 69:34 (68:35 LXX, Vg.); Ps 146:6 (145:6 LXX, Vg.); Acts 14:15. [88]See Rom 1:20-21. [89]FC 93:190.

70:1-5 AN URGENT PRAYER FOR GOD'S HELP

To the choirmaster. A Psalm of David, for the memorial offering.

¹*Be pleased, O God, to deliver me!*
    O LORD, make haste to help me!
²*Let them be put to shame and confusion*
    who seek my life!
Let them be turned back and brought to dishonor
    who desire my hurt!
³*Let them be appalled because of their shame*

who say, "Aha, Aha!"

⁴*May all who seek thee*
    rejoice and be glad in thee!
May those who love thy salvation
    say evermore, "God is great!"
⁵*But I am poor and needy;*
    hasten to me, O God!
Thou art my help and my deliverer;
    O LORD do not tarry!

OVERVIEW: Some verses of Scripture are so profound and broad in their meaning and application that devotional repetition of them can help to unify the mind and to defend against temptations (CASSIAN). Even Satan's most subtle effort to tempt people who have successfully resisted him to take personal credit for their success can be resisted only by attributing their success to the power of God in their lives (AUGUSTINE). Christians must trust in God in times of joy and in times of affliction because the salvation of God is sure in all circumstances of life (PACHOMIUS).

70:1 Prayer for Divine Help

THE POWER OF MEDITATION. JOHN CASSIAN: This, then, is the devotional formula proposed to you[1] as absolutely necessary for possessing the perpetual awareness of God: "O God, incline to my aid; O Lord, make haste to help me."

Not without reason has this verse been selected from out of the whole body of Scrip-

---

[1]Cassian is here quoting the Egyptian anchorite, Abba Isaac, who was speaking to him about the benefits of unceasing prayer.

ture. For it takes up all the emotions that can be applied to human nature and with great correctness and accuracy it adjusts itself to every condition and every attack. It contains an invocation of God in the face of any crisis, the humility of a devout confession, the watchfulness of concern and of constant fear, a consciousness of one's own frailty, the assurance of being heard and confidence in a protection that is always present and at hand, for whoever calls unceasingly on his protector is sure that he is always present. It contains a burning love and charity, an awareness of traps and a fear of enemies. Seeing oneself surrounded by these day and night, one confesses that one cannot be set free without the help of one's defender. This verse is an unassailable wall, an impenetrable breastplate and a very strong shield for all those who labor under the attack of demons. It does not permit those troubled by boredom and anxiety of mind or those depressed by sadness or different kinds of thoughts to despair of a saving remedy, showing that he whom it invokes is always looking on our struggles and is not detached from his suppliants. It warns those of us who are enjoying spiritual successes and are glad of heart that we must never be exalted or puffed up because of our good fortune, which it testifies cannot be maintained without the protection of God, for it begs him to come to our aid not only at all times but also quickly.

This verse, I say, is necessary and useful for each one of us in whatever condition we may live. For whoever desires to be helped always and in all things shows that he needs God as a helper not only in hard and sad affairs but also and equally as much in favorable and joyful ones, so that just as he may be snatched from the former he may abide in the latter, know that in neither instance can human frailty endure without his assistance. CONFERENCES 10.9.2-5.[2]

70:3-5 In Times of Temptation and Affliction

AVOID THE FLATTERIES OF SATAN. AUGUSTINE: Overcoming well means overcoming all the machinations of the devil. He serves up enticements, he is overcome by self-restraint; he inflicts pains and tortures, he is overcome by patience; he suggests errors, he is overcome by wisdom. As a last resort, when all these ploys have been defeated, he suggests to the soul, "Well done, well done, how much you've been able to do! How valiantly you've contended! Who can be compared with you? How well you have overcome!" The holy soul must answer him, "Let them be put to confusion and shame, those who say to me, Well done, well done!" So when do you overcome, if not when you say, "It is in the Lord that my soul shall be praised; let the gentle hear and rejoice"?[3] SERMON 274.[4]

SALVATION IN TIME OF AFFLICTION. PACHOMIUS: Now is the time to act for the Lord, because our salvation is in a time of affliction. If "those who love his salvation" can "know his steps"[5] and "say constantly: God is great";[6] and if they can say, "My hope shall be in you always," will they believe only in time of joy and not believe in time of affliction?

It is written indeed, "What came out of your mouth, do diligently,"[7] and again, "If you have made a prayer to the Lord, do not delay to render [what you have promised], lest the Lord claim it from you and it be for you a sin."[8] If you say, "My hope shall be in you always,"[9] may you be found confident in time of affliction, in which is salvation. LETTER 3.11.[10]

---

[2]ACW 57:379-80*. [3]Ps 34:2 (33:3 LXX, Vg.). [4]*WSA* 3 8:24. [5]Ps 77:19 (76:20 LXX). [6]Ps 70:4 (69:5 LXX). [7]Num 32:24. [8]Deut 23:21-22. [9]Ps 71:1 (70:1 LXX). [10]CS 47 3:57-58.

71:1-24 A PRAYER FOR GOD'S HELP IN OLD AGE

1In thee, O Lord do I take refuge;
let me never be put to shame!
2In thy righteousness deliver me and rescue me;
incline thy ear to me, and save me!
3Be thou to me a rock of refuge,
a strong fortress,[p] to save me,
for thou art my rock and my fortress.

4Rescue me, O my God, from the hand of the wicked,
from the grasp of the unjust and cruel man.
5For thou, O Lord, art my hope,
my trust, O Lord from my youth.
6Upon thee I have leaned from my birth;
thou art he who took me from my mother's womb.
My praise is continually of thee.

7I have been as a portent to many;
but thou art my strong refuge.
8My mouth is filled with thy praise,
and with thy glory all the day.
9Do not cast me off in the time of old age;
forsake me not when my strength is spent.
10For my enemies speak concerning me,
those who watch for my life consult together,
11and say, "God has forsaken him;
pursue and seize him,
for there is none to deliver him."

12O God, be not far from me;
O my God, make haste to help me!
13May my accusers be put to shame and consumed;
with scorn and disgrace may they be covered
who seek my hurt.
14But I will hope continually,
and will praise thee yet more and more.
15My mouth will tell of thy righteous acts,
of thy deeds of salvation all the day,
for their number is past my knowledge.
16With the mighty deeds of the Lord God I will come,
I will praise thy righteousness, thine alone.

17O God, from my youth thou hast taught me,
and I still proclaim thy wondrous deeds.
18So even to old age and gray hairs,
O God, do not forsake me,
till I proclaim thy might
to all the generations to come.[q]
Thy power 19and thy righteousness, O God,
reach the high heavens.

Thou who hast done great things,
O God, who is like thee?
20Thou who hast made me see many sore troubles
wilt revive me again;
from the depths of the earth
thou wilt bring me up again.
21Thou wilt increase my honor,
and comfort me again.

22I will also praise thee with the harp
for thy faithfulness, O my God;
I will sing praises to thee with the lyre,
O Holy One of Israel.
23My lips will shout for joy,
when I sing praises to thee;

my soul also, which thou hast rescued.
²⁴And my tongue will talk of thy righteous help
    all the day long,

for they have been put to shame and disgraced
    who sought to do me hurt.

p Gk Compare 31.3: Heb *to come continually thou hast commanded*   q Gk Compare Syr: Heb *to a generation, to all that come*

OVERVIEW: We do not receive the mercy of God on the basis of our merit; God must first be inclined to help us (CASSIODORUS). John was one of the mountains, that is, the eminent souls who are spiritual blessings to lesser souls as they share their wisdom. When Christians suffer persecution, they should pray for deliverance from their enemies in patient endurance of their ordeal. A Christian who is patient in suffering hardships knows that what has been redeemed by the blood of Christ, such as the bodies of martyrs, will not perish even if they seem to be destroyed in this life (AUGUSTINE).

Business transactions and the possession of wealth do not by themselves corrupt faithful people; they become wrong when conducted and gained in an evil way (CASSIODORUS).

The Psalms testify to the intercommunication of the three persons in the Godhead, thereby witnessing to their divinity and personal distinction (TERTULLIAN).

71:2-3 In Your Righteousness Deliver Me

GOD'S GRACE INCLINES HIM TO SAVE US. CASSIODORUS: "Deliver me in your justice, and rescue me. Incline your ear to me, and deliver me." When he says "in your justice," he seeks divine mercy, for it is the role of divine justice to spare the suppliant, since it has pleased his fairness to pardon the person known to condemn his own actions. He says, "Deliver me from looming dangers, rescue me from the power of the devil"; this is so that he may not be condemned with the devil for eternity. When he says "incline," he proclaims that he is lowly and prostrate. Unless God's grace inclines to deliver us, we cannot attain by our own merits the mercy for which we long. No person's merit touches the Lord unless

in his mercy he bends low to reach sinners. EXPOSITIONS OF THE PSALMS 70.2.[1]

GREATER AND LESSER SOULS. AUGUSTINE: For this John, my dearest brothers, was one of those mountains about which it has been written, "Let the mountains receive peace for your people; and the hills justice." The mountains are eminent souls; the hills are little souls. But the mountains receive peace for this very reason, so that the hills can receive justice. What is the justice that the hills receive? Faith, because "the just person lives by faith."[2] The lesser souls, however, would not receive faith if the greater souls, who were called mountains, were not illuminated by wisdom itself, so that they can convey to the little ones what the little ones are able to grasp, and so that the hills can live by faith because the mountains receive peace. By these very mountains it was said to the church, "Peace be with you." And the mountains themselves, in announcing peace to the church, did not set themselves apart in regard to him from whom they receive peace so that they might announce peace truly and not deceitfully.[3] TRACTATES ON THE GOSPEL OF JOHN 1.2.[4]

71:4-5 Patience from the Lord

PATIENCE IN TIME OF SUFFERING. AUGUSTINE: We saw the martyr so patiently enduring the most monstrous torments; but his soul was submitting itself to God, because it was from him that his patience came. And lest human frailty should fail through lack of patience and deny Christ, and contribute to the enemy's joy, he knew to whom he should say, "My God, rescue

---

[1]ACW 52:167*. [2]Hab 2:4; Rom 1:17; Gal 3:11; Heb 10:38. [3]See Jn 20:19. [4]FC 78:42-43.

me from the hand of the sinner, from the hand of the lawbreaker and the wicked, since you are my patience." In this way, you see, the person who sang these words signified how Christians should ask to be rescued from the hands of their enemies; not, certainly, by suffering nothing but by enduring what they suffer with perfect patience. "Rescue me from the hand of the sinner, from the hand of the lawbreaker and the wicked." But if you ask how he wants to be rescued, look at what follows: "since you are my patience." You will find a glorious passion, wherever there is this devout confession, so that "whoever boasts, may boast in the Lord."[5] SERMON 277A.2.[6]

CHRIST GIVES MARTYRS THE PATIENCE TO ENDURE THEIR SUFFERING. AUGUSTINE: We have been watching a magnificent spectacle with the eyes of faith, the holy martyr Vincent[7] everywhere victorious. He was victorious in his words, victorious in the pains he endured; victorious in his confession, victorious in his tribulations; victorious when burned with fire, victorious when submerged in the waves. When his flesh, which was a kind of tribute to the victorious Christ, was thrown into the sea from the boat, it silently said, "We are cast down but not lost."[8] Who can have endowed this soldier with such patience but the one who first shed his blood for him? The one to whom it says in the psalm, "Since you are my patience, Lord, my hope from my youth." A great contest earns great glory; not human or temporal glory, but divine and eternal. Faith is doing battle; and when faith is doing battle, nobody can overthrow the flesh. Because even if it is mangled and torn to shreds, when can anyone perish who has been redeemed by the blood of Christ? A powerful person cannot lose what he has bought with his gold, and can Christ lose what he bought with his blood? SERMON 274.[9]

71:15 Righteous in Worldly Matters

WEALTH IS NOT EVIL PER SE. CASSIODORUS: "Because I have not known worldly business."

This part of the verse clearly raises a problem unless it is carefully analyzed: if every person of business is to be wholly condemned, those known to practice other occupations do not escape this punishment; for what is business except seeking to retail at a higher price objects that can cost less? Then too we read in the Fathers' lives that the famous Paphnutius, a most holy man, was purchased by a business man who experienced a revelation;[10] and even today we find people in God's church handling merchandise who are persons of the most committed faith. It is the very wicked action, and not honorable property, that is condemned. We read in Scripture that the rich person does not enter the kingdom of heaven,[11] yet the patriarchs Job, Abraham, Isaac and Joseph also had abundant wealth. So the business people who are reckoned as accursed are those who have no thought whatsoever for the Lord's justice, who are corrupted by an uncontrolled desire for money and who sell their goods for a dishonest rather than a just price. Such people as these the Lord cast out of the temple with the words "Make not the house of my Father a house of traffic, a den of thieves."[12] So in my view the meaning to be embraced here is something like this: "My mouth has proclaimed your justice, because I have not known the worldly business that is polluted by evil actions." EXPOSITIONS OF THE PSALMS 70.15.[13]

71:18 Conversation Among the Persons of the Godhead

CHRIST SPEAKS TO THE FATHER. TERTULLIAN: Hear now also the Son's statements about the Father: "The Spirit of the Lord is on me, because

---

[5]1 Cor 1:31. [6]*WSA* 3 8:48. [7]Augustine preached this sermon on the birthday of Vincent, a deacon in Saragossa, Spain, who was martyred in Valencia in 303, during the Diocletian persecution. [8]2 Cor 4:9. [9]*WSA* 3 8:23*. [10]See *Historia Monarchorum* 16 (PL 24.438ff.). Paphnutius was an Egyptian monk, a disciple of Antony. At the Council of Nicaea he created a spectacle at the physical mutilation that he had suffered in the persecutions of 305 to 313. [11]See Lk 16:19-31. [12]Jn 2:16; Mk 11:17; Mt 21:13. [13]ACW 52:173-74*.

he has anointed me to preach the gospel to the poor."[14] He speaks of himself likewise to the Father in the psalm: "Forsake me not, until I have declared the might of your arm to all the generations that are to come." Also with the same substance in another psalm: "O Lord, how many are they that trouble me!"[15] But almost all the psalms that prophesy of the person of Christ, represent the Son as conversing with the Father—that is, represent Christ [as speaking] to God. Observe also the Spirit speaking of the Father and the Son, in the character of a third person: "The Lord said to my Lord, Sit on my right hand, until I make your enemies your footstool."[16] Likewise in the words of Isaiah: "Thus says the Lord to the Lord my anointed."[17] AGAINST PRAXEAS 11.[18]

---

[14]Is 61:1; Lk 4:18. [15]Ps 3:1. [16]Ps 110:1 (109:1 LXX, Vg.). [17]Is 45:1. [18]ANF 3:606**. In this work Tertullian was writing in opposition to one of the advocates of modalistic monarchianism, which denied a trinitarian distinction of persons within the Godhead and advocated only a threefold distinction of operations or roles.

72:1-20 A PRAYER FOR THE KING

A Psalm of Solomon.

[1]Give the king thy justice, O God,
and thy righteousness to the royal son!
[2]May he judge thy people with righteousness,
and thy poor with justice!
[3]Let the mountains bear prosperity for the
people,
and the hills, in righteousness!
[4]May he defend the cause of the poor of the
people,
give deliverance to the needy,
and crush the oppressor!

[5]May he live[r] while the sun endures,
and as long as the moon, throughout all
generations!
[6]May he be like rain that falls on the mown
grass,
like showers that water the earth!
[7]In his days may righteousness flourish,
and peace abound, till the moon be no more!

[8]May he have dominion from sea to sea,
and from the River to the ends of the earth!
[9]May his foes[s] bow down before him,
and his enemies lick the dust!
[10]May the kings of Tarshish and of the isles
render him tribute,
may the kings of Sheba and Seba bring gifts!
[11]May all kings fall down before him,
all nations serve him!

[12]For he delivers the needy when he calls,
the poor and him who has no helper.
[13]He has pity on the weak and the needy,
and saves the lives of the needy.
[14]From oppression and violence he redeems
their life;
and precious is their blood in his sight.
[15]Long may he live,
may gold of Sheba be given to him!
May prayer be made for him continually,
and blessings invoked for him all the day!
[16]May there be abundance of grain in the land;

on the tops of the mountains may it wave;
    may its fruit be like Lebanon;
and may men blossom forth from the cities
    like the grass of the field!
[17]May his name endure for ever,
    his fame continue as long as the sun!
May men bless themselves by him,
    all nations call him blessed!

[18]Blessed be the LORD the God of Israel,
    who alone does wondrous things.
[19]Blessed be his glorious name for ever;
    may his glory fill the whole earth! Amen
    and Amen!

[20]The prayers of David, the son of Jesse, are
    ended.

r Gk: Heb *may they fear thee*   s Cn: Heb *those who dwell in the wilderness*

OVERVIEW: This psalm applies to Christ, who alone rules eternally, exists from eternity and whose justice endures until the end of the world (JUSTIN, ORIGEN, EUSEBIUS). Sometimes the Scriptures use hyperbole to make a point, such as the prophecy of the extent of Solomon's kingdom (THEODORE). Prophecy is compared with the refreshing benefits of rain, the absence of which results in unbelief. Christ ended the drought when he came and gave the world the Holy Spirit (AMBROSE). Christ is prophesied as the Prince of Peace who will shepherd his flock after his birth at Bethlehem (EUSEBIUS). The unusual and quiet nature of Christ's conception and birth were prophesied by David (MAXIMUS).

All Scripture, both the Old and New Testaments, declares that the true church will be spread throughout the world. Prophecies of universal rule can apply only to Christ, whose dominion began at the time of his baptism in the Jordan River. The recognition of Christ and the beginning of his reign occur at the time of John the Baptist's declaration of his identity and baptism of him. The spreading of the Christian church is evidence that Christ has subdued all the kings of the earth and brought them into happy submission. While it may be more honorable to rely on legitimate governments than on heretics, ultimately one's reliance and hope must be in God (AUGUSTINE). Since Christ, like the Father, is God, he should be worshiped throughout the world (FULGENTIUS).

Believers who are afflicted in this world can be cheerful because God has conquered their enemies, delivered them from their oppressors and made their former enemies subject to him (ORIGEN). The magi's gift of gold symbolizes the submission of the Eastern kingdoms to the King of kings (TERTULLIAN).

Christ is God to whom all created things have become subject (JUSTIN). David attests to Christ's eternal existence and therefore to his deity, a fact incomprehensible to the human mind but proclaimed by prophecy (HILARY). Since Christ existed from eternity, it is his human nature that is exalted, not his deity (ATHANASIUS). It is by the power of God that we are transformed spiritually from captives to free persons, from sinful to just and holy, from being disinherited to heirs of God (CHRYSOSTOM). God performs miracles under his own power; when people perform miracles they need God's help in doing so (AUGUSTINE). Some godly people have been so blessed in doing wonderful God-pleasing deeds that they defy human eloquence to describe them (BRAULIO).

72:1-4 The Blessings of Christ and Saints to the Church

CHRIST IS KING. JUSTIN MARTYR: As a further proof of your[1] ignorance of the Scripture, I am

---

[1]Trypho the Jew, whom Justin is trying to convert to Christianity in this dialogue.

going to quote another psalm, dedicated to David by the Holy Spirit, which you erroneously think refers to your king Solomon but which in reality refers to Christ. One cause of your error is that you are misled by the false interpretation of equivocal terms. For when the law of God is called a "blameless law,"[2] you do not understand it as applying to the law that was to come after Moses but to the Mosaic law itself, even though God had promised to establish a new law and a new covenant. And when the psalm says, "Give to the king your judgment, O God," you claim that the words were spoken of Solomon because he was a king, whereas the words clearly proclaim that they were spoken of the eternal King, that is, Christ. I prove from all the Scriptures that Christ is spoken of as a king, and a priest, and God, and Lord, and an angel, and a man, and a leader, and a stone, and a begotten son and as one who at first endured suffering, then ascended into heaven, and as returning to earth with glory and having the eternal kingdom. DIALOGUE WITH TRYPHO 34.[3]

A PROPHECY OF CHRIST. ORIGEN: And I support this[4] from Psalm 71 [LXX], which says, "Give to the king your judgment, O God; and your justice to the king's son, to judge your people with justice, and your poor with judgment." For clearly the psalm, which has been ascribed to Solomon, prophesies of Christ. COMMENTARY ON THE GOSPEL OF JOHN 1.193.[5]

CHRIST, THE SEED OF DAVID, SHALL REIGN FOREVER. EUSEBIUS OF CAESAREA: As this psalm is addressed to Solomon, the first verse of the psalm must be referred to him, and all the rest to the son of Solomon, not Rehoboam, who was king of Israel after him, but him that was of his seed according to the flesh, the Christ of God; for all who are acquainted with the holy Scriptures will agree that it is impossible to connect what is said in this psalm with Solomon or his successors, because of what they reveal about Christ. No, how is it possible to apply to Solomon,

or his son Rehoboam, the burden of the whole psalm?—for instance, "He shall rule from sea to sea, and from the river to the ends of the earth."[6] And "He shall remain as long as the sun, and before the moon for ever,"[7] and other similar statements. Yet the words at the beginning of the psalm are at once seen to apply to Solomon, which say, "O God, you will give judgment to the king," And the addition, "And your justice to the king's son," to the Son of Solomon, not his firstborn who succeeded him in the kingdom (for he only ruled the Jewish nation seventeen years, being a wicked king), nor any of the successors of Rehoboam, but only to one of the seed of David, who could thus be called the son both of David and Solomon. And this is our Lord and Savior Jesus Christ. For his kingdom and its throne will stand as long as the sun. And he alone of people, as the Word of God, existed before the moon and the creation of the world, and he alone came down like dew from heaven on all the earth; and it was said in our quotation a little above, that he had risen on all people and that his justice would remain even until the consummation of life, which is called the removal of the moon. And our Savior's power is supreme from the eastern sea to the west, beginning its activity at the river, which is either the sacrament of baptism, or from Jordan, where he first appeared to benefit humankind. From that time his kingdom has spread and extended through the whole world. PROOF OF THE GOSPEL 7.3.[8]

72:5-7 Prophecies of Christ and the Holy Spirit

SPEAKING HYPERBOLICALLY. THEODORE OF MOPSUESTIA: So that now, concerning the things to be promised to the people through the kingdom of Zerubbabel,[9] who was assigned for this through

---

[2]Ps 19:7 (18:8 LXX). [3]FC 6:197-98*. [4]Origen has just asserted that we know Christ had a kingly nature from the biblical evidence of his divine nature. [5]FC 80:72. [6]Ps 72:8 (71:8 LXX). [7]Ps 72:5 (71:5 LXX). [8]POG 2:89-90*. [9]Zech 4:6-10.

the divine judgment, it was not at all inappropriate for the prophet, speaking, to say, "he comes righteous and saving," so that he might show that he is present with them and that he has been chosen by God for the kingship in order to do these things. It says that those very things, therefore, have successively happened concerning the people through him. But let these things suffice for the most accurate teaching. The prophet is speaking concerning Zerubbabel and prophesying present things concerning him, if also as a prophet himself he had a certain vision concerning things to come, he adds:

He shall govern the waters from sea to sea
And from the River to the ends of the earth.
(Zech 9:10)

This also has apparently been said hyperbolically, that he will prevail over many enemies and that he will occupy much territory, having given it for habitation to the Jews. The seventy-first [seventy-second] psalm by the blessed David is similar; in the form of a prayer it has a figure of the prosperity of Solomon, where it says, "May he live while the sun endures, and as long as the moon throughout all generations! May he have dominion from sea to sea and from the River to the ends of the earth."[10] Is it not obvious that these things are said hyperbolically? COMMENTARY ON ZECHARIAH 9.10-12.[11]

THE HOLY SPIRIT IS LIKE HEAVENLY DEW.
AMBROSE: Nor is it strange that they should suffer the drought of unbelief, whom the Lord deprived of the fertilizing shower of prophecy, saying, "I will command my clouds that they rain not on that vineyard."[12] For there is a health-giving shower of salutary grace, as David also said: "He came down like rain on a fleece and like drops that fall on the earth." The divine Scriptures promised us this rain on the whole earth, to water the world with the dew of the divine Spirit at the coming of the Savior. The Lord, then, has now come, and the rain has come; the Lord has come bringing the heavenly drops with him, and

so now we drink, who before were thirsty, and with an interior draft drink in that divine Spirit. ON THE HOLY SPIRIT 1.8.[13]

A PROPHECY OF THE PRINCE OF PEACE. EUSEBIUS OF CAESAREA: And the oracle in the Psalms, which says about Christ, "There shall rise in his days justice and peace," is in agreement with this.[14] And I think that is why he is called "Prince of Peace" in the prophecy that I quoted before this. And I would ask you to notice that the prophet we are considering says at the outset that the Lord will come from heaven and that the subject of the prophecy will only pasture his flock *after* his birth at Bethlehem. And the Evangelist, whose words I have cited, furnishes the evidence that this was the case with regard to our Lord and Savior. PROOF OF THE GOSPEL 7.2.[15]

CHRIST BECAME INCARNATE QUIETLY. MAXIMUS OF TURIN: Today, then, the Lord was born according to the flesh in such hiddenness and such silence that the world was completely unaware of his birth. The world was unaware because he was both born without the knowledge of a father and conceived outside the order of nature, for Joseph recognized a son whom he did not beget and Mary brought forth one whom she did not conceive in a sexual way. Thus the Lord was born, then, so that no one would suspect his future birth or believe it or perceive it. How would they believe that this would be when they hardly believe what happened after? That the Savior would thus hiddenly and secretly descend into a virgin the prophet David had already prophesied beforehand when he said, "He will descend like rain on fleece." For what takes place with such silence and so noiselessly as a shower on a fleece of wool? It strikes no one's ears with its sound, it sprinkles no one's body with the damp of spattered moisture, but without disturbing

---

[10]Ps 72:5, 8 (71:5, 8 LXX). [11]MFC 9:170-71. [12]Is 5:6. [13]NPNF 2 10:94. [14]The nearly universal peace and government established in the world by the Roman Empire. [15]POG 2:81.

anyone it completely absorbs throughout itself the whole shower that has poured down not knowing a particular course but by its firm softness offering many courses; and what seems to be resistant because of its destiny is open because of its fineness. SERMON 97.3.[16]

72:8-11 God Rules the World

GOD RULES THE EARTH. AUGUSTINE: But the testimonies of the entire Scripture proclaim with one voice that the church, with which the sect of Donatus[17] is not in communion, is indeed spread throughout the entire world. "In your seed shall all the nations of the earth be blessed,"[18] the law of God said. "From the rising of the sun even to the going down, there is offered to my name a clean offering, for my name is great among the Gentiles,"[19] said God through the prophet. "He shall rule from sea to sea, and from the river to the ends of the earth," God said in the psalm. "Bringing forth fruit and growing in the whole world,"[20] God said through the apostle. LETTER 185.5.[21]

SOLOMON WAS A FAINT FORESHADOW OF CHRIST. AUGUSTINE: No doubt a partial reflection of the future reality was shown even in Solomon, in that he did build the temple and that he enjoyed the peace that fits his name—for "Solomon" means "peacemaker."[22] And at the start of his reign he was remarkably praiseworthy. Even so, Solomon in his own person merely gave notice of the coming of Christ, by a foreshadowing of the future; he did not show people the Lord Christ himself. Hence some things are written about him as if they were predictions of Solomon, while in fact holy Scripture, which prophesies by historical events also, sketches, as it were, in him a pattern of the future. For besides the books of sacred history in which the events of his reign were recorded, the seventy-first psalm [LXX] also has his name inscribed in its title. In this psalm there are many sayings that cannot conceivably apply to Solomon but are appropriate—nothing could be clearer—to the Lord Christ. So much so that there is no mistaking the fact that in Solomon there is a kind of shadowy sketch, while in Christ the reality is presented to us. For the limits bounding Solomon's kingdom are well known; yet we read in this psalm, to mention only one point, "His sway will extend from sea to sea, and from the river as far as the bounds of the earth." It is to Christ that we see the fulfillment of these words. It was certainly from the river that he began his lordship; for there, after his baptism by John, he began to be recognized, at John's prompting, by his disciples. And they called him not only "Master" but also "Lord." CITY OF GOD 17.8.[23]

CHRIST'S DOMINION BEGAN AT HIS BAPTISM. AUGUSTINE: Where? At the river Jordan. That, you see, is where Christ's work of teaching began. It was there that the baptism of Christ that was to come was commended to us, because the previous kind of baptism was received there, and the one preparing the way,[24] and saying, "Prepare a way for the Lord, make straight his paths."[25] The Lord, you see, wished to be baptized by the servant, so that those who are baptized by the Lord might appreciate what it is they receive. So he began from the very place where prophecy had very properly preceded him: "He will have dominion from sea to sea, and from the river to the limits of the whole wide world." At the very river where Christ began to have dominion, John saw Christ, recognized him, bore witness to him. SERMON 288.2.[26]

ALL NATIONS WILL SERVE CHRIST. AUGUSTINE: I hear that you[27] often repeat and call

---

[16]ACW 50:261*. [17]The Donatists were a schismatic group that originated in North Africa after the Diocletian persecution (303-311) and insisted that anyone who had denied the faith during the persecution could not be readmitted to the church. [18]Gen 22:18; 26:4. [19]Mal 1:11. [20]Col 1:6. [21]FC 30:145*. [22]A popular etymology; the Hebrew word *shalom* = "peace." [23]CG 735-36. [24]John the Baptist. [25]Mk 1:3. [26]WSA 3 8:111. [27]Donatus, a presbyter in Mutugenna in the diocese of Hippo. He had been a member of the Donatist sect who had been brought forcefully into the church and had attempted to commit suicide.

attention to the passage in the Gospel where it is written that the seventy disciples went back from the Lord and were left to their own choice in their evil and impious separation; and to the twelve who stayed with him he said, "Will you go away also?"[28] You fail to notice that the church then was just beginning to put forth young shoots and that as yet there was no fulfillment of that prophecy: "And all the kings of the earth shall adore him; all nations shall serve him." Surely, the more complete the fulfillment, the greater the authority exercised by the church, not only to invite but to compel people to goodness. This is what the Lord wished to convey by that incident, for, in spite of possessing full power, he chose, instead, to commend humility. He showed this quite clearly in the parable of the wedding feast, in which, after the invited guests had been notified and had refused to come, the servant was told, "Go out into the streets and lanes of the city and bring in the poor and the feeble and the blind and the lame. And the servant said to his lord, It is done as you have commanded and yet there is room. And the lord said to the servant, Go out into the highways and hedges and compel them to come in that my house may be filled."[29] LETTER 173.[30]

CHRIST IS THE TRUE PRINCE OF PEACE.

AUGUSTINE: This and many similar prophecies,[31] which it would take too long to quote, would surely impress the mind of the inquirer. He would see these very kings of the earth now happily subdued by Christ, and all nations serving him. He would also hear the words of the psalm in which this was predicted very long ago: "All the kings of the earth shall bow down to him; all nations shall serve him." And if he were to read the whole of that psalm, which is figuratively applied to Solomon, he would find that Christ is the true King of peace, for Solomon means peaceful; and he would find many things in the psalm applicable to Christ, which have no reference at all to the literal King Solomon. AGAINST FAUSTUS, A MANICHEAN 13.7.[32]

RELY ON GOD.

AUGUSTINE: But we on our side do not rely on any human power, although, no doubt, it would be much more honorable to rely on the emperors than to rely on Circumcellions[33] and to rely on laws than to rely on rioting, but we recall what is written: "Cursed be everyone who puts his hope in man."[34] So, then, if you want to know on whom we rely, think of him whom the prophet foretold, saying, "All the kings of the earth shall adore him; all nations shall serve him." That is why we make use of this power of the church that the Lord both promised and gave to it. LETTER 105.[35]

THE FATHER AND CHRIST ARE ONE GOD.

FULGENTIUS OF RUSPE: Therefore, let them [Arians] say that the Father and the Son are not two lord gods but their one Lord God, if they wish to hold to the truth of the faith and are unwilling to be found in rebellion against the commandments of the law and the gospel. For thus they will be able to preserve equally the understanding and the obligatory force of that text where it is said, "The Lord your God you shall adore, and him alone shall you serve."[36] Nor is it right for anyone to adore the Father as God in such a way that he does not adore the Son as God, for indeed it has been written about the Son in Deuteronomy: "Praise, O heavens, his people; worship him, all you gods."[37] Concerning him as well, the blessed David says in the psalms, "May all kings fall down before him, all nations give him service." LETTER 8.3.8.[38]

---

[28]Jn 6:67. [29]Lk 14:21-23. Augustine used this passage to justify trying to force people to accept Christianity along with the rational argument that the use of force is better than to allow people to go to their eternal perdition without the Christian faith. Augustine changed his earlier evangelical approach to heretics and schismatics after 400 as a result of his dealings with the intransigence of fanatical Donatists, a faulty interpretation of the imperative "compel them to come in," in Luke 14:23, and the rationale that the state has no right to punish other crimes like murder if it does not punish religious errors. [30]FC 30:80*. [31]The reference is to the prophecy given in Psalm 2:7-8. [32]NPNF 1 4:202*. [33]Nomadic, marauding bands of Donatists. [34]Jer 17:5. [35]FC 18:200. [36]Deut 6:13. [37]Deut 32:43 (LXX). [38]FC 95:370-71.

72:12 Deliverance from Oppressors

GOD HELPS THE POOR AND NEEDY. ORIGEN: We are taught, therefore, to be of good cheer when we are afflicted in the world. We learn that the reason for being of good cheer is this: the world has been conquered and, of course, subjected to him who conquered it. For this reason, all the nations, set free from those who formerly controlled them, serve him, because "he delivered the poor from the mighty" through his own passion, "and the needy who had no helper." COMMENTARY ON THE GOSPEL OF JOHN 6.286.[39]

72:15 Gifts and Prayers for the Church

THE GIFTS OF THE MAGI. TERTULLIAN: Besides the generally known fact that the riches of the East, that is to say, its strength and resources, usually consist of gold and spices, it is certainly true of the Creator that he makes gold the riches of the other nations also. Thus he says by Zechariah, "And Judah shall also fight at Jerusalem and shall gather together all the wealth of the nations round about, gold and silver."[40] Moreover, respecting that gift of gold, David also says, "And there shall be given to him of the gold of Arabia"; and again, "The kings of Arabia and Saba shall offer to him gifts."[41] For the East generally regarded the magi as kings; and Damascus was anciently deemed to belong to Arabia, before it was transferred to Syrophoenicia on the division of the Syrias [by Rome]. Its riches Christ then received, when he received the tokens thereof in the gold and spices; while the spoils of Samaria were the magi themselves. The magi discovered him and honored him with their gifts. On bended knee they adored him as their God and King. Through the witness of the star that led them on their way and guided them, they became the spoils of Samaria, that is to say, of idolatry, because, as it is easy enough to see, they believed in Christ. He[42] designated idolatry under the name of Samaria, as that city was shameful for its idolatry, through which it had then revolted from God from the days of King Jeroboam. Nor is this an unusual manner for the Creator [in his Scriptures] figuratively to employ names of places as a metaphor derived from the analogy of their sins. Thus he calls the chief people of the Jews "rulers of Sodom," and the nation itself "people of Gomorrah."[43] AGAINST MARCION 3.13.[44]

72:17-19 The Eternal Nature and Power of God

BLESSED THROUGH CHRIST. JUSTIN MARTYR: While they remained silent, I continued, "My friends, when Scripture through David speaks of Christ, it does not say 'in his seed' shall the Gentiles be blessed, but 'in him.' Here are the words: 'His name shall endure forever; it shall rise above the sun; and all nations shall be blessed in him.' But if all nations are blessed in Christ, and we who are from all nations believe in him, then he is the Christ, and we are they who are blessed through him. It is written that God once allowed the sun to be worshiped,[45] and yet you cannot discover anyone who ever suffered death because of his faith in the sun. But you can find people of every nationality who for the name of Jesus have suffered, and still suffer, all kinds of torments rather than deny their faith in him. For his word of truth and wisdom is more blazing and bright than the might of the sun, and it penetrates the very depths of the heart and mind. Thus Scripture says, 'His name shall arise above the sun.' And Zachariah affirms, 'The East is his name.'[46] And again, 'They shall mourn tribe by tribe.'"[47] DIALOGUE WITH TRYPHO 121.[48]

CHRIST EXISTS FROM ALL ETERNITY. HILARY OF POITIERS: But he who is before the heavens, which, according to you,[49] are also before time, is

---

[39]FC 80:246. [40]Zech 14:14. [41]Ps 72:10 (71:10 LXX, Vg.). [42]Christ. [43]Is 1:10. [44]ANF 3:332*. [45]Deut 4:19. [46]Zech 6:12 (LXX). [47]Zech 12:12 (LXX). [48]FC 6:335*. [49]The Arian heretics who taught the subordination of the Son to the Father.

at the same time before the ages. He is not only before the ages but before all generations that have ever existed. Why do you limit divine and infinite things by those that are perishable, earthly and narrow? Paul knows nothing in Christ except the eternity of the ages. Wisdom states that It[50] is not after something but before all things. In your opinion, the periods of time have been determined from the sun and the moon. But David points out that Christ remains before the sun when he says, "Before the sun [is] his name." And in order that you may not conclude that the things of God had their beginning with the origin of the world, the same one said, "And before the moon [are] the generations of generations." Periods of time are here regarded as of no importance by such outstanding men who were worthy of the Spirit of prophecy, and the human mind has not been afforded any opportunity for reaching into the ages before the birth that transcends the eternal years. Let the faith remain within the limits of the God-fearing teaching, so that the Lord Jesus Christ is the only-begotten God and that he has been born in order that we may confess the perfect birth, and let it not forget that he is eternal when venerating his divinity. ON THE TRINITY 12.34.[52]

THE EXALTATION OF CHRIST'S HUMAN NATURE. ATHANASIUS:

And if, as David says in the seventy-first [LXX] psalm, "His name remains before the sun and before the moon, from one generation to another,"[53] how did he receive what he always had, even before he now received it? Or how is he exalted, being before his exaltation the Most High? Or how did he receive the right of being worshiped, who before he now received it, was always worshiped? It is not an obscure saying but a divine mystery. "In the beginning was the Word, and the Word was with God, and the Word was God"; but for our sakes afterwards the "Word was made flesh."[54] And the term in question, "highly exalted," does not signify that the essence of the Word was exalted, for he always existed and is "equal to God,"[55] but the

exaltation is of the human nature. DISCOURSES AGAINST THE ARIANS 1.11.41.[56]

SPIRITUAL TRANSFORMATION. CHRYSOSTOM:

Let us say again: "Blessed be God, who alone does wonderful things," who does all things and transforms them. Before yesterday you were captives, but now you are free and citizens of the church; lately you lived in the shame of your sins, but now you live in freedom and justice. You are not only free, but also holy; not only holy, but also just; not only just, but also children; not only children, but also heirs; not only heirs, but also brothers of Christ; not only brothers of Christ, but also joint heirs; not only joint heirs, but also members; not only members, but also the temple; not only the temple, but also instruments of the Spirit. BAPTISMAL INSTRUCTIONS 3.5.[57]

GOD ALONE PERFORMS MIRACLES. AUGUSTINE:

So let the blind run to Christ and by receiving their sight be enlightened. Christ, after all, is light in the world, even among the worst of people. Divine miracles were performed, but no one has performed miracles from the beginning of the human race, except the one to whom Scripture says, "Who alone performs marvels." Why does it say "who alone performs marvels"? Surely, because when he wishes to perform them, he has no need of any human beings. But when a human being performs them, he does need God. He, Christ, performed miracles alone. Why? Because the Son is God in the Trinity, together with the Father and the Holy Spirit, one God of course, "who alone performs marvels." SERMON 136B.3.[58]

BY THE POWER OF CHRIST IN US. AUGUSTINE:

But whoever listens with deeper attention to Christ saying, "if I had not done in them[59] the works that no other man has done"[60] (but even if

---

[50]Wisdom or the Son of God. [51]Ps 72:5 (71: 5 LXX, Vg.). [52]FC 25:524*. [53]Ps 72:17, 5 (71:17, 5 LXX, Vg.). [54]Jn 1:1, 14. [55]Phil 2:6. [56]NPNF 2 4:330*. [57]ACW 31:57*. [58]WSA 3 4:364*. [59]People whom Jesus had healed. [60]Jn 15:24.

the Father and the Holy Spirit have done these, no other one has done [them] because there is one substance of the whole Trinity), he will find that he himself did [them] if ever any man of God did any such thing. For indeed, he can in himself do all things by himself; but no one can do anything without him. For Christ together with the Father and the Holy Spirit are not three gods but the one God about whom it has been written, "Blessed be the Lord, the God of Israel, who alone does wonderful things." Therefore, no other individual has done whatever works he has done in them, because whatever another person has done, any one of them has done it by his doing. But he did these things himself, not by their doing. TRACTATES ON THE GOSPEL OF JOHN 91.4.2.[61]

THE INADEQUACY OF HUMAN SPEECH.
BRAULIO OF SARAGOSSA: The marvelous deeds and miracles performed almost in our own day by the apostolic and most upright man, Emilian the priest,[62] are so new that they urge us to relate

them; yet, at the same time, so vast in scope that to recount them is frightening. How can the pen of a man who is bound to earthly things worthily reproduce the acts of a heavenly man, who, when compared with past ages, shines like the brightest star; who, when compared with the present, stands above all in his inimitable virtue? In my opinion, not even if the Tullian springs[63] should flow and come bounding forth in copious veins of eloquence, and multiplicity of thoughts should furnish an abundant supply of words, could all those works of grace be revealed that Christ, "who alone does wondrous deeds," has performed and still is performing through him, from the time he began to despise the world until he departed from his body and from the world. LIFE OF ST. EMILIAN 4.[64]

---

[61]FC 90:167-68. [62]Emilian was a Spanish shepherd who was converted to Christianity and who, except for a brief time as a presbyter, lived as an ascetic hermit along with a small following of disciples. [63]The reference is to Marcus Tullius Cicero (106-43 B.C.), one of the most eloquent of classical Latin authors. [64]FC 63:117.

73:1-14 A PRAYER FOR HELP IN OLD AGE

A Psalm of Asaph.

[1]Truly God is good to the upright,
to those who are pure in heart.[t]
[2]But as for me, my feet had almost stumbled,
my steps had well nigh slipped.
[3]For I was envious of the arrogant,
when I saw the prosperity of the wicked.

[4]For they have no pangs;
their bodies are sound and sleek.

[5]They are not in trouble as other men are;
they are not stricken like other men.
[6]Therefore pride is their necklace;
violence covers them as a garment.
[7]Their eyes swell out with fatness,
their hearts overflow with follies.
[8]They scoff and speak with malice;
loftily they threaten oppression.
[9]They set their mouths against the heavens,
and their tongue struts through the earth.

¹⁰Therefore the people turn and praise them;ᵘ
 and find no fault in them.ᵛ
¹¹And they say, "How can God know?
 Is there knowledge in the Most High?"
¹²Behold, these are the wicked;

always at ease, they increase in riches.
¹³All in vain have I kept my heart clean
 and washed my hands in innocence.
¹⁴For all the day long I have been stricken,
 and chastened every morning.

t Or *Truly God is good to Israel, to those who are pure in heart*   u Cn: Heb *his people return hither*   v Cn: Heb *abundant waters are drained by them*

OVERVIEW: The just person, no matter what his present circumstances, knows that God is always good and that only an individual who has suffered affliction is able to hope for future rewards (AMBROSE). For the righteous to understand why the wicked flourish takes effort and is not fully known until he understands how things will end (AUGUSTINE). Judas provides an example of losing faith (falling from grace); God will keep from falling those who are repentant, understand, and have a zeal for faith and God's commandments (PACHOMIUS, AMBROSE). Even great people of faith, confident of God's providence in all areas of life, are troubled and perplexed by the temporal success of the wicked over the righteous (LEO).

Believers are often sorely afflicted in this life, such as Lazarus, Job and David, so that they may be received as God's children in the next life. God condemns anyone who tries to restrict our knowledge of Christ or understand divine things within the limits of human wisdom (AMBROSE). It is possible for some people, like Pharaoh, to sin so boldly and greatly that God allows their hearts to be hardened against the Holy Spirit so that salvation is no longer possible (CAESARIUS). Pride leads to iniquity, wickedness and loss of virtue; whereas the soul that is properly fed becomes rich in virtue; and the lapse into sacrilege is by conscious intent (AMBROSE). People, such as heretics, who utter vain, shameless, filthy, blasphemous words possess uncircumcised and unclean lips; those who speak the word of God in doctrinal fidelity have circumcised and clean lips (ORIGEN). God leaves open an opportunity for those who lapse into a life of sin, such as the prodigal son, to return to God and receive future

salvation (AMBROSE).

The fact that sinners abound in worldly prosperity should not lead us to deny God's omniscience and providence (AMBROSE, AUGUSTINE). The light of God's truth corrects perverse beliefs and leads us to a correct understanding of life as God's children (AMBROSE).

73:1-3 The Temporal Fortunes of the Wicked Versus the Righteous

GOD IS GOOD TO THE UPRIGHT IN HEART.
AMBROSE: "How good is God to Israel, to them that are right in heart!" Growth in moral perfection is evident as a theme from the beginning of the psalm. Indeed, no one can truly proclaim that God is good but one who knows that goodness is not from his own successes and profits but out of the depth of the heavenly mysteries and the height of God's plan. For it[1] is to be weighed not by the appearance of things present but by the advantage of things to come. Consequently, to the just person God is always good. Whether tormented by bodily pain or overwhelmed by bitter punishments, he always says, "If we have received good things from the hand of the Lord, why do we not bear up under those that are evil?"[2] He rejoices that he is being chastised here, so that he may gain consolation for the future; he knows that one who has received good things in this life has his reward.[3] The person who has not struggled or been tried in the combat of various contests will not be able to hope for future rewards. THE PRAYER OF JOB AND DAVID 3.2.3.[4]

---

[1]Moral perfection. [2]Job 2:10 (LXX). [3]See Mt 6:2. [4]FC 65:369-70*.

ENVY AT THE PEACE OF SINNERS. AUGUSTINE: It was in this way, you see, that the psalmist whose feet were shaken blamed himself, because he had started to find fault with God and was already on the point of doing so; but he was almost on the point of it; he was not quite there yet. He did not deny that God knew,[5] but he staggered, as if his feet were shaken. What does it mean to stagger? To doubt. When he blamed himself, though, for not having an upright heart, what did he say? "Why were my feet disturbed? Because I was envious, he said, of sinners, seeing the peace of sinners. Because I saw that the wicked were rich, I envied them; and I said I have lost out on justice, and for no reason have I made my heart just, and washed my hands among the innocent.[6] And while I am in doubt, this is how I have begun to understand."

"This is how I have begun," he says, "to understand this; there is toil ahead of me." Great toil, to solve this problem. It really is hard labor. All is well with that one, and he is a bad man; all goes badly with this one, and he is a good man; and over them both is God the judge. So the just judge is giving good things to bad people, bad things to good people. "There is toil ahead of me." But for how long is the toil there? "Until I enter into the sanctuary of God and understand about the last things."[7] So if you understand about the last things, you will enjoy the quiet rest of discovery, the toil of inquiry will be over and done with. SERMON 301.7.[8]

WE REMAIN FIRM IN FAITH BY THE GRACE OF GOD. PACHOMIUS: If someone speaks like this: "If ever someone is deceived or snatched away in one of these [abysses], is he already lost and has he no longer repentance," I will tell him that a person who has repentance and a true understanding regarding the faith and God's commandments, with a zeal for this, even if he comes close to falling through negligence, yet the Lord will not let him be lost altogether. As it is written, "My feet were on the point of stumbling." He shows him his grace through the scourge of a

sickness or a grief or the shame of his offense, so that becoming conscious [of his negligence] he may walk in the middle of the narrow path until he arrives and may not wander a single foot off, because the path is four cubits wide.[9] He who wanders off is like Judas, who after receiving great benevolence from the Lord and seeing great signs—even the resurrection of the dead—"having the purse,"[10] was not aware of grace. Because of this he was completely lost through love of money and betrayal. But the good, although as people with free will they may somehow have neglected what is fitting, are still "refined through fire like silver"[11] casting away rust. This is why blessed David says, "I, in the abundance of your mercy, will enter your house."[12] If he says this, how much more we wretches! LIFE OF PACHOMIUS (FIRST GREEK) 141.[13]

DO NOT ENVY THE DECEPTIVE PEACE OF SINNERS. AMBROSE: Indeed, in what follows, David describes his own experience when he says, "But my feet were almost moved, my steps had well nigh slipped, for I was envious in the case of sinners, when I saw the peace of sinners." He is surely not speaking of bodily feet and bodily steps but of the uprightness of the heart and of the step concerning which he says in another passage, "Let not the foot of pride come to me and let not the hand of sinners move me."[14] And so, we ought always to ask that the Lord may direct the footsteps of our spirits. Else they may fall, slip in a kind of morass of error and be unable to maintain their firm hold. Moreover, the reason for David's fall is that he emulated the peace of sinners. But we ought to emulate what is good, not what is filled with shame, even as the apostle Paul also

---

[5]Ps 73:11 (72:11 LXX, Vg.). [6]Ps 73:13 (72:13 LXX, Vg.). [7]Ps 73:16-17 (72:16-17 LXX, Vg.). [8]WSA 3 8:286-87. [9]A width of four cubits indicates a very narrow path. In the previous section Pachomius uses the illustration of a very narrow path of this width over a bottomless abyss; there is no allowance for deviating to one side (the evil lusts of the flesh) or to the other side (the pride of the heart). [10]Jn 12:6. [11]Ps 66:10 (65:10 LXX). [12]Ps 5:7 (5:8 LXX). [13]CS 45:398-99. [14]Ps 36:11 (35:12 LXX, Vg.).

put it when he said, "to emulate the good is always a good thing."[15] THE PRAYER OF JOB AND DAVID 3.3.5.[16]

THE APPARENT SUCCESS OF WICKEDNESS.

LEO THE GREAT: Although the hearts of all the faithful do not doubt that divine providence is never absent in any part of the world or at any time or that success in temporal affairs does not rest on the power of the stars (which is no power) but it acknowledges that all things are disposed according to the most just and most kind decision of the King on High, as it is written: "All the paths of the Lord are mercy and truth."[17] Still, since some things do not happen according to our desires, and since the cause of the wicked is often favored over that of the righteous in the mistakes of human justice, it is a fact very near to us and well known that these things trouble even great souls and drive them to some complaint of an unlawful matter. Even David, most renowned of prophets, confessed himself distressed by these diversities to the point of danger and said, "My feet were almost stumbling, my steps were all but slipping, because I was envious of the arrogant, seeing the prosperity of the sinners." SERMON 43.2.[18]

73:4-9 The Temporary Success of the Wicked

FAITH IS STRENGTHENED BY SCOURGES.

AMBROSE: We have seen that rich man who was clothed in purple and fine linen.[19] In this world, he reclined at table and feasted elegantly every day, while the poor man Lazarus would gather what fell from his table. When he was in torments in hell, he could not lean back and rest; but with great difficulty he lifted up only his eyes to Abraham, not his whole body, and asked him to send Lazarus to dip the tip of his finger in water and to cool his tongue. Therefore "there was no rest to his death nor strength in his affliction."[20] For scourges have no value after death. And so, while David was in this bodily life, he made himself ready for scourges, so that the Lord might

receive him as one that had been chastised. Think again, I ask you, on holy Job. He was covered all over with sores, afflicted in all his limbs and filled with pain over his entire body. He dissolved clods of earth with the corrupt matter and the liquid from his wounds,[21] and since he could not rest in this body, he found death a repose. And so, thinking of his own case, he said, "Death is a repose for a person."[22] He, therefore, was not moved in his affliction, nor did he totter in the morass of his own speech, for "in all those things, he did not sin with his lips," even as Scripture testifies.[23] Rather, he found strength in his affliction, through which he was strengthened in Christ. And thus both Job and David, because they were scourged here, had strength in their afflictions, because "the father scourges the son whom he receives."[24] But those who are not scourged here are not received as sons there. And there "they are not in the toils of people and they shall not be scourged with people," so that they may be scourged forever with the devil. THE PRAYER OF JOB AND DAVID 3.3.8-9.[25]

DANGERS OF A LIMITED KNOWLEDGE OF CHRIST.

AMBROSE: Hence we should know that the Holy Spirit has condemned those detestable people who hold such views. For what other people does he specifically condemn except the Arians, who say that the Son of God does not experience periods of time and years? For there isn't anything with which that God is not familiar. If, however, Christ is God and Christ is the highest God, then he is God above all things. Notice how outraged the blessed David was with such people who limit the Son of God's knowledge. He says, "They do not share the troubles common to human beings, and they will not be plagued like other people. They are burdened with their pride; they are clothed in iniquity and impiety. Their iniquity is proportionate with

---

[15]Gal 4:18. [16]FC 65:372*. [17]Ps 25:10 (24:10 LXX, Vg.). [18]FC 93:187. [19]See Lk 16:19-24. [20]Ps 73:4 (72:4 LXX, Vg.). [21]See Job 2:7-8. [22]Job 3:23 (LXX). [23]Job 2:10. [24]Prov 3:12 (LXX). [25]FC 65:373-74.

their portliness. They extend into the condition of the heart." Without a doubt he condemns those who believe that divine things must be determined from the "condition of the heart." For God is not subject to [any temporal] condition or order because these are things that are peculiar to human beings and according to succeeding generations. But we know that they do not always occur according to some formal plan but more often happen according to some secret and hidden mystery.

"They have thought," he says, "and they have spoken wickedly and sinfully against God. They have set their mouth against heaven." And so we see that he condemns those who are responsible for impious blasphemy and who claim for themselves the right to arrange the secrets of heaven according to the manner of human nature. ON THE CHRISTIAN FAITH 5.16.189-91.[26]

PEOPLE WHOSE HEARTS ARE HARDENED AGAINST GOD. CAESARIUS OF ARLES: Perhaps someone may say, Why did God cause Pharaoh to be hardened by sparing him, and why did he remove his scourges? At this point I reply with assurance: God removed his scourges so often because by the immense number of his sins Pharaoh did not merit to be rebuked as a son for the amendment of his life, but like an enemy he was allowed to become hardened. Such great sins of his had preceded, and he had despised God so often with wicked boldness, that in him was fulfilled what the Holy Spirit said concerning such people: "They are free from the burdens of mortals and are not afflicted like the rest of humanity. So pride adorns them as a necklace; as a robe violence clothes them. Out of their crassness comes iniquity."[27] Behold how a person is hardened if he does not deserve to be chastised by our Lord for his correction. Moreover, what is written concerning those whom God's mercy does not allow to become hardened? "God scourges every son whom he receives";[28] furthermore, "Those whom I love I rebuke and chastise";[29] and again, "For whom God loves he reproves."[30] Concerning this

hardening the prophet also exclaims to the Lord in the person of the people: "Why do you harden our hearts so that we do not fear you?"[31] Surely, this is nothing else than: You have abandoned our heart, that we should not be converted to you. SERMON 101.3.[32]

THE COVERING OF FAITH AND PATIENCE. AMBROSE: "Therefore their pride has gripped them; they are covered with their iniquity and their wickedness."[33] Iniquity affords a bad covering, and if anyone wishes to hold it over us, we ought to remove it; else he may begin to come into judgment with us. And if anyone tries to carry off our spiritual tunic that we have received, remove the cloak of iniquity and take up the covering of faith and of patience, with which David covered himself in fasting, so that he would not lose the garment of virtue. Fasting is itself a covering. Indeed, unless a sober fasting had served to cover the holy Joseph, he would have been stripped by the wanton adulteress.[34] Had Adam chosen to cover himself with that fasting, he would not have been made naked. But because he tasted of the tree of the knowledge of good and evil contrary to heaven's prohibition and violated the fast imposed on him by taking the food of incontinence, he knew that he was naked.[35] Had he fasted, he would have kept the clothing of faith and would not have beheld himself uncovered. Let us not, therefore, clothe ourselves with iniquity and wickedness; else it may be said about one of us, "He clothed himself in cursing."[36] Adam clothed himself badly; while he searched for coverings of leaves, he received the sentence of a curse. The Jews clothed themselves with a curse, for in regard to them it is written, "Their injustice will go forth as from fat; it has passed into the condition of their heart." For from "fat" is derived "fatty," that is, "rich." For just as a soul that is fed on good things and stuffed with virtues

---

[26]CSEL 78:287-88. [27]Ps 73:5-7 (72:5-7 LXX, Vg.). [28]Heb 12:6. [29]Rev 3:19. [30]Prov 3:12. [31]Is 63:17. [32]FC 47:100*. [33]Ps 73:6 (72:6 LXX, Vg.). [34]Gen 39:12. [35]See Gen 3:6-11. [36]Ps 109:18 (108:18 LXX, Vg.).

is filled "as with fat and richness," as it is written,[37] so iniquity, which proceeds, as it were, from fat, is not symbolized as thin and poor but as filled with vices. In fact, they did not fall into error by some chance misstep but passed into sacrilege by plan and intent. THE PRAYER OF JOB AND DAVID 3.4.10-11.[38]

CLEAN AND UNCIRCUMCISED LIPS. ORIGEN: Let us come also, if you wish, to the circumcision of lips. I think that he would be "uncircumcised in lips"[39] who has not yet ceased from silly talk, from obscene language, who disparages good people, who slanders his neighbors, who instigates quarrels, who promotes false accusations, who sets brothers against themselves by making false statements, who utters vain words, inept words, profane words, shameless words, filthy words, injurious words, wanton words, blasphemous words, and other words that are unworthy of a Christian. But if anyone curbs his mouth from all these things and "orders his words with judgment,"[40] if he restrains verbosity, governs his tongue, keeps his words in due bounds, that person deservedly is said to be circumcised in lips. But also those "who speak iniquity on high and stretch out their tongue against heaven," as the heretics do, are to be called uncircumcised and unclean in their lips. But he is circumcised and clean who always speaks the word of God and brings forward sound doctrine fortified with evangelic and apostolic norms. In this way, therefore, also circumcision of lips is given in the church of God. HOMILIES ON GENESIS 3.5.[41]

THE RETURN OF GOD'S PEOPLE FROM WICKEDNESS. AMBROSE: "They have set their mouth against heaven, and their tongue has passed over the earth." We learn the meaning of "to set one's mouth against heaven" from the younger of the two brothers, who returned to his father and said, "Father, I have sinned against heaven and before you."[42] But those who think that freedom to sin is given to them by some inevitability of

birth are setting their mouth against heaven. Such people usually spare neither heaven nor earth, that they may believe that people's lives are governed by the course of the stars, as it were. They leave nothing to providence, nothing to good character. And would that they also had returned like that one of the two young men— the good Lord would not have denied them a remedy! And yet, even if they do not wish to be healed, the Lord keeps open the option of a return, so that those in Israel who were driven out by the blindness of their own hearts may come back through the fullness of the church. Thus they may spend the days of their lives, not in emptiness but filled with good works and faith, when the Lord has filled them with his spiritual favor. Learn how they may return. "A partial blindness only has befallen Israel, until the full number of the Gentiles should enter and thus all Israel should be saved."[43] But it was fitting that the mystery be fulfilled, that God should shut up all things in unbelief,[44] that is, that he should refute and convict them. (For when two parties contend, if one is the stronger, it is said, "He has shut up the other.")[45] And thus, by his mercy, that people indeed went back among the heirs, so that the world might be made subject to God. But they were led astray by the delusion of their late wickedness, so that they would not believe that God had foreknowledge of things hidden. But that they may be redeemed at some time, the Lord has kept open for them the option of future salvation and has said, "Therefore will my people return here."[46] What is "here"? It is "to me, to my equity and justice, to my worship." "And full days will be procured for them."[47] This you will interpret as follows, that the people who have believed are assuredly redeemed. According to this, even though those who have not believed are not

---

[37]Ps 63:5 (62:6 LXX, Vg.). [38]FC 65:374-75. [39]See Ex 6:30. [40]Ps 112:5 (111:5 LXX). [41]FC 71:97*. [42]Lk 15:18. [43]Rom 11:25-26. [44]See Rom 11:32. [45]See 1 Kings 26:8 in the LXX. [46]Ps 73:10 (72:10 LXX, Vg.). [47]Ps 73:10 (72:10 LXX, Vg.).

redeemed, still the redemption of the people is granted as a special favor of God. THE PRAYER OF JOB AND DAVID 3.5.12-13.[48]

73:10-14 God Is All-Knowing

KEEPING THE TEMPORAL PROSPERITY OF SINNERS IN PERSPECTIVE. AMBROSE: Therefore those who were in sin said, "How has God known? And is there all knowledge in the most High?" Indeed, they suppose that knowledge is not in God, because sinners abound in worldly prosperity. And the Scripture still represents such individuals as saying, "Behold, these are sinners, and abounding in the world they have obtained riches." You find this more clearly portrayed in the Gospel where Simon the Pharisee, seeing that the sinful woman had come into his house and had poured ointment over Christ's feet, said to himself, "This man, were he a prophet, would surely know who and what manner of woman this is who is touching him, for she is a sinner."[49] But God's patience is not prejudicial to truth, while his foreknowledge and providence are proved even more by this very fact, that one who is in sin abounds in worldly prosperity and

success. Seeing this, one who is stronger laughs, but one who is incautious is moved and led astray. THE PRAYER OF JOB AND DAVID 3.5.14.[50]

THE DANGER OF SEEKING AN EARTHLY FORTUNE. AUGUSTINE: Why, you have it here in so many words: Look, these are sinners, and prospering always; they have become rich. "Is it to no purpose that I set my heart right or washed my hands among the innocent and was scourged every day?" I worship God; they blaspheme God. For them good fortune, for me misfortune. Where is the justice of it? That is why feet were shaken, that is why steps were almost pulled from under, that is why destruction was looming. Yes, just notice please what a dangerous position he had got into. He adds, "And I said, How did God know? Can there be knowledge in the most High?" Notice what a dangerous position he has got into by looking for earthly good fortune from God as though it were of great value. SERMON 19.4.[51]

---

[48]FC 65:375-77*. [49]Lk 7:39. [50]FC 65:377*. [51]WSA 3 1:381.

73:15-28 THE FATE OF THE WICKED

[15]If I had said, "I will speak thus,"
  I would have been untrue to the generation
    of thy children.
[16]But when I thought how to understand this,
  it seemed to me a wearisome task,
[17]until I went into the sanctuary of God;
  then I perceived their end.
[18]Truly thou dost set them in slippery places;
  thou dost make them fall to ruin.

[19]How they are destroyed in a moment,
  swept away utterly by terrors!
[20]They are[w] like a dream when one awakes,
  on awaking you despise their phantoms.

[21]When my soul was embittered,
  when I was pricked in heart,
[22]I was stupid and ignorant,
  I was like a beast toward thee.

²³*Nevertheless I am continually with thee;*
   thou dost hold my right hand.
²⁴*Thou dost guide me with thy counsel,*
   and afterward thou wilt receive me to
      glory.ˣ
²⁵*Whom have I in heaven but thee?*
   And there is nothing upon earth that
      I desire besides thee.
²⁶*My flesh and my heart may fail,*
   but God is the strengthʸ of my heart and

my portion for ever.
²⁷*For lo, those who are far from thee shall*
   perish;
   thou dost put an end to those who are false
      to thee.
²⁸*But for me it is good to be near God;*
   I have made the Lord GOD *my refuge,*
   that I may tell of all thy works.

w Cn: Heb Lord   x Or honor   y Heb rock

OVERVIEW: God distributes wealth to the wicked by chance, not as a reward for some merit, just as poverty is not a punishment for sin (AMBROSE). Puzzlement at why the wicked prosper and the righteous suffer on earth is solved when we realize that God reverses their fortunes in the next life (AUGUSTINE). God endows some people with great success and wealth so that they are not compelled to sin, their complaining is stifled and their distresses increased. The wicked who perish because of their iniquity leave behind all their good works at death and will possess nothing, like a dream that vanishes in the morning. The righteous will possess the image of God and enter into the city of God; the wicked, however, will be destroyed (AMBROSE).

We become like a beast of burden if we remain silent during a quarrel and refuse to mediate (PASCHASIUS). To have God at one's right hand is to receive divine guidance and assistance in this life. If we possess Christ, we possess all things and therefore seek nothing in this world (AMBROSE). When we reach heaven, we will be grieved that we have been so attracted to earthly pleasures in this life (JEROME). We draw close to God when we leave behind earthly things and enticements to sin, which must come to an end before eternal things can begin. (AMBROSE). The clergy have God as their portion and possession in life; they are content to serve others and do not desire to acquire wealth

and costly possessions (JEROME).

Persons who perish spiritually perish because they have abandoned God and have allowed their iniquities to separate them from God (CHRYSOSTOM, FULGENTIUS). People who fear God's judgment desire to cling to Christ and hope in him who will duly reward them (AMBROSE, AUGUSTINE). In order to cling to God it is necessary to obey God's will and consider the world as nothing. We should sever ourselves from a love of worldly things so that we may cling to our Creator. The Old and New Testaments agree that nothing should separate us from God and that the bond of unity is love. Different philosophical schools have sought happiness in the pleasures of the flesh and in possessing a virtuous soul, but Scripture says happiness comes from one's nearness to God (AUGUSTINE). We should do everything for love of God, not for the sake of human praise (CAESARIUS). Baptism absolves us of all sins, which is a necessary condition for clinging to God (GREGORY THE GREAT).

73:15-20 The Final Destiny of the Wicked Revealed

WEALTH MAY BE GIVEN TO THE WICKED BY CHANCE. AMBROSE: And therefore I conferred with my heart and I said to myself, "if I will speak thus, that I have justified my heart in vain," and the voice of God replied to me and said, "Behold the generation of your children, to which I have made distribution." This means: Behold, you find in the Scriptures, O you son of Adam, that I have made distribution to the generation of your children, that wealth may be granted to the wicked simply by chance and not from some merit. Neither are the rewards of virtue the profits of a treasury, just as poverty . . . is not a punishment for sin. But such things come without distinction, for they roll along on a kind of flow of life that is like a river. THE PRAYER OF JOB AND DAVID 3.6.17.[1]

TEMPORAL CONDITIONS ARE REVERSED IN ETERNITY. AUGUSTINE: But because the psalmist realized afterward—as he goes on to say in the same psalm, "When I tried to understand this," and he added, "it was a wearisome task," why the wicked have all the luck; "it was a wearisome task," he says, "until I went into the sanctuary of God and understood about their latter end," that for the wicked who are now for a time given good fortune, eternal punishment is being saved up for the last day. So when he realized this he became upright of heart and began to praise God for everything, both for the troubles of decent people and for the good fortune of the wicked. For he observed that God is just in his retributions at the end and that he now gives some people temporal good fortune while keeping in store for them at the end everlasting misfortune, and that in the present life he is subjecting some decent people to the rigors of misfortune while saving up for them eternal good fortune in the next. He remarks that they have to change places, like that rich man who used to feast sumptuously every day and that poor man, full of sores, lying at the rich man's gate and longing to fill himself with the crumbs that fell from the rich man's table. But when they were both dead the first began to be in pain in hell, and the second was at rest in Abraham's bosom. When the rich man thought this was unfair and wanted a drop of water dripped on his tongue from Lazarus's middle finger (changing places, he now longed for a drop from the fin-

ger of the man who had longed for a crumb from his table), he heard from Abraham the judgment of the upright God: "Son," he said, "remember that you received good things in your life and Lazarus bad things; but now he is at rest, and you are in torment."[2] SERMON 15A.2.[3]

TEMPORAL GOOD FORTUNE NULLIFIES EXCUSES FOR IMPIETY. AMBROSE: Such, then, is the first supposition of true knowledge, that things in the world happen by chance.[4] The second is that "on account of the subterfuges you have placed before them" prodigious success, worldly profits and an abundance of riches. Otherwise, they might plead by way of excuse that they had been less devout by reason of want or of some bitter pain or grief and had been driven to the guilt of robbery and to the desire to plunder under compulsion of poverty. For they were enriched with wealth and exalted with honors, not for tranquility of life or the enjoyment of delight but that complaining might be foreclosed and distress piled up. THE PRAYER OF JOB AND DAVID 3.7.21.[5]

THE WICKED PERISH BECAUSE OF THEIR INIQUITY. AMBROSE: Therefore, in regard to the latter,[6] David also says, "They have ceased to be and have perished by reason of their iniquity as the dream of one that wakes up." This means: The wicked cease to be, and they disappear as a dream does when one first wakes up from sleep, "because they are in darkness and have walked in darkness";[7] not a trace of their good work remains, but they are like those who see a dream. Now one who dreams, dreams at night, whereas night is in darkness. The children of darkness are deprived of the Sun of justice[8] and the splendor of virtue, for they sleep always and do not keep

---

[1]FC 65:379. [2]Lk 16:25. [3]*WSA* 3 1:332**. [4]Ambrose has been addressing the question of why the wicked prosper; he says that they receive their wealth by chance and not because they have deserved it (see 6.17) and that poverty is not a punishment for sin. [5]FC 65:380-81. [6]People who do not believe in God. [7]Ps 82:5 (81:5 LXX). [8]See Mal 4:2.

watch, and of them it is appropriately said, "They have slept their sleep and have found nothing."[9] For indeed, when their souls are separated from the body, and they are, as it were, released from the sleep of the body, they will find nothing, they will possess nothing, and they will lose what they thought they possessed. For although the unwise and foolish person may overflow with riches, he will leave his riches to strangers, and the glory of his house will not descend to hell together with him.[10] THE PRAYER OF JOB AND DAVID 3.8.23.[11]

THE HEAVENLY JERUSALEM WILL BE INHABITED BY THE GOOD. AMBROSE: Subsequent events also go to show how the image of such a person is not found but perishes, since his image is not found in the city of the Lord, that Jerusalem which is above.[12] For the Lord has painted us in his image and likeness, even as he teaches us, saying, "Behold, O Jerusalem, I have painted your walls."[13] If we have acted well, that heavenly image continues in us; if anyone acts badly, this image is destroyed in him that is the image of him who came down from heaven, and there is in him the image of the earthly. On this account also the apostle says, "Even as we have borne the image of the one that is earthly, let us bear also the image of the other that is heavenly."[14] Therefore, the images of good continue to shine forth in that city of God. But if anyone has turned aside to graver sins and has not done penance, his image is destroyed or else cast out even as Adam was cast out and excluded from paradise. But whoever has conducted himself in a holy and honorable fashion enters into that city of God[15] and brings in his own image so that it may shine in that city of God. "O Lord, in your city you shall reduce their images to nothing," because those who have clothed themselves with the works of darkness cannot shine in the light. Let us adduce an example from the world. See how the images of good rulers continue in cities, whereas the images of tyrants are destroyed. THE PRAYER OF JOB AND DAVID 3.8.24.[16]

73:21-26 God Is My Strength and My Portion

SILENCE DURING A QUARREL. PASCHASIUS OF DUMIUM: Abbot Pimenius asked Abbot Nesteron, who was sitting in the monastery, "Where did you acquire this virtue, brother, that, whenever a quarrel arises in the monastery, you neither speak nor interfere as mediator?" Though he was unwilling to speak, he was compelled by the old man and said, "Forgive me, father, for in the beginning when I entered here I said to my thought: 'Lo, you and this donkey are alike. Just as it gets beaten without speaking and gets thrashed without returning an answer, so you must be also, for the psalm says, "I am become as a beast of burden before you: and I am always with you."'" QUESTIONS AND ANSWERS OF THE GREEK FATHERS 42.3.[17]

HAVE GOD AT YOUR RIGHT HAND. AMBROSE: For this reason David says, as if visited by him," "You have held my right hand, and in your will you have conducted me and have taken me up with glory." This is the text we have received, and it is in accord with the Greek, for the Greek said, *ekratēsas tēs cheiros*, that is, "you have held the hand," *tēs dexias mou*, "my right hand." A person receives good guidance when God takes hold of his right hand with his own hand. Such a one can say, "The Lord is at my right hand, that I be not moved."[18] Had Adam chosen to have the Lord at his right hand, he would not have been deceived by the serpent. But because he forgot God's command and fulfilled the will of the serpent, the devil took hold of his hand and made it to reach out to the tree of the knowledge of good and evil, to pluck things that were forbidden. In him, judgment was passed beforehand on all people, and the adversary began to stand by the right hand of

---

[9]Ps 76:5 (75:6 LXX, Vg.). [10]See Ps 49:17 (48:18 LXX, Vg.). [11]FC 65:382. [12]See Ps 73:20 (72:20 LXX, Vg.). [13]See Is 49:16. [14]1 Cor 15:49. [15]See Rev 3:12. [16]FC 65:382-83. [17]FC 62:163*. [18]Ps 16:8 (15:8 LXX, Vg.).

every person. From this, there also came that model of the curse against Judas, "And may the devil stand at his right hand."[19] If that curse is severe, that blessing, whereby the bonds of the harsh curse are undone, is very momentous. For that reason the Lord Jesus, who had taken up humanity's cause and condition, set the devil at his right hand, just as we read in the book of Zechariah.[20] And so, where the inheritance of Adam stood, there Christ stood. Like a good athlete, he permitted Satan to stand at his right hand so that he could drive him back, and he said, "Be gone, Satan."[21] Consequently, the adversary was cast down from his place and departed; so that the devil may not stand at your right hand, Christ says, "Come, follow me."[22] Therefore, David foresaw the coming of the Lord, who came down from heaven to free us from the power of the adversary, and he said, "The Lord is at my right hand, that I be not moved." But one who had the devil at his right hand was moved. David was justified, then, in saying this also, "You have held my right hand," that is, so that now I cannot sin, so that I can take my stand in a trusty place, while before I was swaying and my step was unsure. How aptly the apostle said this! For the Lord, seeing that he was troubled, stretched out his right hand and did not allow him to falter but steadied him to walk without fear.[23] And on his deliverance, what else did Peter say but these prophetic lines, "You have held my right hand, and in your will you have conducted me and have taken me up with glory"? What is the right hand but the power of the soul in operation? And if it is guided by the will of the Lord, it desires nothing and is in want of nothing; it demands none of the helps or aids of this world. THE PRAYER OF JOB AND DAVID 3.10.27.[24]

POSSESS CHRIST ALONE. AMBROSE: Therefore the holy man says, "For what awaits me in heaven? And besides you what do I desire on earth?" This means: You are my portion, you are abundant to me for all things, I have sought nothing but that I might possess you as my share, I

have not made myself subject to any creature in the heavens, as the Gentiles do, and I have desired none of the wealth and enticing pleasures of this world. I have no want, for I have been taken up by you, and there is nothing further for me to seek in the heavenly bodies. Possessing nothing, I possess all things,[25] because I possess Christ, and him the Father on high "has not spared, but he has delivered him for us all; how has he not, then, given us all things with him?"[26] even as the apostle said. For all things are in Christ, through whom are all things and in whom all things hold together.[27] Therefore, possessing all things in him, I seek no other reward, because he is the reward of all. And so, Christ said to him that was made perfect, "Take up your cross and follow me."[28] For one who follows him is not led to perfection by the reward, but by perfection he is made perfect for the reward. For the imitators of Christ are not good by reason of hope but for their love of virtue; for Christ is good by nature, not by reason of a desire for a reward. And, therefore, he suffered because it pleased him to do good, and not because he sought an increase of glory from his passion. Thus one who desires to imitate him does not do what is for his own advantage but what is for the advantage of others. It is not without reason, therefore, that he fails for himself, while for others he grows strong by the increase of virtue. THE PRAYER OF JOB AND DAVID 3.11.28.[29]

EXCHANGING TEMPORAL POVERTY FOR ETERNAL BLESSEDNESS. JEROME: It is good for us to cleave to the Lord, and to put our hope in the Lord God, so that when we have exchanged our present poverty for the kingdom of heaven, we may be able to exclaim, "Whom have I in heaven but you? and there is none upon earth that I desire beside you." Surely if we can find such

---

[19]Ps 109:6 (108:6 LXX, Vg.). [20]See Zech 3:1. [21]Mt 4:10. [22]Mt 19:21. [23]See Mt 14:30-31. [24]FC 65:385-86. [25]See 2 Cor 6:10. [26]Rom 8:32. [27]See Col 1:16-17. [28]Mk 8:34; Mt 16:24; Lk 9:23; cf. Mt 10:38. [29]FC 65:386-87.

blessedness in heaven we may well grieve to have sought after poor and passing pleasures here on earth. LETTER 43.3.[30]

THE FAILURE OF EARTHLY THINGS. AMBROSE: And the psalmist says, appropriately, "My heart and my flesh have failed, God of my heart." Indeed, abiding things cannot follow unless earthly things have failed. Therefore the flesh falls when fleshly things are put to death. And those who bear about in their flesh the dying of Jesus Christ[31] also fail, for the death of Christ works in them[32] so that every enticement to sin dies. From this it is inferred that the human heart fails when evil thoughts, which proceed from the heart, are put to death. Thus forgetfulness may hide all earthly things, and, for those who are blessed with a clean heart and deserve to see God, there may come the God of their heart[33] that they may draw near to you and not separate themselves. For God, who is near, does not drive back those who draw near to him;[34] he wishes to be for all people a cause of salvation and not of death. Indeed, he rejects no one except one who has decided to remove himself from his sight. THE PRAYER OF JOB AND DAVID 3.11.29.[35]

THE CLERGY'S EARTHLY PORTION. JEROME: A cleric, then, as he serves Christ's church, must first understand what his name means; and then, when he realizes this, must endeavor to be that which he is called. For since the Greek word *klēros* means "lot," or "inheritance," the clergy are so called either because they are the lot of the Lord, or else because the Lord himself is their lot and portion. Now, he who in his own person is the Lord's portion, or has the Lord for his portion, must so bear himself as to possess the Lord and to be possessed by him. He who possesses the Lord and who says with the prophet, "The Lord is my portion,"[36] can hold to nothing beside the Lord. For if he holds to something beside the Lord, the Lord will not be his portion. Suppose, for instance, that he holds to gold or silver, or possessions or inlaid furniture; with such por-

tions as these the Lord will not deign to be his portion. I, if I am the portion of the Lord, and the line of his heritage,[37] receive no portion among the remaining tribes; but, like the priest and the Levite, "I live on the tithe,"[38] and serving the altar, am supported by its offerings.[39] "Having food and raiment, I shall be content with these"[40] and as a disciple of the cross shall share its poverty. I beseech you, therefore, and again and yet again admonish you;[41] do not look to your military experience[42] for a standard of clerical obligation. Do not seek worldly gain through service to Christ, so that, if you should be better off than when you first became clergy, you will not hear people say to your disgrace, "Their portion shall not profit them."[43] Welcome poor people and strangers to dine with you so that with them Christ may become your guest. Avoid as you would a plague a cleric who engages in business and who rises from poverty to wealth and from obscurity to a high position. For "bad company corrupts good character."[44] You despise gold; he loves it. You avoid wealth; he eagerly pursues it. You love silence, meekness, privacy; he takes delight in talking and insolence, in [town] squares and streets and apothecaries' shops. What unity of feeling can there be where there is so wide a divergence of character? LETTER 52.5.[45]

73:27-28 *God Is My Refuge*

GOD DOES NOT ABANDON US UNLESS WE HAVE FIRST ABANDONED HIM. CHRYSOSTOM: Indeed, when we are abandoned by God, we are given over to the devil. When we have been given over to the devil, we are afflicted with countless terrible consequences. Well, then, in order to

---

[30]NPNF 2 6:58. [31]See 2 Cor 4:10. [32]See 2 Cor 4:12. [33]See Mt 4:8. [34]See Jn 6:37; Jas 4:8. [35]FC 65:387-88*. [36]Ps 16:5 (15:5 LXX, Vg.); 73:26 (72:26 LXX, Vg.). [37]Ps 16:5-6 (15:5-6 LXX, Vg.). [38]Num 18:24. [39]1 Cor 9:13. [40]1 Tim 6:8. [41]Virgil *Aeneid* 3:436. [42]Jerome wrote this letter to Nepotian, an individual who had left military service to join the clergy and who had become a presbyter at Altinum, where his uncle, who had also left the military for the ministry, was bishop. [43]Jer 12:13 (LXX). [44]1 Cor 15:33. [45]NPNF 2 6:91**.

frighten his hearers the sacred writer said, "He has hardened" and "He has given up." Listen to what he was really saying, when he said that he himself not only does not give us up but does not abandon us, either, unless we wish it: "Have not your iniquities caused a division between me and you?" And again, "They who withdraw from you perish."[46] Furthermore, Hosea declared, "You have forgotten the law of your God; I also will forget you."[47] And he himself said in the Gospels, "How often would I have gathered your children together, but you would not!"[48] Isaiah, also, in another place said, "I came, and there was no one: I called, and there was no one that would hear."[49] HOMILIES ON THE GOSPEL OF JOHN 68.[50]

PRIDE LEADS TO ABANDONMENT OF GOD.
FULGENTIUS OF RUSPE: Therefore, the human being began to sin in the matter by which he departed from God. For it is written that "the beginning of human pride is to forsake the Lord." And in another place, "Indeed those who are far from you will perish; you put an end to those who are false to you." Therefore, they who are far from God and are false to him indeed perish by sinning through their evil will that is not from God. God will destroy them by his just judgments as is proper to God. For God would not destroy them by his judgment, unless they had perished through their iniquities. For it is written, "How they are destroyed in a moment, swept away utterly by terrors."[51] LETTER TO MONIMUS 1.19.2.[52]

IT IS GOOD TO CLING TO THE LORD.
AMBROSE: "Behold," [the psalmist] says, "people who separate themselves far from you [God] will perish." For every individual either unites or separates himself from your mercy by his deeds. The person who does things he fears will be discovered flees from God, just as the person who is protected by walls or surrounded by darkness[53] thinks he will not be seen by God. On the contrary, he is seen, as it says: "You destroyed everyone who fornicates himself away from you." . . .

And so, whoever does not cling to God but devotes himself to the vain worship of idols separates himself far from the Lord by perverse sacrilege. Whoever is separated from the Lord perishes. Therefore, the saintly person who greatly fears the judgment of God always wants to cling to Christ and to put his hope in him so that he may praise the Lord, to whom belongs honor, glory and infinity from all ages, both now and into all eternity. THE PRAYER OF JOB AND DAVID 3.11.30-31.[54]

IT IS GOOD TO HOLD FAST TO GOD. AUGUS-TINE: For if anyone should have love, he sees God because "God is love," and that eye is cleansed more and more by love so that he may see that unchangeable substance in whose presence he may always rejoice, which he may enjoy forever, joined together with the angels. But let him run now that he may one day rejoice in his homeland. HOMILIES ON 1 JOHN 9.10.[55]

SPIRITUAL ASCENT. AUGUSTINE: So if you want to keep the order of true charity, act justly, love mercy, shun self-indulgence; begin according to the Lord's instruction to love not only friends but also enemies.[56] And when you strive to maintain these standards faithfully with your whole heart, you will be able to climb up by these virtues, as by a flight of steps, to being worthy to love God with your whole mind and your whole strength. And when you reach this happy state of perfection, you will reckon all the desires of this world as nothing but dung, and with the prophet you will be able to say, "But for me to cling to God is good." SERMON 368.5.[57]

YOU CANNOT LOVE GOD FOR THE SAKE OF REWARD. AUGUSTINE: We ought to be on our guard against loving God for any reward. What is

---

[46]Is 58:2. [47]Hos 4:6. [48]Mt 23:37; Lk 13:34. [49]Is 50:2. [50]FC 41:241**. [51]Ps 73:19 (72:19 LXX, Vg.). [52]FC 95:212-13. [53]See Sir 23:18. [54]CSEL 32.2:266-67. [55]FC 92:260*. [56]See Mt 5:44; Lk 6:27. [57]WSA 3 10:302.

the point, after all, of loving God for a reward? What sort of reward is it that God is going to give you? Whatever else he gives you, it is less than he is. You are worshiping him not freely, not gratuitously, in order to receive something from him. Worship him freely, and you will receive God himself; God, you see, is keeping himself for you to enjoy him. And if you love the things he made, what must he that made them be like? If the world is beautiful, what must the architect of the world be like? So tear your heart away from the love of creatures, in order to cling to the creator, and to be able to say what is written in the psalm, "But for me it is good to cling to God." SERMON 385.5.[58]

THE SUPREME GOOD IS TO CLING CLOSELY TO GOD. AUGUSTINE: If you[59] recognize that you have received the virtues that you have, and if you return thanks to him from whom you have received them, directing them to his service even in your secular office; if you rouse the people subject to your authority and lead them to worship God, both by the example of your own devout life and by your zeal for their welfare, whether you rule them by love or by fear; if, in working for their greater security, you have no other aim than that they should thus attain to him who will be their happiness—then yours will be true virtues, then they will be increased by the help of him whose bounty lavished them on you, and they will be so perfected as to lead you without fail to that truly happy life that is none other than eternal life. In that life, evil will no longer have to be distinguished from good by the virtue of prudence, because there will be no evil there; adversity will not have to be borne with fortitude, because there will be nothing there but what we love; temperance will not be needed to curb our passions, because there will be no enticements to passion there; nor shall we have to practice justice by helping the poor out of our abundance, for there we shall find no poor and no needy. There will be but one virtue there, and it will be the same as the reward of virtue, which the speaker in

the sacred writings mentions as the object of his love: "But it is good for me to stick close to my God." This will constitute the perfect and eternal wisdom, as it will constitute the truly happy life, because to attain it is to attain the eternal and supreme good, and to stick close to God forever is the sum of our good. Let this be called prudence because it will cling most providently to the good that cannot be lost, and fortitude because it will cling most stoutly to the good from which it cannot be parted, and temperance because it will cling most chastely to the good in which there is no corruption, and justice because it will cling most uprightly to the good to which it is deservedly subject. LETTER 155.[60]

NOTHING SHOULD SEPARATE US FROM GOD. AUGUSTINE: I will briefly set forth the manner of life according to these virtues,[61] one by one, after I have brought forward, as I promised, passages from the Old Testament parallel to those I have been quoting from the New Testament. For is Paul alone in saying that we should be joined to God so that there should be nothing between to separate us? Does not the prophet say the same most aptly and concisely in the words, "It is good for me to cling to God"? Does not this one word cling express all that the apostle says at length about love? And do not the words "it is good" point to the apostle's statement, "All things issue in good to them that love God"? Thus in one clause and in two words the prophet sets forth the power and the fruit of love. THE CATHOLIC AND MANICHAEAN WAYS OF LIFE 16.26.[62]

THE ONLY TRUE HAPPINESS EXISTS IN NEARNESS TO GOD. AUGUSTINE: There have been some philosophers of this world who have thought that the only happiness is to live according to the flesh, and they have placed human-

---

[58]*WSA* 3 10:388-89*. [59]Macedonius, vicar of Africa, to whom was given the duty of enforcing imperial law against the Donatists. [60]FC 20:313-14*. [61]The four classic virtues of temperance, fortitude, justice and prudence. [62]NPNF 1 4:49*.

kind's good in the pleasures of the body. These philosophers were called Epicureans, from a certain Epicurus, their founder and teacher, and any others like them. However, some proud people came along who claimed to distance themselves from the flesh and set all their hopes of happiness on their souls by placing their supreme good in their own virtue. Your religious feelings, clearly, have recognized in yourself the words of the psalm; you know, realize and recognize how the holy psalm mocks "those who trust in their own virtue."[63] These were the philosophers who were called Stoics. The Epicureans lived according to the flesh, and the Stoics lived according to the soul—neither of the two groups lived according to God.

That is why, when the apostle Paul came to the city of the Athenians, where these philosophical schools engaged in feverish study and wrangling, as you can read in the Acts of the Apostles—and I am glad to see you are already ahead of me in what I am saying, with your quick and lively memories—it is written there, "Certain philosophers of the Epicureans and Stoics conferred with him."[64] Those who were living according to the flesh conferred with him, and those who were living according to the soul conferred with him. He, living according to God, conferred with them. The Epicurean said, "For me to enjoy the flesh is good." The Stoic said, "For me to enjoy my mind is good." The apostle said, "For me, though, to cling to God is good." The Epicurean said, "Blessed is the one who has the enjoyment of the pleasures of his flesh." The Stoic said, "Blessed, rather, is the one who has the enjoyment of the virtue of his mind." The apostle said, "Blessed is the one whose hope is the name of the Lord."

The Epicurean has got it all wrong. I mean, it is simply not true that a person who has the enjoyment of the pleasures of his flesh is blessed. The Stoic, too, is quite mistaken. I mean it is simply not true; it is absolutely incorrect that a person who has the enjoyment of the virtue of his mind is blessed. So, [the psalmist says], "Blessed

is the one whose hope is the name of the Lord."[65] And because those others are vain windbags and liars [he adds], "and who has not paid attention to vanities and lying follies."[66] SERMON 156.7.[67]

DO EVERYTHING FOR LOVE OF GOD. CAESARIUS OF ARLES: What is so finite and limited as a fulfilling [of the law]? Therefore, whatever you do, do it for the love of Christ, and let the intention or end of all your actions look to him. Do nothing for the sake of human praise, but everything for love of God and the desire for eternal life. Then you will see the end of all perfection, and when you have reached it you will wish for nothing more. When the psalm is read and you hear, "Unto the end, a psalm of David,"[68] do not understand it except as Christ, for the apostle says, "Christ is the consummation of the law for the achievement of justice."[69] If you come to anything else, pass beyond it until you reach the end. What is the end? "But for me, to be near God is my good." Have you adhered to God? You have finished your journey and will remain in your true country. SERMON 137.1.[70]

ONLY A SOUL CLEANSED OF SIN CAN CLING TO GOD. GREGORY THE GREAT: But, if there are any who say that sins are only superficially put away in baptism, what can be more against the faith than such preaching, whereby they would willingly undo the very sacrament of faith, wherein principally the soul is bound to the mystery of heavenly cleanness, that, being completely absolved from all sins, it may cleave to him alone of whom the prophet says, "But it is good for me to cling to God"? For certainly the passage of the Red Sea was a figure of holy baptism, in which the enemies behind died but others were found in front in the wilderness. And so to all who are bathed in holy baptism, all their past sins are remitted, since their sins die behind them even as

---

[63]Ps 49:6 (48:7 LXX, Vg.). [64]Acts 17:18. [65]Ps 146:5 (145:5 LXX, Vg.). [66]Ps 40:4 (39:5 LXX, Vg.). [67]WSA 3 5:101**. [68]Ps 4:1 (LXX, Vg.). [69]Rom 10:4. [70]FC 47:270*.

did the Egyptian enemies. But in the wilderness we find other enemies, since, while we live in this life, before reaching the country of promise, many temptations harass us and hasten to bar our way as we are proceeding to the land of the living. Whosoever says, then, that sins are not entirely put away in baptism, let him say that the Egyptians did not really die in the Red Sea. But if he acknowledges that the Egyptians really died, he must acknowledge that sins die entirely in baptism, since surely the truth avails more in our absolution than the shadow of the truth. In the Gospel the Lord says, "He who is washed does not need to wash but is entirely clean."[71] If, therefore, sins are not entirely put away in baptism, how is he that is washed entirely clean? For he cannot be said to be entirely clean if he has any sin remaining. But no one can resist the voice of the truth, "He who is washed is entirely clean." Nothing, then, of the contagion of sin remains to him whom he himself who redeemed him declares to be absolutely clean. LETTER 11.45.[72]

---

[71]Jn 13:10. [72]NPNF 2 13:66**.

74:1-23 A PRAYER FOR HELP AGAINST ENEMIES

A Maskil of Asaph.

[1]*O God, why dost thou cast us off for ever?*
Why does thy anger smoke against the sheep
of thy pasture?
[2]*Remember thy congregation, which thou hast*
gotten of old,
which thou hast redeemed to be the tribe
of thy heritage!
Remember Mount Zion, where thou hast
dwelt.
[3]*Direct thy steps to the perpetual ruins;*
the enemy has destroyed everything in the
sanctuary!

[4]*Thy foes have roared in the midst of thy holy*
place;
they set up their own signs for signs.
[5]*At the upper entrance they hacked*
the wooden trellis with axes.[z]
[6]*And then all its carved wood*

they broke down with hatchets and
hammers.
[7]*They set thy sanctuary on fire;*
to the ground they desecrated the dwelling
place of thy name.
[8]*They said to themselves, "We will utterly*
subdue them";
they burned all the meeting places of God in
the land.

[9]*We do not see our signs;*
there is no longer any prophet,
and there is none among us who knows how
long.
[10]*How long, O God, is the foe to scoff?*
Is the enemy to revile thy name for ever?
[11]*Why dost thou hold back thy hand,*
why dost thou keep thy right hand in[a] *thy*
bosom?

[12]*Yet God my King is from of old,*

working salvation in the midst of the earth.
¹³Thou didst divide the sea by thy might;
    thou didst break the heads of the dragons
      on the waters.
¹⁴Thou didst crush the heads of Leviathan,
    thou didst give him as food^b for the creatures
      of the wilderness.
¹⁵Thou didst cleave open springs and brooks;
    thou didst dry up ever-flowing streams.
¹⁶Thine is the day, thine also the night;
    thou hast established the luminaries and
      the sun.
¹⁷Thou hast fixed all the bounds of the earth;
    thou hast made summer and winter.

¹⁸Remember this, O LORD how the enemy
    scoffs,

and an impious people reviles thy name.
¹⁹Do not deliver the soul of thy dove to the wild
    beasts;
    do not forget the life of thy poor for ever.

²⁰Have regard for thy^c covenant;
    for the dark places of the land are full of the
      habitations of violence.
²¹Let not the downtrodden be put to shame;
    let the poor and needy praise thy name.

²²Arise, O God, plead thy cause;
    remember how the impious scoff at thee
      all the day!
²³Do not forget the clamor of thy foes,
    the uproar of thy adversaries which goes up
      continually!

z Cn Compare Gk Syr: Heb uncertain   a Cn: Heb *consume thy right hand from*   b Heb *food for the people*   c Gk Syr: Heb *the*

OVERVIEW: Christ, who is from eternity, worked out humanity's salvation during his earthly sojourn (AUGUSTINE). Christ is a king in eternity and in time; he accomplished our salvation through his life-giving preaching. Miracles recounted in the Old Testament help explain miracles performed by Christ in the New Testament, namely, the parting of the Red Sea helps explain the cleansing power of holy baptism. Pride is the sin that is most detestable to God because it is the sin that led to the rebellion of Satan and to the fall of Adam in the Garden of Eden (CASSIODORUS).

74:12 In the Midst of the Earth

THE SETTING FOR CHRIST'S REDEMPTIVE WORK. AUGUSTINE: We can appropriately apply the same line of interpretation[1] to a passage in the psalms, where it says, "Now God our king before the ages has achieved salvation in the midst of the earth." We may take "our God" to mean the Lord Jesus, who is before the ages (since the ages were

created by him); for he "achieved salvation in the midst of the earth" when the Word was made flesh and dwelt in a human body. CITY OF GOD 17.4.[2]

CHRIST WAS KING ALREADY IN ETERNITY. CASSIODORUS: "But God is our king before ages; he has worked salvation in the midst of the earth." The understanding of Asaph proclaimed earlier in the heading passes on to the second part, with the spirit of prophecy foretelling that the Lord Savior will come; in order to provide proof of this he recounts all the miracles that the Lord performed in heaven and on earth. Because he intends to speak of his incarnation, he attests that the Lord was already King before the foundation of the world, so that no one would believe that he was a mere lord in time. As he himself

---

[1]Augustine was arguing that a sin can be committed in thought without it involving bodily activity. So here he is saying that God worked out our salvation in eternity, prior to the incarnation of his Son. [2]CG 722-23.

says in the Gospel: "I was born into this world."[3] Ages (*saecula*) are so called because the seasons circle back on themselves (*in se*). Next comes, "He has worked salvation in the midst of the earth." Although this can be interpreted as relating to the miracles he performed, which he is known to have achieved before people's eyes, it would be better for us to understand it as referring to the salvation of souls which he achieved by his life-giving preaching. EXPOSITIONS OF THE PSALMS 73.12.[4]

THE CROSSING OF THE RED SEA PREFIGURED CHRISTIAN BAPTISM. CASSIODORUS: "By your strength you make the sea firm: you crushed the heads of the dragons in the waters."[5] He wishes clearly to demonstrate his earlier statement that the Lord Savior (who deigned to suffer for us, to destroy death by dying, to bestow freedom on captives and rewards on the condemned) was King before the ages, so he recounts the miracles that he earlier performed among the Jewish race. He made the watery depths of the Red Sea firm when the waters on both sides became so motionless that they made a land route out of the ship-bearing deep. Next comes, "You crushed the heads of the dragons in the waters." He appropriately expounds the mystery of that earlier miracle. That crossing of the Red Sea prefigured the waters of holy baptism, in which the heads of dragons—in other words, unclean spirits—are reduced to nothing when the water of salvation cleanses those souls that the spirits corrupted with the filth of sins. EXPOSITIONS OF THE PSALMS 73.13.[6]

74:23 The Clamor of Foes

THE SIN OF PRIDE. CASSIODORUS: Next comes, "Let the pride of them that hate you ascend continuously to you." We note that this is fittingly applied to the Romans, of whom he previously said, "In the midst of your shrine they have set up their ensigns"; he sought to stir up the all-powerful Judge most emphatically against the foes of Jerusalem. Pride is the vice that the Lord particularly abhors. It was through pride that both the angel fell and the blessedness of the first man was lost.[7] Notice how prudently this most cutting vice is placed at the end; he intended to conclude with what could be stored in the confines of the memory. This is the simple and prudent lament of those who are devoted to the Lord in purity of heart; those who show obedience by holy rules of life cannot be seduced in their grief, however severe it is. EXPOSITIONS OF THE PSALMS 73.23.[8]

---

[3]Jn 18:37. [4]ACW 52:217*. [5]Ps 74:13 (73:13 LXX, Vg.). [6]ACW 52:218*. [7]See Gen 3:1-7; 1 Tim 3:6. [8]ACW 52:223*.

75:1-10 A PSALM OF THANKSGIVING

To the choirmaster: according to Do Not Destroy. A Psalm of Asaph. A Song.

we call on thy name and recount[d] thy wondrous deeds.

[1]*We give thanks to thee, O God; we give thanks;*

[2]*At the set time which I appoint I will judge with equity.*

³*When the earth totters, and all its*
    inhabitants,
    it is I who keep steady its pillars.   Selah

⁴*I say to the boastful, "Do not boast,"*
    and to the wicked, "Do not lift up
    your horn;
⁵*do not lift up your horn on high,*
    or speak with insolent neck."

⁶*For not from the east or from the west*
    and not from the wilderness comes lifting
    up;

⁷*but it is God who executes judgment,*
    putting down one and lifting up another.
⁸*For in the hand of the* LORD *there is a cup,*
    with foaming wine, well mixed;
and he will pour a draught from it,
    and all the wicked of the earth
    shall drain it down to the dregs.

⁹*But I will rejoice[e] for ever,*
    I will sing praises to the God of Jacob.
¹⁰*All the horns of the wicked he[f] will cut off,*
    but the horns of the righteous shall
    be exalted.

d Syr Compare Gk: Heb *and near is thy name. They recount*   e Gk: Heb *declare*   f Heb I

OVERVIEW: God condemns what we do because it is evil, but he is graciously willing to save the people whom he had initially made good and in his own image. We insult God if we call on him before cleansing our hearts of wickedness by humble confession (AUGUSTINE). Frequent confession cleanses the heart in preparation for prayer (CASSIODORUS). We speak sinfully against God when we attribute good to ourselves and evil to God. God recognizes two kinds of people, the humble and the proud—the one a bold sinner, the other a confessing penitent—and judges them accordingly (AUGUSTINE). The chalice of salvation is full of a wine mixture that symbolizes the relation of the Old and New Testaments and God's desire to save Jew and Gentile (CASSIODORUS).

75:1 God Is Graciously Ready to Forgive Sin

GOD FINDS NO GOOD IN WHAT HUMANS DO.
AUGUSTINE: Here we have just been singing "We will confess[1] to you, O God, we will confess and call on your name." What does confessing to God mean but humbling oneself before God, not arrogating to oneself any merits? For "we have been saved by his grace," as the apostle says, "not by

works, lest anyone should exalt himself; for it is by his grace that we have been saved."[2] You see, there was not any preexistent good life that he could look down at from up above and admire and love and say, "Come on, let us go down and help these people, because they are leading good lives." He was displeased with our lives, he was displeased with everything we were making of ourselves, but he was not displeased with what he had made in us. So he will condemn what we have made, and what he has made he will save. He will condemn the evil deeds of men and women and save the men and women themselves. SERMON 23A.I.[3]

CLEANSING THE HEART BY CONFESSION.
AUGUSTINE: So he gave us the way of humility. If we keep to it we shall confess to the Lord, and not without reason shall we sing, "We will confess to you, O God, we will confess and call on your name." It is rather shameless to call on his name if you do not confess to him. First confess, in order to prepare a dwelling place for the one you are

---

[1]Augustine apparently used the word *confess* here instead of "praise," as he explains, because confession implies doing something with humility. [2]Eph 2:8-9. [3]*WSA* 3 2:68.

calling on, that is to say calling in. After all, your heart is full of wickedness. But confession sweeps out the uncleanness you are cluttered up with inside and cleans the house into which the one you are calling in is coming. But anyone who calls him in before confessing is deliberately insulting him by asking him in. If you would not dare invite some holy person into your house unless you had first cleaned it out, in case something should offend his eyes, will you have the nerve to call in the name of God into your heart full of wickedness, unless you have first swept out all the iniquity inside by confession? SERMON 23A.4.[4]

FIRST CONFESS, THEN PRAY. CASSIODORUS: "We will confess to you, O God, we will confess to you, and we will call on your name: I will relate all your wondrous works." In this single verse the rule of sacred devotion is explained in due sequence. The Jewish people who were to believe in the Lord Christ, and who the heading warns not to corrupt unto the end, bursts out and with great devotion pledges its praise. As we have often said, confession means the proclamation of something by the combined voices of many; for even if a single person is said to have confessed, it is acknowledged that he is joined to others who preceded him in the faith or to those who follow him. The phrase "we will confess to you" is repeated; this repetition attests the firm nature of the promise, for repetition is never employed casually but is used to denote firm decision, as in the phrase "my heart is ready, O God, my heart is ready,"[5] and similar statements. "To you" was inserted so that the cult of others should be excluded; true devotion is that which most justly reveres the Creator and no other. Let us ponder also that if we confess even once to a crime before an earthly judge, it often entails death; but frequent confession to God results not in hazard of death but in salvation. The run of words is really splendid. First the spokesman says that he is confessing, that is, lamenting his sins, and later that he is calling on the Lord's name; it is apt that we

should first through his gift cleanse our hearts by confession and thus call on the Lord's name to obtain help. To whom will he be able to come except to those who he knows are his own? If one not committed to him calls on him, he appears to be demanding judgment rather than pardon for himself. So we must preface our requests in this way so that we can call on God's clemency with confidence. EXPOSITIONS OF THE PSALMS 74.2.[6]

75:5 Do Not Speak Evil Against God

WHAT GOD DOES IS GOOD; WHAT WE DO IS EVIL. AUGUSTINE: If you say that,[7] you will not be singing to no purpose, "I said, Lord, have mercy on me; heal my soul, for I have sinned against you."[8] If God is blamed for the evil that you do and you take credit for the good, then you are speaking wickedly against God. Listen to what the psalm has to say on this point: "Do not lift your horn on high or speak wickedly against God." The iniquity you were speaking against God is this, that you were wishing to attribute everything good to yourself and everything bad to him. By lifting up the horn of pride, you were speaking wickedly against God. With humility you speak justly. And what is the equity you speak with humility? "I said, Lord, have mercy on me; heal my soul, for I have sinned against you."[9] SERMON 16B.2.[10]

75:6-9 God Executes Judgment

GOD HUMBLES THE PROUD AND EXALTS THE HUMBLE. AUGUSTINE: Thus, after the psalm had said, "Do not lift your horn on high or speak iniquity against God," it went on immediately. "Since neither from the east nor the west, nor from the mountain deserts; since God is judge he humbles this one and that one he exalts."[11] He

---

[4]WSA 3 2:70*. [5]Ps 57:7 (56:8 LXX, Vg.). [6]ACW 52:225*. [7]In the previous paragraphs, Augustine is speaking against the view of people who blame God for the evil that they commit and take credit themselves for the good things that they do. [8]Ps 41:4 (40:5 LXX, Vg.). [9]Ps 41:4 (40:5 LXX, Vg.). [10]WSA 3 1:363. [11]Ps 75:6-7 (74:7-8 LXX, Vg.).

sees two people, that is, two kinds of people. So which two people does he see? One full of pride, the other confessing; one speaking justly, the other speaking unjustly. Who is speaking justly? The one who says "I have sinned." And who is speaking unjustly? The one who says "It is not I who sinned, it is my luck that sinned, my fate that sinned." So when you see two people, one speaking equity, the other iniquity, one humble, the other proud, do not be surprised that it goes on to say, "Since God is judge, he humbles this one and that one he exalts." SERMON 16B.3.[12]

A CHALICE OF MIXED WINE. CASSIODORUS:, The Lord's chalice is "full of well-mixed wine,"[13] so that though continually drunk it is never emptied. "Mixture" points to the New and Old Testaments; the mixture of the two results in the most health-giving drink for souls. The Jews indeed had wine to drink, but it was not mixed because they were unwilling to admit the nourishment of the New Testament. Likewise Manichaeans[14] did not drink mixed wine, because they accepted the New Testament in part but rashly rejected the mysteries of the Old Law. He added, "And he has poured it out from this to that." Here he points unambiguously to the two communities of Jews and Gentiles, for he took from the mouth of unbelieving Jews that which he poured out for the converted peoples of the Gentiles as their drink. It was a blessed and untroubled refreshment to obtain the chalice of salvation from him who always knows how to provide what will be beneficial. This manner of speaking is peculiar to sacred literature, for one can hardly ever find it, I think, in secular writing. EXPOSITIONS OF THE PSALMS 74.9.[15]

---

[12]*WSA* 3 1:364*. [13]Ps 75:8 (74:9 LXX, Vg.). [14]Followers of the Manichaean heresy, which was an extreme form of a Gnostic-type dualism. [15]ACW 52:229*.

76:1-12 A PSALM CELEBRATING GOD'S PROTECTION OF JERUSALEM

To the choirmaster: with stringed instruments. A Psalm of Asaph. A Song.

¹*In Judah God is known,*
  his name is great in Israel.
²*His abode has been established in Salem,*
  his dwelling place in Zion.
³*There he broke the flashing arrows,*
  the shield, the sword, and the weapons
    of war.   Selah

⁴*Glorious art thou, more majestic*

*than the everlasting mountains.*⁸
⁵*The stouthearted were stripped of their spoil;*
  they sank into sleep;
all the men of war
  were unable to use their hands.
⁶*At thy rebuke, O God of Jacob,*
  both rider and horse lay stunned.

⁷*But thou, terrible art thou!*
  Who can stand before thee
  when once thy anger is roused?
⁸*From the heavens thou didst utter judgment;*

the earth feared and was still,
[9] *when God arose to establish judgment*
    to save all the oppressed of the earth.
                                    Selah
[10] *Surely the wrath of men shall praise thee;*
    the residue of wrath thou wilt gird upon
    thee.

[11] *Make your vows to the LORD your God, and*
    perform them;
    let all around him bring gifts
    to him who is to be feared,
[12] *who cuts off the spirit of princes,*
    who is terrible to the kings of the earth.

g Gk: Heb *the mountains of prey*

OVERVIEW: The cruel necessity of death is ame-liorated for believers by the certainty of heaven and the glories and presence of God that will be experienced there (JEROME). We delight in the light and truth that God gives the believer from Scripture as from an everlasting mountain (GREGORY OF NAZIANZUS). Prophets and apostles are granted wisdom to preach true doctrine and therefore do not fade away as heretics do (CAS-SIODORUS). For the unbeliever, this life is like a dream—what he has here vanishes when he awakes in eternity (AUGUSTINE). Gross sinners will be eternally wounded and perish by the jave-lin-like judgments that God hurls down from heaven. God stands when he passes sentence on the wicked to indicate the severity of the punish-ment, but he rewards those who deport them-selves well (CASSIODORUS). Amid all the cruelty and evil in the world we can find consolation in the example of those who do not treasure this life but the next (THEODORET).

76:2 Consolation in the Face of Death

SOULS OF BELIEVERS GO TO HEAVEN. JEROME: Thus when we have to face the hard and cruel necessity of death, we are comforted by this con-solation, that we shall shortly see again those whose absence we now mourn. For their end is not called death but a slumber and a falling asleep. Wherefore also the blessed apostle forbids us to sorrow concerning them which are asleep,[1] telling us to believe that those whom we know to sleep now may hereafter be roused from their sleep and when their slumber is ended may watch once more with the saints and sing with the angels: "Glory to God in the highest and on earth peace among people of good will."[2] In heaven where there is no sin, there is glory and perpetual praise and unwearied singing; but on earth where sedition reigns and war and discord hold sway, peace must be gained by prayer, and it is to be found not among all but only among persons of good will, who pay heed to the apostolic saluta-tion: "Grace to you and peace from God our Father and the Lord Jesus Christ."[3] For "his abode is in peace, and his dwelling place is in Zion," that is, on a watch tower, on the height of doctrines and of virtues, in the soul of the believer; for the angel of this latter[4] daily beholds the face of God and contemplates with unveiled face the glory of God. LETTER 75.1.[5]

76:4-5 The Blessings of the Righteous

GOD SHARES HIS LIGHT WITH THE RIGHT-EOUS. GREGORY OF NAZIANZUS: I will remind you again about Illuminations,[6] and that often, and will reckon them up from holy Scripture. For I myself shall be happier for remembering them (for what is sweeter than light to those who have

---

[1] 1 Thess 4:13. [2] Lk 2:14 (Vg.). [3] Rom 1:7. [4] This is most likely a refer-ence to Lucinius, a wealthy Spaniard of Baetica, who had embraced an ascetic lifestyle and together with his wife, Theodora, had made a vow of continence. Jerome wrote this letter to comfort Theodora at the death of her husband. [5] NPNF 2 6:155*. [6] Illumination (enlighten-ment, *phōtismos*) is one of the most ancient names for baptism, includ-ing the preliminary instruction.

tasted light?). I will dazzle you with my words: "There is sprung up a light for the righteous, and its partner joyful gladness."[7] And, "The light of the righteous is everlasting";[8] and "You are shining wondrously from the everlasting mountains" is said to God, I think of the angelic powers that aid our attempts to do good. You have heard David's words: "The Lord is my light and my salvation, whom shall I fear?"[9] Now he asks that the Light and the Truth may be sent forth for him,[10] now giving thanks that he has a share in it, in that the Light of God is marked on him;[11] that is, that the signs of the illumination given are impressed on him and recognized. On Holy Baptism, Oration 40.36.[12]

True Preachers Are Everlasting Hills. Cassiodorus: "You enlighten wonderfully from the everlasting hills." He passes to the second section, in which he proceeds to expound the various miracles of the Lord. So that we should not ask the source of this enlightenment, he added, "from the everlasting hills," that is, from the preachers who are indeed everlasting hills, for they continue in their enduring and unchangeable loftiness. Earthly mountains are transient and lifeless, but through the Lord's gift the preachers are ever wise and know that they are enduring. The psalmist preserved the order of the truth splendidly: he said that the Lord enlightens through the everlasting hills because he bestows on the prophets and apostles what was spread throughout the whole world by holy preaching. Store in your memory the fact that by the epithet *everlasting* he distinguished true preachers from false heretics who cannot be called everlasting, for once they teach perverse doctrines soon to fade they will be wiped out together with their beliefs. Expositions of the Psalms 75.5.[13]

Temporal Blessings Abandon the Ungodly. Augustine: This life is a dream life; these riches are, as it were, flowing through our sleep. Listen to the psalm, O poorest of the poor, Mr. Rich Man: "They have slept their sleep and

have found nothing in their hands, all the people of riches." Sometimes, too, a beggar lying on the ground, shivering with cold but still overcome with sleep, will dream of untold wealth, and rejoice and grow proud in his sleep and not deign to recognize his ragged old father, and until he wakes up he is rich. So when he goes to sleep, he finds something false and unreal to rejoice in; when he wakes up he finds something only too real and true to grieve over. So the rich person when he dies is like the poor person when he wakes up, after seeing untold wealth in his sleep. I mean, there was that man too, "clothed in purple and fine linen,"[14] a certain rich man who was neither named nor fit to be named, a despiser of the poor man lying at his gate. He was clothed in purple and fine linen, as the Gospel testifies, and he feasted sumptuously every day. He died, he was buried; he woke up and found himself in the flames. So he slept his sleep and found nothing in his hands, that man of riches, because he had done nothing good with his hands. Sermon 345.1.[15]

76:8-9 A God of Judgment

The Judgments of God. Cassiodorus: "He has hurled his judgment from heaven; the earth trembled and was still." Here the very force of the adjudication is described; the judgment comes down from that peak of power like a javelin hurled by the strongest and most unerring hand. But whereas an earthly spear inflicts a temporal blow, the judgment will wound the wicked eternally. Next comes, "The earth trembled and was still." The earth, as has often been remarked, here denotes the most heavy and bloated sinners who will be condemned by the authority of God's judgment. They will tremble when they hear "Go into eternal fire."[16] They will be still when they are admitted to eternal damnation. But this still-

---

[7]Ps 97:11 (96:11 LXX). [8]Prov 13:9. [9]Ps 27:1 (26:1 LXX). [10]Ps 43:3 (42:3 LXX). [11]Ps 4:7 (4:8 LXX). [12]NPNF 2 7:373*. [13]ACW 52:233-34*. [14]Lk 16:19. [15]WSA 3 10:59. [16]Mt 25:41.

ness is without rest; they desist from their evil deeds, but they are not at rest in their pains, for they will be tortured in eternal flames. EXPOSITIONS OF THE PSALMS 75.9.[17]

GOD ROSE IN JUDGMENT. CASSIODORUS: "When God rose in judgment, to save all the meek of the earth." This verse is to be joined to the previous one. The psalmist says, "The earth trembled and was still when God rose in judgment." The phrase "rising in judgment" is splendid, for on earth when Christ was judged, he bore everything in silence, though at the judgment too he will pronounce on all things without anger. The word rise is adopted from the practice of judges on earth, who on passing harsh sentence are said to rise because they appear wrathful when punishing crimes that have been committed. So that you would not think that the judgment was to be held solely to condemn the wicked, he added, "To save all the meek of the earth." The meek of the earth are those who are not carried away with flaming desire by any worldly vices but deport themselves with untroubled self-control, as has been said earlier, and are shown to have placid peace of mind. They are saved when through the Lord's gift they obtain the promised rewards. EXPOSITIONS OF THE PSALMS 75.10.[18]

GOD JUDGES THE WICKED AND THEIR FALSE DOCTRINE. THEODORET OF CYR: If every one had imitated this cruelty,[19] nothing else would have been left then for me in my lifetime but to be wasted by want, and, at my death, instead of being committed to a tomb, to be made meat for dogs and wild beasts. But I have found support in those who care nothing for this present life but await the enjoyment of everlasting blessings, and these furnish me with manifold consolation. But the loving Lord "caused judgment to be heard from heaven; the earth feared and was still, when God arose to judgment." But the wicked shall perish. The falsehood of the new heresy[20] has been proscribed, and the truth of the divine Gospels is publicly proclaimed. I for my part exclaim with the blessed David, "Blessed be the Lord God who alone does wondrous things, and blessed be his glorious name: and let the whole earth be filled with his glory; amen and amen."[21] LETTER 134.[22]

---

[17]ACW 52:235. [18]ACW 52:235-36*. [19]The failure to provide consolation and support for people who had been exiled, deprived of their property and the necessities of life (cf. Letter 32). [20]Eutychianism, a christological heresy that taught that the human nature of the incarnate Christ is effectively absorbed into the divine nature, resulting in Christ having essentially only one nature. [21]Ps 72:18-19 (71:18-19 LXX). [22]NPNF 2 3:305*.

77:1-20 COMFORTING THOUGHTS IN TIME OF DISTRESS

To the choirmaster: according to Jeduthun. A Psalm of Asaph.

[1]*I cry aloud to God,*

aloud to God, that he may hear me.
[2]*In the day of my trouble I seek the Lord;*
in the night my hand is stretched out without wearying;

my soul refuses to be comforted.

³*I think of God, and I moan;*
   I meditate, and my spirit faints.   Selah
⁴*Thou dost hold my eyelids from closing;*
   I am so troubled that I cannot speak.
⁵*I consider the days of old,*
   I remember the years long ago.
⁶*I commune*ʰ *with my heart in the night;*
   *I meditate and search my spirit:*ⁱ
⁷*"Will the Lord spurn for ever,*
   and never again be favorable?
⁸*Has his steadfast love for ever ceased?*
   Are his promises at an end for all time?
⁹*Has God forgotten to be gracious?*
   Has he in anger shut up his compassion?"
                            Selah
¹⁰*And I say, "It is my grief*
   that the right hand of the Most High has
     changed."

¹¹*I will call to mind the deeds of the* LORD
   yea, I will remember thy wonders of old.
¹²*I will meditate on all thy work,*
   and muse on thy mighty deeds.

¹³*Thy way, O God, is holy.*
   What god is great like our God?
¹⁴*Thou art the God who workest wonders,*
   who hast manifested thy might among
     the peoples.
¹⁵*Thou didst with thy arm redeem thy*
     people,
   the sons of Jacob and Joseph   Selah

¹⁶*When the waters saw thee, O God,*
   when the waters saw thee, they were
     afraid,
   yea, the deep trembled.
¹⁷*The clouds poured out water;*
   the skies gave forth thunder;
   thy arrows flashed on every side.
¹⁸*The crash of thy thunder was in the*
     whirlwind;
   thy lightnings lighted up the world;
   the earth trembled and shook.
¹⁹*Thy way was through the sea,*
   thy path through the great waters;
   yet thy footprints were unseen.
²⁰*Thou didst lead thy people like a flock*
   by the hand of Moses and Aaron.

h Gk Syr: Heb *my music*   **i** Syr Jerome: Heb *my spirit searches*

OVERVIEW: Unbelief is a darkness of the heart that motivates us to seek God in a palpable, empirical way (AUGUSTINE). When we take refuge with God in faith, we renounce the world and sin and are spiritually in the presence of God (AMBROSE). In this world we should strive to perform good deeds that please God and benefit our neighbor (CAESARIUS). We should pray early in the morning so that each day is begun with thoughts of God; only then are we prepared to begin the day's tasks (BASIL).

Eternity describes the realm of God's being, but time belongs to created things (PSEUDO-DIONYSIUS). Even in the midst of God's anger against wickedness, he continues to show mercy to good and bad people alike. It is natural for unbelievers to deny the reality of eternal condemnation, but they will be proven wrong in eternity (AUGUSTINE). The "right hand of God" is an expression used for the power of God, to refer to Christ who does the work of God the Father and who assumed a human nature to reveal God to us (GREGORY OF NYSSA). It is God who, sometimes through human agency, turns people's hearts away from heresy to orthodoxy or from iniquity and estrangement to innocence and inheritance in his kingdom (LEO, GREGORY THE GREAT).

David urges us to imitate elements of nature, which knew how to gather, fear and flee at the command of God (AMBROSE). Heretics who deny that the divine nature of Christ is of the same nature as that of the Father are refuted by human and natural testimony (EPHREM).

77:2-3 Reaching Out to God

GOD IS OUR REFUGE IN TIME OF TROUBLE. AUGUSTINE: But now in that part of the reading that sounded most recently in your ears, what did you hear Thomas saying? "I won't believe, unless I touch." And the Lord says to this Thomas, "Come, touch, put your hands into my side, and do not be incredulous but believing."[1] "I," he is saying, "if you do not think it is enough for me to offer myself to your eyes, am also offering myself to your hands. Perhaps, you see, you are one of those who sing in the psalm, 'In the day of my trouble I sought the Lord with my hands in the night in his presence.'" Why was he seeking with his hands? Because he was seeking in the night. What does that mean, was seeking in the night? He was carrying the darkness of unbelief in his heart. SERMON 375C.2.[2]

TAKE REFUGE IN GOD. AMBROSE: Let us flee from here. You can flee in spirit, even though you are kept back in body. You can both be here and be in the presence of the Lord, if your soul clings to him and you walk after him in your thoughts, if you follow his ways, not in pretense but in faith, and take refuge in him. For he is a refuge and a power, and David says to him, "I fled to you for refuge, and I was not deceived." And so, because God is a refuge, and because he is, more-over, in heaven and above the heavens, surely we must flee from here to there, where there is peace and rest from labors and where we can feast upon the great sabbath, even as Moses said, "And the sabbaths of the land shall be food for you."[3] For it is a banquet, and one filled with enjoyment and serenity, to rest in God and to look on his delight.

We have taken refuge with God; shall we return to the world? We have died to sin; shall we seek sins again? We have renounced the world and the use of it; shall we stick fast again in its mire? FLIGHT FROM THE WORLD 8.45.[4]

GOOD DEEDS THAT PLEASE GOD. CAESARIUS OF ARLES: Notice, too, what the psalmist said. When he told them, "On the day of my distress I sought God," he also added, "My hands were stretched out"; further, "by night" and also "before him." What is distress? What does it mean to stretch out one's hands, and what does it mean to do so before God? There is distress when we suffer annoyances and stretching out of hands [when we engage] in good deeds. Searching by night occurs in this world when the truth has not yet shed light. This world will certainly come to an end and will meet Christ [in judg-ment]. And when Christ comes, he will be like the sun shining in the hearts of all people. Why did he add "before him"? The person who stretches out his hands performs good deeds. However, the person who thus performs good deeds in order to please people does not do so before God; that is, in order to please him rather than human beings. Quite rightly, then, "I was not deceived" follows; a person who has sought God in this way [may say,] "I have not been deceived." He has found what he was seeking, and therefore he has told us, "Ask, seek, knock."[5] ADDITIONAL SERMON 3.[6]

BEGIN EACH DAY WITH THOUGHTS OF GOD. BASIL THE GREAT: Prayers are recited early in the morning so that the first movements of the soul and the mind may be consecrated to God and that we may take up no other consideration before we have been cheered and heartened by the thought of God, as it is written: "I remem-bered God and was delighted," and that the body

---

[1]Jn 20:27. [2]WSA 3 10:340. [3]Lev 25:6. [4]FC 65:315-16. [5]Mt 7:7. [6]A Sermon of Augustine on the Gospel Text That Says "It Shall Be Given to You," FC 66:226-27*.

may not busy itself with tasks before we have ful-filled the words "To you will I pray, O Lord; in the morning you shall hear my voice. In the morning I will stand before you and will see."[7] THE LONG RULES 37.[8]

77:5-10 God Has the Power to Change People

THE NATURE OF TIME AND ETERNITY.
PSEUDO-DIONYSIUS: Now, I think we have to be clear about the nature of time and eternity in the Scriptures. When describing things as eternal, the intention of Scripture is not always to suggest that they are absolutely uncreated, everlasting, incorruptible, immortal, unchanging and immu-table. I have in mind here texts such as "Rise up, you eternal doors."[9] Actually, the designation "eternity" is frequently given to something very ancient or, again, to the whole course of earthly time, since it is characteristic of eternity to be very old, unchanging and the measure of being. Time, [by contrast], has to do with the process of change manifested, for instance, in birth, death and variety. Hence theology tells us that we who are bound in by time are destined to have a share of eternity when at last we attain the incorrupt-ible, unchanging eternity.[10] And then Scripture talks sometimes of the splendors of a temporal eternity and of an eternal time. But of course it is clear to us that, strictly speaking, what Scripture discusses and denotes is that eternity is the home of being, while time is the home of things that come to be. Therefore it must not be imagined that things named as eternal are simply co-eternal with the God who precedes eternity. No. Better here to follow carefully the sacred words of Scrip-ture and to take "eternal" and "temporal" in the sense appropriate to them. And we should look on those things that share partly in eternity and partly in time as somehow midway between things that are and things that are coming to be. One can take eternity and time to be predicates of God since, being the Ancient of Days, he is the cause of all time and eternity. Yet he is before time

and beyond time and is the source of the variety of time and of seasons. Or, again, he precedes the eternal ages, for he is there before eternity and above eternity, and "his kingdom is an everlasting kingdom."[11] DIVINE NAMES 10.3.[12]

GOD IS A GOD OF MERCY AND OF JUDGMENT.
AUGUSTINE: No one, therefore, should take this verse of the psalm, "Will God really forget to show mercy? Will he in his wrath restrain his compassion?" and interpret it in such a way as to suggest the notion that God's sentence is true in respect of the good but false in respect of the wicked, or true in respect of good human beings and evil angels but false in respect of evil human beings. In fact, this verse of the psalm refers to the "vessels of mercy" and the "sons of the prom-ise,"[13] one of whom was the prophet; and he first says, "Will God really 'forget to show mercy,' in making his sun shine on the good and bad" and then immediately continues, "Then I said: Now I have begun; this is an alteration of the right hand of God Most High." Here, obviously, he has explained what he meant by "Will God in his wrath restrain his compassion?" For this mortal life is itself part of God's wrath, this life in which "a person becomes like a piece of futility; his days pass by like shadows."[14] Yet even in this manifes-tation of his anger God does not "forget to show mercy," in making his sun shine on the good and bad alike and sending rain on the righteous and the unrighteous,[15] and in this way he does not in wrath restrain his compassion. And this is partic-ularly true in what the psalmist expresses by say-ing, "Now I have begun; this is an alteration of the right hand of God Most High." For in this life, a life full of troubles, which is a manifestation of God's wrath, God changes the "vessels of mercy" into a better state (although his wrath still continues in the misery of this condition of decay) because even in his wrath he does not

---

[7]Ps 5:3 (5:5 LXX). [8]FC 9:309. [9]Ps 24:7 (23:7 LXX). [10]1 Cor 15:53. [11]Ps 145:13 (144:13 LXX). [12]PDCW 120-21. [13]Rom 9:23; Gal 4:28. [14]Ps 144:4 (143:4 LXX, Vg.). [15]Mt 5:45.

restrain his compassion. CITY OF GOD 21.24.[16]

GOD WILL BE MERCIFUL. AUGUSTINE: It is quite in vain, then, that some—indeed very many—yield to merely human feelings and deplore the notion of the eternal punishment of the damned and their interminable and perpetual misery. They do not believe that such things will be. Not that they would go counter to divine Scripture—but, yielding to their own human feelings, they soften what seems harsh and give a milder emphasis to statements they believe are meant more to terrify than to express the literal truth. "God will not forget," they say, "to show mercy, nor in his anger will he shut up his mercy." This is, in fact, the text of a holy psalm. But there is no doubt that it is to be interpreted to refer to those who are called "vessels of mercy," those who are freed from misery not by their own merits but through God's mercy. Even so, if they suppose that the text applies to all people, there is no ground for them further to suppose that there can be an end for those of whom it is said, "Thus these shall go into everlasting punishment." Otherwise, it can as well be thought that there will also be an end to the happiness of those of whom the antithesis was said: "But the righteous into life eternal." ENCHIRIDION 29.112.[17]

THE MEANING OF "THE RIGHT HAND OF GOD HAS CHANGED." GREGORY OF NYSSA: Sufficient defense has been offered on these points, and as for that which Eunomius[18] says by way of calumny against our doctrine, that "Christ was emptied to become himself"[19] there has been sufficient discussion in what has been said above, where he has been shown to be attributing to our doctrine his own blasphemy. For a person who believes that the unchangeable [divine] nature has put on the created and perishable [human nature] is not one who speaks of the transition from like to like but one who believes that the divine nature does not change into the more lowly [human nature]. For if, as their doctrine asserts, he is created, and a human being is created also, the wonder of the doctrine disappears, and there is nothing marvelous in what is alleged, since the created nature comes to be in itself. But we who have learned from prophecy of "the change of the right hand of the Most High"—and by the "Right Hand" of the Father we understand that power of God, which made all things, which is the Lord (not in the sense of depending on him as a part upon a whole but as being indeed from him and yet contemplated in individual existence)—say thus: that neither does the right hand vary from him whose right hand it is, in regard to the idea of its nature, nor can any other change in it be spoken of besides the accommodation to the flesh. For truly the right hand of God was God himself; manifested in the flesh, seen through that same flesh by those whose sight was clear; as he did the work of the Father, being, both in fact and in thought, the right hand of God, yet being changed, in respect of the veil of the flesh by which he was surrounded, as regarded that which was seen, from that which he was by nature, as a subject of contemplation. Therefore he says to Philip, who was gazing only at that which was changed, "Look through that which is changed to that which is unchangeable, and if you see this, you have seen that Father, whom you seek to see; for he that has seen me—not him who appears in a state of change, but my very self, who am in the Father—will have seen that Father in whom I am, because the very same character of Godhead is beheld in both."[20] If, then, we believe that the immortal and impassible and uncreated nature came to be in the nature of the creature that is capable of suffering, and conceive the "change" to consist in this, on what grounds are we charged with saying that he "set aside his divine powers to become incarnate," by those who keep presenting

---

[16]CG 1004. [17]LCC 7:406. [18]Eunomius was bishop of Cyzicus in Cappadocia (360-364). He founded a party called Eunomians, who taught extreme Anomoean teachings of the general comprehensibleness of the divine Essence and the total unlikeness of the Son to the Father. He is often ranked as an extreme Arian. [19]Gregory is speaking here of the view that the incarnate Christ emptied or set aside his divine powers or attributes during his state of humiliation (the period of his earthly life that went from his conception to his burial) in order for the incarnation to be possible. [20]See Jn 14:9-10.

their own statements about our doctrines? For the participation of the created with the created is no "change of the right hand." To say that the right hand of the uncreated nature is created belongs to Eunomius[21] alone and to those who adopt such opinions as he holds. For the person with an eye that looks on the truth will discern the right hand of the Highest to be such as he sees the Highest to be—Uncreated of Uncreated, Good of Good, Eternal of Eternal without prejudice to its eternity by its being in the Father by way of generation. Thus our accuser has unawares been employing against us reproaches that properly fall on himself. AGAINST EUNOMIUS 6.3.[22]

THE MYSTERY OF CONVERSION. LEO THE GREAT: What mind can understand this mystery, what tongue has the capability of explaining this grace? Iniquity turns back into innocence, oldness into newness. Strangers come into adoption, and foreigners enter on an inheritance. Godless people have started to be just, the covetous to be beneficent, the incontinent to be chaste, the "earthly" to be "heavenly."[23] What has effected "this change" but the "right hand of the Most High"? For "the Son of God came to undo the devil's works."[24] He grafted himself into us and us into himself in such a way that God's descent to human affairs became the elevation of human beings to those divine. SERMON 27.2.2.[25]

GOD CHANGES PEOPLE'S HEARTS. GREGORY THE GREAT: I cannot express in words, most excellent son,[26] how much I am delighted with your work and your life. For on hearing of the power of a new miracle in our days, to wit, that the whole nation of the Goths has through your excellency been brought over from the error of the Arian heresy to the firmness of a right faith, one is disposed to exclaim with the prophet, "This is the change wrought by the right hand of the most High." For whose breast, even though stony, would not, on hearing of so great a work, soften in praises of almighty God and love of your excellency? As for me, I declare that it delights me

often to tell these things that have been done through you to my sons[27] who consult with me, and often together with them I marvel at these things. These things also for the most part cause me to become critical of myself, in that I languish sluggish and unprofitable in listless ease, while kings are laboring in the gathering together of souls for the gains of the heavenly country. LETTER 9.122.[28]

77:16-20 God Manifests Himself

NATURE OBEYS GOD. AMBROSE: This is not the only example of the obedience of water available to us, for elsewhere we find it written, "The waters saw you, O God; the waters saw you, and they were afraid." What is said here of the waters does not seem to be without a semblance of truth, since elsewhere the prophet also speaks in the same manner: "The sea saw and fled; Jordan was turned back."[29] Who does not know how in actual fact the sea fled at the crossing of the Hebrews? When the waters were divided, the people crossed over, believing because of the dust under their feet that the sea had fled and that the waters had vanished. Therefore, the Egyptian believed what he saw and entered in, but the waters that had fled returned for him. The waters, then, know how to gather, how to fear and how to flee, when commanded to do so by God. Let us imitate these waters, and let us recognize one congregation of the Lord, one church. SIX DAYS OF CREATION 3.1.2.[30]

HUMANITY AND NATURE TESTIFY TO THE DEITY OF CHRIST. EPHREM THE SYRIAN: "When our Lord had arrived and had entered the

---

[21]He held extreme views regarding the Arian heresy of subordination. [22]NPNF 2 5:185-86**. [23]1 Cor 15:49. [24]1 Jn 3:8. [25]FC 93:112. [26]Gregory is addressing Rechared, the Visigoth king of Spain, who declared himself orthodox in 587 and adopted orthodox Christianity as the faith of the church in Spain at the Council of Toledo in 589. Previously he belonged to the Arian sect. [27]Subservient clergy, such as Probinus, a presbyter who is mentioned later in the letter. [28]NPNF 2 13:35**. [29]Ps 114:3 (113:3 LXX, Vg.). [30]FC 42:67-68*.

boat with Simon, the wind abated."[31] The
Arian,[32] therefore, who contradicts the birth [of
the Lord] is also rejected, through the word that
those who were in the boat spoke, "They came
and worshiped him, and they were saying to him,
'You are indeed the Son of God.'"[33] It is he of
whom it is written, "The waters saw you and
trembled, and the depths too were stirred up.

Your pathways are on many waters, and your
footsteps are not known." So they confessed by
their word that he, concerning whom these
things were spoken, was indeed the Son of God.
COMMENTARY ON TATIAN'S DIATESSARON 12.9.[34]

---

[31]Mt 14:25, 32. [32]An advocate of the Arian heresy, which taught that
Christ was subordinate to God the Father. [33]Mt 14:33. [34]ECTD 194.

78:1-72 A PSALM OF INSTRUCTION

A Maskil of Asaph.

[1]*Give ear, O my people, to my teaching;*
incline your ears to the words of my mouth!
[2]*I will open my mouth in a parable;*
I will utter dark sayings from of old,
[3]*things that we have heard and known,*
that our fathers have told us.
[4]*We will not hide them from their children,*
but tell to the coming generation
the glorious deeds of the LORD and his might,
and the wonders which he has wrought.

[5]*He established a testimony in Jacob,*
and appointed a law in Israel,
which he commanded our fathers
to teach to their children;
[6]*that the next generation might know them,*
the children yet unborn,
and arise and tell them to their children,
[7]*so that they should set their hope in God,*
and not forget the works of God,
but keep his commandments;
[8]*and that they should not be like their fathers,*

a stubborn and rebellious generation,
a generation whose heart was not steadfast,
whose spirit was not faithful to God.

[9]*The Ephraimites, armed with[j] the bow,*
turned back on the day of battle.
[10]*They did not keep God's covenant,*
but refused to walk according to his law.
[11]*They forgot what he had done,*
and the miracles that he had shown
them.
[12]*In the sight of their fathers he wrought*
marvels
in the land of Egypt, in the fields of Zoan.
[13]*He divided the sea and let them pass through*
it,
and made the waters stand like a heap.
[14]*In the daytime he led them with a cloud,*
and all the night with a fiery light.
[15]*He cleft rocks in the wilderness,*
and gave them drink abundantly as from
the deep.
[16]*He made streams come out of the rock,*
and caused waters to flow down like rivers.

[17]Yet they sinned still more against him,
  rebelling against the Most High in the
    desert.
[18]They tested God in their heart
  by demanding the food they craved.
[19]They spoke against God, saying,
  "Can God spread a table in the wilderness?
[20]He smote the rock so that water gushed
    out
  and streams overflowed.
Can he also give bread,
  or provide meat for his people?"

[21]Therefore, when the LORD heard, he was
    full of wrath;
  a fire was kindled against Jacob,
  his anger mounted against Israel;
[22]because they had no faith in God,
  and did not trust his saving power.
[23]Yet he commanded the skies above,
  and opened the doors of heaven;
[24]and he rained down upon them manna to eat,
  and gave them the grain of heaven.
[25]Man ate of the bread of the angels;
  he sent them food in abundance.
[26]He caused the east wind to blow in the
    heavens,
  and by his power he led out the south wind;
[27]he rained flesh upon them like dust,
  winged birds like the sand of the seas;
[28]he let them fall in the midst of their camp,
  all around their habitations.
[29]And they ate and were well filled,
  for he gave them what they craved.
[30]But before they had sated their craving,
  while the food was still in their mouths,
[31]the anger of God rose against them
  and he slew the strongest of them,
  and laid low the picked men of Israel.

[32]In spite of all this they still sinned;
  despite his wonders they did not believe.
[33]So he made their days vanish like a breath,
  and their years in terror.
[34]When he slew them, they sought for him;
  they repented and sought God earnestly.
[35]They remembered that God was their rock,
  the Most High God their redeemer.
[36]But they flattered him with their mouths;
  they lied to him with their tongues.
[37]Their heart was not steadfast toward him;
  they were not true to his covenant.
[38]Yet he, being compassionate,
  forgave their iniquity,
  and did not destroy them;
he restrained his anger often,
  and did not stir up all his wrath.
[39]He remembered that they were but flesh,
  a wind that passes and comes not again.
[40]How often they rebelled against him in the
    wilderness
  and grieved him in the desert!
[41]They tested him again and again,
  and provoked the Holy One of Israel.
[42]They did not keep in mind his power,
  or the day when he redeemed them from
    the foe;
[43]when he wrought his signs in Egypt,
  and his miracles in the fields of Zoan.
[44]He turned their rivers to blood,
  so that they could not drink of their streams.
[45]He sent among them swarms of flies, which
    devoured them,
  and frogs, which destroyed them.
[46]He gave their crops to the caterpillar,
  and the fruit of their labor to the locust.
[47]He destroyed their vines with hail,
  and their sycamores with frost.
[48]He gave over their cattle to the hail,

and their flocks to thunderbolts.
⁴⁹He let loose on them his fierce anger,
    wrath, indignation, and distress,
    a company of destroying angels.
⁵⁰He made a path for his anger;
    he did not spare them from death,
    but gave their lives over to the plague.
⁵¹He smote all the first-born in Egypt,
    the first issue of their strength in the tents
       of Ham.
⁵²Then he led forth his people like sheep,
    and guided them in the wilderness like
       a flock.
⁵³He led them in safety, so that they were not
       afraid;
    but the sea overwhelmed their enemies.
⁵⁴And he brought them to his holy land,
    to the mountain which his right hand had
       won.
⁵⁵He drove out nations before them;
    he apportioned them for a possession
    and settled the tribes of Israel in their tents.

⁵⁶Yet they tested and rebelled against the Most
       High God,
    and did not observe his testimonies,
⁵⁷but turned away and acted treacherously like
       their fathers;
    they twisted like a deceitful bow.
⁵⁸For they provoked him to anger with their
       high places;
    they moved him to jealousy with their
       graven images.

⁵⁹When God heard, he was full of wrath,
    and he utterly rejected Israel.
⁶⁰He forsook his dwelling at Shiloh,
    the tent where he dwelt among men,
⁶¹and delivered his power to captivity,
    his glory to the hand of the foe.
⁶²He gave his people over to the sword,
    and vented his wrath on his heritage.
⁶³Fire devoured their young men,
    and their maidens had no marriage song.
⁶⁴Their priests fell by the sword,
    and their widows made no lamentation.
⁶⁵Then the Lord awoke as from sleep,
    like a strong man shouting because of wine.
⁶⁶And he put his adversaries to rout;
    he put them to everlasting shame.

⁶⁷He rejected the tent of Joseph,
    he did not choose the tribe of Ephraim;
⁶⁸but he chose the tribe of Judah,
    Mount Zion, which he loves.
⁶⁹He built his sanctuary like the high heavens,
    like the earth, which he has founded for
       ever.
⁷⁰He chose David his servant,
    and took him from the sheepfolds;
⁷¹from tending the ewes that had young he
       brought him
    to be the shepherd of Jacob his people,
    of Israel his inheritance.
⁷²With upright heart he tended them,
    and guided them with skilful hand.

j Heb *armed with shooting*

OVERVIEW: Recounting the deeds of great people of faith provides us with examples of godly living and faith in Jesus Christ (PACHOMIUS). God brings judgment on the wicked in the hope of turning them from perversity to faithfulness to God (CLEMENT OF ALEXANDRIA).

David says that the flesh of Christ was like the manna eaten by Israel in the wilderness. It was terrestrial in nature but provided celestial nourishment (TERTULLIAN). When Christ came down as our manna from heaven, he took on himself our sufferings so that we might be born again and live eternally. Through the Word incarnate humanity comes to the Word that was in the beginning with God (AUGUSTINE).

God promises to come to the aid of the righteous who suffer unjustly from the lying and deceit of hypocrites (CLEMENT OF ROME). The divinity of the Holy Spirit and the sameness of his nature with that of the Father and the Son are attested by his divine work of leading and guiding God's people (BASIL). God will punish those who bring false charges against his servants (THEODORET).

78:3 Exemplary Lives

LESSONS AND EXAMPLES OF OUR ANCESTORS IN THE FAITH. PACHOMIUS: Instructed by the holy Scriptures and especially by the gospel, Pachomius endured many temptations from the demons. The holy Scriptures did not mention in detail the saints' struggle, since they used concise language in showing us the way to eternal life. Thus, for example, the law given to our ancestor Abraham was summarized in one saying, "Be well-pleasing before me and be blameless."[1] But since we are like infants, when our parents break the bread for us, we need to be given as well the true water, as it is written.[2] Therefore, "what we have heard and known and our ancestors have told us should not be hidden from the next generation."[3] For, as we have been taught, we know that these words of the psalm are about the signs and portents accomplished by God for Moses and those after him. And after the model of the benefit given by them, we have also recognized in the parents of our time their children and imitators, so that to us and "to the rising generation,"[4] until the end of the world, it might be made known that "Jesus Christ is the same yesterday, today, and forever."[5] LIFE OF PACHOMIUS (FIRST GREEK) 17.[6]

78:7-8 God Is a Refuge and a Source of Mercy

REASONS FOR GOD'S JUDGMENT ON WICKEDNESS. CLEMENT OF ALEXANDRIA: But God's righteousness cried out, "If you will come to me righteous, I will deal with you justly. If you walk treacherously, I will do so also, says the Lord of hosts."[7] He is suggesting that he will punish the treacherous ways of hardened sinners. The righteousness that is his by nature is indicated by the iota of the name Jesus.[8] His goodness to those who believe out of obedience is immoveable and unwavering. "Since I called and you did not obey," the Lord says, "you have disregarded my advice and have not heeded my reprimand."[9] The Lord's reprimand is very beneficial. The Lord also says, through David, that these people are "an unjust and rebellious generation, a generation that does not set its heart straight and whose spirit does not trust in God. They did not keep God's covenant and did not want to walk according to his law."[10] These are the reasons for his frustration and why he will come as a judge to pass judgment on those who do not want to choose to live a good life. On account of this he treats them quite severely in the hope of thwarting their march toward death. At any rate, through David he states very clearly his reason for his threat: "They did not believe in his wondrous deeds. When he killed them, they sought him and returned and came straight to God. They remembered that God was their helper and the most high God their redeemer."[11] In this way, he knew that they repented because of fear after they scorned his love for humankind. As a rule, people who have little regard for what is good behave kindly and remember to love humankind out of fear of justice. CHRIST THE EDUCATOR 1.9.[12]

---

[1]Gen 17:1. [2]Lam 4:4; Is 33:16. [3]Ps 78:3-4 (77:3-4 LXX). [4]Ps 71:18 (70:18 LXX). [5]Heb 13:8. [6]CS 45:308. [7]See Ps 18:25-26 (17:26-27 LXX). [8]The iota is the first letter of the Greek name for Jesus. [9]Prov 1:24-25. [10]Ps 78:8, 10 (77:8, 10 LXX). [11]Ps 78:32-35 (77:32-35 LXX). [12]PG 8:352-53.

78:24-25 The Bread of Angels

CHRIST BECAME MANNA FROM HEAVEN.
AUGUSTINE: Let us turn back to the one who performed these miracles. He is himself the bread that came down from heaven; but bread that nourishes and never diminishes; bread that can be eaten but cannot be eaten up. This bread was also signified by manna, of which it was said, "He gave them the bread of heaven; people ate the bread of angels. Who can the bread of heaven be, but Christ? But for people to eat the bread of angels, the Lord of angels became a human being. Because if he had not become this, we would not have his flesh; if we did not have his flesh, we would not eat the bread of the altar. SERMON 130.2.[13]

PEOPLE ATE THE BREAD OF ANGELS.
AUGUSTINE: This[14] is where you are going; the same one is the way by which you are going. You do not go through one thing to something else; you do not come through something else to Christ. You come through Christ to Christ. How through Christ to Christ? Through Christ the man to Christ the God, through the Word made flesh to the Word which in the beginning was God with God, from that which people ate to that which every day the angels eat. For so it was written, "He gave them the bread of heaven; people ate the bread of the angels." Who is the bread of angels? "In the beginning was the Word, and the Word was with God, and the Word was God."[15] How did people eat the bread of angels? "And the Word was made flesh and dwelt among us."[16] TRACTATES ON THE GOSPEL OF JOHN 13.4.2.[17]

78:36-37 Vain Flattery

HYPOCRITES BLESS WITH THEIR MOUTHS.
CLEMENT OF ROME: Let us, then, attach ourselves to those who are religiously devoted to peace, and not to those who wish for it hypocritically. For somewhere it is said, "This people honors me with its lips, but its heart is far removed from me."[18] And again, "They blessed with their mouth, but they cursed with their heart."[19] And again it says, "They loved him with their mouth, but they lied to him with their tongue. Their heart was not straightforward with him, and they were not faithful to his covenant. Therefore let the deceitful lips that speak evil against the righteous be struck dumb."[20] And again, "May the Lord destroy all deceitful lips and the tongue that boasts unduly and those who say, 'We will boast of our tongues; our lips are our own; who is Lord over us?' Because of the wretchedness of the poor and the groans of the needy I will now arise, says the Lord. I will place him in safety: I will act boldly in his cause."[21] 1 CLEMENT 15.[22]

78:47-66 The Justice of God

GOD LEADS HIS PEOPLE LIKE A FLOCK.
BASIL THE GREAT: The Spirit speaks with the authority of the Lord: "The Spirit said to [Peter], 'Rise and go down, and accompany them without hesitation; for I have sent them.'"[23] Are these the words of an abject inferior? "Set apart for me Barnabas and Saul for the work to which I have called them."[24] Does a slave give commands like this? Isaiah says, "The Lord God and his Spirit have sent me,"[25] and "the Spirit came down from the Lord and led them."[26] Do not try again to convince me that this "leading" by the Spirit is some lowly service. Scripture testifies that it is the work of God: "He led forth his people like sheep," it says, and "You who lead Joseph like a flock,"[27] and "He led them in safety so that they were not afraid." Therefore, when you hear that "the Comforter will bring to remembrance all that I have said to you and will guide you into all truth,"[28] do not quibble over the meaning. ON THE HOLY SPIRIT 19.49.[29]

---

[13]WSA 3 4:311*. [14]"This" refers to Jesus Christ, who said, "I am the way and the truth and the life. No one comes to the Father except through me" (Jn 14:6). [15]Jn 1:1. [16]Jn 1:14. [17]FC 79:48*. [18]Is 29:13; Mk 7:6. [19]Ps 62:4 (61:5 LXX). [20]Ps 31:18 (30:19 LXX). [21]Ps 12:3-5 (11:4-6 LXX). [22]LCC 1:50. [23]Acts 10:20. [24]Acts 13:2. [25]Is 48:16. [26]Is 63:14 (LXX). [27]Ps 80:1 (79:2 LXX). [28]Jn 14:26; 16:13. [29]OHS 78*.

GOD WAKES AND PUNISHES HIS ENEMIES.
THEODORET OF CYR: The blessed David fell into several errors, which God, who wisely orders all things, has caused to be recorded for the good of them that were to come after. But it was not on their account that Absalom,[30] parricide, murderer, impious and altogether vile, started his wild war against his father. The reason of his beginning that most unrighteous struggle was because he coveted the sovereignty. The divine David, however, when these events were coming to pass, began to remember the wrong that he had done. I too am conscious within myself of the guilt of many errors, but I have kept undefiled the dogmatic teaching of the apostles. And they who have trampled on all laws human and divine and condemned me in my absence have not sentenced me for what I have done wrong, for my secret deeds are not made manifest to them; but they have contrived false witness and false charges against me, or rather in their open attack on the doctrines of the apostles have proscribed me for my obedience to them.[31] "So the Lord awoke as one out of sleep; he put his enemies to rout and put them to everlasting disgrace." Counterfeit and spurious doctrines he has scattered to the winds, and he has provided for the free preaching of those which he has handed down

to us in the holy Gospels. To me this suffices for complete delight. I do not even long for a city in which I have passed all my time in hard work; all I long for is to see the establishment of the truth of the Gospels. And now the Lord has satisfied this longing. I am therefore very glad and happy, and I sing praises to our generous Lord, and I invite your honor to rejoice with me, and, with our praises, to put up the earnest prayer that the people who say now one thing and now another and change about to suit the hour, like the chameleons who assume the color of the leaves, may be strengthened by the loving-kindness of the Lord, established on the rocks and, of his mercy, made to pay the highest honor to the truth. LETTER 137.[32]

---

[30]2 Sam 13-18. [31]Theodoret, who was caught up in the controversies between orthodoxy and the Nestorian and Eutychian/Monophysitic heresies, was ordered confined to his diocese as a troublemaker and busybody by an edict of Emperor Theodosius II. He was later condemned by the heretical Robber Synod at Ephesus in 449 and imprisoned. He was exonerated at the Council of Chalcedon in 451, when he yielded to the pressure to personally condemn Nestorius. It is not known whether he returned to his work in Cyrus or went into secluded retirement at Nicerte. [32]NPNF 2 3:306-7*. This letter is addressed to the archimandrite (the head of a monastery) John. There was an archimandrite by this name who was present at the Council of Chalcedon, but there is no evidence that this is the same individual.

79:1-13 A PRAYER FOR FORGIVENESS, HELP AND JUDGMENT ON ENEMY NATIONS

A Psalm of Asaph.

[1]*O God, the heathen have come into thy inheritance;*

> *they have defiled thy holy temple;*
> *they have laid Jerusalem in ruins.*

[2]*They have given the bodies of thy servants*

> *to the birds of the air for food,*
> *the flesh of thy saints to the beasts of the earth.*

[3]*They have poured out their blood like water round about Jerusalem,*

> *and there was none to bury them.*

[4]*We have become a taunt to our neighbors,*

mocked and derided by those round
    about us.

[5]How long, O Lord? Wilt thou be angry for
    ever?
    Will thy jealous wrath burn like fire?
[6]Pour out thy anger on the nations
    that do not know thee,
and on the kingdoms
    that do not call on thy name!
[7]For they have devoured Jacob,
    and laid waste his habitation.

[8]Do not remember against us the iniquities of
    our forefathers;
    let thy compassion come speedily to meet us,
    for we are brought very low.
[9]Help us, O God of our salvation,
    for the glory of thy name;
deliver us, and forgive our sins,

for thy name's sake!
[10]Why should the nations say,
    "Where is their God?"
Let the avenging of the outpoured blood of thy
    servants
    be known among the nations before our eyes!

[11]Let the groans of the prisoners come before
    thee;
    according to thy great power preserve those
    doomed to die!
[12]Return sevenfold into the bosom of our
    neighbors
    the taunts with which they have taunted
    thee, O Lord!
[13]Then we thy people, the flock of thy pasture,
    will give thanks to thee for ever;
    from generation to generation we will
    recount thy praise.

OVERVIEW: In time of great slaughter, the un-buried bodies of Christians attest more to the cruelty of the perpetrator than the plight of the victim (AUGUSTINE). God becomes angry at sin but remains faithful and forgiving to those whom he chastises.

Scripture employs anthropomorphic descriptions of God, which are nonfactual but useful in assisting us in our understanding of God's activity (GREGORY OF NAZIANZUS). While we do not deserve God's pity, God did take pity on us and redeems us in Christ. In times of temporal calamity, God's vengeance on the enemy attests to the reality and presence of the true God (AUGUSTINE).

79:1-4 The Protecting Care of God

UNBURIED BODIES OF BELIEVERS. AUGUSTINE: "But many could not even be buried, in all

that welter of carnage."[1] Religious faith does not dread even that. We have the assurance that the ravenous beasts will not hinder the resurrection of bodies of which not a single hair of the head will perish. He who is the Truth would not say, "Do not fear those who kill the body but cannot kill the soul,"[2] if the future life could be hindered by anything that the foe chose to do with the bodies of the slain. Unless anyone is so absurd as to contend that those who kill the body should not be dreaded before death, for fear that they should kill the body, and yet should be dreaded after death, for fear that they should not allow the corpse to be buried! In that case Christ spoke falsely about "those who kill the body and have nothing that they can do after that,"[3] if they can do so much with the corpses. Perish the thought,

---

[1]The reference is to all the people who were slaughtered and left unburied in Alaric's sack of Rome in 409. [2]Mt 10:28. [3]Lk 12:4.

that the Truth could lie! The reason for saying that they do something when they kill is that there is feeling in the body when it is killed; but after that they have nothing they can do, since there is no feeling in a body that has been killed.

And so many Christian bodies have not received a covering of earth, and yet no one has separated any of them from heaven and earth, and the whole universe is filled with the presence of him who knows from where he is to raise up what he has created. The psalm says, "They have set out the mortal parts of your servants as food for the birds of the sky and the flesh of your saints as food for the beasts of the earth. They have shed their blood like water all round Jerusalem, and there was no one to bury them." But this was said to underline the cruelty of the acts, not to stress the misfortune of the sufferers; for although their sufferings seem harsh and terrible in the eyes of people, yet "the death of his saints is precious in the eyes of God."[4]

Such things as a decent funeral and a proper burial, with its procession of mourners, are a consolation to the living rather than a help to the departed. If an expensive burial is any advantage to the godless, then a cheap funeral, or no funeral at all, will prove a hindrance to the poor religious person. A crowd of dependants provided the rich person in his purple with a funeral that was splendid in the eyes of people, but a funeral much more splendid in God's sight was provided for the poor person by the ministering angels, who did not escort him to a marble tomb but carried him up to Abraham's bosom. CITY OF GOD 1.12.[5]

GOD IS ANGRY AT SIN. GREGORY OF NAZIANZUS: If you shut the heavens, who will open them? And if you let loose your torrents, who will restrain them? It is an easy thing in your eyes to make some people poor and others rich, to make some alive and to kill others, to strike some with illness and to heal others. Whatever you do according to your will is perfect. You are angry, and we have sinned, someone said long ago, in making confession. Now it is time for me to say

the opposite, "We have sinned, and you are angry"; therefore "we have become a reproach to our neighbors." You turned your face from us, and we were filled with dishonor. But stay, Lord; cease, Lord; forgive, Lord; deliver us not up forever because of our iniquities, and let not our chastisements be a warning for others, when we might learn wisdom from the trials of others. ON HIS FATHER'S SILENCE, ORATION 16.12.[6]

79:5-10 God Remembers and Pities His People

DIVINE ACTIVITY IS OFTEN DESCRIBED IN HUMAN TERMS. GREGORY OF NAZIANZUS: Some things mentioned in the Bible are not factual; some factual things are not mentioned; some nonfactual things receive no mention there; some things are both factual and mentioned. Do you ask for my proofs here? I am ready to offer them. In the Bible, God "sleeps,"[7] "wakes up,"[8] "is angered," "walks"[9] and has a "throne of cherubim."[10] Yet when has God ever been subject to emotion? When do you ever hear that God is a bodily being? This is a nonfactual, mental picture. We have used names derived from human experience and applied them so far as we could, to aspects of God. His retirement from us, for reason known to himself into an almost unconcerned inactivity, is his "sleeping." Human sleeping, after all, has the character of restful inaction. When he alters and suddenly benefits us, that is his "waking up." Waking up puts an end to sleep, just as looking at somebody puts an end to turning away from him. We have made his punishing us, his "being angered"; for with us, punishment is born of anger. His acting in different places, we call "walking," for walking is a transition from one place to another. His resting among the heavenly powers, making them almost his haunt, we call his "sitting" and "being enthroned"; this too

---

[4]Ps 116:15 (115:6 LXX, Vg.). [5]CG 21-22*. [6]NPNF 2 7:251**. [7]E.g., Ps 44:23 (43:23 LXX). [8]Jer 31:26 (38:26 LXX). [9]Gen 3:8. [10]Is 37:16; Ps 80:1 (79:2 LXX).

is human language. The divine, in fact, rests nowhere as he rests in the saints. God's swift motion we call "flight;"[11] his watching over us is his "face";[12] his giving and receiving is his "hand."[13] In short every faculty or activity of God has given us a corresponding picture in terms of some thing bodily. ON THE HOLY SPIRIT, THEOLOGICAL ORATION 5[31].22.[14]

GOD'S PITY IS DUE TO HIS GRACE, NOT OUR MERIT.

AUGUSTINE: There, at last, gaze on "In the beginning was the Word."[15] The Word was not, you see, made at some time or other; but it just was in the beginning. Not like creation, of which it is said, "In the beginning God made heaven and earth."[16] As for the Word that was in the beginning, there was no time when it was not. So this that "was in the beginning, and was the Word with God, and the Word itself was God; and all things were made through him, and without him was nothing made"; and in him "what was made is life."[17] This Word came to us. To whom? To us as worthy? Perish the thought! No, but to us as unworthy. After all, "Christ died for the ungodly,"[18] and the unworthy, while being worthy himself. We were unworthy, you see, for him to have pity on; but he was worthy to take pity on us, to be told, "Because of your pity, Lord, deliver us." Not because of any previous merits of ours, but "because of your pity, Lord, deliver us; and be lenient with our sins, because of your name," not because of our merit. Obviously, not because of the merit of our sins, but "because of

your name." I mean, the merit of our sins, of course, is not reward but revenge. So therefore, "because of your name." SERMON 293.5.[19]

GOD IS PRESENT EVERYWHERE.

AUGUSTINE: But there are those who jeer at their[20] integrity. When any temporal disaster comes on God's servants, such people ask, "Where is your God now?"[21] Let those scoffers tell us where their gods are, when the same things happen to them. After all, it is to escape from such evils that they worship their gods—or maintain that they should be worshiped.

The Christian's answer is this: My God is present everywhere and wholly present everywhere. No limits confine him. He can be present without showing himself: he can depart without moving. When I am troubled with adversity, he is either testing my worth or punishing my faults. And he has an eternal reward in store for me in return for loyal endurance of temporal distress. But why should I deign to discuss your God with people like you? Still less should I speak with you about my God, who "is to be feared above all gods; since all the gods of the nations are demons; while the Lord made the heavens."[22] CITY OF GOD 1.29.[23]

---

[11]E.g., Ps 18:10 (17:11 LXX). [12]Ps 4:6 (4:7 LXX); 34:16 (33:17 LXX). [13]Ps 145:16 (144:16 LXX). [14]FGFR 290-91. [15]Jn 1:1. [16]Gen 1:1. [17]Jn 1:1-4. [18]Rom 5:6. [19]WSA 3 8:152. [20]Followers of Christ [21]Ps 42:3 (41:4 LXX, Vg.); 79:10 (78:10 LXX, Vg.). [22]Ps 96:4-5 (95:4-5 LXX, Vg.). [23]CG 41.

80:1-19 A PRAYER FOR RESTORATION

To the choirmaster: according to Lilies. A Testimony of Asaph. A Psalm.

[1]*Give ear, O Shepherd of Israel, thou who leadest Joseph like a flock!*

Thou who art enthroned upon the
    cherubim, shine forth
²before Ephraim and Benjamin
    and Manasseh!
Stir up thy might,
    and come to save us!

³Restore us, O God;
    let thy face shine, that we may be saved!

⁴O LORD God of hosts,
    how long wilt thou be angry with thy
    people's prayers?
⁵Thou hast fed them with the bread of tears,
    and given them tears to drink in full
    measure.
    ⁶Thou dost make us the scornᵏ of our
    neighbors;
and our enemies laugh among themselves.

⁷Restore us, O God of hosts;
    let thy face shine, that we may be saved!

⁸Thou didst bring a vine out of Egypt;
    thou didst drive out the nations and plant it.
⁹Thou didst clear the ground for it;
    it took deep root and filled the land.

¹⁰the mountains were covered with its shade,
    the mighty cedars with its branches;
¹¹it sent out its branches to the sea,
    and its shoots to the River.
¹²Why then hast thou broken down its walls,
    so that all who pass along the way pluck
    its fruit?
¹³The boar from the forest ravages it,
    and all that move in the field feed on it.

¹⁴Turn again, O God of hosts!
    Look down from heaven, and see;
have regard for this vine,
    ¹⁵the stock which thy right hand planted.ˡ
¹⁶They have burned it with fire, they have cut
    it down;
    may they perish at the rebuke of thy
    countenance!
¹⁷But let thy hand be upon the man of thy right
    hand,
    the son of man whom thou hast made strong
    for thyself!
¹⁸Then we will never turn back from thee;
    give us life, and we will call on thy name!

¹⁹Restore us, O LORD God of hosts!
    let thy face shine, that we may be saved!

k Syr: Heb *strife*   l Heb *planted and upon the son whom thou hast reared for thyself*

OVERVIEW: The petitions of the Lord's Prayer have counterparts already in the psalms, and every prayer should be in harmony with it. Our souls should be attracted to God, who is eternal, not to the things of this world, which come into being and in turn cease to exist (AUGUSTINE). We are cleansed from our sins by repentance, not through the endurance of punishments, which are appropriate to the sins committed (CAESARIUS). The conversion of people to faith in Christ is a result of God's grace and mercy, and it comes through humiliation so that they will be motivated to seek him (AUGUSTINE).

The wild beasts (Ps 80:13) also symbolized personal enemies who defame the good reputation of others (JEROME).

While God does not forget his promise to Israel, it is the apostles and the growing number of Gentile converts that constitute God's new vineyard. Both one's coming to faith and one's preservation in the faith is the work of God (AUGUSTINE).

80:1-3 *The Eternal Ruler and Savior*

PRAY IN A SPIRITUAL MANNER. AUGUSTINE: For whatever other words we may say, whatever words the fervor of the suppliant utters at the beginning of his petition to define it[1] or follows up afterward to intensify it, we say nothing that is not found in this prayer of the Lord, if we pray properly and fittingly. But whoever says anything in his prayer that does not accord with this Gospel prayer, even if his prayer is not of the forbidden sort, it is carnal, and I am not sure it ought not to be called forbidden, since those who are born again of the Spirit[2] ought to pray only in a spiritual manner. For instance, he who says, "Be sanctified among all people, as you have been sanctified among us,"[3] and, "May your prophets be found faithful,"[4] what else does he say but "Hallowed be your name"? And he who says, "O God of hosts, convert us and show your face, and we will be saved," what else does he say but "Your kingdom come"? He who says, "Direct my steps according to your word, and let no iniquity have dominion over me,"[5] what else does he say but "Your will be done on earth as it is in heaven"? He who says, "Give me neither poverty nor riches,"[6] what else does he say but "Give us this day our daily bread"? He who says, "O Lord, remember David and all his meekness,"[7] or "Lord, if I have done this thing, if there be iniquity in my hands, if I have rendered to them that have repaid me evils,"[8] what else does he say but "Forgive us our debts as we also forgive our debtors"? He who says, "Take from me the greediness of the belly and let not the lusts of the flesh take hold of me,"[9] what else does he say but "Lead us not into temptation"? He who says, "Deliver me from my enemies, O God, and defend me from them that rise up against me,"[10] what else does he say but "Deliver us from evil"? And if you were to run over all the words of holy prayers, you would find nothing, according to my way of thinking, that is not contained and included in the Lord's Prayer. Hence when we pray, it is allowable to say the same things in different words, but it ought not to be allowable to say different things. LETTER 130.[11]

LOVE NOT THE PERISHABLE THINGS OF THIS WORLD. AUGUSTINE: "O God of hosts, restore us to our own; smile on us, and we shall find deliverance." For wherever the soul of a person may turn, unless it turns to you, it clasps sorrow to itself. Even though it clings to things of beauty, if their beauty is outside God and outside the soul, it only clings to sorrow.

Yet these things of beauty would not exist at all unless they came from you. Like the sun, they rise and set. At their rise they have their first beginning; they grow until they reach perfection; but, once they have reached it, they grow old and die. Not all reach old age, but all alike must die. When they rise, therefore, they are set on the course of their existence, and the faster they climb toward its zenith, the more they hasten toward the point where they exist no more. This is the law they obey. This is all that you have appointed for them, because they are parts of a whole. Not all the parts exist at once, but some must come as others go, and in this way together they make up the whole of which they are the parts. Our speech follows the same rule, using sounds to signify a meaning. For a sentence is not complete unless each word, once its syllables have been pronounced, gives way to make room for the next. Let my soul praise you for these things, O God, Creator of them all; but the love of them, which we feel, through the senses of the body, must not be like glue to bind my soul to them. For they continue on the course that is set for them and leads to their end, and if the soul loves them and wishes to be with them and finds its rest in them, it is torn by desires that can destroy it. In these things there is no place to rest,

---

[1]Augustine wrote this letter in about 412 to Proba, a noble Roman lady who had fled to Africa to escape the barbarian invasion of Italy and asked him to write something on the subject of prayer to God. [2]Jn 3:5. [3]Sir 36:4. [4]Sir 36:18. [5]Ps 119:133 (118:133 LXX, Vg.). [6]Prov 30:8. [7]Ps 132:1 (131:1 LXX, Vg.). [8]Ps 7:3-4 (7:4-5 LXX, Vg.). [9]Sir 23:6. [10]Ps 59:1 (58:2 LXX, Vg.). [11]FC 18:392-94.

because they do not last. They pass away beyond the reach of our senses. Indeed, none of us can lay firm hold of them even when they are with us. For the senses of the body are sluggish, because they are the senses of flesh and blood. They are limited by their own nature. They are sufficient for the purposes for which they were made, but they cannot halt the progress of transient things, which pass from their allotted beginning to their allotted end. All such things are created by your word, which tells them, "Here is your beginning, and here your end." Confessions 4.10.[12]

80:5-7 Divine Punishment and Humanity's Cry for Mercy

Divine Punishment Is Commensurate with People's Sins. Caesarius of Arles: We have said this, brothers, so that you may know that in the Old Testament God's justice orders a year's punishment to make up for the sin of one day. In other words, the people were tormented in the desert for forty years because of the defection of forty days. What will happen to us if, after receiving the grace of Christ who redeemed us with his own blood, we still take pleasure in committing not only slight sins but perhaps even criminal offenses? Therefore, as I have frequently advised, if a person knows he has committed some serious sin, he should have recourse to the remedies of repentance while there is still time and it is within his power to do so. Indeed, conversion in the present life and penance that is fruitfully performed bring a swift cure to wounds of this kind, for repentance not only heals a past wound but also guards the soul against further injury through sin. Now I will add something more. For example, if I am a sinner will I suffer the same punishment if I have offended just once, as I will if I sin twice or a third time and even more frequently? Not at all. The amount of punishment is to be measured according to the manner, number and measure of sin, for God will give us "the bread of tears and tears to drink," but "with ample measure." Every person will then

reap the things he sought in this life by sinning more or less. Sermon 108.4.[13]

A Prayer for Conversion. Augustine: Conversion itself is from the grace of him to whom it is said, "God of hosts, convert us." Perhaps this must also be understood as done out of the mercy of the heavenly medicine so that people who possessed a proud and wicked will and wanted to establish their own justice might be abandoned for the purpose of being blinded. Perhaps they were blinded for the purpose of stumbling on the stone of stumbling and that their face might be filled with shame. Also, so that humbled they might seek the name of the Lord and not their own justice, by which the proud are puffed up, but God's justice by which the ungodly are justified? For this benefited many of them for their good, who, pricked with remorse over their own wrongdoing, afterwards believed in Christ; and for these he had even prayed himself, saying, "Father, forgive them, for they know not what they do."[14] And about this ignorance of theirs the apostle, too, said, "I bear them witness that they have a zeal for God, but not according to knowledge." For then he also added this and said, "For, not knowing God's justice and seeking to establish their own, they have not submitted themselves to the justice of God."[15] Tractates on the Gospel of John 53.11.[16]

80:8-13 God's People and Their Hardships

Wronged by False Accusations. Jerome: What is there in human life that can be safe if innocence is made the object of accusation?[17] I am the householder who finds that while he slept the enemy has sown tares among his wheat. "The wild boar out of the wood has rooted up my vineyard,

---

[12]AC 80-81. [13]FC 47:138*. [14]Lk 23:34. [15]Rom 10:2-3. [16]FC 88:298**. [17]Jerome is responding to claims that he wrote a letter in which he repents of a rash youthful urge to translate the Old Testament into Latin from the Hebrew original instead of from the Septuagint. The claim that the letter was his was an attempt to discredit him.

and the strange wild beast has devoured it." I keep silence, but a letter that is not mine speaks against me. I am ignorant of the crime laid against me, yet I am made to confess the crime all through the world. "Woe is me, my mother, that you have borne me a man to be judged and condemned in the whole earth." AGAINST RUFINUS 2.24.[18]

80:15-19 God Has Regard for His People

THINGS SHALL BE CHANGED. AUGUSTINE: Psalm 79 [LXX] is similarly titled "For the things that shall be changed."[19] In this psalm, among other things, is written, "look down from heaven and see; visit this vineyard and perfect what your right hand has planted and on the son of man whom you have confirmed for yourself."[20] This is the vineyard of which it is said, "You have brought a vineyard out of Egypt."[21] Christ did not plant another; by his coming he changed that one into a better vineyard. Accordingly, we find in the Gospel: "He will utterly destroy those evil men, and will let out the vineyard to other vine dressers."[22] The Gospel does not say, "He will uproot and will plant another," but "this same vineyard he will let out to other vine dressers." The city of God and congregation of the children of promise must be filled with the same community of saints by the death and succession of mortal beings and at the end of the world will receive its due immortality in all people. This same thought is expressed differently by means of the fruitful olive tree in another psalm, which says, "But I as a fruitful olive tree in the house of God, have hoped in the mercy of God forever, yea, for ever and ever."[23] It was not because the unbelievers and the proud had been broken away and the branches were on that account unfruitful and the wild olive of the Gentiles was ingrafted that the root of the patriarchs and prophets died. Isaiah says, "For if your people, O Israel, shall be as the sand of the sea, a remnant of them shall be saved,"[24] but through him about whom the psalm says, "and on the son of man whom you have confirmed for yourself," and about whom is reiter-

ated, "Let your hand be on the man of your right hand: and on the son of man whom you have confirmed for yourself. And we depart not from you." Through this Son of man, Christ Jesus, and from his remnant, that is, the apostles and the many others from among the Israelites who have believed in Christ as God, and with the increasing number of Gentiles, the holy vineyard is being completed. Thus, in the passing of the old rites and in the institution of the new, the title of the psalm, "For the things that shall be changed," is fulfilled. IN ANSWER TO THE JEWS 6.7.[25]

DIVINE PREDESTINATION AND PRESERVATION. AUGUSTINE: This grace he has placed in him "in whom we have obtained our lot, being predestined according to the purpose of him who works all things."[26] And accordingly, just as he likewise brings it about that we should approach him, he brings it about that we not depart from him. For this reason it was said to him by the prophet, "Let your hand be on the man of your right hand, and on the son of man whom you have confirmed for yourself, and we depart not from you." This man is certainly not the first Adam, in whom we departed from God, but the second Adam, on whom is placed the hand of God, that we not depart from him. For Christ is complete, with all his members, because of the church, which is his body and his fullness.[27] So when the hand of God is on him, that we not depart from God, then the work of God (for this is what is meant by his hand) reaches indeed to us. For in Christ "we have obtained our lot, being predestined according to the purpose of him who works all things." Therefore it is by God's hand, not our own, that we depart not from God. This is his hand, I say, who declared, "I will put fear of me into their hearts, that they may not revolt from me."[28] ON THE GIFT OF PERSEVERANCE 7.14.[29]

---

[18]NPNF 2 3:515*. [19]See Ps 79:1 (LXX). [20]Ps 80:14-15 (79:15-16 LXX, Vg.). [21]Ps 80:8 (79:9 LXX, Vg.). [22]Mt 21:41. [23]Ps 52:8 (51:10 LXX, Vg.). [24]Is 10:22. [25]FC 27:399-400**. [26]Eph 1:11. [27]See Eph 1:23. [28]Jer 32:40. [29]FC 86:281-82*.

81:1-16 A FESTIVAL SONG

To the choirmaster: according to The
Gittith. A Psalm of Asaph.

^{1}Sing aloud to God our strength;
  shout for joy to the God of Jacob!
^{2}Raise a song, sound the timbrel,
  the sweet lyre with the harp.
^{3}Blow the trumpet at the new moon,
  at the full moon, on our feast day.
^{4}For it is a statute for Israel,
  an ordinance of the God of Jacob.
^{5}He made it a decree in Joseph,
  when he went out over^m the land of Egypt.

I hear a voice I had not known:
^{6}"I relieved your^n shoulder of the burden;
  your^n hands were freed from the basket.
^{7}In distress you called, and I delivered you;
  I answered you in the secret place of
    thunder;
  I tested you at the waters of Meribah.   Selah
^{8}Hear, O my people, while I admonish you!

O Israel, if you would but listen to me!
^{9}There shall be no strange god among you;
  you shall not bow down to a foreign god.
^{10}I am the LORD your God,
  who brought you up out of the land of Egypt.
  Open your mouth wide, and I will fill it.

^{11}"But my people did not listen to my voice;
  Israel would have none of me.
^{12}So I gave them over to their stubborn hearts,
  to follow their own counsels.
^{13}O that my people would listen to me,
  that Israel would walk in my ways!
^{14}I would soon subdue their enemies,
  and turn my hand against their foes.
^{15}Those who hate the LORD would cringe
    toward him,
  and their fate would last for ever.
^{16}I would feed you^o with the finest of the wheat,
  and with honey from the rock I would
    satisfy you."

m Or *against*   n Heb *his*   o Cn Compare verse 16b: Heb *he would feed him*

OVERVIEW: The use of the trumpet in worship reminds people of God's appearance on Mount Sinai and his great act of deliverance of Israel from Egypt (THEODORET). Ancient secular authors attest not only to the power of music but also to miraculous events in the Old Testament (CASSIODORUS).

Heresies that subordinate the second person of the Trinity to a secondary and intermediate position between God and creation violate the first commandment, because they have created a second god. Christ in his state of humiliation and *kenosis* did not become another god but remained one God, consubstantial with the Father (CYRIL OF ALEXANDRIA). People who forsake God, deny Christ and teach false doctrine bring eternal punishment on themselves (THEODORET). In Canaan, God fed Israel with the fatness of wheat to show the abundance of his grace, and after his resurrection Christ ate honey to show the sweetness of the Gospel message (JEROME).

81:3-4 The Sound of the Trumpet

THE SIGNIFICANCE OF THE TRUMPET. THEODORET OF CYR: "Blow the trumpet at the new moon, on our festival day of good omen. Because it is a command for Israel, a judgment of the God of Jacob." God ordered the priests to use the trumpets. They reminded the people of the trumpets used on the mountain: when the God of all spoke on Mount Sinai, [Scripture] says, there was a loud noise of the trumpet.[1] So when the priests used the trumpets, they reminded the people of that appearance. Consequently, they were right to command those who had been granted return and had enjoyed the divine assistance to make use of the trumpets along with the other instruments. COMMENTARY ON THE PSALMS 81.3.[2]

THE POWER OF MUSIC. CASSIODORUS: "Blow up the trumpet at the beginning of the month, on the day of your noted solemnity." . . . It should be observed that we are enjoined to hymn the Lord and celebrate the solemn day with instruments for musical performance; just as those instruments sweetly combine to produce pleasant melody and a single harmony, so all our actions can be directed to the Lord and offered to his ears with the most pleasant intonation. The discipline of music incorporates great power and knowledge that brings delight; teachers of secular literature, through the generosity of God who grants all that is useful have made it possible through theoretical texts to ascertain what was earlier regarded as hidden from view in the nature of the world.[3] The first division of this discipline, then, is into harmonics, rhythmics and metrics. The second division, that of musical instruments, is between percussion, strings and wind. The third division is into six harmonies, the fourth into fifteen tones. In this way the virtue of this most beautiful discipline is unfolded by distinctions made a long time ago. We read in secular works that many miracles were brought forth by these measures.[4] But we need say nothing of this fabulous material; we read that by means of David's tuneful harp the demon was expelled from Saul.[5] The divine reading attests that the walls of Jericho at once collapsed at the din of trumpets.[6] So there is no doubt that the sounds of music, at the Lord's command or with his permission, have unleashed great forces. EXPOSITIONS OF THE PSALMS 80.4.[7]

81:9 Christ Is Not a Second God

YOU SHALL HAVE NO OTHER GODS. CYRIL OF ALEXANDRIA: Who, then, is this one cast down from his divine preeminence and removed from the limitations of creation?[8] The matter is completely inconceivable, and there is no discernible place or manner of speaking of someone in between creator and creation. Although they dislodged him from the throne of divinity, they have arrived at a point in their teaching that they call him the Son and God and think that he is to be adored although the law openly proclaims, "The Lord your God shall you worship and him only shall you serve,"[9] and although God said to the Israelites through the voice of David, "There shall be no new god among you, nor shall you adore a foreign god." LETTER 1.13.[10]

CHRIST REMAINED GOD DURING HIS STATE OF HUMILIATION. CYRIL OF ALEXANDRIA: That it is none other than God the Word, who exists in the form of God the Father, the impress of his very being,[11] who is equal in all things to the one who begot him, who has emptied himself out. And what is this "emptying out"? It is his life in the form of a slave, in the flesh that he assumes, it is the likeness to us of one who is not as we are in his own nature, since he is above all creation. In this way he humbled himself, economically submitting himself to the limitations of humanity. But even so he was God, for he did not have as a gift what pertained to him by nature. This was

---

[1]Ex 19:16, loosely recalled. [2]FC 102:51-2. [3]See his Institutes 2.5, as well as Augustine's De Musica and Boethius's De Institutione Musica. [4]The playing of musical instruments. There is a good summary of ancient musical theory in Winnington-Ingram's revised article ("Music") in the OCD. [5]See 1 Sam 16:23. [6]Josh 6:20. [7]ACW 52:294-95. [8]Cyril is here referring to the Arian heretics who considered the Son of God to be a middle being, intermediate between God and human beings. [9]Mt 4:10; Deut 6:13. [10]FC 76:18. [11]See Heb 1:3.

why he also said to God the Father who is in heaven, "Father, glorify me with that glory I had with you before the world was."[12] I do not think that they would say that it was David's descendant, born in the last times of this age, who was reclaiming as his own a glory that predated the world, at least if he is a different son and distinct from the true and natural Son? No, surely this is a saying that befits the Godhead? It was necessary, yes necessary, that he should be conformed to us in the limitations of humanity while at the same time he authentically enjoyed transcendent divine status within his own essential being; just as it is with the Father. How can the saying be true: "You must not introduce another god among you," if according to them[13] a man is deified by a conjunction with the Word and is said to be enthroned with God so as to share the Father's dignity? ON THE UNITY OF CHRIST.[14]

81:13-16 God's Judgment on Those Who Are False to Him

THE PENALTY FOR IMPIETY AND FALSE TEACHING. THEODORET OF CYR: "If my people listened to me, if Israel traveled in my ways, I would have reduced their foes to nothing and laid my hand on those afflicting them." If they had adhered to my advice and followed my commandments, I would easily have destroyed their foes. "To nothing" suggests the facility—in other words, easily and without trouble I would have been able to bring about their ruin in an instant. "The Lord's foes were false to him."[15] Aquila . . . put it this way: "in their hatred they will deny the Lord." By denying Christ the Lord, they brought hatred on themselves, and by being false to him and to the existing covenants they made themselves enemies of the Lord. After the giving of the law, [Scripture] says that the people replied, "All that the Lord God has said we will do and listen to."[16] While their promises were of this kind, their words were the direct opposite—they cruci-

fied their own Lord when he appeared and received a penalty for their impiety, namely, eternal ruin. This was true not only of them but also of Arius, Eunomius, Nestorius[17] and the devotees of their teachings. COMMENTARY ON THE PSALMS 81.8.[18]

FED WITH WHEAT AND HONEY. JEROME: "And he fed them with the fat of wheat."[19] He led them into the land of promise. He fed them, not with manna as in the desert, but the wheat that had fallen, that had risen again. "And he fed them with the fat of wheat." Be sure you penetrate the mystery in the scriptural words: "With the finest of wheat." Does wheat have fat? Does it also have intestines? The prophet wanted to show the abundance and richness of spiritual grace, and hence he called it fat. "And with honey from the rock he would fill them." He is the wheat; he also is the rock[20] who quenches the thirst of the Israelites in the desert. He satisfied their thirst spiritually with honey, and not with water, so that they who believe and receive the food taste honey in their mouth. "How sweet to my palate are your promises, sweeter than honey to my mouth!"[21] Lastly, that is why our Lord ate honeycomb after the resurrection and was satisfied with honey from the rock. I am going to tell you something new. The Rock himself ate honey in order to give us honey and sweetness, so that they who in the law had drunk myrrh, or bitterness, might afterwards eat the honey of the Gospel.[22] HOMILIES ON THE PSALMS 13.[23]

---

[12]Jn 17:5. [13]The Nestorian heretics. [14]OUC 86. This is possibly Cyril's last work on Nestorianism. [15]Theodoret is here giving the translation of Symmachus as he contrasts his translation with that of Aquila. Both Symmachus and Aquila translated the Old Testament into Greek. Their translations were reproduced by Origen in his *Hexapla*. [16]Ex 24:3. [17]Three christological heretics who were condemned by the church in the third and fourth centuries. [18]FC 102:54-5**. [19]"The fat of wheat" is usually translated as "the finest of wheat." [20]See 1 Cor 10:4. [21]Ps 119:103 (118:103 LXX, Vg.). [22]See 1 Cor 10:3-4; Ex 16:31. [23]FC 48:100-101*.

82:1-8 A WORD OF JUDGMENT
ON UNJUST RULERS AND JUDGES

A Psalm of Asaph.

¹*God has taken his place in the divine council;*
in the midst of the gods he holds judgment:
²*"How long will you judge unjustly*
and show partiality to the wicked?   Selah
³*Give justice to the weak and the fatherless;*
maintain the right of the afflicted and the
destitute.
⁴*Rescue the weak and the needy;*
deliver them from the hand of the wicked."

⁵*They have neither knowledge nor*
understanding,
they walk about in darkness;
all the foundations of the earth are shaken.

⁶*I say, "You are gods,*
sons of the Most High, all of you;
⁷*nevertheless, you shall die like men,*
and fall like any prince."ᵖ

⁸*Arise, O God, judge the earth;*
for to thee belong all the nations!

p Or *fall as one man, O princes*

OVERVIEW: No human being deserves the name of the transcendent Godhead, but individuals who live very godly lives do deserve to be called divine (PSEUDO-DIONYSIUS). In his eternal kingdom God will govern the redeemed, meting out appropriate honors and heavenly abodes (GREGORY OF NAZIANZUS). Sin is the result of living in spiritual darkness and being ignorant of divine matters (ORIGEN). The Holy Spirit enables us to understand what Scripture means when it says that human beings are gods (CYRIL OF JERUSALEM). God's relation with Old Testament Israel was that of Master, not Father, because they often despised him and disobeyed his law (AUGUSTINE). Scripture used the name God in a fourfold sense; two of those senses are God himself, who is God by nature, and believers, who are called gods in the sense of being children of God by adoption (FULGENTIUS). The title God is appropriate only to the persons of the Holy Trinity, but believers are called children and gods by the grace of God, not by nature (CASSIODORUS). Christ became incarnate so that people who accept him

can become children of God (THEODORET).

God tests the righteous by allowing them to experience sufferings and insults but holds in store for them a future treasure (GREGORY OF NAZIANZUS). We can be heirs of the heritage that God will give us only because Christ died for us, since an inheritance is bestowed only after a death has occurred (JEROME).

82:1-7 People Who Are Called "Gods"

SAINTLY PEOPLE ARE CALLED "GODS."
PSEUDO-DIONYSIUS: You will also notice how God's word gives the title of "gods" not only to those heavenly beings who are our superiors[1] but also to those sacred people among us who are distinguished for their love of God.[2] Now the hiddenness of the Godhead is a transcendent one. It is far above everything. No being can in any way or as a matter of right have a name like it. Yet

[1]See also Ps 95:3 (94:3 LXX); Gen 32:28-30. [2]Ex 4:16; 7:1; Ps 46:5 (Ps 45:6 LXX); Jn 10:34.

every intelligent and reasonable person who returns to God to be united with him, strives to be enlightened by divine matters and tries as hard as possible to imitate God deserves to be called divine. CELESTIAL HIERARCHY 12.3.[3]

THE REDEEMED ARE CONSIDERED "GODS."
GREGORY OF NAZIANZUS: He is said to reign in one sense as the almighty King, both of the willing and the unwilling, but in another as producing in us submission and placing us under his kingship as willingly acknowledging his sovereignty. Of his kingdom, considered in the former sense, there shall be no end. But in the second sense, what end will there be? His taking us as his servants, on our entrance into a state of salvation. For what need is there to work submission in us when we have already submitted? After which he arises to judge the earth and to separate the saved from the lost. After that he is to stand as God in the midst of gods, that is, of the saved, distinguishing and deciding of what honor and of what mansion each is worthy. ON THE SON, THEOLOGICAL ORATION 4[30].4.[4]

PEOPLE WHO WALK IN DARKNESS. ORIGEN: To walk in darkness indicates blameworthy action, and to hate one's own brother is to fall away from that which is properly called knowledge. But also because he who is ignorant of divine matters, by that very ignorance, walks in darkness, David says, "They have not known or understood; they walk in darkness." COMMENTARY ON THE GOSPEL OF JOHN 2.161.[5]

A DIVINE TITLE APPLIED TO HUMAN BEINGS.
CYRIL OF JERUSALEM: Look, I ask you, and see with how great a dignity Jesus favors you. You were called a catechumen, which means one into whom something is drummed from without.[6] You heard of some hope, but you did not know what. You heard mysteries without understanding anything. You heard Scriptures without plumbing their depth. It is not drummed in, any more, but whispered. For the indwelling Spirit is fashioning

your mind into mansions for God. When you hear, in the future, Scriptures concerning mysteries, you will understand things you knew nothing of. And do not esteem as if a trifle what you are receiving. Being but a wretched person, you are recipient of a divine title. For listen to Paul, "God is faithful,"[7] or to another text in Scripture, "God is faithful and just."[8] It was as foreseeing that a divine title would come to be applied to human beings that the psalmist, speaking in the person of God, said, "I have said, you are gods and are all the children of the most High." But see that when the title is faithful, the purpose is not faithless. You have entered the contest; run your course steadfastly. No other chance like this will come your way. If it was your wedding day ahead of you, would you not make light of all else, in preparing the banquet? When, then, you are going to consecrate your soul to the heavenly Bridegroom, will you not leave your physical concerns to chance, so that you may take a firm hold on the things of the spirit? CATECHETICAL LECTURES, PROCATECHESIS 6.[9]

GOD AS MASTER VERSUS GOD AS FATHER.
AUGUSTINE: In every kind of petition we ought first to try to gain the good will of the one we are petitioning and then to state the object of our petition. We usually try to gain the good will by bestowing praise on the one we are petitioning. And the praise is usually placed at the beginning of the prayer, where in this instance our Lord has bidden us to say nothing else than, "Our Father who is in heaven." Praise of God has been expressed in many manners of speech. Anyone can see this as he reads those forms of praise scattered widely here and there throughout the sacred Scriptures. But nowhere is there found any instruction for the people of Israel to say, "Our Father," or to pray to God as to a Father. To

---

[3]PDCW 176**. [4]NPNF 2 7:311*. [5]FC 80:137-38. [6]*Katechein* is to make resound. So a catechumen was literally one who was having the elements drummed into him. Cyril exaggerates a little here in order to raise the status of the *photizomenoi* (those who have been enlightened or instructed). [7]1 Cor 1:9. [8]1 Jn 1:9. [9]LCC 4:68-69**.

them he has been proposed as a Master, for they were servants; that is, they were as yet living according to the flesh. When I say this, I am referring to them when they received the commandments of the law that they were ordered to observe, for the prophets frequently point out that this same Lord of ours would have been their Father as well, if they did not stray from his commandments. For instance, there are the following expressions: "I have reared children and brought them up; but they have despised me,"[10] and, "I have said, 'You are gods, and all of you the children of the most High,'" and, "If I am a Master, where is my fear? And if I am a Father, where is my honor?"[11] Even if we were to disregard those prophetic sayings that refer to the fact that there would be a Christian people who would have God as their Father—in accordance with that saying in the Gospel, "He gave them the power of becoming children of God"[12]—there are still many other expressions whereby they are reproved for the fact that by committing sins they refused to be children. The apostle Paul says, "As long as the heir is a little child, he differs in no way from a slave,"[13] but he reminds us that we have received the spirit of adoption by virtue of which we cry, "Abba, Father."[14] SERMON ON THE MOUNT 2.4.15.[15]

BELIEVERS ARE MADE "GODS" BY GRACE. FULGENTIUS OF RUSPE: We find the name of God in the holy Scriptures, as many as now come to mind, spoken of in four ways. For God is spoken of according to the truth of [his divine] nature, that the holy Trinity is one, true and unchangeable God, who says, "See now that I, even I, am he; there is no God besides me."[16] And concerning whom David says, "For who is God except the Lord? And who is a rock besides our God?"[17] This is the one and only God who alone is God by nature. From this one true God, certain ones, in order that they might be gods, did not have the name by nature but received it by the gift of grace. Concerning such gods, it was Moses to whom that one true God said, "See, I have made

you like God to Pharaoh."[18] Of such people are also those to whom it is said, "I said, 'You are gods, children of the most High, all of you.'" Therefore, these gods received that grace to be gods so that they might become the children of God. The Evangelist says that "to those who did accept him, he gave power to become the children of God, to those who believe in his name, who were born, not by natural generation, or by human choice or by a man's decision, but of God."[19] Likewise, to them it is said, "I said, 'You are gods, children of the most High, all of you.'" LETTER 12.9.[20]

SONS AND GODS ARE TITLES RECEIVED BY GRACE. CASSIODORUS: "The God of gods, the Lord has spoken and called the earth from the rising of the sun to its setting."[21] So that no individual should believe that the Lord's incarnation is to be accorded but modest importance, his power is foretold beforehand, so that the debased nature of all unbelief may be removed. "Gods" is the title accorded to people who in their goodly life receive the grace of the heavenly Majesty; in his words of another psalm, "I have said, 'You are gods, and all of you children of the most High.'" They are called both children and gods because grace, not nature, grants them both titles. The God of gods is the Lord Christ; with the Father and Holy Spirit he is truly called God of gods. However, the title is not entirely appropriate to the Godhead since human language cannot, as we have already said, describe the mystery of the Godhead more than this. EXPOSITIONS OF THE PSALMS 49.1.[22]

BECOMING GOD'S CHILDREN. THEODORET OF CYR: "I have said you are gods and all of you children of the most High, but you shall die like man."[23] This he says to them that did not accept

---

[10]Is 1:2. [11]Mal 1:6. [12]Jn 1:12. [13]Gal 4:1. [14]Rom 8:15. [15]FC 11:122-3*. [16]Deut 32:39. [17]Ps 18:31 (17:32 LXX, Vg.). [18]Ex 7:1. [19]Jn 1:12-13. [20]FC 95:482*. [21]Ps 50:1 (49:1 LXX, Vg.). [22]ACW 51:480**. [23]Ps 82:6-7 (81:6-7 LXX).

the gift of adoption but dishonor the incarnation of the pure generation of the Word of God, deprive humankind of ascent to God and are ungrateful to the Word of God who for their sakes was made flesh. For this cause was the Word made human, that humanity receiving the Word and accepting the adoption should be made God's children.[24] DIALOGUE 1.[25]

82:8 The Hardships of the Faithful Are Temporary

GOD WILL JUDGE THE EARTH. GREGORY OF NAZIANZUS: Often were the righteous given into the hands of the wicked,[26] not that the latter might be honored but that the former might be tested; and though the wicked come, as it is written, to an awful death,[27] nevertheless for the present the godly are a laughing stock, while the goodness of God and the great treasuries of what is in store for each of them hereafter are concealed. Then indeed word and deed and thought will be weighed in the just balances of God, as he arises to judge the earth, gathering together counsel and works and revealing what he had kept sealed up. Of this let the words and sufferings of Job convince you, who was a truthful, blameless, just, God-fearing man, with all those other qualities that are testified of him, and yet he was struck with such a succession of remarkable visitations, at the hands of him who begged for power over him,[28] that, although many have often suffered in the whole course of time, and some have, as is probable, been grievously afflicted, yet none can be compared with him in misfortunes. ON THE GREAT ATHANASIUS, ORATION 21.17.[29]

HEIRS AND COHEIRS. JEROME: "For you shall inherit all the nations." We pray that you be judge because you have compassion on all nations. What was the prophet's intention in saying, "You shall inherit all the nations," instead of, you shall have all the nations? Whenever an inheritance has been bestowed, death has preceded; hence, we are called heirs and coheirs. Heirs, the apostle said, of Christ because Christ died for us; coheirs because Christ will reign with us. HOMILIES ON THE PSALMS 14.[30]

---

[24]*Cont. Haer.* 3.21. [25]NPNF 2 3:177*. [26]Job 9:24. [27]See Job 9:23. [28]Satan. See the temptation of Christ (Mt 4:1-11). [29]NPNF 2 7:274*. [30]FC 48:109.

83:1-18 A PRAYER FOR DESTRUCTION OF ONE'S ENEMY

A Song. A Psalm of Asaph.

[1]*O God, do not keep silence;*
  do not hold thy peace or be still, O God!
[2]*For lo, thy enemies are in tumult;*
  those who hate thee have raised their heads.
[3]*They lay crafty plans against thy people;*

they consult together against thy protected ones.
[4]*They say, "Come, let us wipe them out as a nation;*
  let the name of Israel be remembered no more!"
[5]*Yea, they conspire with one accord;*

against thee they make a covenant—
6*the tents of Edom and the Ishmaelites,*
Moab and the Hagrites,
7*Gebal and Ammon and Amalek,*
Philistia with the inhabitants of Tyre;
8*Assyria also has joined them;*
they are the strong arm of the children of Lot. Selah

9*Do to them as thou didst to Midian,*
as to Sisera and Jabin at the river Kishon,
10*who were destroyed at En-dor,*
who became dung for the ground.
11*Make their nobles like Oreb and Zeeb,*
all their princes like Zebah and Zalmunna,
12*who said, "Let us take possession for ourselves*
of the pastures of God."

13*O my God, make them like whirling dust,*[q]
like chaff before the wind.
14*As fire consumes the forest,*
as the flame sets the mountains ablaze,
15*so do thou pursue them with thy tempest*
and terrify them with thy hurricane!
16*Fill their faces with shame,*
that they may seek thy name, O LORD.
17*Let them be put to shame and dismayed for ever;*
let them perish in disgrace.
18*Let them know that thou alone,*
whose name is the LORD,
art the Most High over all the earth.

q Or *a tumbleweed*

OVERVIEW: God becomes angry with people in order to root out their sinfulness and then takes pity on the same individuals in order to heal and save them (AUGUSTINE). Often the highest offices in the church are filled by heretical and iniquitous individuals who deserve the title "enemies" equal to that of David's lament (THEODORET). The proper interpretation of Scripture requires an understanding of the wide range of meanings and nuances of words, such as David's use of "counsel" (JOHN OF DAMASCUS).

More people can be tempted to evil deeds with less inducement than others can be encouraged to perform good deeds (GREGORY OF NAZIANZUS). We should pray for people who are mired in their malice, since they are like wheels rolling back and forth and never becoming established in what is good so that they may escape from their sinful lives (JEROME).

83:1-4 *Corruption in the Church*

ANGER AND PITY. AUGUSTINE: So let them keep quiet, let them now see that the real Hercules is the God to whom the faithful say, "God, who is like you? Do not keep silent, or grow gentle, God." What I had undertaken was to show how "do not grow gentle" means rooting out errors, not people. He does not grow gentle, so he gets angry. But he is God, so he also takes pity. He gets angry, and he takes pity. He gets angry and strikes; he takes pity and heals. He gets angry and does to death; he takes pity and brings to life. In one person he does this. It is not that he does some people to death and brings others to life, but in the same people he is both angry and gentle. He is angry with errors; he is gentle with bad habits put right. "I will strike, and I will heal; I will kill, and I will make alive."[1] One and the same Saul, afterward Paul, he both laid low and raised up. He laid low an unbeliever, he raised up a believer. He both laid low a persecutor, he raised up a preacher. SERMON 24.7.[2]

[1]Deut 32:39. [2]*WSA* 3 2:77.

Enemies of God. Theodoret of Cyr: When Leontius[3] perceived this,[4] he did not think it safe to try to prevent them, for he saw that the people were exceedingly well-disposed toward these excellent men. However, speaking in a courteous manner, he requested that they would perform this act of worship [antiphonal singing] in the churches. They were perfectly well aware of his evil intent. Nevertheless they set about obeying his request and readily summoned their choir to the church, exhorting them to sing praises to the good Lord. Nothing, however, could induce Leontius to correct his wickedness,[5] but he put on the mask of moderation and concealed the iniquity of Stephanus and Placidus.[6] People who had accepted the corruption of the faith of priests and deacons, although they had embraced a life of vile irregularity, he added to the roll;[7] while others adorned with every kind of virtue and firm adherents of apostolic doctrines, he left unrecognized. Thus it came to pass that among the clergy were numbered a majority of men tainted with heresy, while the mass of the laity were champions of the faith, and even professional teachers lacked courage to lay bare their blasphemy. In truth the deeds of impiety and iniquity done by Placidus, Stephanus and Leontius, in Antioch are so many as to want a special history of their own, and so terrible as to be worthy of the lament of David; for of them too it must be said, "For your enemies make a murmuring, and they that hate you lift up their head. They have imagined craftily against the people and taken counsel against your secret ones. They have said, 'Come and let us root them out that they be no more a people: and that the name of Israel may be no more in remembrance.'" Ecclesiastical History 2.19.[8]

The Meaning of the Word Counsel. John of Damascus: Moreover, one must know that the word *gnōmē*, or opinion, is used in many ways and with many meanings. Thus, it sometimes means "advice" as when the divine apostle says, "Now, concerning virgins, I have no commandment of the Lord; but I give counsel."[9] Sometimes it implies "design," as when the prophet David says, "They have taken a malicious counsel against your people." Sometimes it means "judgment," as when Daniel says: "Why so cruel a sentence has gone forth."[10] And sometimes it is used in the sense of "faith," or "notion," or of "intent"—to put it simply, the word has twenty-eight different meanings. Orthodox Faith 3.14.[11]

83:13 Inducement to Evil Rather Than to Good

Most People Are Disposed to Evil. Gregory of Nazianzus: What does he mean by this?[12] As I take it, that goodness can with difficulty gain a hold on human nature, like fire on green wood; while most people are ready and disposed to join in evil, like stubble, I mean, ready for a spark and a wind, which is easily kindled and consumed from its dryness. For a person will engage more quickly and fully in evil with the slightest inducement than in good with only little encouragement. In Defense of His Flight to Pontus, Oration 2.12.[13]

Make Them Like a Wheel. Jerome: "O my God, make them like a wheel." Notice the mercy of the prophet; he does not pray against them but for them. See what he says: My God, who is the God of all, my very own God, O my God, make them like a wheel. They who lay their foundation in malice, let them have no foundation at all, but let them roll back and forth and never remain fixed in their malice. Homilies on the Psalms 15.[14]

---

[3]Bishop of Antioch, who had made himself a eunuch and tried to conceal his heretical Arian views and who had previously been expelled from being a presbyter. Canon 1 of the Council of Nicaea in 325 forbade mutilated men from being ordained into the ranks of the clergy. [4]Two orthodox laymen, Flavianus and Diodorus, were introducing antiphonal singing of the psalms in the church in Antioch. [5]Concealing his Arian views. [6]Corrupt predecessors of Leontius in the bishopric of Antioch. [7]Ordained such individuals as presbyters or deacons. [8]NPNF 2 3:85-6*. [9]1 Cor 7:25. [10]Dan 2:15. [11]FC 37:303*. [12]Haggai, from whom Gregory quotes in the previous section (Hag 2:11-13). [13]NPNF 2 7:207**. [14]FC 48:116.

84:1-12 A LONGING FOR THE HOUSE
OF THE LORD

*To the choirmaster: according to The
Gittith. A Psalm of the Sons of Korah.*

¹*How lovely is thy dwelling place,
    O LORD of hosts!*
²*My soul longs, yea, faints
    for the courts of the LORD;
my heart and flesh sing for joy
    to the living God.*

³*Even the sparrow finds a home,
    and the swallow a nest for herself,
    where she may lay her young,
at thy altars, O LORD of hosts,
    my King and my God.*
⁴*Blessed are those who dwell in thy house,
    ever singing thy praise!*   Selah

⁵*Blessed are the men whose strength is in thee,
    in whose heart are the highways to Zion.*ʳ
⁶*As they go through the valley of Baca*

*they make it a place of springs;
    the early rain also covers it with pools.*
⁷*They go from strength to strength;
    the God of gods will be seen in Zion.*

⁸*O LORD God of hosts, hear my prayer;
    give ear, O God of Jacob!*   Selah
⁹*Behold our shield, O God;
    look upon the face of thine anointed!*

¹⁰*For a day in thy courts is better
    than a thousand elsewhere.
I would rather be a doorkeeper in the house
        of my God
    than dwell in the tents of wickedness.*
¹¹*For the LORD God is a sun and shield;
    he bestows favor and honor.
No good thing does the LORD withhold
    from those who walk uprightly.*
¹²*O LORD of hosts,
    blessed is the man who trusts in thee!*

r Heb lacks *to Zion*

OVERVIEW: Like birds that have nests in which
to rest after tiring flights, people, wearied by the
troubles of life need an eternal resting place, a
nest for their bodies and souls (JEROME). When
the redeemed receive their eternal reward, they
will live happily in God's presence and eternally
sing his praise (FULGENTIUS).

The church grew gradually in its understanding of the Trinity, understanding the divinity of
the Father, the Son and finally the Holy Spirit
(GREGORY OF NAZIANZUS). God has placed us in
the arena of life with all its struggles so that we
may contend, grow strong and finally be blessed

with the victor's crown in heaven (JEROME).

84:3-4 *A Place to Rest and Dwell*

NEED FOR A RESTING PLACE. JEROME: "Even
the sparrow finds a home, and the turtledove a
nest in which she puts her young." For the
present, let us be satisfied with a simple interpretation. Notice all that the verse implies: I long, O
Lord, for your eternal dwelling places; my soul
yearns and pines for the courts of the Lord; I long
for some place to dwell, a nest for my soul and my
body. The birds that fly about to and fro with no

restraint, nevertheless, after their flight, have a place and a nest in which to rest. How much more ought not my body and soul procure for itself a resting place? Homilies on the Psalms 16.[1]

The Happiness of Our Eternal Dwelling. Fulgentius of Ruspe: In heart, let us migrate from living in this world, from which we are rapidly going to migrate in the body, that that heavenly dwelling may receive us, concerning which the apostle says that we have an eternal dwelling from God, a house not made by hands, in the heavens. Concerning this dwelling it has been written: "Happy are those who live in your house, ever singing your praise." There, just as there is an eternal dwelling, so there is eternal praise. Those who live there always praise God because they are always exulting about God and in God; and just as for those who give praise, there is the sweet eternity of a holy dwelling, so the eternal sweetness of giving praise remains for those who dwell there. Letter 10.56.[2]

84:5-7 From Strength to Strength

Progress from Glory to Glory. Gregory of Nazianzus: The Old Testament proclaimed the Father openly and the Son more obscurely. The New [Testament] manifested the Son and suggested the deity of the Spirit. Now the Spirit dwells among us and supplies us with a clearer demonstration of himself. For it was not safe, when the Godhead of the Father was not yet acknowledged, plainly to proclaim the Son; nor when that of the Son was not yet received to burden us further (if I may use so bold an expression) with the Holy Spirit; lest perhaps people might, like persons loaded with food beyond their strength and presenting eyes as yet too weak to look at the sun's light, risk the loss even of that which was within the reach of their powers; but

that by gradual additions, and, as David says, "Goings up, and advances and progress from glory to glory,"[3] the light of the Trinity might shine on the more illuminated. It was for this reason, I think, that [the Holy Spirit] gradually came to dwell in the disciples, measuring himself out to them according to their capacity to receive him, at the beginning of the Gospel, after the passion, after the ascension, making perfect their powers, being breathed on them and appearing in fiery tongues. On the Holy Spirit, Theological Oration 5[31]. 26.[4]

God Will Give a Blessing. Jerome: "For the lawgiver will give a blessing." Somebody may ask, "Why in the valley of tears, in the place that God has set for the contest—or for the conflict—why has he placed us as athletes? Why has he willed us to fight?" The psalmist gives the answer: He has willed that this place be set for us as an arena that he may reward our victory with a crown. "For the lawgiver will give a blessing." This Lawgiver, our president of the contest,[5] has willed us to contend only that he may bless us. Just consider what the victory means! What are the blessings of this Master of the games? "They go from strength to strength";[6] they win the victory here that they may receive the crown there. If a person of courage gives evidence of strength here, there he becomes stronger. "They go from strength to strength"; hence, unless we are strong here, we cannot have greater strength there. The psalmist did not say, they shall go from weakness to strength, but from strength to strength. Do you want to be a person of fortitude there? Then be one here first. Do you want to be crowned there? Fight here. Homilies on the Psalms 16.[7]

---

[1]FC 48:121. [2]FC 95:471-72. [3]See also 2 Cor 3:18. [4]NPNF 2 7:326*. [5]Cf. Letter 71.2; *Against Jovinianus* 1.12. [6]Ps 84:7 (83:8 LXX, Vg.). [7]FC 48:123-24.

85:1-13 A COMMUNAL PRAYER FOR RENEWAL OF GOD'S MERCIES

To the choirmaster.
A Psalm of the Sons of Korah.

[1]LORD, thou wast favorable to thy land;
  thou didst restore the fortunes of Jacob.
[2]Thou didst forgive the iniquity of thy people;
  thou didst pardon all their sin.   Selah
[3]Thou didst withdraw all thy wrath;
  thou didst turn from thy hot anger.

[4]Restore us again, O God of our salvation,
  and put away thy indignation toward us!
[5]Wilt thou be angry with us for ever?
  Wilt thou prolong thy anger to all
    generations?
[6]Wilt thou not revive us again,
  that thy people may rejoice in thee?
[7]Show us thy steadfast love, O LORD,
  and grant us thy salvation.
[8]Let me hear what God the LORD will speak,
  for he will speak peace to his people,
  to his saints, to those who turn to him
    in their hearts.[s]
[9]Surely his salvation is at hand for those who
    fear him,
  that glory may dwell in our land.

[10]Steadfast love and faithfulness will meet;
  righteousness and peace will kiss each other.
[11]Faithfulness will spring up from the ground,
  and righteousness will look down from
    the sky.
[12]Yea, the LORD will give what is good,
  and our land will yield its increase.
[13]Righteousness will go before him,
  and make his footsteps a way.

s Gk: Heb *but let them not turn back to folly*

OVERVIEW: We are dead until God has compassion on us and restores us to life through the work of our Savior (JEROME). Since nothing happens contrary to God's will, we can rightfully pray that he will keep us from all sinful temptation so that we may receive his salvation. Faith is not a human work but a gift of God, who not only grants us increase in faith but also allows the suffering endured because of it. Believers should pray that God will work in unbelievers the will to believe. Like the land, we would not bear fruit unless God plants his seeds within us and then nurtures them when they have sprouted (AUGUSTINE).

85:4-6 God's Will and Gifts

GIVE US LIFE. JEROME: "Restore us, O God of our salvations."[1] Why did the psalmist not say "our salvation" instead of "our salvations"? If we sinned just once, we would need only one salvation; but we have sinned many times and, therefore, are in need of many salvations. "Will you not instead, O God, give us life?" Until the Lord restores us to life, we are dead. "Show us, O Lord, your kindness, and grant us your salvation." The Savior's descent is the work of God's mercy. He would not have come as a physician if most people were not sick. Because so many were sick, he came as Physician; because we

[1]The LXX 84:5 has *sōtērion* (plural).

were in need of compassion, he came as Savior. HOMILIES ON THE PSALMS 17.[2]

GOD WILL BRING US TO LIFE. AUGUSTINE: But [the objector might continue], "It is by his own will that each person abandons God and is deservedly abandoned by God." Who would ever deny this? And the reason why we ask not to be brought into temptation is that this may not happen. And if we are heard, then this indeed does not happen, because God does not allow it to happen. For nothing happens except what God either does himself or permits to occur. Therefore, he has the power both to turn wills from evil to good and to turn them back when they are inclined toward a fall, as well as to direct their steps in ways that are pleasing to him. It is not in vain that we say to him, "You will turn us, O God, and bring us to life." It is not said in vain, "Do not suffer my feet to be moved."[3] It is not said in vain, "Give me not up, O Lord, from my desire, to the wicked."[4] Finally, not to increase the number of citations, since more may well occur to you, it is not said in vain, "Bring us not into temptation." For whoever is not brought into temptation is evidently not brought into the temptation of his own evil will, and he who is not brought into the temptation of his own evil will is certainly not brought into any temptation at all. ON THE GIFT OF PERSEVERANCE 6.12.[5]

FAITH IS A GIFT OF GOD. AUGUSTINE: But against this error, why do we not instead listen to these words: "Who has first given to him, and what recompense shall be made to him? For of him, and by him and in him are all things."[6] And therefore, that very beginning of our faith—from whom is it if not from him? For it is not the case that, with this excepted, all other things are from him, but "of him, and by him and in him are all things." But who would say that he who has already begun to believe does not merit anything from him in whom he has believed? From which it results that other divine

gifts are said to be added in recompense to him who already has merit, and hence that God's grace is given according to our merits—a statement that Pelagius, when it was raised in objection to him, himself condemned, so that he might not be condemned. Therefore, whoever wishes in every way to avoid this condemnable opinion, let him understand that the apostle spoke truly when he said, "It has been granted to you that for the sake of Christ you should not only believe in him but also suffer for him."[7] Both of these he shows to be the gifts of God, because both he says are given. He does not say, "to believe in him more fully and perfectly," but "to believe in him." Nor does he say that he himself had obtained mercy in order to be more faithful, but to be faithful,[8] because he knew that he had not first given the beginning of his faith to God, and had its increase returned to him by God, but had been made faithful by God, by whom he was also made an apostle. For the beginning of his faith is recorded in Scripture,[9] and the account is very well known, for it is read in our churches on a solemn occasion.[10] Thus, he felt an aversion to the faith to which he was laying waste and, being vehemently adverse toward it, he was suddenly converted to it by a more powerful grace, converted by him to whom, as the one who would do it, the prophet said, "You will turn and bring us to life." Thus, not only from one who refused to believe did he become a willing believer, but even from a persecutor he came to suffer persecution in defense of that faith that he had persecuted. For it was given him by Christ, not only to believe in him but also to suffer for him. PREDESTINATION OF THE SAINTS 2.4.[11]

PRAY FOR UNBELIEVERS. AUGUSTINE: "Why," they say, "does he not teach everyone?" If we reply

---

[2]FC 48:129*. [3]Ps 66:9 (65:9 LXX, Vg.). [4]Ps 140:8 (139:9 LXX, Vg.). [5]FC 86:279-80. [6]Rom 11:35-36. [7]Phil 1:29. [8]See 1 Cor 7:25. [9]Acts 9:1-9. [10]Acts was read on Easter Sunday and immediately afterwards. [11]FC 86:220-21*.

that those whom he does not teach are not willing to learn, we shall be given this answer: "And what happens to that which is said to him, 'You will turn, O God, and bring us to life'"? Or if God does not make people willing who are not willing, why does the church, in accordance with the Lord's commandment, pray for its persecutors?[12] For in this sense also the blessed Cyprian[13] wanted it to be understood when we say, "Your will be done on earth as it is in heaven,"[14] that is just as for those who have already believed and are in a sense "heaven," so too for those who do not believe and for this reason are still "earth." What then do we pray for those who do not will to believe, except that God shall work in them that they will?[15] Certainly, the apostle spoke of the Jews when he said, "Brothers, the good will of my heart indeed, and my prayer to God, is for their salvation."[16] What does he pray for those who do not believe, except that they may believe? For in no other way do they obtain salvation. Therefore if the faith of those who pray precedes the grace of God, then does the faith of those for whom we pray that they might believe precede the grace of God? Not at all, since this is the very thing that is sought for them, that to those who do not believe, that is, those who do not have faith, faith itself be given. Therefore, when the gospel is preached, some believe and some do not, but those who believe, when they hear the voice of the preacher from without, hear from the Father and learn within, while those who do not believe hear the external word but inwardly do not hear nor learn. That is to say, to the former it is given to believe, to the later it is not given. PREDESTINATION OF THE SAINTS 8.15.[17]

85:12 God Is Bountiful

THE LAND WILL YIELD ITS FRUIT. AUGUSTINE: We were wolves. "We too were by nature children of wrath just like the rest."[18] But the sheep died and turned us into sheep. "Behold the Lamb of God, behold him who takes away the sin," not of this person or that, but "of the world."[19] So then, my brothers, let us claim no credit for anything we are, provided it is by faith in him we are whatever we are—let us claim no credit for ourselves, or we may lose what we have received. But for whatever we have received let us give him the glory, him the honor, and may he water the seeds he has sown. What would our land have if he had not sown anything? He too sends the rain. He does not abandon what he has sown. "The Lord will give his sweetness, and our land will yield its fruit." SERMON 26.15.[20]

---

[12]See Mt 5:44. [13]De Dominica Oratione 18. [14]Mt 6:10. [15]See Phil 2:13. [16]Rom 10:1. [17]FC 86:236-37*. [18]Eph 2:3. [19]Jn 1:29. [20]WSA 3 2:101-2.

86:1-17 A PRAYER FOR GOD'S HELP AGAINST THE ATTACKS OF THE ENEMY

A Prayer of David.

[1]*Incline thy ear, O LORD, and answer me,*
for I am poor and needy.

[2]*Preserve my life, for I am godly;*
save thy servant who trusts in thee.
Thou art my God; [3]*be gracious to me, O LORD,*
for to thee do I cry all the day.

⁴*Gladden the soul of thy servant,*
   for to thee, O Lord, do I lift up my soul.
⁵*For thou, O Lord, art good and forgiving,*
   abounding in steadfast love to all who
     call on thee.
⁶*Give ear, O* Lord, *to my prayer;*
   hearken to my cry of supplication.
⁷*In the day of my trouble I call on thee,*
   for thou dost answer me.

⁸*There is none like thee among the gods,*
   O Lord,
   nor are there any works like thine.
⁹*All the nations thou hast made shall come*
   and bow down before thee, O Lord,
   and shall glorify thy name.
¹⁰*For thou art great and doest wondrous things,*
   thou alone art God.
¹¹*Teach me thy way, O* Lord,
   that I may walk in thy truth;
   unite my heart to fear thy name.
¹²*I give thanks to thee, O Lord my God, with*

   my whole heart,
   and I will glorify thy name for ever.
¹³*For great is thy steadfast love toward me;*
   thou hast delivered my soul from the depths
     of Sheol.

¹⁴*O God, insolent men have risen up against*
   me;
   a band of ruthless men seek my life,
   and they do not set thee before them.
¹⁵*But thou, O Lord, art a God merciful and*
   gracious,
   slow to anger and abounding in steadfast
     love and faithfulness.
¹⁶*Turn to me and take pity on me;*
   give thy strength to thy servant,
   and save the son of thy handmaid.
¹⁷*Show me a sign of thy favor,*
   that those who hate me may see and be
     put to shame
   because thou, Lord, *hast helped me and*
   comforted me.

Overview: It is necessary to think of God as holy and awesome; if we know only his holiness we would become indifferent to him, and if we know only his awesomeness, fear of him would lead us to despair (Cassiodorus). The only cure for an ill soul racked by unnatural passions is the Word of God (Clement of Alexandria).

86:2-3 The Soul's Physician

God Is Holy and Terrible. Cassiodorus: They [apostles and Evangelists] added, "Holy and terrible is his name."[1] "Holy" has reference to the incarnation; as he himself says: "Preserve my soul, for I am holy." "Terrible" indicates the omnipotence of the exalted Godhead; as another psalm has, "You are terrible, and who shall resist you?"[2] The two epithets have the purpose of mak-

ing us love our Patron[3] and making us fear our Judge. The two are fittingly combined to ensure that love alone may not make us indifferent and fear alone may not make us despair. Exposi-tions of the Psalms 110.9.[4]

The Medicine of an Ill Soul. Clement of Alexandria: Therefore, the Word is our educa-tor who heals the unnatural passions of our soul with his counsel. The art of healing, strictly speaking, is the relief of the ills of the body, an art learned through human wisdom. Yet, the only true divine healer of human sickness, the holy

---

[1]Ps 111:9 (110:9 LXX, Vg.). [2]Ps 76:7 (75:8 LXX, Vg.). [3]In ancient Roman society, a patron was a man, usually wealthy and of higher social rank, who agreed to protect another individual by making him a client, who was then in a servant relationship to the patron. [4]ACW 53:130*.

comforter of the soul when it is ill, is the Word of the Father. Scripture says, "Save your servant, O my God, who puts his trust in you. Have mercy on me, O Lord, because I have cried to you the whole day through." In the words of Democritus, "The healer, by his art, cures the body of its diseases, but it is wisdom that rids the spirit of its ills."[5] The good educator of little ones, however, Wisdom, the Word of the Father, who created human beings, concerns himself with the whole creation, and as the physician of the whole person heals both body and soul. CHRIST THE EDUCATOR 1.2.6.[6]

[5]*Fragment 50, N. 31. H. Diels, Die Fragmente der Vorsakratiker griechisch und deutsch* (Berlin, 1903). [6]FC 23:7-8*.

87:1-7 A CELEBRATION OF ZION AS THE CITY OF GOD

A Psalm of the Sons of Korah. A Song.

[1]*On the holy mount stands the city he founded;*
  [2]*The LORD loves the gates of Zion*
    more than all the dwelling places of Jacob.
[3]*Glorious things are spoken of you,*
  O city of God.   Selah

[4]*Among those who know me I mention Rahab*
  and Babylon;

behold, Philistia and Tyre, with Ethiopia—
  "This one was born there," they say.
[5]*And of Zion it shall be said,*
  "This one and that one were born in her";
  for the Most High himself will establish her.
[6]*The LORD records as he registers the peoples,*
  "This one was born there."   Selah

[7]*Singers and dancers alike say,*
  "All my springs are in you."

OVERVIEW: In our world, which is bent on destroying God's servants, there still are people like Rahab who will be led to faith and protect God's messengers (JEROME). No matter how great a person's sins are, there is forgiveness and salvation through repentance, as God's mercy to Rahab and Babylon attest (CYRIL OF JERUSALEM).

87:3-4 All Sins Can Be Forgiven

THE CALLING OF THE GENTILES. JEROME: "I will be mindful of Rahab and Babylon among those that know me." Since the psalmist said, "Glorious things are said of you, O city of God,"

and we understand this city to be the church gathered together from the nations, the psalm now speaks of the calling of the Gentiles: "I will be mindful of Rahab and Babylon among those that know me." Let the sinner be at peace; the Lord was mindful of Rahab. I mean, at peace, if the sinner returns to the Lord; otherwise, there is no healing peace in a tearless security. "I will be mindful of Rahab," of Rahab, that harlot[1] who lodged Jesus' secret agents, who lived in Jericho, where Joshua had come and had dispatched the

[1]Josh 2.

two spies. Jericho, that collapsed in seven days, is a type of this world, and as such is determined to kill the secret agents. Because, therefore, Jericho is bent on killing the spies, Rahab, the harlot, alone received them, lodged them not on the ground floor but in the upper story of the roof— or, in other words, in the sublimity of her faith. She hid them under her stalks of flax. Homilies on the Psalms 18.[2]

Testimonies to God's Mercy. Cyril of Jerusalem: Pass now, pray, to the others who were saved by repentance. Perhaps even among the women someone will say, "I have committed fornication and adultery. I have defiled my body with every excess. Can there be salvation for me?" Fix your eyes, woman, on Rahab, and look for salvation for yourself too. For if she who openly and publicly practiced fornication was saved through repentance, will not she whose fornication preceded the gift of grace be saved by repentance and fasting? For observe how she was saved. She said only this: "Since the Lord, your God, is God in heaven above and on earth below."[3] "Your God," she said, for she did not dare call him her God, because of her wantonness. If you want scriptural testimony of her salvation, you have it recorded in the Psalms: "I will think of Rahab and Babylon among those who know me." O the great lovingkindness of God, which is mindful even of harlots in Scripture. He did not say merely, "I shall think of Rahab and Babylon," but added, "among those who know me." The salvation procured by repentance is open to men and women alike. Catechetical Lectures 2.9.[4]

---

[2]FC 48:137-38. [3]Josh 2:11. [4]FC 61:100-101.

88:1-18 A PRAYER OF ONE ON THE VERGE OF DYING

A Song. A Psalm of the Sons of Korah. To the choirmaster: according to Mahalath Leannoth. A Maskil of Heman the Ezrahite.

[1]O Lord, my God, I call for help[1] by day;
I cry out in the night before thee.
[2]Let my prayer come before thee,
incline thy ear to my cry!
[3]For my soul is full of troubles,
and my life draws near to Sheol.
[4]I am reckoned among those who go down to the Pit;
I am a man who has no strength,
[5]like one forsaken among the dead,
like the slain that lie in the grave,
like those whom thou dost remember no more,
for they are cut off from thy hand.
[6]Thou hast put me in the depths of the Pit,
in the regions dark and deep.
[7]Thy wrath lies heavy upon me,
and thou dost overwhelm me with all thy waves.   Selah
[8]Thou hast caused my companions to shun me;
thou hast made me a thing of horror to them.
I am shut in so that I cannot escape;

⁹my eye grows dim through sorrow.
Every day I call upon thee, O LORD;
I spread out my hands to thee.
¹⁰Dost thou work wonders for the dead?
Do the shades rise up to praise thee?
                                    Selah
¹¹Is thy steadfast love declared in the grave,
or thy faithfulness in Abaddon?
¹²Are thy wonders known in the darkness,
or thy saving help in the land of
forgetfulness?

¹³But I, O LORD, cry to thee;

in the morning my prayer comes before thee.
¹⁴O LORD, why dost thou cast me off?
Why dost thou hide thy face from me?
¹⁵Afflicted and close to death from my youth
up,
I suffer thy terrors; I am helpless.ᵘ
¹⁶Thy wrath has swept over me;
thy dread assaults destroy me.
¹⁷They surround me like a flood all day long;
they close in upon me together.
¹⁸Thou hast caused lover and friend to shun
me;
my companions are in darkness.

t Cn: Heb O LORD, God of my salvation   u The meaning of the Hebrew word is uncertain

OVERVIEW: Christ predicted his passion and resurrection already in the words of the psalmist (CYRIL OF JERUSALEM). Christ did not need the help of any human being in the redemption of the world (AMBROSE). David's words in this psalm are seen as a prediction of the burial and resurrection of Christ (CHRYSOSTOM).

88:1 Predictions Regarding Christ

DAY AND NIGHT I HAVE CRIED FOR HELP.
CYRIL OF JERUSALEM: Accept an additional testimony from the eighty-seventh psalm [LXX], where Christ speaks in the prophets—for he who then spoke afterwards came among us: "O Lord, the God of my salvation: I have cried in the day and in the night before you"; and subsequently, "I am become as a man without help, free among the dead."[1] He did not say, "I am become a man without help," but "as a man without help"; for he was crucified, not because of helplessness but because he willed it; his death was not a result of involuntary weakness. "I am numbered with those who go down into the pit."[2] What is the sign? "You have taken my friends away from me"[3] (for the disciples fled away). "Will you work wonders for the dead"?[4] Then, "But I, O Lord, cry out to you;

with my morning prayer I wait on you."[5] See how these verses manifest the actual circumstances of the passion and the resurrection. CATECHETICAL LECTURES 14.8.[6]

88:5-6 Like One Forsaken Among the Dead

I HAVE BECOME AS A MAN WITHOUT HELP.
AMBROSE: Nor was Mary less than was befitting the mother of Christ. When the apostles fled, she stood before the cross and with reverent gaze beheld her Son's wounds, for she awaited not her child's death but the world's salvation. Or perhaps that "regal chamber" knew that through her Son's death would be the world's redemption, and through her own death she thought she would give herself for the common good. But Jesus had no need of a helper in redeeming all, for he saved all without a helper. Therefore he says, "I have become as a man without help, free among the dead." Indeed, he received the devotion of his parent, but he did not seek another's aid. LETTER 59.[7]

¹Ps 88:4-5 (87:5-6 LXX).   ²Ps 88:4 (87:5 LXX).   ³Ps 88:8 (87:9 LXX).   ⁴Ps 88:10 (87:11).   ⁵Ps 88:13 (87:14).   ⁶FC 64:36-37*.   ⁷FC 26:362*.

A PROPHECY OF CHRIST'S BURIAL AND RES-URRECTION. CHRYSOSTOM: Next, David made it clear that Christ would be buried when he said, "They have put me in the lowest pit in the dark places and in the shadow of death." Nor was David silent about the spices used on his shroud. Since the women brought myrrh, spice and cassia, hear what the prophet said: "Your robes are all fragrant with myrrh, spice and cassia, and with them the daughters of kings gladdened you in your honor." See how he also predicted that Christ would rise again. "You will not leave my soul in hell, nor will you allow your holy one to see corruption."[8] Isaiah expressed the same thing in a different way. For he said, "The Lord wishes to cleanse him from his wounds, to show him light, to justify the righteous one who has served many well."[9] DEMONSTRATION AGAINST THE PAGANS 4.12.[10]

---

[8]Ps 16:10 (15:10 LXX). [9]See Is 53:10-11. [10]FC 73:207.

89:1-52 A PRAYER FOR RESTORATION OF THE DAVIDIC DYNASTY

A Maskil of Ethan the Ezrahite.

[1]*I will sing of thy steadfast love, O LORD,[v] for ever;*
with my mouth I will proclaim thy faithfulness to all generations.
[2]*For thy steadfast love was established for ever,*
thy faithfulness is firm as the heavens.
[3]*Thou hast said, "I have made a covenant with my chosen one,*
I have sworn to David my servant:
[4]*"I will establish your descendants for ever,*
and build your throne for all generations.'"
                                                          Selah
[5]*Let the heavens praise thy wonders, O LORD,*
thy faithfulness in the assembly of the holy ones!
[6]*For who in the skies can be compared to the LORD?*
Who among the heavenly beings[w] is like the LORD,

[7]*a God feared in the council of the holy ones,*
great and terrible[x] above all that are round about him?
[8]*O LORD God of hosts,*
who is mighty as thou art, O LORD,
with thy faithfulness round about thee?
[9]*Thou dost rule the raging of the sea;*
when its waves rise, thou stillest them.
[10]*Thou didst crush Rahab like a carcass,*
thou didst scatter thy enemies with thy mighty arm.
[11]*The heavens are thine, the earth also is thine;*
the world and all that is in it, thou hast founded them.
[12]*The north and the south, thou hast created them;*
Tabor and Hermon joyously praise thy name.
[13]*Thou hast a mighty arm;*
strong is thy hand, high thy right hand.

¹⁴Righteousness and justice are the foundation
of thy throne;
steadfast love and faithfulness go before
thee.
¹⁵Blessed are the people who know the festal
shout,
who walk, O LORD, in the light of thy
countenance,
¹⁶who exult in thy name all the day,
and extol^y thy righteousness.
¹⁷For thou art the glory of their strength;
by thy favor our horn is exalted.
¹⁸For our shield belongs to the LORD,
our king to the Holy One of Israel.

¹⁹Of old thou didst speak in a vision
to thy faithful one, and say:
"I have set the crown^z upon one who is mighty,
I have exalted one chosen from the people.
²⁰I have found David, my servant;
with my holy oil I have anointed him;
²¹so that my hand shall ever abide with him,
my arm also shall strengthen him.
²²The enemy shall not outwit him,
the wicked shall not humble him.
²³I will crush his foes before him
and strike down those who hate him.
²⁴My faithfulness and my steadfast love shall be
with him,
and in my name shall his horn be exalted.
²⁵I will set his hand on the sea
and his right hand on the rivers.
²⁶He shall cry to me, 'Thou art my Father,
my God, and the Rock of my salvation.'
²⁷And I will make him the first-born,
the highest of the kings of the earth.
²⁸My steadfast love I will keep for him for ever,
and my covenant will stand firm for him.
²⁹I will establish his line for ever

and his throne as the days of the heavens.
³⁰If his children forsake my law
and do not walk according to my ordinances,
³¹if they violate my statutes
and do not keep my commandments,
³²then I will punish their transgression with
the rod
and their iniquity with scourges;
³³but I will not remove from him my steadfast
love,
or be false to my faithfulness.
³⁴I will not violate my covenant,
or alter the word that went forth from my
lips.
³⁵Once for all I have sworn by my holiness;
I will not lie to David.
³⁶His line shall endure for ever,
his throne as long as the sun before me.
³⁷Like the moon it shall be established for ever;
it shall stand firm while the skies endure."^a
Selah
³⁸But now thou hast cast off and rejected,
thou art full of wrath against thy anointed.
³⁹Thou hast renounced the covenant with thy
servant;
thou hast defiled his crown in the dust.
⁴⁰Thou hast breached all his walls;
thou hast laid his strongholds in ruins.
⁴¹All that pass by despoil him;
he has become the scorn of his neighbors.
⁴²Thou hast exalted the right hand of his foes;
thou hast made all his enemies rejoice.
⁴³Yea, thou hast turned back the edge of his
sword,
and thou hast not made him stand in battle.
⁴⁴Thou hast removed the scepter from his
hand,^b
and cast his throne to the ground.
⁴⁵Thou hast cut short the days of his youth;

thou hast covered him with shame.

Selah

[46]How long, O LORD? Wilt thou hide thyself
    for ever?
  How long will thy wrath burn like fire?
[47]Remember, O Lord,[c] what the measure of life
    is,
  for what vanity thou hast created all the
    sons of men!
[48]What man can live and never see death?
  Who can deliver his soul from the power
    of Sheol?

Selah

[49]Lord, where is thy steadfast love of old,
  which by thy faithfulness thou didst swear to
    David?
[50]Remember, O Lord, how thy servant isscorned;
  how I bear in my bosom the insults[d] of the
    peoples,
[51]with which thy enemies taunt, O LORD,
  with which they mock the footsteps of thy
    anointed.

[52]Blessed be the LORD for ever!
  Amen and Amen.

---

v Gk: Heb *the steadfast love of the* LORD   w Or *sons of gods*   x Gk Syr: Heb *greatly terrible*   y Cn: Heb *are exalted in*   z Cn: Heb *help*   a Cn: Heb *the witness in the skies is sure*   b Cn: Heb *removed his cleanness*   c Cn: Heb *I*   d Cn: Heb *all of many*

OVERVIEW: Even though God punishes his people for their iniquity, he should be praised for his sure promises of future mercy (THEODORET). God is merciful to sinners to lead them to virtue and frightens the righteous so that they do not neglect their zeal (CHRYSOSTOM). Since we suffer the punishments due because of our sins, we must beseech God for the mercy he promises (CYPRIAN). The punishments we receive because of our sins are benevolent chastisements; therefore, we do not lose hope for a remedy (AMBROSE). God, who is gracious and merciful, wants people to repent so that they will not perish (CYPRIAN). David's cry for divine mercy was spoken with the Christian dispensation in mind (AUGUSTINE).

89:1-4 Praise God for His Promises

PRAISE FOR GOD'S UNFAILING PROMISE. THEODORET OF CYR: *Orthodoxos:*[1] Listen now how the prophet praises God at the very beginning of the psalm. He saw with his prophetic eyes the future iniquity of his people and the captivity that was in consequence foredoomed; yet he praised his own Lord for unfailing promises. "I will sing," he says, "of the mercies of the Lord forever; with my mouth will I make known your faithfulness to all generations, for you have said, Mercy shall be built up forever, your faithfulness you shall establish in the very heavens."

Through all this the prophet teaches that the promise was made by God on account of lovingkindness and that the promise is faithful. Then he goes on to say what he promised, and to whom, introducing God as the speaker. ("I have made a covenant with my chosen.") It is the patriarchs that he called chosen; then he goes on, "I have sworn to David my servant," and he states concerning what he swore, "Your descendants will I establish forever, and build up your throne to all generations." DIALOGUE I.[2]

89:7 A God Who Is Feared

GOD IS MERCIFUL TO THE SINNER AND FEARSOME TO THE RIGHTEOUS. CHRYSOSTOM: O such strictness toward the righteous! O such abundant forgiveness toward the sinner! He finds so many different means, without himself changing, to keep the righteous in check and forgive the

---

[1]The name given to the defender of the orthodox faith in a dialogue with Eranistes, who represents heretical views.   [2]NPNF 2 3:169*.

sinner, by usefully dividing his rich goodness. And listen how. If he frightens the sinner who persists in sins, he brings him to desperation and to the exhaustion of hope. If he blesses the righteous, he weakens the intensity of his virtue and makes him neglect his zeal, since he considers himself already blessed. For this reason he is merciful to the sinner and frightens the righteous. "For he is terrible to all who surround him." And, "The Lord is good to the whole world."[3] "He is terrible," David says, "to all who surround him." And who are they but the saints? "For God," David says, "who is glorified in the council of the saints, [is] great and terrible to all who surround him." If he sees someone who has fallen, he extends a loving hand. If he sees someone standing, he brings fear on him. And this reveals righteousness and righteous judgment. He establishes the righteous one with fear, and he raises up the sinner with benevolence. HOMILIES ON REPENTENCE AND ALMSGIVING 7.5.[4]

89:31-34 The Mercy of God

THE PUNISHMENT FOR SIN. CYPRIAN: We suffer these things because of our fault and of our deserving, as the divine judgment has forewarned us, saying, "If they have forsaken my law and have walked not in my judgments, if they have profaned my ordinances and have kept not my commands, I will visit their crime with a rod and their guilt with stripes."[5] We, therefore, who neither please God with our good deeds nor satisfy him for our sins, feel the rods and the lashes. Let us ask from the depth of our heart and with our whole mind the mercy of God because he himself adds this, saying, "Yet my kindness I will not take from them."[6] Let us ask and we receive; and, if there is delay and tardiness in our receiving because we have offended gravely, let us knock because to him who also knocks it is opened,[7] provided only our prayers and groans and tears knock at the door, in which we ought to persist and to employ much time, provided our prayer is also of one mind. LETTER 11.2.[8]

DO NOT DESPAIR OF RECEIVING A REMEDY FOR SIN. AMBROSE: Not without reason was [the soul][9] given horns and hoofs, to bruise all the sheaves of the threshing floor, like the calf of Libanius,[10] for, unless the sheaves are bruised and the straw winnowed, the corn within cannot appear and be separated. Let the soul that would advance in virtue first bruise and thresh out its superfluous passions that at the harvest it may have its fruits to show. How many weeds choke the good seed! These first must be rooted out, so that they will not destroy the fruitful crop of the soul.[11]

The careful guardian of the soul then sees how he may restrain [the soul] in its pleasures and cut off its desires, to prevent it being overwhelmed with delight in them. The correction of the father who does not spare the rod is useful, that he may render his son's soul obedient to the precepts of salvation.[12] He punishes with a rod, as we read: "I shall punish their offenses with a rod." Therefore, one who with a rod strikes an Israelite's soul on the cheek instructs that one by the Lord's punishment in the discipline of patience. No one who is chastened and corrected need lose hope, for one who loves his son chastises him. No one should despair of a remedy. LETTER 45.[13]

EXHORTATION TO RIGHTEOUSNESS. CYPRIAN: The Lord certainly would not exhort to repentance unless he promised pardon to the penitent. In the Gospel the Lord says, "Just so, I tell you, there will be joy in heaven over one sinner who repents, more than over ninety-nine just who have no need of repentance."[14] Since it is written, "God is not the author of death, nor does he rejoice in the destruction of the living,"[15] certainly he, who wishes no one to perish, desires sinners to do penance and to return to life again through

---

[3]Ps 145:9 (144:9 LXX). [4]FC 96:90*. [5]See Ps 89:31-32 (88:32-33 LXX, Vg.). [6]Ps 89:33 (88:34 LXX, Vg.). [7]See Mt 2:7; Lk 11:10. [8]FC 51:29-30*. [9]A soul afflicted with sin. [10]See Mic 4:13. [11]Ambrose is writing about the need to reconvert or restore weak Christians (souls) who lapse into sin and feel the great weight of the burden of their sin. [12]See Prov 13:24. [13]FC 26:233-34. [14]Lk 15:7. [15]Wis 1:13.

penance.[16] And there, through Joel the prophet, he cries out and says, "And now says the Lord, your God, return to me with your whole heart, at the same time with fasting, and weeping and mourning; and rend your hearts and not your garments, and return to the Lord, your God. For gracious and merciful is he, slow to anger, rich in kindness, and he softens the sentence inflicted against malice."[17] In the Psalms we read also of the censure and of the clemency of God, at the same time, threatening and sparing, punishing that he may correct and saving when he has corrected. "I will visit," he says, "their crime with a rod and their guilt with stripes. Yet my kindness I will not take from them." LETTER 55.22.[18]

89:50-52 A Contemporary, Anticipated Cry for Mercy

LORD, WHERE ARE YOUR ANCIENT MERCIES? AUGUSTINE: The rest of the psalm runs like this: "Lord, where are your mercies of ancient times, which you promised to David, swearing an oath on your truth? Remember, Lord, the insult offered to your servants, the insult of many people that I took to heart, the insult whereby your enemies, Lord, have taunted you, whereby they have taunted the transformation of your anointed."[19] Now the question can justly be raised whether this represents the complaint of those Israelites who longed to receive the fulfillment of the promise made to David; or is it rather the appeal of the Christians, who are Israelites not by physical descent but by spiritual kinship? Now these words, as we know, were said or written in the time of Ethan, from whose name the psalm received its title; and this was the time of David's reign. It follows that it would not have been put in this form, "Lord, where are your mercies of ancient times, which you promised to David, swearing an oath on your truth?" unless this prophecy assumed the person of those who were to come long afterwards, for whom the period when those promises were given to David would be "ancient times." CITY OF GOD 17.12.[20]

---

[16]Cyprian believed that people who had committed the more serious sins, such as, apostasy, murder or adultery, needed to submit to the three-step penance system of confessing their sins, making appropriate satisfaction and then being absolved by the church before they could return to proper fellowship in the church. [17]See Joel 2:12-13. [18]FC 51:147-48*. [19]Ps 89:49-52 (88:50-52 LXX, Vg.). [20]CG 740-41.

90:1-17 A PRAYER FOR COMPASSION

A Prayer of Moses, the man of God.

¹*Lord, thou hast been our dwelling place*ᵉ
  in all generations.
²*Before the mountains were brought forth,*
  or ever thou hadst formed the earth and
  the world,
  from everlasting to everlasting thou
  art God.

³*Thou turnest man back to the dust,*
  and sayest, "Turn back, O children of men!"
⁴*For a thousand years in thy sight*
  are but as yesterday when it is past,
  or as a watch in the night.

⁵*Thou dost sweep men away; they are like a*
  dream,
  like grass which is renewed in the morning:

⁶*in the morning it flourishes and is renewed;*
  in the evening it fades and withers.

⁷*For we are consumed by thy anger;*
  by thy wrath we are overwhelmed.
⁸*Thou hast set our iniquities before thee,*
  our secret sins in the light of thy countenance.

⁹*For all our days pass away under thy wrath,*
  *our years come to an end*ᶠ *like a sigh.*
¹⁰*The years of our life are threescore and ten,*
  or even by reason of strength fourscore;
*yet their span*ᵍ *is but toil and trouble;*
  they are soon gone, and we fly away.

¹¹*Who considers the power of thy anger,*
  and thy wrath according to the fear of thee?

¹²*So teach us to number our days*
  that we may get a heart of wisdom.

¹³*Return, O LORD! How long?*
  Have pity on thy servants!
¹⁴*Satisfy us in the morning with thy steadfast love,*
  that we may rejoice and be glad all our days.
¹⁵*Make us glad as many days as thou hast afflicted us,*
  and as many years as we have seen evil.
¹⁶*Let thy work be manifest to thy servants,*
  and thy glorious power to their children.
¹⁷*Let the favor of the Lord our God be upon us,*
  and establish thou the work of our hands upon us,
  yea, the work of our hands establish thou it.

e Another reading is *refuge* f Syr: Heb *we bring our years to an end* g Cn Compare Gk Syr Jerome Tg: Heb *pride*

OVERVIEW: Whenever we experience afflictions in life, we should turn to God for help first and foremost (BASIL). Seeking refuge in God involves lifting our hearts to the resurrected Lord, not to ourselves, which is pride (AUGUSTINE). The co-eternity of Christ with God the Father has ample testimony in Scripture, even in a psalm of David (ATHANASIUS). Immortality has been promised to us because of the transient nature of our temporal life, especially the flesh (AUGUSTINE).

No matter how he may try, humans cannot hide their sins from God (JEROME). All humankind has come under the wrath of God because of original sin and needs Christ as its mediator and reconciler with God (AUGUSTINE). No one escapes ill fortune in this life, and God uses our misfortunes as training for salvation (DIONYSIUS). Whether we live for seventy or eighty years, this life is short compared with life in eternity, and our sufferings here are trifling in light of the promises of heaven (ATHANASIUS). While our sins, even the most grievous ones, are forgiven, God may allow the sinner to live the full length of his life so that his soul can be benefited by confession and penitence (PALLADIUS).

God's right hand is his Son, Jesus Christ, who made God known to humanity when he assumed a human nature in order to save us (JEROME). No person of good sense can doubt the eternity of Christ (ATHANASIUS).

90:1-2 An Everlasting God

GOD IS THE TRUE REFUGE FOR THE RIGHT-EOUS. BASIL THE GREAT: Therefore, "God is our refuge and strength." To him who is able to say, "I can do all things in him," Christ, "who strengthens me,"[1] God is strength. Now, it is the privilege of many to say, "God is our refuge," and "Lord, you have been our refuge." But to say it with the same feelings as the prophet is the privilege of few. For there are few who do not admire human interests but depend wholly on God and breathe him and have all hope and trust in him. And our

[1]Phil 4:13.

actions convict us whenever in our afflictions we run to everything else rather than to God. Is a child sick? You look around for an enchanter or one who puts superstitious marks on the necks of the innocent children; or finally, you go to a doctor and to medicines, having neglected him who is able to save. If a dream troubles you, you run to the interpreter of dreams. And, if you fear an enemy, you cunningly secure some man as a patron. In short, in every need you contradict yourself in word, naming God as your refuge; in act, drawing on aid from useless and vain things. God is the true aid for the righteous person. Just as a certain general, equipped with a noble heavy-armed force, is always ready to give help to an oppressed district, so God is our helper and an ally to everyone who is waging war against the wiliness of the devil, and he sends out ministering spirits for the safety of those who are in need. HOMILIES ON THE PSALMS 18.2.[2]

OUR HOPE IS IN CHRIST'S RESURRECTION.
AUGUSTINE: The resurrection of the Lord is our hope, the Lord's ascension our glorification. Today, you see, we are celebrating the feast of the ascension. So if we are to celebrate the Lord's ascension in the right way, with faith, with devotion, with reverence as God-fearing people, we must ascend with him and lift up our hearts. In ascending, however, we must not get above ourselves. Yes, we should lift up our hearts, but to the Lord. As you know, not lifting up hearts to the Lord is due to pride; lifting up hearts to the Lord is called "taking refuge." After all, we say to the one who has ascended, "Lord, you have become a refuge for us."

He rose again, you see, to give us hope, because what rises again is what first dies. So it [Christ's resurrection] was to save us from despair at dying and from thinking that our whole life ends with death. We were anxious, I mean, about the soul, and he by rising again gave us an assurance even about the flesh. So he ascended—who did? The one who descended.[3] He descended in order to heal you; he ascended in order to lift you up. You will fall if you have lifted yourself up; you remain standing if you have been lifted up by him. So, lift up your hearts, but to the Lord—that is taking refuge. Lifting up your heart, but not to the Lord, that is pride. So let us say to him as he rises again, "Since you, O Lord, are my hope"; and as he ascends, "You have placed your refuge very high."[4] How, I mean, can we possibly be proud, if we lift up our hearts to him, seeing that he humbled himself for our sakes, so that we should not remain proud? SERMON 261.1.[5]

GOD IS FROM EVERLASTING TO EVERLASTING.
ATHANASIUS: It is plain then from the above that the Scriptures declare the Son's eternity; it is equally plain from what follows that the Arian phrases "he was not" and "before" and "when"[6] are in the same Scriptures predicated of creatures. Moses, for instance, in his account of the generation of our world, says, "And every plant of the field, before it was in the earth, and every herb of the field before it grew; for the Lord God had not caused it to rain on the earth, and there was not a man to till the ground."[7] And in Deuteronomy, "When the most High gave to the nations their inheritance."[8] And the Lord said, "If you love me, you will rejoice because I said, I go to the Father, for my Father is greater than I. And now I have told you before it comes to pass, that when it comes to pass, you might believe." And concerning the creation he says in the words of Solomon, "Before the world existed, when there were no depths, I was brought forth; when there were no fountains abounding with water. Before the mountains were settled, before the hills, I was brought forth."[9] And, "Before Abraham was, I am."[10] And concerning Jeremiah he says, "Before I formed you in the womb, I knew you."[11] And

---

[2]FC 46:299-300*. [3]See Jn 3:13. [4]Ps 91:9 (90:9 LXX, Vg.). [5]WSA 3 7:208*. [6]Important terms in the Arian heresy, which claimed that the Son of God did not exist in all eternity. [7]Gen 2:5. [8]Deut 32:8. [9]Prov 8:23-25. [10]Jn 8:58. [11]Jer 1:5.

David in the psalm says, "Before the mountains were brought forth, or ever the earth and the world were made, you are God from everlasting and world without end."[12] And in Daniel,[13] "Susanna cried out with a loud voice and said, O everlasting God, you know the secrets, and know all things before they are."[14] Thus it appears that the phrases "once was not," and "before it came to be," and "when" and the like, belong to things that have an origin and were created, which come out of nothing but are alien to the Word. DISCOURSES AGAINST THE ARIANS 1.4.13.[15]

90:5-6 Life Is Like Grass

LIFE'S TRANSIENCE IS THE REASON FOR NEW LIFE. AUGUSTINE: Whatever there is in the world, it fades away, it passes. As for this life, what is it but what the psalmist said: "In the morning it will pass like the grass; in the morning it will flower and pass away; in the evening it will fall, it grows hard and withers."[16] That is what "all flesh is."[17] That is why Christ, that is why the new life, that is why eternal hope, that is why the consolation of immortality has been promised us and in the flesh of the Lord has already been given us. It was from us, after all, that that flesh was taken that is now immortal and that has shown us what he accomplished in himself. It was on our account, you see, that he had flesh. I mean, on his own account "in the beginning was the Word, and the Word was with God, and the Word was God."[18] Look for flesh and blood; where is it to be found in the Word? Because he wished really and truly to suffer with us and to redeem us, he clothed himself in "the form of a servant"[19] and came down here though he was here, in order to be plainly visible though he had never been absent; and he that had made humanity wished to be made human; to be created of a mother, though he had created his mother. He mounted the cross; he died and showed us what we already knew about, being born and dying. In his humility he went through

with those hoary old experiences of ours, so familiar, so well known. SERMON 359.9.[20]

90:8 God Knows All Our Sins

SINS CANNOT BE HIDDEN FROM GOD. JEROME: "You have kept our iniquities before you." Nothing eludes you; night does not conceal our sins, nor does the darkness cover them; all things are clear before you: "Our life in light of your scrutiny." This is expressed much better in the Hebrew: "our hidden sins in the light of your scrutiny." Whatever we do, whatever we think we are doing in secret, lies open before your eyes. "All our days have passed away."[21] Our life hurries on at a great pace, and when we least expect it, it slips away, and we die. These very words we speak are of death, and we do not take thought. "We have spent our years like a spider."[22] Meditate on these words of the psalmist. In the same way that the spider produces, as it were, a thread and runs to and fro, back and forth, and weaves the whole day long, and his labor, indeed, is great but the result is nil; so, too, human life runs about hither and thither. We search for possessions, and we accumulate wealth; we procreate children; we labor and toil; we rise in power and authority; we do everything; and do not realize that we are spiders weaving a web. HOMILIES ON THE PSALMS 19.[23]

90:9-10 Life Is Full of Toil and Trouble

ALL PEOPLE WERE CHILDREN OF WRATH. AUGUSTINE: And so the human race was held fast in a just condemnation, and all people were children of wrath—of that wrath of which it is written, "All our days are spent; and in your wrath we have fainted away. Our years shall be considered as a spider." Or as Job says of this same wrath, "Man, born of a woman, living for a short time, is

---

[12]Ps 90:3 (89:3 LXX). [13]In both the Septuagint and Vulgate versions of the Bible, the apocryphal *History of Susanna* was added to the book of Daniel. [14]*History of Susanna* 42. [15]NPNF 2 4:313-14*. [16]Ps 90:6 (89:6 LXX, Vg.). [17]Is 40:6. [18]Jn 1:1. [19]Phil 2:7. [20]*WSA* 3 10:206-7. [21]Ps 90:9 (89:9 LXX, Vg.). [22]See Ps 89:9 (LXX). [23]FC 48:149-50.

full of wrath."[24] And of this wrath the Lord Jesus also speaks: "He who believes in the Son has everlasting life; he who does not believe in the Son does not have life, but the wrath of God rests on him."[25] He does not say it "will come" but it "rests" upon him, for everyone is born with it. And that is why the apostle says, "We were by nature children of wrath even as the rest."[26] Since people were lying under this wrath because of original sin—sin still more heavy and destructive in proportion as the sins added on it were great or numerous—there was the need for a mediator, that is, a reconciler, who would placate this wrath by the offering of one sacrifice, of which all the sacrifices under the law and the prophets were foreshadowings. ENCHIRIDION 10.33.[27]

FULL OF LABOR AND TROUBLE. DIONYSIUS OF ALEXANDRIA: For in the most general sense it holds good that it is apparently not possible for any person to remain altogether without experience of ill. For, as one says, "the whole world lies in wickedness";[28] and again, "Most of the days of human life are labor and trouble." But you will perhaps say, "What difference is there between being tempted, and falling or entering into temptation?" Well, if one is overcome by evil—and he will be overcome unless he struggles against it himself and unless God protects him with his shield—that person has entered into temptation, and is in it and is brought under it like one that is led captive. But if one withstands and endures, he is indeed tempted; but he has not entered into temptation or fallen into it. Thus Jesus was led up of the Spirit, not indeed to enter into temptation but to be tempted of the devil.[29] And Abraham, again, did not enter into temptation, neither did God lead him into temptation, but he tried [tested] him; yet he did not drive him into temptation. The Lord, moreover, tested the disciples. Thus the wicked one, when he tempts us, draws us into the temptations, as dealing himself with the temptations of evil. But God, when he tests, presents the tests as one untempted by evil. For God, it is said, "cannot be tempted by evil."[30] The

devil, therefore, drives us on by violence, drawing us to destruction; but God leads us by hand, training us for our salvation. FRAGMENT 2.[31]

A SEVENTY-YEAR LIFE IS SHORT COMPARED WITH ETERNAL LIFE. ATHANASIUS: Let everyone above all have this zeal in common so that having made a beginning they not hesitate or grow fainthearted in their labors or say, "We have spent a long time in ascetic discipline." Instead, as though we were beginning anew each day, let each of us increase in fervor. For the entire lifetime of a human being is very brief when measured against the age to come; accordingly, all our time here is nothing compared with life eternal. Everything in the world is sold according to its value and things of equal value are exchanged, but the promise of eternal life[32] is purchased for very little. For it is written, "The days of our life are seventy years or, if we are strong, perhaps eighty; more than this is pain and suffering." When we persevere in ascetic discipline for all eighty or even one hundred years, we will not reign for the equivalent of those one hundred years. Instead of a hundred years, we will reign forever and ever. And although we are contested on earth, we will not receive our inheritance here; we have promises in heaven instead. Once more: when we lay aside this perishable body we receive it back imperishable.[33] LIFE OF ST. ANTHONY 16.3-8.[34]

THE BENEFIT OF YEARS OF PENITENTIAL SORROW. PALLADIUS OF HELENOPOLIS: They say concerning Abba Apollo, who lived in Scete, that he was originally a rude and brutish herdsman, and that he [once] saw in the fields a woman who was with child and that, through the operation of the devil, he said, "I wish to know the condition of the child that is in the womb of this woman," and that he ripped her open and saw the child in

---

[24]Job 14:1 LXX. [25]Jn 3:36. [26]Eph 2:3. [27]FC 2:398*. [28]1 Jn 5:19. [29]Mt 4:1. [30]Jas 1:13. [31]ANF 6:116*. [32]See 1 Tim 4:8. [33]See 1 Cor 15:42. [34]CS 202:97, 99.

her belly; then straightway he repented, and he purged his heart, and having repented he went to Scete and revealed unto the fathers what he had done. And when he heard them singing the psalms and saying, "The days of our years are threescore years and ten, and with difficulty [we come] to fourscore years," he said to the old men, "I am forty years old this day, and I have never prayed; and now, if I live for forty years more, I will never rest nor cease nor refrain from praying to God continually that he may forgive me my sins." And from that time onwards he did even as he had said, for he never toiled with the work of his hands, but he was always supplicating God and saying, "I, O my Lord, like a man, have sinned, and do you, like God, forgive me"; and he prayed this prayer both by night and by day instead of reciting psalms. And a certain brother who used to dwell with him once heard him say in his prayer, now as he spoke he wept, and groaned from the bottom of his heart and sighed in grief of heart, "O my Lord, I have vexed you; have pity on me, and forgive me so that I may enjoy a little rest." Then a voice came to him that said, "Your sins have been forgiven you, and also the murder of the woman; but the murder of the child is not yet forgiven you." And one of the old men said, "The murder of the child also was forgiven to him, but God left him to work because this would prove beneficial to his soul." LAUSIAC HISTORY 2.38.[35]

90:12 A Heart of Wisdom

GOD'S RIGHT HAND. JEROME: "So make your right hand known that fettered we may gain wisdom of heart." Some codices say "trained"; others "fettered." "Trained" implies one thing; "fettered," another. What, then, is the meaning of "make your right hand known"? Why have you restrained your right hand so long, God? "Why draw back your hand and keep it idle beneath your garment?"[36] says another psalm. Here is its meaning: we are lying prostrate in sickness; we

are powerless in our sins; send forth your right hand and raise us up. Why do you keep your right hand so long idle beneath your cloak? Your heart overflows with a goodly theme;[37] send forth your right hand and set us free. Make known to us the mystery that has been hidden from generation to generation. "Make your right hand known." What are you pilfering, Arius?[38] The psalmist did not say, "Make your right hand," for God was never without his right hand. But what did he say? Your right hand, that you have always had and that has been in your bosom,[39] make it known to us. Because we are not able to know him abiding in his Godhead, he assumes our humanity, and in that way we know him. HOMILIES ON THE PSALMS 19.[40]

90:17 The Favor of the Lord

THE EVERLASTING GOD. ATHANASIUS: Thus, if Isaiah says, "The everlasting God, the Creator of the ends of the earth";[41] and Susanna said, "O everlasting God";[42] and Baruch wrote, "I will cry to the Everlasting in my days," and shortly after, "My hope is in the Everlasting, that he will have you, and joy is come to me from the holy One";[43] yet forasmuch as the apostle, writing to the Hebrews, says, "Who being the radiance of his glory and the expression of his person";[44] and David too in the nineteenth psalm, "And the brightness of the Lord be on us," and, "In your light shall we see light,"[45] who has so little sense as to doubt the eternity of the Son? For when did humankind see light without the brightness of its radiance, that he may say of the Son, "There was once, when he was not," or "Before his generation he was not."[46] DISCOURSES AGAINST THE ARIANS 1.4.12.[47]

---

[35]PHF 1:270*. [36]Ps 74:11 (73:11 LXX, Vg.). [37]See Ps 45:1 (44:2 LXX, Vg.). [38]Jerome is alluding to the heretic Arius's belief that the Son, God's right hand, did not always exist. [39]That the Son had always existed in the very being or mind of God. [40]FC 48:153*. [41]Is 40:28. [42]History of Susanna 42. [43]Bar 4:20, 22. [44]Heb 1:3. [45]Ps 36:9 (35:10 LXX). [46]These were key expressions of Arian subordinationism. [47]NPNF 2 4:313*.

91:1-16 A TESTIMONY TO THE SECURITY OF THE REDEEMED

¹He who dwells in the shelter of the Most
High,
who abides in the shadow of the Almighty,
²will say to the LORD, "My refuge and my
fortress;
my God, in whom I trust."
³For he will deliver you from the snare of the
fowler
and from the deadly pestilence;
⁴he will cover you with his pinions,
and under his wings you will find refuge;
his faithfulness is a shield and buckler.
⁵You will not fear the terror of the night,
nor the arrow that flies by day,
⁶nor the pestilence that stalks in darkness,
nor the destruction that wastes at noonday.

⁷A thousand may fall at your side,
ten thousand at your right hand;
but it will not come near you.
⁸You will only look with your eyes
and see the recompense of the wicked.

⁹Because you have made the LORD your
refuge,ᵇ
the Most High your habitation,
¹⁰no evil shall befall you,
no scourge come near your tent.
¹¹For he will give his angels charge of you
to guard you in all your ways.
¹²On their hands they will bear you up,
lest you dash your foot against a stone.
¹³You will tread on the lion and the adder,
the young lion and the serpent you will
trample under foot.

¹⁴Because he cleaves to me in love, I will
deliver him;
I will protect him, because he knows my
name.
¹⁵When he calls to me, I will answer him;
I will be with him in trouble,
I will rescue him and honor him.
¹⁶With long life I will satisfy him,
and show him my salvation.

h Cn: Heb Because thou, LORD, art my refuge; you have made

OVERVIEW: A person who joins himself closely to God receives divine help and support (GREGORY OF NYSSA). Christ is the "refuge" spoken of by David; he became our refuge by being made man (AUGUSTINE). Only God can save us from the snares laid by Satan, the master of deception; only when we put an end to sin and are in a state of grace can we find peace (JEROME). The just and wise person who keeps God's commandments has no reason to fear any enemy whatsoever (ORIGEN). Since there are disasters in which many people lose their lives, it is not unreasonable to believe that many souls will perish eternally. Bodily afflictions experienced by godly believers are not punishments for specific sins but visitations of a loving, disciplining God (JEROME).

Satan deceived himself by thinking that he could destroy the truth and tempt Christ in the wilderness by quoting Scripture and by acknowledging Christ to be the Son of God (TERTULLIAN, AUGUSTINE). Believers should serve God only, not the demons that seek to destroy them (ORIGEN). Believers should not worship demons instead of God since they are powers who have been conquered by Christ (TERTULLIAN). Lack of faith makes us prey to corruption and should be feared more than wild beasts, which did not harm people of faith in Scripture (BASIL). Beware of Satan, who has not lost his power and especially to be feared when he uses flattery (AUGUSTINE). Sin is like the wild beasts that God as a loving physician tramples under foot so that we will not perish because of them (CAESARIUS).

91:1-6 God Is Our Helper

DWELLING IN THE SHELTER OF THE MOST HIGH. GREGORY OF NYSSA: When the great David heard and understood this,[1] he [David] said to him "who dwells in the shelter of the most High; He will overshadow you with his shoulders," which is the same as being behind God (for the shoulder is on the back of the body). Concerning himself David says, "My soul clings close to you, your right hand supports me."[2] You see how Psalms agree with the history. For as the one[3] says that the right hand is a help to the person who has joined himself close behind God, so the other says that the hand touches the person who waits in the rock on the divine voice and prays that he might follow behind. LIFE OF MOSES 250.[4]

CHRIST BECAME OUR REFUGE. AUGUSTINE: "When the fullness of time had come, God sent his Son, made from a woman, made under the law."[5] People are upset by "made from a woman," because we confess that he was born of a virgin. It is only of man that we confess he was made; God is always the one who makes, he cannot be made in order to be. God cannot be made; but he is made into, or becomes, something for someone, in the way in which it is said of him, "Lord, you have become (or have been made into) a refuge

for us"; and, "The Lord has become (has been made) my helper."[6] How many things he has been made into, though he never was made at all! Now the Lord Christ was made man, . . . in order for him who was always the creator to be a creature. While remaining God, you see, he became man in order to become what he was not, not in order to stop being what he was. SERMON 49A.[7]

THE SNARES OF SATAN, THE HUNTER. JEROME: "Say to the Lord, 'My refuge and my fortress, my God.'" I am hemmed in by enemies. You, therefore, are my refuge. "'In whom I will trust.' For he will rescue you from the snare of the hunters.'" Note carefully that the psalmist did not say "I trust" but "I will trust." As long as we continue in a life of sin, we certainly are not trusting; if we put an end to sin, then our hope is confident. "For he will rescue you from the snare of the hunters." There are many hunters in this world that go about setting traps for our soul. Nimrod the giant was a "mighty hunter before the Lord."[8] Esau, too, was a hunter, for he was a sinner. In all of holy Scripture, never do we find a hunter that is a faithful servant; we do find faithful fishermen.

"For he will rescue you from the snare of the hunters." "We were rescued like a bird from the fowler's snare; broken was the snare, and we were freed."[9] What snare is this that has been broken? "The Lord," says the apostle, "will speedily crush Satan under our feet";[10] "that you may recover yourselves from the snare of the devil."[11] You see, then, that the devil is the hunter, eager to lure our souls unto perdition. The devil is master of many snares, deceptions of all kinds. Avarice is one of his pitfalls, disparagement is his noose, fornication is his bait. "And from the destroying word." As long as we are in the state of grace, our soul is at peace; but once we begin to play with sin, then

---

[1]The fact that God who has made all things invites and commands us to follow him. [2]Ps. 63:8 (62:9 LXX). [3]Ps 63:8 (62:9 LXX). [4]MFC 9:159. [5]Gal 4:4. [6]Ps 30:10 (29:11 LXX, Vg.). [7]WSA 3 2:342*. [8]Gen 10:8-9. [9]Ps 124:7 (123:7 LXX, Vg.). [10]Rom 16:20. [11]2 Tim 2:26.

our soul is in trouble and is like a boat tossed about by the waves. HOMILIES ON THE PSALMS 20.[12]

ONE WHO FEARS GOD IS NOT AFRAID OF DANGER. ORIGEN: He said these things[13] about the just and wise person and these are said in the blessings, "You will sleep and there will not be anyone who frightens you."[14] For if I am made just, no one can frighten me; I am afraid of nothing else, if I fear God. For it says, "the just is confident as a lion,"[15] and for this reason, he does not fear the lion, the devil, or "the dragon," Satan, or "his angels";[16] but, according to David, he says, "I shall not be afraid of the nocturnal fear, nor the dart which flies during the day, nor the terror which walks in the darkness nor the ruin and the midday demon." And he adds that "the Lord is my light and my Savior, whom shall I fear? The Lord is the defender of my life, at what shall I tremble?"[17] And again, "If an army stands against me, my heart will not fear."[18] You see the steadfastness and vigor of the soul that keeps the commandments of God and has confidence in the freedom that God gives. HOMILIES ON LEVITICUS 16.6.1.[19]

MANY WILL PERISH. JEROME: "Nor the attack of the noonday demon." This is better expressed by the Greek. *Symptosis* implies a chance occurrence when something strange happens unexpectedly; or *symptoma* may denote a disaster in which many perish at the same time. Grasp, then, what it means. Even though many have been seduced, nevertheless, you who are in the state of grace may escape seduction. I shall give you an example so that even the more simple[-minded] among you may understand what I mean. If you should go to the city, a monk all by yourself, and while you are strolling about you hear a shout in the circus and someone says to you, "Come and see, it is the circus," and you hold back remonstrating, "I have no permission, I cannot go"; if he should call your attention to the thousands of people there and say to you, "Two hundred thou-

sand people are there, are they all going to be lost, and you alone be saved?" You have to be aware that *symptoma* is the devil's own doing. What I am trying to say is that you have to know that many do perish and are lost. HOMILIES ON THE PSALMS 20.[20]

91:10 *Afflictions Can Be Beneficial*

GOD ALLOWS THE RIGHTEOUS TO BE AFFLICTED FOR A PURPOSE. JEROME: And now that I am writing to you I beseech you. Do not regard the bodily affliction[21] that has befallen you as due to sin. When the apostles speculated concerning the man that was born blind from the womb and asked our Lord and Savior: "Who did sin, this man or his parents, that he was born blind?" they were told "Neither has this man sinned nor his parents, but that the works of God should be made manifest in him."[22] Do we not see numbers of pagans, Jews, heretics and people of various opinions rolling in the mire of lust, bathed in blood, surpassing wolves in ferocity and hawks in rapacity, and "for all this the plague does not come near their dwellings"? They are not struck as other people, and accordingly they grow insolent against God and lift up their faces even to heaven. We know on the other hand that holy people are afflicted with sicknesses, miseries and want, and perhaps they are tempted to say, "Truly I have cleansed my heart in vain and washed my hands in innocence." Yet immediately they go on to reprove themselves, "If I say, I will speak thus; behold, I should offend against the generation of your children."[23] If you suppose that your blindness is caused by sin and that a disease [such as blindness] that physicians are often able

---

[12]FC 48:156-57. [13]The reference is to what Solomon said in Proverbs 3:24-25. [14]Lev 26:6. [15]Prov 28:1. [16]See Rev 12:7. [17]Ps 27:1 (26:1 LXX). [18]Ps 27:3 (26:3 LXX). [19]FC 83:272**. [20]FC 48:159. [21]Jerome wrote this letter to Castrutius, a blind man from Pannonia who had set out to visit Jerome in Bethlehem but was persuaded en route by friends to return home. Jerome wrote this letter to thank him for his intentions and to console him in his blindness. [22]Jn 9:2-3. [23]Ps 73:13, 15 (72:13, 15 LXX, Vg.).

to cure is an evidence of God's anger, you will think Isaac a sinner because he was so wholly sightless that he was deceived into blessing one whom he did not mean to bless.[24] You will charge Jacob with sin, whose vision became so dim that he could not see Ephraim and Manasseh,[25] although with the inner eye and the prophetic spirit he could foresee the distant future and the Christ that was to come of his royal line.[26] Were any of the kings holier than Josiah? Yet he was slain by the sword of the Egyptians.[27] Were there ever loftier saints than Peter and Paul? Yet their blood stained the blade of Nero. And to say no more of people, did not the Son of God endure the shame of the cross? And yet you fancy those blessed who enjoy in this world happiness and pleasure? God's hottest anger against sinners is when he shows no anger. Therefore in Ezekiel he says to Jerusalem, "My jealousy will depart from you, and I will be quiet and will be no more angry."[28] For "whom the Lord loves he chastens, and scourges every son whom he receives."[29] The father does not instruct his son unless he loves him. The master does not correct his disciple unless he sees in him signs of promise. When once the doctor gives up caring for the patient, it is a sign that he despairs. You should answer thus: "as Lazarus in his lifetime[30] received evil things so will I now gladly suffer torments that future glory may be laid up for me." For "affliction shall not rise up the second time."[31] If Job, a man holy and spotless and righteous in his generation, suffered terrible afflictions, his own book explains the reason why. LETTER 68.1.[32]

91:11-13 God Has Power Over Beasts and Demons Who Threaten His People

SATAN TESTIFIES TO CHRIST'S DIVINITY. TERTULLIAN: In various ways has the devil rivaled and resisted the truth. Sometimes Praxeas's[33] aim has been to destroy the truth by defending it. He maintains that there is only one Lord, the almighty Creator of the world, in order that out of this doctrine of the unity he may fabricate a

heresy. He says that the Father himself came down into the Virgin, was himself born of her, himself suffered, indeed was himself Jesus Christ. Here the old serpent has fallen out with himself, since, when he tempted Christ after John's baptism, he approached him as "the Son of God." Surely he was intimating that God had a Son, even on the testimony of the very Scriptures, out of which he was at the moment forging his temptation: "If you are the Son of God, command that these stones be made bread."[34] Again, "If you are the Son of God, cast yourself down from here; for it is written, he shall give his angels charge concerning you"[35]—referring no doubt, to the Father—"and in their hands they shall bear you up, so that you do not hurt your foot against a stone." Or perhaps, after all, he was only reproaching the Gospels with a lie, saying in fact, "Away with Matthew. Away with Luke!" AGAINST PRAXEAS 1.[36]

HERETICS LISTEN TO SATAN, NOT TO CHRIST. AUGUSTINE: Well, the Donatists[37] are not false Christians. They are quite simply not Christians at all, since they listen to what the devil suggested and do not listen to the answer Christ gave him. How, after all, did the Lord, our teacher and savior, answer the devil's suggestion of such things? "Get back, Satan, for it is written: You shall not tempt the Lord your God."[38] The devil, as a matter of fact, had taken his suggestion from Scripture, and the Lord replied from Scripture. The devil had said to the Lord, you see, "Since it is written, He will instruct his angels about you; they will lift you up in their hands, lest you should hurt your foot on a stone." "Hurl

---

[24]Gen 27. [25]Gen 48:10. [26]Gen 49:10. [27]2 Kings 23:29. [28]Ezek 16:42. [29]Heb 12:6. [30]Lk 16:25. [31]Nahum 1:9. [32]NPNF 2 6:140-1**. [33]Praxeas advocated the Sabellian or modalistic view that the Father, Son and Holy Spirit are not separate persons in the Godhead but only three separate modes or manners of expression of the one divine being. [34]Mt 4:3. [35]Mt 4:6. [36]ANF 3:597*. [37]Third-century and later heretics who insisted on church purity and that the validity of the sacraments depended on the integrity of the clergy performing them. [38]Mt 4:10, 7; Deut 6:16.

yourself down," he said, "and if you are the Son of God, the angels are there to catch you; what are you afraid of?" The Lord could indeed both have cast down his body and not allowed it to die; but what the devil was suggesting to Christ at that time is the sort of thing Christ was not teaching future Christians. This, you see, is exactly what the devil is also suggesting to the Donatists, saying, "Hurl yourselves down, the angels are there to catch you. With such a death[39] you do not go to punishment, but you win through to a crown." They would be Christians if they give an ear to Christ and did not trust the devil, who first separated them from the peace of the church and later on gave them cliff-jumpers."[40] SERMON 313E.4.[41]

NOTHING SHALL HARM THE BELIEVER. ORIGEN: His[42] next remark was, "Have not these inferior powers been assigned to them by God different departments, according as each was deemed worthy?" But this is a question that requires a very profound knowledge. For we must determine whether the Word of God, who governs all things, has appointed wicked demons for certain duties, in the same way as in states executioners are appointed, and other officers with cruel but necessary duties to discharge; or whether as among robbers, who infest desert places, it is customary for them to choose out of their number one who may be their leader—so the demons, who are scattered as it were in troops in different parts of the earth, have chosen for themselves a chief under whose command they may plunder and pillage human souls. To explain this fully and to justify the conduct of the Christians in refusing homage to any object except the most high God, and the Firstborn of all creation, who is his Word and God, we must quote this from Scripture: "All that ever came before me are thieves and robbers, but the sheep did not hear them"; and again, "The thief does not come, except to steal, and to kill and to destroy";[43] and other similar passages, as, "Behold, I have given you authority to tread on serpents and scorpions and over all

the power of the enemy, and nothing will by any means hurt you";[44] and again, "You shall tread on the lion and adder: the young lion and the dragon you shall trample under foot." But of these things Celsus knew nothing, or he would not have made use of language like this: "Is not everything that happens in the universe, whether it be the work of God, of angels, of other demons or of heroes, regulated by the law of the most high God? Have these not had assigned to them various duties of which they were severally deemed worthy? Is it not just, therefore, that he who serves God should serve those also to whom God has assigned such power?" To which he adds, "It is impossible, they say, for a man to serve many masters."[45] AGAINST CELSUS 7.70.[46]

CHRIST WILL DEFEAT SATAN. TERTULLIAN: This power[47] the Creator conferred on his Christ first of all, even as the ninetieth psalm [LXX] says of him: "You shall tread on the lion and the cobra; the young lion and the serpent you shall trample under foot." Isaiah also says, "In that day the Lord God shall draw his sacred, great and strong sword" (even his Christ) "against that dragon, that great and tortuous serpent; and he shall slay him in that day."[48] But when the same prophet says, "The way shall be called a clean and holy way; over it the unclean thing shall not pass, nor shall there be any unclean way; but the dispersed shall pass over it, and they shall not err therein; no lion shall be there, nor any ravenous beast shall go up thereon; it shall not be found there,"[49] he points out the way of faith, by which we shall reach

---

[39]The devil was suggesting that if the Donatists would throw themselves off a cliff, they would be protected by an angel. [40]Apparently some of the Donatists were throwing themselves off cliffs in obedience to the devil's suggestions. [41]WSA 3 9:111*. [42]Celsus, a second-century pagan Platonist who wrote *True Word*, which is considered the most literate and competent attack on the Christian faith in the period of the early church. [43]Jn 10:8-10. [44]Lk 10:19. [45]Mt 6:24; Lk 16:13. [46]ANF 4:639*. [47]The ability to tread on and put one's hand into the den of a poisonous animal and not be harmed. [48]Is 27:1 (LXX). [49]Is 35:8-9.

God; and then to this way of faith he promises this utter crippling and subjugation of all harmful animals. AGAINST MARCION 4.24.[50]

WILD ANIMALS ARE PROOF OF OUR FAITH.
BASIL THE GREAT: Wild animals are a proof of our faith. Have you trusted in the Lord? "You shall walk on the asp and the basilisk; and you shall trample under foot the lion and the dragon." You have the power through faith to walk on serpents and scorpions. Or, do you not observe that the viper that fastened onto Paul when he was gathering sticks inflicted no harm because the holy man was found to be full of faith? Yet, if you are incredulous, do not fear the wild beast more than your own lack of faith, through which you have made yourself an easy prey to every form of corruption. HOMILIES ON THE HEXAEMERON 9.6.[51]

TRAMPLE THE LION AND THE SERPENT.
AUGUSTINE: But what is said to Christ? "And you shall trample down the lion and the serpent." The lion because of his open danger, the serpent because of his concealed deception. The serpent drove Adam out of paradise; the very same one, as a lion, persecuted the church, as Peter says: "Your adversary the devil goes about as a roaring lion seeking whom he may devour."[52] Let the devil not appear to you to have lost his rage; when he flatters, he must be feared the more. TRACTATES ON THE GOSPEL OF JOHN 10.1.2.[53]

GOD PRESERVES US FOR REPENTANCE. CAE-SARIUS OF ARLES: However, we should not be without anxiety, dearly beloved, because we know that [God] is keeping his patience for such a long time. The fact that such great things happen in the world and he still does not avenge them indicates patience, not carelessness. God has not lost his power but is preserving us for repentance. Yet, the longer he awaits your amendment, the harsher will be your punishment if you refuse to amend. God indeed holds the sword, and he wishes to strike sin; we, on the contrary, defend our sins because we love them. Thus, we who should be the accusers of our sins become their defenders. Truly, dearly beloved, God does not want to kill the sinner, but his sin. Like a good doctor he wants to strike the disease, not the person who is ill. But, what is worse, we often despise the doctor and love our sickness: we love our sin and despise God. Sin, indeed, is like this, a dragon, a viper; but concerning the Lord it is written, "You shall walk on the lion and the cobra; and you shall trample under foot the young lion and the serpent." We, on the other hand, embrace our sins like lions and dragons. But our God, who wants to punish sin and save the sinner, daily exclaims to humanity: Cast off your sin from you, and without you it will die. If you refuse to throw aside your sin, you will perish with it, for sin cannot go unpunished. God wants to kill sin, not to strike the sinner. SERMON 17.4.[54]

---

[50] ANF 3:388**. [51] FC 46:146*. [52] 1 Pet 5:8. [53] FC 78:211*. [54] FC 31:92*.

92:1-15 A SONG OF PRAISE
FOR GOD'S RIGHTEOUS RULE

A Psalm. A Song for the Sabbath.

[1] *It is good to give thanks to the LORD*
  to sing praises to thy name, O Most High;
[2] *to declare thy steadfast love in the morning,*
  and thy faithfulness by night,
[3] *to the music of the lute and the harp,*
  to the melody of the lyre.
[4] *For thou, O LORD hast made me glad by thy*
  work;
  at the works of thy hands I sing for joy.

[5] *How great are thy works, O LORD!*
  Thy thoughts are very deep!
[6] *The dull man cannot know,*
  the stupid cannot understand this:
[7] *that, though the wicked sprout like grass*
  and all evildoers flourish,
they are doomed to destruction for ever,
  [8] *but thou, O LORD art on high for ever.*
[9] *For lo, thy enemies, O LORD*

for lo, thy enemies shall perish;
  all evildoers shall be scattered.

[10] *But thou hast exalted my horn like that of*
  the wild ox;
  thou hast poured over me[i] fresh oil.
[11] *My eyes have seen the downfall of my*
  enemies,
  my ears have heard the doom of my
  evil assailants.

[12] *The righteous flourish like the palm tree,*
  and grow like a cedar in Lebanon.
[13] *They are planted in the house of the LORD,*
  they flourish in the courts of our God.
[14] *They still bring forth fruit in old age,*
  they are ever full of sap and green,
[15] *to show that the LORD is upright;*
  he is my rock, and there is no
  unrighteousness in him.

i Syr: Heb uncertain

OVERVIEW: Before we sing songs of praise to God, we should first confess our sins to him who is able to forgive them (JEROME). Christ is compared with a unicorn in that he is the horn of our salvation and shares in the oneness of divine power (BASIL). The heart of a righteous person is compared with a palm tree, which is tall, straight and has a heart that is sweet and white (DESERT FATHERS). A person who appears to belong to the church but whose heart does not honor God is not a member of the true church (BASIL).

92:1 It Is Good to Give Thanks

CONFESSION AND PRAISE. JEROME: "It is good to confess to the Lord, to sing praise to your name, most High." The psalmist did not say that it is good to sing and after that confess. Note the order: it is good to confess, and it is good to sing. First repent and wash away sin with your tears; then sing to the Lord. "It is good to confess to the Lord"—not to people but to God. Confess your sins to him who is able to heal you. "And to sing praise to your name, most High." HOMILIES ON THE PSALMS 21.[1]

[1] FC 48:165*.

92:10 *The Power of Christ*

HIS HORN SHALL BE EXALTED. BASIL THE GREAT: Remember the calf in Exodus, which they fashioned through idolatry, which Moses beat to powder and gave to the people to drink.[2] In a manner similar to that calf, he will utterly destroy all Lebanon[3] and the practice of idolatry prevailing in it. "And as the beloved son of unicorns."[4] The only-begotten Son, he who gives his life for the world whenever he offers himself as a sacrifice and oblation to God for our sins, is called both Lamb of God and a sheep. "Behold," it is said, "the lamb of God." And again, "He was led like a sheep to slaughter." But, when it is necessary to take vengeance and to overthrow the power attacking the human race, a certain wild and savage force, then he will be called the Son of unicorns. For, as we have learned in Job, the unicorn is a creature irresistible in might and unsubjected to human beings. "For you cannot bind him with a thong," he says, "nor will he stay at your crib."[5] There is also much said in that part of the prophecy about the animal acting like a free person and not submitting to humans. It has been observed that the Scripture has used the comparison of the unicorn in both ways, at one time in praise, at another in censure. "Deliver," he says, "my soul from the sword . . . and my lowness from the horns of the unicorns."[6] He said these words complaining of the warlike people who in the time of passion rose up in rebellion against him. Again, he says, "My horn shall be exalted like that of the unicorn." It seems that on account of the promptness of the animal in repelling attacks it is frequently found representing the baser things, and because of its high horn and freedom it is assigned to represent the better. On the whole, since it is possible to find the "horn" used by Scripture in many places instead of "glory," as the saying, "He will exalt the horn of his people,"[7] and "His horn shall be exalted in glory,"[8] or also, since the "horn" is frequently used instead of "power," as the saying, "My protector and the horn of my salvation," Christ is the power of God; therefore, he is called the Unicorn on the ground that he has one horn, that is, one common power with the Father. HOMILIES ON THE PSALMS 13.5.[9]

92:12-13 *The Heart of the Believer*

BLOSSOM LIKE THE PALM TREE. DESERT FATHERS: An old man used to say, "It is written, 'The right-eous one shall blossom like the palm tree.'" Now these words make known that the soul acquires height, and straightness of stature and sweetness from beautiful deeds. But there is another quality that is found in the palm, that is, a single, white heart, which is wholly suitable for work (or useful for being worked). And this must be found in the righteous person, for his heart must be single and simple, and it must be accustomed to look toward God only. Now the heart of the palm tree is also white by reason of that fire that it possesses naturally, and all the service of the right-eous person is in his heart; and the hollowness and the evenness of the tops of the leaves [typify] the setting up of sharpness of the soul of the righteous person against the calumniator.[10] SAYINGS OF THE FATHERS 186.[11]

THE BELIEVER FLOURISHES IN GOD'S COURTS. BASIL THE GREAT: Accordingly, it is not proper to adore God outside of this holy court, but only within it, lest anyone who is outside of it and is attracted by those outside of it might lose the right to be in the court of the Lord. Many assume an attitude of prayer, but they are not in the court because of the wandering of their mind and the distraction of their thoughts coming from vain solicitude. It is possible to consider the court in a still loftier sense as the heavenly way of life. Therefore, "They that are planted" here "in the house of the Lord," which is the church of the living God, they "shall

---

[2]See Ex 32:20. [3]See Ps 36:35 (LXX). [4]Ps 29:6 (28:6 LXX). [5]Job 39:10. [6]Ps 22:20-21 (21:21-22 LXX). [7]Ps 148:14. [8]Ps 112:9 (111:9 LXX). [9]FC 46:204-5*. [10]The one who utters maliciously false statements. [11]PHF 2:195*. These questions and answers provide guidelines for monastic living in Egypt in the fifth century.

flourish in the courts of our God." But one who makes his belly a god, or glory, or money or anything else which he honors more than all things, neither adores the Lord nor is in the holy court, even though he seems to be worthy of the visible assemblies. HOMILIES ON THE PSALMS 13.3.[12]

---

[12]FC 46:198*.

93:1-5 A HYMN TO GOD'S ETERNAL REIGN

[1]The LORD reigns; he is robed in majesty;
  the LORD is robed, he is girded with
    strength.
Yea, the world is established; it shall never be
  moved;
  [2] thy throne is established from of old;
  thou art from everlasting.

[3]The floods have lifted up, O LORD,

  the floods have lifted up their voice,
  the floods lift up their roaring.
[4]Mightier than the thunders of many waters,
  mightier than the waves[j] of the sea,
  the LORD on high is mighty!

[5]Thy decrees are very sure;
  holiness befits thy house,
  O LORD, for evermore.

j Cn: Heb *mighty the waves*

OVERVIEW: Christ's session at the right hand of God can be understood only in the light of his incarnation and the eternity of his power (RUFINUS).

93:2 The Throne of God Is from Everlasting

GOD'S THRONE HAS BEEN ESTABLISHED FROM ETERNITY. RUFINUS OF AQUILEIA: To sit at the right hand of the Father is a mystery belonging to the incarnation. For it does not befit that incorporeal nature without the assumption of flesh; neither is the excellency of a heavenly seat sought for the divine nature but for the human. Thus it is said of him, "Your seat, O God, is prepared from thence forward; you are from everlasting." The seat, then, on which the Lord Jesus was to sit, was prepared from everlasting, "in whose name every knee should bow, of things in heaven and things on earth and things under the earth; and every tongue shall confess to him that Jesus is Lord in the glory of God the Father;"[1] of whom also David says, "The Lord said to my Lord, Sit on my right hand until I make your enemies your footstool."[2] Referring to these words the Lord in the Gospel said to the Pharisees, "If therefore David in spirit calls him Lord, how is he his Son?"[3] By which [Jesus Christ] showed that according to the Spirit he was the Lord, according to the flesh he was the Son of David. Also the Lord says in another place, "Truly I say to you, henceforth you shall see the Son of man sitting at the right hand of the power of God."[4] And the apostle Peter says of Christ, "Who is on the right hand of God, seated

---

[1]Phil 2:10-11. [2]Ps 110:1 (109:1 LXX, Vg.). [3]Mt 22:43-45. [4]Mt 26:64; Lk 22:69.

in the heavens."[5] And Paul also, writing to the Ephesians, "According to the working of the might of his power, which he wrought in Christ, when he raised him from the dead and seated him on his right hand." COMMENTARY ON THE APOSTLES' CREED 32.[6]

---

[5]1 Pet 3:22. [6]NPNF 2 3:555-56**.

94:1-23 A PRAYER FOR DIVINE VENGEANCE ON THE WICKED

[1]O LORD thou God of vengeance,
    thou God of vengeance, shine forth!
[2]Rise up, O judge of the earth;
    render to the proud their deserts!
[3]O LORD, how long shall the wicked,
    how long shall the wicked exult?

[4]They pour out their arrogant words,
    they boast, all the evildoers.
[5]They crush thy people, O LORD,
    and afflict thy heritage.
[6]They slay the widow and the sojourner,
    and murder the fatherless;
[7]and they say, "The LORD does not see;
    the God of Jacob does not perceive."

[8]Understand, O dullest of the people!
    Fools, when will you be wise?
[9]He who planted the ear, does he not hear?
He who formed the eye, does he not see?
[10]He who chastens the nations, does he not
    chastise?
He who teaches men knowledge,
    [11]the LORD, knows the thoughts of man,
    that they are but a breath.

[12]Blessed is the man whom thou dost chasten,
    O LORD,
    and whom thou dost teach out of thy law
[13]to give him respite from days of trouble,
    until a pit is dug for the wicked.
[14]For the LORD will not forsake his people;
    he will not abandon his heritage;
[15]for justice will return to the righteous,
    and all the upright in heart will follow it.

[16]Who rises up for me against the wicked?
    Who stands up for me against evildoers?
[17]If the LORD had not been my help,
    my soul would soon have dwelt in the land
    of silence.
[18]When I thought, "My foot slips,"
    thy steadfast love, O LORD, held me up.
[19]When the cares of my heart are many,
    thy consolations cheer my soul.
[20]Can wicked rulers be allied with thee,
    who frame mischief by statute?
[21]They band together against the life of the
    righteous,
    and condemn the innocent to death.
[22]But the LORD has become my stronghold,

and my God the rock of my refuge.
[23]He will bring back on them their
*   iniquity*

and wipe them out for their wickedness;
the LORD our God will wipe them
*   out.*

Overview: God's people should not envy or be upset by the present success of sinners since it will be short-lived (Ambrose). Few people will deny the existence of God, but there are many who will deny his providential involvement in earthly affairs.

God gives people free will and bodily senses so that they may understand what Scripture says and what they accept by faith. The false assumption that God does not know or see what people are in this life leads them to sin openly. It is difficult for people accustomed to believe what they see to believe the miracles and words of God that surpasses our experience. The power granted to humanity in this world is great and can be wielded for the good of society, but it is nothing compared with the power and justice of God.

It is the folly of human pride to think that one can do good on his own and rightly exercise free will without the grace of God. God is not a helpless observer of our lives but one who becomes involved with our daily struggles, especially when we call on him.

God grants us prosperity and adversity—prosperity is a counterweight to adversity so that we are not broken by adversity, and adversity so that we are not weakened in faith by prosperity. If we were not sustained by the Holy Spirit in the trials and tribulations of this life, we would succumb to Satan. This life will not be free of sorrows, but it will be sustained by God, who keeps his promises (Augustine). The expectations of God's law are very demanding; thus, the road to heaven is not an easy one (Jerome). God often allows us to experience pain and afflictions so that, in his mercy, he may heal us (Augustine).

94:3 The Vanity of Worldly Prosperity

The Glory of Sinners Is Temporary.
Ambrose: We have discussed the prayer of holy Job; now let us approach that prayer that we have found in the psalms. David spoke out in many passages in regard to worldly vanity; he often asserted that the supposed goods of this world were vain, especially in the thirty-eighth psalm, in which he says, "And indeed all things are vanity, every one living. Although a person walks in the image of God, yet he is troubled vainly. He stores up, and he knows not for whom he is gathering these things."[1] And in another passage he says, "How long shall sinners, O Lord, how long shall sinners glory?"— because here they have a shadow of glory, but, when they have departed from life, they will not have the benefit of consolation. Still, the same David introduced into the collection Psalm 72 [LXX]. In it he declares, under the title Asaph,[2] that at first he almost fell, being afflicted with great pain. For he saw that sinners were wealthy and rich in this world and enjoyed prosperity and abundance, whereas he, who was just in his heart, was in afflictions and tribulations. He had committed a rather serious offense in the beginning; later he had been corrected and enlightened through the scourges of the Lord and had learned the course of true surrender by the gift of God's knowledge. The Prayer of Job and David 3.1.1.[3]

94:7 God Is Omniscient and Providential

God Exists and Governs the Universe.
Augustine: However, with the other class of unbelievers who either believe that there is no divine power or that it has nothing to do with human affairs, I am not sure that an argument should be undertaken on any subject of dutiful

---

[1]Ps 39:5-6 (38:6-7 LXX, Vg.). [2]Ps 73:1 (72:1 LXX, Vg.). [3]FC 65:368*.

devotion, although hardly anyone can be found nowadays who is so foolish as to dare to say even in his own heart, "There is no God."[4] But other fools are not lacking who have said, "The Lord shall not see," that is, he does not extend his providence to these earthly affairs. Accordingly, in those books which I wish your charity[5] to read, along with the description of the city of God, if God wills and for whom he wills, I shall justify the belief that not only does God exist—and this belief is so ingrained in nature that hardly any impiety ever tears it out—but that he regulates human affairs, from governing human beings to rewarding the just with blessedness in the company of the holy angels and condemning the wicked to the lot of the bad angels. LETTER 184.A.[6]

94:8-11 God Sees and Hears All Things

DIVINE GRACE AND FREE WILL. AUGUSTINE: Take care, then, to avoid what the great apostle sets forth so fearfully, and when you feel that you do not understand, make an immediate act of faith in what is divinely revealed, that there is both free will in humans and grace from God; and pray that what you religiously believe you may also wisely understand. Indeed, it is for this very reason that we have free will that we may wisely understand, for, unless our understanding and wisdom were regulated by free will, we should not be commanded in the words of Scripture: "Understand, you senseless among the people; and you fools be wise at last." The very fact, then, that we are instructed and commanded to understand and be wise is proof of a demand on our obedience, which cannot exist without free will. But, if it were possible for this to be accomplished by free will without the grace of God, namely, that we should understand and be wise, we should not have to say to God, "Give me understanding that I may know your commandments";[7] nor would it be written in the Gospel, "Then he opened their understanding that they might understand the Scriptures";[8] nor would the apostle James have said, "But if any of you lack

wisdom, let him ask of God who gives to all people abundantly and upbraids not: and it will be given to him."[9] LETTER 214.[10]

GOD KNOWS EVERYTHING. AUGUSTINE: When, then, that man,[11] so learned in the Scriptures, was commenting on the psalm where it says, "Understand, you senseless among the people; and you fools be wise at last. He who has planted the ear, shall he not hear? or he who has formed the eye, does he not consider?" He said, among other things, "This passage is directed chiefly against the anthropomorphists who say that God has members such as we have. For example, God is said to have eyes: the eyes of the Lord look on all things;[12] the hand of the Lord makes all things;[13] and it says, "Adam heard the footsteps of the Lord walking in paradise."[14] They take these expressions literally, and they attribute our human inadequacies to the magnificence of God. But I say that God is all eye, he is all hand, he is all foot. He is all eye because he sees all things; he is all hand because he effects all things; he is all foot because he is everywhere present. See, then, what it says, "He who has planted the ear, does he not hear?" It does not say, "He who has planted, does he not then have an ear?" and it does not say, "Does he not then have eyes?" What does it say? "He who has planted the ear, shall he not hear? He who has formed the eye, does he not consider?" He brought together the members, he gave the faculties.[15] LETTER 148.[16]

GOD HEARS AND SEES. AUGUSTINE: What is the topmost pinnacle of the building we are striving to construct? How far does the top of our edifice reach? I'll tell you straightaway: as far as the sight of God. You can see how high that is, what a great thing it is, to see God. Any of you who long

---

[4]Ps 14:1 (13:1 LXX, Vg.). [5]Two monks, Peter and Abraham, to whom the letter is written. [6]FC 30:140-41*. [7]Ps 119:125 (118:125 LXX, Vg.). [8]Lk 24:45. [9]Jas 1:5. [10]FC 32:61-2*. [11]Jerome. [12]See Prov 15:3. [13]See Is 64:8. [14]Gen 3:8. [15]Breviarium in Psalmum 93 (PL 26:1108). [16]FC 20:234-35**.

for this will understand what I am saying and you are hearing. We have been promised the sight of God, of the true God, of the supreme God. This really is a wonderful thing, to see the one who sees.[17]

I mean, those who worship false gods can easily see them, but they see gods who have eyes and do not see. But we have been promised the vision of the God who lives and sees, and so the God we should be yearning to see is the one of whom Scripture says, "Will he who planted the ear not hear? Does he who fashioned the eye not observe?" So does the one who made you something to hear with not hear himself? And does he not see, the one who created the means for you to see with?

In this psalm [the psalmist] very neatly prefaces those words with these: "Understand, therefore, you who are unwise among the people; and you fools, come sooner or later to your senses." You see, this is why many people do wrong, imagining that they are not noticed by God. It is difficult, of course, for them to believe he cannot see, but they assume he does not want to. You won't find many people so totally irreligious that they fulfill the text, "The fool has said in his heart, There is no God."[18] Few hold this crazy idea. Just as there aren't many people who are deeply religious, so there aren't many who are totally irreligious. But what I am going to say now is what the crowd says: "Look, do you really think God takes trouble to know what I do in my house, that God cares two cents what I choose to do in my bed?" Well, who is it that says, "Understand, you who are unwise among the people; and you fools, come sooner or later to your senses"? Being a mere human, it takes you quite a lot of trouble to know everything that goes on in your house and to insure that what your slaves say and do gets back to you; but do you imagine it is any trouble like that for God to pay attention to you, seeing that it was no trouble at all for him to create you? Having made your eyes, will he not turn his own on to you? You did not exist, and he created you, to bring you into being. Now that you do exist,

will he not care for you, he that summons the things that are not, as though they were? SERMON 69.3.[19]

GOD IS ALL-KNOWING. AUGUSTINE: So this Peter, playing the great part I have suggested to you, is questioned by the Lord after the resurrection, as we had it read to us, and he said to him, "Simon of John"—you see, he was called Simon when he was born; he was the son of John— "Simon of John, do you love me more than these?" Who is doing the questioning? The one who knew everything. Is he like someone who does not know, this one "who has passed on knowledge"? It was not that the Lord wanted to be informed, but that he wanted Peter to confess. SERMON 229P.2.[20]

HUMAN THOUGHTS ARE VAIN. AUGUSTINE: People argue against this evident truth. What else, after all, could you expect from mere people, who savor the things of humankind, but to argue about God against God? I mean, he is God, they are mere individuals. But God "knows the thoughts of people, that they are vain."[21] With worldly, materialistic people, what they are in the habit of observing entirely governs their manner of understanding. What they are accustomed to see, they can believe; what they aren't, they can't. God performs miracles that go beyond what we are accustomed to, because he is God. It is in fact a greater miracle, so many people being born every day who did not previously exist, than a few having risen again, who did exist; and yet this kind of miracle is not seriously considered and appreciated, but being so common is disregarded as uninteresting. Christ rose again; the case is complete and closed. He was body, he was flesh, which hung on the cross, gave up the soul, was placed in the tomb. He presented it alive, seeing

---

[17]See Gen 16:13. For Hagar, turned out into the desert, being seen was as important as seeing. [18]Ps 14:1 (13:1 LXX, Vg.); 53:1 (52:2 LXX, Vg.). [19]*WSA* 3 3:236*. [20]*WSA* 3 6:327-28. [21]Ps 94:11 (93:11 LXX, Vg.).

he lived in it. Why are we astonished, why don't we believe? It is God who did it. Reflect on the one who brought it about, and you eliminate all possibility of doubt. SERMON 242.1.[22]

94:12-15 God Is Faithful

GOD WILL NOT FORSAKE HIS PEOPLE.
AUGUSTINE: How much power in any case can mortals have? Let mortals hold on to justice; power will be given them when they are immortal. Compared with this, the power of those people who are called powerful on earth is shown to be ridiculous weakness, and "a pit is dug for the sinner" in the very place where the wicked seem to be able to do most. The just person sings, "Happy is the one whom you instruct, Lord, and teach from your law, in order to comfort him in evil days, until a pit is dug for the sinners. For the Lord will not reject his people or forsake his inheritance, until justice turns into judgment, and those who have it are all of an upright heart." So in this time during which the power of the people of God is being deferred, God will not reject his people or forsake his inheritance, however bitter and humiliating the trials it suffers in its humility and weakness, until the justice that now belongs to the weakness of the godly turns into judgment, that is until it receives the authority to judge, which is being reserved for the just in the end, when power follows in its proper order on the justice that preceded it. ON THE TRINITY 13.13.17.[23]

THE LORD WILL NOT CAST OFF HIS PEOPLE.
AUGUSTINE: What indeed does holy Scripture say in a psalm to those members who endure the wickedness of this age? "The Lord will not cast off his people." His people, in truth, toil among the unworthy, among the wicked, among blasphemers, among murmurers, detractors, persecutors, and, if it be allowed, killers. It toils indeed, but "the Lord will not cast off his people, and he will not forsake his own inheritance until justice is turned to judgment." "Until justice," which the

saints now possess, "is turned to judgment," when what was said to them will be fulfilled: "You will sit on twelve seats judging the twelve tribes of Israel."[24] The apostle possessed justice, but not yet that judgment about which he says, "Do you not know that we shall judge angels?"[25] TRACTATES ON THE GOSPEL OF JOHN 28.6.2.[26]

94:17-19 Without God's Help People Perish

GOD IS OUR HELPER.
AUGUSTINE: But why is there no fear of uttering an indirect lie? We do not deny that free will is healed by the grace of God, but we believe that we make progress through the daily grace of God, and we trust in its help. And people say, "It is in my own power to do good." If only people did do good! O empty boasting of wretchedness! Every day they disclaim sin, and in their boasting they attribute to themselves unaided free will, not scrutinizing their conscience, which cannot be healed but by grace, so as to say, "Be merciful to me, heal my soul, for I have sinned against you."[27] What would those do who boast of their own free will—which is not denied so long as it is helped by the grace of God—if death had now been swallowed up in victory, if our mortal were putting on immortality and our corruptible were putting on incorruption?[28] Behold, their wounds fester, and they seek a remedy in pride. They do not say with the just person, "Unless the Lord had been my helper, my soul had almost dwelled in hell." They do not say with the saint, "Except the Lord guards the city, he watches in vain that guards it."[29] LETTER 216.[30]

GOD COMES TO OUR AID.
AUGUSTINE: The one who arranged the contest helps the contestant. God, you see, does not watch you in the ring in the same way as the populace watch a charioteer; they know how to shout, they do not know

---

[22]WSA 3 7:78-79. [23]FC 45:393**. [24]Mt 19:28; Lk 22:30. [25]1 Cor 6:3. [26]FC 88:7*. [27]Ps 41:4 (40:5 LXX, Vg.). [28]See 1 Cor 15:53-54. [29]Ps 127:1 (126:1 LXX, Vg.). [30]FC 32:72*.

how to help. God does not watch you battling in the ring in the same way as the president at the games watches an athlete and prepares a crown of leaves for the winner; he does not know how to give strength to the man struggling in the arena, and he cannot do it anyhow; after all he is a man, not God. And perhaps while he is watching, he endures more weariness sitting there than the other does as he wrestles. God, you see, when he watches his champions, helps them when they call on him. I mean, it is the voice of his athlete in the psalm, "If I said, my foot is slipping, your mercy, Lord, came to my help." So, my brothers and sisters, do not let us be slow about it; let us ask, let us seek, let us knock. "For everyone who asks receives, and who seeks will find, and who knocks will have the door opened."[31] SERMON 343.10.[32]

GOD IS OUR EVER-PRESENT HELP. AUGUSTINE: All the same, you[33] must not think that you are in every respect or immediately going to be strong or . . . going to fail utterly by despairing. After all, that alternation of failure and of strength in the arms of God's servant Moses was, perhaps, your alternation. Sometimes, you see, you fail in your trials and temptations, but do not totally succumb to them. Moses let his arms droop a little but did not collapse altogether.[34] "If I were to say, my foot has slipped, behold, your mercy, Lord, would come to my help." So do not be afraid; the one is present on the journey to help you along, who was not absent in Egypt to set you free. Do not be afraid, step out along the road, be confident and throw care to the winds. Sometimes he lowered his arms, sometimes he lifted them up; anyway, Amalek was defeated. They were able to wage war, they were not able to win. SERMON 352.6.[35]

PUT YOUR CONFIDENCE IN THE LORD. AUGUSTINE: So, to conclude this sermon where we began it, let us pray and put all our trust in God; let us live as he commands us, and when we stumble and stagger in this life, let us call on him as

the disciples called upon him when they said, "Lord, increase our faith."[36] Peter too was full of confidence and staggered; yet he was not ignored and allowed to drown but given a helping hand and set on his feet. Just what, after all, did he place his confidence in? It was not in himself, it was in the Lord. How is that? "Lord, if it is you, bid me come to you over the water." The Lord, you remember, was walking over the waters. "If it is you, bid me come to you over the water." I know, you see, that if it is you, you have only to command, and it will happen. And he said, "Come." Peter got down from the boat at his command; he began to tremble at his own weakness. And yet when he grew afraid Peter cried out to him: "Lord, deliver me," he said. Then the Lord took him by the hand and said, "Little faith, why did you doubt?"[37] It was Jesus that invited him, he that delivered him when Peter tottered and staggered. "This fulfilled what was said in the psalm, "If I said, My foot has slipped, your mercy, Lord, would come to my help." SERMON 80.6.[38]

94:19 God Consoles Care-Stricken Souls

DIVINE PROVIDENCE BALANCES OUR ADVERSITY AND PROSPERITY. AUGUSTINE: Thus even the devil, the prince of that irreligious city, when he brings his instruments to bear on the city of God on pilgrimage in this world, is permitted to do it no harm. Without any doubt, the providence of God provides it with the consolation of prosperity so that it is not shattered by adversity, and with the discipline of adversity so that it is not corrupted by prosperity. And he so tempers the one with the other that we recognize here the source of that saying in the psalm, "According to the multitude of the sorrows in my heart, your consolations have gladdened my soul." Hence also the words of the apostle, "Rejoicing in hope, steadfast in tribulation."[39] CITY OF GOD 18.51.[40]

---

[31]Lk 11:10. [32]*WSA* 3 10:47. [33]The people to whom Augustine was preaching this sermon. [34]Ex 17:11-13. [35]*WSA* 3 10:145. [36]Lk 17:5. [37]Mt 14:28, 30-31. [38]*WSA* 3 3:354. [39]Rom 12:12. [40]CG 834.

CURBED BY CORRECTION AND CHEERED BY CONSOLATION. AUGUSTINE: This, then, is the way now in which one living according to Christ acts in regard to his flesh when he struggles against his evil lustfulness. He restrains it in order to be healed, but he retains it even though his flesh is not yet healed. Still he nourishes and cherishes his flesh's good nature, since "no one ever hated his own flesh."[41] In this way also Christ regards the church, insofar as we may compare lesser things with the greater. He both curbs it by corrections lest it be dissolved through the inflation of impunity, and he cheers it by consolations lest it succumb to the weight of its infirmity. In reference to this we have both the words of the apostle: "But if we judged ourselves, we should not thus be judged. But, when we are judged, we are being chastised by the Lord, that we may not be condemned with the world,"[42] and those of the psalm: "According to the multitude of my sorrows in my heart, your comforts have given joy to my soul." We must hope for the perfect soundness of our flesh, free from any resistance, because at that time the church of Christ will have a certain security that is free from any fear. ON CONTINENCE 11.25.[43]

GOD'S COMFORTER SAVES US FROM THE PERSECUTOR. AUGUSTINE: Dearly beloved, as I have already said, the devil is always either raging or lying in ambush. So, it behooves us to be always prepared by keeping our hearts fixed on the Lord. It behooves us to exert ourselves to the utmost in beseeching the Lord for fortitude in the midst of those harassing trials and tribulations, for of ourselves we are nothing but little children. What should we say with regard to ourselves? You have heard the answer from the apostle Paul during the reading of the epistle, in which he says, "For as the sufferings of Christ abound in us, so also through Christ does our comfort abound."[44] In the psalm, it is expressed in this way: "According to the multitude of my sorrows in my heart, your encouragements have given joy to my soul." The psalmist expresses it one way, the apostle expresses it in another, but each of them tells us

that if the Comforter were not with us we would yield to the persecutor. SERMON 13.5.[45]

GOD GIVES WHAT HE PROMISES. AUGUSTINE: Remember how often I remind you of this,[46] and let us not think that we ought now, in this life, to be happy and free from all trials; let us not sacrilegiously murmur against God in the straits of our temporal affairs, as if he were not giving us what he has promised. For he promised what we need for this life, but the comforting of the sad is one thing, the joys of the blessed something quite other. "Lord," the psalmist says, "according to the multitude of my sorrows in my heart, your comforts have given joy to my soul." Let us not, then, murmur in our trials, lest we lose the inclusiveness of good cheer, of which it is said, "rejoicing in hope," followed by "patient in tribulation."[47] Therefore, the new life begins now by faith and is carried on by hope, but then will come the time when "death shall be swallowed up in victory,"[48] when that "enemy, death, shall be destroyed last,"[49] when we shall be changed and shall become like the angels, "for we shall all indeed," he says, "rise again, but we shall not all be changed."[50] And the Lord said, "They will be equal to the angels of God."[51] We have now mastered fear by faith, but then we shall have the mastery in love by vision. "For as long as we are in the body, we are absent from the Lord, for we walk by faith and not by sight."[52] LETTER 55.[53]

94:20 God Is Mercifully Angry with Those Who Sin

GOD'S LAW REQUIRES EFFORT. JEROME: "Who cause toil by your law."[54] No one receives a crown

---

[41]Eph 5:29. [42]1 Cor 11:31-32. [43]FC 16:222**. [44]2 Cor 1:5. [45]FC 11:345-46*. [46]In the previous paragraph Augustine was speaking about the hardships we often face in this life and how we should patiently wait for the relief that will come in the next life. [47]Rom 12:12. [48]1 Cor 15:54. [49]1 Cor 15:26. [50]1 Cor 15:51. [51]Lk 20:36. [52]2 Cor 5:6-7. [53]FC 12:281-82*. [54]Cf. Letter 133.7. Earlier in the homily Jerome asserted that obeying God's will, such as giving food to the hungry, water to the thirsty or repenting of one's sins, requires effort.

while he is asleep; no one is secure in his possession of the kingdom of heaven; no one with a full stomach is fit to discourse on fasting.[55] You grasp now the force of the versicle: "who cause toil by your law." All the commandments of the Lord demand effort. Without labor and toil, we cannot possess the kingdom of heaven. Do you want to know why? "If you will be perfect, go, sell what you have and give to the poor, and come, follow me."[56] In other words, a person who desires to attain the kingdom of heaven, let him pray night and day; let him keep watch; let him fast; let him make his bed on rushes, not on down and silk. Penitence has no fellowship with soft luxuries. "For I eat ashes like bread and mingle my drink with tears."[57] HOMILIES ON THE PSALMS 22.[58]

THE LESSON OF SUFFERING. AUGUSTINE: But,

instead, I was in a ferment of wickedness. I deserted you and allowed myself to be carried away by the sweep of the tide. I broke all your lawful bounds and did not escape your lash. For what person can escape it? You were always present, angry and merciful at once, strewing the pangs of bitterness over all my lawless pleasures to lead me on to look for others unallied with pain. You meant me to find them nowhere but in yourself, O Lord, for you teach us by inflicting pain, you smite so that you may heal,[59] and you kill us so that we may not die away from you. CONFESSIONS 2.2.[60]

---

[55]Cf. Letter 52.7. [56]Mt 19:21. [57]Ps 102:9 (101:10 LXX, Vg.). [58]FC 48:180-81. [59]See Deut 32:39. [60]AC 44.

95:1-11 A CALL TO WORSHIP

[1]O come, let us sing to the LORD;
  let us make a joyful noise to the rock of our
    salvation!
[2]Let us come into his presence with
    thanksgiving;
  let us make a joyful noise to him with songs
    of praise!
[3]For the LORD is a great God,
  and a great King above all gods.
[4]In his hand are the depths of the earth;
  the heights of the mountains are his also.
[5]The sea is his, for he made it;
  for his hands formed the dry land.

[6]O come, let us worship and bow down,
  let us kneel before the LORD, our Maker!

[7]For he is our God,
  and we are the people of his pasture,
  and the sheep of his hand.

O that today you would hearken to his voice!
  [8]Harden not your hearts, as at Meribah,
  as on the day at Massah in the wilderness,
[9]when your fathers tested me,
  and put me to the proof, though they had
    seen my work.
[10]For forty years I loathed that generation
  and said, "They are a people who err
    in heart,
  and they do not regard my ways."
[11]Therefore I swore in my anger
  that they should not enter my rest.

OVERVIEW: When we consider what Christ, who holds the world in his hands, endured for us, we should be willing to honor him with our lives if required (JEROME). Every human being is created by God, even though the laws of procreation may seem to leave God out of the picture. Instead of trying to elevate ourselves above God, we should worship him since he alone can heal, save, and recreate us (AUGUSTINE).

The danger of delaying repentance in order to continue in sin for a time is that we may die before conversion and receipt of forgiveness (FULGENTIUS). During their forty-year wilderness journey, Israel turned away from and sinned against God; yet God remained present with and blessed Israel (CHRYSOSTOM). God will reward the faithful with an eternal rest, but he will deny it to the wicked (AMBROSE).

95:4-5 The World Belongs to God

HOW CAN WE REPAY GOD FOR HIS BENEFITS? JEROME: For our salvation the Son of God is made the Son of man. Nine months he awaits his birth in the womb, undergoes the most revolting conditions and comes forth covered with blood, to be swathed in rags and covered with caresses. "He who clasps the world in his fist" is contained in the narrow limits of a manger. I say nothing of the thirty years during which he lives in obscurity, satisfied with the poverty of his parents. When he is scourged, he holds his peace; when he is crucified, he prays for his crucifiers. "What shall I render to the Lord for all his benefits towards me? I will take the cup of salvation and call on the name of the Lord. Precious in the sight of the Lord is the death of his saints."[1] The only fitting return that we can make to him is to give blood for blood; and, as we are redeemed by the blood of Christ, gladly to lay down our lives for our Redeemer. What saint has ever won his crown without first contending for it? Righteous Abel is murdered. Abraham is in danger of losing his wife. And, as I must not enlarge my book unduly, seek for yourself: you will find that all

holy people have suffered adversity. Solomon alone lived in luxury, and perhaps it was for this reason that he fell. For "whom the Lord loves, he chastens, and scourges every son whom he receives."[2] Which is best—for a short time to do battle, to carry stakes for the palisades, to bear arms, to faint under heavy bucklers, that ever afterwards we may rejoice as victors? Or to become slaves forever, just because we cannot endure for a single hour?[3] LETTER 22.39.[4]

95:6 Worship God and Bow Down Before God

GOD MADE AND PRESERVES US. AUGUSTINE: But I do not somehow think that this[5] is what the Holy Spirit was chiefly concerned to remind us of in this psalm, where it says, "Let us weep before the Lord who made us." In another place it says, it is "he who made us, and not we ourselves,"[6] which, as I remarked, no Christian doubts. Because not only did God create the first human being, from whom come all people, but God also creates each and every human being today—he who said to one of his saints, "Before I formed you in the womb, I knew you."[7] So at the beginning he created people without other people; now he creates people from people. Still, whether it is people without people or people from people, it is "he who made us, and not we ourselves."[8]

So at the first and easy sense of these words—still a true one, of course—"let us worship him, brothers, and prostrate ourselves before him and cry before the Lord who made us." He did not, after all, make us and now desert us. He did not go to the trouble of making us only to abandon us. "Let us worship before the Lord who made us," because we did not worship when he made us, and yet he made us all the same. So having made us before we worshiped him, is he going to desert us

---

[1]Ps 116:12-13, 15 (115:3-4, 6 LXX, Vg.). [2]Heb 12:6. [3]See Mt 26:40. [4]NPNF 2 6:40*. [5]The fact that God created humanity in his own image, something which no sensible person can doubt. [6]Ps 100:3 (99:3 LXX, Vg.). [7]Jer 1:5. [8]Ps 100:3 (99:3 LXX, Vg.).

when we worship him? If someone were doubting whether he would be listened to when he prayed, Scripture reassures him when it says, "Let us cry before the Lord who made us." Of course he listens to those he made; of course he cannot fail to care for those he made. Sermon 26.1.[9]

Prostrate Yourself Before God. Augustine: Do not despair. You are sick, approach him[10] and be healed; you are blind, "approach him and be enlightened."[11] Those of you who are healthy, thank him for it; those of you who are sick, run to him to be healed. All of you, say, "Come, let us worship and prostrate ourselves before him, and let us weep before the Lord who made us," made us human beings and saved us. You see, if it was he that made us human beings, while we saved ourselves, it means we have done something better than he has. I mean, a saved human being is better than an unsaved one. So if God made you a human being, and you made yourself a good human being, what you made is better. Do not lift yourself up above God; submit yourself to God, worship, prostrate yourself, confess to the one who made you; because nobody can recreate except the one who creates; nobody can make you new but the one who made you in the first place. Sermon 176.5.[12]

95:7-8 Do Not Harden Your Hearts

The Danger of Delaying Repentance. Fulgentius of Ruspe: Indeed, no one should continue longer time in his sins out of hope for the mercy of God, since no one wishes to be ill for a longer time in the body because of the hope for future health. Those who decline to give up their sins and vices and promise themselves forgiveness from God are thus frequently visited beforehand by the sudden fury of God, so that they find neither time for conversion nor the blessing of forgiveness. Therefore, holy Scripture mercifully forewarns each one of us when it says, "Do not delay to turn back to the Lord, and do not postpone it from day to day; for suddenly the wrath of

the Lord will come on you, and at the time of punishment you will perish."[13] Blessed David also says, "Today, if you hear his voice, do not harden your hearts." The blessed Paul agrees that we should not continue in our sins in these words: "Take care, brothers, that none of you may have an evil and unfaithful heart, so as to forsake the living God. Encourage yourselves daily while it is still 'today' so that none of you may grow hardened by the deceit of sins."[14] To Peter on the Faith 3.40.[15]

95:10-11 *Punishment for Those Who Err*

Forty Years of Mercy for Israel. Chrysostom: Did not the prophet, speaking in behalf of God, say to you, "Forty years I was offended with that generation,[16] and I said, 'These always err in heart.'" How was it, then, that at that time God did not turn away from you? How is it that after you killed your children, after your idolatries, after your many acts of arrogance, after your unspeakable ingratitude, that God even allowed the great Moses to be a prophet among you and that he worked wondrous and marvelous signs himself? What happened in the case of no human being did happen to you. A cloud was stretched over you in place of a roof; a pillar instead of a lamp served to guide you; your enemies retreated of their own accord; cities were captured almost at the first battle shout. You had no need of weapons, no need of an army in array, no need to do battle. You had only to sound your trumpets, and the walls came tumbling down of their own accord. And you had a strange and marvelous food that the prophet spoke of when he exclaimed, "God gave them the bread of heaven. The people ate the bread of angels; he sent them provisions in abundance."[17] Dis-

---

[9]*WSA* 3 2:93-94. [10]Jesus Christ, whom Augustine describes in the previous paragraph as the "good doctor." [11]Ps 34:5 (33:6 LXX, Vg.). [12]*WSA* 3 5:275*. [13]Sir 5:7. [14]Heb 3:12-13. [15]FC 95:85*. [16]The reference is to the apostasy, idolatry, and other sins of the Israelites during their forty-year journey in the Sinai desert. [17]See Ps 78:24-25 (77:24-25 LXX).

courses Against Judaizing Christians 6.2.7.[18]

The Wicked Shall Not Enter God's Rest.
AMBROSE: "See, O people, the grace of Christ about you. Even while you are harassed on earth, you have possessions in heaven. There, then, let your heart be, where your possession is." This is the rest that is due the just and is denied the unworthy. Wherefore says the Lord, "As I swore in my wrath, that they shall not enter into my rest." For they who have not known the ways of the Lord shall not enter into the rest of the Lord, but to the individual who has fought the good fight and has finished his course it is said, "Turn to your rest." It is a blessed rest to pass by the things of the world and to find repose in the celestial fellowship of the mysteries that are above the world. This is the rest toward which the prophet hastened, saying, "Who will give me wings like a dove and I will fly and be at rest?"[19] The holy person knows that his rest is in heaven, and to this rest he says his soul must turn. Therefore his soul was in its rest, to which he says it must return. This is the rest of the great sabbath, in which each of the saints is above the sensible things of the world, devoting himself entirely to deep and invisible mystery and cleaving to God. This is that rest of the sabbath on which God rested from all the works of his world. ON THE DEATH OF THEODOSIUS 29.[20]

---

[18]FC 68:153. [19]Ps 55:6 (54:7 LXX, Vg.). [20]FC 22:320*.

96:1-13 A SUMMONS FOR ALL TO PRAISE GOD

[1]O sing to the LORD a new song;
   sing to the LORD, all the earth!
[2]Sing to the LORD, bless his name;
   tell of his salvation from day to day.
[3]Declare his glory among the nations,
   his marvelous works among all the peoples!
[4]For great is the LORD, and greatly to be
     praised;
   he is to be feared above all gods.
[5]For all the gods of the peoples are idols;
   but the LORD made the heavens.
[6]Honor and majesty are before him;
   strength and beauty are in his sanctuary.

[7]Ascribe to the LORD O families of the peoples,
   ascribe to the LORD glory and strength!
[8]Ascribe to the LORD the glory due his name;

   bring an offering, and come into his courts!
[9]Worship the LORD in holy array;
   tremble before him, all the earth!

[10]Say among the nations, "The LORD reigns!
   Yea, the world is established, it shall never
     be moved;
   he will judge the peoples with equity."
[11]Let the heavens be glad, and let the earth
     rejoice;
   let the sea roar, and all that fills it;
[12]let the field exult, and everything in it!
Then shall all the trees of the wood sing for joy
    [13]before the LORD, for he comes,
   for he comes to judge the earth.
He will judge the world with righteousness,
   and the peoples with his truth.

OVERVIEW: Christ, whose coming is foretold by the psalmist, will bring salvation to all people and will judge the world in righteousness (EUSEBIUS). Believers who are part of the church, the new house God is building, will sing to the Lord a new song when they are dedicated at their resurrection to life everlasting. The church is composed of people who sing, believe, hope, love and have Christ in their hearts. Heretics cut themselves off from the true church, become enemies of love and are cut off from the liturgical life of the church. The rebuilding of the temple foretold the church, especially as God establishes his temple of the Holy Spirit in the lives of those who are baptized (AUGUSTINE). The Holy Spirit enables people to understand the mystery of salvation and to praise God for it (JUSTIN). The sin of Adam made every human being slaves of the devil and created the need for a redeemer (AUGUSTINE). Christ, born of a virgin, existed before time and ushers in the day of eternal salvation (BEDE). Christ's generation from the Father is prophesied in the phrase "from day to day" (AUGUSTINE).

The name "god," if predicated of any being except the true God, must be qualified by adding "their" or "of the pagans" (TERTULLIAN). Demons, whom the pagans worship as gods, are beings who fell away from God and should not be worshiped by true believers (ORIGEN). Scripture uses the name "god" for pagan deities, but restricts other designations, such as of holiness, of eternity, to the true God (BASIL). God forbids sacrifice to all except himself, not only to pagan gods but also to heavenly spirits (AUGUSTINE). God enjoins not only the Hebrews to worship and sacrifice to him, but also the Gentiles (EUSEBIUS).

David prophesied that Christ would be crucified when David said that Christ would reign from a tree (JUSTIN, TERTULLIAN).

Nature is inanimate even though we may speak of it anthropomorphically (JOHN OF DAMASCUS).

96:1-3 Sing to the Lord a New Song

A NEW SONG SHALL BE GIVEN TO THE GENTILES. EUSEBIUS OF CAESAREA: In Psalm 95 [LXX] the coming of the Lord to humankind is again foretold, and that a new song, by which is meant the new covenant, will be sung by the whole earth at his coming, not by the Jewish race; and that the good news will no longer be for Israel but for all the nations, since it says that the Lord who is to come will be their King. Who could this be but God the Word, who, intending to judge the world in righteousness and the human race in truth, considers all people in the world equally worthy of his call, and consequently of the salvation of God? PROOF OF THE GOSPEL 6.5.[1]

THE DEDICATION OF BELIEVERS. AUGUSTINE: And how many more they have joined, by being given birth to by [the church]?[2] How many members have adhered to the head and are adhering now? And these have been baptized, and others will be baptized, and after us will come others. Then, I say, at the end of the world the stones will attach themselves to the foundation, living stones, holy stones, so that at the end the whole building may be built up out of that church; indeed out of this very church, which is now singing the new song, while the house is being built. That, you see, is what this psalm says, "when the house was being built after the captivity."[3] What does it say? "Sing to the Lord a new song; sing to the Lord, all the earth." What a great house it is! But when does it sing the new song? While it is being built? When is it dedicated? At the end of time? Its foundation has already been dedicated, because he has ascended into heaven and dies no more. When we too have risen again, so as never to die anymore, that is

---

[1]POG 2:6**. [2]Augustine had just said, "let a bride be born in purple to the Lord from the blood of the martyrs." He was referring to Tertullian's comment that the blood of the martyrs is the seed of the church (*Apology* 50.13). [3]Psalm 96 had presumably been the responsorial psalm the people had just been singing. "When the house" is the psalm's title in the Septuagint and hence in Augustine's Latin text. [4]WSA 3 4:207.

when we too will be dedicated. SERMON 116.7.[4]

ALL THE EARTH SINGS A NEW SONG. AUGUSTINE: As a door leads into a house, so the title of a psalm leads into understanding. Now this one has a heading as follows: "When the house was being built after the captivity." You ask what house; the psalm shows you straightaway: "Sing to the Lord a new song, sing to the Lord, all the earth." There you are, that is what house it is. When the whole earth sings a new song, it is the house of God. It is built by singing, its foundations are believing, it is erected by hoping, it is completed by loving. So it is being built now, but it is dedicated at the end of the world. Let the living stones, then, come flocking together to the new song, come flocking all together and be fitted together into the fabric of God's temple. Let them recognize their Savior and receive him as their occupant. SERMON 27.1.[5]

HERETICS CANNOT SING A NEW SONG TO THE LORD. AUGUSTINE: The rebaptizing Donatists[6] should not think they belong to the new song. They cannot sing the new song, seeing that with insufferable impiety they have cut themselves off from the church that God willed to exist in every land. After all, the same prophet says somewhere else, "Sing to the Lord a new song, sing to the Lord every land." So anyone who refuses to sing with every land and does not withdraw from the old man,[7] does not sing the new song and does not play on the ten-stringed harp, because he is an enemy of charity, which alone is the fullness of the law and which we say is contained in the ten commandments that pertain to love of God and of neighbor. SERMON 33.5.[8]

THE REBUILT TEMPLE IN JERUSALEM FORESHADOWED THE CHRISTIAN CHURCH. AUGUSTINE: The baptized have, then, something to do in themselves, that is, in the temple of God that is first built and dedicated at the end. It is built after the captivity, as the title of the psalm indicates: when the enemy who had taken them captive has

been expelled. There is something noteworthy in the order of the psalms. The psalm of the dedication of the house precedes in order of numbering the psalm of the building of the house. The psalm of the dedication comes first, because the psalmist is singing of the house of which its Architect says, "Destroy this temple, and in three days I will raise it up."[9] The later psalm, when the house was being built after the captivity, foretold the church. Moreover, its opening words are "Sing to the Lord a new song, sing to the Lord all the earth." Let no one foolishly think that a baptized person is already perfect, therefore, merely because it has been said, "For holy is the temple of God, and this temple you are,"[10] and, "Do you not know that your members are the temple of the Holy Spirit, who is in you, whom you have from God?"[11] AGAINST JULIAN 6.14.42.[12]

PRAISE AND BLESS THE LORD FOR HIS SALVATION. JUSTIN MARTYR: "We are aware," said Trypho,[13] "that you [Justin] have quoted those passages for us at our request. But the psalm of David that you just cited seems to have been spoken of nobody else than the Father, who created the heavens and earth. You, however, claim that it refers to him who suffered, and who you are anxious to prove is the Christ."

"Please meditate," I [Justin] pleaded, "as I repeat the words uttered by the Holy Spirit in this psalm, and you shall understand that I have not spoken maliciously, nor have you in truth been deceived." Besides, you will thus, when you are by yourselves, be able to grasp many other statements of the Holy Spirit. "Sing to the Lord and bless his name; show forth his salvation from day to day, his wonders among all people." With

---

[5]WSA 3 2:104. [6]Donatists were fourth-century heretics who advocated ecclesiastical purity and insisted on the rebaptizing of people who had been baptized by apostasizing or non-Donatist clergy. [7]Adam; see 1 Cor 15:47. [8]WSA 3 2:156-57. [9]Jn 2:19. [10]1 Cor 3:17. [11]1 Cor 3:16. [12]FC 35:349*. [13]A Jewish friend with whom Justin discusses the truth of the Christian faith versus the Jewish faith. Justin has claimed that Jewish teachers had left out the words "from the tree" for Psalm 95:10, along with other passages and sections of Scripture.

these words the Holy Spirit commands all those inhabitants of this globe who know this mystery of salvation [the passion of Christ], through which he saved them, to sing out and constantly praise the Father of all. They should do so since they realize that he is both to be feared and to be praised and is the Creator of heaven and earth. Christ, who redeemed the human race, after he died on the cross, was deemed worthy by him [the Father] to reign over the whole world. As also by[14] . . . of the "land into which it[15] enters; and they will forsake me and will make void the covenant that I have made with them in that day. And I will forsake them and will hide my face from them; and there shall be devouring and many evils and afflictions shall overtake them, so that they shall say in that day: 'In truth it is because the Lord my God is not with us, that these evils have come on us.' But I will hide my face from them in that day, for all the evils that they have done, because they have followed strange gods."[16] DIALOGUE WITH TRYPHO 74.[17]

HUMANKIND BECAME CAPTIVES THROUGH SIN.

AUGUSTINE: We have said what house it is; now we must say after what captivity.[18] The psalm shows you this[19] too. Carry on a little: "Sing to the Lord a new song, sing to the Lord, all the earth. Sing to the Lord, bless his name, proclaim from day to day the gospel of his salvation. Proclaim among the nations his wonders, in all peoples his glory. Since all the gods of the nations are demons." There you are again, that is under whom the house was held in captivity. From the first transgression of the first human being, the whole human race, being born in the shackles of sin, was the property of the devil who had conquered it. After all, if we had not been held in captivity, we would not have needed a redeemer. SERMON 27.2.[20]

THE BIRTH OF CHRIST FORETOLD.

BEDE: "A savior who is Christ the Lord has been born to you today in the city of David."[21] It is good that [the angel] said "has been born today" and did not say "this night," for with heavenly light he

appeared to those who were conducting the watch by night and brought the good news that day was born, namely, the one concerning whom the psalmist foretold, saying, "Announce well his salvation day from day." Indeed the salvation of God, that is, the Lord Jesus, is "day from day" because he who appeared temporally in the city of David as a human being from a virgin mother was, in truth, himself born before all time and without spatial limitation, light from light, true God from true God. Because, therefore, the light of life rose for those of us dwelling in the region of the shadow of death, the herald of this rising suitably says, "A savior has been born to you today,"[22] so that being always advised by this word we may recollect that the night of ancient blindness is gone past and the day of eternal salvation has drawn near, and "let us cast off the works of darkness."[23] And let us walk as children of light, "for the fruit of the light, as the same apostle [Paul] says, is in all justice and holiness."[24] HOMILIES ON THE GOSPELS 1.6.[25]

CHRIST IS THE ETERNAL DAY.

AUGUSTINE: Rightly, then, are we stirred by the voice of the psalmist as by the sound of a heavenly trumpet,[26] when we hear, "Sing to the Lord a new canticle; sing to the Lord, all the earth. Sing to the Lord and bless his name." Let us recognize, then, and proclaim the "Day born of the day" who became incarnate on this day. The Day is the Son born of the Father, the eternal Day, God of God, Light of Light; he is our salvation, of whom the psalmist says elsewhere, "May God have mercy on us and bless us: may he cause the light of his countenance to shine on us. That we may know your way on earth; your salvation in all nations."[27] The

---

[14]The original text is mutilated here, and it is not clear how much is lost. [15]The people of Israel. [16]Deut 31:16-18. [17]FC 6:266-67*. [18]The Babylonian captivity. [19]In the previous section Augustine had said that the house of God is built by singing, referring to the second temple built after the people had returned from captivity. [20]WSA 3 2:104. [21]Lk 2:11. [22]Lk 2:11. [23]Rom 13:12. [24]Eph 5:8-9. [25]CS 110:61. [26]Augustine preached this sermon on the feast of the nativity. [27]Ps 67:1-2 (66:2-3 LXX, Vg.).

idea expressed in "on the earth" he expanded to "in all nations" and the significance of "your way" he repeated in "your salvation." We recall that the Lord said, "I am the way."[28] And only recently, when the Gospel was read, we heard that the thrice-blessed old man, Simeon, had received a divine promise that he would not experience death until he had seen Christ the Lord and that, when he had taken the infant Christ into his hands and had recognized the mighty little One, he said, "Now dismiss your servant, O Lord, according to your word, in peace, because my eyes have seen your salvation."[29] Gladly, then, let us announce his salvation, this Day born of the eternal Day, let us declare "his glory among the Gentiles, his wonders among all people." He lies in a manger, but he holds the world in his hand; he is nourished at the breast, but he feeds the angels; he is wrapped in swaddling clothes, but he clothes us with immortality; he is suckled but is adored; he does not find room in the inn, but he makes a temple for himself in the hearts of believers. For Strength took on weakness that weakness might become strong. Therefore, let us marvel at rather than despise his human birth; from it let us learn the lowliness that such loftiness assumed for our sake. Then let us enkindle our love so that we may come to his eternal day. SERMON 190.3.[30]

96:5 A God Above All Gods

THE WORD GODS CAN BE USED ONLY IN A QUALIFIED SENSE. TERTULLIAN: True, Scripture says, "Make no mention of the name other gods, neither let it be heard out of your mouth."[31] What it stipulates is that we should not call them gods. For in the first part of the law it says, "You shall not take the name of the Lord your God in vain," that is, apply it to an idol. So anyone who honors an idol with the name of God falls into idolatry. If I am compelled to mention gods, I must add something to show that I do not call them gods. Scripture uses the name "gods" but adds "their" or "of the pagans," as when David,

having used the name "gods," says "but the gods of the pagans are demons." ON IDOLATRY 20.[32]

DEMONS MUST NOT BE WORSHIPED. ORIGEN: And it is not we alone who speak of wicked demons, but almost all who acknowledge the existence of demons. Thus, then, it is not true that all observe the law of the most High; for all who fall away from the divine law, whether through heedlessness, or through depravity and vice or through ignorance of what is right, all such do not keep the law of God, but, to use a new phrase that we find in Scripture, "the law of sin."[33] I say, then, that in the opinion of most of those who believe in the existence of demons, some of them are wicked; and these, instead of keeping the law of God, offend against it. But, according to our belief, it is true of all demons that they were not demons originally, but they became so in departing from the true way; so that the name "demons" is given to those beings who have fallen away from God. Accordingly, those who worship God must not serve demons. We may also learn the true nature of demons if we consider the practice of those who call on them by charms to prevent certain things or for many other purposes. For this is the method they adopt, in order by means of incantations and magical arts to invoke the demons and induce them to further their wishes. Wherefore, the worship of all demons would be inconsistent in us who worship the supreme God; and the service of demons is the service of so-called gods, for "all the gods of the pagans are demons." The same thing also appears from the fact that the dedication of the most famous of the so-called sacred places, whether temples or statues, was accompanied by curious magical incantations, which were performed by those who zealously served the demons with magical arts. Hence we are determined to avoid the worship of demons even as we would avoid death; and we hold that the worship,

---

[28]Jn 14:6. [29]Lk 2:29-30. [30]FC 38:26-27*. [31]Ex 23:13. [32]LCC 5:106*. [33]Rom 7:25; 8:2.

which is supposed among the Greeks to be rendered to gods at the altars, and images and temples, is in reality offered to demons. AGAINST CELSUS 7.69.[34]

THE GODS OF THE GENTILES ARE DEVILS. BASIL THE GREAT: But, if he[35] is of too little importance, according to their reasoning, to be capable of the partnership of the term "Godhead" with the Father and the Son, he is not worthy of sharing any other of the terms proper to God. For, if the terms are considered and compared with each other according to the significance observed in each, none will be found to be inferior to the title of "God." And a proof of this is that many inferior things also are called by this name. Moreover, the divine Scripture does not refrain from using this equivocal term, not even in inconsistent matters, as when it calls images by the name of "God." "For," it says, "let the gods who did not make the heaven and the earth be destroyed and be cast under the earth."[36] It also says, "All the gods of the Gentiles are devils." And the witch[37] with her magic arts summoning up the souls sought by Saul said that she saw gods. Furthermore, even Balaam,[38] a certain diviner and soothsayer, who bore his oracles in his hand, as the Scripture says, and who successfully procured for himself instruction from the demons through his divining trickery, is related by the Scripture to have taken counsel with God. And, it is possible, collecting many such passages from the divine Scriptures, to allege that this name has no precedence above the other appellations proper to God, since, as it has been said, we even find it used equivocally in incongruous matters. But the name of holiness, and of eternity, and of righteousness and of goodness, we are taught by the Scriptures, is nowhere communicated to things that are unfit. Therefore, if they do not deny that the Holy Spirit shares with the Son and the Father in the names piously used exclusively in the case of the divine nature alone, what reason is there to try to make out that he has no partnership in this one alone that both evil spirits and

idols have been shown to share through a certain equivocal use? LETTER 189.[39]

SACRIFICE TO GOD ALONE. AUGUSTINE: For in fact the God whom the wise people of the Hebrews worshiped forbids sacrifices to be offered even to the holy angels and the powers of God, those angels and powers whom we venerate and love, in this mortal pilgrimage of ours, as our completely blessed fellow citizens. He forbids this in a voice of thunder in his law, which he gave to his Hebrew people, when he said, in words heavy with menace, "Anyone who sacrifices to other gods will be extirpated."[40] Now it might be supposed that this precept forbids sacrifice to those most evil demons and the earthly spirits, which Porphyry[41] calls "least" or "lesser"; for even these are called "gods" in the sacred Scriptures—of the Gentiles, that is, not in those of the Hebrews. This is made quite clear by the seventy translators in one of the psalms, where they say, "For all the gods of the nations are demons." But to prevent any such supposition that sacrifice, while forbidden to those demons, was allowed to all or some of the heavenly beings, these words immediately follow: "instead of the Lord alone," that is "to the Lord alone." *Domino soli* means "our Lord the sun," to whom sacrifice is to be offered. That this is not the meaning can easily be discovered by a reference to the Greek version. CITY OF GOD 19.23.[42]

96:7-8 Ascribe to the Lord Glory and Strength

GIVE GOD GLORY AND HONOR. EUSEBIUS OF CAESAREA: And if they[43] say that they were chosen to act as priests and to offer worship to God,

---

[34]ANF 4:638-89. [35]The reference here is to the Holy Spirit. In this letter Basil is writing in opposition to those who denied the full divinity of the Holy Spirit. [36]See Jer 10:11. [37]See 1 Sam 28:13. [38]See Num 22:20. [39]FC 28:29-30*. [40]Ex 22:20. [41]Porphyry (234-30) was a Neoplatonist and a fierce critic of Christianity. [42]CG 888-89. [43]Old Testament prophets Jeremiah, Amos, Micah, Zechariah, Malachi and Isaiah, whom he has just quoted.

it can be shown that the Word promised that he would give to the Gentiles an equal share in his service, when he said, "Render to the Lord, O you kindreds of the nations, render to the Lord glory and honor: bring sacrifices and come into his courts." To which the oracle in Isaiah may be conjoined: "There shall be an altar to the Lord in the land of Egypt . . . and the Egyptians will know the Lord. And they shall sacrifice, and say prayers to the Lord and make offering."[44] And in this you will understand that it is prophesied that an altar will be built to the Lord away from Jerusalem in Egypt and that the Egyptians will there offer sacrifice, say prayers and give gifts to the Lord. Yes, and not only in Egypt, but in the true Jerusalem itself, whatever it is thought to be, all the nations, including the Egyptians indeed, the most superstitious of them all, are invited to keep the feast of tabernacles, as a feast of the heart. PROOF OF THE GOSPEL 2.3.[45]

96:10 The Lord Reigns

THE LORD HAS REIGNED FROM A TREE. JUSTIN MARTYR: Furthermore, from a verse of the ninety-sixth psalm of David they[46] have left out the short phrase "from the tree."[47] For they have changed the verse, "Say to the Gentiles: The Lord has reigned from the tree," to "Say to the Gentiles: The Lord has reigned." Now, no one of your people was ever said to have reigned as God and King over the Gentiles, except the crucified One, who (as the Holy Spirit testifies in the same psalm) was freed from death by his resurrection and thus showed that he is not like gods of the Gentiles, for they are but the idols of demons. DIALOGUE WITH TRYPHO 73.[48]

A SYMBOL OF CHRIST'S DOMINION. TERTULLIAN: Come now, when you read in the words of David that "the Lord reigns from the tree," I want to know what you understand by it. Perhaps you think some wooden king of the Jews is meant—and not Christ, who overcame death by his suffering on the cross and thence reigned! Now,

although death reigned from Adam even to Christ, why may not Christ be said to have reigned from the tree, from his having shut up the kingdom of death by dying on the tree of his cross? Likewise Isaiah also says, "For unto us a child is born."[49] But what is there unusual in this, unless he speaks of the Son of God? "To us is given he whose government is on his shoulder."[50] Now, what king is there who bears the ensign of his dominion on his shoulder, and not rather upon his head as a diadem or in his hand as a scepter, or else as a mark in some royal apparel? But the one new King of the new ages, Jesus Christ, carried on his shoulder both the power and the excellence of his new glory, even his cross; so that, according to our former prophecy, he might thenceforth reign from the tree as Lord. AGAINST MARCION 3.19.[51]

96:11-13 The Relationship Between God and Creation

LET ALL CREATION REJOICE AND BE GLAD. JOHN OF DAMASCUS: Furthermore, let no one maintain that the heavens or the heavenly bodies are animate, for they are inanimate and without feeling. So, even though sacred Scripture says, "Let the heavens rejoice, and let the earth be glad," it is really calling on the angels in heaven and the people on earth to rejoice. Of course, Scripture can personify inanimate things and talk about them as if they were alive, as for example, "The sea saw and fled; Jordan was turned back," and, "What ailed you, O sea, that you did flee? and you, O Jordan, that you were turned back?" and again, "Mountains and hills are asked the reason for their skipping."[52] In just the same way it is customary for us to say that "the city was gathered together," not intending to mean the houses but the occupants of the houses. Still

---

[44]Is 19:19-21. [45]POG 1:73*. [46]The Jewish teachers. [47]Justin claimed that the Jewish teachers had left this phrase out of Psalm 96:10. [48]FC 6:264*. [49]Is 9:6. [50]Is 9:6. [51]ANF 3:337*. [52]Ps 114:3, 5-6 (113:3, 5-6 LXX).

again, "the heavens show forth the glory of God"[53] not by speaking in voice audible to sensible ears but by manifesting to us through their own greatness the power of the Creator, and when we make comments about their beauty, we

give glory to their Maker as the best of all artificers. ORTHODOX FAITH 2.6.[54]

---

[53]See Ps 18:2 (17:3 LXX). [54]FC 37:214*.

97:1-12 A CELEBRATION OF GOD'S RIGHTEOUS REIGN

[1]The LORD reigns; let the earth rejoice;
 let the many coastlands be glad!
[2]Clouds and thick darkness are round about
  him;
 righteousness and justice are the foundation
  of his throne.
[3]Fire goes before him,
 and burns up his adversaries round about.
[4]His lightnings lighten the world;
 the earth sees and trembles.
[5]The mountains melt like wax before the
  LORD,
 before the Lord of all the earth.

[6]The heavens proclaim his righteousness;
 and all the peoples behold his glory.
[7]All worshipers of images are put to shame,

who make their boast in worthless idols;
 all gods bow down before him.
[8]Zion hears and is glad,
 and the daughters of Judah rejoice,
 because of thy judgments, O God.
[9]For thou, O LORD, art most high over all the
  earth;
 thou art exalted far above all gods.

[10]The LORD loves those who hate evil;[k]
 he preserves the lives of his saints;
 he delivers them from the hand of the
  wicked.
[11]Light dawns[l] for the righteous,
 and joy for the upright in heart.
[12]Rejoice in the LORD, O you righteous,
 and give thanks to his holy name!

k Cn: Heb You who love the LORD hate evil   l Gk Syr Jerome: Heb is sown

---

OVERVIEW: When God threatens the earth or promises good things, his threats and promises are made to human beings, on whose account the earth suffers. Christ's promise to send fire on earth, a frequent means of divine retribution on wickedness throughout Scripture, is foretold in David's reference to the fire that will consume

God's enemies (TERTULLIAN).

Those who believe in God rejoice in the sufferings and hardships of this life because they belong to this life, not the next (JEROME). To love God means obeying his commands, keeping oneself holy, thinking only divine and heavenly things and shunning all evil. True love of people is a love of God who dwells in them; to love anyone or anything else is evil (AUGUSTINE).

97:1-3 Righteousness and Judgment

LET THE FLESH OF THE SAINTS BE GLAD. TERTULLIAN: For if the earth has to suffer either joy or injury, it is simply on people's account, that they may suffer the joy or the sorrow through the events that happen to their dwelling place, whereby they will rather have to pay the penalty that, simply on their account, even the earth must suffer. When, therefore, God even threatens the earth, I would prefer saying that he threatens the flesh. So likewise, when he makes a promise to the earth, I would rather understand him as promising the flesh; as in that passage of David: "The Lord is King, let the earth be glad," meaning the flesh of the saints, to which appertains the enjoyment of the kingdom of God. ON THE RESURRECTION OF THE FLESH 26.[1]

GOD SAVES BELIEVERS AND CONDEMNS SINNERS. TERTULLIAN: If, however, those whom God has accepted and the believers shall attain salvation, it is necessary that those whom God has rejected and the unbelieving should incur the opposite issue, even the loss of salvation. Now here is a judgment, and those who hold it out before us belong to the Creator. Whom else than the God of retribution can I understand by the one who shall "beat his servants with stripes," either "few or many," and shall exact from them what he had committed to them? Whom is it suitable for me to obey, but him who remunerates? Your Christ proclaims, "I have come to send fire on the earth."[2] That most lenient being, the Lord who has no hell, not long before had restrained his disciples from demanding fire on the churlish village. Whereas he burned Sodom and Gomorrah with a tempest of fire. Of him the psalmist sang, "A fire shall go out before him and burn up his enemies round about." By Hosea he uttered the threat, "I will send a fire on the cities of Judah";[3] and by Isaiah, "A fire has been kindled

in my anger."[4] He cannot lie. If it is not he who spoke even out of the burning bush, it can be of no importance what fire you insist on being understood. AGAINST MARCION 4.29.[5]

97:8-9 Zion Hears and Is Glad

REJOICE IN ALL GOD'S JUDGMENTS. JEROME: But you will say, "I am a girl delicately reared, and I cannot labor with my hands. Suppose that I live to old age and then fall sick, who will take pity on me?"[6] Hear Jesus speaking to the apostles: "Take no thought what you shall eat; nor yet for your body, what you shall put on. Is not the life more than meat, and the body than raiment? Behold the fowls of the air: for they do not sow, neither do they reap or gather into barns; yet your heavenly Father feeds them."[7] If clothing should fail you, set the lilies before your eyes. If hunger should seize you, think of the words in which the poor and hungry are blessed. If pain should afflict you, read, "Therefore I take pleasure in infirmities,"[8] and "There was given to me a thorn in the flesh, the messenger of Satan to buffet me, lest I should be exalted above measure."[9] Rejoice in all God's judgments, for does not the psalmist say, "The daughters of Judah rejoiced because of your judgments, O Lord"? Let the words be ever on your lips: "Naked came I out of my mother's womb, and naked shall I return there";[10] and "We brought nothing into this world, and it is certain we can carry nothing out."[11] LETTER 22.31.[12]

97:10 The Lord Loves Those Who Hate Evil

LOVE THE LORD AND HATE EVIL. AUGUSTINE: I should not pass over without investigating the significance of the phrases, to love God and to love one's neighbor. A person who loves God will

---

[1]ANF 3:564*. [2]Lk 12:49. [3]Hos 8:14. [4]The passage referred to is most likely Jeremiah 15:14 (however, see Is 30:27, 30). [5]ANF 3:399**. [6]These are words that Jerome puts in the mouth of Eustochium, a wealthy widow. [7]Mt 6:25-26. [8]2 Cor 12:10. [9]2 Cor 12:7. [10]Job 1:21. [11]1 Tim 6:7. [12]NPNF 2 6:36*.

do the following: obey his command in all respects; observe his laws and precepts; attempt to sanctify himself because God is holy, as is written: "Be holy, because I the Lord your God am holy";[13] fulfill the direction of the prophet: "You that love the Lord, hate evil"; think of nothing but divine and heavenly subjects, for God is a lover of nothing but holiness, justice and piety; do only what God seems to love. ON THE CHRISTIAN LIFE 9.[14]

LOVE GOOD AND HATE EVIL. AUGUSTINE: Let us love, let us love freely and without any strings attached. It is God, after all, whom we love. We can find nothing better than God. Let us love him for his own sake, and ourselves and each other in him, but still for his sake. You only love your friend truly, after all, when you love God in your friend, either because God is in him or in order that God may be in him. That is true love and respect; if we love ourselves for any other reason, we are in fact hating rather than loving. "Whoever loves iniquity,"[15] you see—what does he hate? Maybe the man next door, maybe the woman next door? It is his turn to be horrified, for they "hate their own soul."[16] Love of wickedness means love of your own soul. "You that love the Lord, hate evil." God is good, what you love is evil, and you love yourself when you are evil; how can you love God, when you still love what God hates? SERMON 336.2.[17]

---

[13]Lev 19:2. [14]FC 16:24*. [15]Ps 11:5 (10:6 LXX, Vg.). [16]Ps 11:5 (10:6 LXX, Vg.). [17]WSA 3 9:267*.

98:1-9 A CALL TO CELEBRATE GOD'S RIGHTEOUS REIGN

A Psalm.

¹O sing to the LORD a new song,
for he has done marvelous things!
His right hand and his holy arm
have gotten him victory.
²The LORD has made known his victory,
he has revealed his vindication in the sight
of the nations.
³He has remembered his steadfast love and
faithfulness
to the house of Israel.
All the ends of the earth have seen
the victory of our God.

⁴Make a joyful noise to the LORD, all the earth;
break forth into joyous song and sing
praises!
⁵Sing praises to the LORD with the lyre,
with the lyre and the sound of melody!
⁶With trumpets and the sound of the horn
make a joyful noise before the King, the
LORD!

⁷Let the sea roar, and all that fills it;
the world and those who dwell in it!
⁸Let the floods clap their hands;
let the hills sing for joy together
⁹before the LORD, for he comes
to judge the earth.
He will judge the world with righteousness,
and the peoples with equity.

OVERVIEW: The church should praise God for his goodness when persecution and hardships end (EUSEBIUS). The awesome and terrifying God of the law becomes a gentle shepherding God who invites and commands us to sing to him joyful praise (PETER CHRYSOLOGUS). God is praised not only with our voices but also with our emotions and good works (CASSIODORUS). Since there is only one God, the same God will judge both the Jews and the Gentiles (EUSEBIUS).

98:1-4 Sing to the Lord

SING A NEW SONG. EUSEBIUS OF CAESAREA: Along with my prayers I now add book 10 to the *Church History* and dedicate it to you, my most consecrated Paulinus,[1] and blazon you as the seal of the whole work. It is appropriate that in a perfect number[2] I shall here provide a completed account in celebration of the restoration of the churches, in obedience to the divine Spirit who urges us:

> Sing to the Lord a new song, for he has done marvelous things;
> His right and his holy arm have wrought salvation for him.
> The Lord has made known his salvation:
> His righteousness he has revealed in the sight of the heathen.

Accordingly, let me now sing the new song, since after those grim and horrifying scenes and narratives, I was now privileged to see and to celebrate what many righteous people and martyrs of God before me desired to see but did not see and to hear but did not hear. But they hurried on to far better things in the heavens, caught up into a paradise of divine bliss, while I, admitting that even the present circumstances are more than I deserve, have been totally astonished at the magnitude of grace he has conferred and offer him my total awe and worship, confirming the truth of the prophecies that declare:

> Come and behold the works of the Lord,
> What wonders he has wrought on the earth,
> Making wars to cease to the ends of the world.
> He will break the bow and shatter the spear,
> And the shields he will burn with fire.[3]

Rejoicing that all this has been clearly fulfilled, let me proceed with my narrative. ECCLESIASTICAL HISTORY 10.1.[4]

SING JOYFULLY TO THE LORD. PETER CHRYSOLOGUS: "Sing joyfully to God, all the earth." What is it that an understanding of this great joy is likely to make clear? Why is it that, after God gave commandments so great, so terrifying and so awesome, he now invites the earth to a shout of joy? "Sing joyfully to God, all the earth," the text reads.

What other reason is there than the following? The awesome God later on chose the role of a very gentle shepherd. He assumed this character in order to act as a merciful shepherd and gather together, like straggling sheep into one fold, those wandering peoples, those straying nations, those tribes scattered far and wide. Yes, more, he wanted to lead back to the use of milk and grass and restore those wild nations that were languishing after the prey of a carcass, the eating of flesh, the drinking of blood and the fury of beasts. Briefly, he desired to make them once more truly humble sheep.

"All the earth sing joyfully to God," he says, and by this command he imposes his shepherdly control on all the earth. The resounding trumpet draws the soldier forth to war; just so does the sweetness of this jubilant call invite the sheep to pasture. How fitting it was to mitigate the din of fighting by shepherdly kindness, in order that such gentle grace might save the nations that their own natural wildness had long been destroying. SERMON 6.[5]

---

[1]The bishop of Tyre who urged Eusebius to write this history. Later he became bishop of Antioch, his native city. [2]Perfect because after ten there are no new numerals, just combinations of the previous ones. [3]Ps 46:8-9 (45:9-10 LXX). [4]ECH 345-46. [5]FC 17:52-53*.

SING, REJOICE, AND HYMN. CASSIODORUS: "Sing, rejoice and hymn." Though these words seem similar, there is some distinction between them. Sing (*cantare*) means to sound praises to the Lord, offering the service of the Christian voice at its most earnest; rejoice (*exultare*), to declare one's desires with great emotional intensity; hymn (*psallere*), to fulfill the Lord's commands by good words. He urges that this action be performed in many ways because we must rejoice in them with a variety of virtues. EXPOSITIONS OF THE PSALMS 97.4.[6]

98:9 God Will Judge the Earth

THE COMING OF THE LORD. EUSEBIUS OF CAESAREA: It is prophesied here[7] that the coming of the Lord will be the cause of great benefits to the nations, which have been proved to have actually accrued to them, through the manifestation of our Savior. For of a truth from then and not before the new song of the new covenant has been sung among all people, and his wonders have been known and heard by all people through the written Gospels. And salvation also, by the resurrection of the Lord from the dead, has been revealed to all nations, and the true righteousness, by which it has been clearly proved that God is not the God of the Jews only, but of the Gentiles. "Since there is one God," in the words of the holy apostle, "who will judge the circumcised from their faith, and the uncircumcised through faith."[8] And the words "for he, comes to judge the earth," might refer also to his second coming." PROOF OF THE GOSPEL 6.6.[9]

---

[6]ACW 52:433. [7]Ps 98:1-9 (97:1-9 LXX). [8]Rom 3:30. [9]POG 2:6-7*.

99:1-9 A HYMN CELEBRATING GOD AS THE GREAT LORD IN ZION

[1]*The* LORD *reigns; let the peoples tremble!*
 He sits enthroned upon the cherubim; let the
 earth quake!
[2]*The* LORD *is great in Zion;*
 he is exalted over all the peoples.
[3]*Let them praise thy great and terrible name!*
 Holy is he!
[4]*Mighty King,*[m] *lover of justice,*
 thou hast established equity;
thou hast executed justice
 and righteousness in Jacob.
[5]*Extol the* LORD *our God;*
 worship at his footstool!

Holy is he!

[6]*Moses and Aaron were among his priests,*
 Samuel also was among those who called
 on his name.
 They cried to the LORD *and he answered*
 them.
[7]*He spoke to them in the pillar of cloud;*
 they kept his testimonies,
 and the statutes that he gave them.
[8]*O* LORD *our God, thou didst answer them;*
 thou wast a forgiving God to them,
 but an avenger of their wrongdoings.

[9]*Extol the LORD our God,*
  and worship at his holy mountain;   *for the LORD our God is holy!*

m Cn: Heb *and the king's strength*

OVERVIEW: The angels, as well as human beings, worship God (AMBROSE).

99:5 Extol the Lord

LET ALL HIS ANGELS WORSHIP HIM.
AMBROSE: And the apostles worshiped, and, therefore, they who bore the testimony of the faith received authority of faith. And the angels worshiped God, of whom it is written: "And let all his angels worship him."[1]

But they worship not only his Godhead but also his footstool, as it is written: "And worship his footstool, for it is holy." Or, if they deny that in Christ the mysteries also of his incarnation are to be worshiped, in which we observe as it were certain express traces of his Godhead and certain ways of the heavenly Word, let them read that even the apostles worshiped him when he rose again in the glory of his flesh. ON THE HOLY SPIRIT 3.11.75-76.[2]

[1]Heb 1:6. [2]NPNF 2 10:145-46*.

100:1-5 A CALL TO PRAISE GOD

A Psalm for the thank offering.

[1]*Make a joyful noise to the LORD, all the lands![n]*
  [2]*Serve the LORD with gladness!*
  Come into his presence with singing!

[3]*Know that the LORD is God!*
  It is he that made us, and we are his;[o]

  we are his people, and the sheep of his pasture.

[4]*Enter his gates with thanksgiving,*
  and his courts with praise!
  Give thanks to him, bless his name!

[5]*For the LORD is good;*
  his steadfast love endures for ever,
  and his faithfulness to all generations.

n Heb *land or earth*   **o** Another reading is *and not we ourselves*

OVERVIEW: Since God is a loving Lord, he can be served and worshiped joyfully (THEODORET). God created humankind and everything that exists (AUGUSTINE). Joyful service involves loving God above everything else, loving other people and living a virtuous life in true humility (CASSIODORUS). God not only created us and blesses us in many ways, but he will mercifully and freely crown us with eternal life (BEDE).

100:2 *Serve the Lord with Gladness*

GOD IS A LOVING LORD. THEODORET OF CYR: "Serve the Lord with gladness," for the kingship of our God and Savior has nothing of the harsh tyranny of the devil; rather, his lordship is mild and loving. COMMENTARY ON THE PSALMS 100.1.[1]

100:3 *Created by God*

GOD MADE ALL THINGS. AUGUSTINE: But what is my God? I put my question to the earth. It answered, "I am not God," and all things on earth declared the same. I asked the sea and the chasms of the deep and the living things that creep in them, but they answered, "We are not your God. Seek what is above us." I spoke to the winds that blow, and the whole air and all that lives in it replied, "Anaximenes[2] is wrong. I am not God." I asked the sky, the sun, the moon and the stars, but they told me, "Neither are we the God whom you seek." I spoke to all the things that are above me, all that can be admitted by the door of the senses, and I asked, "Since you are not my God, tell me about him. Tell me something of my God." Clear and loud they answered, "God is he who made us."[3] I asked these questions simply by gazing at these things, and their beauty was all the answer they gave. CONFESSIONS 10.6.[4]

SERVE THE LORD WITH GLADNESS: CASSIODORUS: "Serve the Lord with gladness. Come in before his presence with exultation."[5] ... This gladness is nothing other than the charity that, in Paul's words, "is not puffed up, deals not perversely, is not ambitious";[6] other statements, too, which retail this outstanding virtue in wondrous description. So those who serve the Lord with gladness are they who love him above all else and show brotherly charity to each other. What free servitude this is! What service, excelling all forms of dominance! Such servants are accorded a gladness such as is not enjoyed by the glory of kingships. Now observe the reward attendant on this gladness that is enjoined on us in this world; he says, "Come in before his presence with exultation." It is much more difficult, much more glorious to rejoice before the presence of the great Judge, where we are warned to gather with moral awareness of the need to manifest the joys of humility, for he is known to be harsh to all people of pride. EXPOSITIONS OF THE PSALMS 99.2.[7]

GOD MADE US TO BE HOLY AND BLESSED PEOPLE. BEDE: We are taught by their[8] testimonies that "it is God himself and not we ourselves who made us"—not only to be human beings but also to be holy and blessed human beings. If by the gift of his grace we pursue him eagerly, always with a pure and untiring heart, he will be propitious toward all our iniquities, according to the promises made to our ancestors. He will satisfy our desire with good things, he will crown us unto eternal life not as a reward for the works of justice that we have done of ourselves but in the compassion and mercy[9] that he has given us, for he lives and reigns in the unity of the Holy Spirit, throughout all ages. Amen. HOMILIES ON THE GOSPELS 2.19.[10]

---

[1]FC 102:144. [2]Anaximenes of Miletus (fl. 530 B.C.) was one of the early Greek philosophers; he taught that air is the first cause of all things and that it is quasi-divine. [3]Ps 100 (99:3 LXX, Vg.). [4]AC 212. [5]Ps 100:2 (99:2 LXX, Vg.). [6]See 1 Cor 13:4-8. [7]ACW 52:444*. [8]Ancestors in the Christian faith, such as biblical authors [9]Ps 103:3-5 (102:3-5 LXX, Vg.). [10]CS 111:200.

101:1-8 A KING'S PLEDGE TO
REIGN RIGHTEOUSLY

A Psalm of David.

¹*I will sing of loyalty and of justice;*
   to thee, O LORD, I will sing.
²*I will give heed to the way that is blameless.*
   Oh when wilt thou come to me?

I will walk with integrity of heart
   within my house;
³*I will not set before my eyes*
   anything that is base.

I hate the work of those who fall away;
   it shall not cleave to me.
⁴*Perverseness of heart shall be far from me;*
   I will know nothing of evil.

⁵*Him who slanders his neighbor secretly*
   I will destroy.

The man of haughty looks and arrogant heart
   I will not endure.

⁶*I will look with favor on the faithful in the*
      land,
   that they may dwell with me;
he who walks in the way that is blameless
   shall minister to me.

⁷*No man who practices deceit*
   shall dwell in my house;
no man who utters lies
   shall continue in my presence.

⁸*Morning by morning I will destroy*
   all the wicked in the land,
cutting off all the evildoers
   from the city of the LORD.

OVERVIEW: In mercy God invites us to his heavenly banquet through the gospel and determines our will to accept, but he brings judgment on those who refuse. All people are evil by nature in God's eyes, but he makes some good through the forgiveness of their sins. No matter how great and numerous our sins, God is a God of mercy first and a God of judgment second; he will forgive our sins and give us the promised reward, but he does expect us to display the same kind of mercy toward other people (AUGUSTINE). Judgment and mercy never exist independently of one another in God's dealings with people (CASSIODORUS). The innocent of heart know how to be patient and tolerant toward those who abuse and revile them (AUGUSTINE). A believer is not du-plicitous but has great integrity between what he does publicly and what he does privately (THEODORET). We sin severely if our dealings with people are based on unsubstantiated suspicion and mere slander—this God clearly forbids (ATHANASIUS, CHRYSOSTOM).

The needs and desires of our physical nature may be satisfied but not to excess or for vainglory (POEMEN). Persecution has been perversely practiced against good and righteous people but also in a just and fair manner by the good and righteous against those who are evil and enemies of God (AUGUSTINE). The psalms, which provide us with holy guidelines and thought, are weapons against evil for godly people (CAESARIUS). Verses such as Psalm 101:8 provide ample proof of the

---

dangers of a strictly literal interpretation of some passages with spiritual interpretation (ORIGEN).

101:1-4 *Loyalty and Justice*

THE ROLES OF MERCY AND JUDGMENT.

AUGUSTINE: In fact, to that prepared feast of which the Lord speaks in the Gospel, not all who were called wanted to come, nor could those come who did come except they were called.[1] Accordingly neither should those who came give themselves the credit, for they came by invitation, nor should those who did not want to come blame it on another, but only on themselves, for they had been invited to come of their free will. Therefore, before merit, the calling determines the will. For this reason, even if someone called takes the credit for coming, he cannot take the credit for being called. And as for him who is called and does not come, just as his calling was not a deserved reward, so his neglecting to come when called lays the foundation for a deserved punishment. There will thus be the following two things: "Of your mercy and judgment will I sing, O Lord." To mercy belongs the calling; to judgment belongs the blessedness of those who did not want to come. ON EIGHTY-THREE VARIED QUESTIONS 68.5.[2]

CHRIST CAME FIRST TO SAVE. AUGUSTINE:

Christ has come, but first to save, afterwards to judge, by pronouncing punishment for those who were unwilling to be saved and by leading those to life, who, by believing, did not spurn salvation. Thus the first dispensation of our Lord Jesus Christ is medicinal, not judicial; for if he had come first to judge, he would have found no one to whom to grant the rewards of justice. Therefore, because he saw that all were sinners and that no one at all was free from the death of sin, his mercy first had to be bestowed and his judgment shown later. For the psalm had sung about him, "Mercy and judgment I will sing to you, Lord." It does not say judgment and mercy. For if judgment were first, there would be no mercy; but

mercy first, judgment afterwards. TRACTATES ON THE GOSPEL OF JOHN 36.4.3.[3]

GOD'S MERCY IS UNDESERVED. AUGUSTINE:

While the reprobate angels and people continue in eternal punishment, the saints will have fuller knowledge of the good conferred on them by grace. Then, through the very facts themselves they will gain a clearer understanding of what is written in the psalm: "Mercy and judgment I will sing to you, O Lord," for it is only through unmerited mercy that anyone is freed and only through deserved judgment that anyone is condemned. Then will be clear what now is dark: When one of two children is through his mercy chosen by God for himself, while the other through his judgment is to be abandoned (the one chosen knowing what would have been his due through judgment had not mercy come to his aid), why the one rather than the other is chosen, when the condition of the two was the same? Or again, why miracles were not worked in the presence of some people who, had they been worked, would have done penance, while miracles were worked in the presence of those who were not going to believe anyway? For this is the Lord's very clear statement: "Woe to you, Korazin! Woe to you, Bethsaida! For if in Tyre and Sidon had been worked the miracles that have been worked in you, they would have repented long ago in sackcloth and ashes."[4] And surely there was no injustice in God's not willing that they be saved, though they could have been saved if he had so willed it. ENCHIRIDION 24.94-95.[5]

REMISSION OF SINS FOR THOSE WHO

BELIEVE. AUGUSTINE: But, inasmuch as "Christ has died for the wicked,"[6] what person has been found good by the Lord? He therefore found all trees bad, but, to those who believe in his name, "he gave the power of becoming children of God."[7] Hence, whoever is now a good person

---

[1]See Lk 14:16-24. [2]FC 70:164-65. [3]FC 88:84. [4]Mt 11:21. [5]FC 2:447*. [6]Rom 5:6. [7]Jn 1:12.

(that is to say, a good tree) was found bad and has been made good. If the Lord had willed to root up the bad trees when he came, what tree would have been left that would not deserve to be rooted up? But he came to dispense mercy beforehand, so that he might afterwards dispense justice, for he is the Lord to whom the psalmist says, "Mercy and judgment I will sing to you, O Lord." He therefore gave remission of sins to those who believe. Of them, he would not even demand an accounting of previous decrees.[8] He gave remission of sins; he made the trees good. He delayed the axe; he removed the threat. SERMON 72.2.[9]

MERCY AND JUDGMENT RECIPROCATED.

AUGUSTINE: Obviously, it is just that those who have pardoned should receive pardon and that it should be given to those who give. It is natural that there should be in God both mercy for him that judges and judgment for him that shows mercy. That is why we say to him, "Mercy and judgment I will sing to you, O Lord." Whoever, presuming on his own justice, expects judgment with mercy as if he were secure provokes the most just anger, of which the psalmist said in fear, "Enter not into judgment with your servant."[10] Therefore, God says to his perverse people, "Why will you contend with me in judgment?"[11] For when "the just king shall sit on his throne, who will boast that he has a chaste heart, or who will boast that he is pure of sin?"[12] What hope is there, then, unless "mercy exalts itself above judgment," but only toward those who have shown mercy by saying sincerely, "Forgive us as we forgive" and by giving without protest? "For God loves a cheerful giver."[13] Finally, in order to comfort those in whom the former sentence had roused extreme fear, James in the sequence to that passage speaks of the works of mercy, when he points out how even daily sins, without which there is no living in this world, are expiated by daily remedies. Without these, the person who becomes guilty of all by offending in one point and by offending in many—"because in many things we all offend"—would drag with

him to the judgment seat of the great judge a mighty load of guilt, gathered up bit by bit, and would not find the mercy that he had not shown. By forgiving and giving, he deserves to have his debts forgiven and the promised reward given to him. LETTER 167.20.[14]

MERCY AND JUDGMENT ARE INTERLINKED.

CASSIODORUS: "Mercy and judgment will I sing: you, O Lord, will I hymn." The heavenly crowd of the blessed on earth uttered the prelude to embrace everything in brief compass, for the Lord's power is always either pitying or judging. But his mercy is never found without judgment or his judgment without mercy. Both are joined in an interlinked association; no act of his ever comes to light that is not seen to be full of all the virtues. Just as the psalmist speaks here of mercy and justice, so elsewhere instead of these two he has "justice and peace,"[15] or again "mercy and truth"[16] or "justice and judgment the preparation of your throne,"[17] so that everywhere he shows God as devoted and just. Undoubtedly this manner of speaking can be counted among the peculiarities of divine Scripture. For on the glorious occasion too of his coming he first mentions mercy when he says, "Come, blessed of my Father,"[18] and the rest; but this is not without equity, for he renders his promises to the faithful. But next follows judgment, when he said to the wicked, "Depart from me, you cursed, into everlasting fire,"[19] though this action is not unloving, for he is known to show vengeance only after much long-suffering. So you see that the two concepts are reconcilable with each other and shine forth in their due places. Sinners who wickedly despair of their salvation must accordingly listen to the Lord of mercy, whereas the proud who think that their wickedness will not be punished must visualize him as Judge. So here the totality

---

[8]Col 2:14. [9]FC 11:287-88. [10]Ps 143:2 (142:2 LXX, Vg.). [11]Jer 2:29. [12]Prov 20:8-9 LXX. [13]2 Cor 9:7. [14]FC 30:48-49*. [15]Ps 85:10 (84:11 LXX, Vg.). [16]Ps 85:10 (84:11 LXX, Vg.). [17]Ps 89:14 (88:15 LXX, Vg.). [18]Mt 25:34. [19]Mt 25:41.

is sung briefly but fully, for in these two words all the Lord's works and the building up of the entire church are clearly told. Expositions of the Psalms 100.1.[20]

A Time to Be Silent. Augustine: "I grew deaf and humbled myself"—that is how it goes on—"and held my peace from good things."[21] "I grew deaf": I did not listen to him talking. What progress such a spirit displays, in that while he rejoices inwardly at his brother's being mistaken and his own conscience being easy, he refrains outwardly from barking! What a fine soul that is, how carefree, how joyful! This is the soul that says to God, "I would walk in the innocence of my heart, in the midst of your house." The rowdies were hammering at the doors, but the house was safe and sound. "I grew deaf and humbled myself," I did not stand up proudly against him. And in humbling myself "I held my peace from good things." In fact it was not the time for saying anything good. It is the time to keep silent now. After the fellow has calmed down, talk then; then he will understand. Sermon 16a.8.[22]

Innocence of Heart. Theodoret of Cyr: "I walked in the innocence of my heart in my house." I continued to live a life of simplicity, I did not practice duplicity, feigning a different appearance to outsiders while bringing myself to do the opposite at home; instead, my private face corresponded to my public one. Commentary on the Psalms 101.3.[23]

101:5-6 The Fates of Sinful and Faithful People Are Different

God Will Destroy Slanderers. Athanasius: And Jezebel was able to injure the most religious Naboth[24] by her false accusations; but then it was the wicked and apostate Ahab who listened to her. But the most holy David, whose example you ought to follow, as all pray that you may, does not favor such people but was apt to turn away from them and avoid them, as raging dogs. He

says, "Whoever secretly slanders his neighbor, him will I destroy." For he kept the commandment that says, "You shall not receive a false report."[25] And false are the reports of these people in your sight. You, like Solomon, have required of the Lord (and you ought to believe yourself to have obtained your desire), that it would seem good to him to remove far from you vain and lying words.[26] Defense Before Constantius 20.[27]

Give No Place to Slander. Chrysostom: I beseech you, let us avoid altogether passing sentence on our neighbor. You see, even though you have no share in judicial authority and yet you still pass judgment in your mind, you have rendered yourself guilty of sin for accepting no proof and acting in many cases only on suspicion and mere slander. This, in fact, was the reason blessed David also cried out in the words, "The one who slanders his neighbor in secret I drove out." Do you see the extraordinary degree of virtue? Not only did he not entertain what was said but he also gave short shrift to the person bent on slandering his brother. So if we, too, want to reduce our own faults, we should be on our guard about this most of all, not to condemn our brothers or to encourage those anxious to slander them, but rather to rebuff them as the inspired author recommended and utterly repel them. In fact, I am inclined to think this is what the inspired author Moses also was indicating in his words, "Do not accept an idle report."[28] Homilies on Genesis 42.14.[29]

Avoid Bodily Gratification and Pride. Poemen: He [Poemen] also said, "If a monk hates two things, he is able to free himself from the world, and these are," he said, "the gratifications of the body and vainglory."

The same old man also said, "Wrath is a natu-

---

[20]ACW 52:447-48*. [21]Ps 39:2 (38:3 LXX, Vg.). [22]WSA 3 1:353. [23]FC 102:146-47. [24]1 Kings 21:10. [25]Ex 23:1. [26]Prov 30:8. [27]NPNF 2 4:246*. [28]Ex 23:1. [29]FC 82:425-26.

ral thing in a person, it is his nature, but it must be used to cut off evil passions. Hunger is natural in a person, but it must be employed [in satisfying] the needs of the body and not [to gratify] the feeling of eager lust [to eat], even as the blessed David said, "With him whose eye is lofty and whose heart is greedy I have not eaten."[30] Sleep "too is natural in humankind, but [it must not be indulged] to satiety." SAYINGS OF THE FATHERS 2.479-80.[31]

RECIPROCATED JUDGMENT. AUGUSTINE: If it were always praiseworthy to suffer persecution, it would have been enough for the Lord to say, "Blessed are they that suffer persecution," without adding "for justice sake."[32] Similarly, if it were always blameworthy to persecute, it would not be written in the sacred Books: "The one that in private speaks ill of his neighbor, him did I persecute." Sometimes, then, the one who suffers persecution is unjust, and the one who persecutes is just. It is clear that the bad have always persecuted the good and the good have persecuted the bad; the former to do harm unjustly, the latter to bring about amendment by punishment; the one without limits, the other within bounds; those as slaves of passion, these out of love. The one who kills does not mind how he butchers his victim, but the one who cures watches carefully how he cuts; he has health as his aim, the other destruction. Impious people killed the prophets; the prophets also killed impious people.[33] The Jews scourged Christ, and Christ scourged the Jews. The apostles were delivered up by people to the civil rulers,[34] and the apostles delivered up people to the power of Satan.[35] In all these cases, what else is to be noted except to ask which of them served the cause of truth, which that of sin; which one wished to injure, which one wished to convert? LETTER 93.[36]

101:7-8 The Wicked Will Be Excluded from the Presence of God

THE PSALMS ARE WEAPONS AGAINST SIN.

CAESARIUS OF ARLES: If we return to our psalms rather frequently, brothers, we shut off the approach to worldly thoughts; the spiritual song dominates, and carnal thoughts depart. The psalms are the weapons of the servants of God. The one who clings to the psalms does not fear the enemy, for our Lord says concerning this adversary, "Your adversary is the devil."[37] The devil suggests adverse thoughts, in order that he may kill us if he can; on the other hand, we have right thoughts, if we read the psalms aloud quite frequently. The devil says, Be proud; I repeat with the psalm what our Lord says: "He shall not dwell within my house who practices pride"; and elsewhere: "God resists the proud";[38] also in Solomon: "A proud person knows nothing. He has a morbid passion for contention."[39] He [the devil] would not encourage pride, if he knew that it had a place among the servants of God in paradise. This is why the devil especially encourages monks to be proud, in order that they may afterwards be excluded from the place from which he was expelled. If he had not been proud, he would have kept his preeminence in heaven. He encourages quarrels, he excites hatred, he himself stirs up people, but you should resist him like the true psalmist by saying, "O Lord, set a watch before my mouth, and let not my heart incline to evil words."[40] SERMON 238.2.[41]

SOME TEXTS MAKE LITTLE SENSE IF ONLY INTERPRETED LITERALLY. ORIGEN: Now if these words in the law, "You shall have dominion over many nations, and no one shall rule over you,"[42] were simply a promise to them[43] of dominion, and if these words contain no deeper meaning than this, then it is certain that the people would have had still stronger grounds for despising the promises of the law.

---

[30]See also Ps 131:1 (130:1 LXX). [31]*PHF* 2:250*. [32]Mt 5:10. [33]See Ex 32:25-28; 1 Kings 18:4. [34]See Acts 16:22-24; 21:33-34. [35]See 1 Cor 5:5. [36]FC 18:64*. [37]1 Pet 5:8. [38]Jas 4:6. [39]1 Tim 6:4. This text is not from Solomon, as Caesarius indicates. [40]Ps 141:3-4 (140:3-4 LXX, Vg.). [41]FC 66:221-22*. [42]Deut 15:6. [43]The people of Israel.

Celsus[44] brings forward another passage, although he changes its terms, where it is said that the whole earth shall be filled with the Hebrew race; which indeed, according to the testimony of history, did actually happen after the coming of Christ, although rather as a result of God's anger, if I may say so, than of his blessing. As to the promise made to the Jews that they should slay their enemies, it may be answered that anyone who examines carefully into the meaning of this passage will find himself unable to interpret it literally. It is sufficient at present to refer to the manner in which in the Psalms the just person is represented as saying, among other things, "Every morning will I destroy the wicked of the land, that I may cut off all workers of iniquity from the city of the Lord." Judge, then, from the words and spirit of the speaker, whether it is conceivable that, after having in the preceding part of the psalm, as anyone may read for himself, he uttered the noblest thoughts and purposes, he should in the sequel, according to the literal rendering of his words, say that in the morning, and at no other period of the day, he would destroy all sinners from the earth and leave none of them alive, and that he would slay every one in Jerusalem who did iniquity. And there are many similar expressions to be found in the law, as this, for example: "We did not leave anything alive."[45] AGAINST CELSUS 7.19.[46]

---

[44]Celsus was a heathen philosopher who wrote a learned attack on the Christian religion in about 180 B.C. It was titled *True Word* and did not receive a Christian rebuttal until Origen published his *Against Celsus* about fifty years later. [45]Deut 2:34. [46]ANCL 23:442-43*.

102:1-17 A PRAYER IN TIME OF DISTRESS

*A prayer of one afflicted, when he is
faint and pours out his complaint
before the LORD.*

¹*Hear my prayer, O LORD;
    let my cry come to thee!*
²*Do not hide thy face from me
    in the day of my distress!
Incline thy ear to me;
    answer me speedily in the day when I call!*

³*For my days pass away like smoke,
    and my bones burn like a furnace.*
⁴*My heart is smitten like grass, and withered;
    I forget to eat my bread.*
⁵*Because of my loud groaning
    my bones cleave to my flesh.*
⁶*I am like a vulture[p] of the wilderness,
    like an owl of the waste places;*
⁷*I lie awake,
    I am like a lonely bird on the housetop.*
⁸*All the day my enemies taunt me,
    those who deride me use my name for
        a curse.*
⁹*For I eat ashes like bread,
    and mingle tears with my drink,*
¹⁰*because of thy indignation and anger;
    for thou hast taken me up and thrown me
        away.*
¹¹*My days are like an evening shadow;
    I wither away like grass.*

¹²*But thou, O LORD, art enthroned for ever;*
  thy name endures to all generations.
¹³*Thou wilt arise and have pity on Zion;*
  it is the time to favor her;
  the appointed time has come.
¹⁴*For thy servants hold her stones dear,*
  and have pity on her dust.

¹⁵*The nations will fear the name of the LORD,*
  and all the kings of the earth thy glory.
¹⁶*For the LORD will build up Zion,*
  he will appear in his glory;
¹⁷*he will regard the prayer of the destitute,*
  and will not despise their supplication.

p The meaning of the Hebrew word is uncertain

OVERVIEW: Just as a person who neglects to nourish his physical body with food becomes weak, so the person who fails to nourish his soul on the Word of God becomes spiritually weak (THEODORET). King David is an exemplar of a truly repentant individual who remained remorseful for his sin even after absolution (CYRIL OF JERUSALEM). True repentance should be accompanied by intense prayer and much weeping (CHRYSOSTOM). A truly penitent person not only confesses his sin but seeks to correct his sinful life and become more godly (PAULINUS). At the right time God manifests his mercy; the most propitious time was the advent of Christ who shed his blood to destroy Satan (AUGUSTINE).

102:4-9 Contrition and Repentance

NOURISHMENT FOR THE SOUL. THEODORET OF CYR: "For I forgot to eat my bread. At the sound of my groaning, my bones stuck to my flesh." I lost appetite for any food, and was completely bereft of my former good condition, my body being consumed by the wasting of discouragement; I am but skin and bones. The word of God, then, is our soul's bread: just as ordinary bread nourishes the body, so the word from heaven [nourishes] the soul's substance. In passing on the prayer,[1] Christ said as much to the apostles, "Give us this day our daily bread."[2] So whoever forgets to eat it, that is, to be active (action, after all, constituting the eating of the spiritual bread, as is clear from the saying of the Lord to the apostles, "Be active, not for the eating, which per-

ishes, but for that which endures to life eternal"),[3] this one's heart is stricken and dried up like hay. How does hay get stricken and dry up? When rain stops falling on it. As the heart, too, when suffering from a dearth of the word, is then stricken and dries up, the flower of virtue no longer has the strength to bloom. COMMENTARY ON THE PSALMS 102.3.[4]

ACTS OF TRUE PENITENCE. CYRIL OF JERUSALEM: So then the prophet comforted David as we have seen, but that blessed man, though he received most gladly the assurance, "The Lord has put away your sin," did not, king as he was, draw back from penitence. Indeed he put on sackcloth in place of his purple robe, and the king sat in ashes on the bare earth instead of on his gilded throne. And in ashes he did not merely sit but took them for eating, as he himself says, "I have eaten ashes as if bread and mingled my drink with weeping." His lustful eye he wasted away with tears; as he says, "Every night I wash my bed and water my couch with my tears."[5] And when his courtiers exhorted him to take bread, he would not, but he prolonged his fast for seven whole days. Now if a king was apt to make confession after this manner, should not you, as a private person, make your confession? Again, after Absalom's rebellion, when David was in flight, with many roads to choose from before him, he chose to make his escape by the Mount of

---

[1]The Lord's Prayer. [2]Mt 6:11. [3]Jn 6:27. [4]FC 102:150*. [5]Ps 6:6 (6:7 LXX).

Olives, as good as invoking in his own mind the Deliverer who should from there ascend into the heavens. And when Shimei cursed him bitterly, he said, "Let him be." For he knew that forgiveness is for those who forgive.[6] CATECHETICAL LECTURES 2.12.[7]

INTENSE PRAYER AND MUCH WEEPING. CHRYSOSTOM: And after humility of mind, there is need of intense prayers, of many tears, tears by day and tears by night, for, he says, " every night will I wash my bed, I will water my couch with my tears. I am weary with my groaning."[8] And again, "For I have eaten ashes as if bread and mingled my drink with weeping." ON THE EPISTLE TO THE HEBREWS 9.8.[9]

CONFESSION AND PENITENCE. PAULINUS OF MILAN: Indeed, to the penitent confession alone does not suffice, unless correction of the deed follows, with the result that the penitent does not continue to do deeds that demand repentance. He should even humble his soul just as holy David, who, when he heard from the prophet, "Your sin is pardoned,"[10] became more humble in the correction of his sin, so that "he did eat ashes like bread and mingled his drink with weeping." THE LIFE OF ST. AMBROSE 9.39.[11]

102:13-14 An Appointed Time for God to Show Mercy

GOD HAD MERCY ON ZION. AUGUSTINE: But what have you heard about Jerusalem in the Psalms? "For its stones are dear to your servants; its very dust moves them to pity," "You," it says, "will arise and have compassion on Zion, for it is time to show favor to it." When the time came for God to show mercy, the Lamb came. What kind of Lamb is it whom the wolves fear? What kind of Lamb is it who, though killed, kills the lion? For the devil has been called a lion, going about and roaring, seeking someone to devour;[12] by the Lamb's blood the lion has been conquered. Behold the spectacles of Christians! TRACTATES ON THE GOSPEL OF JOHN 7.6.3.[13]

---

[6]See 2 Sam 15:30—16:10. [7]LCC 4:88*. [8]Ps 6:6 (6:7 LXX). [9]NPNF 1 14:412*. [10]2 Sam 12:13. [11]FC 15:57*. [12]1 Pet 5:8. [13]FC 78:159*.

102:18-28 THE CREATOR AND HIS CREATION

[18]Let this be recorded for a generation to come,
  so that a people yet unborn may praise the
  LORD:
[19]that he looked down from his holy height,
  from heaven the LORD looked at the earth,
[20]to hear the groans of the prisoners,
  to set free those who were doomed to die;
[21]that men may declare in Zion the name of the
  LORD,

and in Jerusalem his praise,
[22]when peoples gather together,
  and kingdoms, to worship the LORD.

[23]He has broken my strength in midcourse;
  he has shortened my days.
[24]"O my God," I say, "take me not hence
  in the midst of my days,
thou whose years endure

throughout all generations!"

²⁵*Of old thou didst lay the foundation of the
earth,
and the heavens are the work of thy hands.*
²⁶*They will perish, but thou dost endure;
they will all wear out like a garment.
Thou changest them like raiment, and they*

pass away;
²⁷*but thou art the same, and thy years have
no end.*
²⁸*The children of thy servants shall dwell
secure;
their posterity shall be established before
thee.*

OVERVIEW: God measures to each person a span of earthly life but does not reveal the time of its end (ATHANASIUS). The wicked may die untimely, but God promises the righteous the full length of their days and eternal life as a crown of righteousness (ORIGEN, ATHANASIUS). No human being can fully understand God's creation or know the length of his life (DIONYSIUS).

The splendor of the heavens declares God's glory, and humanity does the same through good works. Both are created by God; the first will perish, but the second will become immortal through the work of Christ (AMBROSE). God made the world not by mere appearance or approach but by the labors of his hands. Prophecies of the final dissolution of the created order must be understood literally and not spiritually (TERTULLIAN). David's testimony that this world will perish is confirmed in the words of Christ in the New Testament (AMBROSE). The creation of a new heaven and a new earth are prophetically described in terms of stitching a new garment (AMBROSE, CYRIL OF JERUSALEM). Of all the biblical prophecies of the end of the world, one of the clearest occurs in Psalm 102 (AUGUSTINE).

The triune God is eternal and immutable by nature (FULGENTIUS). In the resurrection our human nature will be changed into something better, namely, a spiritual and incorruptible body (BASIL). The creation of the world is as much the work of the Son as of the Father, and the Son's begottenness does not imply inferiority (CHRYSOSTOM). The divine nature of Christ was not changed as a result of his incarnation. By assuming a human nature, Christ's divine nature was not changed for the worse, but his human nature was changed for the better (AUGUSTINE). The heavens and the earth will perish, but God will remain the same (ATHANASIUS). Mutable humans were created by an immutable God whose immutability is attested in Scripture (AUGUSTINE). God cannot do anything contrary to his nature, but in Christ what is human must be predicated only of his human nature (THEODORET).

102:23-24 A Prayer for a Longer Life

SHORTNESS OF DAYS. ATHANASIUS: Now as these things are written in the Scriptures, the case is clear, that the saints know that a certain time is measured to every person, but that no one knows the end of that time is plainly intimated by the words of David, "Declare to me the shortness of my days." He desired information about that which he did not know. Accordingly the rich man also, while he thought that he had still a long time to live, heard the words, "You fool! This very night your life will be demanded from you. Then who will get what you have prepared for yourself?"[1] And the Preacher speaks confidently in the Holy Spirit and says, "A person also does not know his time."[2] Wherefore the patriarch Isaac said to his son Esau, "Behold, I am old, and I know not the day of my death."[3] DEFENSE OF HIS FLIGHT 15.[4]

CALLED OUT OF THIS LIFE. ORIGEN: That

---

[1]Lk 12:20. [2]Eccles 9:12. [3]Gen 27:2. [4]NPNF 2 4:260*.

which is said is also fulfilled in the saint: "I will recall you from there in the end."[5] For the end is considered to be the perfection of things and the consummation of virtues. Indeed for this reason also another saint said, "Don't recall me in the midst of my days." And again the Scripture bestows testimony on the great patriarch Abraham since "Abraham died full of days."[6] This statement, therefore, "I will recall you from there in the end," is as if he had said, Since "you have fought a good fight, you have kept the faith, you have finished the course,"[7] I will now recall you from this world to the future blessing, to the perfection of eternal life, to "the crown of justice that the Lord will give in the end of the ages to all who love him."[8] HOMILIES ON GENESIS 15.6.[9]

PRAYER FOR LONGER LIFE. ATHANASIUS: For although it is hidden and unknown to all, what period of time is allotted to each and how it is allotted, yet every one knows this, that as there is a time for spring and for summer, and for autumn and for winter, so, as it is written, there is a time to die and a time to live. And so the time of the generation that lived in the days of Noah was cut short, and their years were contracted, because the time of all things was at hand. But to Hezekiah were added fifteen years. As God promises to them that serve him truly, "I will fulfill the number of your days,"[10] Abraham dies "full of days," and David urgently begged God, saying, "Don't take me away in the midst of my days." And Eliphaz, one of the friends of Job, being assured of this truth, said, "You shall come to your grave like ripe corn, gathered in due time, and like as a shock of corn comes in its season."[11] Solomon, confirming his words, says, "The souls of the unrighteous are untimely taken away."[12] And therefore he exhorts in the book of Ecclesiastes, saying, "Don't be too wicked, neither be hard: why should you die before your time?"[13] DEFENSE OF HIS FLIGHT 14.[14]

THE NUMBER OF OUR DAYS IS UNKNOWN TO US. DIONYSIUS OF ALEXANDRIA: And this[15] is true. For no one is able to comprehend the works of God altogether. Moreover, the world is the work of God. No one, then, can find out as to this world what is its space from the beginning and to the end, that is to say, the period appointed for it and the limits before determined for it; in view of the fact that God has set the whole world as a realm of ignorance in our hearts. And thus one says, "Declare to me the shortness of my days." In this manner, and for our profit, the end of this world [age]—that is to say, this present life—is a thing of which we are ignorant. FRAGMENT 1.3.11.[16]

102:25-27 God Created the Heavens and the Earth

THE EARTH PERISHES; HUMANITY BECOMES IMMORTAL. AMBROSE: Heaven is of the world, humanity above the world; the one is part of the world, the other an inhabitant of paradise, Christ's possession. Heaven is considered incorruptible, yet it passes away; humanity is regarded as corruptible and is clothed with incorruption; the figure of the one perishes, the other rises as being immortal. Yet, according to the authority of Scripture, the hands of the Lord fashioned both. We read of the heavens: "The heavens are the works of your hands." Humankind, too, says, "Your hands have made me and formed me,"[17] and "The heavens declare the glory of God."[18] As heaven is lighted with the splendor of the stars, so do humans shine with the light of their good works, and their deeds shine before their Father in heaven.[19] The one is the firmament of heaven on high, the other is a similar firmament of which it is said, "On this rock I will build my church";[20] the one is a firmament of the elements, the other of virtues, and this last is more excellent. They sucked oil out of the hard stone,[21] for the rock is

---

[5]Gen 46:4. [6]Gen 25:8. [7]2 Tim 4:7. [8]2 Tim 4:8; Jas 1:12. [9]FC 71:212*. [10]Gen 25:8. [11]Job 5:26 (LXX). [12]See Prov 10:27. [13]Eccles 7:17. [14]NPNF 2 4:260*. [15]See Eccles 3:11. [16]ANF 6:114*. [17]Ps 119:73 (118:73 LXX, Vg.). [18]Ps 19:1 (18:2 LXX, Vg.). [19]Mt 5:16. [20]Mt 16:18. [21]See Deut 32:13.

Christ's body that redeemed heaven and the entire world.[22] LETTER 49.[23]

THE WORLD IS THE WORK OF GOD'S HANDS.
TERTULLIAN: But it is not thus that the prophets and the apostles have told us that the world was made by God merely appearing and approaching matter. They did not even mention any matter but [said] that Wisdom was first set up, the beginning of his ways, for his works.[24] Then that the Word was produced,[25] "through whom all things were made, and without whom nothing was made."[26] Indeed, "by the Word of the Lord were the heavens made, and all their hosts by the breath of his mouth."[27] He is the Lord's right hand, indeed his two hands, by which he worked and constructed the universe. "For," he says, "the heavens are the works of your hands." Wherewith "he has measured out the heaven, and the earth with a span."[28] Do not be willing so to cover God with flattery, as to contend that he produced by his mere appearance and simple approach so many vast substances, instead of rather forming them by his own energies. For this is proved by Jeremiah when he says, "God has made the earth by his power; he has established the world by his wisdom and has stretched out the heaven by his understanding."[29] These are the energies by the stress of which he made this universe. His glory is greater if he labored. AGAINST HERMOGENES 45.[30]

WHAT COMES FROM NOTHING RETURNS TO NOTHING. TERTULLIAN: In like manner David says, "The heavens, the works of your hands, shall themselves perish. For even as a garment shall he change them, and they shall be changed." Now to be changed is to fall from that primitive state that they lose while undergoing the change. "And the stars too shall fall from heaven, even as a fig tree casts its green figs when it is shaken by a mighty wind."[31] "The mountains shall melt like wax at the presence of the Lord";[32] that is, "when he rises to shake terribly the earth."[33] "But I will dry up the pools";[34] and "they shall seek water,

and they shall find none."[35] Even "the sea shall be no more."[36] Now if any person should go so far as to suppose that all these passages ought to be spiritually interpreted, he will still be unable to deprive them of the true accomplishment of those issues that must come to pass just as they have been written. For all figures of speech necessarily arise out of real things, not out of chimerical ones; because nothing is capable of imparting anything of its own for a similitude, except it actually be that very thing that it imparts in the similitude. I return therefore to the principle that defines that all things that have come from nothing shall return at last to nothing. AGAINST HERMOGENES 34.[37]

A PROPHECY OF THE LAST JUDGMENT.
AMBROSE: But this opinion[38] could not withstand the words of the prophet, which the divine majesty of our Lord Jesus Christ, our God, has confirmed in the Gospel. For David has said, "In the beginning, O Lord, you founded the earth, and the heavens are the work of your hands. They shall perish, but you remain, and all of them shall grow old as a garment. And as a robe you shall change them, and they shall be changed. But you are always the same, and your years shall not fail." To such a degree did the Lord confirm this that he said, "Heaven and earth will pass away, but my words will not pass away."[39] SIX DAYS OF CREATION 1.6.24.[40]

A NEW HEAVEN AND A NEW EARTH. AMBROSE: "When he has gone to sleep, he will not rise again even until the heaven is unstitched."[41] This appears to mean, until heaven is made new. "For there will be a new heaven and a new earth,"[42] just

---

[22]1 Cor 10:4. [23]FC 26:258*. [24]See Prov 8:22-23. [25]Brought forth or begotten. [26]Jn 1:3. [27]Ps 33:6 (32:6 LXX, Vg.). [28]Is 40:12. [29]Jer 51:15. [30]ANF 3:502*. [31]Rev 6:13. [32]Ps 97:5 (96:5 LXX, Vg.). [33]Is 2:19. [34]Is 42:15. [35]Is 41:17. [36]Rev 21:1. [37]ANF 3:497*. [38]The view of some philosophers that the substance of the heavens and the stars is ethereal, composed of a fifth corporeal nature, which gives permanency to the substance of the heavens. [39]Mt 24:35. [40]FC 42:24-25*. [41]Job 14:12. [42]Is 65:17.

as it is written. For what is stitched up is old, and what is old will be changed. Then listen as the psalmist says, "In the beginning, O Lord, you founded the earth, and the heavens are the works of your hands. They shall perish, but you remain; and all of them shall grow old like a garment, and you shall change them like a garment, and they shall be changed." We are able also to weave on the garment, because what is old is stitched on, whereas what is new suffers violence. "From the days of John the Baptist the kingdom of heaven suffers violence, and the violent take it by force."[43] The synagogue stitched on it in the case of a few; the church forces it in the case of thousands. Or else the meaning is that heaven now appears to be stitched on, being often interwoven with clouds and mist and the darkness of night and the golden redness of the rising day, a various and multicolored sight. Then "night shall be no more, and they shall have no need of light of lamp and light of sun, because the Lord will shed light on them,"[44] even as John said. Or else, "Woe to those who sew pillows to overthrow the souls of the people."[45] The prophet was lamenting the wretched frailty of our condition, that has no rest in this life and loses everything by death's sudden onset. For the Holy Spirit revealed to him that man would not arise for so long a time, until he should come who would not stitch the old to the new nor join new material to old material[46] but would make all things new, even as he said, "Behold, I make all things new!"[47] For he is the resurrection, the firstborn from the dead,[48] in whom we have all indeed received the prerogative of a future resurrection; yet till now he alone has risen in a perpetual resurrection. THE PRAYER OF JOB AND DAVID 1.7.24-25.[49]

THE HEAVEN AND THE EARTH WILL BE MADE NEW AGAIN. CYRIL OF JERUSALEM: Our Lord Jesus Christ, therefore, is to come from heaven, and to come with glory at the end of this world, on the last day. For an end of this world there will be; this created world will be made new again. Corruption, theft, adultery and sins of every kind

have flooded the earth, and bloodshed has been paid with blood; so to prevent this wondrous dwelling place from continuing forever filled with iniquity, this world is to pass away, to make room for a fairer world. You want proof of this from Scripture? Listen to Isaiah: "The heavens shall be rolled up like a scroll, and all their hosts shall wither away as the leaf on the vine or as the fig withers on the fig tree."[50] And the Gospel says, "The sun shall be darkened, and the moon will not give its light, and the stars will fall from heaven."[51] Let us not grieve as though we alone were to die, for the stars also will die; but perhaps they will rise again. The Lord shall fold up the heavens, not to destroy them but to raise them up more beautiful. Listen to David the prophet: "Of old you established the earth, and the heavens are the work of your hands. They shall perish, but you remain." But someone will say, "Behold, he says plainly that 'they shall perish.' Ah, but hear in what sense he says, 'they shall perish'; it is clear from what follows: 'though all of them grow old like a garment. Like clothing you change them, and they are changed.'" For just as humankind is said to perish, according to the text, "The just perishes, and no one takes it to heart,"[52] and this is said, though the resurrection is expected, so we look for a "resurrection" of the heavens. CATECHETICAL LECTURES 15.3.[53]

A CLEAR PROPHECY OF THE END OF THE WORLD. AUGUSTINE: The psalms contain many references to the last judgment, most of them being brief statements made in passing. But I shall certainly not fail to mention the most explicit statement in the psalms about the end of the world. "In the beginning you founded the world, Lord, and the heavens are the work of your hands. They will perish, but you endure, and they will all grow old like a piece of clothing, and you will change them like a garment, and

---

[43]Mt 11:12. [44]Rev 22:5. [45]Ezek 13:18 LXX. [46]See Mt 9:16. [47]Rev 21:5. [48]See Col 1:18; Rev 1:5. [49]FC 65:344-45*. [50]Is 34:4. [51]Mt 24:29. [52]Is 57:1. [53]FC 64:55-56.

they will be changed. But you are always the same, and your years will never end." CITY OF GOD 20.24.[54]

GOD IS ETERNAL AND UNCHANGEABLE. FULGENTIUS OF RUSPE: Hold most firmly and never doubt that the holy Trinity, the only true God, just as it is eternal, is likewise the only one by nature unchangeable. God indicates this when he says to his servant Moses, "I am which I am."[55] Hence, it is said in the psalms, "In the beginning you laid the foundation of the earth, and the heavens are the work of your hands. They will perish, but you endure." TO PETER ON THE FAITH 4.50.[56]

A CHANGE FOR THE BETTER. BASIL THE GREAT: For this very reason, a certain one of the interpreters[57] seems to me to have handed over beautifully and accurately the same thought[58] through another title, saying, "For the lilies," in place of, "For them that shall be changed." He thought that it was appropriate to compare the transitoriness of human nature with the early death of flowers. But, since this word has been inflected in the future tense (it is said: "For them that shall be changed," as if at some time later this change will be shown to us), let us consider whether there is suggested to us the doctrine of the resurrection, in which a change will be granted to us, but a change for something better and something spiritual. "What is sown in corruption," he says, "rises in incorruption." Do you see the change? "What is sown in weakness rises in power; what is sown a natural body rises a spiritual body,"[59] when every corporeal creature will change together with us. Also, "The heavens shall grow old like a garment, and as a robe" God "shall change them, and they shall be changed."[60] Then, according to Isaiah, "The sun will be sevenfold, and the moon like the present size of the sun."[61] HOMILIES ON THE PSALMS 17.2.[62]

THE SON IS NOT INFERIOR TO THE FATHER. CHRYSOSTOM: But, if you think the word *through* implies inferiority, listen to [the prophet] saying, "In the beginning you did establish the earth, and heaven is the work of your hands." What is said of the Father as Creator is meant also of the Son; he would not have said it if he had not the same opinion of him as Creator, and as not inferior to anyone. And if the words "through him" are used here, they are employed with no other view than that no one may subscribe to the idea that the Son is unbegotten. HOMILIES ON THE GOSPEL OF JOHN 5.[63]

THE IMMUTABILITY OF CHRIST. AUGUSTINE: Suppose they[64] say, though, that the Lord's own divine substance is not the same when he is with the Father as it was when he wished to show himself on earth without taking a body, then what else have the poor fools committed themselves to, but saying that the divine substance is subject to change in place and time? They do not want to read, or they find it difficult to understand, what is said by the prophet, "They will perish, but you remain; they will all wear out like a garment. Like clothing you will change them, and they will be discarded. But you remain the same, and your years will never end"; and what is written in the book of divine Wisdom about Wisdom: "While remaining in herself, she renews all things."[65] SERMON 12.10.[66]

HUMAN FLESH CHANGED FOR THE BETTER. AUGUSTINE: If, however, they[67] do not say "so impure" but "so weak," we agree entirely. And that is why Christ is our strength, because he was not changed by our weakness. Here I recognize the aptness of the prophet's words, "You will change them, and they shall be changed; but you

---

[54]CG 947. [55]Ex 3:14. [56]FC 95:92. [57]The Benedictine editors believe that Basil is speaking of the translator, Aquila. [58]The idea that living things are constantly subject to change, such as growth and aging, circumstances of life, mood swings. [59]1 Cor 15:42-44. [60]Ps 102:26 (101:27 LXX). [61]See Is 30:26. [62]FC 46:277*. [63]FC 33:62-63*. [64]Augustine here is refuting Manicheans, who held that Christ's body was apparent rather than real. [65]Wis 7:27. [66]WSA 3 1:302-3. [67]Manicheans believed that the body is impure because it consists of matter, which is evil.

yourself are the same, and your years shall not fail." Not only did the weakness of the flesh not change him for the worse, but by him it was changed for the better. SERMON 12.12.[68]

AN UNALTERABLE GOD. ATHANASIUS: Therefore the Image of the unalterable God must be unchangeable; for "Jesus Christ is the same yesterday, today and forever."[69] And David in the psalm says of him, "You, Lord, in the beginning have laid the foundation of the earth, and the heavens are the work of your hands. They shall perish, but you remain; and they all shall grow old as does a garment. And you shall fold them up as a piece of clothing, and they shall be changed, but you are the same, and your years shall not fail." And the Lord says of himself through the prophet, "See now that I, even I am he," and "I change not."[70] DISCOURSES AGAINST THE ARIANS 1.10.36.[71]

GOD IS IMMUTABLE. AUGUSTINE: These things that we hold according to our faith, and which reason also demonstrates, can be supported by testimonies from the divine Scriptures, so that the less intelligent who cannot follow the argument may believe on divine authority and so may deserve to reach understanding. Those who understand, and are less instructed in ecclesiastical sacred books, are not to think that we have produced them[72] out of our heads and that they are not in the Scriptures. That God is immutable is written thus in the Psalms: "You shall change them, and they shall be changed; but you are the same." And in the book of Wisdom it is written of Wisdom: "Abiding in herself she renews all things."[73] The apostle Paul says, "To the invisible, incorruptible, only wise God."[74] The apostle James writes, "Every good gift and every perfect gift is from above and comes down from the Father of lights, with whom is no variableness, neither shadow of turning."[75] Because the Son was not made, but all things were made through him, it is written, "In the beginning was the Word, and the Word was with God, and the Word was God. He was in the beginning with God. All things were made through him, and without him nothing was made."[76] ON THE NATURE OF THE GOOD 24.[77]

GOD IS TRUE TO HIS NATURE. THEODORET OF CYR: Even in the case of our own soul, when we say that it cannot die, we do not predicate weakness of it, but we proclaim its capacity of immortality. And similarly when we confess the immutability, impassibility and immortality of God, we cannot attribute to the divine nature change, passion or death. Suppose they insist that God can do whatever he will, you must reply to them that he wishes to do nothing that it is not his nature to do. He is good by nature; therefore he does not wish anything evil. He is just by nature; therefore he does not wish anything unjust. He is true by nature; therefore he considers falsehood abominable. He is by nature immutable; therefore he does not admit of change. If he does not admit of change, he is always in the same state and condition. This he himself asserts through the prophet: "I am the Lord; I change not."[78] And the blessed David says, "You are the same, and your years shall have no end." If he is the same, he undergoes no change. If he is naturally superior to change and mutation, he has not become mortal from immortal or passible from impassible, for had this been possible he would not have taken on him our nature. But since he has an immortal nature, he took a body capable of suffering, and with the body a human soul. Both of these he kept unstained from the defilements of sin and gave his soul for the sake of the souls that had sinned and his body for the sake of the bodies that had died. And since the body that was assumed is described as the body of the very only-begotten Son of God, he refers the passion of the body to himself. LETTER 144.[79]

---

[68]WSA 3 1:304. [69]Heb 13:8. [70]Deut 32:39; Mal 3:6. [71]NPNF 2 4:327*. [72]The truths on which faith is based. [73]Wis 7:27. [74]1 Tim 1:17. [75]Jas 1:17. [76]Jn 1:1-3. [77]LCC 6:333-34*. [78]Mal 3:6. [79]NPNF 2 3:311**.

103:1-22 A HYMN OF PRAISE FOR GOD'S LOVE AND COMPASSION

A Psalm of David.

1Bless the LORD, O my soul;
and all that is within me, bless his holy name!
2Bless the LORD. O my soul,
and forget not all his benefits,
3who forgives all your iniquity,
who heals all your diseases,
4who redeems your life from the Pit,
who crowns you with steadfast love and mercy,
5who satisfies you with good as long as you live[q]
so that your youth is renewed like the eagle's.

6The LORD works vindication
and justice for all who are oppressed.
7He made known his ways to Moses,
his acts to the people of Israel.
8The LORD is merciful and gracious,
slow to anger and abounding in steadfast love.
9He will not always chide,
nor will he keep his anger for ever.
10He does not deal with us according to our sins,
nor requite us according to our iniquities.
11For as the heavens are high above the earth,
so great is his steadfast love toward those who fear him;
12as far as the east is from the west,
so far does he remove our transgressions from us.
13As a father pities his children,
so the LORD pities those who fear him.
14For he knows our frame;
he remembers that we are dust.

15As for man, his days are like grass;
he flourishes like a flower of the field;
16for the wind passes over it, and it is gone,
and its place knows it no more.
17But the steadfast love of the LORD is from everlasting to everlasting
upon those who fear him,
and his righteousness to children's children,
18to those who keep his covenant
and remember to do his commandments.

19The LORD has established his throne in the heavens,
and his kingdom rules over all.
20Bless the LORD, O you his angels,
you mighty ones who do his word,
hearkening to the voice of his word!
21Bless LORD, all his hosts,
his ministers that do his will!
22Bless the LORD, all his works,
in all places of his dominion.
Bless the LORD, O my soul!

q Heb uncertain

OVERVIEW: Only Christians who cleanse their souls of sinfulness can gain a true understanding of the deeper spiritual meaning of the Bible (ORIGEN). It is sacrilege to believe that God can only forgive past sins; rather, God is an expert, merciful physician who is able to cure all our maladies and forgive all our sins (FULGENTIUS). Sin is like an illness that is alien to human nature as God created it; therefore it must not only be forgiven but also eradicated, even though that will not happen totally in this life. Since we cannot totally get rid of sin in this life, we must strive for it to be diminished. We lack understanding and are terrorized by spiritual darkness and impending punishments until we are spiritually renewed by God. Out of mercy and compassion God promises us a crown of life, not because we deserve it (AUGUSTINE). Like the legendary phoenix that supposedly rose again from its ashes, sinners are born again to a new life in God through the sacrament of baptism. Even before death separates the soul from the body, God teaches us to raise our soul from earthly to heavenly things so that it may be renewed even now as the eagle restores its youthfulness. We possess two legs, suggesting an affinity with birds. So we should set our vision on things above, yet higher than the eagle, that is, those things that are heavenly (AMBROSE). In baptism we are restored to a youthful state of righteousness. Like the eagle, which was believed to revivify itself by shedding its old plumage for new, so through the grace of baptism we put on the new clothing of holiness (MAXIMUS).

Even though people have violated their conscience and God's written law, God did not punish and dishonor them as they deserved but forgave and restored them as his children out of mercy and grace (CHRYSOSTOM). Human beings know God only to the degree that God has enabled them (GREGORY OF NYSSA). God does not deal with us as our sins deserve but according to his underserved mercy, so that we are justified by faith (FULGENTIUS). We should not only separate ourselves from evil persons and events but also support those in authority and try to restrain others from evil deeds so that God may have mercy on them and bring an end to humanity's evil (AUGUSTINE). The words of the psalmist will be fulfilled on the last day when the goats will be separated from the sheep. The wicked will be punished for the wickedness they have done on earth, and the righteous will be rewarded for the good merits bestowed on them by God (FULGENTIUS). God in his goodness and mercy has removed our sins from us as far as the heavens are from the earth (PACHOMIUS). When Paul was thrown on the ground as a persecutor and raised up as a preacher, he acknowledged that he received mercy according to the promise of the psalmist that God does not deal with us according to our sins (CAESARIUS). God does not reject those whom he regards with favor but strengthens them in their weakness and cleanses them of their sins (AMBROSE). In heaven the redeemed will recognize one another and remember things they knew on the earth, but the wicked will not recognize either (APOCRYPHAL REVELATION).

Human life is like the flight of a bird that leaves no trace of its passage in the air and as a ship that leaves no trace of its voyage on the sea—so life begins and ends without much fanfare (GREGORY OF NAZIANZUS). Even good people suffer much hardship, anxiety and brevity of life in this world (AMBROSE). God will judge people who remember his commandments in order to despise and attack rather than obey (AUGUSTINE).

In Psalm 103 David helps us understand that the doing of God's will in heaven means that angels do God's will there as the righteous do on earth (CYRIL OF JERUSALEM). Blessed are the angels who are ministers of God's will because they are instrumental in the salvation of human beings by proclaiming the mystery of the Trinity and effecting the purging of sins (GREGORY OF NYSSA).

103:1-5 A New Life in God

A SPIRITUAL UNDERSTANDING OF WISDOM.
ORIGEN: In like manner, "these fatty parts of the ram that are around the kidneys and these that cover the interior parts"[1] are commanded to be

---

[1] See Lev 7:4.

placed on the altar. So you who hear these things should know you ought to offer on the fire of the altar everything that is more sinful within you and hides your "inner being" so that all your "inner being" may be cleansed and you also may say, as David said, "Bless the Lord, my soul, and all that is within me, bless his holy name." For unless that sinfulness that touches your "inner being" should be removed, your inner being cannot lay hold of the subtle and spiritual sense and cannot receive the understanding of wisdom; therefore, it cannot praise the Lord. HOMILIES ON LEVITICUS 5.4.3.[2]

ALL SINS CAN BE FORGIVEN. FULGENTIUS OF RUSPE: Who does not see how impious and how sacrilegious it is if a person, who has been converted to good things through penance for his past evils, believes that there can be no forgiveness for any sin?[3] What else is being done with these words than that the hand of the all-powerful physician is being pushed away by the vice of despair, from effecting human salvation? For the physician himself says, "Those who are healthy do not need a physician, but the sick do."[4] If our physician is an expert, he can cure all maladies. If God is merciful, he can forgive all sins. A goodness that does not conquer every evil is not a perfect goodness, nor is a medicine perfect for which any disease is incurable. It is written in the sacred writings, "Against wisdom, evil does not prevail";[5] and the omnipotence of our physician is made known by such words in the psalm: "Bless the Lord, O my soul, and all that is within me, bless his holy name. Bless the Lord, O my soul, and do not forget all his benefits—who forgives all your iniquity, who heals all your diseases, who redeems your life from the pit, who crowns you with steadfast love and mercy, who satisfies you with good as long as you live so that your youth is renewed like the eagle's." What, I ask, do we think cannot be forgiven us when the Lord forgives all our iniquities? Or what do we think cannot be healed in us, when the Lord heals all our diseases? Or how is there anything still lacking to

the healed and justified person whose desire is satisfied with good things? Or how is he not believed to gain the benefit of complete forgiveness to whom a crown is given together with love and mercy? Therefore, let no one despairing of the physician remain in his infirmity; let no one, downplaying the mercy of God, waste away in iniquities. The apostle calls out that "Christ died for the ungodly."[6] LETTER 7.4.[7]

OUR NATURES NEED TO BE HEALED. AUGUSTINE: If you[8] did not wish to be contentious, I think you would now see how correctly we understand what you are trying to explain differently. When the prophet said, "who forgives all your faults"—something that is done by the remission of all sins—he immediately added "who heals all your diseases." He wants us to understand the evils with which the saints will never finish their internal warfare until those evils are healed or, as far as possible in this life, progressively diminished. Not even when the virtue of chastity stands unshaken is there no sickness by which the flesh lusts against the spirit. When there is no sickness, the spirit does not lust against it, because it lusts in order at least by not consenting to obtain health, since it is unable to do so by not fighting. We are speaking of that whose resistance to us we perceive within us; if an alien nature, we must get rid of it; if our own, it must be healed. If we say it is an alien nature and must be gotten rid of, we agree with the Manichaeans.[9] Let us, then, confess it is our own nature that must be healed, and thus we shall at the same time be clear of Manichaeans and Pelagians.[10] AGAINST JULIAN 6.18.57.[11]

---

[2]FC 83:97*. [3]It was a common belief in the early church that mortal sins, especially those committed after baptism, could not be absolved by the church. [4]Lk 5:31. [5]Wis 7:30. [6]Rom 5:6. [7]FC 95:355-56*. [8]Julian, a Pelagian heretic. [9]The Manichaeans held a strong dualistic view of the world in which matter was absolutely evil and the spiritual was altogether good. [10]The Pelagians denied original sin. They affirmed that a person is saved by good works alone, even apart from the redemption of Jesus Christ. [11]FC 35:367*.

Forgiveness and the Fulfillment of God's Promises. Augustine: He is the Beginning, O God, in which you made heaven and earth. In this wonderful way you spoke and created them in your Word, in your Son, who is your strength, your wisdom and your truth.

Who can understand this mystery or explain it to others? What is that light whose gentle beams now and again strike through to my heart, causing me to shudder in awe yet firing me with their warmth? I shudder to feel how different I am for it: yet in so far as I am like it, I am aglow with its fire. It is the light of Wisdom, Wisdom itself, which at times shines on me, parting my clouds. But when I weakly fall away from its light, those clouds envelop me again in the dense mantle of darkness that I bear for my punishment. For "my strength ebbs away for very misery,"[12] so that I cannot sustain my blessings. And so I shall remain until you, O Lord, who "have pardoned all my sins," also "heal all my mortal ills." For you will "rescue my life from deadly peril, crown me with the blessings of your mercy, content all my desire for good, restore my youth as the eagle's plumage is restored." "Our salvation is founded on the hope of something,"[13] and in endurance we await the fulfillment of your promises. Let those who are able listen to your fulfillment of your promises. Let those who are able listen to your voice speaking to their hearts. Trusting in your inspired words, I shall cry out, "What diversity, Lord, in your creatures! What wisdom has designed them all!"[14] The Beginning is Wisdom, and Wisdom is the Beginning in which you made heaven and earth. Confessions 11.9.[15]

The Crown of Life. Augustine: Finally, after redemption from all decay, what remains but the crown of justice? Certainly that remains; but even with that, or rather under that, take care the head is not too swollen to receive the crown. Listen, pay attention to the psalm, and see how the crown refuses to fit a swollen head. After saying, "who redeems your life from decay," he went on, "who crowns you." Now here you were on the point of saying, "Crowns you: that means my merits are being acknowledged; my virtue has brought this about; a debt is being paid, not a gift being presented." Listen rather to the psalm. After all, here is something you also say: "Every person is a liar."[16] So listen to what God is saying: "Who crowns you with compassion and mercy." So it is out of mercy that he crowns you, out of compassion that he crowns you. I mean to say, you did not deserve to be called, and being called to be justified, and being justified to be glorified. Sermon 131.8.[17]

New Birth in Baptism. Ambrose: And that the writer[18] was speaking of baptism is evident from the very words in which it is stated that it is impossible to renew to repentance those who were fallen, inasmuch as we are renewed by means of the laver of baptism, whereby we are born again, as Paul says: "For we are buried with him through baptism into death, that, as Christ rose from the dead through the glory of the Father, so we, too, should walk in newness of life."[19] And in another place: "Be renewed in the spirit of your mind, and put on the new person that is created after God."[20] And elsewhere again: "Your youth shall be renewed like the eagle," because the phoenix after death is born again from its ashes, as we being dead in sin are through the sacrament of baptism born again to God and created anew. So, then, here as elsewhere, he teaches one baptism. "One faith," he says, "one baptism."[21] Concerning Repentance 2.2.8.[22]

Strive for What Is Eternal. Ambrose: But let us speak of death as common to all people. Why should we be afraid of it, when it generally

---

[12]Ps 31:10 (30:11 LXX, Vg.). [13]Rom 8:24. [14]See Ps 104:24 (103:24 LXX, Vg.). [15]AC 260-61. [16]Ps 116:11 (115:2 LXX, Vg.). [17]WSA 3 4:320-21. [18]The author of the book of Hebrews (whom Ambrose thought was Paul). Hebrews 6:4-6 was used by Montanists and Novatians to support their view that there is no (second) forgiveness of mortal sins. [19]Rom 6:4. [20]Eph 4:23-24. [21]Eph 4:5. [22]NPNF 2 10:346*.

does not harm the soul? For it is written, "Do not be afraid of those who kill the body but cannot kill the soul."[23] Now through death the soul is freed, while it separates itself from the dwelling place of the body and divests itself of the wrappings of disquiet. And so let us too, while we are in the body, following the way of death, raise up our bodies from this fleshly couch and arise from the tomb, as it were. Let us withdraw from the bond of the body and leave all things whatsoever that are of earth, so that when the adversary comes he may find nothing of his in us.[24] Let us strive for the eternal and fly up to the divine on the wings of love and the oars of charity. Let us rise up from here, that is, from the things of the age and those of the world. For the Lord has said, "Arise, let us go from here,"[25] teaching that each one should arise from the earth, raise up his soul that lies on the ground, lift it to the things that are above and call forth his eagle, the eagle of whom it is said, "Your youth will be renewed like the eagle's." DEATH AS A GOOD 5.16.[26]

OUR CITIZENSHIP IS IN HEAVEN. AMBROSE: That humans should have two legs and not more is altogether fitting. Wild animals and beasts have four legs, while birds possess two. Hence humans have kinship with the winged flock in that with his vision he aims at what is high. He flies as if "on the propulsion of wings" by reason of the sagacity of his sublime senses. Hence it was said of him, "Your youth is renewed like the eagle's," because he is near what is celestial and is higher than the eagle, as one who can say, "But our citizenship is in heaven."[27] SIX DAYS OF CREATION 6.9.74.[28]

RENEWED THROUGH BAPTISM. MAXIMUS OF TURIN: Your holiness[29] recalls, brothers, how I preached very recently that the human person is reformed into a more youthful state through righteousness and, although worn out by age, is born again into childhood by innocent behavior so that, once the mystery [baptism] has taken place, we may see old people turned into babes.

For it is a kind of renewal to cease what you were and to take up what you had once been. This renewal, I say, is why new converts are called neophytes, since in a kind of newness they cast off the stains of oldness and receive the grace of simplicity, as the apostle says: "Laying aside the old person with his practices, put on the new, which has been created according to God."[30] Hence also holy David says, "Your youth shall be renewed like an eagle's." It is understood that by the grace of baptism what is failing in our life can live again and what had broken down in us by reason of the old age of sin can be renewed by a certain youthfulness. But in order for you to see that the prophet speaks of the grace of baptism, he compares this very renewal with an eagle, a bird that by a continual changing of its garment is said to live to a great age. Its old and already decayed plumage it makes youthful with a new set of feathers so that, once renewed, when it has laid down its old covering it clothes itself in fresh garments. From this we understand that it is not an eagle's body but its plumage that feels old age. Therefore it reclothes itself, and as her feathers sprout an old mother bird becomes an eaglet again. She is to be compared with a young bird when, with pinions outspread, she has to practice flying again and gain control over the once seasoned apparatus of her wings, just as if she were a newly hatched bird lying sluggish in its nest. For although she is well accustomed to flying, nonetheless she lacks confidence because of the sparsity of her feathers. The holy psalmist, therefore, prophesied this with the grace of baptism in mind. For, indeed, our newly baptized neophytes have laid aside their old garment like eagles and have put on the new clothing of holiness! They have shed their former sins like light feathers, and they are adorned with the new grace of immortality. Thus in them the feeble sins of old age grow old, but life does not grow old, for as an eagle

---

[23]Mt 10:28. [24]See Jn 14:30. [25]Jn 14:31. [26]FC 65:82. [27]Phil 3:20. [28]FC 42:281*. [29]This was a common form of address used in sermons. [30]Col 3:9-10.

becomes an eaglet so they become babes. From their way of life they are familiar with the world, but thanks to their renewal they are secure in righteousness. SERMON 55.1.[31]

103:6-14 God Is Abounding in Love

GOD IS GOOD AND RIGHTEOUS. CHRYSOSTOM: Further, the restoration of this [unwritten natural law[32]] by a written law, after it had been corrupted, was the work of grace. Moreover, the logical consequence was that they who transgressed the precept, once it had been given, be punished and dishonored; this, however, was not what took place. Rather, reinstatement once more and pardon: not due, of course, but given out of mercy and grace. In proof that it was given out of mercy and grace, listen to what David says: "The Lord works deeds of mercy and judgment for all that suffer wrong. He has made known his ways to Moses, his deeds to the children of Israel." And again: "The Lord is good and righteous; he will give a law to sinners in the way."[33] HOMILIES ON THE GOSPEL OF JOHN 14.[34]

GOD'S NAME AND ATTRIBUTES DERIVE FROM HIS ACTIVITIES. GREGORY OF NYSSA: God is not an expression, and he does not have his essence in voice or utterance. God is of himself what also he is believed to be. He is named by those who call on him, not what he is essentially (for the nature of him who alone is unspeakable), but he receives his names from what are believed to be his works in regard to our life. To take an instance ready at hand, when we speak of him as God, we so name him from his overlooking and surveying all things and seeing through the things that are hidden. But if his essence is prior to his works, and if we understand his works by our senses and express them in words as we are best able, why should we be afraid of calling things by words of later origin than themselves? For if we stop interpreting any of the attributes of God until we understand them, and if we understand them only by what his works

teach us, and if his power precedes its exercise and depends on the will of God, while his will resides in the spontaneity of the divine nature, are we not clearly taught that the words that represent things are of later origin than the things themselves and that the words that are framed to express the operations of things are reflections of the things themselves? And that this is so, we are clearly taught by holy Scripture, by the mouth of great David, when, as by certain peculiar and appropriate names, derived from his contemplation of the works of God, he thus speaks of the divine nature: "The Lord is full of compassion and mercy, long-suffering, and of great goodness." Now what do these words tell us? Do they indicate his operations or his nature? No one will say that they indicate anything but his operations. At what time, then, after showing mercy and pity, did God acquire his name from the display of his works? Was it before a person's life began? But who was there to be the object of pity? Was it, then, after sin entered into the world? But sin entered after humankind. The exercise, therefore, of pity, and the name itself, came after humanity. What then? Will our adversary [Eunomius], wise as he is above the prophets, convict David of error in applying names to God derived from his opportunities of knowing him? Or, in contending with him, will he use against him the pretense in his stately passage as out of a tragedy, saying that "he glories in the most blessed life of God with names drawn from human imagination, whereas it gloried in itself alone, long before people were born to imagine them"? The psalmist's advocate will readily admit that the divine nature gloried in itself alone even before the existence of human imagination but will contend that the human mind can speak only so much in respect of God as its capacity, instructed by his works, will allow. "For," as says the Wisdom of Solomon, "by the greatness and beauty of the creatures

---

[31]ACW 50:133-34*. [32]A person's conscience. [33]Ps 25:8 (24:8 LXX, Vg.). [34]FC 33:136*.

proportionably the Maker of them is seen."[35] ANSWER TO EUNOMIUS'S SECOND BOOK.[36]

GOD'S FREE GIFTS TO PEOPLE. FULGENTIUS OF RUSPE: He is the one about whom the psalm says, "The Lord is merciful and gracious, slow to anger and abounding in steadfast love. He will not always accuse, nor will he keep his anger forever. He does not deal with us according to our sins or repay us according to our iniquities. For as the heavens are far above the earth, so great is his steadfast love toward those who fear him. As far as the east is from the west, so far does he remove our transgressions from us. As a father has compassion for his children, so the Lord has compassion for those who fear him." In all of these great, good things that the Lord gives to the wicked, what else is being sung than undeserved mercy? What else other than free piety is being proclaimed? For in this, that "he does not deal with us according to our sins or repay us according to our iniquities," the free justification of the impious is displayed. And in this that "as a father has compassion for his children, so the Lord has compassion for those who fear him,"[37] the free adoption of children shines through by the same justification by faith. For not as a father has compassion on his children unless becoming our father through grace, he deigned to make us his children. "To those who did accept him, he gave power to become children of God."[38] LETTER TO MONIMUS 1.21.3.[39]

RESTRAIN ONESELF AND OTHERS FROM SERIOUSLY EVIL ACTIVITIES. AUGUSTINE: So let us at last wind up this sermon. My brothers and sister, I urge you, I beseech you by the Lord and his gentleness, be gentle in your lives, be peaceful in your lives. Peacefully permit the authorities to do what pertains to them, of which they will have to render an account to God and to their superiors. As often as you have to petition them, make your petitions in an honorable and quiet manner. Do not mix with those who do evil and rampage in a rough and disorderly manner; do not desire to be present at such goings-on even as spectators. But as far as you can, let each of you in his own house and his own neighborhood deal with the one with whom you have ties of kinship and charity, by warning, persuading, teaching, correcting; also by restraining him from such seriously evil activities by any kind of threats, so that God may eventually have mercy, and put an end to human evils and "may not deal with us according to our sins or requite us according to our iniquities, but as far as the east is from the west may cast our sins for away from us," and that he "may be gracious to our sins, lest the nations perhaps should say, Where is their God?"[40] SERMON 302.21.[41]

GOD DOES NOT REPAY US ACCORDING TO OUR INIQUITIES. FULGENTIUS OF RUSPE: The shepherd's most certain knowledge of merits,[42] by which the sheep will be separated from the goats, is so great that no goat will be placed on the right, just as no sheep will be located on the left. Those merits with which people go forth from this life will remain ceaselessly and unchangeably with them in that other life, whether they are good merits that here divine piety has bestowed or demerits that human wickedness has procured here below. And for this reason, there will be no removal of evil demerits, although there will be an advancement for good merits. The former will remain for punishment; the latter will be perfected in glory. Therefore, that is the time in which God, as it is written in the psalm, "does not deal with us according to our sins or repay us according to our iniquities. For as the heavens are high above the earth, so great is his steadfast love toward those who fear him; as far as the east is from the west, so far he removes our transgressions from us." ON THE FORGIVENESS OF SINS 2.10.4.[43]

---

[35]Wis 13:5. [36]NPNF 2 5:265**. [37]Ps 103:13 (102:13 LXX, Vg.). [38]Jn 1:12. [39]FC 95:215-16. [40]Ps 79:9-10 (78:9-10 LXX, Vg.). [41]WSA 3 8:310. [42]Fulgentius believed that faith and works are both necessary for salvation. God freely justifies people according to his mercy, but individuals will be rewarded with glory in the next life according to the merits they have won by their good works during their temporal life. [43]FC 95:163-64.

God Delights in Mercy. Pachomius: "O wretched person, you have estranged yourself completely from the Lord. But the Lord is good, and he never 'kept his anger for a testimony, for he delights in mercy,' and he is 'able to sink our sins in the depths of the sea,' for 'as far as the heavens are from the earth, so far away does he set our sins from us. For he desires not the death of the sinner but his repentance,'[44] and that the person who has fallen should not remain in his fallen condition but should rise up, and that he who has turned away should not go far off but return quickly to him. Therefore, despair not of yourself; 'there is hope' of salvation. For, as it is said, 'if a tree is cut down, it will sprout again.'[45] Then, if you will even now listen to me in everything I say to you, you shall have forgiveness from God." He[46] answered with tears, "In all things I will listen to you from now on, O father!" Paralipomena 5.11.[47]

Deal Not with Us as Our Sins Deserve. Caesarius of Arles: You[48] do nothing with regard to the reward; you do not act alone in the deed. Your crown comes from him, but the work is yours, although it does not happen without his help. When the apostle Paul, who was first Saul, was an exceedingly cruel and fierce persecutor, he merited nothing good at all but rather a great deal of evil; he deserved to be damned, and not chosen among the elect. Then suddenly, while he was doing evil and meriting evil, he was thrown to the ground by a voice from heaven. The persecutor was cast to the ground, and the preacher was lifted up. Listen to him admitting his own condition: "I was once a blasphemer, a persecutor, a man filled with arrogance, but I have been treated mercifully."[49] Did he say there: "The just judge will give an award to me"? "I have been treated mercifully," he said; I deserved evil but received good. "Not according to our sins does he deal with us." I obtained mercy; what was due to me was not given to me, for if what was due had been rendered, punishment would have been given. I did not receive what was due to me, he says; I

have been treated mercifully. "Not according to our sins does he deal with us." Sermon 226.2.[50]

We Need God's Strength. Ambrose: Therefore do not forget one who is weak. Remember, Lord, that you have made me weak. Remember that "you have fashioned me as dust."[51] How will I be able to stand, unless you direct your care always so as to strengthen this clay, so that my strength may proceed from your countenance? "When you turn away your face, all things will be troubled."[52] If you exercise your care, woe is me! You have nothing to behold in me but the contagion of sins. It is no use either to be abandoned or to be examined, for even while we are being looked on, we are committing offenses. Still, we can hold that God does not reject those whom he looks on, because he makes clean those whom he beholds. A fire blazes before him that burns away sin.[53] The Prayer of Job and David 4.6.22.[54]

Recognition and Remembrance in Eternity. Apocryphal Revelation: And again I said, Lord, will it be possible in heaven for people to recognize one another, a brother his brother, a friend his friend, a father his own children, or the children their own parents? And I heard a voice saying to me, Hear, John. To the righteous there will be recognition, but to the sinners there will not be. Sinners will not be able to recognize each other in hell. And again I, John, said, Lord, will there be recollection of the things that exit in this world, either fields or vineyards, or other things here? And I heard a voice saying to me, Hear, righteous John. The prophet David speaks, saying, I remembered that we are dust: as for [a] man, his days are as grass; as a flower of the field, so he shall flourish, "for a wind has passed over it, and it shall be no more, and it shall no longer remember its

---

[44]Ezek 33:11. [45]Job 14:7. [46]Pachomius is addressing an unnamed monk who wanted to join his monastic community and who wanted to become a martyr. [47]CS 46:32-33*. [48]The audience to whom the sermon was being preached. [49]1 Tim 1:13. [50]FC 66:158-59. [51]See also Job 10:9. [52]See Ps 104:29 (103:29 LXX, Vg.). [53]See Joel 2:3. [54]FC 65:406*.

place." And again the same said, "His spirit shall go forth, and he returns to his earth; in that day all his thoughts shall perish."[55] APOCRYPHAL REVELATION OF JOHN THE THEOLOGIAN.[56]

103:15-18 God's Love Is Eternal

HUMAN LIFE IS BRIEF. GREGORY OF NAZIANZUS: Our life on earth, brothers, is such that our existence is very transitory. We play, as it were, a game on earth: we do not exist, and we are born, and being born we are dissolved. We are like a fleeting dream,[57] an apparition without substance, the flight of a bird that passes, a ship that leaves no trace on the sea.[58] We are dust, a vapor, the morning dew, a flower growing but a moment and withering in a moment.[59] "[A] man's days are as grass: as the flower of the field, so shall he flourish." Beautifully has blessed David meditated on our weakness. Again he says, "Declare to me how few are my days."[60] He defines the days of humankind as the measure of a handbreadth.[61] What would you say to Jeremiah, who, complaining of his birth, even blames his mother, and that, for the failings of others?[62] "I have seen everything,"[63] says Ecclesiastes. I have reviewed in my mind all human things, wealth, luxury, power, glory that is not stable, wisdom that eludes us more often that it is mastered. ON HIS BROTHER ST. CAESARIUS, ORATION 7.19.[64]

THE BREVITY AND VANITY OF LIFE. AMBROSE: Concerning the resurrection more will be said later; but now let us return to our immediate subject. We have shown that even holy people have, without any consideration for their merits, suffered many difficult things in this world, together with toil and misery. So David, in self-reflection, says, "Remember, Lord, that we are dust; as for [a] man, his days are but as grass"; and in another place, "[A] man is like a breath, his days pass away as a shadow."[65] For what is more wretched than we, who are sent into this life as it were plundered and naked, with frail bodies, deceitful hearts, weak minds, anxious in regard to cares,

slothful as to labor, prone to pleasures. ON HIS BROTHER SATYRUS 2.29.[66]

REMEMBER GOD'S COMMANDMENTS. AUGUSTINE: Applicable to this difference[67] is what has been written: "And to those who retain his commandments in memory, that they may do them." For many retain them in memory that they may despise them or even deride and attack them. The words of Christ do not abide in those who in a way barely touch him [and] do not take firm hold of him. And therefore [these words] will not be a benefit for those people but a witness [against them]. And because [the words] are in them in such a way that they do not abide in them, for this reason [those people] are bound by them so that they may be judged in accordance with them. TRACTATES ON THE GOSPEL OF JOHN 81.4.3.[68]

103:20-21 Bless the Lord

ANGELS DO GOD'S WILL. CYRIL OF JERUSALEM: "Your will be done on earth as in heaven." God's divine and blessed angels do the will of God, as David said in the psalm, "Bless the Lord, all his angels, mighty in strength, that do his pleasure." So then in effect this is what you[69] mean when you pray, "as in the angels your will is done, so likewise be it done on earth by human beings, O Lord." MYSTAGOGICAL LECTURES 23.14.[70]

BLESS THE LORD. GREGORY OF NYSSA: Under "thrones" [Paul] includes the cherubim, giving them this Greek name, as more intelligible than the Hebrew name for them. He knew that "God sits upon the cherubim," and so he calls these

---

[55]Ps 146:4 (145:4 LXX). [56]ANF 8:583**. This document is a mid-second century product of Sethian Gnosticism that was pseudonymously attributed to the apostle John. [57]See Job 20:8. [58]See Wis 5:10-11. [59]See Hos 13:3. [60]Ps 102:23 (101:24 LXX). [61]See Ps 39:5 (38:6 LXX). [62]See Jer 15:10. [63]Eccles 1:14. [64]FC 22:19-20**. [65]Ps 144:4 (143:4 LXX, Vg.). [66]NPNF 2 10:178*. [67]Augustine refers to the difference of the words of Jesus that are held in memory and those that are put into action in one's life. [68]FC 90:123*. [69]The catechumens. [70]NPNF 2 7:155**.

powers the thrones of him who sits on them. In the same way there are included in the list of Isaiah's seraphim,[71] by whom the mystery of the Trinity was clearly proclaimed, when they uttered that marvelous cry "holy," being awestruck with the beauty in each person of the Trinity. They are named under the title of "powers" both by the great Paul and by the prophet David—the latter says, "Bless you the Lord all you his powers, you ministers of his that do his pleasure," and Isaiah instead of saying "Bless you" has written the very

words of their blessing, "Holy, holy, holy, Lord God of hosts: the whole earth is full of his glory," and he has revealed by what one of the seraphim did [to him] that these powers are ministers that do God's pleasure, effecting the "purging of sin" according to the will of him who sent them: for this is the ministry of these spiritual beings, namely, to be sent forth for the salvation of those who are being saved. AGAINST EUNOMIUS 1.23.[72]

---

[71]Is 6:6-7. [72]NPNF 2 5:64**.

104:1-17 A HYMN TO THE CREATOR

[1]Bless the LORD, O my soul!
   O LORD my God, thou art very great!
Thou art clothed with honor and majesty,
   [2]who coverest thyself with light as with
      a garment,
who hast stretched out the heavens like a tent,
   [3]who hast laid the beams of thy chambers on
      the waters,
who makest the clouds thy chariot,
   who ridest on the wings of the wind,
[4]who makest the winds thy messengers,
   fire and flame thy ministers.

[5]Thou didst set the earth on its foundations,
   so that it should never be shaken.
[6]Thou didst cover it with the deep as with a
      garment;
   the waters stood above the mountains.
[7]At thy rebuke they fled;
   at the sound of thy thunder they took
      to flight.
[8]The mountains rose, the valleys sank down

to the place which thou didst appoint
   for them.
[9]Thou didst set a bound which they should not
      pass,
   so that they might not again cover the earth.

[10]Thou makest springs gush forth in the valleys;
   they flow between the hills,
[11]they give drink to every beast of the field;
   the wild asses quench their thirst.
[12]By them the birds of the air have their
      habitation;
   they sing among the branches.
[13]From thy lofty abode thou waterest the
      mountains;
   the earth is satisfied with the fruit of thy
      work.

[14]Thou dost cause the grass to grow for the
      cattle,
   and plants for man to cultivate,[r]
that he may bring forth food from the earth,

¹⁵and wine to gladden the heart of man,
oil to make his face shine,
   and bread to strengthen man's heart.
¹⁶The trees of the LORD are watered

   abundantly,
   the cedars of Lebanon which he planted.
¹⁷In them the birds build their nests;
   the stork has her home in the fir trees.

r Or *fodder for the animals that serve man*

OVERVIEW: God put form before function when he created human beings. Function will cease, but human beauty will induce us to give glory to God, who clothes himself in praise and beauty (AUGUSTINE). At his incarnation Christ came humbly, dressed in swaddling clothes; when he returns in judgment he will be clothed in glory and escorted by angels (CYRIL OF JERUSALEM). Regardless of how the world is constituted, we know it was made by God's will and command (JOHN). The world began and will end by divine command, not by its own nature, and its constitution does not depend on human understanding of it (PETER CHRYSOLOGUS). Christ is clothed in the depths of knowledge and the light of wisdom, which are his holy garments (ORIGEN). Christ, the source of our immortality, is greater than the angels, who are his ministering spirits (CLEMENT OF ROME). Moses, David in the Psalms and Isaiah all attribute creation to God but from different perspectives and with different facts (JACOB, JOHN OF DAMASCUS). Only those who are receptive to the Holy Spirit can understand in depth the teachings of holy Scripture.

God created the world and all its creatures, provides for them and gave each a purpose or reason for existence (ORIGEN). When David spoke of bread strengthening a person's heart, he was prophesying the Lord's Supper and its spiritual blessings (CYRIL OF JERUSALEM). Intelligent people who are not deceived by scientific learning know that true nourishment for the mind comes from the word of God (CYRIL OF ALEXANDRIA).

104:1-4 Clothed in Honor and Majesty

THE BEAUTY AND FUNCTION OF THE HUMAN BODY. AUGUSTINE: There are some details in the body that are there simply for aesthetic reasons and for no practical purpose—for example, the nipples on a man's chest and the beard on his face, the latter being clearly for a masculine ornament, not for protection. This is shown by the fact that women's faces are hairless, and since women are the weaker sex, it would surely be more appropriate for them to be given such a protection. Now if it is true (and it is scarcely a matter of debate) that there is no visible part of the body that is merely adapted to its function without being also of aesthetic value, there are also parts that have only aesthetic value without any practical purpose. Hence it can, I think, readily be inferred that in the design of the human body dignity was a more important consideration than utility. For practical needs are, of course, transitory; and a time will come when we shall enjoy one another's beauty for itself alone, without any lust. And this above all is a motive for the praise of the Creator, to whom the psalm says, "You have clothed yourself in praise and beauty." CITY OF GOD 22.24.[1]

CHRIST'S TWO COMINGS COMPARED. CYRIL OF JERUSALEM: What we proclaim is not one single coming of Christ but a second as well, much fairer than the first. For the first presented a demonstration of long-suffering, but the second wears the crown of the kingdom of God. Most things about our Lord Jesus Christ are twofold. His birth is twofold, once of God before the ages and once of the Virgin in the end of the ages. Twice he comes down, once all unseen like dew on a fleece[2] and a second time still future and manifest. When first he came, he was swaddled in a manger. When next he comes he will "clothe himself

---

[1]CG 1074. [2]A conflation of Ps 72:6 (71:6 LXX) and Judg 6:37.

with light as with a garment." At his first coming "he endured the cross, despising the shame";[3] at his second, he comes surrounded with glory and escorted by hosts of angels. We do not therefore simply rest on Christ's first coming, by itself, but let us look forward also to his second; and as we say of his former coming, "Blessed is he that comes in the name of the Lord,"[4] so also we will say the same words again at his second coming, that we may meet our Master in company with angels and say, "Blessed is he that comes in the name of the Lord"[5] as we worship him. The Savior comes again, but not to be judged again, for he will pass judgment on those who passed judgment on him, and he who before kept silence as they judged him now reminds those lawless people who did their outrageous deeds to him on the cross and says, "These things you have done, and I kept silence."[6] He adapted himself when he came then and taught people by persuasion, but this time it is they who will be forced to bow to his rule, whether they want to or not. CATE-CHETICAL LECTURES 15.1.[7]

ALL THINGS WERE CREATED BY GOD. JOHN OF DAMASCUS: Others [unspecified pagan philosophers], however, have imagined the heavens to have the form of a hemisphere, because the inspired David says, "Who stretches out the heaven like a pavilion" which means a tent; and the blessed Isaiah: "He that establishes the heavens like a vault";[8] and because the sun, the moon and the stars, when they set, go round the earth from west to north and return again to the east. However, whichever way it may be, all things have been made and established by the command of God and have their foundation in the divine will and desire. "For he spoke, and they were made; he commanded, and they were created. He has established them for ever, and for ages of ages; he has made a decree, and it shall not pass away."[9] ORTHODOX FAITH 2.6.[10]

THE EARTH CONTINUES TO EXIST BY DIVINE COMMAND. PETER CHRYSOLOGUS: The sky that

you behold, O man [a listener who is a sensible person], made completely of air, carries many waters and is not itself supported by anything else, since a mere command hung it up and the sole force of a precept supports it. The divine revelation states, "Who stretches out the heaven like a pavilion, who covers the higher rooms thereof with water." The great weight and burden of the mountains rests on the earth, which is made solid by its own mass; and that earth floats on a foundation of liquid, as the prophet testifies: "Who established the earth above the waters."[11] Consequently, the fact that it stands arises from a commandment, not from nature. "He spoke, and they were made; he commanded, and they were created."[12] Therefore, the fact that the world holds together is a matter of divine operation, not of human understanding. The sea rolls along with the high crest of its own waves and is raised aloft toward the clouds. Yet, light sands hem it in. Hence we see that its great might yields not to the sand but to a precept. All the beings in the sky and earth and sea move and live after they have been made by one sole command. The prophet affirms that they will be dissolved again by a mere command when he says, "In the beginning, O Lord, you founded the earth, and the heavens are the works of your hands. They shall perish, but you remain; and all of them shall all grow old like a garment, and as a garment shall you change them, and they shall be changed."[13] How? In such a way that their great age may fail through time but not that creation will perish before the eyes of its Creator. SERMON 101.[14]

GOD'S HOLY GARMENTS. ORIGEN: And, therefore, about this one [Jesus Christ] it is rightly said, "He has perfect hands to put on the holy things."[15] For this one is truly he who "put on holy things," not those who were "bad exam-

---

[3]Heb 12:2. [4]Mt 21:9. [5]Mt 23:39. [6]Ps 50:21 (49:21 LXX). [7]LCC 4:147-48*. [8]Ps 104:2 (103:2 LXX); Is 40:22 LXX. [9]Ps 148:5-6. [10]FC 37:212-13*. [11]Ps 136:6 (135:6 LXX). [12]Ps 148:5. [13]Ps 102:25-27 (101:26-28 LXX). [14]FC 17:163-64*. [15]See Lev 21:10.

ples"[16] but these that are truly "holy." But if you want to hear about his more lofty garments, take the prophetic words, "Clothed with light as a garment, the abyss as a garment is his clothing."[17] This is the appearance of my great high priest who is declared clothed with the depths of knowledge and the light of wisdom that truly are "holy" garments. HOMILIES ON LEVITICUS 12.3.3.[18]

GOD IS GREATER THAN THE ANGELS. CLEMENT OF ROME: This is the way, dear friends, in which we found out salvation, namely Jesus Christ, the high priest of our offerings, the guardian and helper of our weakness. Through him let us look steadily into the heights of heaven; through him we see as in a mirror his faultless and transcendent face; through him the eyes of our hearts have been opened; through him our foolish and darkened mind springs up into the light; through him the Master has willed that we should taste immortal knowledge, for "he, being the radiance of his majesty, is as much superior to angels as the name he has inherited is more excellent."[19] For so it is written: "He makes his angels winds and his ministers flames of fire." But of his Son the Master spoke thus: "You are my Son; today I have begotten you. Ask of me, and I will give you the Gentiles for your inheritance and the ends of the earth for your possession."[20] And again he says to him, "Sit at my right hand, until I make your enemies a footstool for your feet."[21] Who, then, are these enemies? Those who are wicked and resist his will. 1 CLEMENT 36.[22]

ANGELS WERE CREATED BY GOD. JACOB OF SARUG:

That through visible things the world might learn who is its Lord[23]
And what Moses omitted from his account, and what was not written,
David expressed in the book of his psalm.
"He made his angels and his ministers of fire and wind."

Thus David caused to be written in his excellent book of Psalms
So that the world might learn that angels too were created works
And with the created things they come to birth from the Creator.
For what the great Moses did not write about concerning the angels
David wrote down, but single is the spirit of their revelations.
And the world learned through Moses as well as through David
That he is one who created all creatures with his gesture.
And David showed on what day the angels came into being
For their creation was made plain to the world, when and how
In that gesture with which heaven and earth were created.
In it all the hosts of heavenly beings arose.
Through the word of the Lord heaven was made, David showed.
And together with it [his word] were the hosts made through the Spirit from his mouth.
Moses demonstrated that the Lord created the heaven and the earth
And David demonstrated how the hosts came into being. Isaiah, too, through that revelation of his prophecy, brought to the world an account of that power of the seraphim.
ON THE ESTABLISHMENT OF CREATION.[24]

MINISTERING SPIRITS. JOHN OF DAMASCUS: [God] is the maker and creator of the angels. He brought into being and made them after his own image into a bodiless nature, some sort of spirit, as it were, and immaterial fire—as the divine David says: "Who makes his angels spirits and his ministers a burning fire." And he determined their lightness, fieriness, heat, extreme acuity,

---

[16]See 1 Cor 10:11. [17]Ps 104:2, 6 (103:2, 6 LXX). [18]FC 83:222*. [19]Heb 1:3-4. [20]Heb 1:5; Ps 2:7-8. [21]Heb 1:13. [22]AF 69. [23]See Rom 1:20. [24]MFC 9:194.

their keenness in their desire for God and his service and their being raised up and removed from every material consideration. ORTHODOX FAITH 2.3.[25]

104:6 *The Earth Clothed with Water*

THE DEEP THINGS OF GOD. ORIGEN: Now, according to a Hebrew figure of speech, it is said of God in the eighteenth psalm that "he made darkness his secret place,"[26] to signify that those notions that should be worthily entertained of God are invisible and unknowable, because God conceals himself in darkness, as it were, from those who cannot endure the splendors of his knowledge or are incapable of looking at them, partly owing to the pollution of their understanding, which is clothed with the body of mortal lowliness, and partly owing to its feebler power of comprehending God. And in order that it may appear that the knowledge of God has rarely been vouchsafed to people and has been found in very few individuals, Moses is related to have entered into the darkness where God was.[27] And again, with regard to Moses it is said, "Moses alone shall come near the Lord, but the rest shall not come near."[28] And again, that the prophet may show the depth of the doctrines that relate to God and that are unattainable by those who do not possess the "Spirit that searches all things, even the deep things of God,"[29] he added, "The abyss like a garment is his covering." No, our Lord and Savior, the Logos of God, manifesting that the greatness of the knowledge of the Father, is appropriately comprehended and known preeminently by him alone, and in the second place by those whose minds are enlightened by the Logos and God, declares, "No one knows the Son but the Father; neither does any one know the Father but the Son, and he to whoever the Son will reveal him."[30] For no one can worthily know the "uncreated" and firstborn of all created nature like the Father who begat him, nor any one the Father like the living Logos, and his Wisdom and Truth. By sharing in him who takes away from

the Father what is called "darkness," which he "made his secret place," and "the abyss," which is called his "covering," and by unveiling the Father in this way, every one knows the Father who is capable of knowing him. AGAINST CELSUS 6.17.[31]

104:14-15 *The Produce of the Earth*

GOD PROVIDES A HOME FOR PEOPLE AND ANIMALS. ORIGEN: Let Celsus[32] then say distinctly that the great diversity among the products of the earth is not the work of Providence but that a certain fortuitous concurrence of atoms gave birth to qualities so diverse, and that it was owing to chance that so many kinds of plants and trees and herbs resemble one another, and that no disposing reason gave existence to them, and that they do not derive their origin from an understanding that is beyond all admiration. We Christians, however, who are devoted to the worship of the only God, who created these things, feel grateful for them to him who made them, because not only for us but also (on our account) for the animals that are subject to us, he has prepared such a home, seeing "he causes the grass to grow for the cattle, and herb for the service of humans, that they may bring forth food out of the earth and wine that makes glad the heart of people, and oil to make their faces to shine, and bread that strengthens humans' hearts." But that he should have provided food even for the most savage animals is not a matter of surprise, for these very animals are said by some who have philosophized [on the subject] to have been created for the purpose of affording exercise to the rational creature. And one of our own wise men says somewhere, "Do not say, What is this? or Wherefore is that? for all things have been made for their uses. And do not say, What is this? or Wherefore is that? for

---

[25]FC 37:205. [26]Ps 18:11 (17:12 LXX). [27]See Ex 20:21. [28]Ex 24:2. [29]1 Cor 2:10. [30]Mt 11:27. [31]ANF 4:581*. [32]A second-century Platonist who wrote one of the most competent literary attacks on Christianity in antiquity, his *True Word*.

everything shall be sought out in its season."[33] AGAINST CELSUS 4.75.[34]

CHRIST'S BODY AND BLOOD FORESHADOWED.
CYRIL OF JERUSALEM: Having learned these things and been fully assured that what seems to be bread is not bread, though sensible to taste, but the body of Christ; and that what seems to be wine is not wine, though the taste will affirm that it is so, but the blood of Christ; and that of this David sang long ago, saying, "And bread strengthens a person's heart, to make his face to shine with oil," "strengthen you your heart," by partaking of it as spiritual, and "make the face of your soul to shine." And so having it unveiled with a pure conscience, may you "reflect as a mirror the glory of the Lord"[35] and proceed from

glory to glory, in Christ Jesus our Lord, to whom be honor and might and glory for ever and ever. Amen. MYSTAGOGICAL LECTURES 22.9.[36]

FOOD FOR MIND AND SOUL. CYRIL OF ALEXANDRIA: People of true and good sense, who have intellectually gathered that knowledge that gives life, are never jaded by the sacred sciences. Indeed it is written that "humankind shall not live by bread alone but by every word that comes from the mouth of God."[37] The word of God is food for the mind and a spiritual "bread that strengthens the heart of humankind," as the book of Psalms sings. ON THE UNITY OF CHRIST.[38]

---

[33]See Sir 39:21, 16-17. [34]ANF 4:531. [35]2 Cor 3:18. [36]NPNF 2 7:152*. [37]Mt 4:4; Deut 8:3. [38]OUC 49.

104:18-35 GOD'S CARE FOR HIS CREATION

[18]The high mountains are for the wild goats;
 the rocks are a refuge for the badgers.
[19]Thou hast made the moon to mark the seasons;
 the sun knows its time for setting.
[20]Thou makest darkness, and it is night,
 when all the beasts of the forest creep forth.
[21]The young lions roar for their prey,
 seeking their food from God.
[22]When the sun rises, they get them away
 and lie down in their dens.
[23]Man goes forth to his work
 and to his labor until the evening.

[24]O LORD, how manifold are thy works!
 In wisdom hast thou made them all;
 the earth is full of thy creatures.

[25]Yonder is the sea, great and wide,
 which teems with things innumerable,
 living things both small and great.
[26]There go the ships,
 and Leviathan which thou didst form
 to sport in it.

[27]These all look to thee,
 to give them their food in due season.
[28]When thou givest to them, they gather it up;
 when thou openest thy hand, they are filled
 with good things.
[29]When thou hidest thy face, they are
 dismayed;
 when thou takest away their breath, they
 die

and return to their dust.
³⁰When thou sendest forth thy Spirit,[s] they are
    created;
and thou renewest the face of the ground.

³¹May the glory of the LORD endure for ever,
    may the LORD rejoice in his works,
³²who looks on the earth and it trembles,
    who touches the mountains and they smoke!

³³I will sing to the LORD as long as I live;
    I will sing praise to my God while I have
    being.
³⁴May my meditation be pleasing to him,
    for I rejoice in the LORD.
³⁵Let sinners be consumed from the earth,
    and let the wicked be no more!
Bless the LORD, O my soul!
Praise the LORD!

s Or breath

OVERVIEW: The hedgehogs spoken of by the psalmist are symbolic of people who live simple and nonaggressive lives intent on spiritual meditation (CASSIAN). The heavenly bodies witness to their creator by their brilliant beauty and persevere to do his will (AMBROSE). The sun, which knows its setting, refers to Christ, who willingly endured his passion (CAESARIUS). Prayer is like the sunrise, which dispels darkness, drives off Satan, enlightens our minds and dissipates our sinful passions (CHRYSOSTOM). The universe was made by the Son of God, who is co-eternal with his Father (ATHANASIUS). The universe gives evidence of the majesty and wisdom of its creator and lifts our eyes from the visible world around us to the invisible God above (AMBROSE). People have many reasons to thank God—their creation in God's image, including their call to repentance and the incarnation of God's Son. The psalmist testifies that the triune nature of God is clearly attested already in the opening verses of Genesis. Christ is the Wisdom of God and God's instrument of creation (AUGUSTINE). The dangers of the sea are symbolic of the dangers that Christians face in the world (ATHANASIUS). The vastness and beauty of the sea and its inhabitants and the fact that the sea abides by its divinely imposed limitations attests to the wisdom of its creator (CYRIL OF JERUSALEM). The sea represents the world filled with countless sinful people; the ship represents the church, which sails toward its destiny; the port, paradise; and the dragon, Satan (CAESARIUS). When God created the devil, he foreknew that he would become an instrument of good as well as evil.

Just as God provides for the needs of the body, he also feeds the soul through sermons if we pay attention (AUGUSTINE). Since only God is good, everything that is good comes from him even if it is deferred for a time (AMBROSE, AUGUSTINE). The resurrection and revivification of believers by the Spirit was prophesied by David (GREGORY OF NYSSA). David gives witness to the mortality of the body and the immortality of the soul of the faithful (JOHN, GREGORY OF NYSSA). In creation the Holy Spirit gave beauty to unformed matter, and neither can anything continue to exist nor can there be a resurrection without him (AMBROSE, GREGORY OF NAZIANZUS). When this universe is destroyed, a new one will be created where people will live physically without sorrow and death and will have a life that resembles the life of angels (METHODIUS, BASIL). We cannot praise the Holy Spirit enough when we remember that he is the one who raises us from the dead and will enable us to adjust to the new spiritual life in heaven (BASIL). The Holy Spirit was and is instrumental in the three creations—the creation of the world, baptismal regeneration and the re-creation or resurrection to life everlasting (NICETAS). The Holy Spirit shared in the work of creation, fills the world and dwells in us—all this is proof of his divinity (FULGENTIUS).

The animal sacrifices in the Old Testament have been replaced by sacrifices of prayer, meditation and righteous living (ATHANASIUS). Prayer is conversation with God, which God desires but which is not absolutely necessary for God to bestow on us his providential care (CHRYSOSTOM). God's judgment falls on sinners who deny him by their deeds as well as those who deny him by their words (AUGUSTINE).

104:18-26 Seasons and Times

A Pious Christian Is Like the Hedgehog. JOHN CASSIAN: Ascending thus to the manifold knowledge of God, thanks to his illumination, from then on he begins to be filled with more sublime and more sacred mysteries, according to the words of the prophet: "The mountains are for stags, the rocks are a refuge for hedgehogs." This very aptly fits the sense that we have spoken of, because whoever abides in simplicity and innocence is harmful and troublesome to no one. Content with his simplicity alone, he desires merely to defend himself from being the prey of those who lie in ambush for him. Having become as it were a spiritual hedgehog, he is protected by the constant shelter of that gospel rock that is the recollection of the Lord's passion, and, fortified by continual meditation on the aforesaid verse, he resists the snares of the attacking enemy. Concerning these spiritual hedgehogs it is also said in Proverbs, "A feeble race are the hedgehogs, who have made their homes in the rocks."[1] CONFERENCES 10.11.2-3.[2]

The Heavenly Bodies Have Set Purposes. AMBROSE: Consider that the sun, the moon and the stars, the lights of the sky which, though they shine with brilliant splendor, are yet creatures, and, whether they rise or fall in their daily performance of duty, they serve the will of the eternal Creator, bringing forth the beauty with which they are clothed and shining by day and by night. How often is the sun covered by clouds or taken from the gaze of the earth when the ray of its light is dispelled in the sky or an eclipse occurs, and as Scripture says: "The moon knows its going down." It knows when it should shine in full light or weakened light. The stars, which are engaged in service to this world's advantage, disappear when they are covered by clouds, not willingly, surely, but in hope, because they hope for gratitude for their labor from him who made them subject [to him]. Thus, they persevere for his sake, that is, for his will. LETTER 51.[3]

Christ Is the True Sun of Justice. CAESARIUS OF ARLES: As you know, that psalm [104 (103 LXX)] contains the words "The sun knows the hour of its setting. You bring darkness, and it is night." What person, though unlettered, does not understand and know that when the sun reaches its setting, immediately night and darkness appear? Why, then, was it necessary for the prophet to say what is evidently understood by everyone? Likewise what follows: "Then all the beasts of the forest roam about. Young lions roar for the prey and seek their food from God." Can there be found anyone who does not know this? Truly, it is known to everyone that when night comes all the beasts roam about everywhere. Since, as you see, we ought not receive this according to the letter, listen attentively, as is your custom, to their spiritual significance.

Now what the psalmist said, "The sun knows the hour of its setting," is not to be taken concerning the sun but with regard to him of whom the prophet says, "For those who fear your name there will arise the sun of justice with its healing rays."[4] Of him we read in Solomon that the wicked will say, "The sun did not rise for us."[5] Therefore, Christ is the true sun of justice. He knew his setting when he yielded to his passion for our salvation; for when he was crucified, night and darkness took hold of the souls of his disciples. Truly, brothers, how was there not darkness in those who did not believe Christ was risen from the dead? Finally,

---

[1]Prov 30:26 LXX. [2]ACW 57:383-84. [3]FC 26:274-75*. [4]See Mal 4:2. [5]Wis 5:6.

when the women reported that they had seen the Lord, "this talk seemed to the apostles to be nonsense, and they did not believe the women."[6] Moreover, on another occasion the two disciples spoke thus to the Lord who was talking to them: "But we were hoping that it was he who should redeem Israel."[7] When the apostles spoke these words, then was fulfilled those others: "The sun knows the hour of its setting. You bring darkness, and it is night." Sermon 136.2-3.[8]

Prayer Is Like the Sun's Rays. Chrysostom: Then, even if anger boils up, it is easily cooled. If passion flares forth, the flames are readily quenched. If envy consumes us, it is not difficult to drive it away. The same thing happens that the prophet says happens when the sun rises. What did he say? "You made the darkness, and it was night. In it all the wild beasts of the forest will go forth, even young lions roaring for prey and to seek meat for themselves from God. The sun arose, and they were gathered together and shall lie down in their dens." At sunrise, then, every wild beast is driven off and slinks away to its lair. So, too, when a prayer, like a ray of the sun, arises from our tongue and comes forth from our mouth, our mind is enlightened, all the savage passions that destroy our reason slink away and flee to their own lairs, if only our prayer is diligent, if only it comes from a watchful soul and sober mind.[9] Should the devil be on hand when we pray, he is driven off; should a demon be there, he slinks away. Against the Anomoeans 7.59.[10]

God Made the World in Wisdom. Athanasius: But their doctrine is false.[11] Truth witnesses that God is the eternal fountain of his proper wisdom; and, if the Fountain is eternal, the Wisdom also has to be eternal. For in it were all things made, as David says in the psalm, "In wisdom you have made them all"; and Solomon says, "The Lord by wisdom has formed the earth, by understanding he has established the heavens."[12] And this Wisdom is the Word, and by

him, as John says, "all things were made," and "without him not one thing was made."[13] Discourses Against the Arians 1.6.19.[14]

The Work of God's Hand. Athanasius: Doubtless the things that came to be through the Word, these are "founded in wisdom" and what are "founded in wisdom," these are all made by the Hand and came to be through the Son. And we have proof of this, not from external sources, but from the Scriptures; for God says by Isaiah the prophet, "My hand also has laid the foundation of the earth, and my right hand has spanned the heavens."[15] And again, "And I will cover you in the shadow of my hand, by which I planted the heaven, and laid the foundations of the earth."[16] And David, who was taught this and knew that the Lord's hand was nothing else than wisdom, says in the psalm, "In wisdom you have made them all; the earth is full of your creation." Defense of the Nicene Definition 4.17.[17]

Creation Declares the Glory of God. Ambrose: This world is an example of the workings of God, because, while we observe the work, the Worker is brought before us. The arts may be considered in various aspects. There are those that are practical. These relate to the movement of the body or to the sound of the voice. When the movement or the sound has passed away, there is nothing that survives or remains for the spectators or the hearers. Other arts are theoretical. These display the vigor of the mind. There are other arts of such a nature that, even when the processes of operation cease, the handiwork remains visible. As an example of this we have buildings or woven material that, even when the craftsman is silent, still exhibit his skill, so that testimony is presented of the craftsman's own work. In a similar way, this work[18] is a distinctive

---

[6]Lk 24:11. [7]Lk 24:21. [8]FC 47:264-65*. [9]See 1 Pet 5:8. [10]FC 72:209. [11]The Arian teaching of the subordination of the Son of God. [12]Prov 3:19. [13]Jn 1:3. [14]NPNF 2 4:317*. [15]Is 48:13. [16]Is 51:16. [17]NPNF 2 4:161*. [18]The world that God created.

mark of divine majesty from which the wisdom of God is made manifest. On beholding this, raising the eyes of his mind at the same time to the things invisible, the psalmist says, "How great are your works, O Lord; you have made all things in wisdom." SIX DAYS OF CREATION 1.5.17.[19]

REASONS FOR THANKING GOD. AUGUSTINE: In case any of us should struggle with this,[20] there are just two commands: God and neighbor; the one who made you, and the one he made you to be with. No one has told you "Love the sun, love the moon, love the earth and everything that has been made." These are the things in which God is to be praised, the Maker to be blessed. "How magnificent are your works!" we say; "in wisdom you have made them all." They are yours, you have made them all. Thanks be to you! But you have made us over all of them. Thanks be to you! For we are your image and likeness. Thanks be to you! We have sinned, we have been sought. Thanks be to you! We have been negligent, we have not been neglected. Thanks be to you! When we despised you, we were not despised; in case we should have forgotten your divinity and should lose you, you even took upon yourself our humanity. Thanks be to you! When and where can there not be thanks? SERMON 16A.6.[21]

GOD CREATED THE WORLD THROUGH HIS SON. AUGUSTINE: This Word, through which heaven and earth were made, this Word was not itself made. I mean, if it was made, through what was it made? "All things were made through it."[22] So if whatever has been made was made through the Word, the Word itself, clearly, through which all things were made, was not made. One more point: the narrator of the works of creation, God's servant Moses, says, "In the beginning, God made heaven and earth." He made heaven and earth in the beginning. By what means did he make it? Through the Word. Did he also make the Word? No; well what, then? "In the beginning was the Word";[23] that through which he made

things already was; that is how he made what as yet was not. We can understand it, and rightly understand it, in the sense that heaven and earth were made in the only-begotten Word itself. They were made in, you see, that through which they were made. This can be, and be understood as, the beginning in which God made heaven and earth. This Word, after all, is also the wisdom of God, about which it is said, "You have made all things in wisdom." If God made all things in wisdom, and his only-begotten Son is without a shadow of doubt that wisdom of God, let us not doubt that whatever we have learned was made through the Son, was also made in the Son. The Son himself, after all, is certainly the beginning. When the Jews were questioning him and saying, "Who are you? he answered, The beginning."[24] There you have, "In the beginning, God made heaven and earth."[25] SERMON 223A.1.[26]

REFERENCES TO THE TRINITY IN GENESIS 1. AUGUSTINE: I would not attempt to refute this position, especially because I am delighted with the idea that the Trinity is emphasized even in the very first chapter of the sacred book of Genesis. For first we have the statement: "In the beginning, God created heaven and earth,"[27] by which it can be understood that the Father created "in the Son," an interpretation that is supported by one of the psalms, where we read, "How glorified are your works, Lord; you have made all things in wisdom." Then shortly afterwards we find a most appropriate mention of the Holy Spirit. CITY OF GOD 11.32.[28]

GOD MAKES ALL THINGS IN WISDOM. AUGUSTINE: "All things" then, my brothers, "all things"—each and every one—"were made through him, and without him was nothing made."[29] But how were all things made through

---

[19]FC 42:16-17*. [20]Augustine had just been speaking of the twofold summary of the law (Mt 22:37, 39-40). [21]WSA 3 1:351*. [22]Jn 1:3. [23]Jn 1:1 [24]Jn 8:25. [25]Gen 1:1. [26]WSA 3 6:212-13. [27]Gen 1:1. [28]CG 467. [29]Jn 1:3.

him? "That which was made, in him is life."[30] Now this can be taken as follows: "That which was made in him, is life." And if we express the sentence in this way, everything is life. For what was not made in him? For he himself is the wisdom of God, and in the psalm it is said, "You have made all things in wisdom." If, then, Christ is the wisdom of God and the psalm says, "You have made all things in wisdom," as all things were made through him, so they were made in him. TRACTATES ON THE GOSPEL OF JOHN 1.16.1.[31]

THE WORLD IS FULL OF DANGERS. ATHANASIUS: Let us, therefore, in the faith of the disciples, converse frequently with our Master. For the world is like the sea to us, my brothers, of which it is written, "This is the great and wide sea, there go the ships; the Leviathan, which you have created to play therein." We float on this sea, as with the wind, through our own free will, for everyone directs his course according to his will, and either, under the pilotage of the Word, he enters into rest, or, laid hold on by pleasure, he suffers shipwreck and is in peril by storm. For as in the ocean there are storms and waves, so in the world there are many afflictions and trials. FESTAL LETTERS 19.7.[32]

GOD SETS LIMITS FOR THE OCEANS. CYRIL OF JERUSALEM: "This great and wide sea, in it there are creeping things without number." Who can describe the beauty of the fishes therein? Who can describe the greatness of the whales and the nature of the amphibious animals, how they live on the dry land and in the waters? Who can describe the depth and breadth of the sea or the shock of its tumultuous waves? The sea stays within its confines because of him who said, "This far shall you come but no farther, and here shall your proud waves be stilled!"[33] It clearly reveals the decree imposed on it, when running out it leaves on the sands a distinct line marked by its waves, as though to signify to those who see it that it has not transgressed its appointed bounds. CATECHETICAL LECTURES 9.11.[34]

THE CHURCH IS LIKE A SHIP. CAESARIUS OF ARLES: After this the prophet added the words "The sea also, great and wide, in which are schools without number of living things." The sea is understood as the world, which is full of storms and dangerous waves, even full of bitterness and saltiness. It also has quite large fish that do not cease to devour the smaller ones. There are numberless creeping things, so-called because they creep over the earth. For this reason carnal people and those who are too fond of the world, because they think only of the present life and continuously apply themselves to its pursuits out of love for it, are not unfittingly called creeping things. Furthermore, the words "The sea also, great and wide, where ships move about" are not to be understood relative to the ships of wood that are carried over the sea by the force of the wind but to the catholic church. While the latter desires to reach the port of paradise by holy, just works, it is beaten by many waves of tribulation and the winds of various storms. Moreover, although it is tossed by the violent beating of the winds, it is so well directed by the oars of holy discipline, so well driven by the breath of the Holy Spirit, that it is carried to eternal life by the very adversities that oppose it. In this sea there is also that dragon of which it is written: "This sea dragon that you formed to make sport of it." That dragon is understood as the devil. He is apt to play in the wicked in such a way that not only does he persuade them to sin but, using them as his ministers, he does not cease to persecute even those who are holy and just. This dragon was made a good angel by God, but since he exalted himself against God by pride and fell from that happy angelic state, deceiving himself by pride, through God's hidden but just judgment he is permitted to deceive with his cunning careless people. SERMON 136.6.[35]

GOD MAKES USE OF THE DEVIL'S WICKED-

---

[30]See Jn 1:4. [31]FC 78:55. [32]NPNF 2 4:547*. [33]Job 38:11. [34]FC 61:191. [35]FC 47:267.

ness. Augustine: Now God, when he created the devil, was without doubt, well aware of his future wickedness and had foreseen the good that he himself would bring out of that evil. That is why the psalm says, "This is the dragon that you fashioned for him to mock at." In the very creation of the devil, though by God's goodness he was made in a state of good, God had already, in virtue of his foreknowledge, laid plans for making good use of him even in his evil state; and this is the message of the passage in the psalm. City of God 11.17.[36]

The Devil Was Condemned After He Had Sinned. Augustine: Then there is the passage in the book of Job, when the devil is under discussion, "This is the beginning of the Lord's handiwork, and he made him to be mocked by angels"[37] (which seems to be echoed by the psalm, "This is the dragon, whom you fashioned for him to mock at"). This is not to be taken as implying that we should imagine that he was created at the start as a fit object for angelic mockery but that he was consigned to this punishment after his sin. To start with, then, the devil is the Lord's handiwork. For there is nothing in nature, even among the last and least of the little creatures, that is not brought into being by him, from whom comes all form, all shape, all order; and without those definitions nothing can be found in nature or imagined in the mind. How much more must the angelic creation derive from him; for the angels take precedence, in natural worth, over all the works of God. City of God 11.15.[38]

104:27-30 When God Opens His Hand

God Is the Great Provider. Augustine: Let us all therefore fix our gaze on him, that he may feed our hungry souls; he himself was hungry for our sake, seeing that "he became poor though he was rich, in order that by his poverty we might be enriched."[39] How appropriate that we sang to him just now, "All things look to you to give them their food at the proper time."[40] If all

things, then all people; if all people, then us too. So if I am going to give you anything good in this sermon, it is not I who shall be giving it but he from whom we all receive because we all look to him. It is time for him to give, but we must do what he said if he is to give, namely, we must look to him. Let us gaze on him with our minds, because just as the eyes and ears of your bodies are turned to me, so the eyes and ears of your minds should be turned to him. Sermon 2.6.[41]

God Provides Us with Goodness. Ambrose: One who has sought God and has found him exists among those good things.[42] For where a person's heart is, there also is his treasure;[43] the Lord is not accustomed to deny his good gift to those who pray. And so, because the Lord is good and especially good to those who await him, let us cling to him and be with him with our whole soul, our whole heart and our whole strength[44] that we may be in his light and see his glory and enjoy the gift of heavenly joy. Accordingly, let us lift up our spirits to that good and be in it and live in it; let us cling to it, for it is above every thought and every reflection and enjoys an everlasting peace and tranquility, and that peace, moreover, is beyond every thought and every understanding.[45] This is the good that enters into all things; in it we all live and on it we all depend;[46] moreover, it possesses nothing beyond itself but is of God, for "no one is good but only God."[47] Therefore, what is good is of God, and what is of God is good. And for that reason it is said, "When you open your hand, all things shall be filled with goodness." For, through God's goodness, all good things are deservedly granted to us, and in them there is no admixture of evil.[48] Scripture promised these good things to the faithful when it said, "You shall eat the good things of the land."[49] That we may obtain the

---

[36]CG 449. [37]Job 40:19 LXX. [38]CG 447. [39]2 Cor 8:9. [40]Ps 104:27 (103:27 LXX, Vg.). [41]WSA 3 1:179. [42]The good that always endures, that cannot be destroyed by change of time or of age. See Ps 27:13 (26:23 LXX). [43]Mt 6:21. [44]See Deut 6:5; Mt 22:37. [45]See Phil 4:7. [46]See Acts 17:28. [47]Mk 10:18. [48]See Jas 1:17. [49]Is 1:19.

good things, let us be like that good, the good that is without iniquity and without deceit and without severity but is with grace and holiness and purity and benevolence and love and justice. Thus goodness, like a prolific mother, embraces all the virtues. FLIGHT FROM THE WORLD 6.36.[50]

GOD IS A PRUDENT PROVIDER. AUGUSTINE: Don't we see such things every day in human affairs—a kind of hard and inexorable mercy? How many things sick people ask the doctors for, counter to their health, and how many things the doctors, in mercy, refuse them! They refuse them and so spare them; if they grant them, they are being cruel. The doctor knows this; and doesn't God? The one who was created like you knows how to deal with you in this way; and doesn't the one who created you both know how to deal with you both? Accordingly, dearly beloved, in all your troubles, all your fears, all your joys, beg God to grant you, of temporal goods, what he knows is best for you. As for eternal things, though, such as "hallowed be your name, your kingdom come, your will be done as in heaven also on earth," and others of that sort, ask for them without a qualm or qualification; they cannot possibly be to your disadvantage.

Choose, cherish, gather; he opens his hand, after all, and fills every soul with blessing. "And when you give," it says, "they gather." None of us should have any doubts about heavenly good things; even if they are deferred, they will be given. The reward is not being refused, but desire is being whetted. We must go on desiring day after day, because it is a great thing we are going to receive. We must go on thirsting day after day, because it is the fountain of life we shall be drinking from. All the same, dearly beloved, there is something it is not an impudence for us to ask for, because the apostle taught us; let us ask that "we may spend a quiet and tranquil life, and with all piety and charity."[51] SERMON 306C.8.[52]

THE MYSTERY OF THE RESURRECTION. GREGORY OF NYSSA: But she[53] said, "I think that we

should first run briefly through what is set forth in various places by the divine Scripture concerning this doctrine [the resurrection], so that from there we may approach the conclusion of our discourse. I have heard, indeed, what David sings in his divine odes, when he has made the ordering of the universe the subject of his hymn. Near the end of Psalm 103 [LXX] he says, "You will take away their spirit, and they will die and turn to their dust. You will send out your Spirit, and they will be created, and you will renew the face of the earth." He is saying that the power of the Spirit, accomplishing everything in everything, both gives life to those whom it enters and removes from life those from whom it departs. He says that the death of the living happens by the departure of the Spirit, and by its presence the renewal of the dead takes place. Because the death of those who are being renewed comes first in the order of the words, we can say that the mystery of the resurrection is being proclaimed to the church, as David has foretold this grace by his spirit of prophecy. ON THE SOUL AND THE RESURRECTION 10.[54]

GOD IS GOD OF THE LIVING. JOHN OF DAMASCUS: And again to Moses: "I am the God of Abraham and the God of Isaac and the God of Jacob."[55] God "is not the God of the dead,"[56] of those who have died and will never be again. Rather, he is the God of the living, whose souls live in his hand[57] and whose bodies will by the resurrection live again. And David, the ancestor of God, says to God, "You shall take away their breath, and they shall fail and shall return to their dust." See how it is a question of their bodies. Then he adds, "You shall send forth your spirit, and they shall be created; and you shall renew the face of the earth." ORTHODOX FAITH 4.27.[58]

THE HOLY SPIRIT'S ROLE IN CREATION AND

---

[50]FC 65:308-9. [51]1 Tim 2:2. [52]WSA 3 9:41-2*. [53]Macrina, Gregory's sister. [54]GNSR 104. [55]Ex 3:6. [56]Mt 22:32. [57]See Wis 3:1. [58]FC 37:402*.

RESURRECTION. AMBROSE: So when the Spirit was moving on the water, the creation was without grace; but after this world being created underwent the operation of the Spirit, it gained all the beauty of that grace wherewith the world is illuminated. And that the grace of the universe cannot abide without the Holy Spirit the prophet declared when he said, "You will take away your Spirit, and they will fail and be turned again into their dust. Send forth your Spirit, and they shall be made, and you will renew all the face of the earth." Not only, then, did he teach that no creature can stand without the Holy Spirit but also that the Spirit is the Creator of the whole creation. ON THE HOLY SPIRIT 2.5.33.[59]

THE AUTHOR OF SPIRITUAL RENEWAL. GREGORY OF NAZIANZUS: This Spirit shares with the Son in working both the creation and the resurrection, as you may be shown by this Scripture: "By the Word of the Lord were the heavens made, and all the power of them by the breath of his mouth";[60] and this, "The Spirit of God that made me, and the breath of the Almighty teaches me";[61] and again, "You shall send forth your Spirit, and they shall be created, and you shall renew the face of the earth." And he is the author of spiritual regeneration. ON PENTECOST, ORATION 41.14.[62]

A NEW WORLD WITHOUT SORROW. METHODIUS: But if our opponents say, How then is it, if the universe will not be destroyed, that the Lord says that "heaven and earth shall pass away";[63] and the prophet, that "the heaven shall perish as smoke, and the earth shall grow old as a garment";[64] we answer, because it is usual for the Scriptures to call the change of the world from its present condition to a better and more glorious one, destruction; as its earlier form is lost in the change of all things to a state of greater splendor; for there is no contradiction or absurdity in the holy Scriptures. For not "the world" but the "fashion of this world" passes away,[65] it is said; so it is usual for the Scriptures to call the change from an earlier form to a better and more comely

state, destruction; just as when one calls by the name of destruction the change from a childish form into a perfect adult, as the stature of the child is turned into adult size and beauty. We may expect that the creation will pass away, as if it were to perish in the burning, in order that it may be renewed, not however that it will be destroyed, that we who are renewed may dwell in a renewed world without taste of sorrow; according as it is said, "When you let your breath go forth, they shall be made, and you shall renew the face of the earth." ON THE RESURRECTION 1.9.[66]

THE THREE CREATIONS. BASIL THE GREAT: But, if we must go on with our discussion and make a deeper study, let us, from this point, contemplate especially the divine power of the Holy Spirit. We find three creations mentioned in the Scripture; the first, the bringing forth from nonexistence into existence; the second, the change from worse to better; and the third, the resurrection of the dead. In these you will find the Holy Spirit co-operating with the Father and the Son. Take, for instance, the calling into existence of the heavens. And what does David say? "By the word of the Lord the heavens were established, and all their power by the spirit of his mouth."[67] Now, humankind is created a second time through baptism, "for if anyone is in Christ, he is a new creature."[68] And what does the Savior say to the disciples? "Go, make disciples of all nations, baptizing them in the name of the Father and of the Son and of the Holy Spirit."[69] You see here, also, the Holy Spirit present with the Father and the Son. But what would you say concerning the resurrection of the dead, when we shall have departed and returned into our dust, "for we are dust and to dust we shall return"?[70] "And he will send forth the Holy Spirit, and he will create us, and he shall renew the face of the earth." For what Paul

---

[59]NPNF 2 10:118-19*. [60]Ps 33:6 (32:6 LXX). [61]Job 33:4. [62]NPNF 2 7:384*. [63]Mt 24:35. [64]Is 51:6. [65]1 Cor 7:31. [66]ANF 6:366*. [67]Ps 33:6 (32:6 LXX). [68]2 Cor 5:17. [69]Mt 28:19. [70]Gen 3:19.

spoke of as the resurrection, David called renewal. LETTER 8.[71]

THE SPIRIT CREATES AND RENEWS. NICETAS OF REMESIANA: One may concede that, in regard to the Word, it is clear that he created, but have doubts in regard to the Spirit. My reply to this is the testimony of Job, the righteous man of old, who wrote, "The spirit of God made me."[72] So, too, David in one of his psalms says to God, "You shall send forth your spirit, and they shall be created; and you shall renew the face of the earth." But if creation and renewal are to be attributed to the Spirit, certainly the beginning of creation did not occur apart from the Spirit. However, those who are opposed to the truth resort to the evasion of saying that, wherever there is mention of the Spirit as creator, the name and person of the Spirit belong to the Son. The Son is a Spirit, they say, just as the Father is a Spirit. This is a fallacy that should deceive no one. It is enough merely to remember that David clearly distinguishes the Son, whom he calls the Word of the Lord, from the holy One, whom he calls the Spirit. It is the Word who "makes the heavens"; it is the Spirit who "adorns" them, who gives them their power. Anyone who reads these words must believe—else, if he insists on being obstinate, why does he bother to read? Let no one imagine that, somehow, our faith dims the glory of the Father. Rather, it adds to the glory of the Father to refer the creation of all things to a Word of which he is the Father or to a Spirit of which he is the source. The fact remains that when his word and Spirit create, it is he who creates all things. THE POWER OF THE HOLY SPIRIT 8.[73]

THE GIVER OF NEW LIFE. BASIL THE GREAT: Resurrection from the dead is accomplished by the operation of the Spirit: "You send forth your Spirit, and they are created; and you renew the face of the earth." If "creation" means the conversion of sinners to a better way of life (the Scripture often understands it this way; for example, the words of Paul: "If any one is in Christ, he is a new cre-

ation."[74]), and the renewal of this earthly life and changing our earthly, passionate life into heavenly citizenship, then we should know that our souls attain such a high degree of exaltation through the Spirit. Understanding all this, how can we be afraid of giving the Spirit too much honor? We should instead fear that even though we ascribe to him the highest titles we can devise or our tongues pronounce, our ideas about him might still fall short. ON THE HOLY SPIRIT 19.49.[75]

THE HOLY SPIRIT ALSO PARTICIPATED IN CREATION. FULGENTIUS OF RUSPE: Hence it is that the true faith asserts that the Holy Spirit as well is the Creator, not created. How is the Spirit to be denied as Creator, by which the power of the heavens has been strengthened, as David says, "By the word of the Lord the heavens were made and all their host by the breath of his mouth."[76] And in another text: "When you send forth your spirit, they are created." Indeed it is the Creator of all things who is the maker of human beings. Concerning it, the blessed Job says, "The Spirit of God has made me."[77] The Holy Spirit, then, as it has created all things, so, as infinite, it fills all things. And the one who fills all things is by nature true God. It is written that "the Spirit of the Lord has filled the whole world."[78] The blessed David as well bears witness that the Spirit of God is everywhere, saying to God, "Where can I go from your Spirit, or where can I flee from your presence?"[79] How do the Arians[80] deny that the Holy Spirit is God since we are the temple of the Holy Spirit, just as we are the temple of the Father and the Son? For the apostle says, "Do you not know that you are the temple of God and that the Spirit of God dwells in you? If anyone destroys God's temple, God will destroy that person; for the temple of God, which you are, is holy."[81] The apostle asserts that we are

---

[71]FC 13:36-37*. [72]Job 33:4. [73]FC 7:31*. [74]2 Cor 5:17. [75]*OHS* 77-78*. [76]Ps 33:6 (32:6 LXX, Vg.). [77]Job 33:4. [78]Wis 1:7. [79]Ps 139:7 (138:7 LXX, Vg.). [80]Heretics who believed that the Son was subordinate to and not co-eternal with God the Father. [81]1 Cor 3:16-17.

the temple of God in such a way that in the same letter he also says that we are the temple of the Holy Spirit. For he says, "Do you not know that your body is a temple of the Holy Spirit within you, whom you have from God?"[82] And in order that he may show that the Holy Spirit is God, he immediately added, "Therefore glorify God in your body."[83] LETTER 8.8.17.[84]

104:34-35 Meditation That Pleases God

OFFER GOD SACRIFICES OF PRAYER. ATHANA-SIUS: Thus then, being before instructed and taught, they [the people of Israel] learned not to do service to any one but the Lord. They began to know how long the shadow[85] would last and not to forget the time that was at hand, in which no longer should the bullock of the herd be a sacrifice to God, or the ram of the flock or the he-goat,[86] but all these things should be fulfilled in a purely spiritual manner and by constant prayer and upright conversation, with godly words; as David sings, "May my meditation be pleasing to him. Let my prayer be set forth before you as incense, and the lifting up of my hands as the evening sacrifice." The Spirit also, who is in him, commands, saying, "Offer to God the sacrifice of praise, and pay to the Lord your vows. Offer the sacrifice of righteousness, and put your trust in the Lord."[87] FESTAL LETTERS 19.4.[88]

PRAYER IS CONVERSATION WITH GOD. CHRY-SOSTOM: Prayer is a great good: someone conversing with a virtuous person gains no little advantage from the experience, so how much good will the one communing with God be granted? Prayer, after all, is conversing with God. For proof of this, listen to the words of the inspired author: "Let my meditation be pleasing to God," that is, may my words seem acceptable to God. I mean, he is able to offer help before we ask for it, isn't he? Still, he wants so as to take occasion from us for daily bestowing on us providential care from himself. Accordingly, whether we have our requests granted or not, let us persist in asking,

and render thanks not only when we gain what we ask but also when we do not. Failure to gain, you see, when that is what God wants, is not worse than succeeding; we do not know what is to our advantage in this regard in the way he does understand. The result is, then, that succeeding or failing we ought to give thanks. HOMILIES ON GENESIS 30.16.[89]

GOD CAN BE DENIED BY DEED AS WELL AS BY WORD. AUGUSTINE: If God does not punish the sinner, what about the prophecy, "If the just person scarcely will be saved, where will the impious and the sinner appear?"[90] And elsewhere: "Truly the wicked shall perish";[91] and again: "Let sinners be consumed out of the earth, and the unjust, so that they be no more"; and finally: "As smoke vanishes, so let them vanish away: as wax melts before the fire, so let the wicked perish at the presence of God."[92] In these passages it is not so much the incredulous and the unfaithful whom I hear condemned, but the sinners. In a certain passage I read that our Savior said, "Not everyone who says to me, 'Lord, Lord,' shall enter the kingdom of heaven; but he who does the will of my Father who is in heaven."[93] Yet, those people believed in Christ and even called him Lord. Nevertheless, on that account alone the gate of the heavenly kingdom is not opened to them, because by their deeds they deny him whom they praise with their lips. Moreover, the apostle asserts that God is denied by deeds no less than by words: "They profess to know God, but by their works they disown him."[94] And the Lord himself says in the Gospel, "Many will say to me in that day, 'Lord, Lord, did we not prophesy in your name, and cast out devils in your name and work many miracles in your name?' And then I will declare to them, 'I never knew you. Depart from me, all you workers of iniquity.'"[95] It is related that they were

---

[82]1 Cor 6:19. [83]1 Cor 6:20. [84]FC 95:376-77. [85]The pre-Christian era. [86]See Ex 12:5. [87]Ps 50:14 (49:14 LXX); 4:5 (4:6 LXX). [88]NPNF 2 4:546*. [89]FC 82:232*. [90]1 Pet 4:18; cf. Prov 11:31. [91]See Ps 37:20 (36:20 LXX, Vg.). [92]Ps 68:2 (67:3 LXX, Vg.). [93]Mt 7:21. [94]Tit 1:16. [95]Mt 7:22-23.

so strong in their faith that they worked miracles in the name of the Lord; nevertheless, their faith will not profit them, because they have not performed works of justice. So, if faith alone suffices, why are they eternally confined with the minions of Satan in the flames of hell, since they are condemned not because of unbelief but because they did nothing good, as is written: "And the king will say to those on his left hand, 'Depart from me, accursed ones, into the everlasting fire that my Father prepared for the devil and his angels. For I was hungry, and you did not give me to eat,'" etc.?[96] He did not say "because you have not believed in me." Hence, we may conclude that they were condemned for lack of good works, not because of unbelief. ON THE CHRISTIAN LIFE 13.[97]

---

[96]Mt 25:41-42. [97]FC 16:37-39*.

105:1-45 AN EXHORTATION TO TRUST IN AND WORSHIP GOD

[1]O give thanks to the LORD, call on his name,
  make known his deeds among the peoples!
[2]Sing to him, sing praises to him,
  tell of all his wonderful works!
[3]Glory in his holy name;
  let the hearts of those who seek the LORD
    rejoice!
[4]Seek the LORD and his strength,
  seek his presence continually!
[5]Remember the wonderful works that he has
    done,
  his miracles, and the judgments he uttered,
[6]O offspring of Abraham his servant,
  sons of Jacob, his chosen ones!

[7]He is the LORD our God;
  his judgments are in all the earth.
[8]He is mindful of his covenant for ever,
  of the word that he commanded, for a
    thousand generations,
[9]the covenant which he made with Abraham,
  his sworn promise to Isaac,
[10]which he confirmed to Jacob as a statute,
  to Israel as an everlasting covenant,
[11]saying, "To you I will give the land of Canaan
  as your portion for an inheritance."

[12]When they were few in number,
  of little account, and sojourners in it,
[13]wandering from nation to nation,
  from one kingdom to another people,
[14]he allowed no one to oppress them;
  he rebuked kings on their account,
[15]saying, "Touch not my anointed ones,
  do my prophets no harm!"

[16]When he summoned a famine on the land,
  and broke every staff of bread,
[17]he had sent a man ahead of them,
  Joseph, who was sold as a slave.
[18]His feet were hurt with fetters,
  his neck was put in a collar of iron;

¹⁹until what he had said came to pass
  the word of the LORD tested him.
²⁰The king sent and released him,
  the ruler of the peoples set him free;
²¹he made him lord of his house,
  and ruler of all his possessions,
²²to instruct^t his princes at his pleasure,
  and to teach his elders wisdom.

²³Then Israel came to Egypt;
  Jacob sojourned in the land of Ham.
²⁴And the LORD made his people very fruitful,
  and made them stronger than their foes.
²⁵He turned their hearts to hate his people,
  to deal craftily with his servants.

²⁶He sent Moses his servant,
  and Aaron whom he had chosen.
²⁷They wrought his signs among them,
  and miracles in the land of Ham.
²⁸He sent darkness, and made the land dark;
  they rebelled^u against his words.
²⁹He turned their waters into blood,
  and caused their fish to die.
³⁰Their land swarmed with frogs,
  even in the chambers of their kings.
³¹He spoke, and there came swarms of flies,
  and gnats throughout their country.
³²He gave them hail for rain,
  and lightning that flashed through their
    land.
³³He smote their vines and fig trees,

and shattered the trees of their country.
³⁴He spoke, and the locusts came,
  and young locusts without number;
³⁵which devoured all the vegetation in their
    land,
  and ate up the fruit of their ground.
³⁶He smote all the first-born in their land,
  the first issue of all their strength.

³⁷Then he led forth Israel with silver and gold,
  and there was none among his tribes who
    stumbled.
³⁸Egypt was glad when they departed,
  for dread of them had fallen upon it.
³⁹He spread a cloud for a covering,
  and fire to give light by night.
⁴⁰They asked, and he brought quails,
  and gave them bread from heaven in
    abundance.
⁴¹He opened the rock, and water gushed forth;
  it flowed through the desert like a river.
⁴²For he remembered his holy promise,
  and Abraham his servant.

⁴³So he led forth his people with joy,
  his chosen ones with singing.
⁴⁴And he gave them the lands of the nations;
  and they took possession of the fruit of the
    peoples' toil,
⁴⁵to the end that they should keep his statutes,
  and observe his laws.
Praise the LORD!

t Gk Syr Jerome: Heb *to bind*   u Cn Compare Gk Syr: Heb *they did not rebel*

OVERVIEW: David called his patriarchal ancestors prophets and types of Christ because they had received the Holy Spirit prior to the time of Moses and the giving of the law (EUSEBIUS). Only transgressors of the law are punished with death; Christ came to fulfill the law and avenge those who have been oppressed by the violence of death (ARCHELAUS). There is only one Christ who is the Son of God, although the name Christs is used of prophets and apostles because of their anointing and divinely appointed work (CYRIL OF ALEXANDRIA).

One becomes a slave to sin and Satan by foolishness and yielding to temptation; one is freed from such slavery by divine grace (AMBROSE). The cloud on Mount Sinai symbolizes the divine protection that God provided not only to Moses but to all who fear him (BEDE).

105:4-5 Seek the Lord

PATRIARCHS AND THE OUTPOURING OF THE HOLY SPIRIT. EUSEBIUS OF CAESAREA: In Psalm 104 [LXX],[1] David, when referring to the stories of Abraham, Isaac and Jacob, the very men who were his godly ancestors, who lived before Moses' day, calls them Christs, only because they all received the outpouring of the Holy Spirit. And when he tells how they were hospitably received by foreigners, and how they learned that God was their Savior when plots were devised against them, following Moses' account, he names them prophets also and Christs, before Moses had been born and before he had laid down the rule that such men should be anointed with oil. PROOF OF THE GOSPEL 4.15.[2]

105:15 Do Not Harm God's Prophets

THE LAW DOES NOT HARM THOSE WHO KEEP IT. ARCHELAUS: But after Moses had made his appearance, and had given the law to the children of Israel, and had made them aware of all the requirements of the law and everything that it required people to observe and to do, and when he declared that only those who should transgress the law would die, then death no longer reigned over all people. For death then reigned only over sinners, as the law said, "Do not touch those who keep my precepts." Moses therefore served the ministration of this word on death, while he delivered up to destruction all others who were transgressors of the law. For Moses did not come so that death would not reign anywhere at all, since multitudes were definitely held under

the power of death even after Moses. The law was called a "ministration of death" from the fact that then only transgressors of the law were punished, and not those who kept it and who obeyed and observed the things that the law requires, as Abel did, whom Cain, who was made a vessel of the wicked one, killed. However, even after these things death wanted to break the covenant that had been made through the instrumentality of Moses and to reign again over the righteous—and in keeping with this intent it did indeed assail the prophets, killing and stoning those who had been sent by God, down to Zacharias. But my Lord Jesus, maintaining the righteousness of the law of Moses, was angry with death for its transgression of the covenant and of that whole ministration, and he condescended to appear in a human body, for the purpose of avenging not himself but Moses and those who in a continuous succession after him had been oppressed by the violence of death. THE ACTS OF THE DISPUTATION WITH THE HERESIARCH MANES 30.[3]

PROPHETS ARE CALLED CHRISTS (ANOINTED ONES). CYRIL OF ALEXANDRIA: You[4] are right to conclude that he [Jesus] is called Christ only because of the anointing, just as an apostle is so called because of his apostolic function and an angel from his office as messenger. Names like these clearly indicate certain functions rather than individual realities or specific persons. Even the prophets are called Christs, as it is sung in the Psalms: "Do not touch my Christs, and do not harm my prophets" The prophet Habbakuk also said, "You came forth for the salvation of your people, to save your Christs."[5] But tell me this: Is it not true that even they would admit that there is only one Christ and Son, who is the Lord made man, the Only Begotten of God made flesh? ON THE UNITY OF CHRIST.[6]

---

[1]Ps 105:5-15 (104:5-15 LXX). [2]POG 1:195**. [3]ANF 6:203**. [4]An unnamed Nestorian individual with whom Cyril is in dialogue in this treatise. [5]Hab 3:13. [6]OUC 65*.

105:17-19 *Joseph Overcame Temptations*

JOSEPH OVERCAME SATAN WITH THE WORD OF GOD. AMBROSE: Not nature but foolishness makes the slave. Not manumission but learning makes a person free. Esau was born free, but he became a slave; Joseph was sold into slavery,[7] but he was raised to power[8] so that he might rule those who had purchased him. Yet he did not slight his obligation to work zealously; he clung to the heights of virtue; he preserved the liberty of innocence, the stronghold of blamelessness. So the psalmist beautifully says, "Joseph had been sold into slavery. They had bound his feet with fetters." "He had been sold into slavery," he says; he did not become a slave. They had bound his feet, but not his soul.

How is his soul bound when he says, "The iron pierced his soul"? Although the souls of others were pierced with sin (iron is sin, because it pierces within), the soul of blessed Joseph did not lie open to sin but pierced through sin. He was not swayed by the beauty of his mistress's charms, and so he did not experience the flames of passion, for he was aflame with the greater flame of divine grace. Thus, it is said very aptly of him, "Because the word of the Lord burned him," and with this he quenched the fiery darts of the devil. LETTER 53.[9]

105:39 *A Cloud for Protection and a Fire for Light*

THE CLOUD SYMBOLIZES THE LAW AND DIVINE PROTECTION. BEDE: "And when Moses had gone up, a cloud covered the mountain."[10] Just as the mountain on which Moses received the law designates the height of the perfection that was written down in that law, so does the cloud that covered the mountain suggest the grace of divine protection, which is enjoyed more and more the higher one ascends in order to search out the wonders of God's law, as the eyes of one's heart are opened. For surely the cloud covered not only the mountain on which Moses went up, but also the people who were traveling through the wilderness. They were by no means able to ascend to the higher regions, but the cloud sent from heaven overshadowed them nevertheless.[11] Hence it is written that "he spread out a cloud for their protection," since the Lord surely protects with heavenly benediction "all those who fear him, both small and great."[12] ON THE TABERNACLE 1.1.[13]

---

[7]Gen 37:28. [8]Gen 41:41. [9]FC 26:288-89*. [10]Ex 24:15. [11]Ex 13:21-22. [12]Ps 115:13 (113:21 LXX, Vg.). [13]TTH 18:4.

106:1-48 A CONFESSION OF REBELLION AND A PRAYER FOR SALVATION

[1]*Praise the LORD!*
O give thanks to the LORD, for he is good;
  for his steadfast love endures for ever!
[2]*Who can utter the mighty doings of the LORD,*
  or show forth all his praise?

[3]*Blessed are they who observe justice,*
  who do righteousness at all times!

[4]*Remember me, O LORD, when thou showest*
  favor to thy people;

help me when thou deliverest them;
⁵that I may see the prosperity of thy chosen
ones,
that I may rejoice in the gladness of thy
nation,
that I may glory with thy heritage.

⁶Both we and our fathers have sinned;
we have committed iniquity, we have done
wickedly.
⁷Our fathers, when they were in Egypt,
did not consider thy wonderful works;
they did not remember the abundance of thy
steadfast love,
but rebelled against the Most High^v at the
Red Sea.
⁸Yet he saved them for his name's sake,
that he might make known his mighty
power.
⁹He rebuked the Red Sea, and it became dry;
and he led them through the deep as through
a desert.
¹⁰So he saved them from the hand of the foe,
and delivered them from the power of the
enemy.
¹¹And the waters covered their adversaries;
not one of them was left.
¹²Then they believed his words;
they sang his praise.

¹³But they soon forgot his works;
they did not wait for his counsel.
¹⁴But they had a wanton craving in the
wilderness,
and put God to the test in the desert;
¹⁵he gave them what they asked,
but sent a wasting disease among them.

¹⁶When men in the camp were jealous of Moses

and Aaron, the holy one of the Lord,
¹⁷the earth opened and swallowed up Dathan,
and covered the company of Abiram.
¹⁸Fire also broke out in their company;
the flame burned up the wicked.

¹⁹They made a calf in Horeb
and worshiped a molten image.
²⁰They exchanged the glory of God
for the image of an ox that eats grass.
²¹They forgot God, their Savior,
who had done great things in Egypt,
²²wondrous works in the land of Ham,
and terrible things by the Red Sea.
²³Therefore he said he would destroy them—
had not Moses, his chosen one,
stood in the breach before him,
to turn away his wrath from destroying
them.

²⁴Then they despised the pleasant land,
having no faith in his promise.
²⁵They murmured in their tents,
and did not obey the voice of the Lord.
²⁶Therefore he raised his hand and swore to
them
that he would make them fall in the
wilderness,
²⁷and would disperse^w their descendants among
the nations,
scattering them over the lands.

²⁸Then they attached themselves to the Baal of
Peor,
and ate sacrifices offered to the dead;
²⁹they provoked the Lord to anger with their
doings,
and a plague broke out among them.
³⁰Then Phinehas stood up and interposed,

and the plague was stayed.
³¹And that has been reckoned to him as
righteousness
from generation to generation for ever.

³²They angered him at the waters of Meribah,
and it went ill with Moses on their account;
³³for they made his spirit bitter,
and he spoke words that were rash.

³⁴They did not destroy the peoples,
as the LORD commanded them,
³⁵but they mingled with the nations
and learned to do as they did.
³⁶They served their idols,
which became a snare to them.
³⁷They sacrificed their sons
and their daughters to the demons;
³⁸they poured out innocent blood,
the blood of their sons and daughters,
whom they sacrificed to the idols of Canaan;
and the land was polluted with blood.
³⁹Thus they became unclean by their acts,
and played the harlot in their doings.

⁴⁰Then the anger of the LORD was kindled
against his people,
and he abhorred his heritage;
⁴¹he gave them into the hand of the nations,
so that those who hated them ruled over
them.
⁴²Their enemies oppressed them,
and they were brought into subjection under
their power.
⁴³Many times he delivered them,
but they were rebellious in their purposes,
and were brought low through their iniquity.
⁴⁴Nevertheless he regarded their distress,
when he heard their cry.
⁴⁵He remembered for their sake his covenant,
and relented according to the abundance of
his steadfast love.
⁴⁶He caused them to be pitied
by all those who held them captive.

⁴⁷Save us, O LORD our God,
and gather us from among the nations,
that we may give thanks to thy holy name
and glory in thy praise.

⁴⁸Blessed be the LORD the God of Israel,
from everlasting to everlasting!
And let all the people say, "Amen!"
Praise the LORD!

---

v Cn Compare 78.17, 56: Heb *at the sea*　w Syr Compare Ezek 20.23: Heb *cause to fall*

OVERVIEW: No one should be afraid to confess his sins because God already knows them and is both good and willing to forgive them (AUGUSTINE). It is important to read or hear the Scriptures read and expounded by the pastor in church so that one may know God's will, live devoutly in the world and attain the bliss of heaven (CAESARIUS). It is important to remember not only the person but also the words, deeds and prayers of God's servants who labored among us and are now departed (Pachomius).

People who have contempt for God's commands will suffer his judgment (PACHOMIUS).

The crucified Christ was not an impostor or a transgressor of the law (CHRYSOSTOM). God sent Jesus' twelve disciples and Paul, the greatest of the apostles, to evangelize the nations so that they might confess God's name and glory in his praise (AUGUSTINE).

106:1-3 Declaring the Mighty Deeds and Praise of God

CONFESSION OF SINS AND RECEPTION OF DIVINE MERCY. AUGUSTINE: [Jesus] was granting pardon; but while he was granting it he raised his face to her[1] and said, "Has no one stoned you?" And she did not say, "Why? What have I done, Lord? I am not guilty, am I?" She did not say that; what she said was, "No one, Lord."[2] She accused herself. They had been unable to prove it against her and had withdrawn. But she confessed, because her Lord was aware of her guilt but was nonetheless seeking her faith and her confession. "Has no one stoned you?" "No one, Lord." "No one"—that is confession of sins; and "Lord"—that is pardon of the punishment that she deserved. "No one, Lord. I acknowledge both things. I know who you are, I know who I am. It is to you I am confessing. You see, I have heard the words, "Confess[3] to the Lord, for he is good." I know my confession, I know your mercy. SERMON 16A.5.[4]

THE IMPORTANCE OF KNOWING, REMEMBERING AND KEEPING GOD'S WORD. CAESARIUS OF ARLES: I implore, you, dearly beloved, always to call to mind and remember what we have mentioned for the salvation of your soul. Do not accept it only in passing; our sermon ought to fasten its roots in your heart, so that on judgment day it may happily bear the fruits of eternal life. If a person can retain all that we say, he should thank God and always teach others what he remembers. If he cannot remember the whole, let him remember a part of it. If one cannot retain the whole, then let each one remember three or four thoughts. If one then tells another what he heard, by informing each other you can not only remember it all but even with Christ's help fulfill it in deed. One may say to another, "I heard my bishop talking about chastity." Another may say, "I remember that he preached on almsgiving." Still another says, "There has remained in my mind what he said about cultivating our soul like we till our land." Another may report, "I recall that my bishop said that a person who knows letters should be eager to read sacred Scripture, and

one who does not should look for someone and ask him to read God's precepts to him so that with God's help he may fulfill what was read." Again, another may say, "I heard my bishop say that just as merchants who are illiterate hire learned mercenaries so that they may acquire wealth, so Christians should seek, ask and, if necessary, pay for someone to read the sacred Scriptures to them; that just as a trader gets money by having someone else read, so Christians should obtain eternal life in this way." If you do this and admonish each other, you can both live devoutly in this world and afterwards attain to the bliss of eternal life. If you immediately forget all that you heard from the bishop as soon as you leave church, you have come to church without profit and return to your home empty and without fruit. Far be this from you, brothers; may there rather be fulfilled in you what is written: "Blessed are they who keep judgment and do justice at all times." Moreover, "The mercy of the Lord is from eternity and to eternity on them that fear him, and his justice to children's children to such as keep his covenant and are mindful of his commandments, to do them."[5] May the Lord in his goodness bring you to this mercy. SERMON 6.8.[6]

106:13 They Forgot His Works

REMEMBERING THE DEEDS OF THE FAITHFULLY DEPARTED. PACHOMIUS: Three days after our father Theodore died, when all the brothers were in deep mourning, our father Horsiesi became ill from grief over the death of our father Theodore of happy memory. Then some of the elderly brothers, including Apa [Pgentaesi] and Apa Pachomius, strongly urged Apa Horsiesi to go and speak some words of comfort to the brothers. He consented, arose and went out weeping. He sat in the midst of the brothers, who were all gathered together weeping and

---

[1]The woman accused of adultery (Jn 8:3-11). [2]Jn 8:11. [3]The Greek word can also be translated "to give thanks or to praise." [4]WSA 3 1:350-51*. [5]Ps 103:17-18 (102:17-18 LXX, Vg.). [6]FC 31:44-45*.

grieving over our father Theodore. He began to speak to them sorrowfully and tearfully, saying, "God has certainly taken from us in Apa Theodore a righteous father who encouraged us with the word of the Lord. And this great grief of ours is all the greater because it is we who have grieved him so much that he asked the Lord to take him from us quickly and we have been orphaned. Indeed, you all know his great love for us and how he always interceded with God on our behalf to save us from the hands of the devil who is envious of us. Now then, my beloved brothers, let us always remember his labors, his ascetic practices and the tears that he shed in the Lord's presence day and night on our behalf, that this word of Scripture may not apply to us: "They quickly forgot his deeds and did not keep his counsels," and that we may not come under judgment. For this I truly believe: that if we walk in accordance with the directions he gave us, he will be an ambassador for us in the presence of God and of our father Pachomius. It is, in fact, just as our Lord Jesus told his holy disciples and his holy apostles: "I am going before you to prepare a place for you." He also said, "We have one who intercedes for us in the presence of the Father, Jesus Christ our Lord, who loved us and gave himself as a ransom for our sins."[7] It was not on account of ours alone but on account of those of the whole world that he suffered for us. Indeed, during all the days he was with us in the body, our righteous father Pachomius prayed to the Lord day and night for the salvation of our souls and those of the whole world. LIFE OF PACHOMIUS (BOHARIC) 208.[8]

106:17 Putting God to the Test

THE PRICE OF CONTEMPT FOR GOD'S COMMANDS. PACHOMIUS: What shall I say of Adam who, at the beginning of the human race, gave the first example of disobedience and contempt? To him was given power over all the beasts of the earth, just as everything is to be given twofold to the firstborn. But after he held God's order[9] in contempt he did not only lose his power but was cast out of the place he had received for his dwelling—just as the fornicator is cast out of the church and will be deprived of his glory. Everything he endured, those who hold God's commands in contempt will suffer, and walking with pride they will experience the word of Scripture, "He spoke, and the earth swallowed them."[10] LETTER 5.7.[11]

106:30 Divine Punishment Avoided

MANY WERE SAVED BY THE DEATH OF ONE. CHRYSOSTOM: Tell me this.[12] Will you still dare to call Jesus an imposter and lawbreaker? Will you not instead go off and bury yourselves somewhere, when you look the facts in the face, since their truth is so obvious? If Jesus were an imposter and lawbreaker, as you say he was, you should have been held in high honor for putting him to death. Phinehas killed a man and put an end to all God's wrath against the people.[13] The psalmist said, "Then Phinehas stood up and propitiated him, and the slaughter stopped." He rescued a great many ungodly people from the wrath of God by slaying a single lawbreaker. This should have happened all the more in your case, if indeed the man you crucified was a transgressor of the law. DISCOURSES AGAINST JUDAIZING CHRISTIANS 6.3.1.[14]

106:47 Save Us, O Lord

GATHER TOGETHER THE NATIONS. AUGUSTINE: You see, while Jesus did not go to the nations himself, he sent the disciples. That was the fulfillment of what the prophet said, "A people I never knew has served me."[15] Notice how profound, how clear, how explicit a prophecy this is: "A people I never knew"—that means

---

[7]1 Jn 2:1-2. [8]CS 45:260-61. [9]God's command forbidding Adam and Eve to eat of the tree of the knowledge of good and evil. [10]Num 16:32; Deut 11:6. [11]CS 47:65*. [12]Chrysostom is addressing Judaizing Christians in this discourse. [13]See Num 25:6-13. [14]FC 68:154-55*. [15]Ps 18:43 (17:44 LXX, Vg.).

one I had not presented myself to in person—"has served me." How? It goes on, "The moment it heard, it obeyed me";[16] that is, it was not by seeing but by hearing that they came to believe. And it was to call and gather together the nations that the apostle Paul was sent, so fulfilling what we have just been singing, "Gather us from the nations, that we may confess to your name and glory in your praise." That man Tiny,[17] made into the Greatest, not by his own efforts but by the one he used to persecute, was sent to the nations, a sheep stealer turned shepherd, a wolf turned sheep. That least of the apostles was sent to the nations and labored much among the Gentiles, and it was by means of him that the Gentiles came to believe. His letters are the proof of this. SERMON 77.5.[18]

---

[16]Ps 18:44 (17:45 LXX, Vg.).   [17]The allusion is to the apostle Paul's name, which means "small" or "small one."   [18]*WSA* 3 3:319-20*.

107:1-43 AN EXHORTATION TO PRAISE GOD FOR HIS UNFAILING LOVE

[1]*O give thanks to the LORD, for he is good;*
for his steadfast love endures for ever!
[2]*Let the redeemed of the LORD say so,*
whom he has redeemed from trouble
[3]*and gathered in from the lands,*
from the east and from the west,
from the north and from the south.

[4]*Some wandered in desert wastes,*
finding no way to a city to dwell in;
[5]*hungry and thirsty,*
their soul fainted within them.
[6]*Then they cried to the LORD in their trouble,*
and he delivered them from their distress;
[7]*he led them by a straight way,*
till they reached a city to dwell in.
[8]*Let them thank the LORD for his steadfast love,*
for his wonderful works to the sons of men!
[9]*For he satisfies him who is thirsty,*
and the hungry he fills with good things.

[10]*Some sat in darkness and in gloom,*
prisoners in affliction and in irons,
[11]*for they had rebelled against the words of God,*
and spurned the counsel of the Most High.
[12]*Their hearts were bowed down with hard labor;*
they fell down, with none to help.
[13]*Then they cried to the LORD in their trouble,*
and he delivered them from their distress;
[14]*he brought them out of darkness and gloom,*
and broke their bonds asunder.
[15]*Let them thank the LORD for his steadfast love,*
for his wonderful works to the sons of men!
[16]*For he shatters the doors of bronze,*
and cuts in two the bars of iron.

[17]*Some were sick[x] through their sinful ways,*
and because of their iniquities suffered affliction;

¹⁸*they loathed any kind of food,*
  and they drew near to the gates of death.
¹⁹*Then they cried to the* LORD *in their trouble,*
  and he delivered them from their distress;
²⁰*he sent forth his word, and healed them,*
  and delivered them from destruction.
²¹*Let them thank the* LORD *for his steadfast*
    love,
  for his wonderful works to the sons of men!
²²*And let them offer sacrifices of thanksgiving,*
  and tell of his deeds in songs of joy!

²³*Some went down to the sea in ships,*
  doing business on the great waters;
²⁴*they saw the deeds of the* LORD,
  his wondrous works in the deep.
²⁵*For he commanded, and raised the stormy*
    wind,
  which lifted up the waves of the sea.
²⁶*They mounted up to heaven, they went down*
    to the depths;
  their courage melted away in their evil plight;
²⁷*they reeled and staggered like drunken men,*
  and were at their wits' end.
²⁸*Then they cried to the* LORD *in their trouble,*
  and he delivered them from their distress;
²⁹*he made the storm be still,*
  and the waves of the sea were hushed.
³⁰*Then they were glad because they had quiet,*
  and he brought them to their desired haven.
³¹*Let them thank the* LORD *for his steadfast*

love,
  for his wonderful works to the sons of men!
³²*Let them extol him in the congregation of the*
    people,
  and praise him in the assembly of the elders.

³³*He turns rivers into a desert,*
  springs of water into thirsty ground,
³⁴*a fruitful land into a salty waste,*
  because of the wickedness of its inhabitants.
³⁵*He turns a desert into pools of water,*
  a parched land into springs of water.
³⁶*And there he lets the hungry dwell,*
  and they establish a city to live in;
³⁷*they sow fields, and plant vineyards,*
  and get a fruitful yield.
³⁸*By his blessing they multiply greatly;*
  and he does not let their cattle decrease.

³⁹*When they are diminished and brought low*
  through oppression, trouble, and sorrow,
⁴⁰*he pours contempt upon princes*
  and makes them wander in trackless wastes;
⁴¹*but he raises up the needy out of affliction,*
  and makes their families like flocks.
⁴²*The upright see it and are glad;*
  and all wickedness stops its mouth.
⁴³*Whoever is wise, let him give heed to these*
    things;
  let men consider the steadfast love of the
    LORD.

x Cn: Heb *fools*

OVERVIEW: Christ did not eat during the forty days of his temptation in the wilderness and was not in need of food for the forty days after his resurrection to signify the spread of the grace of Christ throughout the world (the Ten Commandments were spread to the four corners of the world: 10 x 4 = 40) (AUGUSTINE). The conversion of people in error, the comforting of the afflicted and the restoration of those in distress are the works of God (GREGORY OF NYSSA). In his mercy God definitely forgives the postbaptismal sins of those who continue in the apostolic faith and are truly penitent (AMMON). Christ was crucified through the weakness of his human nature; he enlivened it by the power of his divine nature (THEODORET).

Just as some people abandon a life of wickedness for a virtuous life of philosophy, so those who experience the love of Christ and the regeneration of the Holy Spirit forsake a life of sin in order to live as followers of Christ. The pagan polemicist Celsus recognized universal sinfulness of the human race, but he failed to understand that God therefore extends his invitation to eternal salvation to every human being (ORIGEN). The psalmist affirms that Christ's incarnation was real, not merely apparent, and that as God incarnate he was also active in the Old Testament period. God sent his Son to redeem those who lived before and those who lived after his incarnation, as well as to bless the church of the Gentiles with abundance (EUSEBIUS). God first offered salvation to the people of Israel, but when they turned away from him, salvation was proclaimed to the Gentiles, who received it, became fruitful and were blessed by God (ORIGEN).

107:2-3 Those Whom God Has Redeemed

THE SAME NUMBER OF DAYS. AUGUSTINE: And that is why Jesus fasted when he was tempted, when he was still in need of food before his death. Although he ate and drank when he was glorified, he was not in need of food after his resurrection.[1] On the first occasion, you see, he was demonstrating in himself our pain. On the second he was demonstrating in us his consolation.[2] Both instances occurred within a period of forty days. I mean, he fasted for forty days, when he was being tempted in the desert, as it is written in the Gospel, before his death in the flesh;[3] and again he was with the disciples for forty days, as Peter puts it in the Acts of the Apostles, going out and coming in, eating and drinking[4] after his resurrection in the flesh.

This number forty seems to signify the course

of this age in those who are being called to grace, through the one who did "not come to undo the law but to fulfill it."[5] There are, after all, ten commandments of the law, now spread by the grace of Christ throughout the world (and the world is four-cornered, and ten multiplied by four makes forty); since "those who have been redeemed by the Lord, from the regions he has gathered them together, from east and west and north and the sea."[6] And so by fasting for forty days before his death in the flesh, it is as though he was crying out, "Hold yourselves in check from the desires of this world"; while by eating and drinking for forty days after his resurrection in the flesh, it is as though he was crying out, "Behold, I am with you until the end of the world."[7] SERMON 263A.4.[8]

107:4-8 God Delivered Them from Their Distress

CONVERSION OF THE WICKED IS THE WORK OF GOD. GREGORY OF NYSSA: Prophetic language affirms that the conversion of those in error is the work of God. For "they went astray in the wilderness in a thirsty land," the psalmist says, and then he adds, "So he led them forth by the right way, that they might go to the city where they dwelled," and "when the Lord turned again the captivity of Zion."[9] In like manner also the comfort of the afflicted is ascribed to God, Paul thus says, "Blessed be God, even the Father of our Lord Jesus Christ, who comforts us in all our tribulation."[10] Again, the psalmist says, speaking in the person of God, "You called on me in trou-

---

[1]In the preceding paragraph Augustine was pointing out the importance of believing that the Christ who descended without a body and the Christ who ascended with a body are one and the same; so here the Christ who ate food out of necessity before his resurrection and the Christ who ate food without having a need for it after his resurrection are one and the same. [2]The prize of eternal life that awaits those who believe. [3]See Mt 4:2. [4]See Acts 10:41. [5]Mt 5:17. [6]The Hebrew text has this strange reading, east, west, north, sea. Modern textual critics have emended sea to south, but ancient exegetes and translators would never have taken such a liberty with the sacred text. [7]Mt 28:20. [8]*WSA* 3 7:224*. [9]Ps 126:1 (125:1 LXX). [10]2 Cor 1:3-4.

ble, and I delivered you."[11] And the setting upright of those who stumble is ascribed innumerable times by Scripture to the power of the Lord: "You have held me by the hand that I might fall, but the Lord was my help,"[12] and "Though he fall, he shall not be cast away, for the Lord upholds him with his hand," and "The Lord helps them that are fallen."[13] And the recovery of the distressed admittedly belongs to the lovingkindness of God, if Eunomius[14] means the same thing of which we learn in prophecy, as the Scripture says, "You laid burdens on our backs; you allowed people to ride over our heads; we went through fire and water, and you brought us to a place of abundance."[15] AGAINST EUNOMIUS 2.15.[16]

CONFESS TO THE LORD HIS MERCIES.
AMMON: Many other monks coming from Phbow[17] by boat reached the island, and we were three hundred in number. About the eighth hour of the twenty-sixth of the month of Athyr,[18] Theodore called all of us and gathered us near himself, and he told Theodore the Alexandrian to interpret what he was going to say to all: "God revealed to me long ago what I have to say but told me to keep silence for a while. Now, as I was standing, I have just been ordered to say it to you, and it is this: In almost every place where the name of Christ is being preached, many of those who have sinned after holy baptism have kept the apostolic faith in which we also stand and have wept for their sins. The Lord, accepting the genuineness of their repentance, has wiped away their sins.[19] Therefore all those among you who up to this day have wept truly over the sins committed after your baptism shall know that you have received forgiveness. Let each of you, therefore, confess to the Lord his mercies and say, You have changed my grief into joy; you have stripped off my sackcloth and girded me with gladness."[20] LETTER OF BISHOP AMMON 28.[21]

107:16 God Breaks Down the Barriers

CHRIST WAS CRUCIFIED IN THE WEAKNESS

OF THE FLESH. THEODORET OF CYR: Let the word *weakness* teach us that Jesus was not nailed to the tree as the Almighty, the uncircumscribed, the immutable and invariable, but that the nature enlivened by the power of God, according to the apostle's teaching, died and was buried—both death and burial being proper to the nature of a servant. "He broke the gates of brass and cut the bars of iron in sunder" and destroyed the power of death and in three days raised his own temple. These are proofs of the divine nature in accordance with the Lord's words "Destroy this temple and in three days I will raise it up." Thus through the sufferings of the one Christ we contemplate the manhood and through the miracles we apprehend the godhead. LETTER 151.[22]

107:20 He Sent Forth His Word

GOD HEALS AND DELIVERS THE REDEEMED.
ORIGEN: Now among the Greeks I know there was only one Phaedon, not a second, and one Polemon,[23] who devoted themselves to philosophy, after a licentious and most wicked life. However, with Jesus there were not only at the time we are speaking of, the twelve disciples, but many more at all times, who, becoming a band of temperate people, speak in the following way of their former lives: "For we ourselves also were sometimes foolish, disobedient, deceived, serving divers lusts and pleasures, living in malice and envy, hateful and hating one another. But after that the kindness and love of God our Savior toward humankind appeared, by the washing of

---

[11]Ps 34:4 (33:5 LXX)   [12]Ps 37:24 (36:24 LXX).   [13]Ps 146:8 (145:8 LXX).
[14]Eunomius was the leader of a staunch group of Arians who subordinated Christ to the Father.   [15]Ps 66:11-12 (65:11-12 LXX).   [16]NPNF 2 5:134**.   [17]Phbow was a town on the Nile River in the Thebaid area of Egypt, where there was a concentration of Christians practicing the ascetic and monastic lifestyles.   [18]November 22, 354.   [19]It was a common belief in the early church that baptism absolved a person only of prebaptismal sins. Postbaptismal sins had to be absolved through individual penance, which included contrition, confession and absolution by a church official.   [20]Ps 30:11 (29:12 LXX).   [21]CS 46:97.   [22]NPNF 2 3:328*.   [23]Two Greek individuals, flourishing in the fourth century, who devoted themselves to living a life according to Greek philosophy.

regeneration and renewing of the Holy Spirit, which he shed on us richly,"[24] we became such as we are. For "God sent forth his Word and healed them and delivered them from their destructions," as the prophet taught in the book of Psalms. AGAINST CELSUS 1.64.[25]

GOD HAS INVITED ALL PEOPLE TO AN ETERNAL REST. ORIGEN: Becoming confused by his efforts to accuse us, Celsus[26] contradicts himself, appearing at one time to know a person "without sin" and "a righteous individual who can look up to God [adorned] with virtue from the beginning." At another time he accepts our statement that there is no human being who is altogether righteous or without sin. He seems to admit this truth when he remarks, "This is indeed apparently true, that somehow the human race is naturally inclined to sin." In the next place, as if all people were not invited by the word, he says, "All people, then, without distinction, ought to be invited, since all indeed are sinners." And yet, in the preceding pages, we have pointed out the words of Jesus: "Come to me, all you who labor and are heavy laden, and I will give you rest."[27] All people, therefore, laboring and being heavily burdened on account of the nature of sin, are invited to the rest spoken of in the word of God, "for God sent his Word,[28] and healed them and delivered them from their destructions." AGAINST CELSUS 3.63.[29]

THE WORD BECAME FLESH. EUSEBIUS OF CAESAREA: For, if it would be unreasonable to suppose that the unbegotten and immutable substance of God the Almighty was changed into the form of man and, in turn, that the eyes of the beholders were deceived by the illusion of something created and that such things were falsely invented by the Scripture, who else could be proclaimed God and the Lord who judges all the earth and passes sentence, appearing in the shape of a man—if it is not proper to call him the first cause of all things—than his preexistent word alone?" And concerning him it was also said in

the Psalms: "He sent his word and healed them and delivered them from their destructions." Of him Moses speaks very clearly, calling him a second Lord after the Father, when he says, "The Lord rained upon Sodom and Gomorrah brimstone and fire from the Lord."[30] The divine Scripture also calls him God, when he again appeared to Jacob in the form of a man, saying to Jacob: "Your name shall not be called Jacob, but your name shall be Israel, because you have been strong with God," when also he called the name of the place "the Vision of God," saying, "For I have seen God face to face, and my soul has been saved."[31] ECCLESIASTICAL HISTORY 1.2.[32]

GOD SENT HIS SON AND HEALED HUMANKIND. EUSEBIUS OF CAESAREA: This[33] clearly proclaims the good news of the descent of God the Word from heaven . . . and of the result of his coming. For it says, "He sent his Word and healed them." And we say distinctly that the Word of God was he who was sent as the Savior of all humankind, whom we are taught by the holy Scriptures to consider divine. And it sadly suggests that he even came down to die for the sake of those who had died before him. By revealing the redemption of those who would be saved by him, it gives the reason of his coming. For he saved without assistance from any one of those who had gone before him even to the gates of death; he healed and rescued them from their destruction. He did this simply by breaking what are called the gates of death and crushing the bars of iron. And then the prophecy proceeds to predict the state of desolation of those who rejected him when he came. For it says, "He turned rivers into a wilderness and rivers of waters into thirst,

---

[24]Tit 3:3-6. [25]ANF 4:425*. [26]Celsus was a heathen philosopher who wrote one of the most competent and thorough literary attacks against Christianity about 180 in his work titled *True Word*. About 230 Origen responded to it in his writing *Against Celsus*. [27]Mt 11:28. [28]Jesus Christ. [29]ANCL 23:143**. [30]Gen 19:24. [31]Gen 32:28, 30 (the allusion is to v. 30 in LXX). [32]FC 19:40-41*. [33]The reference here is to Eusebius's discussion of Psalm 107:1-8 in the previous chapter, in which the psalmist prophesied the coming of Christ to judge all humankind.

a fruitful land into a salty waste for the wickedness of them that dwell therein."[34] You will understand this if you think of Jerusalem of old, the famous city of the Jewish race, its glory and its fruitfulness, devoid now of its saintly citizens and pious people. For after the coming of Christ it became, as the prophet truly says, without fruit or water and quite deserted, "a salty waste for the wickedness of them that dwell therein."[35]

To this is added very much in the prophetic manner a veiled prediction of the change of the longtime desert and thirsty land, referring either to the individual soul or to the turning of the Gentile church to holiness and of its fertility in divine words. This is clearly predicted in a veiled way when it says, "He made the desert into pools of water," and that which follows. But to understand this, one must have wisdom from God; according to the admonition at the end of the psalm, which says, "Who is wise, and he will keep this?"[36] and that which follows. Proof of the Gospel 6.7.[37]

107:33-38 God Turns a Desert into a Land of Plenty

The Fruitfulness of the Gentiles. Origen: The city near the desert, which Jesus entered when he no longer walked boldly among the Jews, is Ephraim.

Now Ephraim means "fruitfulness." He was the brother of Manasseh, the elder of the people "because of forgetfulness."[38]

For after the people "because of forgetfulness" have been left behind, the fruitfulness of the Gentiles has come about, when God "turned" the rivers in Israel "into a desert and the sources of the waters" there "into dry ground" and "their fruitful land into barrenness, for the wickedness of those who dwell in it." But he "turned the desert" from the Gentiles "into pools of waters" and "their dry land into sources of waters."

"And he has placed there the hungry, and they made a city for their habitation," the church. There he sowed fields, according to the seed that fell on the beautiful and good ground and produced a hundredfold, and he planted vineyards, for the Lord's disciples are branches, which also "yielded fruit of produce, and he blessed them and they were multiplied exceedingly."[39] Commentary on the Gospel of John 28.212-15.[40]

---

[34]Ps 107:33-36 (106:33-36 LXX). [35]Ps 107:34 (106:34 LXX). [36]Ps 107:43 (106:43 LXX). [37]POG 2:7-8**. [38]Gen 41:51-52. See verse 51, which says, "It is because God has made me forget all my trouble and all my father's household." [39]Ps 107:37-38 (106:37-38 LXX). [40]FC 89:336*.

108:1-13 PRAISE OF GOD'S LOVE AND PRAYER FOR HIS HELP AGAINST THE ENEMY

A Song. A Psalm of David.

¹*My heart is steadfast, O God,*
 my heart is steadfast!
I will sing and make melody!
 Awake, my soul!

²*Awake, O harp and lyre!*
 I will awake the dawn!
³*I will give thanks to thee, O Lord among the peoples,*
 I will sing praises to thee among the nations.
⁴*For thy steadfast love is great above the*

heavens,
  thy faithfulness reaches to the clouds.

[5]*Be exalted, O God, above the heavens!*
  Let thy glory be over all the earth!
[6]*That thy beloved may be delivered,*
  give help by thy right hand, and answer me!

[7]*God has promised in his sanctuary:*[y]
  "With exultation I will divide up Shechem,
  and portion out the Vale of Succoth.
[8]*Gilead is mine; Manasseh is mine;*
  Ephraim is my helmet;
  Judah my scepter.

[9]*Moab is my washbasin;*
  upon Edom I cast my shoe;
  over Philistia I shout in triumph."

[10]*Who will bring me to the fortified city?*
  Who will lead me to Edom?
[11]*Hast thou not rejected us, O God?*
  Thou dost not go forth, O God, with
  our armies.
[12]*O grant us help against the foe,*
  for vain is the help of man!
[13]*With God we shall do valiantly;*
  it is he who will tread down our foes.

y Or *by his holiness*

OVERVIEW: It is sheer delusion to think that God's power and activity are limited to heaven and do not extend to things on earth (CYRIL OF JERUSALEM). The church has been promised to all nations, even to those who had not seen Christ, so that God would be exalted and glorified throughout the world, but especially in the true catholic church. The true glory of Christ is proclaimed by the power of the Holy Spirit only in the true catholic church (AUGUSTINE).

108:4 God's Love Is Higher Than the Heavens

GOD CANNOT BE LIMITED. CYRIL OF JERUSALEM: Of the Greeks,[1] some have said that God is the soul of the world; others that his power does not extend to earth but only to heaven. Some, laboring under a similar delusion, misinterpret the text "and your faithfulness to the skies" and have dared to limit the providence of God to the skies and heaven and to alienate from God the things on earth, forgetting the psalm that says, "If I go up to the heavens, you are there; if I sink to the underworld, you are present there."[2] For if there is nothing higher

than heaven and the underworld is deeper than the earth, he who rules the lower regions reaches the earth also. **CATECHETICAL LECTURES 8.2.**[3]

108:5 God's Glory Extends Throughout the Earth

GOD IS EXALTED ABOVE THE HEAVENS. AUGUSTINE: But, when once they[4] had become submissive after reflecting on that thought, they would find the church promised to all nations, not in slanders and in human fables but in the sacred Books, and they would see it set before their eyes. Then they would not doubt that Christ, as promised in those Books, though unseen, is now above the heavens. Why in the world, then, should I begrudge them salvation, by recalling my colleagues from this sort of fatherly duty, when it is through this that we see many renouncing their former blindness? Yet some who believed, without seeing, that Christ is raised

[1]Ancient Greek philosophers. [2]Ps 139:8 (138:8 LXX). [3]FC 61:180-81*. [4]Followers of Rogatus, a Donatist bishop of Cartenna in Mauretania, who had rejoined the orthodox church.

above the heavens, still denied his glory over all the earth, which they did see, although the prophet, with strong significance, included both in one sentence when he said, "Be exalted, O God, above the heavens, and your glory over all the earth." LETTER 93.[5]

CHRIST'S TRUE GLORY. AUGUSTINE: Therefore, nothing needs to be said in this place about those who censure and blaspheme Christ (since we are speaking about his glory, by which he was glorified in the world), since the Holy Spirit glorified him with true glory only in the holy catholic church. For elsewhere, that is, either among the heretics or among certain pagans, he cannot be truly glorified on earth, even when he seems to be repeatedly praised. His true glory, therefore, in the catholic church, is sung by the prophet in this way: "Be exalted above the heavens, O God, and above all the earth your glory." And so, because after his exaltation the Holy Spirit will come and will glorify him, this the sacred psalm, this the Only-Begotten himself promised would happen, which we see fulfilled. TRACTATES ON THE GOSPEL OF JOHN 100.3.4.[6]

---

[5]FC 18:57*. [6]FC 90:232**.

109:1-31 A PRAYER FOR GOD'S HELP AGAINST FALSE ACCUSATIONS

To the choirmaster. A Psalm of David.

[1]*Be not silent, O God of my praise!*
[2]*For wicked and deceitful mouths are opened*
   against me,
   speaking against me with lying tongues.
[3]*They beset me with words of hate,*
   and attack me without cause.
[4]*In return for my love they accuse me,*
   even as I make prayer for them.[z]
[5]*So they reward me evil for good,*
   and hatred for my love.

[6]*Appoint a wicked man against him;*
   let an accuser bring him to trial.[a]
[7]*When he is tried, let him come forth guilty;*
   let his prayer be counted as sin!

[8]*May his days be few;*
   may another seize his goods!
[9]*May his children be fatherless,*
   and his wife a widow!
[10]*May his children wander about and beg;*
   may they be driven out of[b] *the ruins they*
   inhabit!
[11]*May the creditor seize all that he has;*
   may strangers plunder the fruits of his toil!
[12]*Let there be none to extend kindness to him,*
   nor any to pity his fatherless children!
[13]*May his posterity be cut off;*
   may his name be blotted out in the second
   generation!
[14]*May the iniquity of his fathers be*
   remembered before the LORD,
   and let not the sin of his mother be

blotted out!

[15]*Let them be before the* LORD *continually;*
  and may his[c] memory be cut off from the
    earth!
[16]*For he did not remember to show kindness,*
  but pursued the poor and needy
  and the brokenhearted to their death.
[17]*He loved to curse; let curses come on him!*
  He did not like blessing; may it be far
    from him!
[18]*He clothed himself with cursing as his coat,*
  may it soak into his body like water,
  like oil into his bones!
[19]*May it be like a garment which he wraps*
    round him,
  like a belt with which he daily girds himself!

[20]*May this be the reward of my accusers from*
    the LORD,
  of those who speak evil against my life!
[21]*But thou, O God my Lord,*
  deal on my behalf for thy name's sake;
  because thy steadfast love is good, deliver
    me!
[22]*For I am poor and needy,*

and my heart is stricken within me.
[23]*I am gone, like a shadow at evening;*
  I am shaken off like a locust.
[24]*My knees are weak through fasting;*
  my body has become gaunt.
[25]*I am an object of scorn to my accusers;*
  when they see me, they wag their heads.

[26]*Help me, O* LORD *my God!*
  Save me according to thy steadfast love!
[27]*Let them know that this is thy hand;*
  thou, O LORD, *hast done it!*
[28]*Let them curse, but do thou bless!*
  Let my assailants be put to shame;[d] may thy
    servant be glad!
[29]*May my accusers be clothed with dishonor;*
  may they be wrapped in their own shame as
    in a mantle!

[30]*With my mouth I will give great thanks to*
    the LORD;
  I will praise him in the midst of the throng.
[31]*For he stands at the right hand of the needy,*
  to save him from those who condemn him to
    death.

---

z Syr: Heb *I prayer*   a Heb *stand at his right hand*   b Gk: Heb *and seek*   c Gk: Heb *their*   d Gk: Heb *they have arisen and have been put to shame*

OVERVIEW: Peter's words in Acts 1 affirm that the opening verses (Acts 1:1-8) are a prophecy of Judas's betrayal of Jesus in Gethsemane. It is possible for sin to be committed within a worship setting (ORIGEN). The judgment against Judas for his betrayal of Christ is applicable to all who betray him in various ways. Since sin has its origin in the will of people, not in their nature as created by God, people are dependent on divine grace in order to do good and to be saved. Contempt for vainglory and praise can lead to love for and pursuit of them (AUGUSTINE).

109:1-9 Wicked and Deceitful Mouths

JUDAS'S BETRAYAL OF CHRIST FORETOLD.
ORIGEN: And if we must make a statement regarding Judas that may overwhelm our opponents with shame, we would say that, in the book of Psalms, the whole of Psalm 108 [LXX] contains a prophecy about Judas, the beginning of which is this: "O God, whom I praise, do not remain silent; for the mouths of the sinner and the mouth of the deceitful man are opened against me." And it is predicted in this psalm both that Judas separated himself from the number of the

apostles on account of his sins and that another was selected in his place; and this is shown by the words "and let another man take his position." But now suppose that he had been betrayed by one of his disciples, who was possessed by a worse spirit than Judas and who had completely poured out, as it were, all the words that he had heard from Jesus, what would this contribute to an accusation against Jesus or the Christian religion? And how will this demonstrate its doctrine to be false? We have replied in the preceding chapter to the statements that follow this, showing that Jesus was not taken prisoner when attempting to flee but that he gave himself up voluntarily for the sake of us all. Therefore it follows, that even if he were bound, he was bound agreeably to his own will, thus teaching us the lesson that we should undertake similar things for the sake of religion in a spirit of willingness. AGAINST CELSUS 2.11.[1]

WHEN WORSHIP BECOMES SINFUL. ORIGEN: This[2] is certainly what David also says in the Psalms. "Let his prayer become sin," when not only is there nothing of worth sought in his sacrifices but even much of blame. For you hear the Lawgiver decree that if anyone eats from that "which was left over to the third day, he will incur the sin." From this we must understand how great a destruction of sins is imminent for the human condition when sin arises even in that place where the offering of the atonement is sought. HOMILIES ON LEVITICUS 5.9.2.[3]

A SENTENCE ON THE ONE WHO BETRAYS CHRIST. AUGUSTINE: Petilianus[4] said, "We must consider, I say, and declare how far the treacherous *traditor*[5] is to be considered dead while he was still living. Judas was an apostle when he betrayed Christ; and the same man was already dead, having spiritually lost the office of an apostle, being destined afterwards to die by hanging himself, as it is written: 'I have sinned,' he says, " 'in that I have betrayed innocent blood'; and he departed, went out, and hanged himself."[6] The traitor per-

ished by the rope: he left the rope for others like himself, of whom the Lord Christ cried aloud to the Father, "Father, those that you gave me I have kept, and none of them is lost, but the son of perdition; that the Scripture might be fulfilled."[7] For David of old had passed this sentence on him who was to betray Christ to the unbelievers: "Let another take his office. Let his children be fatherless and his wife a widow." See how mighty is the spirit of the prophets, that it was able to see all future things as though they were present, so that a traitor who was to be born hereafter should be condemned many centuries before. Finally, that the said sentence should be completed, the holy Matthias received the bishopric of that lost apostle. Let no one be so dull, no one so faithless, as to dispute this: Matthias won for himself a victory, not a wrong, in that he carried off the spoils of the traitor from the victory of the Lord Christ. LETTERS OF PETILIAN THE DONATIST 2.8-17.[8]

109:17 *Cursing and Blessing*

SIN ORIGINATES IN HUMAN WILL. AUGUSTINE: For in that same *Book of Testimonies*,[9] in order to justify somehow his assertion that "all are ruled by their own will," Pelagius[10] has cited this passage from the psalm, "And he loved cursing, and it will come to him, and [he] would not have blessing, and it shall be far from him." But who does not know that this is a fault, not of nature, as God created it, but of the human will, which turned away from God? Even if he[11] had not loved cursing, had desired blessing, and, in this instance, denied that his will was helped by

[1]ANCL 23:16**. [2]Eating flesh left over from a sacrifice on the third day, which was considered an abomination. [3]FC 83:106-7. [4]A member of the Donatists, a separatist sect that advocated purity of church membership. [5]A term given to those who had renounced their faith and turned over copies of Scripture and/or other highly regarded Christian writings during the Diocletian persecution (303-311). [6]Mt 27:4-5. [7]Jn 17:12. [8]NPNF 1 4:532-33*. [9]A lost work containing single assertions of Pelagius followed by biblical passages that supposedly support them. [10]Pelagius was a fifth-century heretic who denied original sin and taught that people can be saved apart from faith in Jesus Christ. [11]The wicked and deceitful accuser mentioned in the psalm.

divine grace, the fact is that, in his ingratitude and impiety, he would be abandoned to be ruled by himself. The result of being deprived of divine guidance and brought to ruin is that he would discover through punishment that he was incapable of being ruled by himself. PROCEEDINGS OF PELAGIANS 3.7.[12]

109:22 Poor and Needy

SELF-SERVING HUMILITY. AUGUSTINE: "I am poor and needy," and I am better only when in sorrow of heart I detest myself and seek your mercy, until what is faulty in me is repaired and made whole and finally I come to that state of peace that the eye of the proud cannot see. Yet in what others say about us and in what they know of our deeds there is grave danger of temptation. For our love of praise leads us to court the good opinion of others and hoard it for our personal glorification. And even when I reproach myself for it, the love of praise tempts me. There is temptation in the very process of self-reproach, for often, by priding himself in his contempt for vainglory, a person is guilty of even emptier pride; and for this reason his contempt of vainglory is an empty boast, because he cannot really hold it in contempt as long as he prides himself on doing so. CONFESSIONS 10.38.[13]

---

[12]FC 86:117**. [13]AC 247-48*.

110:1-7 ORACLES CONCERNING THE MESSIANIC HIGH PRIEST

A Psalm of David.

[1]*The LORD says to my lord:*
    "Sit at my right hand,
till I make your enemies your footstool."

[2]*The LORD sends forth from Zion*
    your mighty scepter.
    Rule in the midst of your foes!
[3]*Your people will offer themselves freely*
    on the day you lead your host
    upon the holy mountains.[e]
From the womb of the morning
    like dew your youth[f] *will come to you.*

[4]*The LORD has sworn*
    and will not change his mind,
"You are a priest for ever
    after the order of Melchizedek."

[5]*The Lord is at your right hand;*
    he will shatter kings on the day of his wrath.
[6]*He will execute judgment among the nations,*
    filling them with corpses;
he will shatter chiefs[g]
    over the wide earth.
[7]*He will drink from the brook by the way;*
    therefore he will lift up his head.

e Another reading is *in holy array*   f Cn: Heb *the dew of your youth*   g Or *the head*

OVERVIEW: David called the Son of God his Lord, not his son (EPISTLE OF BARNABAS). David's reference to Christ's session at the right hand of God is a prophecy of his resurrection and of his return in judgment at the end times and is the place of honor of one who defeated Satan (NOVATIAN). No one should be ashamed of the cross of Christ because it is the symbol of his conquest over Satan and death, as well as his ascension (CYRIL OF JERUSALEM). Christ was always fully God and Lord and the fit instrument of our salvation; he did not change from a lesser to a greater god, nor was he a mere man or adopted for messiahship. Before his incarnation, Christ was the everlasting King and Lord, Image and Word of the Father; in time he became man and redeemed all people (ATHANASIUS). The Father's invitation to his Son to sit at his right hand is a sign of his love and esteem for his Son (AMBROSE). Christ, who now sits at the Father's right hand, will come to award the just with eternal life and to mete out eternal punishment to the wicked (NICETAS). The descent of the Holy Spirit on the disciples at Pentecost was proof that Christ ascended and now sits at the Father's right hand (MAXIMUS). While Christ reigns in heaven waiting the end times, God sends his servants (fearless of death itself) to spread the gospel throughout the world. The opening verses of this psalm refer not to Hezekiah, as the Jews supposed, but to Christ, who is a priest after the order of Melchizedek (JUSTIN).

Christ is the true Son of God by nature, not by the exercise of or increase in virtue (ALEXANDER). Christ is the same person who is called the Son of God, who was put to death for humankind and who rules over all nations until the end of the earth (EUSEBIUS). The source of Christ's being in the Father is described in bodily terminology of human reproduction as an aid to our understanding and to show that he did not come from someone else (HILARY). The womb, as spoken of by the psalmist, in which Christ was begotten was not the corporeal womb of Mary but refers to the eternal begetting of the Son by the Father. Christ cannot be called a Son and a creature; the two are antithetical (ATHANASIUS). Christ is called "firstborn" because there was none born before him, and he is called only-begotten because there is none begotten of the Father after him. The fact that Christ was begotten from all eternity means that he is not included in anyone else's existence but that he is the source of the existence of everything else (AMBROSE). The priesthood of Christ was manifested in his personal sacrifice on the cross (ACTS OF PETER AND PAUL). Christ is called a prophet and priest (after the order of Melchizedek) not only by the apostles but already by Moses and David—this plus his ascension strengthens our faith (THEODORET). In his birth and death Christ took part in the normal course of human life (AUGUSTINE).

110:1 Sit at My Right Hand

JESUS IS CALLED SON OF GOD. EPISTLE OF BARNABAS: Observe again that it is Jesus, not a son of a man but the Son of God, and revealed in the flesh by a symbol.[1]

Since, however, they[2] were going to say that the Messiah is the son of David, David himself, fearing and understanding the error of sinners, prophesied, "The Lord said to my Lord, 'Sit at my right hand until I make your enemies a footstool for your feet.'" And again, Isaiah says as follows: "The Lord said to the Messiah my Lord, whose right hand I held, that the nations would obey him, and I will shatter the strength of kings."[3] Observe how David calls him "Lord" and does not call him "son." EPISTLE OF BARNABAS 12.10-11.[4]

HE WILL SIT AT THE FATHER'S RIGHT HAND. NOVATIAN: He [Christ] foretells that he would

---

[1] *Epistle of Barnabas*, after referring to the brazen serpent as a symbol of Christ, is here referring to Joshua (the Greek of whose name is "Jesus"), the son of Nun and one of the spies sent into the land of Canaan, as a symbol of Jesus. [2] *Epistle of Barnabas* has been speaking about the people of Israel at the time of Moses. [3] See Is 45:1. [4] AF 309.

rise again from the dead: "And in that day there shall be a root of Jesse and one who shall rise to rule the Gentiles: in me shall the Gentiles hope, and his resting place shall be worthy of honor."[5] The time of his resurrection is indicated: "We shall find him ready, as it were, at daybreak."[6] He shall sit at the right hand of the Father: "The Lord says to my Lord, 'Sit at my right hand till I make your enemies your footstool,'" and he is represented as the possessor of all things: "Ask of me, and I will give you the nations for your inheritance and the ends of the earth for your possession."[7] Finally, he is shown to be the Judge of all: "O God, give the King your judgment, and your justice to the king's son."[8] I shall not pursue the matter further at this point; for the things proclaimed about Christ are known to all heretics and are more than familiar to those who hold the truth. ON THE TRINITY 9.8-9.[9]

THE FATHER SUMMONED CHRIST TO RETURN TO HEAVEN. CYRIL OF JERUSALEM: So let us not be ashamed of the cross of Christ, but even if someone else keeps it secret, you should openly sign it upon your forehead, so that evil spirits beholding the royal symbol may fly far from you, terrified. Make this sign as you eat and drink, when you sit down, when you go to bed, when you get up again, while you are talking, while you are walking, in brief, at your every undertaking. He who was crucified then is now in heaven above. For we would have cause to be ashamed if, after he had been crucified and buried, he had remained in the grave. But now, he who was crucified on this very Golgotha ascended to heaven from the Mount of Olives there to the east. For from there he went down into hell and came again to us here. Again he went up from us into heaven, when the Father called him saying, "Sit on my right hand, until I make your enemies your footstool." CATECHETICAL LECTURES 4.14.[10]

I WILL MAKE YOUR ENEMIES YOUR FOOT-STOOL. ATHANASIUS: God, when "becoming a God and a defense" and saying, "I will be a God

to them," does not then become God more than before, nor does he then begin to become God. Rather, what he had always been, that he then becomes to those who need him, when it pleases him. So Christ, also being by nature Lord and King everlasting, does not become Lord more than he was at the time he is sent forth, nor does he then begin to be Lord and King but what he has always been, that he then is made according to the flesh. Having redeemed all, he thereby becomes again Lord of the living and the dead. Thereafter everything serves him, and this is David's meaning in the psalm, "The Lord said to my Lord, 'Sit on my right hand, until I make your enemies your footstool.'" For it was fitting that the redemption should take place through none other than him who is the Lord by nature, lest, though created by the Son, we should name another Lord, and fall into the Arian and Greek folly[11] of serving the creature beyond the all-creating God.[12] DISCOURSES AGAINST THE ARIANS 2.15.14.[13]

THE EVERLASTING KING AND LORD. ATHANASIUS: If then they[14] suppose that the Savior was not Lord and King, even before he became man and endured the cross, but then began to be Lord, let them know that they are openly reviving the statements of the Samosatene.[15] But if, as we have quoted and declared above, he is the everlasting Lord and King, seeing that Abraham worships him as Lord and Moses says, "Then the Lord rained on Sodom and on Gomorrah brimstone and fire from the Lord out of heaven";[16] and David in the Psalms, "The Lord said to my Lord, 'Sit on my right hand'"; and "Your throne, O God, is forever and ever; a scepter of right-

---

[5]Is 11:10. [6]Hos 6:3. [7]Ps 2:8. [8]Ps 72:1 (71:1 LXX, Vg.). [9]FC 67:44*. [10]LCC 4:106-7**. [11]The reference is to the Arian and Greek view of Christ being a secondary or subordinate being. [12]See Rom 1:25. [13]NPNF 2 4:355-56**. [14]The Arians, who taught that the Son was subordinate to the Father and not co-eternal with him. [15]Paul of Samosata, a bishop of Antioch, who was condemned in the late 260s as a supporter of dynamic monarchianism, which supported an adoptionistic view of the incarnate Christ. [16]Gen 19:24.

eousness is the scepter of your kingdom";[17] and "Your kingdom is an everlasting kingdom";[18] it is plain that even before he became man, he was King and Lord everlasting, being Image and Word of the Father. And since the Word is everlasting Lord and King, it is very clear again that Peter did not say that the essence of the Son was made but spoke of his lordship over us, which "became" when he became man, and redeeming all by the cross, became Lord of all and King. DISCOURSES AGAINST THE ARIANS 2.15.13.[19]

CHRIST'S SESSION AT THE RIGHT HAND IS A SIGN OF HONOR. AMBROSE: If reasoning does not move you, at least let the plain aspect of the judgment move you! Raise your eyes to the Judge, see who it is that is seated, with whom he is seated, and where. Christ is sitting at the right hand of the Father. If you cannot perceive this with your eyes, hear the words of the prophet: "The Lord said to my Lord, 'Sit on my right hand.'" The Son, therefore, sits at the right hand of the Father. Tell me now, you who hold that the things of God are to be judged as the things of this world are judged, whether you think that he who sits at the right hand is lower? Is it any dishonor to the Father that he sits at the Son's left hand? The Father honors the Son, and you make it to be an insult! The Father would have this invitation to be a sign of love and esteem, and you would make it an overlord's command! Christ has risen from the dead and sits at the right hand of God. ON THE CHRISTIAN FAITH 2.12.102.[20]

THE SON OF MAN AWAITS HIS SECOND COMING IN JUDGMENT. NICETAS OF REMESIANA: "He ascended into heaven," from where he had descended. "No man has ascended into heaven, but he who descended from heaven, the Son of man who is in heaven."[21] "He sits at the right hand of the Father," according to what was said to David, typifying God the Father speaking to his Son: "Sit at my right hand until I make your enemies your footstool." "Thence he shall come to judge both the living and the dead." Believe that

Christ himself, our God, will come with the angels and powers of heaven to judge both the living and the dead, to give to each according to his works, that is, to award eternal life to the just and to subject the wicked to eternal punishment. EXPLANATION OF THE CREED 6.[22]

CHRIST ASCENDED TO HEAVEN AS VICTOR OVER SATAN. MAXIMUS OF TURIN: All these things[23] are brought about in us by Christ the Lord who, before he returned to heaven, made this promise to his disciples: "But when I ascend I shall ask my Father and he will send you another Paraclete, who will be with you forever, the Spirit of truth."[24] Thus it must be believed that Christ has ascended to the Father when we see that the Paraclete has descended on the apostles. It must be believed, I tell you, that he sits at the right hand of God, as David says of the Savior, because we see the Holy Spirit, as the Lord promised, exulting in the disciples. Consequently the prophetic psalm says, "The Lord said to my Lord: Sit at my right hand." According to our custom the right of sitting is offered to one who, like a victor returning from having accomplished a great deed, deserves to be seated for the sake of honor. And so the man Jesus Christ, who overcame the devil by his suffering and unlocked the underworld by his resurrection, returning to heaven like a victor after having accomplished a great deed, hears from God the Father, "Sit at my right hand." And it is not to be wondered at that sitting on the same seat is offered to the Son by the Father, since by nature he is of one substance with the Father. But perhaps someone is puzzled that the Son is said to be on the right. For although there are no degrees of dignity where the fullness of divinity is concerned, nonetheless the Son sits on the right not because he is preferred to the Father but so that he not be believed

---

[17]Ps 45:6 (44:7 LXX). [18]Ps 145:13 (144:13 LXX). [19]NPNF 2 4:355**. [20]NPNF 2 10:237**. [21]Jn 3:13. [22]FC 7:47*. [23]Maximus is referring to the fact that God provided for our salvation and unlocked the underworld and through the Paraclete has unlocked heaven so that we may go from death to life. [24]Jn 16:7; 14:16-17.

to be inferior. And the Son is on the right because, according to the Gospel, the sheep will be gathered on the right but the goats on the left.[25] SERMON 40.2.[26]

UNTIL THE QUOTA OF THE PREDESTINED IS FILLED. JUSTIN MARTYR: That God the Father of the universe would bring Christ to heaven after his resurrection from the dead and would keep him there until he destroyed his enemies, the demons, and until the quota of those whom he foreknows to be good and virtuous was complete, because of whom he has always delayed the consummation of the world, listen to the words spoken through David the prophet: "The Lord said to my Lord: 'Sit at my right hand, until I make your enemies your footstool.' The Lord shall send to you the scepter of power out of Jerusalem; and rule you in the midst of your enemies. With you is the government in the day of your power, in the brightness of your saints. From the womb have I begotten you before the morning star."[27] The words "he shall send to you the scepter of power out of Jerusalem" signified the powerful teaching that the apostles, going out from Jerusalem, preached everywhere. And although those who teach, or even profess, the name of Christ, will be martyred, we everywhere both accept and teach it. But, if you also should read these words with hostile mind, you can do nothing more, as we already stated, than kill us, which does no real harm to us, but does bring the eternal punishment of fire to you and to all who unjustly hate and do not repent. FIRST APOLOGY 45.[28]

CHRIST IS A PRIEST FOREVER. JUSTIN MARTYR: For instance, your teachers[29] have presumed to refer the words, "The Lord said, to my Lord: Sit at my right hand, till I make your enemies your footstool," to Hezekiah as if he were ordered to sit on the right side of the temple, when the Assyrian king sent men to him with menacing messages and he was warned by Isaiah not to be afraid. Now, we all know and acknowledge that what Isaiah predicted did actually happen, and

that in the days of Hezekiah the Assyrian king was stopped from waging war on Jerusalem and that an angel of the Lord put to death about 185,000 in the Assyrian camp. But, it is evident that the quoted psalm does not refer to Hezekiah, for thus is it worded: "The Lord said to my Lord: Sit at my right hand, till I make your enemies your footstool. He shall send forth the scepter of power on Jerusalem, and he shall rule in the midst of your enemies. In the brightness of the saints, before the morning star I begat you. The Lord has sworn, and he will not repent: You are a priest forever according to the order of Melchizedek."[30] Now, who will not concede that Hezekiah was not a priest forever according to the order of Melchizedek? And who is not aware that he was not the redeemer of Jerusalem? And who does not know that he did not send the scepter of power on Jerusalem and did not rule in the midst of his enemies? (For was it not God who turned his enemies away while he wept and moaned?) But, although our Jesus has not yet returned in glory, he has sent forth into Jerusalem the scepter of power, namely, the call to repentance to all the nations over which the demons used to rule, as David testifies: "The gods of the Gentiles are demons."[31] And the power of his word compelled many to abandon the demons whom they used to obey and through him to believe in almighty God, because the gods of the Gentiles are demons. Furthermore, we have proved earlier that the words, "In the brightness of the saints, from the womb before the morning star I begot you," were addressed to Christ! DIALOGUE WITH TRYPHO 83.[32]

110:3-4 The Eternal Begetting of the Son

CHRIST IS THE ONLY TRUE AND GENUINE SON OF THE FATHER. ALEXANDER OF ALEXAN-

---

[25]Mt 25:33. [26]ACW 50:99-100*. [27]Ps 110:1-3 (109:1-3 LXX). [28]FC 6:82-83**. [29]Since this work is addressed to Trypho, the Jew, the reference is to the teachers of Judaism. [30]Ps 110:1-4 (109:1-4 LXX). [31]Ps 96:5 (95:5 LXX). [32]FC 6:280-81*.

DRIA: And Paul has declared his [Christ's] proper and peculiar, natural and excellent sonship when he thus says of God: "Who spared not his own Son, but for us," who were not his natural sons, "delivered him up."[33] For to distinguish him from those who are not properly sons, he said that he was his own Son. And in the Gospel we read, "This is my beloved Son, in whom I am well pleased."[34] Moreover, in the Psalms the Savior says, "The Lord has said to me, You are my Son."[35] Where, showing that he is the true and genuine Son, he signifies that there are no other genuine sons besides himself. And what, too, is the meaning of this: "From the womb before the morning I begat you"? Does he not plainly indicate the natural sonship of paternal begetting, which he obtained not by the careful framing of his manners, not by the exercise of and increase in virtue, but by property of nature? Wherefore, the only-begotten Son of the Father, indeed, possesses a flawless sonship; but the adoption of rational sons belongs not to them by nature but is prepared for them by the uprightness of their life and by the free gift of God. And it [human nature] is mutable, as Scripture recognizes: "For when the sons of God saw the daughters of men, they took for themselves wives,"[36] etc. And in another place: "I have nourished and brought up children, but they have rebelled against me,"[37] as we find God speaking by the prophet Isaiah. EPISTLES ON THE ARIAN HERESY 1.8.[38]

CHRIST IS THE SON OF GOD ACCORDING TO PROPHECY. EUSEBIUS OF CAESAREA: And what follows in the psalm would agree with him alone, where it says, "The Lord said to me, You are my Son. Today have I begotten you. Ask of me, and I will give you the heathen for your inheritance and the utmost parts of the earth for your possession."[39] For surely only in him has this part of the prophecy received an indubitable fulfillment, since the voice of his disciples has gone forth into all the earth and their words to the ends of the world. And the passage distinctly names Christ,

saying as in his own person, that he is the Son of God, when it says, "The Lord said to me, You are my Son. Today I have begotten you."[40] With which you may compare the words in the Proverbs, also spoken in his own person: "Before the mountains were established, before all the hills he brings me forth."[41] And also the address by the Father to him in Psalm 109 [LXX]: "I begat you from my womb before the morning star." Understand then how the holy Scriptures prophesy that one and the same being, Christ by name, who is also Son of God, is to be plotted against by people, to receive the nations for his inheritance and to rule over the ends of the earth, showing his dispensation among people by two proofs: the one being the attacks on him and the other the subjection of the nations to him. PROOF OF THE GOSPEL 4.16.[42]

THE INEFFABLE BIRTH OF GOD'S SON. HILARY OF POITIERS: Meanwhile, I ask each one's opinion about the interpretation of "from him." Are we to understand these words in the sense of coming from another person, or from no one else, or are we to believe that he himself was the one to whom he was referring? They are not from another person, because they are "from him," that is, in the sense that God does not come from anywhere else except than from God. They are not from nothing, because they come "from him," for a nature is revealed from which the birth is derived. He himself is not meant, because "from him" refers to the birth of the Son from the Father. Moreover, when it is pointed out that he is "from the womb," I ask whether it is possible to believe that he was born from nothing, since the true nature of the birth is revealed by applying the terminology of bodily functions? God was not composed of bodily members when he spoke of the generation of the Son in these words: "From the womb before the day star I begot you." He spoke in order to enlighten our understanding

---

[33]Rom 8:32. [34]Mt 3:17. [35]Ps 2:7. [36]Gen 6:2. [37]Is 1:2. [38]ANF 6:294**. [39]Ps 2:7-8. [40]Ps 2:7. [41]Prov 8:25. [42]POG 1:204-5*.

while he confirmed that ineffable birth of the only-begotten Son from himself with the true nature of the godhead, in order that he might impart to the faculties of our human nature the knowledge of the faith concerning his divine attributes in a manner adapted to our human nature, in order that he might teach us by the expression "from the womb" that the existence of his Only-Begotten was not a creation from nothing but a natural birth from himself. Finally, has he left us in any doubt whatsoever that his words "I came forth from the Father and have come" are to be understood in the sense that he is God, that his being does not come from anywhere else except from the Father? When he came forth from the Father, he did not have a different nature or no nature, but he bears testimony to the fact that he is his author from whom, as he says, he has gone forth. ON THE TRINITY 6.16.[43]

THE SON WAS BEGOTTEN IN ETERNITY.

ATHANASIUS: But since there are poorly instructed people[44] who, while resisting the doctrine of a Son, think little of the words "from the womb before the morning star I begat you," as if this referred to his relation to Mary, alleging that he was born of Mary "before the morning star." Since to say that "womb" could not refer to his relation toward God, we must address the issue briefly here. If then, because the "womb" is human, therefore it is foreign to God; "heart" too clearly has a human meaning, for that which has heart has womb also. Since then both are human, we must deny both or seek to explain both. Now as a word is from the heart, so is an offspring from the womb; and as when the heart of God is spoken of, we do not conceive of it as human, so if Scripture says "from the womb," we must not understand it in a corporeal sense. For it is usual with divine Scripture to speak and signify in the way of humankind what is above humankind. Thus speaking of the creation it says, "your hands made me and fashioned me," and, "your hand made all these things," and, "he commanded, and they were created."[45] Scripture's lan-

guage is suitable then about everything; attributing to the Son "propriety" and "genuineness" and to the creation "the beginning of being." For the one God makes and creates, but him [the Son] he begets from himself, Word or Wisdom. Now "womb" and "heart" plainly declare what is proper and the genuine, for we too have this from the womb, but our works we made by our hands. DISCOURSES AGAINST THE ARIANS 4.27.[46]

CHRIST IS THE SON OF GOD, NOT A CREATURE.

ATHANASIUS: Plainly, divine Scripture, which knows better than any the nature of everything, says through Moses, of the creatures, "In the beginning God created the heaven and the earth";[47] but of the Son it introduces not another but the Father himself saying, "I have begotten you from the womb before the morning star"; and again, "You are my Son, this day have I begotten you."[48] And the Lord says of himself in Proverbs, "Before all the hills he begets me";[49] and concerning things originated and created John says, "All things were made by him";[50] but speaking of the Lord, he says, "The only-begotten Son, who is in the bosom of the Father, he declared him."[51] If then he is a son, therefore he is not a creature; if a creature, his is not a son; for the difference between them is great, and son and creature cannot be the same, unless his essence is considered to be at once from God and external to God. DEFENSE OF THE NICENE DEFINITION 3.13.[52]

THE MEANING OF "FIRSTBORN" AND "ONLY-BEGOTTEN."

AMBROSE: We read that the Son is begotten, inasmuch as the Father says, "I brought you forth from the womb before the morning star." We read of the "firstborn" Son,[53] of the "only-begotten"[54]—firstborn, because there is none before him; only-begotten, because there is none after him. Again, we read, "Who shall declare his generation?"[55] "Generation," mark

---

[43]FC 25:184-85*. [44]The Arians. [45]Ps 119:73 (118:73 LXX). [46]NPNF 2 4:444**. [47]Gen 1:1. [48]Ps 2:7. [49]Prov 8:25. [50]Jn 1:3. [51]Jn 1:18. [52]NPNF 2 4:158*. [53]Col 1:15. [54]Jn 1:14. [55]Is 53:8.

you, not "creation." What argument can be brought to meet testimonies so great and mighty as these? ON THE CHRISTIAN FAITH 1.14.89.[56]

THE ETERNITY OF GOD. AMBROSE: Again, immediately before the declaration "the Lord created me," he says, "I will tell of the things that are from eternity," and before saying, "he begat," he said, "In the beginning, before he made the earth, before all hills." In its extent, the preposition "before" reaches back into the past without end or limit, and so "Before Abraham was, I am,"[57] clearly need not mean "after Adam," just as "before the morning star" need not mean "after the angels." But when he said "before," he intended not that he was included in anyone's existence but that all things are included in his, for thus it is the custom of holy Scripture to show the eternity of God. Finally, in another passage you may read, "Before the mountains were brought forth, or ever the earth and the world were made, you are from everlasting to everlasting."[58]

Before all created things, then, the Son is begotten; within all and for the good of all is he made; begotten of the Father, above the law, brought forth of Mary, under the law. ON THE CHRISTIAN FAITH 3.9.61-62.[59]

SO THAT ALL MAY HAVE LIFE AND SALVATION. ACTS: Just as, therefore, from the side of Adam Eve was created, so also from the side of Christ was created the church, which has no spot or blemish. In him, therefore, God has opened an entrance to all the sons of Abraham, and Isaac and Jacob, in order that they may profess their faith in him and have life and salvation in his name. Turn, therefore, and enter into the joy of your father Abraham, because God has fulfilled what he promised to him. Whence also the prophet says, The Lord has sworn, and will not repent: "You are a priest forever, after the order of Melchizedek." Christ became a priest on the cross, when he offered the whole burnt offering of

his own body and blood as a sacrifice for all the world. ACTS OF THE HOLY APOSTLES PETER AND PAUL.[60]

A PRIEST AFTER THE ORDER OF MELCHIZEDEK. THEODORET OF CYR: He is named Christ from being as man anointed with the Holy Spirit, and called our high priest, apostle, prophet and king. Long ago the divine Moses exclaimed, "The Lord your God will raise up to you a prophet, from the midst of you, of your brethren, like to me."[61] And the divine David cries, "The Lord has sworn and will not repent, you are a priest forever after the order of Melchizedek." This prophecy is confirmed by the divine apostle.[62] And again "seeing then that we have a great high priest who has passed into the heavens, Jesus the Son of God, let us hold firmly to the faith we profess."[63] LETTER 146.[64]

110:7 He Will Drink from the Brook

THE STREAM OF HUMAN BEINGS. AUGUSTINE: So, dearly beloved, "he rejoiced as a strong man to run the course."[65] Which course, if not the course of our mortality, which he was willing to share with us? This course is the way along which the human race passes. They all pass along it, you see, starting on it when they are born, finishing it when they die. And this stream of the human race from beginning to end is constantly issuing from the hidden sources of nature. It was from this rapid and turbulent stream that Christ was willing to drink. You heard just now in the psalm, "From the torrent he drank in the way." This torrent has brought us to birth, has carried us on to death. As though from the hidden source of a spring, Christ has taken to himself the very depths of the sea. Each for our sake—he was both born and died. SERMON 372.3.[66]

---

[56]NPNF 2 10:216*. [57]Jn 8:58. [58]Ps 90:3 (89:3 LXX, Vg.). [59]NPNF 2 10:251*. [60]ANF 8:479**. [61]Deut 18:15. [62]Heb 7:21. [63]Heb 4:14. [64]NPNF 2 3:318**. [65]Ps 19:5 (18:6 LXX, Vg.). [66]WSA 3 10:317-18*.

111:1-10 PRAISE OF GOD FOR HIS UNFAILING RIGHTEOUSNESS

¹*Praise the LORD!*
I will give thanks to the LORD with my whole
  heart,
    in the company of the upright, in the
    congregation.
²*Great are the works of the LORD,*
    studied by all who have pleasure in them.
³*Full of honor and majesty is his work,*
    and his righteousness endures for ever.
⁴*He has caused his wonderful works to be*
    remembered;
    the LORD is gracious and merciful.
⁵*He provides food for those who fear him;*
    he is ever mindful of his covenant.
⁶*He has shown his people the power of his*

works,
    in giving them the heritage of the nations.
⁷*The works of his hands are faithful and just;*
    all his precepts are trustworthy,
⁸*they are established for ever and ever,*
    to be performed with faithfulness
    and uprightness.
⁹*He sent redemption to his people;*
    he has commanded his covenant for ever.
    Holy and terrible is his name!
¹⁰*The fear of the LORD is the beginning of*
    wisdom;
    a good understanding have all those who
    practice it.
His praise endures for ever!

OVERVIEW: Wherever people acknowledge and believe in God there is fear of God, gravity in life and the various virtues and qualities that enhance life (TERTULLIAN). The wisdom of God is more beautiful and valuable than anything we have ever seen or can imagine (GREGORY OF NAZIANZUS). Reverential fear is the main distinguishing mark of our respect for God, and it has its beginning in divine wisdom (AMBROSE). The Holy Spirit works in us his sevenfold gifts, beginning with the wisdom of God and ending in the fear of the Lord (AUGUSTINE).

111:10 *The Fear of the Lord*

FEAR OF GOD AFFECTS THE QUALITY OF HUMAN LIFE. TERTULLIAN: It has also been a subject of discussion, how extremely frequent is the intercourse that heretics hold with magicians, with charlatans, with astrologers, with philoso-

phers; and the reason is that they are people who devote themselves to curious questions. "Seek, and you shall find," is everywhere in their minds. Thus, from the very nature of their conduct may be estimated the quality of their faith. In their discipline we have an index of their doctrine. They say that God is not to be feared; therefore all things are in their view free and unchecked. Where, however, is God not feared, except where he is not, there truth also is not. Where there is no truth, then, naturally enough, there is also such a discipline as the heretics. But where God is, there exists "the fear of God, which is the beginning of wisdom." Where the fear of God is, there is seriousness, an honorable and yet thoughtful diligence, as well as an anxious carefulness and a well-considered admission [to the sacred ministry], a safely guarded communion, promotion after good service, a scrupulous submission [to authority], a devout attendance, a modest gait, a united church and God in all things. PRESCRIPTIONS AGAINST HERETICS 43.[1]

DEEDS ARE BETTER THAN WORDS. GREGORY OF NAZIANZUS: Fairer in my eyes is the beauty that we can gaze on than that which is painted in words; of more value the wealth that our hands can hold, than that which is imagined in our dreams; and more real the wisdom of which we are convinced by deeds, than that which is set forth in splendid language. For "a good understanding," he said, "have all they who act accordingly," not they who proclaim it. Time is the best touchstone of this wisdom, and "the gray head is a crown of glory."[2] ON HIS FATHER'S SILENCE, ORATION 16.3.[3]

WHOEVER FEARS GOD IS BLESSED. AMBROSE: I think I shall not seem to be taking too much on myself, if, in the midst of my children, I yield to my desire to teach, seeing that the master of humility himself has said, "Come, you children, listen to me: I will teach you the fear of the Lord."[4] Therein one may observe both the humility and the grace of his reverence for God. For in saying "the fear of the Lord," which seems to be common to all, he has described the chief mark of reverence for God. As, however, fear itself is the beginning of wisdom and the source of blessedness—for they that fear the Lord are blessed—he has plainly marked himself out as the teacher for instruction in wisdom and the guide to the attainment of blessedness. DUTIES OF THE CLERGY 1.1.[5]

WE BEGIN WITH FEAR AND END IN VIRTUE. AUGUSTINE: Nobody fulfills these ten commandments[6] by his own strength of character, unless helped by the grace of God. So if nobody fulfills the law by his own strength of character, unless God helps with his Spirit; now call to mind how the Holy Spirit is presented to us under the number seven; as the holy prophet says that a person is to be filled with "the Spirit of God, the spirit of wisdom and understanding, of counsel and courage, of knowledge and piety, with the Spirit of the fear of the Lord."[7] These seven activities present the Holy Spirit under the number seven; he, coming down on us as it were from above, begins from wisdom and ends with fear. We, however, going up from below, begin from fear and are perfected in wisdom. "The beginning of wisdom," after all, "is the fear of the Lord." SERMON 248.5.[8]

---

[1]ANF 3:264*. [2]Prov 16:31. [3]NPNF 2 7:248*. [4]Ps 34:11 (33:12 LXX, Vg.). [5]NPNF 2 10:1*. [6]Ex 20:1-17. [7]Is 11:2-3. [8]WSA 3 7:114*.

112:1-10 A EULOGY TO THE GODLY PERSON

[1]*Praise the LORD!*
Blessed is the man who fears the LORD,
    who greatly delights in his commandments!
[2]*His descendants will be mighty in the land;*
    the generation of the upright will be blessed.
[3]*Wealth and riches are in his house;*

and his righteousness endures for ever.
[4]*Light rises in the darkness for the upright;*
    the LORD is gracious, merciful, and
    righteous.
[5]*It is well with the man who deals generously*
    and lends,

who conducts his affairs with justice.
⁶For the righteous will never be moved;
  he will be remembered for ever.
⁷He is not afraid of evil tidings;
  his heart is firm, trusting in the LORD.
⁸His heart is steady, he will not be afraid,
  until he sees his desire on his adversaries.
⁹He has distributed freely, he has given

  to the poor;
  his righteousness endures for ever;
  his horn is exalted in honor.
¹⁰The wicked man sees it and is angry;
  he gnashes his teeth and melts away;
  the desire of the wicked man comes
  to nought.

h Gk: Heb lacks *the* LORD

OVERVIEW: An individual who dies in faith, having delighted in and kept God's commands, has an eternal abode in heaven—a fact that brings joy (ATHANASIUS). What the psalmist says about a man who fears God being blessed applies to women also (AUGUSTINE). Long before David, pagan philosophers knew that obedience to the commands of God brought eternal rewards (AMBROSE). While the earthly life of the righteous may seem cursed, they will be rewarded eternally by God for their fear of the Lord and their delight in God's commands (AUGUSTINE). The light that surrounded the angels at Christ's nativity was unique and a glorious tribute at the birth of humanity's Creator and Redeemer (BEDE).

The church's annual commemoration of the faithfully departed is justified already by the psalmist as a means of providing the living with examples of just and holy lives for their imitation. Prophecies of judgment day are to be seen as assurances that such events as the resurrection and final judgment will indeed occur (AUGUSTINE). Reason, under the tutelage of Christ, teaches generosity, which is a product and the true wealth of the soul (CLEMENT OF ALEXANDRIA). A posthumous reputation is best achieved not by the accumulation of temporal possessions but by the distribution of one's material wealth to the poor (GREGORY OF NAZIANZUS, CHRYSOSTOM, CAESARIUS). The craving pursuit of wealth is a disease, but the distribution of one's wealth to the poor is good and brings a lasting reward.

God's invitation to come to faith must be extended to all, although some will reject it and receive their just reward (AUGUSTINE).

112:1-4 Blessed Is One Who Fears the Lord

BLESSED ARE THEY WHO DIED IN THE FEAR OF THE LORD. ATHANASIUS: I have heard about the death of the blessed Theodorus,[1] and the news caused me great anxiety, knowing as I did his value to you.[2] Now if it had not been Theodorus, I would have spoken to you at greater length, with tears, considering what follows after death. But since it is Theodorus whom you and I have known, what need I say in my letter except "Blessed is" Theodorus, "who has not walked in the counsel of the ungodly"?[3] But if "he is blessed who fears the Lord," we may now confidently call Theodorus blessed, having the firm assurance that he has reached as it were a haven and has a life without care. Would that the same had also befallen each one of us; would that each of us in his running might thus arrive; would that each of us, on his voyage, might anchor his own ship there in the stormless haven, so that, at rest with the fathers, he might say, "here will I dwell, for I have a delight therein."[4] Wherefore, brother beloved and most longed for, weep not for Theodorus, for he "is not dead but is sleeping."[5] SECOND LETTER TO ORSISIUS 58.[6]

---

[1]An Egyptian monk who died on April 27, 364. [2]Orsisius, an abbot of a monastery at Tabenne in Upper Egypt, to whom this letter is addressed. [3]Ps 1:1. [4]Ps 132:14 (131:14 LXX). [5]Mt 9:24. [6]NPNF 2 4:569**.

TERMS ARE SOMETIMES USED INCLUSIVELY.
AUGUSTINE: If, however, this passage is to be
referred to the form of the resurrected body, what
is there to prevent our supposing that the mention of "man" implies "woman" also, *vir* being
used here for *homo* ("human being")? There is a
similar use in the verse, "Blessed is the man (*vir*)
who fears the Lord," which obviously includes the
women who fear him. CITY OF GOD 22.18.[7]

KNOWLEDGE OF GOD BRINGS ETERNAL LIFE.
AMBROSE: Let no one think that this[8] was said
only recently and that it was spoken of by the philosophers before it was mentioned in the gospel.
For the philosophers, that is to say, Aristotle and
Theophrastus, as also Zeno and Hieronymus,
certainly lived before the time of the gospel, but
they came after the prophets. Let them rather
think how long before even the names of the philosophers were heard of, both of these [Aristotle
and Theophrastus] seem to have found open
expression through the mouth of the holy David;
for it is written, "Blessed is the man whom you
instruct, O Lord, and teach him out of your law."[9]
We find elsewhere also, "Blessed is the man who
fears the Lord, he will rejoice greatly in his commandments." We have proved our point as
regards knowledge, the reward for which the
prophet states to be the fruit of eternity, adding
that in the house of the one who fears the Lord or
is instructed in his law and rejoices greatly in the
divine commandments "is glory and riches; and
his justice abides for ever and ever."[10] He has further also in the same psalm made statements
about good works, that they gain for an upright
man the gift of eternal life. He speaks thus:
"Blessed is the man who shows pity and lends; he
will guide his affairs with discretion, surely he
shall not be moved for ever, the righteous shall be
in everlasting remembrance."[11] And further, "He
has dispersed, he has given to the poor, his justice
endures forever."[12] DUTIES OF THE CLERGY
2.2.6.[13]

THE EARTHLY AND ETERNAL FORTUNES OF

THE FAITHFUL. AUGUSTINE: Your fourth question is, "Why David said, 'His seed shall be
mighty on the earth, the generation of the righteous shall be blessed,' when we know that the
children of the just were and are cursed and those
of the unjust were and are blessed." I answer this
question from an exposition of the same psalm[14]
that I gave to the people. For, "Blessed is the one
who fears the Lord; he shall delight exceedingly
in his commandments." God, who alone judges
rightly and mercifully, shall see how much he
excels in his commandments, since, as holy Job
says, "The life of [a person] on earth is a warfare."[15] And again it is written, "For the corruptible body is a load on the soul, and the earthly
habitation presses down the mind that muses on
many things."[16] But he who judges us is the Lord,
and we should not judge before the time until the
Lord shall come and bring to light the hidden
things of darkness and make manifest the counsels of the heart.[17] Then shall each person have
praise from God. Therefore, [God] shall see how
much each person excels in his commandments,
yet each person shall delight exceedingly who
truly loves the peace of the cobuilding, nor
should each person despair now, since "in his
commandments he shall delight exceedingly," and
there will be "peace in the land to men of good
will."[18] EIGHT QUESTIONS OF DULCITIUS 4.[19]

A LIGHT HAS ARISEN IN THE DARKNESS.
BEDE: "Behold, an angel of the Lord stood by
them, and the brightness of God shone around
them."[20] What does it mean that, as the angel was
appearing to the shepherds, the splendor of
divine brightness also enclosed them, something
that we have never discovered in the whole course
of the Old Testament? Though in countless cases
angels appeared to prophets and just people,

---

[7]CG 1059. [8]What Jesus said in Jn 17:3 and Mt 19:20, two passages that
Ambrose quoted at the end of the preceding section. [9]Ps 94:12 (93:12
LXX, Vg.). [10]Ps 112:3 (111:3 LXX, Vg.). [11]Ps 112:5-6 (111:5-6 LXX,
Vg.). [12]Ps 112:9 (111:9 LXX, Vg.). [13]NPNF 2 10:44**. [14]Exposition
of Psalm 112:2-3 (111:2-3 LXX, Vg.). [15]Job 7:1. [16]Wis 9:15. [17]See
1 Cor 4:4-5. [18]See Lk 2:14. [19]FC 16:450-51*. [20]See Lk 2:9.

nowhere do we read of angels enclosing the human beings with the brightness of divine light. [Why is this], unless it is because the privilege was properly kept for the dignity of this time? For when the true Light of the world was born in the world, it was unquestionably fitting that the herald of his nativity should also bathe the bodily sight of human beings with the freshness of heavenly light. Now the prophet says concerning his nativity, "A light has arisen in the darkness for those who are righteous in heart." And as though we were asking what the light was to which he refers, he immediately goes on, "He is a merciful and compassionate and just Lord." Therefore, when the merciful and just Maker and Redeemer of the human race deigned to illuminate the world by the glory of a wondrous nativity, it was entirely proper that the brightness of a wondrous light should fill that very region in which he was born. HOMILIES ON THE GOSPELS 1.6.[21]

112:6-9 The Steadfastness and Generosity of the Righteous

A JUST PERSON WILL BE REMEMBERED FOREVER. AUGUSTINE: Today we are celebrating the memory of a just man.[22] So in this sermon that I owe your graces in carrying out my ministry, I must say something about what we have been singing to the Lord with full and harmonious hearts and voices: "The just person will be held in eternal memory, he will not be afraid of an evil hearing." The psalm, clearly, was read in order to remind us what good purpose is served by this sort of solemn celebration. The reason, you see, that holy church celebrates every year the anniversary of the last days of the just and holy people who have departed from this world is not thereby to increase the honor enjoyed by these just persons but to set before us an example to be imitated. SERMON 335L.1.[23]

PROPHECIES ARE PROMISES OF THE FUTURE. AUGUSTINE: So "the just person will be remembered forever; and he will not be afraid of an evil

hearing." The judge is coming, you see, of the living and the dead, as we read in the Gospel. And it is true; since in fact the things we now see had not yet occurred, when it was foretold they would happen. The fact that you can now see the name of Christ being proclaimed throughout all nations, people converted to the one God, idols being forsaken, temples pulled down, images smashed; none of these things had yet happened, and yet they were spoken of, and now they can be seen. So in the Scriptures in which these things we can now see were written about (they were written, though, at a time when they could not be seen, but they were being promised for the future), in the very same Scriptures we read of what has not yet come about.

I mean, the day of judgment has not yet come, the resurrection of the dead has not yet happened, the one who is going to judge has not yet come, who came the first time to be judged. SERMON 328.5.[24]

TRUE WEALTH IS IN THE SOUL. CLEMENT OF ALEXANDRIA: However, in my opinion, he who possesses things of higher value is the one, and the only one, who is truly wealthy, without passing for such. A gem is not worth much, nor is silver, nor clothes nor beauty of body; but virtue is, because it is reason translated into deeds under the guidance of the Educator [Christ]. This is reason forbidding luxuriousness, stimulating independent service of self and singing the praises of frugality, offspring of self-control. "Receive instruction," Scripture says, "and not money, and choose knowledge rather than gold. For wisdom is better than precious stones, and all that is priceless cannot be compared with it." And, again, "My fruit is better than gold and precious stone and silver; and my blossoms than choice silver."[25] If we must make distinctions, let the person with a fortune be considered the wealthy one,

---

[21]CS 110:60. [22]"Just man" is to be understood generically as any just and holy person. [23]WSA 3 9:260. [24]WSA 3 9:178. [25]Prov 8:10-11, 19.

loaded down as he is with gold like a dingy purse; but the holy one is the discreet one, for discretion is the quality that maintains a properly balanced moderation between spending and giving. "Some distribute their own goods," it is written, "and become richer."[26] Of such people, Scripture says, "He has distributed, he has given to the poor; his justice remains forever."[27] Therefore, it is not he who possesses and retains his wealth who is wealthy but he who gives; it is giving, not receiving, that reveals the happy person. Generosity is a product of the soul; so, true wealth is in the soul. CHRIST THE EDUCATOR 3.6.35.[28]

A TRUE EXAMPLE OF GENEROSITY AND HOSPITALITY. GREGORY OF NAZIANZUS: Who, more than she [Gregory's sister], threw open her house, with a courteous and generous welcome to those who live according to God? And, better still, who received them with such modesty or advanced to meet them in a manner so pleasing to God? Further, who displayed a mind more tranquil in misfortune or a heart more sympathetic to those in distress? Who was more liberal to those in want? I would not hesitate to praise her in the words of Job: "Her door was open to every traveler, the stranger did not stay without."[29] "She was an eye to the blind, and a foot to the lame and a mother to orphans."[30] Of her compassion toward widows, what more need I say than that she received as its fruit never to be called a widow herself? Her house was a common hospice for all her needy relatives, and her goods were as common to all the needy as their own personal belongings. "She has distributed, she has given to the poor." Because of the infallible truth of the divine promise, she stored up many treasures in the heavenly coffers and often received Christ himself in the person of the many to whom she had shown kindness. Best of all, she was more truly what she was than she appeared to be, and in secret she cultivated piety for him who sees secret things. She snatched everything from the prince of this world, and she transferred it to safe storehouses. She left nothing behind to earth except her body. She exchanged all things for the hopes above. The only riches she left to her children were imitation of her example and emulation of her virtues. ON HIS SISTER ST. GORGIANA, ORATION 8.12.[31]

GENEROSITY PRODUCES AN HONORABLE REPUTATION. CHRYSOSTOM: There are many people even today who in imitation of them[32] want to be remembered for such achievements, by building splendid homes, baths, porches and avenues. I mean, if you were to ask each of them why they toil and labor and lay out such great expense to no good purpose, you would hear nothing but these very words—so as to ensure their memory survives in perpetuity and to have it said that "this is the house belonging to so-and-so," "this the property of so-and-so." This, on the contrary, is worthy not of commemoration but of condemnation: hard on those words come other remarks equivalent to countless accusations—"belonging to so-and-so the grasping miser, despoiler of widows and orphans." So such behavior is calculated not to earn remembrance but to encounter unremitting accusations, achieve notoriety after death and incite the tongues of onlookers to calumny and condemnation of the person who acquired these goods. But if you are quite anxious for undying reputation, I will show you the way to succeed in being remembered for every achievement and also, along with an excellent name, to provide yourself with great confidence in the age to come. How, then, will you manage both to be remembered day after day and also become the recipient of tributes even after passing from one life to the next? If you give away these goods of yours into the hands of the poor, letting go of precious stones, magnificent homes, properties and baths. This is undying reputation; this remembrance proves that you are a provider of countless

---

[26]Prov 11:24. [27]Ps 112:9 (111:9 LXX). [28]FC 23:228-29*. [29]Job 31:32, with a substitution of "his" for "my" to suit the context. [30]Job 29:15-16, with a shift from "I" to "she." [31]FC 22:108-9*. [32]The people who built the tower of Babel (Gen 11:3-4).

treasures; this remembrance relieves you of the burden of sins and procures for you great confidence with the Lord. After all, consider, I ask you, even the very words everybody would be likely to say about the dispenser of such largesse—so generous and kind, so gentle and good. Scripture says, remember, "He distributed his goods as gifts to the poor; his righteousness lasts forever." That, after all, is what material wealth is like: the more it is given away, the more it remains, whereas if it is clung to and locked up in safe keeping, it destroys even the people who cling to it. "He distributed his goods as gifts to the poor," it says, remember. But listen to what follows as well: "His righteousness lasts forever." It took one day for him to distribute his wealth, and his goodness continues for all time and earns an undying remembrance. HOMILIES ON GENESIS 30.7.[33]

DESIRE ONLY WHAT IS NECESSARY. CAESARIUS OF ARLES: For our part, beloved brothers, when we recognize our kind Redeemer and reflect on our price, let us not love "the world or the things that are in the world";[34] but according to the apostle, "having food and sufficient clothing, with these let us be content."[35] Let us seek the use of what is necessary but not have greedy desires. If we lack riches, let us not seek them in the world by evil deeds or unjust gains. However, if we have them, let us transmit them to heaven by good works, so that there may be fulfilled in us what is written: "Lavishly he gives to the poor; his generosity shall endure forever"; with the help of our Lord Jesus Christ, who lives and reigns forever and ever. Amen. SERMON 141.6.[36]

DOING GOOD WITH ONE'S GOODS. AUGUSTINE: So there is a good that can make [you] good, and there is a good with which you can do good. The good that makes [you] good is God, for only the one who is always good can make people good. In order that you, therefore, may be good, call on God. There is, however, another good with which you can do good, anything, that

is, that you may have. It is gold, it is silver, it is good, not such that can make you good but such that you can do good with.

You have gold, you have silver, and you are lusting for gold, and you are lusting for silver. You have it, and you are lusting for it, you are full, and you are still thirsty. It is a disease you have, not prosperity. There are people with a disease that makes them full of moisture and yet always thirsty; they are full of moisture, and they are thirsting for moisture! So how can you enjoy your prosperity when your lust for money suggests a bad case of dropsy?

So you have gold, it is good; you have something to do good with but not something to be good with. "What good," you ask, "am I going to do with gold?" Haven't you heard the psalm, "He has distributed," it says, "he has given to the poor his justice abides forever and ever." This is the good, this is the good you are good with, justice. If you have the good you can be good with, do good with the good you are not good with. You have some money, disburse it. By disbursing your money, you increase your justice. "He has distributed," you see, he has disbursed, "he has given to the poor; his justice abides forever and ever." Notice what gets less and what increases; what gets less is money, what increases is justice. It is what you are going to say goodbye to that gets less, what you are going to leave behind that gets less; what increases is what you are going to possess forever. SERMON 61.3.[37]

112:10 The Wicked Shall See and Be Angry

HUMBLY INVITE THE WICKED TO COME TO GOD. AUGUSTINE: Dearly beloved, whether the Jews receive these divine testimonies with joy or with indignation, nevertheless, when we can, let us proclaim them with great love for the Jews. Let us not proudly glory against the broken branches; let us rather reflect by whose grace it is, and by

---

[33]FC 82:224-25. [34]1 Jn 2:15. [35]1 Tim 6:8. [36]FC 47:291*. [37]WSA 3 3:143*.

much mercy, and on what root, we have been ingrafted. Then, not savoring of pride but with a deep sense of humility, not insulting with presumption but rejoicing with trembling,[38] let us say, "Come and let us walk in the light of the Lord,"[39] because his "name is great among the Gentiles." If they hear him and obey him, they will be among them to whom Scripture says, "Come to him and be enlightened, and your faces shall not be confounded."[40] If, however, they hear and do not obey, if they see and are jealous,[41] they

are among them of whom the psalm says, "The wicked shall see and shall be angry, he shall gnash with his teeth and pine away." "But I," the church says to Christ, "as a fruitful olive tree in the house of God, have hoped in the mercy of God for ever, yea forever and ever."[42] IN ANSWER TO THE JEWS 10.15.[43]

---

[38]See Ps 2:11. [39]Is 2:5. [40]Ps 34:5 (33:6 LXX, Vg.). [41]See Rom 11:11. [42]Ps 52:8 (51:10 LXX, Vg.). [43]FC 27:414*.

113:1-9 CELEBRATING A GOD OF MAJESTY AND MERCY

[1]*Praise the LORD!*
Praise, O servants of the LORD,
*   praise the name of the LORD!*

[2]*Blessed be the name of the LORD*
*   from this time forth and for evermore!*
[3]*From the rising of the sun to its setting*
*   the name of the LORD is to be praised!*
[4]*The LORD is high above all nations,*
*   and his glory above the heavens!*

[5]*Who is like the LORD our God,*
*   who is seated on high,*
[6]*who looks far down*
*   upon the heavens and the earth?*
[7]*He raises the poor from the dust,*
*   and lifts the needy from the ash heap,*
[8]*to make them sit with princes,*
*   with the princes of his people.*
[9]*He gives the barren woman a home,*
*   making her the joyous mother of children.*
Praise the LORD!

OVERVIEW: The name of God is blessed when we wait on the needs of others, in imitation of Christ's human servanthood (EUGIPPIUS). The holy church consists of everyone throughout the world who praises God (AUGUSTINE). The law was given to one nation, Israel, but the gospel was given to all people, as the gift of tongues at Pentecost clearly attests (BEDE).

God remembers all people of low estate but

especially the martyrs, who are the princes and exemplars of the church. One cannot gain Christ unless he is humbled by suffering and hardship (AMBROSE). We may not understand the reasons of the divine will, but we know that God raises up the humble according to his will and justice (JEROME). While there is joy in the bearing of children, the greatest of which belongs to the Virgin Mary, virgins limit death by not bringing into this world new life, which is the starting point of death (GREGORY OF NYSSA).

113:2-4 God's Name Is Blessed Forever

BLESSED BE THE NAME OF THE LORD. EUGIPPIUS: After the destruction of the towns in the upper region of the Danube, Severin[1] constantly warned all the people who, obeying his instructions, had migrated to the town of Lauriacum not to trust in their own power but, being intent on prayer, fasts and almsgiving, to fortify themselves rather with spiritual weapons. One day the man of God ordered all the poor to be assembled in a basilica in order to deal them out their ration of oil. This commodity [spice] was hard to obtain in those places because merchants had great difficulty in importing it. Now, as if a blessing was to be gained, a big crowd of needy people had gathered; since this liquid was precious food, it had greatly increased the number of beggars. When the holy man had finished the prayer and had made the sign of the cross, in the presence of all he uttered the words of sacred Scripture: "Blessed be the name of the Lord!" Then he began to deal out the oil with his own hand to the ministers who carried it around, imitating, as a faithful servant, his Lord, who had come not to be served but to serve,[2] and, following in the footsteps of the Savior, he saw to his joy that the substance that his right hand poured out without his left hand knowing[3] was increased. For while the vessels of the poor were filling, there was no less in the hands of his ministers. THE LIFE OF SAINT SEVERIN 28.1-3.[4]

THE LORD IS PRAISED EVERYWHERE. AUGUSTINE: Now follows what concerns us: *In the holy church.* The holy church is what we are; but I do not mean "we" in the sense of just those of us who are here, you who are listening to me now; as many of us as are by the grace of God Christian believers in this church, that is in this city, as many as there are in this region, as many as there are in this province, as many as there are also

across the sea, as many as there are in the whole wide world, since "from the rising of the sun to its setting the name of the Lord is praised." Such is the catholic church, our true mother, the true consort of that bridegroom. SERMON 213.8.[5]

THE GOSPEL HAS BEEN GIVEN TO ALL NATIONS. BEDE: There [on Sinai], after all the legal decrees had been heard, the entire people answered with one voice, "We will hear and do all the words that the Lord has spoken."[6] Here [in the upper room], after the assembly of the church, which was being born, had received the enlightenment of the Spirit, they spoke of the wonders of God in the languages of all countries. Doubtlessly it was thanks to a certain discernment that the observance of the law was given to only one nation, that of the Jews, while the word of the gospel was to be proclaimed to all nations throughout the world, and that the proclamations of the Christian faith were to be spoken in the languages of all peoples, fulfilling the prophecy that says, "From the rising of the sun to its setting, praise the name of the Lord; the Lord is high above all nations." HOMILIES ON THE GOSPELS 2.17.[7]

113:5-6 God Looks Down on Heaven and Earth

GOD LOOKS ON THE LOWLY. AMBROSE: Another psalm that was read says, "Who is as the Lord our God who dwells on high and looks down on the low things in heaven and in earth?" God, no doubt, casts his eyes on the lowly, he who laid bare the relics of the holy martyrs of his church, lying hid under the lowly turf, their souls in heaven, their bodies in the earth: "Raising up the needy person out of the dust, lifting up the poor person out of the dunghill,"[8] placing him, as you see, with the princes of his people. Whom are

---

[1]A fifth-century monk and apostle of Noricum (Austria). [2]Mt 20:28; Mk 10:45. [3]Mt 6:3. [4]FC 55:83-84. [5]WSA 3 6:144-45*. [6]Ex 24:3. [7]CS 111:172-73*. [8]Ps 113:7 (112:7 LXX, Vg.).

we to think of as the princes of his people if not the holy martyrs in whose number long ago the unknown Protase and Gervase[9] were given place? They now cause the church at Milan, barren of martyrs, now the mother of many children, to rejoice in the glory and examples of their suffering. Letter 61.[10]

113:7-9 God Watches Over and Helps the Downtrodden

God Raises Up the Needy and the Lowly. Ambrose: It is written that "there is no glory, if when you sin, you are punished and endure it, but if when you do good and suffer, this is a grace with God. To this, indeed, you have been called, because Christ also has died for you, leaving you an example, that you may follow in his steps, who did no sin, neither was deceit found in his month; who, when he was reviled, did not revile in return, when he suffered, did not threaten."[11] And so the just person, even if he is on the rack, is always just. Because he justifies God and says that his suffering is less than his sins warrant, he is always wise. For true and perfect wisdom is not taken away by the torments of the rack, nor does it lose its nature, because it casts out fear by its zealous and loving purpose,[12] even as the wise person knows that he should say that our sufferings in this body are unworthy of the reward of future glory and that all the sufferings of this time cannot equal the reward that is to come.[13] And thus, to him, God, who knows the time of the harvest, is always good. Therefore, like a good farmer, he plows his field here with the ploughshare of a rather severe abstinence, as it were. He clears his land here with the scythe of virtues that cuts off the vices, so to speak. He manures here by humbling himself even to the earth, for he knows that "God raises up the needy from the earth and lifts up the poor out of the dunghill." Indeed, unless the apostle Paul had been counted as dung, he could never have gained Christ for himself. Such a person keeps watch over his crops here, so that he may store them away there

without concern. And so, to him, God is always good because he always hopes for good things from God. The Prayer of Job and David 3.2.3.[14]

We Do Not Know the Reasons of the Divine Will. Jerome: Daniel, the prophet, says to Nebuchadnezzar, that the most High rules in the kingdom of humankind, and he will give it to whomsoever it shall please him, and he will appoint the lowest and the basest person over it.[15] Ask him the reason why he appoints the lowest and the basest person as king and does what he wills; question the justice of the will of him of whom it is written, "He raises up the needy from the earth and lifts up the poor out of the dung-hills, that he may place him with the princes, with the princes of his people." Is he, perhaps, according to your [the Pelagians'] view, seeking glory and popular acclaim without judgment and justice, so that he raises the lowly to royal power and humiliates the powerful in exchange? Listen to the prophet, who says, "All the inhabitants of the earth are reputed as nothing before him."[16] For he has done whatsoever he wished in heaven and on earth, and there is no one who will resist his will or who can say to him, "Why have you done this?" His works are all true and his ways justice, and he can humiliate the proud. Against the Pelagians 2.3.[17]

God Blesses the Barren Woman. Gregory of Nyssa: What lesson, then, results from these remarks?[18] This: that we should wean ourselves from this life in the flesh, which has an inevitable follower, death; and that we should search for a manner of life that does not bring death in its train. Now the life of virginity is such a life. We will add a few other things to show how true this is. Everyone knows that the propagation of mor-

---

[9]They were two martyrs whose bones were believed to have been discovered in Milan at the time of Ambrose. [10]FC 26:378*. [11]1 Pet 2:20-23. [12]See 1 Jn 4:18. [13]See Rom 8:18. [14]FC 65:370-71. [15]See Dan 4:14. [16]Dan 4:32. [17]FC 53: 344-45. [18]Such as Jesus' comment to Nicodemus (Jn 3:6), as well as comments about the flesh being susceptible to death and the spirit having the potential for life.

tal bodies is the work of sexual intercourse; whereas for those who are joined to the Spirit, life and immortality instead of children are produced by this latter intercourse; and the words of the apostle beautifully suit their case, for the joyful mother of such children as these "shall be saved in childbearing";[19] as the psalmist in his divine songs thankfully cries, "He makes the barren woman to keep house and to be a joyful mother of children." Truly a joyful mother is the virgin mother who by the operation of the Spirit conceives the deathless children and who is called by the prophet barren because of her modesty only. This life, then, which is stronger than the power of death, is, to those who think, the preferable one. The physical bringing of children into the world—I speak without wishing to offend—is as much a starting point of death as of life, because from the moment of birth the process of

dying commences. But those who by virginity have desisted from this process have drawn within themselves the boundary line of death and by their own deed have checked his advance; they have made themselves, in fact, a frontier between life and death, and a barrier too, which thwarts him. If, then, death cannot pass beyond virginity but finds his power checked and shattered there, it is demonstrated that virginity is a stronger thing than death; and that body is rightly named undying that does not lend its service to a dying world or allow itself to become the instrument of a succession of dying creatures. In such a body the long unbroken career of decay and death, which has intervened between the first man and the lives of virginity that have been led, is interrupted. ON VIRGINITY 13.[20]

---

[19]1 Tim 2:15. [20]NPNF 2 5:359.

114:1-8 A CELEBRATION OF THE EXODUS

[1]*When Israel went forth from Egypt,*
the house of Jacob from a people of strange
language,
[2]*Judah became his sanctuary,*
Israel his dominion.

[3]*The sea looked and fled,*
Jordan turned back.
[4]*The mountains skipped like rams,*
the hills like lambs.

[5]*What ails you, O sea, that you flee?*
O Jordan, that you turn back?
[6]*O mountains, that you skip like rams?*
O hills, like lambs?

[7]*Tremble, O earth, at the presence of the*
LORD,
at the presence of the God of Jacob,
[8]*who turns the rock into a pool of water,*
the flint into a spring of water.

OVERVIEW: When David said that the Jordan turned back, he ultimately meant that the grace of baptism begins not just at its institution in the New Testament but flows back to touch with its benefits all who believed from the beginning and to render judgment on those who have not believed (MAXIMUS). Scripture contains many instances of nature obeying God's command (AMBROSE). David's words about the Jordan River being turned back are also understood to mean that the benefits of baptism begin even with infants (AUGUSTINE).

114:3 The Waters Turned Back

THE CLEANSING NATURE OF WATER. MAXIMUS OF TURIN: Although it had been harsh and cold, the water is purged and endowed with the warmth of the Lord's blessing, so that what had removed material stains a little before now cleanses the spiritual stains of souls. Nor should we be surprised that we speak of water, which is something of bodily substance, as cleansing the soul. There is no doubt that it comes and penetrates into all that is secret in the conscience. For although it is already subtle and fine, yet, having become even more subtle by Christ's blessing, it passes through the hidden tissues of life to the recesses of the soul like a spiritual dew. For the current of blessings is more subtle than the flow of waters. Hence we have also said that in the baptism of the Savior the blessing that flowed down like a spiritual stream touched the outpouring of every flood and the course of every stream. When Christ stood in the Jordan, the flood of waters moved wondrously, but the flood of blessings also flowed. In the one the river's stream was borne more violently, while in the other the most pure font of the Savior diffused itself. And in a certain wonderful way the consecration of that baptism went back to the source of the Jordan, and the flow of blessings was carried in the opposite direction to the flow of the waters, which is the reason, I think, that David said, "The Jordan turned back." For in the baptism of Christ it was not the waters of the Jordan that turned back but the grace of the sacrament, and it returned to the source of its own being in blessing rather than in substance, and inasmuch as the grace of consecration was dispersed to every stream, it may be seen that its own onrush was called back to the beginning of its flow. SERMON 13B.2.[1]

THE RESPONSE OF NATURE TO DIVINE COMMANDS. AMBROSE: Nor ought it to appear at all improbable that at the command of God the bones were fitted again to their joints,[2] since we have numberless instances in which nature has obeyed the commands of heaven; as the earth was commanded to produce the green herb[3] and did produce it; as the rock at the touch of the rod produced water for the thirsting people;[4] and the hard stone poured forth streams by the mercy of God for those parched with heat. What else did the rod changed into a serpent[5] signify than that at the will of God living things can be produced from those that are without life? Do you think it more incredible that bones should come together when commanded than that streams should be turned back or the sea flee? For thus does the prophet testify: "The sea saw it and fled; Jordan was driven back." Nor can there be any doubt about this fact, which was proved by the rescue of one and the destruction of the other of two peoples, that the waves of the sea stood restrained and at the same time surrounded one people and poured back on the other for their death, that they might overwhelm the one but preserve the other.[6] And what do we find in the Gospel itself? Did not the Lord himself prove there that the sea grew calm at a word, the clouds were driven away, the blasts of the winds yielded, and that on the quieted shores the dumb elements obeyed God? ON HIS BROTHER SATYRUS 2.74.[7]

INFANTS ARE TRANSFORMED THROUGH BAPTISM. AUGUSTINE: But, again, listen to another excellent steward[8] of God, whom I reverence as a father, for in Christ Jesus he begat me through the gospel,[9] and from this servant of Christ I received the laver of regeneration. I speak of the blessed Ambrose, whose grace, constancy, labors,

---

[1]ACW 50:36-37. [2]See Ezek 37:7. [3]Gen 1:11. [4]Num 20:11. [5]Ex 4:3. [6]Ex 14:22-31. [7]NPNF 2 10:185-86*. [8]Ambrose. [9]See 1 Cor 4:15.

dangers, whether in works or in speech, for the catholic faith, I myself have experienced, and together with me the Roman world does not hesitate to proclaim them. When this man was explaining the Gospel according to Luke, he said, "The Jordan turned backwards" signified the

future mysteries of the laver of salvation, through which infants who are baptized at the beginning of their natural life are reformed from badness. AGAINST JULIAN 1.3.10.[10]

---

[10]FC 35:10*.

115:1-18 PRAISE GOD FOR HIS LOVE AND FAITHFULNESS

[1]Not to us, O LORD, not to us, but to thy
name give glory,
for the sake of thy steadfast love and thy
faithfulness!
[2]Why should the nations say,
"Where is their God?"

[3]Our God is in the heavens;
he does whatever he pleases.
[4]Their idols are silver and gold,
the work of men's hands.
[5]They have mouths, but do not speak;
eyes, but do not see.
[6]They have ears, but do not hear;
noses, but do not smell.
[7]They have hands, but do not feel;
feet, but do not walk;
and they do not make a sound in their
throat.
[8]Those who make them are like them;
so are all who trust in them.

[9]O Israel, trust in the LORD!
He is their help and their shield.
[10]O house of Aaron, put your trust in the

LORD!
He is their help and their shield.
[11]You who fear the LORD trust in the LORD!
He is their help and their shield.

[12]The LORD has been mindful of us; he will
bless us;
he will bless the house of Israel;
he will bless the house of Aaron;
[13]he will bless those who fear the LORD,
both small and great.

[14]May the LORD give you increase,
you and your children!
[15]May you be blessed by the LORD,
who made heaven and earth!

[16]The heavens are the LORD's heavens,
but the earth he has given to the sons
of men.
[17]The dead do not praise the LORD,
nor do any that go down into silence.
[18]But we will bless the LORD
from this time forth and for evermore.
Praise the LORD!

Overview: We are nothing without God, but when he looks on us we are forgiven and give glory to God alone (Augustine). God can do whatever he pleases because God's power can perfectly accomplish his will (Flugentius). What God made is good in itself but may be abused when put to bad use, such as the making of idols (Tertullian). Whatever God promises to do, he has both the power and the will to keep his promises (Fulgentius). Pagan idols are incapable of doing any of the things their humanlike representations suggest, such as having eyes that cannot see and ears that cannot hear (Athanasius).

People of common rank are blessed by God along with people of greater achievements; it is fitting that heroes of faith should be rightfully honored (Augustine).

We should lay up our treasures in heaven since heaven belongs to God and is a safe place for our treasures (Augustine). Christ's suffering and death can be celebrated only by those who live in him (Athanasius).

115:1 Give Glory to God's Name

We Are Nothing Without God. Augustine: When Jesus was entrusting Peter with his sheep, he was entrusting him with us. When he was entrusting Peter with us, he was entrusting the church with his members. So, Lord, entrust your church to your church, let your church entrust itself to you. After all, we say, "Not to us, Lord, not to us, but to your name give the glory." I mean, what are we without you? Only Peter when he denied you three times. To show up Peter to himself, that is to show up Peter to Peter, the Lord turned his face away from him for a while—and Peter denied him. He turned his face toward him when he looked around—and he wept. Peter washed away his fault with his tears; he poured water from his eyes and baptized his conscience. Sermon 229p.4.[1]

115:3-8 The True God Versus Idols

God Does Whatever He Pleases. Fulgentius of Ruspe: Therefore, there is no falseness in God's promises because for the all-powerful there is no problem about doing things. And so the effects of the will are never lacking because the will itself is nothing other than power. Whatever God wills, he can do; he can do as much as he wishes.

So it is rightly said of him alone, "He does whatever he pleases." And again, "For you have power to act whenever you choose."[2] So we have said that there is as much power of will there as there is will itself for the power. Since for the one to whom it is subject, when he shall will, he can, willing being nothing other than power. Letter to Monimus 1.12.4-5.[3]

The Reality of the True God. Athanasius: But this[4] all inspired Scripture also teaches more plainly and with more authority, so that we in our turn write boldly to you as we do, and you, if you refer to Scripture, will be able to verify what we say. For an argument when confirmed by higher authority is irresistibly proved. From the first then the divine Word firmly taught the Jewish people about the abolition of idols when it said, "You shall not make for yourself a graven image or the likeness of anything that is in the heaven above or in the earth beneath."[5] But the cause of their abolition another writer declares, saying, "The idols of the heathen are silver and gold, the works of human hands; they have a mouth and will not speak, they have eyes and will not see, they have ears and will not hear, they have noses and will not smell, they have hands and will not handle, they have feet and will not walk." Nor has it passed over in silence the doctrine of creation; but, knowing well its beauty, lest any attending solely to this beauty should worship things as if they were gods, instead of God's

---

[1]*WSA* 3 6:329*. [2]Wis 12:18. [3]FC 95:204*. [4]Athanasius was just asserting that the Word [the Son] is from the Father and that if a person knows the Son, he also knows the Father. [5]Ex 20:4.

works, it teaches people firmly beforehand when it says, "And do not, when you look up with your eyes and see the sun and moon and all the host of heaven, go astray and worship them, which the Lord your God has given to all nations under heaven."[6] But he gave them, not to be their gods but that by their agency the Gentiles should know, as we have said, God the Maker of them all. Against the Heathen 45.2-3.[7]

115:13 God Blesses All Who Fear Him

God Will Bless the Little with the Great. Augustine: So then, let us celebrate their feasts,[8] as indeed we are doing, with the utmost devotion, soberly cheerful, gathered in a holy assembly, thinking faithful thoughts, confidently proclaiming their sanctity. It is no small part of imitation to rejoice together in the virtues of those who are better than we are. They are great, we are little; but "the Lord has blessed the little with the great." They have gone ahead of us, they tower over us like giants. If we are not capable of following them in action, let us follow in affection; if not in glory, then certainly in joy and gladness; if not in merit, then in desire; if not in suffering, then in fellow feeling; if not in excellence, then in our close relationship with them. Sermon 280.6.[9]

115:16-18 The Heavens Belong to God

The Heavens Are the Lord's. Augustine: Because the Lord insists that our heart be cleansed, he therefore goes further and gives a command, saying, "Do not collect treasure on earth, where the moth and corrosion destroy, and where thieves dig up and steal; but lay up for yourselves treasures in heaven, where neither moth nor corrosion destroys, nor thieves dig up and steal. For where your treasure is, there your heart also will be."[10] Now, if a person does something with the intention of gaining earthly profit, his heart is on the earth. And how can a heart be clean while it is wallowing on the earth? On the other hand, if it is in heaven it will be clean, for whatsoever things are heavenly are clean. A thing becomes defiled if it is mixed with a baser substance, even though that other substance is not vile in its own nature; for instance, gold is debased by pure silver if it is mixed with it. So also is our mind defiled by a desire for the things of earth, although the earth itself is pure in its own class and in its own order. Let us not think that in this text the word *heaven* signifies the universe of heavenly bodies, for the word *earth* includes every kind of body, and a person ought to disregard the whole world when he is laying up treasure for himself in heaven. Therefore, the reference is to that heaven of which it is said, "The heaven of heaven is the Lord's." Moreover, since we ought to fix our treasure and our heart on that which will abide forever and not on something that will pass away, the heaven here mentioned means the spiritual firmament, for "heaven and earth will pass away." Sermon on the Mount 2.13.44.[11]

The Saints Will Bless the Lord Forever. Athanasius: The festival of Easter does not consist in pleasant conversation at meals, or splendor of clothing or days of leisure but in the acknowledgment of God and the offering of thanksgiving and of praise to him. Now this belongs to the saints alone, who live in Christ; for it is written, "The dead shall not praise you, O Lord, neither all those who go down into silence; but we who live will bless the Lord, from henceforth even forever." So it was with Hezekiah, who was delivered from death and therefore praised God, saying, "Those who are in hades cannot praise you; the dead cannot bless you; but the living shall bless you, as I also do."[12] For to praise and bless God belongs to those only who live in Christ, and by means of

---

[6]Deut 4:19. [7]NPNF 2 4:28*. [8]The feasts commemorating the martyrdom of Perpetua and Felicity. [9]WSA 3 8:75. [10]Mt 6:19-21. [11]FC 11:152-53. [12]Is 38:18-19.

this they go up to the feast; for the Passover is not of the Gentiles or of those who are yet Jews in the flesh but of those who acknowledge the truth in Christ, as he declares who was sent to proclaim such a feast: "Our Passover, Christ, is sacrificed."[13] Festal Letters 7.3.[14]

---

[13]1 Cor 5:7. [14]NPNF 2 4:524*.

116:1-19 PRAISE OF GOD FOR DELIVERANCE FROM DEATH

[1]I love the Lord, because he has heard
  my voice and my supplications.
[2]Because he inclined his ear to me,
  therefore I will call on him as long as I live.
[3]The snares of death encompassed me;
  the pangs of Sheol laid hold on me;
  I suffered distress and anguish.
[4]Then I called on the name of the Lord:
  "O Lord, I beseech thee, save my life!"

[5]Gracious is the Lord and righteous;
  our God is merciful.
[6]The Lord preserves the simple;
  when I was brought low, he saved me.
[7]Return, O my soul, to your rest;
  for the Lord has dealt bountifully with you.
[8]For thou hast delivered my soul from death,
  my eyes from tears,
  my feet from stumbling;
[9]I walk before the Lord
  in the land of the living.
[10]I kept my faith, even when I said,
  "I am greatly afflicted";

[11]I said in my consternation,
  "Men are all a vain hope."

[12]What shall I render to the Lord
  for all his bounty to me?
[13]I will lift up the cup of salvation
  and call on the name of the Lord,
[14]I will pay my vows to the Lord
  in the presence of all his people.
[15]Precious in the sight of the Lord
  is the death of his saints.
[16]O Lord, I am thy servant;
  I am thy servant, the son of thy handmaid.
  Thou hast loosed my bonds.
[17]I will offer to thee the sacrifice of thanksgiving
  and call on the name of the Lord.
[18]I will pay my vows to the Lord
  in the presence of all his people,
[19]in the courts of the house of the Lord,
  in your midst, O Jerusalem.
Praise the Lord!

Overview: The true object of our love should be God, and it is that love that motivates us to endure sufferings and hardships because we know that he will hear our prayer in time of need. God hears our prayers—those that remain unuttered in our hearts and those uttered in ill-fortune as well as in good (Basil). In the severe sorrows and tribulations of life God enables us to overcome them so that we may gain the crown that he gives (Ambrose). The "sorrows of death" and "pride of hell" have been variously interpreted to refer to the pains of childbirth, the separation of soul and body at death, sorrow over great sins and the suffering experienced during penance.

In God judgment and mercy are intertwined, and he measures out his mercy to people no matter how far they have fallen from what they once were, as is evidenced in God seeking fallen Adam in the Garden of Eden. No child could survive the traumatic change of environment at birth unless preserved by God. Each person who finished his life in faith receives an eternal rest not on the basis of his works but as a gift of God's grace.

God blesses the immortal soul of his people at death with release from the body and sin and in the next life with mastery of the soul over the body and possession of heavenly promises (Basil). The soul does not die with the body but lives on free of sin and guilt (Ambrose). Life in heaven, in many ways, will be the opposite of life on earth (Basil). Since the soul is different in nature from the body, it will not die, and, if it fears God, it will experience good things in this life and in the next. Sin, sorrow and death belong to life in this world, but they will not be experienced in heaven (Ambrose).

Prayers and the guidance of the Holy Spirit are necessary in order to understand the truths of God's word (Basil). The main events of Christ's incarnate life have been prophesied by prophets and apostles. Failure to believe what God says results in failure to speak, as in the case of Zachariah. The church's faith remains the same from generation to generation because all generations proclaim the same faith. It is ingratitude not to proclaim the truths God has given us in Scripture. The only way that humans, who by nature

are liars, can tell the truth is to believe God's truth (Augustine). The fact that all people lie shows their need of God's mercy and that truthfulness is ascribed to God alone (Epiphanius). Since "liar" is a synonym for "sinner," David here attests to the universality of sin within humanity and to the fact that the crown of eternal life is a gift not a merit.

The more we love God, the less toilsome a life of faith becomes. Since God has given us everything, we have nothing to give him except a portion of what he has given us. If we give ourselves to the Lord, we are only giving him what he has made (Augustine). We should praise God not only in good fortune but also in times of great difficulty (Theodoret).

God's goodness is manifest in his deliverance of us from all our afflictions (Tertullian). The death of the elect is the beginning of rest, a glorious sleep. God was pleased with the loyalty and willing sacrifice of martyrs whose blood helped end the persecutions (Cyprian). Death is better than life; this is evident in the benefit that the church receives from the death of martyrs (Ambrose). The death of martyrs is grounded in the death of Christ and is proof of their faith. God has not abandoned the bodies of martyrs, but he has preserved them so that they may bring honor to his glory. God gives those who are persecuted the strength to persevere in life and protects them in their transit to the next life. The martyrs gave their lives to spread the gospel—a kind of repayment to God for their salvation. The blood of God's people is made precious by the blood that Christ shed for them (Augustine). Since the blood of saints is precious to God, the enemies of the church cannot destroy it (Leo). When we die to sin and all manner of evil, we put to death sin and a multitude of vices (Leo). Martyrs give a more powerful witness when dead than when alive (Augustine).

People are God's servants and children in a different sense than Christ is (Athanasius). Christ became a servant by assuming a complete human nature and by experiencing its weaknesses (AMBROSE). The love of temporal life and wealth leads to a loss of eternal life and riches. Only God can enable us to free ourselves from the shackles that prevent us from following him (AUGUSTINE). Once God has freed us from bondage to sin and we become certain of our salvation, it is our obligation to worship him (CAESARIUS). If God had not saved us from the temptations of the flesh, our souls would dwell in hell (CASSIAN). Humankind's sacrifice of praise will be completed when we enter into eternal life (AMBROSE). When God unfetters us from the things of this world, we become sure of our eternal salvation (AUGUSTINE).

116:1-4 Pray to the Lord

THE LORD WILL HEAR MY PRAYER. BASIL THE GREAT: "I have loved," the psalmist says, "because the Lord will hear the voice of my prayer." It is not in the power of everyone to say "I have loved," but of him who is already perfect and beyond the fear of slavery and who has been formed in the spirit of adoption as children. He does not add to "I have loved" the word *someone*, but we supply in thought "the God of the universe." For, that which is properly beloved is God, since they define "beloved" as that at which all things aim. Now, God is a good and the first and most perfect of good things. Therefore, I have loved God, who is the highest of objects to be desired, and I have received with joy sufferings for his sake. What these things are, the psalmist goes through in detail a little later—the pangs of death, the dangers of hell, the affliction, the pain, all things whatsoever that are desirable to him because of the love of God—and he demonstrates the hope that was stored up for those who receive sufferings because of their devoutness. For I did not endure the contests, he says, contrary to my will or by force or constraint, but I accepted the sufferings with a certain love and affection, so that I was able to say, "Because for your sake we are killed all the day long."[1] And these words

seem to have equal weight with the words of the apostle and to be spoken by him with the same feeling: "Who shall separate us from the love of Christ? Shall tribulation, or distress, or persecution, or hunger, or nakedness, or danger or the sword?"[2] Therefore, I have loved all these things, knowing that I endure the dangers for the sake of piety under the hands of the Lord of the universe who sees and bestows the reward. "Because the Lord will hear the voice of my prayer." So, each one of us is able to perform the difficult tasks enjoined by the commandments whenever he displays his conduct of life to the God of the universe as if to a spectator. HOMILIES ON THE PSALMS 22.[3]

I WILL CALL ON THE LORD. BASIL THE GREAT: "Because he has inclined his ear to me." "He inclined," he said, not that you might take some corporeal notion about God having ears and inclining them to a gentle voice, as we do, putting our ear close to those who speak low, so that by the nearness we may perceive what is said. But he said, "he inclined," in order that he might point out to us his own weakness. Because through kindness God came down to me while I was lying on the ground, as if, when some sick person is not able to speak clearly because of his great weakness, a kind physician, bringing his ear close, should learn through the nearness what was necessary for the sick person. Therefore, "He has inclined his ear to me." The divine ear, indeed, does not need a voice for perception; it knows how to recognize in the movements of the heart what is sought. Or, do you not hear how Moses, although he said nothing but met the Lord with his inexpressible groanings, was heard by the Lord, who said, "Why do you cry to me?"[4] God knows how to hear even the blood of a just person,[5] to which no tongue is attached and of which no voice pierces the air. The presence of good works is a loud voice before God.

"And in my days I will call on him."[6] If we have

---

[1]Ps 44:22 (43:22 LXX). [2]Rom 8:35. [3]FC 46:351-52*. [4]Ex 14:15. [5]See Gen 4:10. [6]Ps 116:2 (114:2 LXX).

prayed on one day, or if in one hour for a brief time we were saddened by our sins, we are carefree as if we had already made some compensation for our wickedness. However, the holy person says that he is disclosing his confession, which is measured by the whole time of his life, for he says, "In all my days I will call on him." Then, in order that you may not think that he called on God because he was fortunate in this life and because all his affairs were successful, he describes in detail the magnitude and difficulty of the circumstances in which, when he was involved, he did not forget the name of God. HOMILIES ON THE PSALMS 22.[7]

THE SORROWS OF DEATH OVERCOME ME.

AMBROSE: Do you hear him [the psalmist] saying, "The sorrows of death have compassed me"? "Still, I have loved the Lord even in the sorrows of death. The perils of hell have found me, not fearing indeed, but loving, but hoping, because no distress, no persecution, no dangers, no sword shall separate me from Christ."[8] Therefore, he accepted tribulation and sorrow willingly, knowing that "suffering produces endurance, and endurance produces character, and character produces hope."[9] As a good athlete, he sought the contest that he might gain the crown, but he knew that this was given to him not through his own strength but by the aid of God. He could not have been victorious had he not called on him who helps contenders. ON THE DEATH OF THEODOSIUS 23.[10]

TROUBLE AND SORROW ARE EXPERIENCED IN MANY DIFFERENT WAYS.

BASIL THE GREAT: "The sorrows of death," he says, "have compassed me; and the perils of hell have found me." Properly the sorrows of death have been agreed on as the pains of childbirth, when the womb, distended with its burden, thrusts out the fetus; then, the generative parts, being compressed and stretched around the fetus by spasms and contractions of the muscles, produce in the mothers the sharpest pains and most bitter pangs. He

transferred the name of these pains to those that besiege the animal in the division of soul and body at death. He says that he has suffered nothing moderately but that he has been tried even to the sorrows of death and has arrived at the peril of the descent into hell. Now, did he endure only these things for which he is exalted, or did he endure these things frequently and unwillingly? Nothing that is forced is praiseworthy. But, look at the nobility of nature of the athlete. When the sorrows of death compassed me and the perils of hell found me, I was so far from succumbing to these trials that I willingly proposed to myself even much greater trials than these. Trouble and sorrow, I, as it were, willingly devised for myself; I was not unwillingly seized by them.

Indeed, in the preceding words we read, "The perils of hell have found me," but here, "I met with trouble and sorrow." For, since I was found to be unyielding there in regard to what was brought on by the tempter, in order that I might show the abundance of my love toward God, I added trouble to trouble and sorrow to sorrow, and I did not rise up against these sufferings by my own power, but I called upon the name of the Lord. Such is also the declaration of the apostle, who says, "But in all these things we overcome because of him who has loved us."[11] For he conquers who does not yield to those who lead on by force, but he is more than conqueror, who voluntarily invites sorrows for a demonstration of his endurance. Let him who was in some sin to death[12] say, "The sorrows of death have compassed me." "For everyone," he says, "who commits sin has been born of the devil."[13] Now, when I, he says, committed sin and was pregnant by death, then also I was found by the perils of hell. How, then, did I cure myself? Because I devised trouble and sorrow through penance. I contrived for myself a suffering of penance proportionate to the greatness of the sin, and thus I dared to call on the name of the Lord. But, what was it that I

---

[7]FC 46:352-53*. [8]See also Rom 8:35. [9]Rom 5:3. [10]FC 22:317*. [11]Rom 8:37. [12]See 1 Jn 5:17. [13]1 Jn 3:8.

said? "O Lord, deliver my soul." I am held in this captivity, so you give ransom for me and deliver my soul. HOMILIES ON THE PSALMS 22.[14]

116:5-6 God Is Gracious, Righteous and Merciful

IN GOD MERCY AND JUSTICE ARE INTERTWINED. BASIL THE GREAT: "The Lord is merciful and just." Everywhere Scripture joins justice with the mercy of God, teaching us that neither the mercy of God is without judgment nor his judgment without mercy. Even while he pities, he measures out his mercies judiciously to the worthy; and while judging, he brings forth the judgment, having regard to our weakness, repaying us with kindness rather than with equal reciprocal measurement.

"And our God shows mercy." Mercy is an emotion experienced toward those who have been reduced beyond their desert and that arises in those sympathetically disposed. We pity the person who has fallen from great riches into the uttermost poverty, one who has been overthrown from the peak of vigor of body to extreme weakness, one who gloried in the beauty and grace of body and who has been destroyed by most shameful passions. Though we at one time were held in glory, living in paradise, yet we have become inglorious and humble because of our banishment; "our God shows mercy," seeing what sort of people we have become from what we were. For this reason he summoned Adam with a voice of mercy, saying, "Adam, where are you?"[15] He who knows all things was not seeking to be informed, but he wished to perceive what sort Adam had become from what he had been. "Where are you?" instead of "to what sort of a ruin have you descended from so great a height?" HOMILIES ON THE PSALMS 22.[16]

GOD PRESERVES THE CHILD AT BIRTH. BASIL THE GREAT: "The Lord is the keeper of little ones; I was humbled, and he delivered me." According to natural reason human nature would

not stand unless the little ones and those still infants were kept by the Lord. For, unless it was preserved by the custody of God, how could the fetus in the mother be nourished or moved while it was in such narrow spaces, with no room for turning, and while it lived in dark and moist places, unable to take a breath or to live the life of people, but, on the contrary, was borne around in liquids like the fish? And how would it last even for a short time after it had come out into this unaccustomed place and, lacking the warmth within the mother, had become chilled all over by the air, unless it was preserved by God? Therefore, "the Lord is the keeper of little ones; I was humbled, and he delivered me." Or, you may understand these words thus. When I was turned and became as a little child and received the kingdom of heaven as a child and through innocence brought myself down to the humility of children,[17] "the Lord, the keeper of little ones," since I was humbled, "delivered me." HOMILIES ON THE PSALMS 22.[18]

116:7-9 God Has Delivered My Soul from Death

ETERNAL REST. BASIL THE GREAT: "Turn, O my soul, into your rest: for the Lord has been bountiful to you." The brave contestant applies to himself the consoling words, very much like Paul, when he says, "I have fought the good fight, I have finished the course, I have kept the faith. For the rest, there is laid up for me a crown of justice."[19] These things the prophet also says to himself: Since you have fulfilled sufficiently the course of this life, turn henceforth into your rest, "for the Lord has been bountiful to you." For eternal rest lies before those who have struggled through the present life observant of the laws, a rest not given in payment for a debt owed for their works but provided as a grace of the munificent God for those who have hoped in him. Then,

---

[14]FC 46:353-55*. [15]Gen 3:9. [16]FC 46:355-56*. [17]See Mt 18:3-4. [18]FC 46:356*. [19]2 Tim 4:7-8.

before he describes the good things there, telling in detail the escape from the troubles of the world, he gives thanks for them to the Liberator of souls, who has delivered him from the varied and inexorable slavery of the passions. HOMILIES ON THE PSALMS 22.[20]

THE LORD KEPT ME FROM FALLING. AMBROSE: For it is clear that the soul does not die with the body, because it is not of the body. And that it is not of the body Scripture teaches us in many ways. For Adam received the breath of life from the Lord God "and became a living soul,"[21] and David says, "Turn, O my soul, into your rest, for the Lord has been good to me." And learn the nature of God's goodness: "For he has freed my feet from falling." You see that David rejoices in the remedy of such a death, because an end has been put to error, because guilt has perished but not nature. And so he says, as if liberated and free, "I shall please the Lord in the land of the living." For that[22] is the land. . . . Further, he says that the land of the living is that resting place of souls,[23] where sins do not enter in and where the glory of the virtues lives. Now that land is filled with the dead, because it is filled with sinners, and it was rightly said, "Leave the dead to bury their own dead."[24] But likewise he also said above, "His soul shall dwell in good things, and his seed shall inherit the land";[25] that is, the soul of one who fears God will dwell in good things, so that it is always in them and in conformity with them. The passage can also be taken to refer to one who is in the body, so that he too, if he fears God, dwells in good things and is in heavenly things, for he possesses his body and enjoys mastery over it as if it had been reduced to slavery, and he possesses the inheritance of glory and of the heavenly promises. DEATH AS A GOOD 9.38-39.[26]

HEAVENLY REST COMPARED WITH TEMPORAL THINGS. BASIL THE GREAT: "For he has delivered my soul from death: my eyes from tears, my feet from falling." He describes the future rest by a comparison with things here. Here, he says, the sorrows of death have compassed me, but there he has delivered my soul from death. Here the eyes pour forth tears because of trouble, but there, no longer is there a tear to darken the eyes of those who are rejoicing in the contemplation of the beauty of the glory of God. "For God has wiped away every tear from every face."[27] Here there is much danger of a fall; wherefore, even Paul said, "Let him who thinks he stands take heed lest he fall."[28] But there the steps are firm; life is immutable. No longer is there the danger of slipping into sin. For there is neither rebellion of the flesh nor cooperation of a woman in sin. Therefore, there is no male and female in the resurrection, but there is one certain life, and it is of one kind, since those dwelling in the country of the living are pleasing to their Lord. This world itself is mortal and is the place of mortals. Since the substance of visible things is composite and every composite thing is apt to be destroyed, we who are in the world, being part of the world, necessarily possess the nature of everything. Therefore, even before the soul is separated from the body by death, we people frequently die.[29] HOMILIES ON THE PSALMS 22.[30]

GOD SNATCHED HIS SOUL FROM DEATH. AMBROSE: Theodosius,[31] now at peace, rejoices that he has been snatched away from the cares of this world, and he lifts up his soul and directs it to that great and eternal rest. He declares that he has been admirably cared for, "since God has snatched his soul from death," the death that he frequently withstood in the treacherous conditions of this world, when he was disturbed by the waves of sin. And God has snatched his eyes from tears, for sorrow and sadness and mourning shall flee away.[32] And elsewhere we have, "He shall wipe away every tear from their eyes; and death shall be no more; neither shall there

---

[20]FC 46:356-57*. [21]Gen 2:7. [22]The land of the living. [23]See Ps 27:13 (26:13 LXX, Vg.). [24]Mt 8:22. [25]Ps 25:13 (24:13 LXX, Vg.). [26]FC 65:97-98. [27]Is 25:8. [28]1 Cor 10:12. [29]They die in the sense of the many sorrows and sufferings they experience in life. [30]FC 46:357*. [31]Theodosius I (Roman emperor, 378-395). [32]See Is 51:11.

be mourning or crying or pain."[33] If, then, death will be no more, he cannot suffer a fall when he is in that rest, "but he will please God in the land of the living." For while humankind is here enveloped in a mortal body subject to falls and transgressions, that will not be so there. Therefore, that is the land of the living where the soul is, for the soul has been made to the image and likeness of God; it is not flesh fashioned from earth.[34] Hence, flesh returns to earth, but the soul hastens to celestial rest, and to it is said, "Turn, my soul, to your rest." ON THE DEATH OF THEODOSIUS 30.[35]

116:10-11 Keep the Faith

I HAVE BELIEVED, THEREFORE I HAVE SPOKEN. BASIL THE GREAT: He further commanded them, "Going, teach all nations, baptizing them in the name of the Father and of the Son and of the Holy Spirit."[36] I think that we must by faith grasp and understand each of these words and speak, according as words are granted us in answer to the prayers of all, at the opening of our mouth. It is written, "If you do not believe, you shall not understand,"[37] and also, "I have believed, therefore have I spoken." Now, I am of the opinion that the nouns and verbs and the content of the holy Scriptures do not have as regards God and his Christ or the holy prophets and evangelists and apostles the simple and conventional understanding of them. On the contrary, we should examine the words and content under the guidance of the Holy Spirit and with a pious intention, not all together but by parts, according as each may contribute to the exposition of sound doctrine. We should reflect on them devoutly and direct our thoughts to a consideration of the rules and teachings of the devout life. It is most important that we be observant and attentive to every word and choose the sense that is in keeping with our heavenly calling. This we shall accomplish if, through the prayers of all, Jesus Christ, the only-begotten Son of God, strengthen us, so that the words of the apostle may be realized in us: "I can do all things in Christ who strengthens me."[38] CONCERNING BAPTISM 1.2.[39]

IN THE COMPANY OF THE FAITHFUL. AUGUSTINE: We believe that the Lord Jesus Christ was born of a virgin, came in the flesh, suffered, arose, ascended into heaven; we now believe that all of this has been fulfilled, as you hear words of past time. With us in the company of this faith are also those ancestors who believed that he would be born of a virgin, would suffer, would arise, would ascend into heaven. For the apostle pointed to them when he said, "But having the same spirit of faith, as has been written, 'I have believed and because of this I have spoken,' we also believe, and because of this we also speak."[40] The prophet said, "I have believed, and because of this I have spoken." The apostle says, "We also believe, and because of this we also speak." But, that you may know that the faith is one, hear him saying, "Having the same spirit of faith, we also believe."[41] TRACTATES ON THE GOSPEL OF JOHN 45.9.2.[42]

DISBELIEF RESULTS IN AN INABILITY TO SPEAK. AUGUSTINE: The same angel comes to Mary, announces to her that Christ is going to be born of her in the flesh, and Mary says something of the same kind. Zachariah, you see, had said, "How shall I know this? For I am an old man, and my wife is advanced in years."[43] And he is told, "Behold, you shall be dumb, and you will not be able to speak until the day when these things are fulfilled, because you have not believed my words." And he was given the punishment of dumbness, earned by his unbelief. What had the prophet said about John? "The voice of one crying in the desert."[44] Zachariah is dumb, and he is going to beget the voice. It was because he did not believe that he was made speechless; rightly was he struck dumb, until the voice should be born.

---

[33]Rev 21:4. [34]Gen 1:27; 2:7. [35]FC 22:320-21*. [36]Mt 28:19. [37]Is 7:9. [38]Phil 4:13. [39]FC 9:356-57**. [40]2 Cor 4:13. [41]2 Cor 4:13. [42]FC 88:194. [43]Lk 1:18. [44]Is 40:3.

After all, if it rightly says, or rather because it certainly does rightly say in the holy psalm "I have believed, therefore have I spoken"; then because Zachariah did not believe, he very properly did not speak. SERMON 290.4.[45]

THE SAME FAITH. AUGUSTINE: So it was the same Lord Christ, not only as Word but also as "mediator between God and humanity the man Christ Jesus,"[46] in whom the ancient fathers believed. They also handed on this same faith to us by their proclamation of it and by their prophesying. That is why the apostle says, "Since we have the same spirit of faith, of which it was written: I have believed, therefore have I spoken."[47] So, "having the same spirit of faith," he says, of which it was written by the ancients, "I have believed, therefore have I spoken," "we too believe, therefore we too speak."[48] SERMON 19.3.[49]

WE MUST DECLARE WHAT WE RECEIVE. AUGUSTINE: You see, if there is faith in you, Christ is living in you. You heard the psalm: "I have believed, therefore have I spoken." It was impossible for him both to believe and remain dumb. It is being ungrateful to the one who fills you, if you do not pour out; so the fuller you are, the more you ought to pour out. A fountain, you see, is being born in you of a kind that is able to flow, unable to dry up: "It will become in him a fountain of water leaping up to eternal life."[50] You need have no qualms about preaching, because you are not lying about the fountain of truth; you have received what comes bubbling off your tongue. I mean, if you want to say something of your very own, you will be liars. That is what is said in this very psalm: "I said in my ecstasy, Everyone is a liar." What is "Everyone is a liar?" Every Adam a liar. Strip yourself of Adam, and put on Christ, and you won't be a liar. SERMON 260E.2.[51]

EVERY MAN IS A LIAR. AUGUSTINE: So this is what Scripture wished to demonstrate, that every human being, absolutely every single one pre-

cisely as human, is a liar. You see, what makes us liars is what we have of our own, and all we have of our very own is the capacity to be liars; not that we cannot be true but that we cannot be true in virtue of what we are in ourselves. Therefore, in order to be true, "I believed, wherefore I also spoke." Deprive him of "I believed" —"everyone is a liar." For when he moves away from the truth of God, he will remain in his lying, because whoever "speaks a lie speaks from what is his own."[52] Say therefore, "What shall I give back to the Lord for everything he has given to me?"[53] After all, "it was in my panic that I said"—and what I said was true—"everyone is a liar." But he gave me back not punishment for lying but good for evil, and by justifying the wicked he made of a liar a speaker of the truth. SERMON 28A.1.[54]

TRUTHFULNESS BELONGS TO GOD ALONE. EPIPHANIUS OF SALAMIS: And if we must also comment on the statement, "I said in my ecstasy, Everyone is a liar," its meaning again is different. It is not at all like that of a person who is out of his senses and mentally deranged (God forbid), but of one who is greatly astonished and who thinks with the powers of reason customary to those who see and act in the proper way. For since the prophet was astonished, he also speaks here because of his astonishment. Now the prophets have experienced ecstasy, but not an ecstasy of their powers of reasoning. Peter, for example, experienced ecstasy, not that he did not understand rationally but that he saw phenomena different from the everyday order among people. "For he saw a large piece of cloth being lowered, bound at its four corners, and in it all the four-footed beasts and creeping things and birds of heaven." And notice that the holy Peter understands and was not out of his wits. For when he hears, "Rise, kill, and eat," he did not obey as one not having a sound mind, but he says in the Lord, "By no

---

[45]WSA 3 8:127. [46]1 Tim 2:5. [47]2 Cor 4:13. [48]2 Cor 4:13. [49]WSA 3 1:380. [50]Jn 4:14. [51]WSA 3 7:207. [52]Jn 8:44. [53]Ps 116:12 (115:3 LXX, Vg.). [54]WSA 3 2:115.

means, Lord; for never has anything common or unclean entered my mouth."[55]

And the holy David, too, said, "[I said] Everyone is a liar." But when he said, "I said," he spoke on his own, and he said of people that they lie. He himself, therefore, did not lie, but being amazed and astounded at God's love for humanity and the things that had been announced to him by the Lord, he marveled exceedingly, and when he saw every person in need of God's mercy and recognized that every person is subject to punishment, he ascribed truthfulness to the Lord alone, to make known the true Spirit who spoke in the prophets and revealed to them the depths of the accurate knowledge of God. PANARION 48.7.1-7.[56]

LYING IS SYNONYMOUS WITH SINNING.

AUGUSTINE: Such an individual,[57] then, guards against lying just as against sinning. Sometimes, in fact, the word *lie* is used for the word *sin*; whence the saying "Everyone is a liar." So it was said as the equivalent of "Everyone is a sinner." Similarly: "if through my lie the truth of God has abounded."[58] Thus, when he lies as people do, he sins as people do and will be bound by the judgment that says "Everyone is a liar," and "if we say that we have no sin, we deceive ourselves, and the truth is not in us."[59] But when nothing false proceeds from his mouth, it will be in consequence of that grace about which it has been said, "Whoever is born of God does not commit sin."[60] For if this birth alone were in us, no one would sin; when it alone will be in us, no one will sin. But we now are still failing, because we are born corruptible, although, if we walk well there where we have been reborn, day by day our inner person is being renewed.[61] When this corruptible body also puts on incorruption, life will absorb all, and no sting of death will remain. But the sting of death is sin.[62] AGAINST LYING 20.40.[63]

116:12-13 Return to God a Token of What He Has Given

WE ARE OBLIGED TO LOVE OUR REDEEMER.

AUGUSTINE: I am certainly obliged to love the Redeemer, and I know what he said to Peter: "Peter, do you love me? Feed my sheep."[64] This was said once, said again, said a third time. Love was being questioned and toil commanded, because where the love is greater, the toil is less. "What shall I pay back to the Lord for all that he has paid back for me?" If I say that what I am paying back is my herding his sheep, even here it is "not I who am doing it but the grace of God with me."[65] So when can I be found to be paying him back, since he gets in first every time? And yet, because we love freely, because we are herding his sheep, we look for a reward.

How shall this be? How can "I love freely and that's why I'm herding sheep" be consistent with "I request a reward, because I'm herding sheep"? This could not possibly happen; in no way at all could a reward be sought from one who is loved freely, unless the reward were the very one who is being loved. I mean, if what we are paying back for his having redeemed us is our herding his sheep, what are we paying back for his having made us shepherds? Being bad shepherds, you see—which God preserve us from—is something we are by our own badness; whereas good shepherds—which God grant we may be—is something we can be only by his grace. SERMON 340.2.[66]

THROUGH HIS PROMISES GOD BECOMES OUR

DEBTOR. AUGUSTINE: So let us praise the Lord, brothers and sisters, because we are holding his trustworthy promises, though we have not yet received the things promised. Do you imagine it is not enough to hold him to his promises and that we should be demanding the payment of his debts? By making promises, God has become our debtor. It is out of his goodness, not our rights,

---

[55]Acts 10:10-14. [56]MOT 37-39*. [57]A righteous person; see Prov 29:17. [58]Rom 3:7. [59]1 Jn 1:8. [60]1 Jn 3:9. [61]See 2 Cor 4:16. [62]See 1 Cor 15:53-56. [63]FC 16:177-78**. [64]Jn 21:16. [65]1 Cor 15:10. [66]WSA 3 9:293.

that he has become a debtor. What have we ever given him, that we should be able to hold him in our debt? Or perhaps because you heard in the psalm, "What shall I render to the Lord?" First of all, when he says, "What shall I render to the Lord?" they are the words of a debtor, not of someone demanding repayment of a debt. Something had been advanced to him. "What shall I render the Lord?" What is "What shall I render?" What shall I pay back? What for? "For all the things he has rendered to me." What has he rendered to me? To begin with, I was nothing, and he made me; I had gotten lost, and he looked for me; looked for me and found me; I was a captive, and he redeemed me; having bought me, he set me free; from a slave he made me into a brother. "What shall I render to the Lord?" You haven't got anything you can tender.

When you look for absolutely everything from him, what have you got that you can render to him? But wait. There is something or other the psalmist wants to say, when he asks, "What shall I render to the Lord for all the things he has rendered to me?" He looks around everywhere for something he can tender, pay back, and he seems to find it. What does he find? "I will take the cup of salvation." Even though you were thinking of paying something back, you are still looking for something to take. Look here, please. If you are still looking for something to take, you will still be a debtor. When are you going to be a someone who pays back? So if you are always going to be a debtor, when will you ever pay back? You won't find anything you can pay back; you won't have anything apart from what he has given. SERMON 254.6.[67]

ALL THE THINGS GOD HAS DONE FOR US. AUGUSTINE: Christ loved you before you existed; he created you; he predestined you before the foundation of the world; once created through the agency of your father and mother, he has reared you. It is not your parents, you see, who made you, though they hand on to you their family characteristics. He loved you, he created you,

he reared you, he gave himself up for you, he listened to insults for you, he endured wounds for you, he redeemed you with his blood. Aren't you overwhelmed, and won't you say, "What shall I give back to the Lord for all that he has given to me?" What will you give back to the Lord for all that he has given to you? Listen to his saying, "Whoever has loved father or mother more than me is not worthy of me."[68] Listen to him saying it, fear the menace contained in it, love the promise implied in it.

What have you given back to the Lord for all that he has given to you? So, all right, you have already given something back, eh? Well, *what* have you given back? Have you saved him as he has saved you? Have you opened up eternal life for him, as he has done for you? Have you created him, as he did you? Did you make him the Lord as he made you a person? Have you given anything back to him that does not come back to you? If you look frankly at the truth of the matter, you have not given him anything. . . . "For what do you have that you have not received?"[69] Why don't you find something you can give back to the Lord? Give him back yourself, give him back what he has made. Give him back yourself, not what is yours, his creation, not your perversion. SERMON 65A.12.[70]

GRATEFUL IN ALL CONDITIONS OF LIFE. THEODORET OF CYR: For it is absurd, the height of stupidity, no, of extreme insanity, for those only to sing the praises of the pilot who ride the rough waves and are borne on the breakers and who pass their lives in great misfortune, while those who are situated outside the range of fire, as the proverb has it, being spectators rather than contestants, hurl their blasphemous taunts at the ringmaster when they cannot pelt him literally. That those who cultivate virtue praise the God of the universe not merely when they are borne on favorable winds, but even when they are struggling with billow and storm, can be perceived

---

[67]WSA 3 7:155*. [68]Mt 10:37. [69]1 Cor 4:7. [70]WSA 3 3:205.

from the exclamation of the blessed David, a man who spent a lifetime in warfare and struggle with countless misfortunes: "What shall I render to the Lord for all the things that he has rendered to me?" ON DIVINE PROVIDENCE 10.7.[71]

116:15 Precious Is the Death of God's Saints

ABUNDANT PROOF OF GOD'S GOODNESS. TERTULLIAN: "For the eyes of the Lord are on those who fear him, on those who hope in his mercy, to deliver their souls from death," even eternal death, "and to nourish them in their hunger," that is, after eternal life.[72] "Many are the afflictions of the righteous, but the Lord delivers them out of them all."[73] "Precious in the sight of the Lord is the death of his saints." "The Lord keeps all their bones; not one of them shall be broken."[74] The Lord will redeem the souls of his servants. We have adduced these few quotations from a mass of the Creator's Scriptures; and no more, I suppose, are needed to prove him to be a most good God, for they sufficiently indicate both the precepts of his goodness and the firstfruits of it. AGAINST MARCION 2.19.[75]

DEATH IS THE PRICE OF IMMORTALITY. CYPRIAN: Oh, what was that spectacle of the Lord, how sublime, how exalted, how acceptable to the eyes of God in the solemn pledge and devotion of his army,[76] as it is written in the Psalms when the Holy Spirit speaks to us likewise and warns, "Precious in the sight of God is the death of his faithful ones"! This death that has bought immortality at the price of its blood, that has received the crown from the consummation of its valor, is precious. LETTER 10.2.[77]

THE FRUITS OF INEXTINGUISHABLE FAITH. CYPRIAN: There they stood, victims of torture yet stronger than their tormentors. Their battered and lacerated limbs overcome the "claws" that tore and ripped at them. The savage, oft-repeated lashes could not defeat the martyrs' inextinguishable faith, though once their entrails were prized

apart it was not the limbs of God's servants but their open wounds that were racked. It was as though their blood flowed to extinguish the fires of the persecution, to damp down the flames and burning coals of hell with its glorious streams. O what a marvelous sight it was before the Lord, how sublime, how precious! How welcome a sight to God's eyes is the allegiance and self-offering of his legionaries! So it is written in the Psalms, when the Holy Spirit speaks likewise reminding us, "How precious in the sight of the Lord is the death of his just." LETTER 8.[78]

DEATH IS BETTER THAN LIFE. AMBROSE: By the death of the martyrs, religion has been defended, the faith spread and the church strengthened. The dead have been victorious, and the persecutors have been vanquished. Accordingly, we celebrate the deaths of those of whose lives we know nothing. So, too, David in prophecy rejoiced at the departure of his own soul, saying, "Precious in the sight of the Lord is the death of the saints." He held death in more esteem than life. The death itself of the martyrs is the prize of life. Furthermore, even the hatreds of enemies are dissolved by death. ON HIS BROTHER SATYRUS 2.45.[79]

THE GLORIOUS DEEDS OF MARTYRS. AUGUSTINE: Through such glorious deeds of the holy martyrs, with which the church blossoms everywhere, we prove with our own eyes how true what we have just been singing is, that "precious in the sight of the Lord is the death of his saints"; seeing that it is precious both in our sight and in the sight of him for the sake of whose name it was undertaken. But the price of these deaths is the death of one man. How many deaths were bought by one dying man, who was the grain of wheat that would not have been multiplied if he had not

---

[71]ACW 49:137*. [72]Ps 33:18-19 (32:18-19 LXX, Vg.), slightly altered. [73]Ps 34:19 (33:20 LXX, Vg.). [74]Ps 34:20 (33:21 LXX, Vg.). [75]ANF 3:312**. [76]The army of martyrs who suffer for their faith. [77]FC 51:25-26. [78]MFC 17:128. [79]FC 22:215.

died! You heard his words when he was drawing near to his passion, that is, when he was drawing near to our redemption: "Unless the grain of wheat falls into the ground and dies, it remains alone; but if it dies, it bears much fruit."[80]

On the cross, you see, he transacted a grand exchange; it was there that the purse containing our price was untied; when his side was laid open by the lance of the executioner, there poured out from it the price of the whole wide world. The faithful were bought and the martyrs; but the faith of the martyrs has been proved; blood is the witness to it. They have paid back what was spent for them, and they have fulfilled what John says: "Just as Christ laid down his life for us, so we too should lay down our lives for the brothers."[81] And in another place it says, "You have sat down at a great table; consider carefully what is set before you, since it behooves you to prepare the same kind of things yourself."[82] It is certainly a great table, where the lord of the table is himself the banquet. Nobody feeds his guests on himself; that is what the Lord Christ did, being himself the host, himself the food and drink. So the martyrs recognized what they ate and drank, so that they could give back the same kind of thing. SERMON 329.1[83]

THE GRAVES OF MARTYRS. AUGUSTINE: The Lord, though, bears striking witness to his witnesses [martyrs], when after stiffening their hearts for the struggle, he does not abandon their bodies once they are dead, like the outstanding miracle he performed over the body of blessed Vincent.[84] The enemy desired and took all necessary steps to ensure that the body should completely disappear; but a divine sign gave its whereabouts away and revealed it for religious burial and veneration so promptly that it would continue as a lasting memorial to the victory of piety and impiety's defeat. Indeed, "how precious in the sight of the Lord must be the death of his saints," when not even the earth of the flesh is ignored after the life has gone out of it; and when, as the invisible soul withdraws from its visible

home, this dwelling of his servant is preserved by the Lord's care and honored for the Lord's glory by his faithful fellow servants. SERMON 275.3.[85]

MARTYRS CONQUER IN LIFE AND IN DEATH. AUGUSTINE: So Vincent vanquished Dacian[86] while he lived; he vanquished him also when he was dead. Living he trampled on the torments, dead he swam across the sea. But the one who guided and steered the lifeless corpse through the waves was the same one who had granted him an invincible spirit among the torturer's iron claws. The torturer's flames did not intimidate his heart, the waters of the sea did not sink his body. But all these things occurred just to show that "precious in the sight of the Lord is the death of his saints." To this glory may the Lord bring us too under his protection, whose is the honor and the empire for ever and ever. SERMON 276.4.[87]

THE BLOOD OF CHRIST AND THE BLOOD OF MARTYRS COMPARED. AUGUSTINE: But the truth was revealed to the man[88] who pointed out the things that were discovered. The place,[89] you see, was indicated by preceding signs; and it was discovered to be just as it had been revealed in them. Many people received relics from there, because that was God's will, and they came as far as here.[90] So both this place and this day is being commended to your graces'[91] devotion; each is to be celebrated to the honor of God,

---

[80]Jn 12:24. [81]1 Jn 3:16. [82]Prov 23:1-2 (LXX). [83]WSA 3 9:182*. [84]Vincent was a deacon in Saragossa, Spain, who was martyred in Valencia in 303, by the Spanish governor Dacian during the Diocletian persecution. According to reports his flesh was pierced with iron hooks, roasted on a gridiron, thrown into a dungeon strewn with broken pottery. His lifeless body was disposed of at sea, weighed down with a heavy rock; however, it did not sink but floated back to shore and was buried by fellow Christians. The commemoration of his birthday was the occasion for this sermon. [85]WSA 3 8:27-28. [86]See footnote on Vincent in previous entry. [87]WSA 3 8:31*. [88]Lucianus, a priest from Palestine who supposedly discovered the bones of Stephen, the church's first martyr, about twenty miles from Jerusalem in the December 415. Augustine acquired a few of Stephen's relics in 424 for his church in Hippo Rhegius, where an annex was added to the main basilica as a memorial chapel. [89]Palestine. [90]Hippo Rhegius. [91]The audience that Augustine is addressing in the sermon.

whom Stephen confessed. After all, we have not built an altar in this place to Stephen, but an altar to God from Stephen's relics. Altars of this kind are pleasing to God. You ask why? Because "precious in the sight of the Lord is the death of his saints." Those who shed their blood for their Redeemer were redeemed by his blood. He shed his as the redemptive price of their salvation; the martyrs shed theirs as a means of spreading his gospel. They gave him something in exchange, but not from their own resources; their ability to do so, after all, was his gift; and for that to be done that could be done by them was his gift. As a mark of his favor, he proved them with the occasion of their martyrdom. It happened, they suffered, they trampled on the world. SERMON 318.1.[92]

CHRIST'S BLOOD MAKES OUR BLOOD PRECIOUS.

AUGUSTINE: Yet he himself also made precious the blood of his people for whom he gave the price of his blood; for if he did not make precious the blood of his people, it would not be said, "Precious in the sight of the Lord is the death of his saints."[93] And so also in regard to what Jesus says, "The good shepherd lays down his life for his sheep."[94] He is not the only one who did this; and yet, if those who did [so] are Christ's members, he himself alone likewise did this. For he could do [something] without them, but how could they do [anything] without him since he himself said, "Without me you can do nothing"?[95] From this we show, however, what the others also did: because John the apostle himself, who preached this Gospel that you have heard, said in his epistle, "As Christ laid down his life for us, so we, too, ought to lay down our lives for our brothers."[96] "We ought to," he said; he who first showed the way made us debtors. Therefore in a certain place it has been written, "If you sit to dine at the table of the ruler, wisely understand what is set before you. And put forth your hand, knowing that you ought to prepare such things."[97] You know what the table of the ruler is; thereupon is the body and blood of

Christ. He who approaches such a table, let him prepare such things. What is, let him prepare such things? "As he laid down his life for us, so we, too, ought," for edifying the people and defending the faith, "to lay down our lives for our brothers." TRACTATES ON THE GOSPEL OF JOHN 47.2.2.[98]

PERSECUTION CANNOT DESTROY A RELIGION BUILT ON THE MYSTERY OF THE CROSS.

LEO THE GREAT: Your[99] blessed co-apostle, Paul, "vessel of election" and special teacher of the nations, coming to this city, was your associate at that time when all innocence, all honor, all liberty was suffering under the will of Nero. Nero's rage, inflamed by an excess of all vices, in this time drove him up to such a flood of insanity that he was the first to bring on the honor of a general persecution for the name of Christian. He seemed to think that the grace of God might be cut off through the slaughter of God's holy ones. Nero did not know that the religion founded on the mystery of the cross cannot be extinguished by any kind of cruelty, since "precious in the sight of the Lord is the death of his saints." This does not diminish, but it increases, the church. As if the grace of God could be blotted out by the slaughter of his holy ones, for whom it was the greatest profit that the contempt of this failing life brought the knowledge of eternal happiness. Therefore this failing life brought the knowledge of eternal happiness. Therefore "precious in the sight of the Lord is the death of his saints." SERMON 82.6.[100]

THE DEATH OF MARTYRS WAS A MANY-SIDED VICTORY.

LEO THE GREAT: Renounce pleasure, turn away from uncleanness, dispel luxury, flee unrighteousness, resist falsehood. When you see that you are waging a battle on many fronts, then you must also, in imitation of the

---

[92]WSA 3 9:147*. [93]Ps 115:15 (116:6 LXX, Vg.). [94]Jn 10:11. [95]Jn 15:5. [96]1 Jn 3:16. [97]Prov 23:1-2 (LXX). [98]FC 88:213-14. [99]Peter. The sermon was preached on the feast of Peter and Paul. [100]FC 93:355*.

martyrs, pursue a many-sided victory. Every time we die to sins, the sins die in us, and this "death of his holy ones is precious in the sight of the Lord," because a "human being" dies "to the world" not by the destruction of senses but by the death of vices. SERMON 84B.2.[101]

THE SEED OF THE CHURCH. AUGUSTINE: The earth has been filled with the blood of the martyrs as with seed, and from that seed have sprung the crops of the church. They have asserted Christ's cause more effectively when dead than when they were alive. They assert it today, they preach him today; their tongues are silent, their deeds echo round the world. They were arrested, bound, imprisoned, brought to trial, tortured, burned at the stake, stoned to death, run through, fed to wild beasts. In all their kinds of death they were jeered at as worthless, but "precious in the sight of the Lord is the death of his saints." SERMON 286.3.[102]

116:16-17 A Servant of the Lord

SERVANT AND SON OF GOD. ATHANASIUS: When we read this,[103] we correctly understand that Solomon was a natural and genuine son and do not consider him a servant just because we hear him so called. So also concerning the Savior, who is confessed to be in truth the Son and to be the Word by nature, as the saints say, "Who was faithful to him that made him," or if he says of himself, "The Lord created me," and, "I am your servant and the Son of your handmaid," and similar claims. Let no one on this account deny that he is the true Son of the Father and from him. As in the case of Solomon and David, let them have a correct understanding of the Father and the Son. DISCOURSES AGAINST THE ARIANS 2.14.4.[104]

THE SERVANTHOOD OF CHRIST. AMBROSE: Learn, then, what this means: "He took on himself the form of a servant." It means that Christ took on himself all the perfections of humanity in

their completeness and obedience in its completeness. And so it says in the thirtieth psalm, "You have set my feet in a large room. I am made a reproach above all mine enemies. Make your face to shine on your servant."[105] "Servant" means the Man in whom he was sanctified; it means the Man in whom he was anointed; it means the Man in whom he was made under the law, made of the Virgin; and, to put it briefly, it means the Man in whose person he has a mother, as it is written: "O Lord, I am your servant, I am your servant and the son of your handmaid"; and again: "I am cast down and deeply humbled."[106] ON THE CHRISTIAN FAITH 5.8.108.[107]

LIVE FOR ETERNITY. AUGUSTINE: He [the psalmist] must not give into his panic; in his panic he is likely to be mistaken. And while he was trembling with fear, he was given courage, where he said, "O Lord, I am your servant and the son of your maidservant; you have burst my chains asunder." My biggest chain was the love of staying alive, and therein was the cause of my dying. Many, you see, for love of staying alive, have died eternally. And again, many martyrs, by thinking nothing of life that has an end, have gained life without end. Just as the person who loves money often disregards money for love of money, so as to gain more money by disregarding money.[108] So we have the dictum of a well-known personage,[109] "On occasion to take no account of money is now and then extremely profitable." And that is what moneylenders do; they amass money by giving it away, as though sowing a little of it in order to reap a large quantity. In the same way, too, the martyrs for love of life disregarded life. By fearing death, they would have died; by wishing to live, they would have refused to live. SERMON 335E.3.[110]

---

[101]FC 93:364*. [102]WSA 3 8:102. [103]References to Solomon as servant by his mother, Bathsheba, and Nathan the prophet (see 1 Kings 1:19, 26). [104]NPNF 2 4:350**. [105]Ps 31:8, 15-16 (30:8, 15-16 LXX, Vg.). [106]Ps 38:8 (37:9 LXX, Vg.). [107]NPNF 2 10:298*. [108]As Augustine explains a little later, moneylenders make money by lending it. [109]His identity is not known. [110]WSA 3 9:235-36.

CHAINED BY THE CARES OF THIS WORLD.
AUGUSTINE: But after the Lord cried out through the Gospel, "Come to me, all you who labor and are burdened, and I will refresh you. Take my yoke on you, and learn from me, for I am meek and humble of heart,"[111] how many, when they heard the Gospel did what the rich man,[112] when he heard it from the Lord's own mouth, did not do? Therefore, let us now do it, let us follow the Lord. Let us loose the shackles by which we are prevented from following. And who is suited to loose such knots, if that one should not help to whom it was said, "You have broken my bonds"? And about him another psalm says, "The Lord releases those that were fettered, the Lord raises up those that were bowed down."[113] TRACTATES ON THE GOSPEL OF JOHN 34.8.[114]

GOD HAS BROKEN OUR CHAINS OF INIQUITY.
CAESARIUS OF ARLES: Our Savior, dearly beloved, has ascended into heaven; therefore let us not be disturbed on earth. Let our spirit be in heaven, and peace will be here. Meanwhile let us ascend with Christ in heart, and when his promised day comes, we shall also follow in body. Nevertheless, we ought to know that pride or avarice or dissipation did not ascend with Christ. No vice of ours ascended with our physician. And for this reason, if we desire to ascend and follow the physician, let us strive here to lay aside our vices and sins. For all of our iniquities surround us as if with chains, and they strive to bind us in the network of our sins. Therefore with God's help, according to what the psalmist says, "Let us break their chains."[115] Then we will be able to say to the Lord with assurance, "You have loosed my bonds, to you will I offer sacrifice of thanksgiving." The resurrection of the Lord is our hope; his ascension is our glory. SERMON 210.1.[116]

SAVED BY GOD'S PROTECTIVENESS. JOHN CASSIAN: And so, whoever attains by way of this love to the image and likeness of God will take delight in the good because of pleasure in the good itself.

Since he likewise possesses a similar disposition of patience and mildness, he will no longer be angered by the vices of sinners. On the contrary, with sorrow and compassion he will beg pardon for their frailty. Remembering that he himself was for a long time assailed by the urges of similar passions until he was saved by the Lord's pity, he will realize that, since he was not freed from assaults of the flesh by his own effort but was saved by the protection of God, it is not wrath but mercy that must be shown to those in error, and he will repeat this verse to God with utter tranquility of heart: "You have broken my chains. To you will I offer a sacrifice of praise." And, "Unless the Lord had helped me, my soul would soon have dwelt in hell."[117] CONFERENCES 11.9.2.[118]

I WILL OFFER SACRIFICE AND PRAISE.
AMBROSE: While we often read that sacrifices were offered by David to the Lord, he adds this passage: "To you I will offer sacrifice of praise." He does not say "I offer sacrifice" but "I will offer sacrifice," meaning that the sacrifice will have been completed when each one stands before the Lord, freed of the chains of this body, and offers himself as a victim of praise. For before death no praise is completed, nor could anyone in this life be praised with final praise, since his later actions are uncertain. Death then is the freeing of the soul from the body. And so we have taught what was written by the apostle: "by far the better to be dissolved and to be with Christ."[119] And what is the effect of that dissolution? The body is released and at rest, while the soul turns to its place of repose and is free; if it is devout, it is going to be with Christ. DEATH AS A GOOD 3.8.[120]

CERTAIN OF SALVATION. AUGUSTINE: My God, let me be thankful as I remember and acknowl-

---

[111]Mt 11:28-29. [112]Mk 10:17-22. [113]Ps 146:7 (145:7 LXX, Vg.). [114]FC 88:67. [115]Ps 2:3. [116]FC 66:93-94. [117]Ps 94:17 (93:17 LXX). [118]ACW 57:415. [119]Phil 1:23. [120]FC 65:75*.

edge all your mercies. Let my whole self be steeped in love of you and all my being cry, "Lord, there is none like you!"[121] "You have broken the chains that bound me; I will sacrifice in your honor." I shall tell how it was that you broke them and, when they hear what I have to tell, all who adore you will exclaim, "Blessed be the Lord in heaven and on earth. Great and wonderful is his name." CONFESSIONS 8.1.[122]

[121]Ps 35:10 (34:10 LXX, Vg.). [122]AC 157.

117:1-2 A HYMN OF PRAISE

[1]*Praise the LORD, all nations!*
     Extol him, all peoples!
[2]*For great is his steadfast love toward us;*

and the faithfulness of the LORD endures
     for ever.
Praise the LORD!

OVERVIEW: God exhorts the entire church to praise him collectively so that none can claim that they were judged unfairly on the last day. We must confess that the Son of God is co-eternal and consubstantial with the Father—to confess less is sacrilege (CASSIODORUS).

117:1-2 Praise the Lord, Who Is Eternal

PRAISE UTTERED IN UNISON. CASSIODORUS: Next comes "And praise him together, all you people." Collective praise is that uttered in unison by all the faithful and is seen to befit the catholic church assembled from different parts of the world. All nations in common are exhorted among the people so that none at the Lord's judgment may claim that they were not included. EXPOSITIONS OF THE PSALMS 116.1.[1]

THE LORD REMAINS FOREVER. CASSIODORUS: He added, "And the truth of the Lord remains forever." The truth of the Lord here means the Son; as he himself says: "I am the way, the truth and the life."[2] In the view of the utterly mad Arian,[3] there was a time—this is a sacrilege to utter—when the Son was not. That means that there would have been a time when the Father was without the Truth, the Way and the Life. But since we must believe that the Father was never without them [the Son and the Holy Spirit], it befits our salvation and truth itself to confess the Son as co-eternal and consubstantial with the Father through all things. EXPOSITIONS OF THE PSALMS 116.2.[4]

[1]ACW 53:160*. [2]Jn 14:6. [3]The Arian heresy taught that the Son was neither co-eternal nor of the same nature or substance with the Father. [4]ACW 53:161.

118:1-18 A HYMN OF THANKSGIVING
FOR DELIVERANCE FROM THE ENEMY

¹*O give thanks to the L*ORD*, for he is good;*
his steadfast love endures for ever!

²*Let Israel say,*
"His steadfast love endures for ever."
³*Let the house of Aaron say,*
"His steadfast love endures for ever."
⁴*Let those who fear the L*ORD *say,*
"His steadfast love endures for ever."

⁵*Out of my distress I called on the L*ORD
*the L*ORD *answered me and set me free.*
⁶*With the L*ORD *on my side I do not fear.*
What can man do to me?
⁷*The L*ORD *is on my side to help me;*
I shall look in triumph on those who
hate me.
⁸*It is better to take refuge in the L*ORD
than to put confidence in man.
⁹*It is better to take refuge in the L*ORD
than to put confidence in princes.

¹⁰*All nations surrounded me;*
*in the name of the L*ORD *I cut them off!*
¹¹*They surrounded me, surrounded me on*
every side;
*in the name of the L*ORD *I cut them off!*
¹²*They surrounded me like bees,*
they blazed ⁱ *like a fire of thorns;*
*in the name of the L*ORD *I cut them off!*
¹³*I was pushed hard,* ʲ *so that I was falling,*
*but the L*ORD *helped me.*
¹⁴*The L*ORD *is my strength and my song;*
he has become my salvation.

¹⁵*Hark, glad songs of victory*
in the tents of the righteous:
*"The right hand of the L*ORD *does valiantly,*
¹⁶*the right hand of the L*ORD *is exalted,*
*the right hand of the L*ORD *does valiantly!"*
¹⁷*I shall not die, but I shall live,*
*and recount the deeds of the L*ORD*.*
¹⁸*The L*ORD *has chastened me sorely,*
but he has not given me over to death.

i Gk: Heb *were extinguished*   j Gk Syr Jerome: Heb *thou didst push me hard*

OVERVIEW: God admonishes and commands us to confess our sins to him because of his goodness (AUGUSTINE).

One who longs for eternal life considers lengthening of life a burden (GREGORY OF NYSSA). Christ, who admonishes us not to fear, himself did not fear death when captured in the garden (ATHANASIUS). Persecutions should not be feared because God is more capable of protecting us than Satan is of assaulting us (CYPRIAN). In the face of temptation and evil thoughts, God will aid the person who weeps in the face of God's goodness (ASCETIC MONKS OF EGYPT). Pastors can serve effectively only if they follow Christ's example of self-denial and of humble station (JEROME). God will ultimately destroy all human dominion and authority (AUGUSTINE). God will watch over us and strengthen us whenever we are oppressed (PACHOMIUS). Strength in the face of all adversity comes from God and from our love for him (AUGUSTINE).

Anthropomorphic descriptions of God are

not to be understood literally but are expressions of the unity that exists in the godhead (AMBROSE). Only the righteous can properly celebrate Easter and proclaim God's marvelous deeds (ATHANASIUS). Eternal life and the resurrection are declared in both Testaments and cannot be denied as they are by many non-Christians (AUGUSTINE). God chastises and educates his people so that they may be delivered from death, and examples provide the most effective lesson. God allows us to experience hardship and suffering so that he may teach us his statutes and judgments (CLEMENT OF ALEXANDRIA). Certain biblical passages offer power and encouragement in the face of temptation. God chastens his people in this life so that they do not suffer the eternal torments of hell (SYNCLETICA).

118:1 God Is Good

CONFESS TO THE LORD BECAUSE HE IS GOOD. AUGUSTINE: We have been admonished to confess to the Lord, and indeed commanded to do so by the Spirit of God. And we have been told the reason for confessing to the Lord: "since he is good." It is said very briefly; it can be thought about very deeply. "Confess to the Lord," he says. And as though we asked him "Why?" the answer comes, "since he is good." What more can you ask for, if you ask for anything, than the good? Such is the power of the good, that the good is what is sought even by the bad. SERMON 29.1.[1]

118:4-5 The Lord Set Me Free

GOD SET ME FREE. GREGORY OF NYSSA: Therefore, if one examines these matters and because of this despises whatever is held in honor among people and longs only for the divine life, knowing that "all flesh is grass and all the glory of people is as the flower of grass,"[2] is he likely to think of grass, which exists today and is gone tomorrow, as something worth striving for? The one who has examined well the divine things

knows that not only human affairs have no stability but also that the whole world itself has not remained forever unchanged. Therefore, he despises this life as alien and impermanent, since "heaven and earth will pass away,"[3] according to the word of the Savior, and all things of necessity undergo a transformation. Therefore, as long as he is "in the tent, burdened"[4] by the present life, as the apostle says to illustrate its impermanence, he laments the lengthening of his stay, as the psalmist says in his divine songs. For they truly live in darkness who spend their life in these quarters. Because of this, the prophet groans over the extension of his sojourn here and says: "Alas, my stay is lengthened." But he attributes the cause of his dejection to darkness, for in Hebrew darkness is equivalent to qedar, as we learn from the scholars. Is it not true that people overcome by some night blindness are thus dim-sighted in recognizing delusions, not knowing that whatever is considered honorable in this life, or even whatever is assumed to be the opposite, is understood thus only on the assumption of the foolish? Of themselves they are never anything at all. ON VIRIGINITY 4.[5]

118:6-7 The Lord Is on My Side

I WILL NOT FEAR. ATHANASIUS: And how should Christ, who said to Abraham, "Fear not, for I am with you," and encouraged Moses against Pharaoh and said to the son of Nun, "Be strong and of a good courage,"[6] himself be terrified before Herod and Pilate? Furthermore, did he who helps others overcome fear (for "the Lord," says Scripture, "is on my side, I will not fear what people shall do to me"), fear governors, who are mortals? Was he who himself encountered death terrified of death? Is it not both unseemly and irreligious to say that he was terrified of death or hades, whom the keepers of the gates of hades saw and shuddered? But if, as you would main-

---

[1]*WSA* 3 2:116. [2]1 Pet 1:24. [3]Mt 24:35. [4]See 2 Cor 5:4. [5]FC 58:23-24. [6]Gen 15:1; 26:24; Ex 4:23; Josh 1:18 (LXX).

tain, the Word was afraid, wherefore, when he spoke long before of the conspiracy of the Jews, did he not flee, no, said when actually sought, "I am he," for he could have avoided death, as he said, "I have power to lay down my life, and I have power to take it again"; and "No one takes it from me."[7] DISCOURSES AGAINST THE ARIANS 3.29.54.[8]

OUR GOD IS MIGHTIER THAN OUR ENEMIES. CYPRIAN: The injuries and punishments of persecutions are not to be feared, because the Lord is greater in protecting than the devil in assaulting. John in his epistle approves, saying, "Greater is he who is in you than he who is in the world."[9] Likewise in Psalm 117 [LXX]: "I shall not fear what people do to me; the Lord is my helper." And again: "Those are strong in chariots, these in horses, but we, in the name of our God. They with their feet bound have fallen, but we are risen up and stand erect."[10] EXHORTATION TO MARTYRDOM 5.10.[11]

GOD IS MY HELPER. DESERT FATHERS: A brother asked an old man, "What shall a man do in every temptation that comes on him and in every thought sent by the enemy?" He replied, "He must weep in the sight of the goodness of God, that he may aid and assist him. For it is written, 'The Lord is with me to help me, and I shall avenge myself upon my foes.'" SAYINGS OF THE EGYPTIAN FATHERS 36.[12]

118:8-9 Take Refuge in the Lord

HOLINESS IS OF GREATER VALUE THAN EARTHLY WEALTH. JEROME: Avoid entertaining people of the world, especially those whose honors make them swell with pride. You are the priest of a crucified Lord who was poor and lived on the bread of strangers. It is a disgrace to you if the consul's lictors or soldiers keep watch before your door and if the governor of the province has a better dinner with you than in his own palace. If you plead as an excuse your wish to intercede

for the unhappy and the oppressed, I reply that a secular magistrate will defer more to a pastor who is self-denying than to one who is rich; he will pay more regard to your holiness than to your wealth. Or if he is a man who will only listen to the clergy over a glass, I will readily forego his aid and will appeal to Christ, who can help more effectively than any judge. Truly "it is better to trust in the Lord than to put confidence in people. It is better to trust in the Lord than to put confidence in princes." LETTER 52.11.[13]

ALL AUTHORITY COMES FROM GOD. AUGUSTINE: Moreover, he will destroy every dominion and authority through the express manifestation of the kingdom of the Father so that all may know that no ruler and no authority, whether they are heavenly or earthly, have possessed any dominion and authority of themselves but by him from whom are all things, not only in respect of their existing but also in respect of their ordering. For in that appearing[14] there will remain no hope for anyone in any ruler or in any person. This is said even now by way of prophecy: "It is good to hope in the Lord rather than to hope in people; it is good to hope in the Lord rather than to hope in princes." Thus, with this meditation, the soul rises up even now to the kingdom of the Father, neither placing much value in the power of anyone besides him, nor, to its own destruction, flattering itself about its own. ON EIGHTY-THREE VARIED QUESTIONS 69.4.[15]

118:11-14 God Is Our Strength and Salvation

WHEN OPPRESSED, TRUST IN GOD'S IMMINENT HELP. PACHOMIUS: When a thought oppresses you, do not be downhearted but put up with it in courage, saying, "They swarmed

---

[7]Jn 18:5; 10:18. [8]NPNF 2 4:423**. [9]1 Jn 4:4. [10]Ps 20:7-8 (19:8-9 LXX, Vg.). [11]FC 36:329. [12]FC 62:24*. These sayings were translated into Latin by Martin of Braga in the sixth century. [13]LCC 5:326. [14]The appearing of the kingdom of God when Christ will show that the Father reigns. [15]FC 70:170.

around me closer and closer, but I drove them back in the name of the Lord." Divine help will arrive at your side immediately, and you will drive them away from you, and courage will compass you round about, and the glory of God will walk with you; and "you will be filled to your soul's desire."[16] For the ways of God are humility of heart and gentleness. It is said indeed, "Whom shall I consider if not the humble and the meek?"[17] If you move ahead in the ways of the Lord, he will watch over you, will give you strength and will fill you with knowledge and wisdom. Your remembrance will remain before him at all times. He will deliver you from the devil, and in your dying day he will grant you his peace. INSTRUCTIONS 9.[18]

THE LORD IS MY STRENGTH. AUGUSTINE: The strength, the fortitude, of Christ's martyrs, men and women alike, is Christ. If men alone, you see, stood out as being brave and strong in suffering, their courage would be attributed to their being the stronger sex. The reason the weaker sex, too, had been able to suffer bravely is that God was able to make it possible in people of all sorts. Accordingly, whether they are men or women, in their tribulations they all ought to say, "The Lord is my strength," and "I will love you, Lord, my might."[19] Love is itself might, or courage; I mean, if you really know how to love, you can endure anything and everything for what you love. And if the lewd kind of love has persuaded lovers to suffer many things bravely for the sake of their frivolities and delinquencies, and if those who set traps for someone else's chastity do not take any danger into consideration, how much braver in the charity of God ought those to be who love him, since neither alive nor dead can they be separated from him! The unchaste lover obviously loses what he loves, if he is killed for the sake of his beloved; but the brave and just lover of God not only does not lose what he has loved because he dies, but in fact by dying he finds what he has loved. Finally, the lover of delinquency is afraid to con-

fess it; the lover of God is afraid to deny him. SERMON 299E.1.[20]

118:16-18 The Right Hand of the Lord

THE LORD HAS DONE MIGHTY THINGS. AMBROSE: And there are some who suppose that God is fashioned after a bodily manner, when they read of his hand or finger, and they do not observe that these things are written not because of any fashion of a body, since in the godhead there are neither members nor parts, but they are expressions of the oneness of the godhead, that we may believe that it is impossible for either the Son or the Holy Spirit to be separated from God the Father; since the fullness of the godhead dwells as it were bodily in the substance of the Trinity. For this reason, then, is the Son also called the right hand of the Father, as we read: "The right hand of the Lord has done mighty things, the right hand of the Lord has exalted me." ON THE HOLY SPIRIT 2.7.69.[21]

GOD IS NOT ASHAMED TO BE THE GOD OF THE RIGHTEOUS. ATHANASIUS: Thus it is that sinners, and all those who are aliens from the catholic church, heretics and schismatics, since they are excluded from glorifying [God] with the saints, cannot properly even continue to be observers of the feasts. But the righteous person, although he appears dying to the world, uses boldness of speech, saying, "I shall not die but live and narrate all your marvelous deeds."[22] For even God is not ashamed to be called the God of those who truly mortify their members that are on the earth but live in Christ; for he is the God of the living, not of the dead. And he by his living Word quickens all people and gives him to be food and life to the saints; as the Lord declares, "I am the bread of life."[23] FESTAL LETTERS 7.4.[24]

---

[16]Is 58:11. [17]Is 66:2. [18]CS 47:14-15. [19]Ps 18:1 (17:2 LXX, Vg.). [20]WSA 3 8:263. [21]NPNF 2 10:123*. [22]Ps 118:17 (117:17 LXX). [23]Jn 6:48. [24]NPNF 2 4:525*.

The Righteous Will Live Forever.

Augustine: I am disposed, after careful examination, to doubt whether the expression so often used by the Lord, "the kingdom of heaven," can be found in these books [Old Testament]. It is said, indeed, "Love wisdom, that you may reign forever."[25] And if eternal life had not been clearly made known in the Old Testament, the Lord would not have said, as he did even to the unbelieving Jews, "Search the Scriptures, for in them you think that you have eternal life, and they are they that testify of me."[26] And to the same effect are the words of the psalmist: "I shall not die but live and declare the works of the Lord." And again: "Enlighten my eyes, lest I sleep the sleep of death."[27] Again, we read, "The souls of the righteous are in the hand of the Lord, and pain shall not touch them"; and immediately following, "They are in peace; and if they have suffered torture from people, their hope is full of immortality; and after a few troubles, they shall enjoy many rewards."[28] Again, in another place: "The righteous shall live forever, and their reward is with the Lord, and their concern with the Highest; therefore shall they receive from the hand of the Lord a kingdom of glory and a crown of beauty."[29] These and many similar declarations of eternal life, in more or less explicit terms, are found in these writings. Even the resurrection of the body is spoken of by the prophets. The Pharisees, accordingly, were fierce opponents of the Sadducees, who disbelieved the resurrection. This we learn not only from the canonical Acts of the Apostles, which the Manichaeans[30] reject, because it tells of the advent of the Paraclete promised by the Lord, but also from the Gospel, when the Sadducees question the Lord about the woman who married seven brothers, one dying after the other, whose wife she would be in heaven.[31] As regards, then, eternal life and the resurrection of the dead, numerous testimonies are to be found in these Scriptures. But I do not find there the expression "the kingdom of heaven." This expression belongs properly to the revelation of the New Testament, because in the resurrection our earthly bodies shall, by that change that Paul fully describes, become spiritual bodies, and so heavenly, that thus we may possess the kingdom of heaven. And this expression was reserved for him whose advent as king to govern and priest to sanctify his believing people was ushered in by all the symbolism of the old covenant, in its genealogies, its typical acts and words, its sacrifices and ceremonies and feasts and in all its prophetic utterances and events and figures. He came full of grace and truth, in his grace helping us to obey the precepts and in his truth securing the accomplishment of the promises. He came not to destroy the law but to fulfill it. Against Faustus, a Manichaean 19.31.[32]

Chastened, but Not Forsaken by God.

Clement of Alexandria: Consider the carefulness and the wisdom and the power of this Educator [Christ]: "He shall not judge according to appearance or reprove according to gossip, but he shall render judgment with humility and shall reprove the sinners of the earth."[33] And through the lips of David, he says, "The Lord chastising has chastised me, but he has not delivered me over to death." Indeed, the very act of being chastised, and being educated by the Lord as a child, means deliverance from death. Again, he says through the same psalmist: "You shall rule them with a rod of iron."[34] Similarly, the apostle exclaimed when he was aroused by the Corinthians: "What is your wish? Shall I come to you with a rod, or in love and in the spirit of meekness?"[35] By another psalmist, the Lord says again: "The Lord will send forth the rod of power out of Zion."[36] Christ the Educator 1.7.61.[37]

The Lord Will Educate You. Clement of

Alexandria: "When we are judged by the Lord," says the apostle, "it is for our education, so that

---

[25]Wis 6:21. [26]Jn 5:39. [27]Ps 13:3 (12:4 LXX, Vg.). [28]Wis 3:3-5. [29]Wis 5:15-16. [30]A Gnostic-like sect in the early church. [31]Mt 22:23-28. [32]NPNF 1 4:252*. [33]Is 11:3-4. [34]Ps 2:9. [35]1 Cor 4:21. [36]Ps 110:2 (109:2 LXX). [37]FC 23:55-56*.

we may not be condemned along with the world."[38] Earlier the prophet said, "The Lord has given me a stern lesson but not handed me over to death." Scripture says, "It is to teach you his righteousness that he taught you a lesson, tested you and exposed you to hunger and thirst in a desolate land, for you to know in your heart all his statutes and judgments that I am laying on you today. The Lord your God will educate you just as a human will educate his son."[39] Scripture again emphasizes the lesson taught by a good example: "It is a great education when a malefactor sees a criminal punished,"[40] for "the fear of the Lord breeds wisdom."[41] STROMATEIS 1.27.172.[42]

GOD'S WORDS ARE WORDS OF POWER AND ENCOURAGEMENT. SYNCLETICA: Rejoice because God has visited you. Keep saying the famous text: "The Lord has chastened and corrected me, but he has not given me over to death."... A messenger from Satan is given to you to be a thorn in your flesh.[43] Lift up your heart, for you see that you have received a gift like that of St. Paul. If you suffer from fever and cold, remember the text of Scripture, "We went through fire and water," and then, "you brought us out to a place of rest."[44] ... Threefold suffering like this will make you perfect. He also said, "You set me at liberty when I was in trouble."[45] Thus, let us test our souls by this kind of self-discipline, for we have our enemy before our eyes. SAYINGS OF THE FATHERS 7.16.[46]

SUFFERING STRENGTHENS US. SYNCLETICA: When the devil does not use the goads of poverty to tempt, he uses wealth for the purpose. When he cannot win by scorn and mockery, he tries

praise and flattery. If he cannot win by providing health, he tries illness; if he cannot win by comfort, he tries to ruin the soul by vexations that lead a person to act against the monastic vow. He inflicts severe sicknesses on people whom he wants to tempt, and so makes them weak and thereby shakes the love that they feel toward God. But although the body is shattered and running high temperatures and thirsting unbearably—yet you who endure all this are a sinner, and remember the punishments of the next world, and the everlasting fire and the torments of the judgment. So you will not fail in the sufferings of this present time; indeed you should rejoice because God has visited you. Keep saying the famous text: "The Lord has chastened and corrected me, but he has not given me over to death." Iron is cleaned of rust by fire. If you are righteous and suffer, you grow to a yet higher sanctity. Gold is tested by fire. A messenger from Satan is given to you to be a thorn in your flesh. Lift up your heart, for you see that you have received a gift like that of Paul. If you suffer from fever and cold, remember the text of Scripture, "We went through fire and water"—and then "you brought us out into a place of rest."[47] If you have endured the suffering, you may expect the place of rest, provided you are following what is good. Cry aloud the prophet's words, "I am poor and destitute and in misery"—for the threefold suffering shall make you perfect. SAYINGS OF THE FATHERS 7.16.[48]

---

[38]1 Cor 11:32. [39]Deut 8:2-3. [40]Prov 21:11. [41]Prov 15:33. [42]FC 85:149. [43]2 Cor 12:7. [44]Ps 66:12 (65:12 LXX). [45]Ps 4:3 (4:4 LXX). [46]LCC 12:86*. [47]Ps 66:12 (65:12 LXX). [48]LCC 12:85-86*.

118:19-29 THE STONE THE BUILDERS REJECTED

¹⁹Open to me the gates of righteousness,
   that I may enter through them
   and give thanks to the LORD.

²⁰This is the gate of the LORD;
   the righteous shall enter through it.

²¹I thank thee that thou hast answered me
   and hast become my salvation.
²²The stone which the builders rejected
   has become the head of the corner.
²³This is the LORD's doing;
   it is marvelous in our eyes.
²⁴This is the day which the LORD has made;
   let us rejoice and be glad in it.
²⁵Save us, we beseech thee, O LORD!

O LORD, we beseech thee, give us success!

²⁶Blessed be he who enters in the name of the
      LORD!
   We bless you from the house of the LORD.
²⁷The LORD is God,
   and he has given us light.
Bind the festal procession with branches,
   up to the horns of the altar!

²⁸Thou art my God, and I will give thanks to
      thee;
   thou art my God, I will extol thee.

²⁹O give thanks to the LORD for he is good;
   for his steadfast love endures for ever!

OVERVIEW: Christ is the path to righteousness through whom we are reconciled and restored (CLEMENT OF ROME). There are two gates through which people can enter—one is the gate of death that leads to dissolution and the other the gate of Zion that leads to righteousness. The gate of death, which is sin, leads to eternal destruction, and the gate of righteousness, which is virtue, leads to eternal life (ORIGEN). Christ is the gate to heaven as already symbolized by Jacob's dream at Bethel (APHRAHAT).

The church is built on the foundation of the ancient prophets, Christ as its cornerstone (TERTULLIAN). A theme of stone imagery runs from the rejected stone of this verse to the stone placed at the entrance to the tomb of Christ (EPHREM). Christ, called the stone in the prophets, was rejected by his people before Pilate and then became the foundation stone of the church of the Gentiles (APHRAHAT). The church of the Jews and the church of the Gentiles are the two walls

that come together in Christ, the cornerstone. Christ is called the cornerstone because he united the two walls, Jews and Gentiles, in his peace (AUGUSTINE). The stone the builders rejected then becomes the cornerstone is a prophecy of the rejection of Christ and his later glorification (TERTULLIAN). Christ, originator of the first and second giving of the law, joins together Judaism and Christianity as two buildings in one (EUSEBIUS). Since Christ is the true Sun and the true Day, there is no time of day exempted from prayer (CYPRIAN).

The advent of Christ ushered in the eternal day, prophesied by the psalmist, and its twelve hours of daylight are symbolized by the twelve apostles (PETER CHRYSOLOGUS). Easter is the day of Christ's resurrection and should be a day of joy and gladness as the prophet declared (AMBROSE). Christ the cornerstone enables us to experience the eternal day that will have a beginning but no end. The church of the Jews and the church of the Gentiles are the two walls that come together in Christ, the cornerstone (Augustine).

The church should accept into its midst only those people who come in the name of the Lord (Didache). Christ is the one who has come in the name of God, not the antichrist or any other imposter (Bede). As the psalmist foretold, Christ appeared in human form to save us, and he established the church with its leaders to feed the souls of future generations(pachomius). If the Gentiles had unwittingly honored the true God, they would not have failed to acknowledge the incarnation (Athanasius). Only the one who has experienced the need of mercy can truly be merciful to others in imitation of God's mercy to us (Augustine).

118:19-20 The Gates of Righteousness

Open for Me the Gates of Righteousness. Clement of Rome: Let us therefore root this out quickly,[1] and let us fall down before the Master and entreat him with tears, that he may show himself propitious and be reconciled to us and may restore us to the seemly and pure conduct that belongs to our love of the brothers. For this is a gate of righteousness opened to life, as it is written: "Open to me the gates of righteousness, that I may enter in thereby and praise the Lord. This is the gate of the Lord; the righteous shall enter in thereby." Seeing then that many gates are opened, this is that gate that is in righteousness, even that which is in Christ, whereby all are blessed who have entered in and direct their path in holiness and righteousness, performing all things without confusion. Let a person be faithful, let him be able to expound a deep saying, let him be wise in the discernment of words, let him be strenuous in deeds, let him be pure; for so much the more ought he to be lowly in mind, in proportion as he seems to be the greater; and he ought to seek the common advantage of all, and not his own. 1 Clement 48.[2]

The Gate of Death Versus the Gate of Righteousness. Origen: In this place,[3] then,

the gates of hades are spoken of; but in the Psalms the prophet gives thanks saying, "He who lifts me up from the gates of death that I may declare all your praises in the gates of the daughter of Zion."[4] And from this we learn that it is never possible for anyone to be fit to declare the praises of God, unless he has been lifted up from the gates of death and has come to the gates of Zion. Now the gates of Zion may be conceived as opposed to the gates of death, so that there is one gate of death, dissoluteness, but a gate of Zion, self-control; and so a gate of death, unrighteousness, but a gate of Zion, righteousness, which the prophet shows forth saying, "This is the gate of the Lord, the righteous shall enter into it." And again there is cowardice, a gate of death, but courage, a gate of Zion; and want of prudence, a gate of death, but its opposite, prudence, a gate of Zion. But to all the gates of the "knowledge that is falsely so called" one gate is opposed, the gate of knowledge which is free from falsehood. But consider if, because of the saying, "our wrestling is not against flesh and blood,"[5] etc., you can say that each power and world ruler of this darkness and each one of the "spiritual hosts of wickedness in the heavenly places"[6] is a gate of hades and a gate of death. Let, then, the principalities and powers with which our wrestling is, be called gates of hades, but the "ministering spirits"[7] gates of righteousness. But as in the case of the better things many gates are first spoken of, and after the gates, one, in the passage, "Open to me the gates of righteousness, I will enter into them and will make full confession to the Lord," and "this is the gate of the Lord, by it the righteous shall enter"; so also in the case of those gates that are opposed, many are the gates of hades and death, each a power; but over all these the wicked one himself. Commentary on Matthew 12.13.[8]

---

[1]The schism that existed in the church in Corinth and that was the occasion for Clement writing this letter. [2]AF 83. [3]Mt 16:18. [4]Ps 9:13-14 (9:14-15 LXX). [5]Eph 6:12. [6]Eph 6:12. [7]Heb 1:14. [8]ANF 9:457-58*.

THE GATE OF DEATH IS SIN AND THE GATE OF RIGHTEOUSNESS IS VIRTUE. ORIGEN: And it is not incredible that the gates that are said to open spontaneously are referred obscurely by some to the words "Open to me the gates of righteousness, that I may go into them and praise the Lord; this gate of the Lord, into it the righteous shall enter"; and again, to what is said in the ninth psalm, "You that lift me up from the gates of death, that I may show forth all your praise in the gates of the daughter of Zion."[9] The Scripture further gives the name of "gates of death" to those sins that lead to destruction, as it calls, on the contrary, good actions the "gates of Zion." So also "the gates of righteousness," which is an equivalent expression to "the gates of virtue." These are ready to be opened to one who follows after virtuous pursuits. AGAINST CELSUS 6.36.[10]

THE GATE OF HEAVEN IS CHRIST. APHRAHAT: Our father Jacob too prayed at Bethel and saw the gate of heaven opened, with a ladder going up on high.[11] This is a symbol of our Savior that Jacob saw: the gate of heaven is Christ, in accordance with what he said: "I am the gate of life; every one who enters by me shall live forever."[12] David too said, "This is the gate of the Lord, by which the righteous enter." Again, the ladder that Jacob saw is a symbol of our Savior, in that by means of him the just ascend from the lower to the upper realm. The ladder is also a symbol of our Savior's cross, which was raised up like a ladder, with the Lord standing above it; for above Christ is the Lord of all, just as the blessed apostle said: "The head of Christ is God."[13] Now Jacob called that place Bethel;[14] and Jacob raised up there a pillar of stone as a testimony, and he poured oil over it. Our father Jacob did this too in symbol, anticipating that stones would receive anointing—for the peoples who have believed in Christ are the stones that are anointed; just as John says of them: "From these stones God is able to raise up children for Abraham."[15] For in Jacob's prayer the calling of the nations was symbolized. DEMONSTRATIONS 4.5.[16]

118:22-23 The Cornerstone

THE CHURCH OF CHRIST. TERTULLIAN: Thus we find from this passage also, that Christ possessed a body of flesh, such as was able to endure the cross. "When, therefore, he came and preached peace to them that were near and to them which were afar off," we both obtained "access to the Father," being "now no more strangers and foreigners but fellow citizens with the saints and of the household of God" (even of him from whom, as we have shown above, we were aliens and placed far off), "built on the foundation of the apostles"[17]—[the apostle added] "and the prophets"; these words, however, the heretic erased,[18] forgetting that the Lord had set in his church not only apostles but prophets also. He feared, no doubt, that our building was to stand in Christ on the foundation of the ancient prophets, since the apostle himself never fails to build us up everywhere with [the words of] the prophets. For whence did he learn to call Christ "the chief cornerstone"[19] but from the figure given him in the psalm: "The stone that the builders rejected is become the head [stone] of the corner"? AGAINST MARCION 5.17.[20]

THE STONE AT CHRIST'S TOMB AND CHRIST THE CORNERSTONE. EPHREM THE SYRIAN: "A stone was placed at the entrance to the tomb."[21] Thus, one stone [was placed] against another stone, so that [this] stone might be keeping guard over "the stone that the builders rejected."[22] This [stone], lifted "up by" [human] hands, had to keep guard over that which was "detached, without [human] hands";[23] this [stone], on which "the

---

[9]Ps 9:13-14 (9:14-15 LXX). [10]ANF 4:589*. [11]Gen 28:12. [12]Jn 10:9. [13]1 Cor 11:3. [14]Gen 28:18. [15]Lk 3:8. [16]CS 101:8-9*. [17]Eph 2:17-20. [18]Marcion rejected the entire Old Testament and everything in the New Testament that he believed reflected Jewish influence. This left him with a New Testament canon that included a shortened version of Luke's Gospel and ten of Paul's letters. He did not include 1 and 2 Timothy and Titus because he did not think they had been written by Paul. [19]Eph 2:20. [20]ANF 3:467*. [21]Mt 27:60. [22]See also Mt 21:42. [23]See Dan 2:34, 45.

angel was sitting,"[24] [had to keep guard] over that which "Jacob had placed under his head";[25] this [stone] with its seal [had to keep guard] over that which, through its seal, watches over the faithful. Thus did the gate of life go forth from the gate of death. "For this is the gate of our Lord, through which the just enter." When it was closed, it delivered those closed in. Through its death the dead lived. Through its voice the silent cried out. Through its resurrection, there was an earthquake.[26] Its emergence forth from the tomb introduced the Gentiles into the church.[27] COMMENTARY ON TATIAN'S DIATESSARON 21.21.[28]

THOSE WHO REJECT CHRIST, THE CORNERSTONE, WILL BE CRUSHED BY HIM. APHRAHAT: But I must proceed to my former statement that Christ is called the stone in the prophets. For in ancient times David said concerning him, "The stone that the builders rejected has become the head of the building." And how did the builders reject this stone that is Christ? How else than that they so rejected him before Pilate and said, "This man shall not be king over us."[29] And again in that parable that our Lord spoke that a certain nobleman went to receive kingly power and to return and rule over them; and they sent after him envoys saying, "This man shall not be king over us."[30] By these things they rejected the stone that is Christ. And how did it become the head of the building? How else than that it was set up over the building of the Gentiles and on it is reared up all their building. And who are the builders? Who but the priests and Pharisees who did not build a sure building but were overthrowing everything that he was building, as is written in Ezekiel the prophet: "He was building a wall of partition, but they were shaking it, that it might fall."[31] And again it is written, "I looked for a man among them who would build up the wall and stand before me in the gap on behalf of the land, that I might not destroy it, but I did not find one."[32] And furthermore Isaiah also prophesied beforehand with regard to this stone. For he said, "Thus says the Lord, 'Behold, I lay in Zion a cho-

sen stone in the precious corner, the heart of the wall of the foundation.'"[33] And he said again there, "Every one who believes on it shall not fear. And whosoever falls on that stone shall be broken, and every one on whom it shall fall, it will crush."[34] For the people of the house of Israel fell on him, and he became their destruction forever. And again "it shall fall on the image and crush it."[35] And the Gentiles believed on it and do not fear. DEMONSTRATIONS 1.6.[36]

TWO PEOPLE JOINED TOGETHER IN THE LORD. AUGUSTINE: So there were sheep from among the Jews, and many sheep. But not the only ones. The Lord had others from among the Gentiles. These two peoples coming as it were from different directions are also represented by two walls. The church of the Jews comes from the circumcision; the church of the Gentiles comes from the uncircumcision. Coming from different directions, they are joined together in the Lord. That is why the Lord is called the cornerstone. Thus the psalm says, "The stone that the builders rejected, this very one has become the head of the corner." And the apostle says, "Christ Jesus being himself the chief cornerstone."[37] Where there is a corner, two walls connect; two walls do not meet in a corner unless they come from different directions; if they only come from one direction, they do not make a corner. So then, the two goats are the two peoples, so are the two sheepfolds, so are the two walls, so are the two blind men who sat by the road,[38] so are the two boats into which the fish were hauled.[39] There are many places in Scripture where the two peoples are to be understood—but they are one thing in Jacob. SERMON 4.18.[40]

CHRIST UNITES JEWS AND GENTILES IN GRACE. AUGUSTINE: A symbolic statement: "The stone that the builders rejected, this has

---

[24]Mt 28:2. [25]Gen 28:18. [26]Mt 27:51, 54. [27]See Mt 27:54. [28]*ECTD* 327-28*. [29]Lk 19:14. [30]Jn 19:15. [31]Ezek 13:10-11. [32]Ezek 22:30. [33]Is 28:16. [34]Mt 21:44. [35]Dan 2:34. [36]*NPNF* 2 13:347*. [37]Eph 2:20. [38]Mt 20:30. [39]See Lk 5:7. [40]*WSA* 3 1:195.

become the head of the corner."[41] If we understand "stone" in the proper sense, what stone did the builders reject, and it became the head of the corner? If we take "corner" in the proper sense, of what corner did this stone become the head? If we admit it is said symbolically, and you take it symbolically, the cornerstone is Christ, head of the corner, head of the church. Why is the corner the church? Because he called the Jews from this side, the Gentiles from that; and like two walls coming from different directions and coming together in him, he tied them together by the grace of his peace. "For he is our peace, who made of both one."[42] SERMON 89.4.[43]

THE STONE THAT THE BUILDERS REJECTED.
TERTULLIAN: For Jesus tells them [the disciples] that "the Son of man must suffer many things and be rejected," before his coming,[44] at which his kingdom will be really revealed. In this statement he shows that it was his own kingdom that his answer to them had contemplated and that was now awaiting his own sufferings and rejection. But having to be rejected and afterwards to be acknowledged and taken up and glorified, he borrowed the very word *rejected* from the passage where, under the figure of a stone, his twofold manifestation was celebrated by David—the first in rejection, the second in honor. "The stone," he says, "that the builders rejected is become the headstone of the corner. This is the Lord's doing." Now it would be idle, if we believed that God had predicted the humiliation, or even the glory, of any Christ at all, that he could have designed his prophecy for any but him whom he had foretold under the figure of a stone and a rock and a mountain.[45] AGAINST MARCION 4.35.[46]

THE BUILDING OF MOSES AND THE BUILDING OF THE GOSPEL. EUSEBIUS OF CAESAREA: [Christ] ordained that the former law should stand till he came, and he was revealed as the originator of the second law of the new covenant preached to all nations, as being responsible for the law and influence of the two religions, I mean Judaism and Christianity. And it is wonderful that divine prophecy should accord:

> "Behold, I lay in Zion a stone, choice, a cornerstone; precious, and he that believes on him shall not be ashamed."[47]

Who could be the cornerstone but he, the living and precious stone who supports by his teaching two buildings and makes them one? For he set up the Mosaic building, which was to last till his day, and then fitted on to one side of it our building of the gospel. Hence he [Christ] is called the cornerstone. And it is said in the Psalms:

> "The stone that the builders refused, the same is become the head of the corner. This is of the Lord, and it is marvelous in our eyes."

This oracle too indubitably indicates the Jewish conspiracy against the subject of the prophecy, how he has been set at naught by the builders of the old wall, meaning the scribes and Pharisees, the high priests and all the rulers of the Jews. And it prophesied that though he should be despised and cast out he would become the head of the corner, regarding him as the originator of a new covenant, according to the preceding proofs. PROOF OF THE GOSPEL 1.7.[48]

CHRIST IS THE TRUE SUN AND THE TRUE DAY.
CYPRIAN: Likewise at the setting of the sun and at the end of the day necessarily there must again be prayer. For since Christ is the true Sun and the true Day, as the sun and the day of the world recede, when we pray and petition that the light come on us again, we pray for the coming of Christ to provide us with the grace of eternal light. Moreover, the Holy Spirit in the Psalms declares that Christ is called the Day. He says, "The stone that the builders rejected has become the cornerstone. This is the Lord's doing; it is

---

[41]See also Mt 21:42. [42]Eph 2:14. [43]*WSA* 3 3:443. [44]Lk 17:25. [45]See Is 8:14; 1 Cor 10:4. [46]*ANF* 3:409*. [47]Is 28:16. [48]*POG* 1:45-46*. [49]Ps 118:22-24 (117:22-24 LXX, Vg.).

wonderful in our eyes. This is the day that the Lord has made; let us exalt and rejoice therein."[49] Malachi the prophet also testifies that he is called the Sun when he says, "But to you who fear my name, the Sun of justice shall arise with healing in his wings."[50] But if in holy Scripture Christ is the true Sun and the true Day, no hour is appointed for Christians, by whom God should be adored frequently and always, so that we who are in Christ, that is, in the true Sun and in the true Day, should be insistent throughout the whole day in our petitions and should pray. When, by the law of nature, the revolving night, recurring in its alternating cycle, follows the day, there can be no harm from the darkness for those who pray, because to the sons of light even in the night there is day. For when is he without light who has light in his heart? Or when does he not have sun and day, to whom Christ is Sun and Day? THE LORD'S PRAYER 35.[51]

118:24-25 The Day That the Lord Has Made

EASTER IS A DAY OF JOYFUL CELEBRATION. AMBROSE: We must keep the law regarding Easter in such a way that we do not observe the fourteenth as the day of the resurrection; that day or one very close to it is the day of the passion, because the feast of the resurrection is kept on the Lord's day.[52] Moreover, we cannot fast on the Lord's day; fasting on this day is what we criticize in the Manichaeans.[53] One shows disbelief in the resurrection of Christ if he proposes a law that we fast on the day of the resurrection, since the law says that the Passover should be eaten with bitterness, that is, with sorrow because the author of our salvation was slain by humanity's great sacrilege. On the Lord's day the prophet bids us rejoice, saying, "This is the day that the Lord has made; let us be glad and rejoice at it." LETTER 36.[54]

THE DAY THAT THE LORD HAS MADE. AUGUSTINE: We have just been singing to God, "This is the day that the Lord has made." Let us talk about

it, seeing that the Lord has presented us with it. This obviously prophetic Scripture wanted us to understand something, some day not of the common sort, not visible to eyes of flesh; not the kind of day that has a sunrise and sunset but a day that could know a dawn but never know a setting. Let us see what the same psalm had said just before: "The stone that the builders rejected, this has been made into the head of the corner. It was made by the Lord; this is wonderful in our eyes."[55] And it continues, "This is the day that the Lord has made." Let us take the cornerstone as introducing us to this day. SERMON 258.1[56]

THIS IS THE DAY THE LORD HAS MADE. PETER CHRYSOLOGUS: "And he summoned the twelve,"[57] the text says. After the long centuries of dreadful night, the eternal day, our Christ, shone forth. The world had long awaited the splendor of his dawning. In the case of his twelve apostles he desired to signify the twelve hours of this day. The blessed psalmist saw this day in spirit when he sang, "This is the day that the Lord has made; let us be glad and rejoice in it." Consequently, the apostle, too, calls the believers children of light and of faith: "You are children of the light and children of the day."[58] SERMON 170.[59]

118:26-27 God Has Given Us Light

HELP THOSE WHO TRAVEL, BUT USE DISCRETION. DIDACHE: Let everyone who "comes to you in the name of the Lord"[60] be received; but, after testing him, you will know him, for you know

---

[50]Mal 4:2. [51]FC 36:158-59**. [52]A major controversy in the early church was when to celebrate Easter. Christ was crucified on a Friday, which was the fourteenth day of the month of Nisan in the Jewish calendar. One view generally maintained in the Eastern church was to commemorate Christ's crucifixion on the fourteenth of Nisan no matter on which day of the week it occurred and to celebrate Easter two days later. The other view, generally held in the Western church, was to commemorate Christ's crucifixion always on a Friday and to celebrate his resurrection always on the following Sunday. [53]A Gnostic-like sect in the early church. [54]FC 26:193-94*. [55]Ps 118:22-23 (117:22-23 LXX, Vg.). [56]WSA 3 7:174. [57]Mk 6:7. [58]1 Thess 5:5. [59]FC 17:278-79*. [60]Mt 21:9.

right and wrong. If the one who comes to you is a traveler, help him as much as you can; but he shall remain with you no more than two or three days, unless there is need. But, if he wishes to settle among you and is a craftsman, let him work and eat. But, if he has no trade, provide according to your conscience, so that no Christian shall live among you idle. But, if he does not agree to do this, he is trading on the name of Christ; beware of such people. DIDACHE 12.1-5.[61]

CHRIST CAME IN THE NAME OF GOD THE FATHER. BEDE: "Blessed is he who comes in the name of the Lord." "In the name of the Lord" signifies "in the name of God the Father," just as [our Lord] himself said elsewhere to the unbelieving Jews, "I have come in the name of my Father, and you do not receive me; another will come in his own name, him you will receive."[62] Christ came in the name of God the Father, because in everything that he did and said he was concerned with glorifying his Father and with proclaiming to human beings that he is to be glorified. The antichrist will come in his own name, and although he may be the most wicked person of all and a convivial companion of the devil, he will see fit to call himself the Son of God while "being opposed to and raised above everything that is said to be God and is worshiped."[63] The crowd took this verse of praise from Psalm 117 [LXX], and there is no one who doubts that it is sung about the Lord. Hence it is appropriate that there is previously sung of him in the same psalm, "The stone that the builders rejected has become the cornerstone." For Christ, whom the Jews rejected as they were building the decrees of their own traditions, became a memorial for believers from among both peoples, namely, the Jews and the Gentiles. For as to the fact that Christ is called the cornerstone in this psalm, this is what was being chanted in high praise in the gospel by the voice of those who followed and those who went ahead. HOMILIES ON THE GOSPELS 2.3.[64]

THE NEED FOR SPIRITUAL SHEPHERDS.

PACHOMIUS: As for us, brothers, understanding these things, let us keep each to his own measure, the one who is considered a shepherd of souls as well as the one who is considered a sheep. Yet let us all pray to be sheep, for no one is the shepherd save he who said, "I am the good Shepherd."[65] But when he appeared, as David had foretold and signified, "God is the Lord, and he has appeared to us," God the Word appearing in human form saved us, bestowing on us knowledge of the faith. And before going up into heaven, he established the apostles as his successors, saying to Peter, "Feed my lambs"[66] and "Look after my sheep."[67] For this reason there is need now too for people who, generation after generation, feed the souls in the Lord, who says, "I am with you."[68] For we know that after the apostles it is the bishops who are the fathers. But all those who listen to Christ who is in them are also their children, although they do not belong to the clergy and have no ecclesiastical rank. LIFE OF PACHOMIUS (FIRST GREEK) 135.[69]

CHRIST HAS COME. ATHANASIUS: But if the Gentiles are honoring the same God who gave the law to Moses and made the promise to Abraham and whose word the Jews dishonored—why are they [the Jews] ignorant of, or rather why do they choose to ignore, that what the Lord foretold in the Scriptures has been revealed in the world and appeared to it in bodily form, as the Scripture said: "The Lord God has shined on us"; and again: "He sent his Word and healed them";[70] and again: "Not a messenger, not an angel but the Lord himself saved them"?[71] Their state may be compared to that of one out of his right mind, who sees the earth illumined by the sun but denies the sun that illumines it. ON THE INCARNATION 40.[72]

118:29 God Is Good

[61]FC 1:181-82. [62]Jn 5:43. [63]2 Thess 2:4. [64]CS 111:28-29*. [65]Jn 10:14. [66]Jn 21:15. [67]Jn 21:16. [68]Mt 28:20. [69]CS 45:394-95. [70]Ps 107:20 (106:20 LXX). [71]Is 63:9 (LXX). [72]LCC 3:94*.

EMULATE GOD'S MERCY TO OTHER PEOPLE.
AUGUSTINE: Let us commend ourselves to God, my brothers, by works of mercy. "O praise the Lord, for he is good: for his mercy endures forever." Give praise, for God is merciful, and he wishes to forgive the sins of those who give praise. In addition, offer sacrifice to him. O man, be merciful to your fellow mortals, and God will show mercy to you. You are a mortal; the other person is a mortal also; you are both in need of mercy. On the other hand, God is not in need of mercy, but he is merciful. If, however, the person who is in need of mercy does not show mercy to another who is in need of mercy, how does he expect mercy from One who will never be in need of mercy? Think over what I am saying, brothers. For example, whoever is pitiless in regard to a shipwrecked person remains pitiless until he himself suffers shipwreck. But if he has been shipwrecked, whenever he sees a shipwrecked person he recalls his former experience and he experiences a sympathetic feeling of mercy. Hence, a personal experience of misfortune softens the one whom the common bond of human nature was not able to incline to mercy. How readily he who has been in service in the past has compassion on a servant! How readily he who was once a hired laborer feels sorry for a laborer deprived of his pay! The person who has once suffered a similar loss sympathizes most sincerely with a parent lamenting the loss of a child. Therefore, a similarity of suffering softens any degree of hardness in a human heart. If, then, you who either have been in need of mercy or who fear that you may be in such need (for, as long as you are on this earth, you ought to fear what you have not been, to remember what you have been and to consider what you may be)—if, then, encompassed with the memory of your former need of mercy, with the fear of future needs and with the suffering of present miseries, you do not have mercy on a person who is in trouble and in need of your help, do you expect him whom misery has never afflicted to have mercy on you? And do you fail to give of the abundance that you have received from God and then wish God to give to you from that which he has not received from you? SERMON 259.3.[73]

---

[73]FC 38:372-73*.

119:1-24 A DEVOTION ON THE WORD OF GOD
(ALEPH—GIMEL)

[1]Blessed are those whose way is blameless,
   who walk in the law of the LORD!
[2]Blessed are those who keep his testimonies,
   who seek him with their whole heart,
[3]who also do no wrong,
   but walk in his ways!
[4]Thou hast commanded thy precepts
   to be kept diligently.
[5]O that my ways may be steadfast
   in keeping thy statutes!
[6]Then I shall not be put to shame,
   having my eyes fixed on all thy
      commandments.
[7]I will praise thee with an upright heart,
   when I learn thy righteous ordinances.
[8]I will observe thy statutes;

O forsake me not utterly!

[9]*How can a young man keep his way pure?*
  By guarding it according to thy word.
[10]*With my whole heart I seek thee;*
  let me not wander from thy commandments!
[11]*I have laid up thy word in my heart,*
  that I might not sin against thee.
[12]*Blessed be thou, O* LORD*;*
  teach me thy statutes!
[13]*With my lips I declare*
  all the ordinances of thy mouth.
[14]*In the way of thy testimonies I delight*
  as much as in all riches.
[15]*I will meditate on thy precepts,*
  and fix my eyes on thy ways.
[16]*I will delight in thy statutes;*
  I will not forget thy word.

[17]*Deal bountifully with thy servant,*
  that I may live and observe thy word.
[18]*Open my eyes, that I may behold*
  wondrous things out of thy law.
[19]*I am a sojourner on earth;*
  hide not thy commandments from me!
[20]*My soul is consumed with longing*
  for thy ordinances at all times.
[21]*Thou dost rebuke the insolent, accursed ones,*
  who wander from thy commandments;
[22]*take away from me their scorn and contempt,*
  for I have kept thy testimonies.
[23]*Even though princes sit plotting against me,*
  thy servant will meditate on thy statutes.
[24]*Thy testimonies are my delight,*
  they are my counselors.

OVERVIEW: Christ, who has risen from the dead, enables us to know the Father, become pure in heart and eventually see God (ATHANASIUS). Blessedness and happiness come from knowing and living an undefiled life (BEDE). God requests and strongly commends obedience to his commandments (AUGUSTINE). We are always at the crossroads between good and evil, and when we sin, we should immediately correct our life by listening to and following the Word of God (AMBROSE). The only way to stay on the straight and narrow path is to obey the Word of God (CLEMENT OF ALEXANDRIA).

Although the work of giving us new life is attributed to the Holy Spirit, it is also the work of the Father and the Son (AMBROSE). Whenever the Word of God is read, we should pray that God would enable us to understand it. Only God can remove the veil from our eyes so that we may gain a spiritual understanding of his Word (ORIGEN). The only way we can comprehend the Word of God is if God enables us to understand it. When we fail to understand things correctly,

we must pray to God for enlightenment (JEROME). It is not sufficient merely to hear the Word of God; we must reflect or meditate on it (CHRYSOSTOM). We cannot understand what God reveals in his Scripture unless he enlightens us (JEROME). When we are terrified by our sins or discouraged in heart, we should turn to the Word of God for help. On earth we live in someone else's home so that God is our landlord—it is up to God to tell us when to leave. Desire for justification, or as Paul says, "to be with Christ" is a good love, and the object desired will bring joy and pleasure (AUGUSTINE).

119:1-8 Walk in the Law of the Lord

BLESSED ARE THEY WHOSE WAYS ARE BLAMELESS. ATHANASIUS: And as he is First-born among brothers and rose from the dead "the firstfruits of them that slept";[1] so, since it became him "in all things to have the preeminence,"[2]

---

[1]1 Cor 15:20. [2]Col 1:18.

therefore he is created "a beginning of ways," that we, walking along it and entering through him who says, "I am the Way" and "the Door" and partaking of the knowledge of the Father, may also hear the words, "Blessed are the undefiled in the Way,"[3] and "Blessed are the pure in heart, for they shall see God."[4] DISCOURSES AGAINST THE ARIANS 2.21.64.[5]

HUMANITY'S GREATEST HAPPINESS. BEDE: Jesus said, "If you know these things, you will be blessed if you do them." This statement of our Savior is very helpful for salvation, and we must ponder it attentively. We will be blessed if we know the heavenly commands, yet still more so if we eagerly pursue in our works the things that we know. One who neglects to keep his known commandments is not capable of being happy; one who scorns finding out about these [commandments] is separated much further away from the heritage of the blessed. The psalmist agrees with this. Weighing the hearts of mortals and in like manner perceiving that everyone loves happiness but few ask where it is, he clearly testified as to what is the greatest happiness of human beings in this life, saying, "Blessed are those who are undefiled in the way, who walk in the Lord's law." And lest it be supposed that this way of the undefiled and blessed can be laid hold of indiscriminately by the ignorant and the untaught, he subsequently continued and said, "Blessed are they who search his testimonies and seek him with their whole heart." HOMILIES ON THE GOSPELS 2.5.[6]

GOD'S COMMANDMENTS ARE TO BE KEPT DILIGENTLY. AUGUSTINE: What is so generally or so forcefully commanded as obedience, by which the commandments of God are observed? Yet we find that it is the object of petition. "You have commanded your commandments to be kept most diligently." Then follows, "O! that my ways may be directed to obey your decrees. Then shall I not be confounded, when I shall look into all your commandments." He [the psalmist] begged that this thing be fulfilled by him, which he stated God

had commanded. HOLY VIRGINITY 41.42.[7]

119:9 Live According to God's Word

ONE REMAINS PURE BY KEEPING GOD'S WORD. AMBROSE: Let us listen, then, to the master of precaution: "I said, I will pay attention to my ways"; that is, "I said to myself: in the silent biddings of my thoughts, I have enjoined on myself, that I should pay attention to my ways." Some ways there are that we ought to follow; others as to which we ought to pay attention. We must follow the ways of the Lord and pay attention to our own ways, lest they lead us into sin. One can pay attention if one is not hasty in speaking. The law says, "Hear, O Israel, the Lord your God."[8] It said not "speak" but "hear." Eve fell because she said to the man what she had not heard from the Lord her God. The first word from God says to you, Hear! If you hear, pay attention to your ways; and if you have fallen, quickly amend your way. For "how does a young person amend his way; except by paying attention to the word of the Lord?" Be silent therefore first of all, and listen, so that you do not fail in your tongue. DUTIES OF THE CLERGY 1.2.7.[9]

DO NOT FOLLOW THE EXAMPLE OF THE GENTILES. CLEMENT OF ALEXANDRIA: To sum up, David in the Psalms speaks about obedience: "How shall a young person keep his path straight?" The answer comes immediately: "By keeping your Word with his whole heart." Jeremiah says, "These are the Lord's words: do not follow the paths of the Gentiles."[10] STROMATEIS 3.4.33.4-5.[11]

119:17-21 Deal Bountifully with Your Servant

THE HOLY SPIRIT GIVES US NEW LIFE. AMBROSE: And what wonder is it the Spirit

---

[3]Ps 119:1 (118:1 LXX). [4]Mt 5:8. [5]NPNF 2 4:383*. [6]CS 111:49. [7]FC 27:195-96*. [8]Deut 6:4. [9]NPNF 2 10:2**. [10]Jer 10:2. [11]FC 85:276.

works life, who enlivens as does the Father and as does the Son? And who can deny that giving new life is the work of the eternal Majesty? For it is written, "Give life to your servant." He, then, is enlivened who is a servant, that is, a person, who before he did not have life but received the privilege of having it.

Let us then see whether the Spirit is enlivened, or himself giving life. Now it is written, "The letter kills, but the Spirit gives life."[12] So, then, the Spirit enlivens.

But that you may understand that the enlivening of the Father, Son and Holy Spirit is no separate work, read how there is a oneness of quickening also, since God gives life through the Spirit, for Paul said, "He who raised up Christ from the dead shall also give life to your mortal bodies because of his Spirit who dwells in you."[13] ON THE HOLY SPIRIT 2.4.29-31.[14]

PRAY AT THE READING OF GOD'S WORD. ORIGEN: We should ask the Father of the Word during each individual reading "when Moses is read,"[15] that he might fulfill even in us that which is written in the Psalms: "Open my eyes, and I will consider the wondrous things of your law." For unless he himself opens our eyes, how shall we be able to see these great mysteries that are fashioned in the patriarchs, that are pictured now in terms of wells,[16] now in marriages,[17] now in births,[18] now even in barrenness?[19] HOMILIES ON GENESIS 12.1.[20]

TAKE THE VEIL FROM OUR EYES: ORIGEN: Therefore, let us fall, if it is necessary, into your[21] detractions so long as the church, which has already turned to Christ the Lord, may know the truth of the Word that is completely covered under the veil of the letter. For thus the apostle said, "if anyone turns to the Lord, the veil will be removed; for where the Spirit of the Lord is, there is freedom."[22] Thus, the Lord, the Holy Spirit, must be entreated by us to remove every cloud and all darkness that obscures the vision of our hearts hardened with the stains of sins in

order that we may be able to behold the spiritual and wonderful knowledge of his law, according to him who said, "Take the veil from my eyes, and I shall observe the wonders of your law." HOMILIES ON LEVITICUS 1.1.4.[23]

OPEN MY EYES TO THE WONDERFUL THINGS IN YOUR LAW. JEROME: Now it was in the law and in the prophets that he was foreordained and prefigured. For this reason too the prophets were called seers,[24] because they saw him whom others did not see. Abraham saw his day and was glad.[25] The heavens that were sealed to a rebellious people were opened to Ezekiel. "Open my eyes," David says, "that I may behold wonderful things out of your law." For "the law is spiritual,"[26] and a revelation is needed to enable us to comprehend it and, when God uncovers his face, to behold his glory. LETTER 53.4.[27]

UNLOCKING THE MEANING OF SCRIPTURE. JEROME: Hear me, therefore, my fellow servant, my friend, my brother; give ear for a moment that I may tell you how you are to walk in the holy Scriptures. All that we read in the divine books, while glistening and shining without, is yet far sweeter within. "He who desires to eat the kernel must first break the nut."[28] "Open my eyes," says David, "that I may behold wondrous things out of your law." Now, if so great a prophet confesses that he is in the darkness of ignorance, how deep, do you think, must be the night of misapprehension with which we, mere babes and unweaned infants, are enveloped! Now this veil rests not only on the face of Moses[29] but on the Evangelists and the apostles as well. To the multitudes the Savior spoke only in parables and, to make it clear that his words had a mystical meaning, said, "He who has ears to hear, let him hear."[30] Unless all

---

[12]2 Cor 3:6. [13]Rom 8:11. [14]NPNF 2 10:118**. [15]2 Cor 3:15. [16]Gen 24:11-20. [17]Gen 29:22-27. [18]Gen 25:21-26. [19]See Gen 11:30; 29:31. [20]FC 71:176*. [21]People who follow the literal, rather than an allegorical, interpretation of Scripture. [22]2 Cor 3:16-17. [23]FC 83:30. [24]1 Sam 9:9. [25]Jn 8:56. [26]Rom 7:14. [27]NPNF 2 6:98*. [28]Plautus *Curc.* 1.1.55. [29]2 Cor 3:14-15. [30]Lk 8:8.

things that are written are opened by him "who has the key of David, who opens and no one shuts, and shuts and no one opens,"[31] no one can undo the lock or set them before you. LETTER 58.9.[32]

LISTEN AND MEDITATE ON GOD'S WORD.
CHRYSOSTOM: God does not wish us merely to listen to the words and phrases contained in the Scriptures but to do so with a great deal of prudent reflection. Therefore, blessed David frequently prefixed to his psalms the expression "a meditation" and also said, "Open my eyes, and I will consider the wondrous things of your law." And after him, his son also pointed out by way of instruction that one must seek for wisdom even as for silver, or, rather, to trade in it more than in gold. HOMILIES ON THE GOSPEL OF JOHN 15.[33]

GOD MUST ENLIGHTEN US AS TO THE MEANING OF HIS WORD. JEROME: This is true wisdom in a person: to know that he is imperfect; and, if I may say so, the perfection of all the just, living in the flesh, is imperfect. Whence, also, we read in Proverbs: "To understand true justice."[34] For unless there were also false justice, the justice of God would never be referred to as true justice. And the apostle continues in the same passage: "And if in any point you think otherwise, this also God will reveal to you."[35] It is a strange thing that I hear. He who but a moment ago had said "Not that I have already obtained it or have already been made perfect"; he, who was the chosen vessel, who dared to say with the confidence of Christ dwelling within him, "Do you seek a proof of Christ who speaks in me?"[36] and yet frankly confessed that he had not been made perfect, now ascribes to the multitude something that he specifically denied to himself, and he associates himself with the others and says, "Let us then, as many as are perfect, be of this mind."[37] But he explains in the following verses what he meant by this statement. Let us, he says, who wish to be perfect, according to the measure of human frailty, be of

this mind, that we have not yet obtained it; that we have not yet laid hold of it; that we have not yet been made perfect. And because we have not yet been made perfect, and, perhaps, think otherwise than is demanded by true and perfect perfection, if we think of and understand anything that is different from what is consistent with the knowledge of God, this, also, God will reveal to us, so that we may pray with David and say, "Open my eyes, and I will consider the wondrous things of your law." AGAINST THE PELAGIANS 1.14.[38]

CONSIDER THE WONDERS OF GOD'S WORD.
AUGUSTINE: Terrified by my sins and the dead weight of my misery, I had turned my problems over in my mind and was half determined to seek refuge in the desert. But you forbade me to do this and gave me strength by saying, "Christ died for us all, so that being alive should no longer mean living with our own life but with his life who died for us."[39] Lord, I cast all my troubles on you and from now on "I shall contemplate the wonders of your law." You know how weak I am and how inadequate is my knowledge: teach me and heal my frailty. Your only Son, "in whom the whole treasury of wisdom and knowledge is stored up,"[40] has redeemed me with his blood. "Save me from the scorn of my enemies,"[41] for the price of my redemption is always in my thoughts. I eat it and drink it and minister it to others; and as one of the poor I long to be filled with it, to be one of those who "eat and have their fill." And "those who look for the Lord will cry out in praise of him."[42] CONFESSIONS 10.43.[43]

GOD IS OUR LANDLORD. AUGUSTINE: Our wish, you see, is to attain to eternal life. We wish to reach the place where nobody dies, but if possible

---

[31]Rev 3:7. [32]NPNF 2 6:122*. [33]FC 33:141*. [34]Prov 1:3 (LXX). [35]Phil 3:15. [36]2 Cor 13:3. [37]Phil 3:15. [38]FC 53:252*. [39]2 Cor 5:15. [40]Col 2:3. [41]Ps 119:122 (118:122 LXX, Vg.). [42]Ps 22:26 (21:27 LXX, Vg.). [43]AC 251-52.

we do not want to get there via death. We would like to be whisked away there while we are still alive and see our bodies changed, while we are alive, into that spiritual form into which they are to be changed when we rise again. Who wouldn't like that? Isn't it what everybody wants? But while that is what you want, you are told, *Quit.* Remember what you have sung in the psalm: "A lodger am I on earth." If you are a lodger, you are staying in someone else's house; if you are staying in someone else's house, you quit when the landlord bids you. And the landlord is bound to tell you to quit sooner or later, and he has not guaranteed you a long stay. After all, he did not sign a contract with you. Seeing that you are lodging with him for nothing, you quit when he tells you to. And this, too, has to be put up with, and for this, too, patience is very necessary. SERMON 359A.8.[44]

THE SOUL IS CONSUMED WITH LONGING FOR

GOD'S LAW. AUGUSTINE: And so a rightly directed will is love in a good sense and a perverted will is love in a bad sense. Therefore a love that strains after the possession of the loved object is desire; and the love that possesses and enjoys that object is joy. The love that shuns what opposes it is fear, while the love that feels that opposition when it happens is grief. Consequently, these feelings are bad, if the love is bad, and good if the love is good.

Let me prove this statement from Scripture. The apostle "desires to depart and to be with Christ";[45] and, "My soul has desired to long for your judgments,"[46] or (to put it more appropriately), "My soul has longed to desire your judgments"; and, "The desire for wisdom leads to sovereignty."[47] CITY OF GOD 14.7.[48]

---

[44]*WSA* 3 10:215. [45]Phil 1:23. [46]Ps 119:20 (118:20 LXX, Vg.). [47]Wis 6:20. [48]CG 557-58.

119:25-48 A DEVOTION ON THE WORD OF GOD (DALETH—WAW)

[25]*My soul cleaves to the dust;*
revive me according to thy word!
[26]*When I told of my ways, thou didst answer*
me;
teach me thy statutes!
[27]*Make me understand the way of thy precepts,*
and I will meditate on thy wondrous works.
[28]*My soul melts away for sorrow;*
strengthen me according to thy word!
[29]*Put false ways far from me;*
and graciously teach me thy law!
[30]*I have chosen the way of faithfulness,*
I set thy ordinances before me.

[31]*I cleave to thy testimonies, O* LORD;
let me not be put to shame!
[32]*I will run in the way of thy commandments*
when thou enlargest my understanding!

[33]*Teach me, O* LORD, *the way of thy statutes;*
and I will keep it to the end.
[34]*Give me understanding, that I may keep thy*
law
and observe it with my whole heart.
[35]*Lead me in the path of thy commandments,*
for I delight in it.
[36]*Incline my heart to thy testimonies,*

and not to gain!

³⁷Turn my eyes from looking at vanities;
    and give me life in thy ways.
³⁸Confirm to thy servant thy promise,
    which is for those who fear thee.
³⁹Turn away the reproach which I dread;
    for thy ordinances are good.
⁴⁰Behold, I long for thy precepts;
    in thy righteousness give me life!

⁴¹Let thy steadfast love come to me, O Lord,
    thy salvation according to thy promise;
⁴²then shall I have an answer for those who
    taunt me,

for I trust in thy word.
⁴³And take not the word of truth utterly out of
    my mouth,
    for my hope is in thy ordinances.
⁴⁴I will keep thy law continually,
    for ever and ever;
⁴⁵and I shall walk at liberty,
    for I have sought thy precepts.
⁴⁶I will also speak of thy testimonies before kings,
    and shall not be put to shame;
⁴⁷for I find my delight in thy commandments,
    which I love.
⁴⁸I revere thy commandments, which I love,
    and I will meditate on thy statutes.

Overview: Even the mightiest of people must become penitent suppliants in the presence of God (Theodoret). Creation and divine miracles, as recounted in Scripture, should not be seen as natural processes but be believed because they are attested to in Scripture (Ambrose). Security and strength for this life can be found only in the Word of God and by faith and obedience to God's will (Caesarius). The word *useful* should suggest not money or business success but Christ and godliness with contentment (Ambrose). We should follow King David's example and not be interested in the empty values of the theater and the arena if we want deliverance from this world (Cyril of Jerusalem). People who want to be saved must turn to Christ and away from the vanities of this world (Ambrose).

119:25-28 Revive, Teach and Strengthen Me

I Am Laid Low in the Dust. Theodoret of Cyr: Now the very faithful emperor[1] came boldly within the holy temple but did not pray to his Lord standing, or even on his knees, but lying prone upon the ground he uttered David's cry, "My soul cleaves to the dust; you give me life according to your word." Ecclesiastical History 5.17.[2]

Trust God's Word Above Reason or Natural Explanation. Ambrose: I bid you, therefore, be considerate enough to regard in a natural sense our plausible discourse and to weigh our statements in simplicity of mind and with attentive intellect. Do not follow the traditions of philosophy or those who gather the semblance of truth in the "vain deceit"[3] of the arts of persuasion. Rather, accept, in accordance with the rule of truth, what is set forth in the inspired words of God and is poured into the hearts of the faithful by the contemplation of such sublimity. For it is written: "Strengthen me in your words." "The wicked have told me fables but not as your law, O Lord. All your statutes are truth."[4] Therefore, not the nature of the elements but Christ himself, who created the world in the abundance and plenitude of his divinity, should be our standard in the examination of what was created and in the question as to what natural power is able to achieve. The people who beheld with their own eyes the miracles related in the Gospel of the healing of the leper and that of giving sight to the blind did not regard these as a medical process

---

[1]Theodosius I. [2]NPNF 2 3:144*. [3]Col 2:8. [4]Ps 119:85-86 (118:85-86 LXX, Vg.).

but rather, marveling at the power of the Lord, "gave praise to God," as it is written.[5] Moses did not follow the calculations of the Egyptians and the conjunctions of the stars and the relations of the elements when he stretched out his hand to divide the Red Sea, but he was complying with the commands of divine power. Hence, he says, "Your right hand, O Lord, is magnified in strength. Your right hand, O Lord, has broken the enemy."[6] To him, therefore, you faithful people, lift up your mind and bring to him all your heart. God does not see as people do: God sees with his mind; people see with their eyes. Therefore, people do not see as God does. Pay attention to what God saw and what he praised. Do not, therefore, estimate with your eyes or weigh with your mind the problem of creation. Rather, you should not regard as a subject for debate what God saw and approved of. Six Days of Creation 2.1.3.[7]

Strengthened by God's Word. Caesarius of Arles: "And you," it says, "may dwell securely in your land."[8] The wicked person is never secure but is always disturbed and wavering. He is tossed about by every wind of doctrine to deceitful error, by the craftiness of people. However, the just person who observes God's law dwells in security on his land, because he governs his body in fear of God and brings it into subjection. His understanding is firm when he says to God, "Strengthen me according to your words, O Lord." Strengthened, secure and well-rooted, he dwells on the earth, founded in faith. His house is not built on sand but is established on solid ground. Sermon 105.4.[9]

119:36-40 Give Me Life in Your Righteousness

That Which Is Useful. Ambrose: Therefore, as I am about to speak of what is useful, I will take up those words of the prophet: "Incline my heart to your testimonies and not to covetousness," that the sound of the word *useful* may not

rouse in us the desire for money. Some indeed put it thus: "Incline my heart to your testimonies and not to what is useful," that is, that kind of usefulness that is always on the watch for making gains in business and has been bent and diverted by the habits of people to the pursuit of money. For as a rule most people call useful only what is profitable, but we are speaking of that kind of usefulness that is sought in earthly loss "that we may gain Christ,"[10] whose gain is "godliness with contentment."[11] Great, too, is the gain whereby we attain to godliness, which is rich with God, not indeed in fleeting wealth but in eternal gifts, and in which rests no uncertain trial but constant and unending grace. Duties of the Clergy 2.6.26.[12]

Turn My Eyes from Worthless Things. Cyril of Jerusalem: Next you say,[13] "and all his pomp." The pomp of the devil is the craze for the theater, the horse races in the circus, the wildbeast hunts and all such emptiness, from which the saint prays to God to be delivered in the words, "Turn away my eyes that they may not behold worthless things." Avoid an addiction to the theater, with its portrayal of sinful conduct, the lewd and unseemly antics of actors and the frantic dancing of degenerates. Not for you, either, the folly of those who, to gratify their miserable appetite, expose themselves to wild beasts in the combats in the amphitheater. They pamper their belly at the cost of becoming themselves, in the event, food for the mouths of savage beasts; of these gladiators it is fair to say that in the service of the belly that is their god they court death in the arena. Shun also the bedlam of the races, a spectacle in which souls as well as riders come to grief. All these follies are the pomp of the devil. Mystagogical Lectures 1.6.[14]

---

[5]Mt 8:2; 9:30; Lk 18:43. [6]Ex 15:6. [7]FC 42:46-48**. [8]Lev 26:5. [9]FC 47:121*. (For a similar quote see Origen *Homily* 165 [FC 83:271].) [10]Phil 3:8. [11]1 Tim 6:6. [12]NPNF 2 10:47-48*. [13]Cyril was just speaking of all sin being the work of Satan and that all temptations that are contrary to a person's baptismal promise must be renounced. [14]FC 64:156-57**.

SEEK CHRIST AND FLEE WORLDLY THINGS.
AMBROSE: Therefore David, who had experienced those very glances that are dangerous for a man,[15] aptly says that the one is blessed whose every hope is in the name of God.[16] For such a person does not have regard to worthless things and follies if he always strives toward Christ and always looks on Christ with his inner eyes. For this reason David turned to God again and said, "Turn away my eyes, that they may not see vanity." The circus is vanity, because it is totally without profit; horse racing is vanity, because it is counterfeit as regards salvation; the theater is vanity, every game is vanity. "All things are vanity!"[17] as Ecclesiastes said, all things that are in this world. Accordingly, let one who wishes to be saved ascend above the world, let him seek the Word who is with God, let him flee from this world and depart from the earth. For one cannot comprehend that which exists and exists always, unless he has first fled from here. On this account also, the Lord, wishing to approach God the Father, said to the apostles, "Arise, let us go from here."[18] FLIGHT FROM THE WORLD 1.4.[19]

---

[15]2 Sam 11:2-5. [16]See Ps 40:5 (39:6 LXX, Vg.). [17]Eccles 1:2. [18]Jn 14:31. [19]FC 65:282-83*.

119:49-80 A DEVOTION ON THE WORD OF GOD (ZAYIN—YODH)

[49]Remember thy word to thy servant,
  in which thou hast made me hope.
[50]This is my comfort in my affliction
  that thy promise gives me life.
[51]Godless men utterly deride me,
  but I do not turn away from thy law.
[52]When I think of thy ordinances from of old,
  I take comfort, O LORD.
[53]Hot indignation seizes me because of the
    wicked,
  who forsake thy law.
[54]Thy statutes have been my songs
  in the house of my pilgrimage.
[55]I remember thy name in the night, O LORD,
  and keep thy law.
[56]This blessing has fallen to me,
  that I have kept thy precepts.

[57]The LORD is my portion;
  I promise to keep thy words.
[58]I entreat thy favor with all my heart;
  be gracious to me according to thy promise.
[59]When I think of thy ways,
  I turn my feet to thy testimonies;
[60]I hasten and do not delay
  to keep thy commandments.
[61]Though the cords of the wicked ensnare me,
  I do not forget thy law.
[62]At midnight I rise to praise thee,
  because of thy righteous ordinances.
[63]I am a companion of all who fear thee,
  of those who keep thy precepts.
[64]The earth, O LORD, is full of thy steadfast
    love;
  teach me thy statutes!

⁶⁵Thou hast dealt well with thy servant,
  O LORD, according to thy word.
⁶⁶Teach me good judgment and knowledge,
  for I believe in thy commandments.
⁶⁷Before I was afflicted I went astray;
  but now I keep thy word.
⁶⁸Thou art good and doest good;
  teach me thy statutes.
⁶⁹The godless besmear me with lies,
  but with my whole heart I keep thy precepts;
⁷⁰their heart is gross like fat,
  but I delight in thy law.
⁷¹It is good for me that I was afflicted,
  that I might learn thy statutes.
⁷²The law of thy mouth is better to me
  than thousands of gold and silver pieces.

⁷³Thy hands have made and fashioned me;
  give me understanding that I may learn thy
commandments.
⁷⁴Those who fear thee shall see me and rejoice,
  because I have hoped in thy word.
⁷⁵I know, O LORD, that thy judgments are
  right,
  and that in faithfulness thou hast afflicted
  me.
⁷⁶Let thy steadfast love be ready to comfort me
  according to thy promise to thy servant.
⁷⁷Let thy mercy come to me, that I may live;
  for thy law is my delight.
⁷⁸Let the godless be put to shame,
  because they have subverted me with guile;
  as for me, I will meditate on thy precepts.
⁷⁹Let those who fear thee turn to me,
  that they may know thy testimonies.
⁸⁰May my heart be blameless in thy statutes,
  that I may not be put to shame!

OVERVIEW: God gives us strength and fortitude to bear the trials and weaknesses we experience in this life (HILARY). The church must not be allowed to be undone by people who bring in heresies and schisms; they must be tolerated rather than separated since separation will occur at the final judgment (AUGUSTINE).

The inheritance that we receive from God is his commands, his words and precepts (AMBROSE). Our souls can find rest and quiet by remembering the example of saintly people (BASIL). Nighttime is a good time to pray because our minds are relieved of many of the troubles and pressures of daytime activities (CHRYSOSTOM). Great people of faith prayed at night when they were free of the burdens of the day and received answers to their prayer (ISAAC). We should offer different kinds of prayer suitable to various needs and occasions—petitions, thanksgiving, praise (APHRAHAT). When the soul embraces the Word of God, it has unlimited joy and delight. Knowledge of sin should humble us and thereby sever the bond of transgression we have with Adam and Eve (AMBROSE).

Christ assumed a human nature that was made like that of other human beings (ATHANASIUS). We may speak words of divine truth to one another, but it is God who enables us to understand them (AUGUSTINE). God is the author of our birth and life (PETER CHRYSOLOGUS).

119:50-53 Comfort in My Afflictions

YOUR WORD HAS GIVEN ME LIFE. HILARY OF POITIERS: We are instructed in all this, but the prophet has already experienced it.[1] He says, "This hope has consoled me in my humility, for your word has given me life." The hope is the hope that God has implanted in him. It has con-

---

[1]Consolation during times of trials and indignities with God's promise of a future life in heaven.

soled him "in his humility," that is, when he is spurned, mocked, vexed by injustices, dishonored by insults, for he knows that he is soldiering through his present trials. But the hope instilled by the Lord consoles him in these wars endured in his weakness, and he is lent life by the utterances of God. By these he knows that the glory of his weakness is outstanding in heaven. He knows that his soul, renewed by the utterances of God, contains within it, so to say, the nourishment of eternal life. He lives by God's utterances and is untroubled by the empty fame of the proud, for he knows that his need is richer than their wealth. He knows that his fasting is abundantly fed by the blessing of heaven and the gospel, that his humility will be rewarded by the glorious prize of honor. So he added, "The arrogant mock me without restraint, but I do not turn from your law." HOMILY ON PSALM 118.[2]

WEARINESS HAS TAKEN HOLD OF ME.

AUGUSTINE: So there you are, I have said a few words to prevent the boats from sinking.[3] Something much more dreadful happened at that catch of fish,[4] and that is that the nets were broken. The nets were broken, heresies arose. What else, after all, are schisms, but tears of the fabric? The first catch of fish has to be endured and tolerated in such a way that nobody grows weary, even though it is written, "Weariness has taken hold of me because of sinners who forsake your law." It is the boat crying out that it is being overloaded by the mob, as though the boat itself is giving voice to these words, "I have become weary because of sinners who forsake your law." Even if you are being overloaded, always see to it that you do not sink. Bad people are to be put up with now, not to be separated and cut off. "Mercy and judgment we shall sing to the Lord."[5] First of all mercy is extended, and later on judgment is exercised; separation will happen at the judgment. Now may the good person listen to me and become better; may the bad person too listen and become good, while it is the time for repentance, not for sentence. SERMON 250.2.[6]

119:57-62 Hasten to Keep God's Commandments

GOD IS MY INHERITANCE.

AMBROSE: The possession of God is owed to such as these, as Isaiah says: "This is the inheritance of those who believe in the Lord."[7] Very aptly does he say, "This is the inheritance," for that alone is the inheritance; there is no other. The inheritance is not a treasure that people stumble on blindly, and passing things have not the quality of an inheritance. The only inheritance is that in which God is the portion, as the Lord's holy one says: "God is my inheritance," and again: "I have become an heir of your precepts."[8] You see what are the possessions of the just person: God's commandments, his words, his precepts. In these he is rich; on these he feeds; with these he is delighted as if by all riches. LETTER 82.[9]

I AM NOT TROUBLED IN MY SOUL.

BASIL THE GREAT: Let each of these considerations find entrance into your mind and check the swollen growth of wrath. By such preparations and by acquiring such dispositions, we quiet the leaping and throbbing of the heart and restore it to tranquil steadiness. This, indeed, is the implication in the words of David: "I am ready and am not troubled." You must, therefore, repress the violent and frenzied movement of the soul by recalling the example of saintly people. How gently, for instance, the mighty David bore the fury of Shimei. He did not allow himself to grow angry but turned his thoughts to God, saying, "The Lord has bid him curse David."[10] HOMILY AGAINST THOSE PROVE TO ANGER.[11]

[2]MFC 17:184*. [3]Augustine had just been speaking about the large number of people joining the church. Since some of them are not sincere in their faith but continue in their wickedness and seem to prosper and be happy, the true believers are tempted to follow the lifestyle of the wicked and fall from faith—too many unregenerate people in the church is analogous to too large a catch of fish breaking the nets and sinking a boat. [4]Large number of converts. [5]Ps 101:1 (100:1 LXX, Vg.). [6]WSA 3 7:122. [7]Is 54:17. [8]Ps 119:57, 111 (118:57, 111 LXX, Vg.). [9]FC 26:459-60*. [10]2 Sam 16:10. [11]FC 9:455*.

PRAYER AT MIDNIGHT. CHRYSOSTOM: Accordingly, let us condition ourselves to not be easily distracted from the task of approaching God constantly with our prayers day and night, and especially at night. Night is the time when there is no one to hinder us, when there is great peace of mind, when there is complete repose. It is also the time when all turmoil is left outside the house, when no one is likely to put us off or distract us from entreaty, and when our mind happens to be set at rest and is able to propose everything precisely to the physician of souls. I mean, if blessed David, king as he was as well as inspired author and beset with so many worries, clad in mantle and crown, could say, "At midnight I rise to praise you for the rulings of your justice," what should we say who, despite leading a private and carefree life, do not even do the same as he? In other words, since by day he had much on his mind, a great mass of business, terrible confusion, and could not find a suitable time for the proper kind of prayer, he prayed during the time of respite that others devote to sleep, lying on soft beds, tossing and turning. On the contrarythe king, though caught up in such responsibility, devoted the time to prayer, conversing privately with God, directing sincere entreaties to him of the most intense kind, and thus he achieved whatever he set his mind to. Through these prayers he was successful in wars, inflicting defeat and adding victory to victory. He enjoyed, you see, an invincible weaponry, an ally from on high sufficient not merely for battles conducted by human beings but also for the cohorts of the demons. HOMILIES ON GENESIS 30.17.[12]

RIGHTEOUS PEOPLE PRAY AT NIGHT. ISAAC OF NINEVEH: Prayer offered up at night possesses a great power, more so than the prayer of the daytime. Therefore all the righteous prayed during the night, while combating the heaviness of the body and the sweetness of sleep and repelling corporeal nature. And this the prophet also says, "I toiled in my groaning; every night I will wash my bed, with tears will I water my couch,"[13] while he sighed in fervent prayer. And again, "At midnight I arose to give thanks unto Thee for the judgments of Thy righteousness." And for every entreaty for which they urgently besought God, they armed themselves with the prayer of night vigil, and at once they received their request. ASCETICAL HOMILIES 75.[14]

DIFFERENT KINDS OF PRAYER. APHRAHAT: In petition one asks for mercy for one's sins, in thanksgiving you give thanks to your Father who is in heaven, while in praise you praise him for his works. At a time when you are in trouble, offer up petition, and when you are well supplied with good things, you should give thanks to the Giver, and when your mind rejoices, offer up praise. Make all these prayers of yours with discernment to God. See how David was always saying, "I have risen to give thanks to you for your judgments, O just One." And in another psalm he said, "Praise the Lord in heaven, praise him in the heights."[15] Again he says, "I will bless the Lord at all times, and at all times his praises are in my mouth."[16] Do not pray using only one kind of prayer, but pray them at different times. DEMONSTRATIONS 4.17.[17]

119:68-71 Teach Me Your Statutes

DESIRE AND LOVE GOD ABOVE EVERYTHING. AMBROSE: If the soul, with its capacity for pleasure and delight, has tasted this true and highest good and has adhered to both[18] with the means at its disposal, putting away sorrow and fear, then it is wonderfully inflamed. Having embraced the Word of God, it knows no bounds, it knows no satiety, and says, "You are sweet, O Lord, and in your joy teach me your laws." Having embraced the Word of God, the soul desires him above every beauty; it loves him above every

---

[12]FC 82:234**. [13]Ps 6:6 (6:7 LXX). [14]*AHSIS* 372. [15]Ps 148:1. [16]Ps 34:1 (33:2 LXX). [17]CS 101:22**. [18]*The true goodness and the highest goodness, both of which describe Jesus Christ.*

joy; it is delighted with him above every perfume; it wishes often to see, often to gaze, often to be drawn to him that it may follow. "Your name," it says, "is as oil poured out,[19] and that is why we maidens love you and vie with one another but cannot attain to you. Draw us that we may run after you, that from the odor of ointments we may receive the power to follow you. LETTER 79.[20]

IT IS GOOD TO BE HUMBLED. AMBROSE: Sin abounded by the law because through the law came knowledge of sin,[21] and it became harmful for me to know what through my weakness I could not avoid. It is good to know beforehand what one is to avoid, but, if I cannot avoid something, it is harmful to have known about it. Thus was the law changed to its opposite, yet it became useful to me by the very increase of sin, for I was humbled. And David therefore says, "It is good for me that I have been humbled." By humbling myself I have broken the bonds of that ancient transgression by which Adam and Eve had bound the whole line of their succession. Hence, too, the Lord came as an obedient man to loose the knot of human disobedience and deception. And as through disobedience sin entered, so through obedience sin was remitted. Therefore, the apostle says, "For just as by the disobedience of one man the many were constituted sinners, so also by the obedience of the one the many will be constituted just."[22] LETTER 83.[23]

119:73 Let Me Learn God's Commandments

IT IS GOD WHO HAS MADE ME. ATHANASIUS: But though we were to allow some prerogative to the Protoplast[24] as having been deemed worthy of the hand of God, still it must be one of honor, not of nature. For he came from the earth, as other people, and the hand that then fashioned Adam is also both now and ever fashioning and giving entire consistency [same human nature] to those who come after him. And God declares this to Jeremiah, as I said

before: "Before I formed you in the womb, I knew you";[25] and so he says of all, "All those things have my hand made";[26] and again by Isaiah, "Thus says the Lord, your redeemer, and he that formed you from the womb, I am the Lord that makes all things; that stretches forth the heavens alone; that spreads abroad the earth by myself."[27] And David, knowing this, says in the psalm, "Your hands have made me and fashioned me"; and he who says in Isaiah, "Thus says the Lord who formed me from the womb to be his servant,"[28] signifies the same. Therefore, in respect of nature, Christ differs nothing from us though he precede us in time, so long as we all consist and are created by the same hand. DEFENSE OF THE NICENE DEFINITION 3.9.[29]

UNDERSTANDING IS A GIFT OF GOD. AUGUSTINE: Without doubt, if what I said is true and you not only heard this true thing but also understood it, two things happened there; distinguish them, hearing and understanding. Hearing occurred through me; through whom did understanding occur? I spoke to the ear that you might hear; who spoke to your heart that you might understand? Without a doubt, someone also said something to your heart so that not only did that sound of words strike your ear but something of truth descended into your heart. Someone spoke also to your heart, but you did not see him. If you understand, brothers, your heart has also been spoken to. Understanding is a gift of God. If you understood, who spoke this in your heart? He to whom the psalm says, "Give me understanding that I may learn your commands." TRACTATES ON THE GOSPEL OF JOHN 40.5.3.[30]

FORMED BY THE HANDS OF GOD. PETER CHRYSOLOGUS: Futile is the act of the father and mother, unless the Creator's work and will also

---

[19]Song 1:2. [20]FC 26:441-42*. [21]Rom 7:7. [22]Rom 5:19. [23]FC 26:466-67. [24]Adam as the first human being created by God. [25]Jer 1:5. [26]Is 66:2. [27]Is 44:24. [28]Is 49:5. [29]NPNF 2 4:155*. [30]FC 88:128.

touch the offspring. "Your hands have made me and formed me." And elsewhere it is written, "You have formed me and have laid your hand on me."[31] Therefore, we do not owe our birth and life to ourselves, but we owe them entirely to our Creator. SERMON 6.[32]

---

[31]Ps 139:5 (138:5 LXX, Vg.). [32]FC 17:55*.

119:81-104 A DEVOTION ON THE WORD OF GOD (*KAPH-MEM*)

[81]My soul languishes for thy salvation;
  I hope in thy word.
[82]My eyes fail with watching for thy promise;
  I ask, "When wilt thou comfort me?"
[83]For I have become like a wineskin in the
  smoke,
  yet I have not forgotten thy statutes.
[84]How long must thy servant endure?
  When wilt thou judge those who persecute
  me?
[85]Godless men have dug pitfalls for me,
  men who do not conform to thy law.
[86]All thy commandments are sure;
  they persecute me with falsehood; help me!
[87]They have almost made an end of me on
  earth;
  but I have not forsaken thy precepts.
[88]In thy steadfast love spare my life,
  that I may keep the testimonies of thy mouth

[89]For ever, O LORD, thy word
  is firmly fixed in the heavens.
[90]Thy faithfulness endures to all generations;
  thou hast established the earth, and
  it stands fast.
[91]By thy appointment they stand this day;

  for all things are thy servants.
[92]If thy law had not been my delight,
  I should have perished in my affliction.
[93]I will never forget thy precepts;
  for by them thou hast given me life.
[94]I am thine, save me;
  for I have sought thy precepts.
[95]The wicked lie in wait to destroy me;
  but I consider thy testimonies.
[96]I have seen a limit to all perfection,
  but thy commandment is exceedingly broad.

[97]Oh, how I love thy law!
  It is my meditation all the day.
[98]Thy commandment makes me wiser than my
  enemies,
  for it is ever with me.
[99]I have more understanding than all my
  teachers,
  for thy testimonies are my meditation.
[100]I understand more than the aged,
  for I keep thy precepts.
[101]I hold back my feet from every evil way,
  in order to keep thy word.
[102]I do not turn aside from thy ordinances,
  for thou hast taught me.

*[103]How sweet are thy words to my taste,
      sweeter than honey to my mouth!*

*[104]Through thy precepts I get understanding;
      therefore I hate every false way.*

OVERVIEW: The Scriptures declare God's providential care and ordering of the world (ATHANASIUS). The day of judgment is fully established by God (AMBROSE). The summary of God's law is brotherly love. Whoever loves Christ will extend his love to everyone throughout the world; to love less is to divide the body of Christ, the church. When we come to Christ (are in Christ) we see love as the fulfillment of the commandments (AUGUSTINE). The soul that has tasted the sweetness of God's Word can desire nothing more than to remain or be with God continually (AMBROSE). The Old Testament law was harsh and bitter until it was tempered and sweetened by the mystery of the cross proclaimed in the gospel (MAXIMUS).

119:81-86 *A Prayer for Help*

MY SOUL LONGS FOR YOUR SALVATION. BEDE: "And Joseph called his name Jesus." "Jesus" in Hebrew means "saving" or "savior" in Latin.[1] It is clear that the prophets most certainly call on his name. Hence these things are sung in great desire for a vision of him: "My soul will exult in the Lord and take delight in his salvation."[2] "My soul pines for your salvation." "I, however, will glory in the Lord; I will rejoice in God my Jesus."[3] And especially that [verse]: "God in your name save me!"[4] as if the [prophet] would say, "You who are called Savior, make bright the glory of your name in me by saving [me]." HOMILIES ON THE GOSPELS 1.5.[5]

LOVE GOD AND ONE ANOTHER. AUGUSTINE: What order does God impose on you? "Love me. You love gold, you will seek gold, and perhaps you will not find it. Whoever seeks me, I am with him. You will love honor, and perhaps you will not find it. Whoever seeks me, I am with him. Who has loved me and has not attained

me?" God says to you, "You wish to make [someone] a patron or a powerful friend of yours; you solicit him through someone else inferior. Love me," God says to you, "there is no soliciting of me through anyone; love itself makes me present to you." What is sweeter than this love, brothers? Not without reason you just heard in the psalm, "The unjust have told me of delights, but not as your law, Lord." What is the law of God? The commandment of God. What is the commandment of God? That new commandment that is called new for the very reason that it renews: "A new commandment I give to you, that you love one another."[6] Hear that this is the law of God. The apostle says, "Bear one another's burdens, and so you will fulfill the law of Christ."[7] This is the consummation of all our works, love. There is the end. Because of this we are running; to this we are running. When we come to it, we shall rest. HOMILIES ON 1 JOHN 10.4.[8]

TRUE VERSUS FALSE MARTYRS. AUGUSTINE: The true martyrs are those of whom the Lord says, "Blessed are they who suffer persecution for justice's sake."[9] Therefore, it is not those who suffer for the sake of injustice and the impious division of Christian unity, but those who suffer persecution for justice's sake who are truly martyrs. Hagar suffered persecution from Sarah, yet the one who persecuted was holy and she who suffered was sinful.[10] Is that any reason for comparing the persecution suffered by Hagar to that with which the wicked Saul afflicted holy David?[11] Obviously, there is a very great difference, not because David suffered, but because he suffered for justice's sake. And the Lord himself

---

[1]Isidore. *Etymol.* 7.2.7. [2]Ps 35:9 (34:9 LXX, Vg.). [3]See Phil 4:4. [4]Ps 54:1 (53:1 LXX, Vg.). [5]CS 110:49-50*. [6]Jn 13:34. [7]Gal 6:2. [8]FC 92:267*. [9]Mt 5:10. [10]Gen 16:6. [11]1 Sam 18:8-29.

was crucified among thieves.[12] But, though they were alike in suffering, they were different in the reason for suffering. Therefore, in the psalm we must understand the voice of the true martyr wishing to be distinguished from false martyrs: "Judge me, O God, and distinguish my cause from the nation that is not holy."[13] He does not say "distinguish my punishment" but "distinguish my cause." For the punishment of the wicked can be the same, but the cause of the martyrs is not the same, and their cry is, "They have persecuted me unjustly; help me." The psalmist thinks himself worthy of being justly helped because they persecuted unjustly, for, if they persecuted justly, he would not be worthy of help but of chastisement. LETTER 185.9.[14]

119:90-96 God's Faithfulness Endures

GOD HAS LAID THE FOUNDATIONS OF THE WORLD. ATHANASIUS: But that the providence and ordering power of the Word also, over all and toward all, is attested by all inspired Scripture, this passage suffices to confirm our argument, where people who speak of God say, "You have laid the foundation of the earth, and it abides. The day continues according to your ordinance." AGAINST THE HEATHEN 46.2.[15]

THE DAY OF JUDGMENT IS CERTAIN. AMBROSE: If we are to believe this [that God knows the past, present and future] about the ages, much more must we believe it about the day of judgment, on the ground that the Son of God has knowledge of it, as being already made by him. For it is written, "According to your ordinance the day will continue." He did not merely say "the day continues" but even "will continue," so that the things that are to come might be governed by his ordinance. Does he not know what he ordered? "He who planted the ear, shall he not hear? He who formed the eye, shall he not see?"[16] ON THE CHRISTIAN FAITH 5.4.198.[17]

GOD'S COMMANDS KNOW NO LIMIT. AUGUS-

TINE: We answer them: You have Christ's baptism; come, in order to have Christ's Spirit as well. Be afraid of what is written: "But anyone who does not have the Spirit of Christ, that person does not belong to him."[18] You have put on Christ in the form of the sacrament; put him on by imitating his example, "since Christ suffered for us, leaving us an example, so that we might follow his footsteps."[19] Do not be people who "have the form of piety but deny its power."[20] What greater power could piety have than the love of unity? It says in the Psalms, "I have seen the end of every consummation; your commandment is exceedingly broad." Which commandment, if not the one about which it says, "A new commandment I give you, that you should love one another"?[21] Why "broad," if not because "the love of God has been poured out in our hearts"?[22] Why "an end of every" consummation, if not because "the fullness of the law is love; and the whole law is summed up in this" that is written: You shall love "your neighbor" as "yourself"?[23] The way you people, though, love your neighbors as yourselves, is that while you do not want anything bad to be believed about you, which has neither been seen nor proved, you are happy to believe about the whole world what you have neither seen nor received any proof of. SERMON 269.3.[24]

LOVE KNOWS NO BOUNDARIES. AUGUSTINE: Let us run, therefore, my brothers, let us run and let us love Christ. What Christ? Jesus Christ. Who is this? The Word of God. And how does he come to the sick? "The Word was made flesh and dwelled among us."[25] What Scripture foretold was, therefore, accomplished: "Christ will suffer and rise from the dead on the third day."[26] Where does his body lie? Where do his members toil? Where ought

---

[12]Mt 27:38; Mk 15:27; Lk 23:33. [13]Ps 43:1 (42:1 LXX, Vg.). [14]FC 30:149-50*. [15]NPNF 2 4:28*. [16]Ps 94:9 (93:9 LXX, Vg.). [17]NPNF 2 10:309*. [18]Rom 8:9. [19]1 Pet 2:21. [20]2 Tim 3:5. [21]Jn 13:34. [22]Rom 5:5. [23]Rom 13:9-10. [24]WSA 3 7:285. [25]Jn 1:14. [26]Lk 24:46.

you to be so that you may be under the head? "And penance and remission of sins is to be preached in his name through all the nations, beginning from Jerusalem."[27] Let your love be spread about there. Christ and the psalm, that is, the Spirit of God, say, "Exceedingly broad is your commandment"—and someone or other puts in Africa the boundaries of love! Extend love through the whole world if you wish to love Christ, because Christ's members lie throughout the world. If you love apart, you have been divided. If you have been divided, you are not in the body. If you are not in the body, you are not under the head. HOMILIES ON 1 JOHN 10.8.1.[28]

LOVE IS THE END OF ALL THE COMMAND-MENTS. AUGUSTINE: You have heard in the psalm, "I have seen an end to all perfection." What had this person seen? Had he climbed, do we suppose, to the peak of some very high and very sharp mountain and had he looked out and seen the perimeter of the earth and the circles of the whole world and therefore said, "I have seen an end of all perfection"? If this is praiseworthy, let us seek from God eyes of flesh so sharp that we may look for some exceedingly lofty mountain that is on earth from whose top we may see an end of all perfection. Do not go far. Look, I say to you, climb onto the mountain and see the end. Christ is the mountain. Come to Christ; you see from there an end of all perfection. What is this end? Ask Paul. "Now the end of the command-ment is love, from a pure heart and a good con-science and an unfeigned faith."[29] And in another place, "But love is the fulfillment of the law."[30] HOMILIES ON 1 OF JOHN 10.5.1.[31]

119:103 God's Words Are Sweeter Than Honey

THE SWEETNESS OF GOD'S WORD. AMBROSE: The soul presses forward for a glimpse of hidden mysteries, to the very abode of the Word, to the very dwelling place of that highest Good, and

his light and brightness. In that bosom and secret dwelling place of the Father the soul has-tens to hear his words, and having heard them, it finds them sweeter than all things. Let the prophet who has tasted this sweetness teach you, when he says, "How sweet are your words to my lips, above honeycomb to my mouth." What else can a soul desire when it has once tasted the sweetness of the Word, when it has once seen its brightness? When Moses remained on the mountain forty days to receive the law, he had no need of food for the body.[32] Elijah, rest-ing [under a broom tree], asked that his life be taken away from him.[33] Even Peter, foreseeing on the mountain the glory of the Lord's resur-rection, did not wish to come down and said, "Lord, it is good for us to be here."[34] How great is the glory of that divine Essence, how great the graces of the Word at which even angels wish to gaze! LETTER 79.[35]

THE SWEETENING EFFECT OF THE GOSPEL. MAXIMUS OF TURIN: In this mystical number,[36] I say, the children of Israel, arriving at Marah and being unable to draw the water because of its bit-terness (for the well had water but no sweetness, and it was pleasing to the eye but polluted to the taste), drank water that became sweet and mild as soon as wood was thrown into it by Moses.[37] The sacrament of the wood removed the harsh-ness that the noxious water bore. I believe that this happened as a sign,[38] for I think that the bit-ter water of Marah is the Old Testament law, which was harsh before it was tempered by the Lord's cross. For it used to command "an eye for an eye and a tooth for a tooth"[39] and, austere as it was, it offered none of mercy's consolation. But,

---

[27]Lk 24:47. [28]FC 92:273*. [29]1 Tim 1:5. [30]Rom 13:10. [31]FC 92:267-68*. [32]See Ex 34:28. [33]1 Kings 19:4. [34]Mt 17:4. [35]FC 26:442*. [36]The number 42. See Numbers 33:1-49, where Moses rescued the Israelites from Egypt and led them to the promised land in stages of forty-two days. Also, in fifth-century Turin, Lent extended over the six weeks preceding Easter Sunday. Thus, it took stages of forty-two days to reach the Jordan River and forty-two days of preparation for bap-tism. [37]Ex 15:23-25. [38]See 1 Cor 10:6. [39]Ex 21:24.

when it had been tempered by the wood of gospel suffering,[40] at once it changed its bitterness into mildness and presented itself as a sweet drink to all, as the prophet says: "How sweet are your words to my taste, more than honey and the honeycomb to my mouth!" For sweet are the words that command, "If anyone strikes you on your cheek, offer him the other as well; if anyone takes your tunic from you, leave him your cloak too."[41] This, then, is the bitterness that has been changed into sweetness: the austerity of the law has been tempered by the grace of the gospel. For the letter of the law is bitter without the mystery of the cross; about this the apostle says, "The letter kills."[42] But when the sacraments of the passion are joined to it, all its bitterness is spiritually buried, and about that the apostle says, "But the Spirit gives life."[43] SERMON 67.4.[44]

---

[40]That the wood thrown into the waters of Marah symbolizes the cross is an image that dates back to Justin Martyr (see *Dialogue with Trypho the Jew* 86). [41]Mt 5:39-40. [42]2 Cor 3:6. [43]2 Cor 3:6. [44]ACW

119:105-136 A DEVOTION ON THE WORD OF GOD (NUN—PE)

[105]Thy word is a lamp to my feet
  and a light to my path.
[106]I have sworn an oath and confirmed it,
  to observe thy righteous ordinances.
[107]I am sorely afflicted;
  give me life, O LORD, according to thy word!
[108]Accept my offerings of praise, O LORD,
  and teach me thy ordinances.
[109]I hold my life in my hand continually,
  but I do not forget thy law.
[110]The wicked have laid a snare for me,
  but I do not stray from thy precepts.
[111]Thy testimonies are my heritage for ever;
  yea, they are the joy of my heart.
[112]I incline my heart to perform thy statutes
  for ever, to the end.

[113]I hate double-minded men,
  but I love thy law.
[114]Thou art my hiding place and my shield;
  I hope in thy word.
[115]Depart from me, you evildoers,
  that I may keep the commandments of my
    God.
[116]Uphold me according to thy promise, that I
    may live,
  and let me not be put to shame in my hope!
[117]Hold me up, that I may be safe
  and have regard for thy statutes continually!
[118]Thou dost spurn all who go astray from thy
    statutes;
  yea, their cunning is in vain.
[119]All the wicked of the earth thou dost count
    as dross;
  therefore I love thy testimonies.
[120]My flesh trembles for fear of thee,
  and I am afraid of thy judgments.

[121]I have done what is just and right;
  do not leave me to my oppressors.

¹²²*Be surety for thy servant for good;*
  let not the godless oppress me.
¹²³*My eyes fail with watching for thy salvation,*
  and for the fulfilment of thy righteous
    promise.
¹²⁴*Deal with thy servant according to thy*
    steadfast love,
  and teach me thy statutes.
¹²⁵*I am thy servant; give me understanding,*
  that I may know thy testimonies!
¹²⁶*It is time for the LORD to act,*
  for thy law has been broken.
¹²⁷*Therefore I love thy commandments*
  above gold, above fine gold.
¹²⁸*Therefore I direct my steps by all thy*
    precepts;[k]
  I hate every false way.

¹²⁹*Thy testimonies are wonderful;*
  therefore my soul keeps them.
¹³⁰*The unfolding of thy words gives light;*
  it imparts understanding to the simple.
¹³¹*With open mouth I pant,*
  because I long for thy commandments.
¹³²*Turn to me and be gracious to me,*
  as is thy wont toward those who love thy
    name.
¹³³*Keep steady my steps according to thy*
    promise,
  and let no iniquity get dominion over me.
¹³⁴*Redeem me from man's oppression,*
  that I may keep thy precepts.
¹³⁵*Make thy face shine upon thy servant,*
  and teach me thy statutes.
¹³⁶*My eyes shed streams of tears,*
  because men do not keep thy law.

k Gk Jerome: Heb uncertain

OVERVIEW: As a lamp God's Word enlightens us in this world, but as a light it shows us the way to a spiritual future (ORIGEN). The light of God's Word is the gospel, which brings light to the darkness of the world (AMBROSE). The light of God's Word guides our way and keeps us from falling into the snares of Satan (PRUDENTIUS). If the priests put the light of God's Word under a bushel, they hide true doctrine from the church and some will fall into error and sin; the true Word should not be hidden for temporal gain (CAESARIUS). No one has both the will and ability to do God's commands unless God mercifully grants it. When we praise God or eulogize a martyr, we must ask God to grant us acceptable words.

God rejects those who apostasize or reject him. Everyone enters this life as a sinner, not first by actual sin but through original sin, sin transmitted from one generation to the next. Everyone sins by transgressing the law written on their hearts (AUGUSTINE). Fear of God and faith in the power of the cross are more powerful than the threat of punishment (AMBROSE). No adversary can overpower the soul that is rooted in the fear of God and knowledge of Christ's teachings (CHRYSOSTOM). God commands us to be wise and to have understanding and graciously gives them to us when we pray for them (AUGUSTINE). Nature grants understanding, and knowledge of God's law is available in Scripture; yet we should pray for a better grasp of God's law (CASSIAN). Free will must be submissive to divine mercy and grace. Sin has no dominion over the person who finds his strength in God (AUGUSTINE).

119:105-108 Give Me Life, O Lord

THE DIFFERENCE BETWEEN LAMP AND LIGHT. ORIGEN: Nevertheless, I remember, when we explained that verse of Psalm 118

[LXX], in which it is written, "Your law, Lord, is a lamp to my feet and a light to my paths," we showed the difference between "lamp" and "light" as best we could. For we said that "the lamp" was allotted "for the feet," that is, the lower parts of the body; but "the light" was given "for the paths," which "paths" are called in another passage "eternal paths." Therefore, because according to such a mystical understanding this world is understood as the lower parts of creation, therefore "the lamp" of the law is mentioned as having been lit for these who are in this world as the feet of the whole creation. But the eternal "light" will be for those "paths" through which each one in accordance with his merits will advance into the future age. HOMILIES ON LEVITICUS 13.2.3.[1]

GOD'S WORD IS A LAMP TO MY FEET.

AMBROSE: "Therefore will I remember you, O Lord, from the land of Jordan and Hermon."[2] Therefore, one who is troubled, if he takes good counsel, goes out from Egypt and follows the way of light, for Hermon is interpreted to mean "way of the lamp." And so, go out first from Egypt, if you wish to see Christ's light. The Canaanite woman went out from the territory of the pagans and found Christ; she said to him, "Have pity on me, O son of David!"[3] Moses went out from Egypt and was made a prophet and sent back to the people, that he might free their souls from the land of affliction.[4] Moreover, the lamp is in the body of Christ, and this is the lamp that shows you the way. For this reason also holy David says, "Your word is a lamp to my feet," a lamp, because it has enlightened the souls of all people[5] and shown the way in the darkness. The way of the lamp is the gospel; it shines in the darkness, that is, in the world. THE PRAYER OF JOB AND DAVID 4.4.14.[6]

THE LAMP OF FAITH. PRUDENTIUS:

Behold a stone is set for us, a stumbling block,[7]
    Against which vanity may strike,
A sign unto the faithful, scandal to the lax,
    The one it fells, the other guides.
The blind one feels his way with slow
        uncertain step
    And runs into what'er he meets.
The lamp of faith alone must shine before our
        feet,
    That footsteps may unswerving be.
The foe assails and carries off the wanderers
    Who in the darkness go astray,
A demon who devours the wheat speeds on the
        way
    For pilgrims passing to and fro,
A thief who tampers with the fertile fields of
        Christ
    By sowing in them barren oats.[8]
A demon who devours the wheat spread on the
        way
    For pilgrims passing to and fro,
A thief who tampers with the fertile fields of
        Christ
    By sowing in them barren oats.[9]
THE DIVINITY OF CHRIST 33-46.[10]

DO NOT HIDE THE LIGHT OF GOD'S WORD.

CAESARIUS OF ARLES: If we notice carefully, we will realize that what our Lord said to the blessed apostles also refers to us: "You are the light of the world," he says, "and no one lights a lamp and puts it under a bushel but on the lampstand, so as to give light to all in the house."[11] Now, if the head's bodily eyes refuse to show the way to the rest of the members, the whole body walks in darkness. Similarly, if priests, who seem to have the function of eyes in the body of Christ the head, have been put on a lampstand in the church but are unwilling to shine in God's house and have ceased to show the light of doctrine to the whole church, it is to be feared that some of the people may become involved in the darkness of error and fall into some abyss of sin. The fact that the Lord said his word is a lamp is not a trite

---

[1]FC 83:234-35. [2]Ps 42:6 (41:7 LXX, Vg.). [3]Mt 15:22. [4]Ex 2:11-4:17. [5]Jn 1:9. [6]FC 65:398-99*. [7]See 1 Pet 2:7-8. [8]See Mt 13:25. [9]See Mt 13:25. [10]FC 52:4-5. [11]Mt 5:14-15.

utterance, for we read, "Your word is a lamp to my feet, O Lord." Now, profits of the present world are understood in the nature of a bushel. Who, indeed, puts a lamp under a bushel, except the person who darkens the light of doctrine with the profits of material advantages and fears to preach the truth lest he have less of the temporal possessions he desires? Thus, a person puts a lamp under a bushel if he prefers material to spiritual gains. SERMON 1.16.[12]

THE WILL AND ABILITY TO BE GODLY. AUGUSTINE:

Is anybody, I mean to say, in a position to have both the will and the ability, unless the one who granted us the will by calling us also helps us to have the ability by inspiring us? The fact is, his mercy gets in ahead of us every single time; to call us when we were lacking the will and then to ensure we obtain the ability to do what we will. So let us say to him, "I have sworn and determined to keep the judgments of your justice." I have indeed determined, and promised obedience because you have ordered it; but because "I can see another law in my members fighting back against the law of my mind and taking me prisoner to the law of sin that is in my members,"[13] "I have been utterly humbled, Lord; give me life according to your word." Look, "to will is available to me";[14] therefore, "approve, Lord, the voluntary offering of my mouth," so that your peace may come on earth to people of good will. SERMON 193.2.[15]

PRAYER FOR ACCEPTABLE WORSHIP. AUGUSTINE:

A most holy and solemn day[16] has dawned for us to rejoice in, and one that is very special and glorious for this church as its crowning ornament, seeing the most blessed Cyprian filled it with the light for us by the glory of his sufferings. For praising this revered bishop and venerable martyr no tongue would be sufficient, not even were he to praise himself. So in this sermon of mine, which I am paying to your ears as something owed you on his account, please acknowledge the loving readiness of my will, rather than demanding an effective display of any skill. Thus

it is, you see, that when the holy praise singer perceived himself to be less than capable of praising God—for which, indeed, not just speech but even any thought is insufficient—he said, "Make the voluntary offerings of my mouth acceptable, Lord." Let me too say the same; let this also be a sign of my devotion, and even if I am not equal to explaining what I wish, may there be an acceptable offering in the fact that I do wish. SERMON 313.1.[17]

119:118-120 God's Judgments Are to Be Feared

REJECTION OF THOSE WHO STRAY. AUGUSTINE:

For even Job himself is not silent concerning his own sins, and certainly our friend [Hilary] is right in his judgment that humility can by no means be placed on the side of falsehood. Therefore, whatever Job confesses, since he is a true worshiper of God, he undoubtedly confesses it sincerely. And Hilary, when he explains the verse of the psalm, in which it is written, "You have despised all them that fall off from your judgments," says, "For if God were to despise sinners, the judgments would indeed despise everyone, for no one is without sin. But he despises those who fall away from him, who are called apostates."[18] Notice how he does not say that no one *was* without sin, as if he were speaking of people of the past, but no one *is* without sin. On this point, as I have said, I have no quarrel. But if someone does not yield to the apostle John, who does not himself say, "if we say that we *had* no sin," but, "If we say that we *have* no sin,"[19] how will he be ready to yield to Bishop Hilary? I raise my voice in the defense of the grace of Christ, without which no one is justified, as though the free will of our nature were sufficient. Indeed, it is Christ who raises his voice in defense of this;

---

[12]FC 31:18-19**. [13]Rom 7:23. [14]Rom 7:18. [15]WSA 3 6:51. [16]The day commemorating the birthday of Cyprian, bishop of Carthage, who was martyred in 258. [17]WSA 3 9:86. [18]Hilary *Tractatus super Psalmos* 118.15.10. [19]1 Jn 1:8.

let us submit to him when he says, "Without me you can do nothing."[20] ON NATURE AND GRACE 62.73.[21]

EVERYONE IS A SINNER. AUGUSTINE: But the first covenant, made with the first man, is certainly this: "On the day you eat, you will surely die."[22] Hence the statement in the book called Ecclesiasticus: "All flesh grows old like a garment. For the covenant from the beginning is, 'You will surely die.'"[23] Now, seeing that a more explicit law was given later, and the apostle says, "Where there is no law, there is no law breaking,"[24] how can the psalm be true, where we read, "I have counted all sinners on earth as lawbreakers"? It can only be true on the assumption that those who are held bound by any sin are guilty of a breach of some law.

Therefore if even infants, as the true faith holds, are born sinners, not on their own account but in virtue of their origin (and hence we acknowledge the necessity for them of the grace of remission of sins), then it follows that just as they are sinners, they are recognized as breakers of the law that was given in paradise. And so both passages in Scripture are true, "I have counted all sinners on earth as lawbreakers" and "Where there is no law, there is no law breaking." Thus the process of birth rightly brings perdition on the infant because of the original sin by which God's covenant was first broken, unless the rebirth sets him free; and circumcision was instituted as a sign of rebirth. Therefore, those divine words must be interpreted as saying in effect, "He who has not been reborn, his soul will perish from his people, because he broke God's covenant: when, in Adam, he himself also sinned, along with all the rest of humankind. CITY OF GOD 16.27.[25]

TRANSGRESSING THE LAW OF GOD WRITTEN ON OUR HEARTS. AUGUSTINE: After those words on which we have been commenting, Paul continues and says, "Now the law entered in that sin might abound,"[26] but this does not apply to the sin that is derived from Adam, of which he said above: "Death reigned through one."[27] Clearly, we must understand by it either the natural law that was known in those ages among all who had the use of reason or the written Law that was given by Moses but that could not give life or set people free "from the law of sin and death"[28] that came down from Adam. Rather, it added an increase of transgression: "For where there is no law," says the same apostle, "neither is there transgression."[29] Since there is a law in human reason, written by nature in the heart of everyone who enjoys the use of free will, and this law suggests that a person do no evil to another that he would not wish to suffer himself, therefore, according to this law all are transgressors, even those who have not received the law given by Moses, of whom the psalmist says, "I have accounted all the sinners of the earth liars." Not all the sinners of the earth have transgressed against the law given by Moses, but unless they had committed some transgression they would not be called liars, "for where there is no law, neither is there transgression."[30] LETTER 157.[31]

NAILS OF FEAR AND FAITH. AMBROSE: O the divine mystery of that cross, on which weakness hangs, might is free, vices are nailed and triumphal trophies raised. So that a certain saint said, "Pierce my flesh with nails for fear of you"; he says not with nails of iron but of fear and faith. For the bonds of virtue are stronger than those of punishment. Lastly, Peter was bound by his faith, when he had followed the Lord as far as the hall of the high priest; no one had bound and punishment had not loosened Peter, who had been bound by faith. Again, when Peter was bound by the Jews, prayer loosed him, punishment did not hold him, because he had not gone back from Christ. OF THE HOLY SPIRIT 1.9.108.[32]

---

[20]Jn 15:5. [21]FC 86:79. [22]Gen 2:17. [23]Sir 14:17. [24]Rom 4:15. [25]CG 688-89. [26]Rom 5:20. [27]Rom 5:17. [28]Rom 8:2. [29]Rom 4:15. [30]Rom 4:15. [31]FC 20:331-32*. [32]NPNF 2 10:107-8*.

Nail My Flesh with Your Fear. Chrysostom: In our affairs, beloved, we have great need of perseverance. And perseverance is the fruit when [Christ's] teachings become deeply rooted in us. No assault of the wind will be strong enough to uproot the oak that has sent its roots deep down into the depths of the earth and has become firmly encompassed by them. Similarly, no one will be strong enough to overpower the soul that is nailed down by the fear of God, because to be nailed down is to be more securely fastened than to be rooted. In fact, the prophet prayed for this when he said, "Nail my flesh with your fear." Homilies on the Gospel of John 54.[33]

119:125 I Am Your Servant

God Requires and Graciously Gives Wisdom and Understanding. Augustine: There has to be a distinction between the law and grace. The law knows how to command; grace, how to help. The law would not command if there were no free will, nor would grace help if the will were sufficient. We are commanded to have understanding when the Scripture says, "Do not become like the horse and the mule that have no understanding,"[34] yet we pray to have understanding when it says, "Give me understanding that I may learn your commandments." We are commanded to have wisdom when it says, "You fools, be wise at last,"[35] but we pray to have wisdom when it says, "If any of you want wisdom, let him ask of God who gives to all generously and without reproach."[36] We are commanded to have continence when it says, "Be prepared for action,"[37] but we pray to have continence when it says, "As I knew that no one could be continent except God gave it, and this also was a point of wisdom to know whose gift it was, I went to the Lord and besought him."[38] Finally, not to be too lengthy in listing all the rest, we are commanded not to do evil when it says, "Decline from evil,"[39] but we pray not to do evil when it says, "We pray the Lord that you do no evil."[40] We are com-

manded to do good when it says, "Decline from evil and do good,"[41] but we pray to do good when it says, "We cease not to pray for you, asking,"[42] and among other things that he asks he mentions, "That you may walk worthy of God in all things pleasing, in every good work and good word."[43] As then we acknowledge the part played by the will when these commands are given, so let him acknowledge the part played by grace when these petitions are offered. Letter 177.[44]

A Better Understanding of God's Will. John Cassian: This very understanding, whereby he may recognize God's commands that he knew were prescribed in the book of the law, is what blessed David asks to acquire from the Lord when he says, "I am your servant; give me understanding so that I may learn your commands." Indeed, he possessed an understanding that had already been given him by nature, also a knowledge of God's commands, which were discussed in the law; it was at his fingertips, in fact. And yet he begged the Lord that he might receive it more fully, knowing that what nature had given would never suffice for him if his intelligence were not enlightened by the Lord and by his daily illumination, so that he might understand the law spiritually and acknowledge its commandments more clearly. Conferences 3.15.1.[45]

119:133 Keep Me Steadfast

One Who Calls on the Lord Will Be Saved. Augustine: This free will will be free in proportion as it is sound, and sound in proportion as it is submissive to divine mercy and grace. Therefore, it prays with faith and says, "Direct my paths according to your word, and let no iniquity have dominion over me." It prays, it does not promise; it confesses, it does not declare itself; it

---

[33]FC 41:64*. [34]Ps 32:9 (31:9 LXX, Vg.). [35]Ps 94:8 (93:8 LXX, Vg.). [36]Jas 1:5. [37]See Lk 12:35. [38]Wis 8:21. [39]Ps 37:27 (36:27 LXX, Vg.). [40]2 Cor 13:7. [41]Ps 37:27 (36:27 LXX, Vg.). [42]Col 1:9. [43]Col 1:10. [44]FC 30:97-98. [45]ACW 57:133.

begs for the fullest liberty, it does not boast of its own power. It is not everyone who trusts in his own strength, but everyone who calls on the name of the Lord will be saved. "How then shall they call on him in whom they have not believed?"[46] Therefore, those who believe rightly believe that they may call on him in whom they have believed and may be strong to do what they have learned in the precepts of the law, since faith obtains what the law commands. LETTER 157.[47]

LET SIN HAVE NO DOMINION OVER ME.
AUGUSTINE: When, however, you hear, "Sin shall have no dominion over you,"[48] do not trust in yourself in order that sin may not dominate you, but trust in him to whom that holy one was praying when he said, "Direct my steps according to your word, and let no iniquity have dominion over me." Lest, perhaps, when we have heard, "Sin shall not have dominion over you," we should exalt ourselves and attribute this to our

own strength, the apostle saw this and added at once, "Since you are not under the law but under grace."[49] Grace therefore causes sin not to have power over you. Do not, then, trust in yourself, lest thereby sin have much more dominion over you. And when we hear, "If by the Spirit you put to death the deeds of the flesh, you shall live,"[50] let us not attribute this good to our spirit alone, as if through itself it could do these things. For, lest we enjoy that carnal feeling, our spirit being dead rather than a death-dealing one, he immediately added, "For whoever are led by the Spirit of God, they are the children of God."[51] So, when by our spirit we put to death the works of the flesh, we are impelled by the Spirit of God, which grants the continence by which we restrain, master and overcome sexual desire. ON CONTINENCE 5.12.[52]

---

[46]Rom 10:14. [47]FC 20:323-24*. [48]Rom 6:14. [49]Rom 6:14. [50]Rom 8:13. [51]Rom 8:14. [52]FC 16:202-3**.

119:137-176 A DEVOTION ON THE WORD OF GOD
(TSADHE—TAW)

[137]Righteous art thou, O LORD,
    and right are thy judgments.
[138]Thou hast appointed thy testimonies in
        righteousness
    and in all faithfulness.
[139]My zeal consumes me,
    because my foes forget thy words.
[140]Thy promise is well tried,
    and thy servant loves it.
[141]I am small and despised,
    yet I do not forget thy precepts.
[142]Thy righteousness is righteous for ever,

and thy law is true.
[143]Trouble and anguish have come upon me,
    but thy commandments are my delight.
[144]Thy testimonies are righteous for ever;
    give me understanding that I may live.

[145]With my whole heart I cry; answer me,
        O LORD!
    I will keep thy statutes.
[146]I cry to thee; save me,
    that I may observe thy testimonies.
[147]I rise before dawn and cry for help;

I hope in thy words.
¹⁴⁸My eyes are awake before the watches of the
    night,
  that I may meditate upon thy promise.
¹⁴⁹Hear my voice in thy steadfast love;
  O Lᴏʀᴅ, in thy justice preserve my life.
¹⁵⁰They draw near who persecute me with
    evil purpose;
  they are far from thy law.
¹⁵¹But thou art near, O Lᴏʀᴅ,
  and all thy commandments are true.
¹⁵²Long have I known from thy testimonies
  that thou hast founded them for ever.

¹⁵³Look on my affliction and deliver me,
  for I do not forget thy law.
¹⁵⁴Plead my cause and redeem me;
  give me life according to thy promise!
¹⁵⁵Salvation is far from the wicked,
  for they do not seek thy statutes.
¹⁵⁶Great is thy mercy, O Lᴏʀᴅ;
  give me life according to thy justice.
¹⁵⁷Many are my persecutors and my
    adversaries,
  but I do not swerve from thy testimonies.
¹⁵⁸I look at the faithless with disgust,
  because they do not keep thy commands.
¹⁵⁹Consider how I love thy precepts!
  Preserve my life according to thy steadfast
    love.
¹⁶⁰The sum of thy word is truth;
  and every one of thy righteous ordinances
    endures for ever.

¹⁶¹Princes persecute me without cause,

but my heart stands in awe of thy words.
¹⁶²I rejoice at thy word
  like one who finds great spoil.
¹⁶³I hate and abhor falsehood,
  but I love thy law.
¹⁶⁴Seven times a day I praise thee
  for thy righteous ordinances.
¹⁶⁵Great peace have those who love thy law;
  nothing can make them stumble.
¹⁶⁶I hope for thy salvation, O Lᴏʀᴅ,
  and I do thy commandments.
¹⁶⁷My soul keeps thy testimonies;
  I love them exceedingly.
¹⁶⁸I keep thy precepts and testimonies,
  for all my ways are before thee.

¹⁶⁹Let my cry come before thee, O Lᴏʀᴅ;
  give me understanding according to
    thy word!
¹⁷⁰Let my supplication come before thee;
  deliver me according to thy word.
¹⁷¹My lips will pour forth praise
  that thou dost teach me thy statutes.
¹⁷²My tongue will sing of thy word,
  for all thy commandments are right.
¹⁷³Let thy hand be ready to help me,
  for I have chosen thy precepts.
¹⁷⁴I long for thy salvation, O Lᴏʀᴅ,
  and thy law is my delight.
¹⁷⁵Let me live, that I may praise thee,
  and let thy ordinances help me.
¹⁷⁶I have gone astray like a lost sheep; seek
    thy servant,
  for I do not forget thy commandments.

Overview: The Holy Spirit inflames the hearts
of believers (Oʀɪɢᴇɴ). God defends his people
and enables them to withstand all the troubles
that beset them (Aᴛʜᴀɴᴀsɪᴜs). Strive to overcome all evil passions and evil thoughts so that
you may pray to God without distractions (Jᴏʜɴ

of Damascus). Prayers should be offered frequently and at different times of the day (Ambrose). To praise God seven times a day means to praise him continually. Believers do not scandalize their brothers because of their unity and brotherly love (Augustine).

119:137-143 God's Righteousness

The Spirit Ignites the Hearts of Believers. Origen: Do you want me to show you how the fire goes out from the words of the Holy Spirit and ignites the hearts of believers? Hear David speaking in the psalm: "The declaration of the Lord has set him on fire." And again in the Gospel it was written, after the Lord spoke to Cleopas, "Was not our heart burning within us when he opened the Scriptures to us?"[1] Whence will you burn? Whence will "the coals of fire" be bound in you who are never set on fire by the declaration of the Lord, never kindled by the words of the Holy Spirit? Homilies on Leviticus 9.9.7.[2]

Overcome by Affliction. Athanasius: For this is the divine promise: "The Lord shall fight for you."[3] Henceforth, although afflictions and trials from without overtake them, yet, being fashioned after the apostolic words and "being steadfast in tribulations and persevering in prayers"[4] and in meditation on the law, they stand against those things that befall them, are well-pleasing to God and give utterance to the words that are written, "Afflictions and distresses are come on me, but your commandments are my meditation." Festal Letters 11.6.[5]

119:163-165 Love God's Law

Hate Falsehood, Love God's Law. John of Damascus: Obtain the same thing for yourself and strive to advance toward it;[6] for it is able to raise you from earth to heaven. You will not advance in it without preparation or [solely] by chance. First cleanse your soul of every passion and wipe it as clean of every evil as a newly cleansed mirror. Remove far from you every recollection of wrong and anger, which most of all prevents our daily prayers from reaching God. Also remove from your heart the offenses of everyone who has ever sinned against you. Giving wings to your prayer with mercy and compassion for the poor, approach God with fervent tears. Praying in this way you will be able to say with the blessed David, who, although he was king and burdened with countless cares, cleansed his soul of all passions: "I hated and abhorred iniquity, but I loved your law. Seven times a day I praised you because of the judgments of your righteousness." My soul kept your testimonies and I loved them very much. Let my prayer draw near to you, Lord; enable me to understand your word.[7] Barlaam and Joseph 20.175-76.[8]

Appropriate Times for Prayer. Ambrose: Frequent prayer also commends us to God. For if the prophet says, "Seven times a day have I praised you," though he was busy with the affairs of a kingdom, what ought we to do, who read, "Watch and pray that you enter not into temptation"?[9] Certainly our customary prayers ought to be said with giving of thanks, when we rise from sleep, when we go forth, when we prepare to receive food, after receiving it and at the hour of incense,[10] when at last we are going to rest. Concerning Virgins 3.4.18.[11]

Praise God Seven Times a Day. Augustine: The seven loaves signify the sevenfold working of the Holy Spirit;[12] the four thousand people,[13] the church established under the four Gospels; the seven baskets of fragments,[14] the perfection of the church. This number, you see, stands for perfection extremely often. I mean, how come it says,

---

[1]Lk 24:32. [2]FC 83:198*. [3]Ex 14:14. [4]Rom 12:12. [5]NPNF 2 4:535*. [6]Prayer that is proper and prayed directly to God. [7]See Ps 119:27 (118:27 LXX). [8]PG 96:1041. [9]Mt 26:41. [10]It is doubtful whether incense was burned in connection with Christian worship as early as the time of Ambrose, and the reference here may be to burning incense at evening in the Jewish temple. [11]NPNF 2 10:384*. [12]See Is 11:2-3. [13]Mt 15:38 [14]Mt 15:37.

"Seven times a day shall I praise you"? Is a person going wildly astray who does not praise God that number of times? So what else can be the meaning of "seven times a day shall I praise you," but "I shall never cease from praising"? You see, when he says seven times he signifies the whole of time; that is why the ages unfold in the weekly round of seven days. So what else can "seven times a day shall I praise you" mean but his "praise is always in my mouth"?[15] SERMON 95.2.[16]

THERE IS NO SCANDAL IN BELIEVERS. AUGUSTINE: But whom does the church burn as the moon by night?[17] They who have caused schisms. Hear this very same thing stated by the apostle: "Who is weak and I am not weak? Who is scandalized and I am not burned?"[18] How then is there no scandal in him who loves his brother? Because he who loves his brother endures all things for the sake of unity, because in the unity of love is brotherly loving. If some wicked person or other, or someone supposedly or allegedly wicked, offends you, do you desert so many good people? What sort of brotherly loving is it as has appeared in these people?[19] When they accuse the Africans, they have deserted the world. Were there no saints in the world? Or was it possible for them to be condemned by you unheard? But, if you loved your brother, there would be no scandal in you. Hear the psalm, the one that says, "Much peace have they who love your law and there is no scandal to them." It said that they who love the law of God have much peace and for that reason there is no scandal to them. Those therefore who suffer scandal lose peace. And who did it say do not suffer scandal or do not cause it? Those loving the law of God. HOMILIES ON 1 JOHN 1.12.3.[20]

---

[15]Ps 34:1 (33:2 LXX, Vg.). [16]WSA 3 4:24. [17]See Ps 120:6 (LXX): "By day the sun will not burn you, nor the moon by night." People who are scandalized by Christ are burned as by the sun; those who are scandalized by the church are burned as by the moon. [18]2 Cor 11:29. [19]Schismatic Donatists. [20]FC 92:137-38*.

120:1-7 A PRAYER FOR DELIVERANCE FROM FALSE ACCUSERS

A Song of Ascents.

[1]*In my distress I cry to the LORD,*
that he may answer me:
[2]*"Deliver me, O LORD,*
from lying lips,
from a deceitful tongue."

[3]*What shall be given to you?*
And what more shall be done to you,
you deceitful tongue?

[4]*A warrior's sharp arrows,*
with glowing coals of the broom tree!

[5]*Woe is me, that I sojourn in Meshech,*
that I dwell among the tents of Kedar!
[6]*Too long have I had my dwelling*
among those who hate peace.
[7]*I am for peace;*
but when I speak,
they are for war!

OVERVIEW: The one to whom David prayed for help and from whom he received deliverance was none other than the true God (ATHANASIUS). Death is a blessing and possibly a protection from future misfortune for believers; longer life is a greater hardship than death (JEROME).

120:1-2 I Cried to the Lord

AN ANSWER TO PRAYER FOR DELIVERANCE. ATHANASIUS: Therefore it was none other than God whom David too implored for his deliverance: "When I was in trouble, I called on the Lord, and he heard me; deliver my soul, O Lord, from lying lips and from a deceitful tongue." To him also giving thanks he spoke the words of the song in the seventeenth psalm [LXX], in the day in which the Lord delivered him from the hand of all his enemies and from the hand of Saul, saying, "I will love you, O Lord, my strength; the Lord is my strong rock and my defense and deliverer."[1] And Paul, after enduring many persecutions, to none other than God gave thanks, saying, "Out of them all the Lord delivered me; and he, in whom we trust, will deliver me."[2] DISCOURSES AGAINST THE ARIANS 3.25.13.[3]

120:5-6 Woe Is Me

A LONGING TO BE WITH GOD. JEROME: But why should that be hard to bear which we must one day ourselves endure? And why do we grieve for the dead? We are not born to live forever. Abraham, Moses and Isaiah, Peter, James and John, Paul, the "chosen vessel,"[4] and even the Son of God have all died; and are we vexed when a soul leaves its earthly tenement? Perhaps he is taken away, "lest wickedness should alter his understanding . . . for his soul pleased the Lord;

therefore he hastened to take him away from the people"[5]—lest in life's long journey he should lose his way in some trackless maze. We should indeed mourn for the dead, but only for one whom Gehenna[6] receives, whom Tartarus[7] devours and for whose punishment the eternal fire burns. But we who, in departing, are accompanied by an escort of angels and met by Christ, should rather grieve that we have to tarry yet longer in this tabernacle of death.[8] For "while we are at home in the body, we are absent from the Lord."[9] Our one longing should be that expressed by the psalmist: "Woe is me that my pilgrimage is prolonged, that I have dwelled with them who dwell in Kedar, that my soul has made a far pilgrimage." Kedar means darkness, and darkness stands for this present world (for, we are told, "the light shines in darkness; and the darkness comprehends it not"[10]). Therefore we should congratulate our dear Blaesilla,[11] that she has passed from darkness to light,[12] and has in the first flush of her dawning faith received the crown of her completed work. Had she been cut off (as I pray that none may be) while her thoughts were full of worldly desires and passing pleasures, then mourning would indeed have been her due, and no tears shed for her would have been too many. As it is, by the mercy of Christ she, four months ago, renewed her baptism in her vow of widowhood, and for the rest of her days spurned the world and thought only of the religious life. LETTER 39.3.[13]

---

[1]Ps 18:1-2 (17:2-3 LXX). [2]See 2 Tim 3:11; 2 Cor 1:10. [3]NPNF 2 4:401*. [4]Acts 9:15. [5]Wis 4:11, 14. [6]A place of misery or hell. [7]A section of hades (hell) reserved for the punishment of the wicked. [8]2 Cor 5:4. [9]2 Cor 5:6. [10]Jn 1:5. [11]A young Roman widow whom Jerome influenced to pursue the ascetic life and who died young. [12]Eph 5:8. [13]NPNF 2 6:50-51*.

121:1-8 A DIALOGUE OF CONFESSION AND ASSURANCE

A Song of Ascents.

¹I lift up my eyes to the hills.
  From whence does my help come?
²My help comes from the LORD,
  who made heaven and earth.

³He will not let your foot be moved,
  he who keeps you will not slumber.
⁴Behold, he who keeps Israel
  will neither slumber nor sleep.

⁵The LORD is your keeper;
  the LORD is your shade
  on your right hand.
⁶The sun shall not smite you by day,
  nor the moon by night.

⁷The LORD will keep you from all evil;
  he will keep your life.
⁸The LORD will keep
  your going out and your coming in
  from this time forth and for evermore.

OVERVIEW: Our eyes must not be set on physical mountains but on God, Scripture, the lofty angels and the lives of saints; it is from them that we receive real spiritual help (CASSIODORUS). Our help does not come from the mountains but from God, who made heaven and earth. John, in his bearing witness to Christ, is considered the mountain from whom our help comes. "Heaven and earth" are inclusive terms and refer to everything that is contained in them (AUGUSTINE).

We ask God to arise from sleep when he considers us unworthy of his watchfulness because of our slothful behavior (BASIL). God, who does not sleep, is our creator and guard (AUGUSTINE). To ascribe conflicting attributes to Christ, such as sleeping and not sleeping, is not a contradiction, but the attributes must be understood as appropriate to one or the other of Christ's two natures, divine or human (THEODORET).

God will protect us when we enter and exit from trials and temptations (AUGUSTINE).

121:1-2 I Lift Up My Eyes to the Hills

I LIFT UP MY EYES TO THE MOUNTAINS. CAS-

SIODORUS: When the psalmist says, "I have lifted up," he shows that he has advanced to a kind of contemplation; lifting up means raising something to a higher level. "My eyes" means nothing other than the heart's vision, of which Scripture says, "Open my eyes, and I will consider the wondrous things of your law";[1] and again, "The precept of the Lord is bright, enlightening the eyes."[2] If you were to interpret these as the eyes of the body, what advantage could they gain by deciding to focus on mountains planted with woodland or dotted with unsightly rocks? But if you investigate the phrase in the spiritual sense, it is clearly helpful; we can believe that he has raised his inward eyes to holy people, or to the divine books or to the lofty angels who in their greatness and strength are truly mountains and from whom fitting help was also obtained. But in case we perhaps set our hope in the mountains mentioned, the second verse reveals the true Source of possible help to us, the Source who orders all things by a saving dispensation; thus our hope in the

---

[1]Ps 119:18 (118:18 LXX, Vg.). [2]Ps 19:9 (18:9 LXX, Vg.).

mountains is such that we realize that it is the Lord who lends help through them. It is from him that the necessary benefit, the saving protection, the unshakeable blessing comes. As Paul says, "Neither he that plants is anything, nor he that waters, but God that gives the increase."[3] So that you would not think that this was some other Lord—for the term is ambiguous—he says, "who made heaven and earth," thus denoting the Word by which all things were made. EXPOSITIONS OF THE PSALMS 120.1-2.[4]

MY HELP IS FROM THE LORD. AUGUSTINE: And say, "I have lifted my eyes to the mountains from which help shall come to me" in such a way that you add to it immediately, "My help is from the Lord, who made heaven and earth." Therefore let us lift our eyes to the mountains from which help shall come to us. Yet it is not the mountains themselves in which our hope is to be placed, for the mountains receive what they may present to us. Therefore we must put our hope in that place from which the mountains also receive [what they give to us]. When we lift our eyes to the Scriptures, because the Scriptures were delivered through people,[5] we lift our eyes to the mountains from which help will come to us; and yet since they who wrote the Scriptures were themselves people, they were not providing enlightenment from themselves. Rather, Christ was the true light who enlightens everyone coming into the world.[6] TRACTATES ON THE GOSPEL OF JOHN 1.6.2.[7]

THOSE WHO BEAR WITNESS TO THE LIGHT. AUGUSTINE: However just people may be, however preeminent in grace, however luminous their wisdom, however great the merits that set them on a pinnacle, they are only mountains. Pay attention to the psalm: "I lifted up my eyes to the mountains, from where my help shall come," because "there was a man sent by God, whose name was John; this man came to bear witness to the light."[8] So you have lifted up your eyes to the mountain John, from where your help may come, because he is bearing witness to the light. Con-

tinue with the psalm; do not stop on the mountain: "My help is from the Lord, who made heaven and earth." That is Christ; "all things were made through him."[9] He is the constructor of the world; he is, you see, the Word of the Father; the Father made all things through the Word. SERMON 379.7.[10]

THE LORD MADE HEAVEN AND EARTH. AUGUSTINE: The Son of God, the only begotten of the Father, God always, man for our sake, having become what he made—I mean, he became man, having made humankind—says to the Father, "I confess to you, Father, Lord of heaven and earth."[11] "You are my Father, Lord of heaven and earth"; Father of the one through whom all things were made. The whole of creation, you see, is briefly unfolded in these two words, heaven and earth. That is why it says in the first book of God's Scriptures, "In the beginning, God made heaven and earth"[12]; and also, "My help is from the Lord, who made heaven and earth." But by the word *heaven* is to be understood whatever is in the heavens, and by the word *earth* whatever is on the earth; so by naming these two parts of creation, you do not leave out a single creature, because it is either here, or it is there. SERMON 68.2.[13]

121:4 The God Who Keeps Israel

GOD DOES NOT SLUMBER. BASIL THE GREAT: We attribute to God, as it were, every state that corresponds to our circumstances. For this reason, when we are half asleep and behaving slothfully, God, since he judges us unworthy of his observant watchfulness over us, is said to be asleep. But, when, after noticing at some time the harm that comes from his sleeping, we shall say, "Arise, why do you sleep, O Lord?"[14] "Behold, he shall neither slumber nor sleep at that time, that keeps Israel." Some others, as it were, turn their

---

[3]1 Cor 3:7. [4]ACW 53:266-67*. [5]See 2 Cor 3:3. [6]Jn 1:9. [7]FC 78:45-46*. [8]Jn 1:6-7. [9]Jn 1:3. [10]WSA 3 10:358-59. [11]Mt 11:25. [12]Gen 1:1. [13]WSA 3 3:222. [14]Ps 44:23 (43:23 LXX).

eyes away from God because of their shameful deeds and their acts unworthy of the eyes of God. These, on repenting, say, "Why do you turn your face away?"[15] Besides these, there are others who have cast out the memory of God and, as it were, are producing in him forgetfulness of themselves, and these say, "Why do you forget our want and our trouble?"[16] In a word, people do the very things that are humanly spoken about God, making God behave in ways appropriate to the manner in which they have been made. Therefore, "I will extol you, O Lord; for you have upheld me; and you have not made my enemies to rejoice over me."[17] And I will suffer nothing low or abject in my life. Homilies on the Psalms 14.2.[18]

God Watches Over Those Whom He Has Redeemed.

Augustine: Not without reason, brothers. For Samaritan is interpreted as guard.[19] He knew that he was our guard. For "he neither slumbers nor sleeps, who guards Israel," and "Unless the Lord guard the city, in vain do they who guard watch."[20] He who is our Creator is our guard. For did it suit him that we be redeemed but not that we be saved? Tractates on the Gospel of John 43.2.2.[21]

Christ Sleeps and Yet Does Not Sleep.

Theodoret of Cyr: Regarding the divine nature the prophet David says, "Behold, he who keeps Israel shall neither slumber nor sleep." But the narrative of the Evangelist describes the Master Christ as sleeping in the boat. Now not sleeping and being asleep are two contrary ideas, so the prophet contradicts the Gospels if, as they argue, the Master Christ was God alone. There is no contradiction, for both prophecies and Gospels flow from one and the same spirit. The Master Christ therefore had a body, akin to all other bodies, affected by the need of sleep. So the argument for the confusion is proved a fable.

Regarding the divine nature the prophet Isaiah said, "He shall neither be hungry nor weary" and so on.[22] But the Evangelist says, "Jesus, being weary with his journey, sat thus by the well";[23] and "shall not be weary" is contrary to "being weary." Therefore the prophecy is contrary to the narrative of the Gospels. But they are not contrary, for both are descriptive of one God. Not being weary is proper to the uncircumscribed nature that fills all things. But moving from place to place is proper to the circumscribed nature. When that which moves is constrained to travel, it is subject to the weariness of the wayfarer. Therefore what walked and was weary was a body, for the union did not confound the natures. Dialogue 6-7.[24]

121:8 God Will Guard You During Trials

God Protects Our Coming and Going.

Augustine: "May the Lord protect your coming in and your going out." Now look at the coming out of the furnace and the going into it; "Reckon it all joy, my brothers, when you fall into various trials."[25] There you are, you have heard about the entrance; now find the exit. It is easy enough to go in; coming out is the big thing. But do not worry: "God is faithful"—because you have gone in, you are naturally thinking about getting out— "God is faithful and does not allow you to be tempted above what you are able to bear, but with the temptation he will also make a way out."[26] What is the way out? "That you may be able to endure."[27] You have gone in, you have fallen in, you have endured, you have come out. Sermon 15.4.[28]

---

[15]Ps 43:24 (43:24 LXX). [16]Ps 44:24 (43:24 LXX). [17]Ps 30:1 (29:2 LXX). [18]FC 46:214-15**. [19]The context is Augustine's discussion of John 8:48-59, where Jesus is accused of being a Samaritan and demon-possessed. Augustine's definition of Samaritan as guard is one of the two meanings given the name by the Fathers; the other is observer or keeper of the law. [20]Ps 127:1 (126:1 LXX, Vg.). [21]FC 88:163-64. [22]Is 40:28 (LXX). [23]Jn 4:6. [24]NPNF 2 3:247**. [25]Jas 1:2. [26]1 Cor 10:13. [27]1 Cor 10:13. [28]WSA 3 1:325-26.

122:1-9 A HYMN OF JOY OVER JERUSALEM

A Song of Ascents. Of David.

[1]*I was glad when they said to me,*
  "Let us go to the house of the LORD!"
[2]*Our feet have been standing*
  within your gates, O Jerusalem!

[3]*Jerusalem, built as a city*
  which is bound firmly together,
[4]*to which the tribes go up,*
  the tribes of the LORD,
as was decreed for Israel,

to give thanks to the name of the LORD.
[5]*There thrones for judgment were set,*
  the thrones of the house of David.

[6]*Pray for the peace of Jerusalem!*
  "May they prosper who love you!
[7]*Peace be within your walls,*
  and security within your towers!"
[8]*For my brethren and companions' sake*
  I will say, "Peace be within you!"
[9]*For the sake of the house of the LORD our God,*
  I will seek your good.

OVERVIEW: The foot that we have in heaven while still living on earth is the foot of the soul (AMBROSE). The church welcomes and urges those who have fallen into sin or wandered into heresy to return to the true church, where there is peace, strength and love (AUGUSTINE).

122:2 Standing Within Jerusalem

STANDING IN THE COURTS OF JERUSALEM. AMBROSE: These are the feet[1] that David washes in spirit when he teaches you how to keep them unsoiled, saying, "Our feet have been standing in your courts, O Jerusalem." Certainly, here "feet" is to be understood not as of the body but as of the soul. For how could a person on earth have his physical feet in heaven? Since Jerusalem, as Paul tells you, is in heaven, he also shows you how to stand in heaven when he says, "But our abode is in heaven":[2] the "abode" of your behavior, the "abode" of your deeds, the "abode" of your faith. ON VIRGINITY 9.59.[3]

122:6-7 Pray for Peace in the Church

PEACE IS THE STRENGTH OF THE CITY. AUGUSTINE: Let them,[4] then, have a bitter sorrow for their former detestable wrongdoing, as Peter had for his cowardly lie, and let them come to the true church, that is, their catholic mother, and let them be clerics or bishops in it with as much service for it as they formerly used against it. We do not begrudge it to them; on the contrary, we embrace them, we beg them, we exhort them, we compel them to come in when we find them in the highways and hedges. Even so, we do not yet persuade some of them that we seek them, not their possessions. When the apostle Peter denied the Savior and wept and remained an apostle, he had not yet received the Holy Spirit who had been promised,[5] but much less have they received him when, severed from the unity of the body to which alone the Holy Spirit gives life,[6] they have maintained the sacraments of the church outside the church and in opposition to

---

[1]Ambrose had an unusual view of foot washing, which he considered a sort of sacrament and necessary to salvation. [2]Phil 3:20. [3]AOV 28-29. [4]Schismatic Donatists. [5]See Jn 14:26; 16:13. [6]2 Cor 3:6.

the church and have fought a kind of civil war, setting up our own banners and our own arms against us. Let them come; "let there be peace in the strength of Jerusalem," the strength that is charity, as it was said to the holy city: "Let peace be in your strength and abundance in your towers." Let them not rise up against the motherly anxiety that she had and has to gather them in, and with them so many throngs of people whom they deceive or did deceive. Let them not be proud, because she thus welcomes them. Let them not turn to the evil purpose of self-esteem what she does for the good purpose of peace. LETTER 185.46.[7]

---

[7]FC 30:185*.

123:1-4 A PRAYER FOR GOD'S MERCY AND TO FOIL THE CONTEMPT OF THE PROUD

A Song of Ascents.

[1]*To thee I lift up my eyes,*
   O thou who art enthroned in the heavens!
[2]*Behold, as the eyes of servants*
   look to the hand of their master,
as the eyes of a maid
   to the hand of her mistress,
so our eyes look to the LORD our God,

till he have mercy upon us.

[3]*Have mercy upon us, O LORD, have mercy*
   upon us,
   for we have had more than enough of
      contempt.
[4]*Too long our soul has been sated*
   with the scorn of those who are at ease,
   the contempt of the proud.

OVERVIEW: People who trust in God follow the urging of Scripture and the example of Christ in lifting their eyes to heaven in anticipation of receiving God's mercy (ORIGEN). We attract the attention of God when we look toward him in reverential awe (BASIL). The word *until* does not imply that God will cease to reign or cease to have mercy; it implies the beginning of the fullness of God's reign or the fullness of his mercy (JEROME). The arrogant error of the rich is that they assume that true patience derives from their own will power and not from divine assistance, not heeding the words of Scripture (AUGUSTINE).

123:1-2 *Our Eyes Look to Our God*

LOOK UP TO HEAVEN. ORIGEN: The tax collector in the Gospel, therefore, acting properly, "did not wish even to lift up his eyes,"[1] but on the other hand, the disciple who is present with Jesus would reasonably lift them up when he is given the command, "Lift up your eyes and see the fields, that they are already white to harvest."[2]

   The prophet, too, says, "Lift up your eyes on

---

[1]Lk 18:13. [2]Jn 4:35.

high."[3] But in addition, in Psalm 122 (LXX), which is the fourth song of the gradual psalms,[4] the prophet, when he has lifted up his eyes to God in a fitting manner, says, "To you who dwell in heaven I have lifted up my eyes. Behold as the eyes of servants are on the hands of their masters, as the eyes of a handmaid are on the hands of her mistress, so our eyes are on the Lord our God, until he has mercy on us."

And if we must also show more clearly for whom it is now proper to imitate Jesus by lifting up his eyes, in that he also lifts up his eyes, and for whom this is not proper, but who, like the tax collector, should not only stand far away from the temple but also not wish to lift up his eyes, we will quote the words of Daniel about the lawless elders who lusted after Susanna. The words are as follows: "And they perverted their own mind and turned their eyes away that they might not look to heaven or remember just judgments."[5] These words should be taken along with the following remarks made about Susanna, "But she, weeping, looked up to heaven, for her heart trusted in the Lord."[6] Notice in these words that those who perverted their own mind turned their eyes away that they might not look to heaven, but she who trusted in the Lord looked up to heaven as a result of her trust in the Lord. COMMENTARY ON THE GOSPEL OF JOHN 28.32-34.[7]

THE EYES OF THE LORD. BASIL THE GREAT: "Behold the eyes of the Lord are on them that fear him."[8] Elsewhere, it says, "The eyes of the Lord are on the just,"[9] but here, "on those that fear him." When we look upon the Lord and our eyes are on him, so that we say, "Behold as the eyes of the servants are on the hands of their masters, so are our eyes unto the Lord our God," then, we, as it were, draw the eye of the Lord to watch over us. HOMILIES ON THE PSALMS 15.10.[10]

THE MEANING OF "UNTIL." JEROME: What does he mean then by saying, "for he must reign

until he has put all enemies under his feet"? Is the Lord to reign only until his enemies begin to be under his feet, and once they are under his feet will he cease to reign? Of course his reign will then commence in its fullness when his enemies begin to be under his feet. David also in the fourth Song of Ascents speaks thus, "Behold, as the eyes of servants look to the hand of their master, as the eyes of a maiden unto the hand of her mistress, so our eyes look to the Lord our God, until he has mercy on us." Will the prophet, then, look to the Lord until he obtains mercy, and when mercy is obtained will he turn his eyes down to the ground, although elsewhere he says, "My eyes fail, looking for your salvation, and for your righteous promise"?[11] I could accumulate countless instances of this usage and cover the verbosity of our assailant[12] with a cloud of proofs; I shall, however, add only a few and leave the reader to find similar ones for himself. THE PERPETUAL VIRGINITY OF MARY 6.[13]

123:4 The Scorn and Contempt of the Proud

TRUE PATIENCE COMES FROM GOD. AUGUSTINE: We must find out whence true patience, worthy of the name, is to be had. There are those who attribute it to the powers of human will, not those that people have from divine assistance but from their own free will.[14] But that is an arrogant error. It is the error of the rich about which the psalm speaks, "a reproach to the rich and contempt to the proud." It is not the patience of the poor, which "shall not perish forever."[15] For the poor receive it from the wealthy One to whom it is said, "You are my

---

[3]Is 40:26. [4]Ps 123. Psalms 120-134 are considered gradual or ascent psalms. [5]Sus (Theod.) 9. [6]Sus (Theod.) 35. [7]FC 89:298-99*. [8]Ps 33:18 (32:18 LXX). [9]Ps 34:15 (33:16 LXX). [10]FC 46:244. [11]Ps 119:123 (118:123 LXX, Vg.). [12]Helvidius, who denied the perpetual virginity of Mary, and the individual against whom this treatise was written. [13]NPNF 2 6:337*. [14]Here, Augustine is refuting the errors of the Pelagians without naming them specifically, as was his consistent custom prior to their condemnation in 418. [15]Ps 9:18 (9:19 LXX, Vg.).

God, for you have no need of my goods,"[16] from whom "is every best gift and every perfect gift,"[17] on whom the poor and needy person calls, who praises his name and by seeking, by asking, by knocking, says, "Deliver me, O my God, out of the hand of the sinner and out of the hand of the transgressor of the law and of the unjust. For you are my patience, O Lord: my hope, from my youth."[18] The rich and those who disdain being needy before the Lord should not receive true patience from him. Glorying in their own false patience, they wish "to confound the counsel of the poor person, but the Lord is his hope."[19] Since they are human and attribute so much to themselves, that is, to their human will, they do not tend to apply to themselves the words of Scripture: "Cursed is everyone that trusts in man."[20] For, even if sometimes in order not to displease people or to suffer worse ills,

they bear up under things that are hard and rugged, or else in pleasing themselves and loving their own presumption they suffer these same evils with an arrogant will, that which the blessed James the apostle said about wisdom must be said to them about their patience: "This is not the wisdom that descends from above. It is earthly, sensual, devilish."[21] For, why is there not a false patience of the proud just as there is a false wisdom of the proud? He who is the source of true wisdom is also the source of true patience. And to him the one who is poor in spirit sings, "My soul is subject to God, for from him is my patience."[22] ON PATIENCE 15.12.[23]

---

[16]Ps 16:2 (Ps 15:2 LXX, Vg.). [17]Jas 1:17. [18]Ps 71:4-5 (70:4-5 LXX, Vg.). [19]Ps 14:6 (13:6 LXX, Vg.). [20]Jer 17:5. [21]Jas 3:15. [22]Ps 62:5 (61:6 LXX, Vg.). [23]FC 16:249-50*.

124:1-8 PRAISE FOR DELIVERANCE
FROM ENEMIES

A Song of Ascents. Of David.

[1]*If it had not been the* Lord *who was on our side,*
   let Israel now say—
[2]*if it had not been the* Lord *who was on our side,*
   when men rose up against us,
[3]*then they would have swallowed us up alive,*
   when their anger was kindled against us;
[4]*then the flood would have swept us away,*
   the torrent would have gone over us;
[5]*then over us would have gone*

the raging waters.

[6]*Blessed be the* Lord,
   who has not given us
   as prey to their teeth!
[7]*We have escaped as a bird*
   from the snare of the fowlers;
the snare is broken,
   and we have escaped!

[8]*Our help is in the name of the* Lord,
   who made heaven and earth.

OVERVIEW: Believers are spiritually victorious, like the martyrs, because God strengthens them with faith and patience (AUGUSTINE). Easter is an occasion for thanking God for delivering us from the edict of death and the opponents of Christ (ATHANASIUS). God is blessed when the church thanks him for his gift to the church of martyrs who were victorious over their enemies (AUGUSTINE). The soul can soar like a bird on wings of good works, wings that are reminiscent of the outstretched arms of Christ on the cross (AMBROSE).

Since God created the heaven and the earth, we should not belittle what God has made—that is something unbelievers do (AUGUSTINE).

124:1-3 The Lord Is on Our Side

SPIRITUAL VICTORY. AUGUSTINE: The holy martyrs, you see, did not rely on themselves but asked for relief from Christ. That is why they were also victorious. Listen to the voices of those who do not rely on themselves; it is the voice of the holy martyrs: "Unless the Lord were among us, let Israel now say; unless the Lord were among us when people rose up against us, they would perhaps have swallowed us alive." The martyrs say, "Unless the Lord were among us," unless he had helped us, unless he had strengthened our hearts with faith, unless he had endowed us with patience, unless he had provided us with power as we fought, "they would perhaps have swallowed us alive." SERMON 335F.2.[1]

124:5-7 Thank God for Victory over Your Enemies

EASTER IS A FEAST OF DELIVERANCE. ATHANASIUS: What then is our duty, my brothers, for the sake of these things, but to praise and give thanks to God, the king of all? And let us first exclaim in the words of the psalms, "Blessed be the Lord, who has not given us over as a prey to their teeth." Let us keep the feast in that way that he has dedicated for us unto salvation—the holy day Easter—so that we may celebrate the feast which is in heaven with the angels. Thus anciently, the people of the Jews, when they came out of affliction into a state of ease, kept the feast, singing a song of praise for their victory. So also the people in the time of Esther, because they were delivered from the edict of death, kept a feast to the Lord,[2] considering it a feast, returning thanks to the Lord and praising him for having changed their condition. Therefore let us, performing our vows to the Lord and confessing our sins, keep the feast to the Lord, in conversation, moral conduct and manner of life; praising our Lord, who has chastened us a little but has not utterly failed or forsaken us or altogether kept silence from us. For if, having brought us out of the deceitful and famous Egypt of the opponents of Christ, he has caused us to pass through many trials and afflictions, as it were in the wilderness, to his holy church, so that from hence, according to custom, we can send to you, as well as receive letters from you; on this account especially I both give thanks to God myself and exhort you to thank him with me and on my behalf, this being the apostolic custom, which these opponents of Christ, and the schismatics, wished to put an end to and to break off. The Lord did not permit it but both renewed and preserved that which was ordained by him through the apostle, so that we may keep the feast together, and together keep holy day, according to the tradition and commandment of the fathers. FESTAL LETTER 10.11.[3]

GRATITUDE FOR THE GIFTS OF GOD. AUGUSTINE: We have sung a psalm: "Blessed is the Lord, who has not given us as a quarry to their teeth." A proper expression of gratitude for the gifts of God. "Blessed is the Lord, who has not given us as a quarry to their teeth." It is certainly the voice of gratitude, and a very fitting gratitude. And when can human gratitude ever match such divine gifts? When the blessed martyr shed his

---

[1]WSA 3 9:240. [2]See Esther 3:9; 9:21. [3]NPNF 2 4:531-32*.

sacred blood in this place,[4] I do not know whether there was as big a crowd here of people raging against him, as there is now a multitude of people praising him. I repeat—I am delighted, after all, to see in the house of the Lord the people converging so religiously on this place and to compare times with times—which is why I say again and repeat, and so far as I can I devoutly commend to your consideration; when the blessed martyr shed his blood in this place, I do not know whether there was such a big crowd here raging against him as there now is a multitude of people praising him.

But even if there was, "blessed is the Lord, who has not given us as a quarry to their teeth." When they killed, they imagined they had conquered; they were being conquered by the people who were dying, and they rejoiced. If they were being conquered, they were naturally raging. So the raging crowd has departed, and the praising multitude has taken its place. Let them say, let them say, the praising multitude, "Blessed is the Lord, who has not given us as a quarry to their teeth." Whose teeth? The teeth of the enemies, the teeth of the godless, the teeth of those persecuting Jerusalem, the teeth of Babylon, the teeth of the enemy city, the teeth of the crowd gone stark, staring mad in their villainy, the teeth of a crowd persecuting the Lord, forsaking the Creator, turning to the creature, worshiping things made by hand, ignoring the one by whom they were made. "Blessed is the Lord, who has not given us as a quarry to their teeth." SERMON 313B.1.[5]

THE SOUL IS DESCRIBED AS A BIRD. AMBROSE: It is the same with David. Where the soul is supported with spiritual wings, he has chosen to describe the soul as a bird, as he has said in one place, "My soul has escaped like a bird from the snare of the fowlers"; and again, In the Lord I take refuge; how can you say to my soul, "Flee like a bird to the mountain."[6] Thus the soul has its wings by which it can raise itself free from the earth. But this movement of the wings is not of something constructed of feathers but a continuing series of good works, like those of the Lord of whom it is well said, "And in the shadow of your wings I shall take refuge."[7] In the first place, the hands of our Lord fixed on the cross were extended like something in flight, and, second, the actions of God are like a refreshing shadow of eternal salvation that can regulate the conflagration raging in our world. ON VIRGINITY 18.116.[8]

124:8 Lord of Heaven and Earth

OUR HELP IS IN THE NAME OF THE LORD. AUGUSTINE: So this heaven and earth is called the world. In saying "Do not love the world," he is not disparaging that world; whoever disparages that world, after all, is disparaging the maker of the world. Listen to the world mentioned twice in one place in different senses: it was said of the Lord Christ, "He was in this world, and the world was made through him, and the world did not know him."[9] The world was made through him: "Our help is in the name of the Lord, who made heaven and earth." The world was made through him: "I lifted up my eyes to the mountains; from where will help come to me? My help is from the Lord, who made heaven and earth."[10] This world was made by God, and the world did not know him. Which world did not know him? The lover of the world, the lover of the work, the scorner of the workman. SERMON 313A.2.[11]

---

[4]Augustine preached this sermon in Carthage on the birthday of Cyprian, who had been martyred in 258. [5]WSA 3 9:96*. [6]Ps 11:1 (10:2 LXX, Vg.). [7]Ps 57:1 (56:2 LXX, Vg.). [8]AOV 51. [9]Jn 1:10. [10]Ps 121:1-2 (120:1-2 LXX, Vg.). [11]WSA 3 9:91.

125:1-5 ISRAEL'S PEACE

A Song of Ascents.

[1]*Those who trust in the LORD are like Mount Zion,*
  which cannot be moved, but abides for ever.
[2]*As the mountains are round about Jerusalem,*
  so the LORD is round about his people,
  from this time forth and for evermore.
[3]*For the scepter of wickedness shall not rest*
  upon the land allotted to the righteous,
lest the righteous put forth
  their hands to do wrong.
[4]*Do good, O LORD, to those who are good,*
  and to those who are upright in their hearts!
[5]*But those who turn aside upon their crooked ways*
  the LORD will lead away with evildoers!
Peace be in Israel!

Overview: A righteous person, like an indestructible mountain, is safe from any power of wickedness, including Satan (Chrysostom). God protects his people who trust in him from Satan and the divisions that he seeks to create among God's people (Athanasius).

Although both sinners and righteous people have been baptized, they will be separated in the final judgment (Apocryphal Revelation). God's attributes of goodness and justice are so intertwined that he is neither merciful without judgment nor judging without being merciful (Basil). Satan and evil are figuratively located in the north and God and his grace in the south (Augustine).

125:1 Members of the Church Trust in the Lord

The Nature of a Righteous Person. Chrysostom: Such,[1] however, is not the nature of the righteous person. But what manner of person is he? Hear the same prophet, saying, "They that trust in the Lord are as Mount Zion." What does the phrase "as Mount Zion" mean? "He shall not be shaken forever," he says. For whatever engines [instruments of warfare] you bring up, whatever darts you hurl, desiring to overturn a mountain, you will never be able to prevail. For how can you? You will break in pieces all your engines and exhaust your own strength. Such also is the righteous person. Whatever blows he may receive, he suffers no evil therefrom but destroys the power of those who take counsel against him, and not of human beings only but of demons. You have heard often what engines the devil brought up against Job. But not only did he fail to overthrow that mountain but drew back exhausted, his darts broken to pieces and his engines rendered useless, by that assault! Homilies Concerning the Statues 8.4.[2]

People Who Trust in the Lord. Athanasius: For to those who thus examine themselves and conform their hearts to the Lord, nothing adverse shall happen; for indeed, their hearts are strengthened by confidence in the Lord, as it is written, "They who trust in the Lord are as Mount Zion; he who dwells in Jerusalem shall not be moved forever."[3] For if at any time, the crafty one shall be presumptuously bold against them, chiefly that he may break the rank of the saints and cause a division among brethren; even in this the Lord is with them, not only as an avenger on their behalf but also when they have already been beaten, as a

---

[1]Being subject to temptation, in conflict with himself and conscience-stricken. [2]NPNF 1 9:397**. [3]Ps 125:1-2 (124:1-2 LXX).

deliverer for them. FESTAL LETTER 11.6.[4]

125:3 The Righteous Will Be Separated from the Unrighteous

SINNERS WILL NOT SHARE THE LOT OF THE RIGHTEOUS. APOCRYPHAL REVELATION: And again I said, Lord, and what of those who have received baptism? And I heard a voice saying to me, Then the race of the Christians shall be examined, who have received baptism. And then the righteous shall come at my command, and the angels shall go and collect them from among the sinners, as the prophet David foretold: "The Lord will not allow the scepter of the sinners in the lot of the righteous"; and all the righteous shall be placed on my right hand[5] and shall shine like the sun. As you see, John, the stars of heaven were all made together but differ in light.[6] So shall it be with the righteous and the sinners— the righteous shall shine as lights and as the sun, but the sinners shall stand in darkness. APOCRYPHAL REVELATION OF JOHN THE THEOLOGIAN.[7]

125:4-5 God Is Merciful and Just

MERCIFUL AND JUST. BASIL THE GREAT: God is good, but he is also just, and it is the nature of the just to reward in proportion to merit, as it is written: "Do good, O Lord, to those that are good and to the upright of heart. But such as turn aside to their own crooked ways, the Lord shall lead out with the workers of iniquity." He is merciful, but he is also a judge, for "the Lord loves mercy and judgment," says the psalmist.[8] And he therefore also says, "Mercy and judgment I will sing to you, O Lord."[9] We have been taught who they are on whom he has mercy: "Blessed are the merciful," says the Lord, "for they shall obtain mercy."[10] You see with what discernment he bestows mercy, neither being merciful without judgment nor judging without mercy, for "the Lord is merciful and just."[11] Let us not, therefore, know God by halves or make his loving-kindness an excuse for our indolence; for this, his thunders, for this,

his lightnings—that his goodness may not be held in dispute. He who causes the sun to rise[12] also strikes people with blindness.[13] He who sends the rain[14] also causes the rain of fire.[15] By the one he manifests his goodness; by the other, his severity. For the one let us love him, for the other let us fear, that it may not be said also to us, "Or do you despise the riches of his goodness and patience and longsuffering? Do you not know that the kindness of God leads you to penance? But according to your hardness and impenitent heart, you store up for yourself wrath against the day of wrath."[16] THE LONG RULES, PREFACE.[17]

NORTH VERSUS SOUTH, FIGURATIVELY. AUGUSTINE: Therefore, the devil and his angels, by turning from the light and warmth of charity and going over to pride and envy, were made numb as by an icy hardness. Therefore they are figuratively located in the north. Thus, while the devil weighed down the human race, the future grace of the Savior was spoken of in the Canticle of Canticles thus: "Arise, O north wind, and come, O south wind, blow through my garden and let the aromatical spices thereof flow."[18] Arise, you who did rush in, who does weigh on the conquered, who does oppress those whom you own, arise, that those whose souls you have pressed on and bowed down may be relieved of your weight and may lift up their heads. "And come, O south wind," he says, calling on the spirit of grace, breathing from the south, as from a warm and luminous quarter, "that the aromatical spices may flow." Hence the apostle says, "We are the good odor of Christ in every place."[19] Hence, also, it says in another psalm, "Turn again our captivity, O Lord, as a stream in the south"; doubtless, the captivity in which they were held

---

[4]NPNF 2 4:535*. [5]Mt 25:33. [6]1 Cor 15:41. [7]ANF 8:585*. This document is a mid-second century product of Sethian Gnosticism that was pseudonymously attributed to the apostle John. [8]Ps 33:5 (32:5 LXX). [9]Ps 101:1 (100:1 LXX). [10]Mt 5:7. [11]Ps 116:5 (114:5 LXX). [12]Mt 5:45. [13]2 Kings 6:18. [14]Zech 10:1. [15]Gen 19:24. [16]Rom 2:4-5. [17]FC 9:229-30*. [18]Song 4:16. [19]2 Cor 2:14.

under the devil, as under the north wind, where they were chilled by abounding iniquity, and were, so to speak, frozen. Hence, also, the Gospel says, "And because iniquity has abounded, the charity of many shall grow cold."[20] But, truly, when the south wind blows, the ice is melted and the streams flow; that is, when their sins are for-

given the people flock to Christ by charity. Hence, also, it is written elsewhere, "And your sins are melted away as the ice in the fair, warm weather."[21] LETTER 140.22.[22]

---

[20]Mt 24:12. [21]Sir 3:15. [22]FC 20:103-4*.

126:1-6 A SONG OF JOY FOR RESTORATION

A Song of Ascents.

[1]*When the LORD restored the fortunes of Zion,*[1]
  we were like those who dream.
[2]*Then our mouth was filled with laughter,*
  and our tongue with shouts of joy;
then they said among the nations,
  "The LORD has done great things for them."
[3]*The LORD has done great things for us;*

we are glad.

[4]*Restore our fortunes, O LORD,*
  like the watercourses in the Negeb!
[5]*May those who sow in tears*
  reap with shouts of joy!
[6]*He that goes forth weeping,*
  bearing the seed for sowing,
shall come home with shouts of joy,
  bringing his sheaves with him.

1 Or *brought back those who returned to Zion*

OVERVIEW: People may find joy in their acquaintanceship with others on earth, but the joy of knowing one another in heaven will be much greater (AUGUSTINE).

We may abstain from things that provide sensual pleasures for the sake of receiving a heavenly harvest, but we must not mandate of others matters that are morally indifferent (CYRIL OF JERUSALEM). People who are grieved by their sins will rejoice in the life to come (BASIL). A final harvest of souls will be reaped at the end of the world when angels will be the reapers (AUGUSTINE). True joy and happiness cannot exist on earth, but we will experience them in heaven (CAESARIUS). All believers know that they must experience the

sorrows of this life before they reach their heavenly joy (BEDE). We all have an example in Christ of experiencing sorrows and tribulations in life, but after death we will experience joy. If we are willing to die for God and consider the joys of our eternal reward, we will not be reluctant to die.

When we sow the seeds of good works among the poor and needy, we must trust God to provide the harvest. The fruits of our labors are not harvested in this life but in the life to come (AUGUSTINE). It is necessary to read and hear God's Word, to pray and to perform good works so that we may plant in our hearts the seeds that will yield a harvest of justice and mercy on the day of retribution (CAESARIUS).

126:2 *Joy in Hope*

JOY IN THE FELLOWSHIP OF HEAVEN. AUGUSTINE: The Lord our God has granted me the favor of seeing you and being seen by you, and we can all give him thanks together. And if this is the reason that "our mouth is filled with joy and our tongue with exultation," that we have seen each other in the mortal flesh, imagine what our joy will be when we have seen each other in that place, where we will have nothing at all to fear from each other. The apostle says, "Rejoice in hope."[1] So our present joy is in hope, not yet in the thing itself. "But hope which is seen," he says, "is not hope; for why does anyone hope for what he can see? But if we are hoping for what we cannot see, we wait for it with patience."[2] But if travelers rejoice in each other's company on the way, what joy they will obtain in their home country! SERMON 306B.1.[3]

126:5 *True Happiness Exists Only in Heaven*

PLEASURES OF THE SENSES VERSUS SPIRITUAL DELIGHTS. CYRIL OF JERUSALEM: Concerning food. Let the body have its victuals, that it may live and render its services unimpeded, but not so as to be given to daintiness. Let these be your rules regarding food, since many trip up over meat. There are those who eat things sacrificed to idols without taking any notice. There are others who practice abstinence and then pass judgment on those who eat. And so the soul of this person or that is soiled in different ways, all in connection with the question of meats, through their not knowing the sensible reasons for eating or not eating. For we fast by abstaining from wine and from meat, not as though these things were abominations that we must hate but as expecting a reward for doing so, namely, that in spurning sensuous things, we may enjoy a spiritual and heavenly feast, "that sowing now in tears, we may reap in joy," in the world to come. But do not, in fasting, despise those who are eating such food, and eating it

because of bodily infirmity. Do not blame those "who use a little wine for their stomach's sake, and their frequent infirmities,"[4] and certainly do not adjudge them to be sinners. Do not abhor flesh meats as if they were taboo, for the apostle evidently knew people like that, since he says that there are [those] "who forbid to marry, and command to abstain from meats, which God has created to be received with thanksgiving by those who believe."[5] If therefore you are abstaining from these things, let it not be as from things abhorred, or your reward is lost, but as good things let them be transcended, in the quest of the fairer spiritual rewards that are set before you. CATECHETICAL LECTURES 4.27.[6]

OUR JOY IS IN THE FUTURE. BASIL THE GREAT: "Blessed are they who weep, for they shall laugh."[7] They, therefore, who spend the days of their life, which is already at its consummation and declining toward its setting, in weeping for their sins, these will be glad in that true morning that is approaching. "They that sow in tears shall reap in joy," of course, in the future. HOMILIES ON THE PSALMS 14.4.[8]

CHRIST DIED FOR US THAT WE MIGHT DIE FOR HIM TO LIVE FOREVER. AUGUSTINE: I sympathize with you,[9] because the Lord our God also sympathized with us, suffered with us. You see, he revealed himself in you, and you in himself, when he said, "My soul is sad to the point of death."[10] He suffered for us, let us suffer for him; he died for us, let us die for him, in order to live forever with him. But perhaps you are hesitant to die, O mortal creature, though you are bound to die sometime or other, precisely because you are mortal. Would you like not to fear death? Die for God. But perhaps the

---

[1]Rom 12:12. [2]Rom 8:24-25. [3]*WSA* 3 9:28. [4]1 Tim 5:23. [5]1 Tim 4:3. [6]LCC 4:113-14*. [7]Lk 6:21. [8]FC 46:220. [9]Cyprian. The sermon is a discourse on the occasion of commemorating Cyprian's birthday. [10]Mk 14:34.

reason you are afraid to die is that death is such a sad business. Consider the harvest; the time for sowing is cold; but if the farmer declines to be made miserable by sowing in the cold in winter, he won't rejoice in the summer. Take a look at yourself, and see whether the reason you are reluctant to sow is that there is the sadness and misery of the cold at seed time.

Look at the psalm: "Those who sow in tears shall reap in joy. Going, they were going and weeping, casting their seed;"[11] That is what we were singing just now; let us do what we have sung. Let us sow our souls in this time, like corn in winter, so that we may reap them in eternal time, like corn in summer time. That is the way the holy martyrs, the way all the just, toiling away on earth, weeping cast their seed; this life, after all, is full of tears. And what follows? "But coming, they will come with exultation, carrying their lapfuls."[12] Your seed is the shedding of your blood; your lapful the reception of your crown. SERMON 313D.3.[13]

PRESENT AND FUTURE HARVESTS. AUGUSTINE: Who labored? Abraham, Isaac and Jacob. Read their labors! In all their labors [there was] prophecy of Christ; and thus [they were] the sowers. Moses and the rest of the patriarchs and all the prophets, how much did they endure in that cold when they were sowing! Therefore in Judea the harvest was now ready. Rightly there the crop was, so to speak, ripe, when so many thousands of people were bringing the price of their possessions and laying it at the feet of the apostles; their shoulders freed of worldly baggage, they were following Christ, the Lord.[14] Truly a ripe harvest. What came of it? From that harvest a few grains were cast out, and they sowed the world, and there arises another harvest that is to be reaped at the end of the world. About this harvest it is said, "They who sow in tears shall reap in joy." To this harvest, therefore, not apostles but angels will be sent; he says, "The reapers are the angels."[15] TRACTATES ON THE GOSPEL OF JOHN 15.32.3.[16]

JOY AFTER SORROW. CAESARIUS OF ARLES: Let no one believe that he possesses any happiness or true joy in this world. Happiness can be prepared for, but it cannot be possessed here. Two times succeed each other in their own order, "a time to weep, and a time to laugh."[17] Let no one deceive himself, brethren; there is no time to laugh in this world. I know, indeed, that everyone wants to rejoice, but people do not all look for joy in the place where it should be sought. True joy never did exist in this world, it does not do so now, and it never will. For thus the Lord warned his disciples in the Gospel when he said, "You will suffer in the world,"[18] and again, "While the world rejoices, you will grieve for a time, but your grief will be turned into joy."[19] For this reason, with the Lord's help let us do good in this life through labor and sorrow, so that in the future life we may be able to gather the fruits of our good deeds with joy and exultation according to that sentence: "Those who sow in tears shall reap rejoicing." SERMON 215.2.[20]

EARTHLY SORROWS PRECEDE HEAVENLY JOYS. BEDE: But this discourse of the Lord is also appropriate to all believers who are striving to arrive at eternal joys through the tears and distress of the present [life]; who rightly lament and weep and are sorrowful during the present [time], since they are not yet capable of seeing him whom they love. As long as they are in their body they recognize that they are on a journey and [absent] from their fatherland and kingdom. They have no doubt that they must reach their crown by labors and contests. Their sorrow will be changed to joy when, after the struggle of this present life is over, they receive the prize of everlasting life, about which it is said in the psalm, "Those who sow in tears will reap in joy." HOMILIES ON THE GOSPELS 2.13.[21]

---

[11]Ps 126:5-6 (125:5-6 LXX, Vg.). [12]Ps 126:6 (125:6 LXX, Vg.). [13]WSA 3 9:106. [14]See Acts 4:34-35. [15]Mt 13:39. [16]FC 79:98-99. [17]Eccles 3:4. [18]Jn 16:33. [19]Jn 16:20. [20]FC 66:114. [21]CS 111:119.

THEY SOW IN TEARS AND REAP IN JOY.
AUGUSTINE: So [Christ] transposed the weak
members of his body [the church] into himself.
And perhaps it was of them that it is said,
"Those who sow in tears shall reap in joy," that is
to say, of the weaker ones. After all, that great
herald of Christ was not sowing in tears when he
said, "For I indeed am already being sacrificed,
and the time of my casting off is at hand. I have
fought the good fight, I have completed the
course, I have kept the faith. For the rest, there is
being kept for me the crown of justice—a crown
made of sheaves. There is being kept for me," he
says, "the crown of justice, which the Lord, the
just judge, will render to me on that day."[22] As
though to say, "He will render me the harvest,
for whom I am spending myself in sowing."
These words, brothers, as I understand them,
are the words of someone merrymaking, not of
someone crying. You don't suppose he was in
tears, do you, when he said this? Wasn't he exactly like the cheerful giver, whom God loves? So
let us refer these words [Jesus' words] to the
weak, in order that not even those who have
sown in tears need despair, because even if they
have sown in tears, the pain and the sighing will
pass away. Sadness passes at the end, and gladness comes without end.

And yet for all that, dearly beloved, this finally
is how it seems to me that these words refer to
everyone, "Those who sow in tears shall reap in
joy. Going they were going and weeping, casting
their seed. But coming they shall come with merrymaking, carrying their sheaves."[23] Listen, if
with the Lord's assistance I am able to explain it,
how "going they were going and weeping" belongs
to everyone. From the moment we are born, we
are going. Is there anyone, after all, who stands
still? Is there anyone who, from the moment he
enters life, is not forced to get moving? An infant
is born; it gets moving by growing. Death is the
end. We have still got to come to the end—but
with merrymaking. SERMON 31.3-4.[24]

126:6 Fruits of Our Labors

**TRUST GOD TO GRANT THE HARVEST OF OUR
LABORS.** AUGUSTINE: So it is only proper, brothers and sisters, that you should be told these
things. Attend to the poor, whether they are lying
there or whether they are walking about; attend
to the poor, do good works. If you are in the habit
of doing so, do so; if you are not in the habit of
doing so, do so. Let there be an increase in the
number of do-gooders, because there is an
increase, certainly, in the number of the faithful.
When you do something, you cannot yet see the
quantity of the good you do; just as when the
countryman sows he cannot yet see the crop, but
he trusts the earth. You then, why don't you trust
God? Our harvest is coming. Imagine that we are
now toiling away in what we do, toiling away as
we work, only to reap the benefit in due course, as
it is written: "Going they were going and weeping, casting their seed; but coming they shall
come with rejoicing, carrying their sheaves." SER-
MON 102.5.[25]

WORDS FOR ALL BELIEVERS. AUGUSTINE: This
psalm [126], being sung to the Lord, seems to fit
the holy martyrs; but if we are members of
Christ, as we ought to be, we can take these
words as referring to all of us: "Those who sow in
tears shall reap in joy. Going they shall go and
weep, casting their seed. But coming they shall
come with merrymaking, carrying their
sheaves."[26] Where are they going, and where are
they coming from? What are they sowing in
tears? What is the seed, what are the sheaves?
Going into death, coming from death; going by
being born, coming by rising again. Sowing is
whatever good we have done; our sheaves, what
we shall receive at the end. So if the seed is good,
the works are good, why "in tears," seeing that
God loves a cheerful giver?[27]

The first thing to notice, dearly beloved, is
how these words above all suit the blessed martyrs. Nobody, after all, has spent as much as those

---

[22]2 Tim 4:6-8. [23]Ps 126:5-6 (125:5-6 LXX, Vg.). [24]WSA 3 2:132-33.
[25]WSA 3 4:75. [26]Ps 126:5-6 (125:5-6 LXX, Vg.). [27]See 2 Cor 9:7.

who have spent their very selves, as the apostle Paul says: "And I myself will be spent for your souls."[28] They spent themselves by confessing Christ and by carrying out with his help the saying "You have sat at a great table; know that you must prepare similar things yourself."[29] What is the meaning of "know that you must prepare similar things yourself," if not what the blessed John explains: "Just as Christ laid down his life for us, so we too ought to lay down our lives for the brethren"?[30] There you are, that is how much they spent. SERMON 31.1-2.[31]

THE HARVEST OF OUR LABORS IN HEAVEN. AUGUSTINE: I say this so that we should not nurse hopes of receiving the fruits of our sowing during this time in which we have done the sowing. Here we sow with toil a harvest of good works, but it is in the time to come that we shall garner its fruits with joy, according to what is written: "Going they sent and wept, scattering their seed; but coming they will come with rejoicing, carrying their sheaves."[32] SERMON 11.3.[33]

PREPARATION FOR ENDLESS BLISS. CAESARIUS

OF ARLES: I beseech you with fatherly solicitude, equally admonishing and exhorting you, as was already said, to endeavor continually to read the sacred lessons yourselves or willingly to listen to others read them. By thus always thinking over in the treasury of your heart what is just and holy, you may prepare for your souls an eternal spiritual food that will bring you endless bliss. Christ does not lie when he says in the person of his apostle, "What a person sows, that he will also reap."[34] With God's help let us endeavor to continually plant in the field of our heart by reading, praying and performing good works those deeds whereof we may reap a harvest of justice and mercy on the future day of retribution. Then will be fulfilled in us what is written: "Going, they went and wept, casting their seeds. But coming, they shall come with joyfulness, carrying their sheaves." To this happiness may the good Lord lead you, who, together with the Father and the Holy Spirit, lives and reigns world without end. SERMON 8.5.[35]

---

[28] 2 Cor 12:15. [29] Sir 31:12. [30] 1 Jn 3:16. [31] *WSA* 3 2:131. [32] Ps 126:5-6 (125:5-6 LXX, Vg.). [33] *WSA* 3 1:295. [34] Gal 6:7. [35] FC 31:54*.

127:1-5 GODLY WISDOM CONCERNING HOME AND HEARTH

A Song of Ascents. Of Solomon.

¹*Unless the* LORD *builds the house,*
    those who build it labor in vain.
Unless the LORD *watches over the city,*
    the watchman stays awake in vain.
²*It is in vain that you rise up early*
    and go late to rest,

eating the bread of anxious toil;
    *for*ᵐ *he gives to his beloved sleep.*

³*Lo, sons are a heritage from the*
    LORD,
    the fruit of the womb a reward.
⁴*Like arrows in the hand of a warrior*
    are the sons of one's youth.

*[5]Happy is the man who has
    his quiver full of them!*

*He shall not be put to shame
    when he speaks with his enemies in the gate.*

m Another reading is *so*

OVERVIEW: It is the Holy Spirit specifically who protects our faith (CHRYSOSTOM). We cannot by ourselves preserve the faith that God has given us; rather it is also our ever-watchful God who guards and protects our faith (AUGUSTINE). Contrary to the wisdom of the philosophers, nothing happens by chance; everything happens by the disposition of God (JEROME). Humility is instilled in us and pride rooted out when we recognize that we can do nothing good without the help of God (EVAGRIUS).

127:1 God Watches Over the City

THE HOLY SPIRIT AND FAITH. CHRYSOSTOM: "That good thing that was committed to you to keep"—how?—"by the Holy Spirit, who dwells in us." For it is not in the power of a human soul, when instructed with things so great, to be sufficient for keeping them [of himself]. And why? Because there are many robbers and thick darkness, and the devil is still at hand to plot against us; and we know not what is the hour, what the occasion for him to set on us. How then, he means, shall we be sufficient for keeping them? "By the Holy Spirit"—that is if we have the Spirit with us, if we do not expel grace, he will stand by us. For, "Except the Lord build the house, they labor in vain who build it. Except the Lord keep the city, the watchman wakes but in vain." This is our wall, this our castle, this our refuge. If therefore he dwells in us and is himself our guard, what need is there for the commandment? That we may hold him fast, may keep him and not banish him by our evil deeds. HOMILIES ON 2 TIMOTHY 3.[1]

GOD PRESERVES OUR FAITH. AUGUSTINE: But someone, perhaps, will say, "I did indeed receive faith, but it is I who have guarded and kept it."

You perhaps say this, whoever you are, listening to all this and having no sense: "I received faith, but it is I who have guarded and kept it." It is not what our Paul says, "It is I who have guarded and kept it." He had his eyes, you see, on [the words] "unless the Lord keeps watch over the city, he labors in vain who guards it." Labor, by all means, guard it; but it is good for you that you are being guarded. Because you are not up to guarding yourself. If you are left to yourself, you will doze off and fall asleep. "He," though, "does not doze nor sleep, the one who guards Israel."[2] SERMON 297.7.[3]

NOTHING HAPPENS BY CHANCE. JEROME: He claims that this is how an Epicurus[4] would speak, or an Aristippus[5] and his Cyrenian flowers,[6] or the other philosophers who preach carnal pleasures. But when I diligently reconsider the question, I find nothing to support such vile conclusions that everything happens by chance and that fortune has free rein in human affairs. Rather the truth is that everything is under God's judgment. The fleet of foot ought not to think that the footrace is his, any more than the strong person should confide in his brute strength. Nor should the wise person reckon that wealth and opulence go with prudence, nor should the learned orator reckon that he can find favor with the crowd because of his learning and eloquence. Rather, everything happens by the disposition of God, and except he govern everything by his will and build the house, they labor in vain who build it. And unless he guard the city,

---

[1]NPNF 1 13:484**. [2]Ps 121:4 (120:4 LXX, Vg.). [3]*WSA* 3 8:220*. [4]Epicurus (341-270 B.C.) was the Greek philosopher who founded the philosophy emphasizing the pursuit of pleasure that bears his name. [5]Aristippus (435-366 B.C.) was a student of Socrates and the Greek philosopher who founded the Cyrenaic school of hedonism. [6]The disciples of Aristippus.

they keep watch in vain who set a guard over it. COMMENTARY ON ECCLESIASTES.[7]

GOD'S HELP FOR EVERY HUMAN ACT. JEROME: Atticus:[8] Therefore, they are wrong in their thinking who rule out the help of God in every single action that we perform and who seek to twist the true meaning to other meanings by putting forth interpretations that are perverted, nay more, worthy of ridicule, on the following passage: "Except the Lord build the house, they labor in vain that build it. Except the Lord keep the city, he watches in vain who keeps it." AGAINST THE PELAGIANS 1.2.[9]

DEPENDENCE ON GOD INSTILLS HUMILITY. EVAGRIUS OF PONTUS: The cowl[10] is a symbol of the charity of God our Savior. It protects the

most important part of the body and keeps us, who are children in Christ, warm. Thus it can be said to afford protection against those who attempt to strike and wound us. Consequently, all who wear this cowl on their heads sing these words aloud: "If the Lord does not build the house and keep the city, in vain does the builder labor and the watchman stand his guard." Such words as these instill humility and root out that long-standing evil, which is pride and which caused Lucifer, who rose like the day star in the morning, to be cast down to the earth. PRAKTIKOS, INTRODUCTORY LETTER TO ANATOLIUS.[11]

---

[7]MFC 17:185*. [8]The name of the orthodox disputant in this dialogue with the Pelagian Critobulus. [9]FC 53:237*. [10]A hood or hooded cloak of a monk. [11]CS 4:13*.

128:1-6 THE BLESSEDNESS OF THE GODLY PERSON

A Song of Ascents.

[1]*Blessed is every one who fears the LORD,*
  who walks in his ways!
[2]*You shall eat the fruit of the labor of your*
    hands;
  you shall be happy, and it shall be well with
    you.

[3]*Your wife will be like a fruitful vine*
  within your house;

your children will be like olive shoots
    around your table.
[4]*Lo, thus shall the man be blessed*
  who fears the LORD.

[5]*The LORD bless you from Zion!*
  May you see the prosperity of Jerusalem
    all the days of your life!
[6]*May you see your children's children!*
  Peace be upon Israel!

OVERVIEW: People are saved, not by nominal membership in those known as God's people, but by virtue of their fear of the Lord and by their walking in his ways (THEODORET). People who fear loss of temporal possessions are not blessed, but those who fear the Lord experience true joy.

When the psalmist says that the man who fears the Lord is blessed, he also included the female (CASSIODORUS).

128:1 Fear God and Walk in His Ways

DIVINE FEAR. THEODORET OF CYR: "Blessed are all who fear the Lord." The inspired word declared blessed not the one from Abraham's stock or from Israel's seed but the person adorned with the fear of God. Blessed Peter also says this in the book of Acts: "In truth I grasp the fact that God shows no partiality, but in every nation the person fearing him and performing righteousness is acceptable to him."[1] The inspired word also gave a glimpse of the character of the fear of God, adding "those walking in his ways":[2] "Not everyone saying to me, Lord, Lord, will enter the kingdom of heaven, but the one doing the will of my Father who is in heaven."[3] So it is typical of those fearing the Lord not to stray from the ways of God but to travel in them without fail. COMMENTARY ON THE PSALMS 128.2.[4]

FEAR OF GOD IS BORN OF CHARITY. CASSIODORUS: His words, "blessed are all they who fear the Lord," reveal that those who with troubled mind are apprehensive of the world's dangers in loss of temporal possessions are not blessed. These dangers make people wretched, torturing them with empty fear, so that they do not experi-

ence growth but a diminution, no ascent but a headlong fall. By contrast, fear of the Lord is the offspring of love, is born of charity, is sprung from sweetness. What devoted fear, consoling the fearful, refreshing the afflicted, experiencing no absence of joy unless the benefit of such fear is laid aside! Scripture says of this fear: "Come, children, hearken to me: I will teach you the fear of the Lord."[5] How advantageous the fear is by which children are instructed, how splendid the training bestowed with sweet affection! EXPOSITIONS OF THE PSALMS 127.1.[6]

128:3 Blessed Are They Who Fear the Lord

INCLUSIVE LANGUAGE. CASSIODORUS: Next comes "Your sons as olive plants round about your table." Wisdom as wife is rightly said to have sons and not daughters. The male sex usually denotes mental strength; in other cases, when the male sex is referenced, it embraces both male and female. When the psalmist says elsewhere, "Blessed is the man that fears the Lord,"[7] it is not just the man who fears the Lord that is blessed; the woman too who fears the Lord is blessed. EXPOSITIONS OF THE PSALMS 127.3.[8]

---

[1]Acts 10:34-35. [2]Acts 10:35. [3]Mt 7:21. [4]FC 102:297*. [5]Ps 34:11 (33:12 LXX, Vg.). [6]ACW 53:302*. [7]Ps 112:1 (111:1 LXX, Vg.). [8]ACW 53:304*.

129:1-8 ISRAEL'S PRAYER FOR THE DEMISE OF ITS ENEMIES

A Song of Ascents.

[1]*"Sorely have they afflicted me from my youth,"*
*   let Israel now say—*

[2]*"Sorely have they afflicted me from my youth,*
*   yet they have not prevailed against me.*
[3]*The plowers plowed upon my back;*
*   they made long their furrows."*

⁴*The LORD is righteous;*
  he has cut the cords of the wicked.
⁵*May all who hate Zion*
  be put to shame and turned backward!
⁶*Let them be like the grass on the housetops,*
  which withers before it grows up,

⁷*with which the reaper does not fill his hand*
  or the binder of sheaves his bosom,
⁸*while those who pass by do not say,*
  "The blessing of the LORD be upon you!
  We bless you in the name of the LORD!"

OVERVIEW: Although the church may have seemed defeated many times throughout history, it has and always will survive (AUGUSTINE). The church is constantly under attack from its enemies, but it prevails and gains many for eternal life. Aggressive sinners seem to flourish for a time, but their faith dies from pride and lack of proper nourishment (CASSIODORUS). People who cannot constrain their sinning try to shift the blame to God for creating the good things of this world, such as the gold that induces them to become greedy (AUGUSTINE).

129:1-3 They Have Not Prevailed

THE TRIUMPHANT CHURCH. AUGUSTINE: "Many a time have they fought against me from my youth up." The church speaks of those whom it tolerates, and as if it were asked, "Is it now?" The church is of ancient birth. As long as saints have been so called, the church has been on earth. At one time the church was in Abel only, and he was fought against by his wicked and lost brother Cain.[1] At one time the church was in Enoch alone, and he was translated from the unrighteous.[2] At one time the church was in the house of Noah alone and endured all who perished by the flood, and the ark alone swam on the waves and escaped to shore.[3] At one time the church was in Abraham alone, and we know what he endured from the wicked. The church was in his brother's son, Lot, alone, and in his house, in Sodom; and he endured the iniquities and perversities of Sodom, until God freed him from their midst.[4] The church also began to exist in the people of Israel: they endured Pharaoh and the Egyptians.

The number of the saints began to be also in the church, that is, in the people of Israel. Moses and the rest of the saints endured the wicked Jews, the people of Israel. We come to our Lord Jesus Christ: The gospel was preached in the Psalms.[5] . . . For this reason, lest the church wonder now, or lest any one wonder in the church who wishes to be a good member of the church, let him hear the church his mother saying to him, Marvel not at these things, my child: "many a time have they fought against me from my youth up." EXPLANATIONS OF THE PSALMS 129.2.[6]

THE CHURCH IS ATTACKED BUT NEVER DEFEATED. CASSIODORUS: "Often have they fought against me from my youth, but they could not prevail over me." There was a similar exordium in the fifth of these psalms of the steps;[7] this figure is called *anaphora*, the recital of the same expression at the start of several verses. We must interpret this period as the church's old age. As the apostle says, "Little children, it is the last hour";[8] for whatever occurs at the end of the world is most suitably called its old age. So the church says that it has been fiercely warred on from its youth, so that you may realize that it is never brought to an end, since it is under constant attack. So it grows under the

---

[1]Gen 4:8. [2]Gen 5:24. [3]Gen 6-8. [4]Gen 13-20. [5]Ps 40:5 (39:6 LXX, Vg.); Heb 4:2. [6]NPNF 1 8:611*. [7]See Ps 124 (123 LXX). The heading before each of the Psalms 120 (119 LXX, Vg.) – 134 (133 LXX, Vg.) is *Canticum Graduum*, usually rendered in English as "Gradual Canticle." Cassiodorus accepts Jerome's explanation in his *commentariolus*: The fifteen psalms of the steps lead up to the heights by a kind of progression. The fifteen steps are the stairs from the Women's Court to the Men's Court in the temple in Jerusalem. They are mounted on the first day of the feast of tabernacles by the levitical singers (ACW 53:501). [8]1 Jn 2:18.

persecution of the wicked and grows through its grief. Even though it seems to lose holy ones in this life, it is seen to gain them for the fatherland to come; so it cannot be brought to an end, since it is clearly increased by the losses that it sustains. This is what the following words make clear: "But they could not prevail over me." It says that those who it earlier states had warred against it could not prevail over it; for the warring that develops into further conflict is not brought to an end, and victory must not be pronounced when it is certain that the conflict can be renewed. Expositions of the Psalms 128.2.[9]

God Is Not the Cause of People's Sins.
Augustine: You accuse a person of greed, and he accuses God on the ground that he made gold.[10] Do not be covetous. And God, you reply, should not make gold. This now remains, because you can not restrain your evil deeds, you accuse the good works of God: the creator and architect of the world displeases you. He ought not to make the sun either; for many contend concerning the lights of their windows and drag each other before courts of law.[11] Oh, if we could restrain our vices! For all things are good, because a good God made all things; and his works praise him,

when their goodness is considered by him who has the spirit of discerning them, the spirit of piety and wisdom.[12] Explanations of the Psalms 129.5.[13]

129:6 Like Grass on the Top of Buildings

Persistent Sinners Die Spiritually Before They Die Physically. Cassiodorus: "Let them be as grass on the tops of buildings, which withers before it is plucked up." Abandoned buildings often sprout momentarily with grass on their tops. Before it can be gathered it withers and dies because it has insufficient roots to give it strength. Aggressive sinners are linked with such grass in a most apt association, for they also often die off here before they are taken from this world's light, for they sprout on the heights of pride where they are not firmly based, whereas if they sprouted in the vale of tears, they could with the Lord's help bring their harvest to fullness. Expositions of the Psalms 128.6.[14]

---

[9]ACW 53:308*. [10]These comments are made in reference to Psalm 129:3 (128:3 LXX, Vg.). [11]People sue other people because of the conduct they observe through unshaded windows. [12]Song of Three Children 35, etc. [13]NPNF 1 8:611-12**. [14]ACW 53:309*.

130:1-8 A SUPPLICATION FOR FORGIVENESS AND REDEMPTION

A Song of Ascents.

[1]*Out of the depths I cry to thee, O Lord!*
   [2]*Lord, hear my voice!*
Let thy ears be attentive
   to the voice of my supplications!

[3]*If thou, O Lord, shouldst mark iniquities,*
   Lord, who could stand?
[4]*But there is forgiveness with thee,*
   that thou mayest be feared.

[5]*I wait for the Lord my soul waits,*
   and in his word I hope;

⁶my soul waits for the LORD
  more than watchmen for the morning,
  more than watchmen for the morning.

⁷O Israel, hope in the LORD!

For with the LORD there is steadfast love,
  and with him is plenteous redemption.
⁸And he will redeem Israel
  from all his iniquities.

OVERVIEW: Sinners who repent and are ashamed of their sins should be reconciled to the church with proper admonition and discipline (APOSTOLIC CONSTITUTIONS). When repentance is genuine, absolution should be granted immediately, just as God's mercy has no limit or fixed time (LEO).

130:3-4 If God Should Mark Iniquities

PRAYER FOR MERCY. APOSTOLIC CONSTITUTIONS: When you see the offender,[1] with severity command him to be cast out. As he is going out, let the deacons also treat him with severity, and then let them go and seek for him and keep him out of the church. When they come in, let them entreat you for him. For our Savior entreated his Father for those who had sinned, as it is written in the Gospel: "Father, forgive them; for they know not what they do."[2] Then order the offender to come in. And if on examination you find that he is penitent and fit to be received at all into the church when you have assigned him his days of fasting, according to the degree of his offense—as two, three, five or seven weeks—so set him at liberty and speak such things to him as are fit to be said by way of reproof, instruction and exhortation to a sinner for his reformation, so that he may continue privately in his humility and pray to God to be merciful to him, saying: "If you, O Lord, should mark iniquities, O Lord, who shall stand? For with you there is forgiveness." This sort of statement contains what is said in the book of Genesis to Cain: "You have sinned; be quiet";[3] that is, do not continue in sin. That a sinner ought to be ashamed for his own sin, the oracle of God delivered to Moses concerning Miriam is a suffi-

cient proof, when he prayed that she might be forgiven. For God said to him, "If her father had spit in her face, should she not be ashamed? Let her be shut out of the camp for seven days, and afterwards let her come in again."[4] We therefore ought to do the same with offenders, when they profess their repentance, namely, to separate them for a period of time, according to the degree of their offense; and afterwards, as fathers deal with their children, receive them again on their repentance. CONSTITUTIONS OF THE HOLY APOSTLES 2.3.16.[5]

130:7 Steadfast Love and Plenteous Redemption

THERE ARE NO LIMITATIONS ON GOD'S MERCY. LEO THE GREAT: But satisfaction must not be ruled out or absolution denied to those who in time of necessity or in the moment of pressing danger beg for the protection of penance followed by absolution. For we cannot put limitations on the mercy of God or fix limits to times. With him there is no delaying of pardon when the conversion is genuine, as the Spirit of God says through the prophet: "If being converted you lament, you will be saved";[6] and elsewhere: "Tell me your sins first in order that you may be justified";[7] and again: "Because with the Lord there is mercy; and with him plentiful redemption." Consequently, we must not be stingy in dispensing the gifts of God or disregard the tears and groans of those accusing

---

[1]A person who has sinned. In the immediately preceding context, the author quotes Jer 12:10; Zech 10:3; Mal 1:6. [2]Lk 23:34. [3]Gen 4:7 (LXX). [4]Num 12:14. [5]ANF 7:402**. [6]See Is 30:15. [7]Is 43:26.

themselves, since, in our opinion, the very desire for penance was conceived through the inspiration of God, as the apostle says: "Lest by chance God give them repentance . . . so that they may recover themselves from the snare of the devil, at whose pleasure they are held captive."[8] LETTER 108.[9]

---

[8]2 Tim 2:25-26. [9]FC 34:192*.

131:1-3 A CONFESSION OF HUMBLE TRUST IN GOD

A Song of Ascents. Of David.

[1]*O LORD, my heart is not lifted up,*
  my eyes are not raised too high;
I do not occupy myself with things
  too great and too marvelous for me.

[2]*But I have calmed and quieted my soul,*
  like a child quieted at its mother's breast;
  like a child that is quieted is my soul.

[3]*O Israel, hope in the LORD*
  from this time forth and for evermore.

OVERVIEW: Even if a person's humility is sincere, there is always the danger that it may become the source of a new sense of pride (JEROME). We must build in our hearts a temple to the Holy Spirit, made from stones of humility, so that we may offer him the psalmist's song of humility for all he has given us (MARTIN). Humility was taught by the psalmist before Plato but reaches its fullest expression and exemplification in Jesus Christ (ORIGEN). Humility is the virtue that is the opposite of pride, which destroys not only humility but all virtues (CASSIAN). The authority of great people and our ancestors should not be resisted but followed in true humility (BRAULIO).

131:1-2 A Spirit of Humility

DO NOT BE PROUD OF HUMILITY. JEROME: I know your[1] humility. I know that you can say with sincerity, "Lord, my heart is not haughty or my eyes lofty"; I know that in your heart as in that of your mother the pride through which the devil fell has no place. It would be time wasted to write to you about it; for there is no greater folly than to teach a pupil what he knows already. But now that you have despised the boastfulness of the world, do not let the fact inspire you with new boastfulness. Harbor not the secret thought that having ceased to court attention in garments of gold you may begin to do so in mean attire. And when you come into a room full of brothers and sisters, do not sit in too low a place or plead that you are unworthy of a footstool. Do not deliberately lower your voice as though worn out with fasting; or, leaning on the shoulder of another, mimic the tottering gait of one who is faint. Some women, it is true, disfigure their faces so that they may appear to other people to fast.[2] As soon as they catch sight of any one, they groan, they look down; they cover up their faces, except for one eye, which they keep free to see with. Their dress is somber, their girdles are of

---

[1]Eustochium, to whom this letter is addressed. She was the daughter of Paula, one of the wealthy Roman widows whom Jerome had befriended. [2]Mt 6:16.

sackcloth, their hands and feet are dirty; only their stomachs—which cannot be seen—are hot with food. Of these the psalm is sung daily: "The Lord will scatter the bones of them that please themselves."[3] Others change their garb and assume the appearance of men, being ashamed of being what they were born to be—women. They cut off their hair and are not ashamed to look like eunuchs. Some clothe themselves in goat's hair, and, putting on hoods, pretending to become children again by making themselves look like so many owls.[4] LETTER 22.27.[5]

A HUMBLE PERSON GIVES ALL CREDIT TO GOD. MARTIN OF BRAGA: Now your goodness must listen briefly while I explain how this virtue may be obtained. First of all, if you intend to start a good work, you will begin it not with the intention of acquiring praise but for the love and desire of doing good. Then, when this good task, whatever it is, has been completed, you will guard your heart most cautiously, lest you fall under the influence of human favors and overestimate yourself, thus trying to please yourself or to look for some renown from any deed. For glory is like the human shadow: if you follow it, it runs away; if you run away, it follows. Always value yourself least of all and remember, whenever any good befalls you throughout your life, ascribe it all to God who gave it, not to yourself who received it, convincing yourself with these words of the apostle Paul: "What have you that you have not received? And if you have received it, why do you boast as if you had not received it?"[6] And also reflecting on these words of the apostle: "Every good gift and every perfect gift is from above, coming down from the Father of lights."[7] And when you have built in your heart a temple to the Holy Spirit, using these most precious stones of holy humility, then pray in it, using the song of the prophet David. Not in words only but in deeds shall you sing: "O Lord, my heart is not proud, nor are my eyes haughty; I busy not myself with great things or with things too sublime for me." This song you will truly be able to

offer to God when you humiliate yourself and praise him alone, to whom truly with all the faithful you may every day say, "To you we owe a hymn of praise,"[8] glorifying him alone. EXHORTATION TO HUMILITY 8.[9]

THE DOCTRINE OF HUMILITY. ORIGEN: Celsus,[10] . . . as one who has heard the subject of humility greatly talked about but who has not been at pains to understand it, would wish to speak evil of that humility that is practiced among us, and imagines that it is borrowed from some words of Plato imperfectly understood, where he expresses himself in the *Laws* as follows: "Now God, according to the ancient account, having in himself both the beginning and end and middle of all existing things, proceeds according to nature and marches straight on. He is constantly followed by justice, which is the avenger of all breaches of the divine law: he who is about to become happy follows [justice] closely in humility, and becomingly adorned."[11] He did not observe, however, that in writers much older than Plato the following words occur in a prayer: "Lord, my heart is not haughty or my eyes lofty, neither do I walk in great matters, nor in things too wonderful for me; if I had not been humble," etc. Now these words show that one who is of humble mind does not by any means humble himself in an unseemly or inauspicious manner, falling down on his knees or casting himself headlong on the ground, putting on the dress of the miserable or sprinkling himself with dust. But he who is of humble mind in the sense of the prophet, while "walking in great and wonderful things," which are above his capacity—namely, those doctrines that are truly great and those thoughts that are wonderful—"humbles himself under the mighty hand of God."[12] If there are

---

[3]Ps 53:5 (52:6 LXX, Vg.). [4]The Latin has *noctuas et bubones*, the first being a night owl and the second a horned owl, whose cry was considered an ill omen. [5]NPNF 2 6:33-4. [6]1 Cor 4:7. [7]Jas 1:17. [8]Ps 65:1 (64:2 LXX, Vg.). [9]FC 62:57*. [10]A Platonist who wrote the most capable and reasoned attacks on early Christianity in 180. [11]Plato, *De Legibus* 4. [12]1 Pet 5:6.

some, however, who through their stupidity have not clearly understood the doctrine of humiliation and act as they do, it is not our doctrine that is to be blamed; but we must extend our forgiveness to the stupidity of those who aim at higher things and owing to their foolishness of mind fail to attain them. He who is "humble and becomingly adorned," is so in greater degree than Plato's "humble and becomingly adorned" individual: for he is humble and becomingly adorned on the one hand, because "he walks in things great and wonderful," which are beyond his capacity; and humble, on the other hand, because, while being in the midst of such, he yet voluntarily humbles himself, not under anyone at random but under "the mighty hand of God," through Jesus Christ, the teacher of such instruction, "who did not deem equality with God a thing to be eagerly clung to, but made himself of no reputation and took on him the form of a servant, and being found in fashion as a man, humbled himself and became obedient unto death, even the death of the cross."[13] And so great is this doctrine of humiliation that it has no ordinary individual as its teacher; but our great Savior says, "Learn of me, for I am meek and lowly of heart, and you shall find rest for your souls."[14] AGAINST CELSUS 6.15.[15]

THE VIRTUE OF HUMILITY. JOHN CASSIAN: And so it is very clearly shown from scriptural examples and texts that, although the disgrace of pride is last in the order of battle, it is nonetheless first in terms of origin and is the source of all sins and misdeeds, and that, unlike the other vices, it does not do away merely with its opposite virtue—that is, humility—but is actually the destroyer of all the virtues together, and that it tries not only the middling and the small but in particular those who stand at the summit of strength. For so the prophet says of this spirit, "His foods are choice."[16] Hence, although blessed David guarded the recesses of his heart with great care (so that he boldly declared to him from

whom the secrets of his conscience were not hidden: "Lord, my heart has not grown proud, nor have my eyes been lifted up; neither have I walked in great matters or in marvels beyond me. If I did not feel humble"; and again, "He who does what is proud shall not dwell within my house"[17]), he knew nonetheless how difficult it was even for the perfect to keep up this guard, and he did not presume on his own effort alone but, in order to be able to escape unharmed this enemy's dart, prayerfully implored the Lord's help and said, "Let the foot of pride not come on me."[18] And he was terrified and frightened lest there befall him what was said of the proud: "God is set against the proud."[19] And again: "Everyone whose heart grows proud is unclean in the sight of God."[20] INSTITUTES 12.6.1-2.[21]

THINK HUMBLE THOUGHTS AS OUR ANCESTORS DID. BRAULIO OF SARAGOSSA: Nor can I think otherwise against the authority of so great a man,[22] but I can only follow his steps and, in Christian humility, not deviate from the paths of our ancestors; as David says, "Neither have I walked with great things or with things too sublime for me." He is raised up above himself who departs from the traces of his elders and tries to have vision in things that are beyond his powers. Hence, it follows, "If I was not humbly minded, but exalted my soul: as a child that is weaned is towards his mother, so will you reward my soul." And so it is useful for us to think humble thoughts, in the words of the apostle: "Not setting your mind on high things but condescending to the lowly";[23] and to receive weaning with Isaac, that we may share stronger food rather than with Ishmael, son of the slave girl, to carry a bottle with water instead of wine[24] and to be driven from the eternal inheritance. LETTER 44.[25]

---

[13]Phil 2:6, 8. [14]Mt 11:29. [15]ANCL 23:352-53*. [16]Hab 1:16 (LXX). [17]Ps 101:7 (100:7 LXX). [18]Ps 36:11 (35:12 LXX). [19]Jas 4:6. [20]Prov 16:5 (LXX). [21]ACW 58:257-58. [22]Jerome. In the previous paragraph a reference is made to Jerome's letter (Letter 72) to a priest named Vitalis. [23]Rom 12:16. [24]See Gen 21:9-18. [25]FC 63:109*.

132:1-18 A PRAYER FOR GOD'S FAVOR

A Song of Ascents.

¹*Remember, O LORD, in David's favor,*
    all the hardships he endured;
²*how he swore to the LORD*
    and vowed to the Mighty One of
        Jacob,
³*"I will not enter my house*
    or get into my bed;
⁴*I will not give sleep to my eyes*
    or slumber to my eyelids,
⁵*until I find a place for the LORD,*
    a dwelling place for the Mighty One
        of Jacob."

⁶*Lo, we heard of it in Ephrathah,*
    we found it in the fields of Jaar.
⁷*"Let us go to his dwelling place;*
    let us worship at his footstool!"

⁸*Arise, O LORD, and go to thy resting*
        place,
    thou and the ark of thy might.
⁹*Let thy priests be clothed with*
        righteousness,
    and let thy saints shout for joy.
¹⁰*For thy servant David's sake*
do not turn away the face of thy anointed
    one.

¹¹*The LORD swore to David a sure oath*
    from which he will not turn back:
"One of the sons of your body
    I will set on your throne.
¹²*If your sons keep my covenant*
    and my testimonies which I shall teach
        them,
their sons also for ever
    shall sit upon your throne."

¹³*For the LORD has chosen Zion;*
    he has desired it for his habitation:
¹⁴*"This is my resting place for ever;*
    here I will dwell, for I have desired it.
¹⁵*I will abundantly bless her provisions;*
    I will satisfy her poor with bread.
¹⁶*Her priests I will clothe with salvation,*
    and her saints will shout for joy.
¹⁷*There I will make a horn to sprout for*
        David;
    I have prepared a lamp for my anointed.
¹⁸*His enemies I will clothe with shame,*
    but upon himself his crown will shed its
        luster."

OVERVIEW: As David went without sleep to find a place for the tabernacle of God, the saints teach us the virtue of observing night vigils in celebration of our salvation (NICETAS). We must resist Satan by never resting until we have made a place for God to dwell in our souls (SAHDONA).

The church must be adorned with the garments of faith, proclamation of the Word, patience, knowledge, purity, virginity, suffering, love and especially Jesus Christ (ORIGEN).

Mary was of the lineage of King David, to whom God had promised that there would be no end of his descendants (CYRIL OF JERUSALEM).

Joshua, who led Israel into the promised land, and John, the forerunner of Christ, are called angels because they are ministers of God's power and lamps who illumine the minds of people that they may understand Christ (TERTULLIAN). Christ, as lamp, has sought us so that we might not be lost, and the church now seeks those who have already been found by Christ. David predicted the coming of our Lord and Savior, Jesus Christ, as well as John, who would prepare the way for his advent. The psalmist already foretold that many would not accept Christ and would become his enemies. Christ will confound his enemies but unite and sanctify those who believe in him (AUGUSTINE).

132:3-5 A Dwelling Place for the Lord

VIGILS ARE TESTS OF ONE'S LOVE FOR GOD. NICETAS OF REMESIANA: The more I meditate on the mind of the saints, the more I am reminded of something that is high and hard and beyond the powers of human nature. Call to mind what the same psalmist [David] has said: "If I shall go up into the bed wherein I lie; if I shall give sleep to my eyes, or slumber to my eyelids or rest to my temples; until I find out a place for the Lord, a tabernacle for the God of Jacob." Who would not be amazed at such a love of God, such dedication of soul, that a king and prophet should deny himself all sleep—the very essential of bodily vigor—until he should find a place to build a temple to the Lord? This fact should be a strong admonishment to us who long to be a dwelling place of the Lord and to be considered his tabernacle and temple forever. "You are," as Paul reminds us, "the temple of the living God."[1] Let us, then, be moved by the example of the saints to love vigils to the utmost of our power. And let it not be said of us what is said in the psalm: "They have slept their sleep and . . . found nothing."[2] Rather, let each of us be glad to say, "In the day of my trouble I have sought God and with my hands lifted up to him in the night and was not deceived."[3] The reason is that "it is good to give praise to the Lord and to sing to your name, O most High; to show forth your mercy in the morning and your truth in the night."[4] These and many other such

thoughts the saints have left us in song and other writings, so that we who are their heirs may be moved by such examples to celebrate at night the vigils of our salvation. VIGILS OF THE SAINTS 5.[5]

DO NOT REST UNTIL YOUR SOUL FINDS ITS REST IN GOD. SAHDONA: Girded with such things to serve as invincible armor, let us take our stand against the evil one, being wakeful and well prepared, as though it was day. Let us pierce him with the mighty arrows of the Spirit's words and cut off all his hopes, joining David, the son of Jesse, in adjuring him by the covenant that does not fail: "Depart from us and go to your ill fate, you mad *dog*"[6] that audaciously barks against its master, for we have sworn to the Lord and make our vow to the God of Jacob that we shall "not allow sleep to touch our eyes, or drowsiness our eyelids, until we have found a place for the Lord to rest in our souls, a tent for the God of Jacob" to dwell in our hearts. We will certainly not cease from vigil, prayer, toil and labor until the Lord is pleased at our soul and chooses it as a place in which to live, saying, "This is my resting place for eternal ages; here shall I reside, for I have desired it." BOOK OF PERFECTION 72.[7]

132:9 Clothed with Righteousness

GARMENTS OF MERCY. ORIGEN: But lest we linger too long on the forms of individual virtues, we can briefly say that they indicate those things by which the church is adorned. Its faith can be compared with gold; the word of preaching with silver; bronze with patience; incorruptible wood with the knowledge that comes through the wood or to the incorruptibility of purity that never grows old; virginity with linen; the glory of suffering with scarlet; the splendor of love with purple; the hope of the kingdom of heaven with the blue. Let those, however, be the materials from

---

[1]1 Cor 3:16. [2]Ps 76:5 (75:6 LXX). [3]Ps 77:2 (76:3 LXX). [4]Ps 92:1-2 (91:2-3 LXX). [5]FC 7:59. [6]See 1 Sam 17:43. [7]CS 101:231-32*.

which the whole tabernacle is constructed, the priests are clothed and the high priest is adorned. The prophet speaks in another passage about the nature and quality of their clothing: "Let your priests be clothed with justice." All those garments, therefore, are garments of justice. And again the apostle Paul says, "Put on heartfelt mercy."[8] They are also, therefore, garments of mercy. But the same apostle no less also designates other more noble garments when he says, "Put on the Lord Jesus Christ, and give no attention to the flesh for lusting."[9] Those, therefore, are the garments with which the church is adorned. HOMILIES ON EXODUS 9.3.[10]

132:11 God Swore an Oath to David

THE VIRGIN MARY'S ROYAL LINEAGE. CYRIL OF JERUSALEM: That the Lord was to be born of a virgin we know clearly; now we must show of what stock the virgin was. "The Lord swore to David a firm promise from which he will not withdraw: 'Your own offspring I will set on your throne.'" Again, "I will make his posterity endure forever and his throne as the days of heaven."[11] Then, "Once by my holiness I have sworn; I will not be false to David: his posterity shall continue forever, and his throne shall be like the sun before me; like the moon, which remains forever."[12] You see that the words concern Christ, not Solomon, for Solomon's throne did not endure as the sun. But if anyone should object that Christ did not sit on the wooden throne of David, let us produce that saying: "The scribes and Pharisees have sat on the chair of Moses."[13] For this signifies not the chair of wood but the authority of his teaching. CATECHETICAL LECTURES 12.23.[14]

132:17-18 A Lamp for His Anointed

A LAMP REVEALING CHRIST. TERTULLIAN: For Joshua was to lead the people into the land of promise, not Moses. Now he called him an "angel," on account of the magnitude of the mighty deeds that he was to achieve (which mighty deeds Joshua the son of Nun did, and you yourselves have read about) and on account of his office of prophet announcing the divine will. Just as the Spirit, speaking in the person of the Father, calls the forerunner of Christ, John, a future "angel," through the prophet: "Behold, I sent my angel before your"—that is, Christ's—"face, who shall prepare your way before you."[15] Nor is it a novel practice to the Holy Spirit to call those "angels" whom God has appointed as ministers of his power. For the same John is called not merely an "angel" of Christ but also a "lamp" shining before Christ. For David predicts, "I have prepared the lamp for my Christ"; and so Christ, coming "to fulfill the prophets,"[16] referred to him [John] [when speaking] to the Jews. "He was," he says, "the burning and shining lamp,"[17] being the one who not only prepared his ways in the desert" but, by pointing out "the Lamb of God,"[18] enlightened the minds of people by his proclaiming, so that they understood him to be that Lamb whom Moses was accustomed to announce as destined to suffer. AN ANSWER TO THE JEWS 9.[19]

SOUGHT BY GOD. AUGUSTINE: What is the woman?[20] The flesh of Christ. What is the lamp? "I have prepared a lamp for my anointed." Therefore we were sought in order that we might be found; having been found, we speak. Let us not be proud because, before we were found, if we were not sought for, we would have been lost. Therefore let not those whom we love and whom we wish to win over to the peace of the catholic church say to us, "Why do you want us? Why do you seek us if we are sinners?"[21] We seek you precisely that you may not be lost; we seek you because we were sought; we wish to find you because we were found. TRACTATES ON THE GOSPEL OF JOHN 7.21.3.[22]

---

[8]Col 3:12. [9]Rom 13:14. [10]FC 71:340. [11]Ps 89:29 (88:30 LXX). [12]Ps 89:35-36 (88:36-37 LXX). [13]Mt 23:2. [14]FC 61:241-42*. [15]Mal 3:1. [16]Mt 5:17. [17]Jn 5:35. [18]Jn 1:29, 36. [19]ANF 3:163-64**. [20]See Lk 15:8-9, the woman in the parable of the lost coin. [21]See Tractate 6.22. [22]FC 78:175*.

PROPHECIES OF CHRIST AND HIS FORERUN-NER JOHN. AUGUSTINE: Let me talk to your graces[23] in the house of God about what this psalm here has reminded us of; who it is who says, "I have prepared a lamp for my Christ; his enemies I will clothe with confusion, but on him my sanctification shall flower"; and what that lamp may be, which he prepared for his Christ; and who the enemies of his Christ may be, whom he has clothed with confusion by means of that lamp; and what the sanctification is of the one who prepared a lamp for his Christ, which will flower on his Christ. In all these words, after all, the only thing that seems plain and open is what he says here, "my Christ"; none other, I mean, is to be understood, but Christ our Lord and Savior. SERMON 308A.1.[24]

THE ENEMIES OF GOD ARE CONFUSED. AUGUSTINE: And, because they[25] had shut themselves up against him, by asserting that they did not know what they knew, the Lord did not open up to them because they did not knock. For it has been said, "Knock, and it will be opened to you."[26] But they not only had not knocked that it might be opened, but by their denial they barricaded the door itself against themselves. And the Lord said to them, "Neither do I tell you by what authority I do these things."[27] And they were confounded through John, and in them was fulfilled the prophecy, "I have prepared a lamp for my Christ; his enemies I will clothe with confusion." TRACTATES ON THE GOSPEL OF JOHN 2.9.2.[28]

UNITY AND SANCTIFICATION. AUGUSTINE: So a lamp was prepared for Christ our Lord in the person of John the Baptist. His enemies, trying to trap him with their questions, withdrew in confusion when this lamp was brought out. Thus was fulfilled [the prophecy] "I will clothe his enemies with confusion." Let us, though, brothers and sisters, acknowledge the Lord by means of John the Baptist his forerunner. Indeed by the Lord's own witness, of which he said, "I have a greater witness than John,"[29] let us believe in Christ and in this way be formed into the body of him the head, so that head and body may be the one Christ. And so in all of us, having been made one, shall be fulfilled, "but on him my sanctification shall flower." SERMON 308A.8.[30]

---

[23]A common form of address for the people to whom the sermon is preached. [24]*WSA* 3 9:55. [25]The people who did not accept Jesus. [26]Mt 7:7. [27]Mt 21:27; Mk 11:29; Lk 20:8. [28]FC 78:68. [29]Jn 5:36. [30]*WSA* 3 9:61**.

133:1-3 PRAISE OF THE UNITY AMONG GOD'S PEOPLE

A Song of Ascents.

[1]*Behold, how good and pleasant it is*
    when brothers dwell in unity!
[2]*It is like the precious oil upon the head,*
    running down upon the beard,
upon the beard of Aaron,
    running down on the collar of his robes!
[3]*It is like the dew of Hermon,*
    which falls on the mountains of Zion!
For there the LORD *has commanded the*
    blessing,
    life for evermore.

OVERVIEW: Since God unites his people, they must be willing to assist one another in matters of faith and deeds of love (ZEPHYRINUS). The psalmist, in advocating that believers live together in mutual charity, anticipated the Christian community taught by the apostles (HORSIESI). We must pray for unity of faith and for those who cause divisions so that they may also receive the salvation of God (AUGUSTINE). Christ came for all people and to unite everyone in faith, as the psalmist foretold (PETER CHRYSOLOGUS). The greatest good in life is the peace that results from people being united in the triune God (VALERIAN). Spiritual knowledge can be attained only by those who have been cleansed of the filth of sin (CASSIAN).

133:1 It Is Good and Pleasant to Dwell in Unity

UNITY AMONG BELIEVERS. ZEPHYRINUS: Assist, therefore, one another in good faith, and by deed and with a hearty will; nor let any one remove his hand from the help of a brother, since "by this," says the Lord, "shall all people know that you are my disciples, if you have love one toward another." Wherefore, too, he speaks by the prophet, saying, "Behold how good and how pleasant it is for brethren to dwell together in unity!" In a spiritual dwelling, I interpret it, and in a concord that is in God, and in the unity of the faith that distinguishes this pleasant dwelling according to truth, which indeed was illustrated more beautifully in Aaron and the priests clothed with honor, as ointment on the head, nurturing the highest understanding and leading even to the end of wisdom. For in this dwelling the Lord has promised blessing and eternal life. Apprehending, therefore, the importance of this utterance of the prophet, we have spoken this present brotherly word for love's sake and by no means seeking, or meaning to seek, our own things. EPISTLES OF ZEPHYRINUS 2.1.[1]

A COMMUNITY OF MUTUAL CHARITY. HORSIESI: The apostle taught us that our community,

the communion by which we are joined to one another, springs from God, when he said, "Do not forget good works and communion, for God takes pleasure in such sacrifices."[2] We read the same thing in the Acts of the Apostles: "For the multitude of believers had one heart and soul, and no one called anything his own. They held everything in common. And the apostles gave witness to the resurrection of the Lord Jesus with great power."[3] The psalmist is in agreement with these words when he says, "Behold, how good and how delightful it is for brothers to live together." And let us who live together in the *Koinonia* and who are united to one another in mutual charity, so apply ourselves that, just as we deserved fellowship with the holy fathers in this life, we may also be their companions in the life to come. We know that the cross of our life is also the foundation of our doctrine and that "we must share Christ's sufferings,"[4] and we must realize that without trials and difficulties no one attains victory. "Happy the one who endures trial,[5] for when he has proved himself, he shall receive the crown of life."[6] THE TESTAMENT OF HORSIESI 50.[7]

PRAY FOR UNITY IN THE CHURCH. AUGUSTINE: Perform your duties in the church faithfully and joyfully, as they fall to your lot according to your rank, and fulfill your ministry[8] with uprightness, because of that God under whom we are fellow servants and to whom we understand that we shall render an account of our actions. Therefore, his mercy ought to abound in us, because "judgment without mercy to him that has not done mercy."[9] For this reason pray with us for those who still cause us sadness,[10] that the sickness of their carnal mind, intensified and concentrated by long custom, may be healed.[11] For who does not understand "how good and how pleasant it is

---

[1]ANF 8:61*. [2]Heb 13:16. [3]Acts 4:32-33. [4]Rom 8:17. [5]See Acts 14:22. [6]Jas 1:12. [7]CS 47:208-9. [8]2 Tim 4:5. [9]Jas 2:13. [10]The reference here is to the Donatists, who were still creating difficulties for the church. [11]This is another lacuna in the text here. The emended verse has been followed.

for brethren to dwell together in unity" if that pleasure touches a palate from which the mind has spit out all the bitterness of division and that loves the sweetness of charity? The God to whom we pray for them is powerful and merciful enough to use any sort of occasion to draw them even now to salvation. May the Lord preserve you in peace. LETTER 142.[12]

IMPORTANCE LIES IN ECCLESIAL UNITY.

PETER CHRYSOLOGUS: The law was given not for one, but for all. So, too, Christ came not for one or to one but to all and for all. He desired to bring all things together into a unity that alone is good and pleasant. The prophet, aware of the future, assures us, "Behold, how good and pleasant it is for brethren to dwell together in unity." For not singularity but unity is acceptable to God. The Holy Spirit descended on the apostles with all his welling fountain when they were assembled together.[13] This occurred after the apostles had been instructed by the Lord's own commandment to wait in a group for the Spirit's coming. SERMON 132.[14]

THE BLESSING OF SHARING A COMMON FAITH.

VALERIAN OF CIMIEZ: The prophet said in praise of fraternal charity: "Behold, how good and how pleasant it is for brethren to dwell together in unity." What good is there in the life of people except peace, in which upright pursuits make progress and religious activities are fostered? What is more joyful than all nations serving the one God in peace and the prayers of all people converging to the praise of the one Lord?

To dwell together in unity is this: to believe in God and faithfully to remain in the one Son of God. This is the one profitable and joyful union for mortals: our not dividing, as the heretics do, the Father from the Son, or the Son from the Father or the Holy Spirit from both, but, rather, our believing that these three names are distributed among the persons and that the persons rejoice in the participation of the one godhead.

Thus it comes to pass that, when there is agreement to unity, there will be no shattering of charity in the church. HOMILY 12.6.[15]

133:2 Like Precious Ointment on the Head

CORRUPTION OF PURITY VERSUS PURIFICATION OF CORRUPTION.

JOHN CASSIAN: But it is impossible, as we have already said, for someone who is inexperienced to know or teach this. For if someone is really incapable of receiving something, how will he be fit to pass it on? Yet even if he presumes to teach something about these matters, his words will only get as far as his hearers' ears, and they will be ineffective and useless. Produced out of inactivity and barren vanity, they will be unable to penetrate their hearts because they come not from the treasury of a good conscience but from vain and arrogant boastfulness. For it is impossible for the impure soul, with whatever effort it may have toiled in reading, to acquire spiritual knowledge. No one pours a choice ointment or the finest honey or any kind of precious liquid into a foul-smelling and filthy vessel. A pot that has once been filled with horrid, foul-smelling odors spoils the most aromatic myrrh more easily than it received any sweetness or pleasantness from it, for clean things are more quickly filthied than filthy things are made clean. Likewise, therefore, unless the vessel of our heart has first been cleansed of every foul-smelling vice, it will not deserve to receive the oil of blessing that is spoken about by the prophet: "Like oil on the head, which ran down to Aaron's beard, which ran down to the edge of his garment." Nor will it preserve unspoiled that spiritual knowledge and the words of Scripture that are "sweeter than honey and the honeycomb."[16] "For what do righteousness and wickedness have in common? Or what fellowship is there between light and darkness? Or what agreement is there between Christ and Beliel?"[17] CONFERENCES 14.14.1-3.[18]

---

[12]FC 20:149. [13]Acts 2:1-4. [14]FC 17:218-19*. [15]FC 17:381*. [16]Ps 19:10 (18:11 LXX). [17]2 Cor 6:14-15. [18]ACW 57:519.

134:1-3 A LITURGY OF PRAISE

A Song of Ascents.

[1]*Come, bless the LORD,*
all you servants of the LORD,
who stand by night in the house of
the LORD!

[2]*Lift up your hands to the holy place,*
and bless the LORD!

[3]*May the LORD bless you from Zion,*
he who made heaven and earth!

OVERVIEW: We stand for worship because it is a position of alertness and guardedness against our spiritual enemies (AMBROSE). Christ accepts only alms given by faithful Christians, and they must give all credit for their charity to God, who enriched them (CASSIODORUS).

134:1-2 Lift Up Your Hands and Bless the Lord

WHY WE STAND IN GOD'S HOUSE. AMBROSE: People sit when they disparage, but they stand when they bless the Lord, to whom it is said, "Behold, now bless you the Lord, all you servants of the Lord, who stand in the house of the Lord." One who sits (to speak of the bodily habit) is, as it were, unnerved, when the body is idle and when he relaxes the tension of his mind. But a cautious watchman, an active searcher, a wide-awake guard before the camp, stands. The soldier on duty, who wishes to anticipate the enemy's designs, stands in the battle line before he is expected. LETTER 59.[1]

SACRED PRAISES AND DEVOTED WORKS: CASSIODORUS: Notice the significance of "lift up"; it means "give alms more abundantly," for the Lord demands of us not only words of devotion but also deeds. He added, "In the holy house," so that the hand that plants the alms should belong to the Christian. If heretics or pagans do this, their hands are not lifted up in the holy house; Christ accepts only the alms that the faithful Christian offers to his name. But he says that in performing this action the Lord must be blessed, so that no one may claim any credit for himself, since it is the Lord who bestows both a merciful spirit and more generous wealth. In this way he teaches the love of the Lord is to be fulfilled both by sacred praises and by devoted works. When these have been performed, observe how worthy a recompense follows. EXPOSITIONS OF THE PSALMS 133.1-2.[2]

---

[1]FC 26:336-37*. [2]ACW 53:339-40.

135:1-21 A CALL TO PRAISE GOD

¹Praise the LSORD!
Praise the name of the LORD,
    give praise, O servants of the LORD,
²you that stand in the house of the LORD,
    in the courts of the house of our God!
³Praise the LORD, for the LORD is good;
    sing to his name, for he is gracious!
⁴For the LORD has chosen Jacob for himself,
    Israel as his own possession.

⁵For I know that the LORD is great,
    and that our Lord is above all gods.
⁶Whatever the LORD pleases he does,
    in heaven and on earth,
    in the seas and all deeps.
⁷He it is who makes the clouds rise at the end
        of the earth,
    who makes lightnings for the rain
    and brings forth the wind from his
        storehouses.

⁸He it was who smote the first-born of Egypt,
    both of man and of beast;
⁹who in thy midst, O Egypt,
    sent signs and wonders
    against Pharaoh and all his servants;
¹⁰who smote many nations
    and slew mighty kings,

¹¹Sihon, king of the Amorites,
    and Og, king of Bashan,
    and all the kingdoms of Canaan,
¹²and gave their land as a heritage,
    a heritage to his people Israel.

¹³Thy name, O LORD, endures for ever,
    thy renown, O LORD, throughout all ages.
¹⁴For the LORD will vindicate his people,
    and have compassion on his servants.

¹⁵The idols of the nations are silver and gold,
    the work of men's hands.
¹⁶They have mouths, but they speak not,
    they have eyes, but they see not,
¹⁷they have ears, but they hear not,
    nor is there any breath in their mouths.
¹⁸Like them be those who make them!—

    yea, every one who trusts in them!
¹⁹O house of Israel, bless the LORD!
    O house of Aaron, bless the LORD!
²⁰O house of Levi, bless the LORD!
    You that fear the LORD, bless the LORD!
²¹Blessed be the LORD from Zion,
    he who dwells in Jerusalem!
Praise the LORD!

OVERVIEW: The command to praise God applies only to individuals who are his servants, who stand firm in the faith and who enter the open court of God's house (CASSIODORUS). In this life we become weary and distracted in our worship and praise of God, but in heaven our praise will be continuous.

While it might seem contradictory to the omnipotence of God to claim that there are things he cannot do, such as die, change or be deceived, there are things he cannot do because he does not will to do them. Since God does what he wills, it is impossible for people to resist doing what God wills (AUGUSTINE). God not only created the world because he willed to do so, but it is also his will to provide for it (JOHN OF DAMASCUS). It is important to remember that all aspects of creation are the works of God (PRUDENTIUS).

The first commandment forbidding idolatry was first spoken by Moses and then reiterated by all the prophets thereafter (TERTULLIAN). While songbirds are excellent paradigms for people's praise of God, we should not be like the owl and see the darkness of the world but be blind to the light of our Savior and divine matters (MAXIMUS).

135:1-2 Praise the Lord, You His Servants

PRAISE THE CREATOR CONTINUOUSLY. CAS-SIODORUS: Following on the previous psalms, as has been said, in which the prophet through God's pity has mounted to the peak of all the virtues, he addresses those who stand in the Lord's house, urging that after the bestowal of such great benefits they should praise unceasingly the Creator of heaven and earth. Observe too in these two verses [1-2] how these instructions mount to a climax by the distinctions that are made. First he said, "Praise the name of the Lord." So that you would not think that this command was imposed on each and every one, he added, "You servants, praise the Lord," in other words, "You who are his servants, you who are committed to him with steadfast will and believe that you have a Lord whom you do not despise through any superstition." Third, he says, "You who stand in the house of the Lord," that is, "You who stand fast in your holy belief in him with constant and unshakeable will"; doubtless this is said to contrast with those who suffered sudden eclipse and fell from the distinction bestowed on them. Next comes, "In the courts of the house of our God." The court is the front entrance to a house of grand dimensions, in which dwellers, as we know, used to fashion a fireplace for themselves to drive out the cold; tradition relates that such places were called atria or courts because they were black (atra) from the most dense masses of smoke. Because there is no expression that does not apparently contain some arcane meaning, he says that

they too must praise the Lord who are seen to have entered the first chamber of the Lord's house. EXPOSITIONS OF THE PSALMS 134.1-2.[1]

WE WILL PRAISE GOD IN HEAVEN. AUGUS-TINE: But you say to me, "What am I going to do? If there will be no use for my members there, what am I going to do?" Does existing, seeing, loving, praising seem idleness to you? Behold! These holy days that are celebrated after the resurrection of the Lord signify the life that is to come after our resurrection. For just as the forty days before Easter symbolized the life full of suffering in this mortal period of distress, so these joyful days point to the future life, where we are destined to reign with the Lord. The life that is signified by the forty days before Easter is our burden now; the life that is symbolized by the fifty days after Easter is not possessed now but is an object of hope and is loved while it is hoped for. By that very love we praise God, who promised this eternal life to us, and our praises are Alleluias. For what does "Alleluia" mean? It is a Hebrew word signifying "praise God," allelu meaning "praise" and Ia meaning "God." Therefore, by our "Alleluia" we cry out, "Praise God," and we arouse one another to praise God. We sing praises to God, we chant our "Alleluias" with hearts attuned to harmony far better than with the chords of the lyre. When we have sung our praises, impelled by our weakness we withdraw to refresh our bodies. Why do we do this, except because we are faint? Furthermore, the weakness of the flesh is so great and the annoyance of this life so oppressive that everything, no matter how great it be, eventually leads to aversion. When these days were drawing to a close, how we longed for those of the coming year, and with how much eagerness we approached them after a lapse of time! But, if we were given the command "Sing Alleluias without ceasing," we would excuse ourselves. Why? Because in our weariness we would not be able to do so, because even in the

---

[1]ACW 53:342-43.

face of such a good we would be overcome by our distaste. There [in the risen life] no weakness, no aversion will exist. Stand and give praise, you "who stand in the house of the Lord, in the courts of the house of our God." Why do you question what you are going to do there? The psalmist says, "Blessed are they who dwell in your house, O Lord; they shall praise you forever and ever."[2] SERMON 243.9.[3]

135:6 God Does Whatever He Pleases

GOD IS AND DOES WHAT HE WILLS TO BE AND DO. AUGUSTINE: But as I said that the only thing the Almighty cannot do is what he does not will, in case anybody should consider it was very rash of me to say that the Almighty cannot do something, the blessed apostle said it too: "If we do not believe, he remains faithful, he cannot deny himself." But it is because he does not wish to that he cannot do it, because he cannot even have the will to. Justice, after all, cannot have the will to do what is unjust, or wisdom will what is foolish or truth will what is false.

Thus we are advised that almighty God not only, as the apostle says, "cannot deny himself," but cannot do many things as well. Here I am saying it, and it is by his truth I dare to say what I dare not deny: almighty God cannot die, cannot change, cannot be deceived or mistaken, cannot be miserable, cannot be defeated. Perish the thought that the Almighty should be able to do these and similar things. And so it is that truth not only shows he is almighty because he cannot do these things but also requires anyone who can do them not to be almighty. God, you see, is willingly whatever he is; so he is willingly eternal, unchangeable, truthful, blessed and undefeatable. So if he can be what he does not wish, he is not almighty; but he is almighty, which is why he is capable of whatever he wishes. And therefore what he does not will he cannot be, the reason he is called almighty is that he is capable of whatever he wishes. As the psalm says about him, "In heaven and on earth he has done whatever he has willed." SERMON 214.4.[4]

GOD'S WILL IS IRRESISTIBLE. AUGUSTINE: Accordingly, there is no doubt that human wills cannot resist the will of God, "who has done whatsoever he pleased in heaven and on earth" and who has even "done the things that are to come."[5] Nor can the human will prevent him from doing what he wills, seeing that even with the wills of people he does what he wills, when he wills to do it. Take, for instance, the case of Saul. When God willed to give the kingdom to Saul, was it in the power of the Israelites to subject themselves to him or not to subject themselves? In a sense, yes; but not in such a way that they were able to resist God. As a matter of fact, God carried the matter through by means of the wills of people themselves, having, as he undoubtedly does, the almighty power to bend human hearts whithersoever he pleases. So it is written, "And Samuel sent away all the people, everyone to his own house. Saul also departed to his own house in Gabaa; and there went with him a part of the army, whose hearts God had touched. But the children of Belial said, Shall this fellow be able to save us? And they despised him and brought him no presents."[6] Surely, no one will say that any one of those whose hearts God had touched, that they should go with Saul, failed to go with him, or that any of the children of Belial, whose hearts God had not so touched, did go with him. ADMONITION AND GRACE 14.45.[7]

GOD IS CREATOR AND PROVIDER. JOHN OF DAMASCUS: *Providence*, then, is the solicitude that God has for existing things. And again, providence is that will of God by which all existing things receive suitable guidance through to their end. But, if providence is God's will, then, according to right reason, everything that has come about through providence has quite necessarily come about in the best manner and that most befitting God, so that it could not have happened in a better way. Now, the Maker of existing things must be the same as their Pro-

---

[2]Ps 84:4 (83:5 LXX, Vg.). [3]FC 38:278-79*. [4]*WSA* 3 6:152-53**. [5]Is 45:11 (LXX). [6]1 Sam 10:25-27. [7]FC 2:299*.

vider, for it is neither fitting nor logical that one should be their creator and another their provider, because in such a case they would both be definitely wanting—the one in the matter of creating and the other in that of providing. Hence, God is both Creator and Provider, and his power of creating, sustaining and providing is his good will. For "whatsoever the Lord pleased he has done, in heaven and in earth," and none resisted his will. He willed all things to be made, and they were made; he wills the world to endure, and it does endure; and all things whatsoever he wills are done. ORTHODOX FAITH 2.29.[8]

135:7 The True God Created the World

ASPECTS OF GOD'S CREATION. PRUDENTIUS:
The sky above, the earth and ocean's mightydepths,
The orbs presiding over day and over night,
The winds and tempests, lightnings, showers of
    rain and clouds,
The polar stars, the star of evening, heat and snow,
The fountains, hoarfrosts, precious veins of ore
    and streams,

One in their might one both the Father and the
    Son,
And that one splendor generated by one light
With all the Godhead's plenitude of brightness
    shone.
In God one undivided being operates,
And by one power was created all that is,

The rugged cliffs and level plains and mountain
    dells,
Wild beasts, the fowl of air and reptiles, all that
    swim,
The beasts of burden, cattle, oxen, mammoth
    brutes,
The flowers and shrubs, the vines, the herbs and
    woodland groves,
All plants that shed their fragrance, plants that
    food supply.
BOOK OF THE MARTYRS' CROWNS 10.325-35.[9]

135:15-16 Idols of Silver and Gold

THE FALSENESS OF IDOLS. TERTULLIAN: "I am the Lord your God. You shall not make for yourselves idols fashioned by the hand, neither set up a graven image. Nor shall you set up a remarkable stone in your land [to worship it]: I am the Lord your God."[10] These words indeed were first spoken by the Lord by the lips of Moses, being applicable certainly to whomsoever the Lord God of Israel may lead forth in like manner from the Egypt of a most superstitious world and from the place of human slavery. But from the mouth of every prophet in succession sounds forth also utterances of the same God, augmenting the same law of his by a renewal of the same commands, and in the first place announcing no other duty in so special a manner as being on guard against all making and worshiping of idols; as when by the mouth of David he says, "The gods of the nations are silver and gold: they have eyes, and see not; they have ears, and hear not; they have a nose, and smell not; a mouth, and they speak not; hands, and they handle not; feet and they walk not. Like to them shall be they who make them and trust in them." SCORPIACE 2.[11]

IMITATE THE SINGING OF BIRDS. MAXIMUS OF TURIN: What human being, then, would not blush to end the day without praying the Psalms, when the birds themselves burst out with the sweetness of the Psalter in order to give pleasure, and who would not, with the loveliness of verses, sound forth the glory of him whose praise the birds pronounce in delightful song? Imitate, then, the smallest birds, brother, by giving thanks to the Creator morning and evening. And if you are more devout, imitate the nightingale which, since the day alone is not sufficient for praise, runs through the night hours with wakeful song. And you, then, binding the day together with your praises, add the course of the night to your work and lighten the sleepless activity of the toil that

---

[8]FC 37:260*. [9]FC 43:205. [10]Lev 25:55-26:1. [11]ANF 3:635-36*.

you have taken up with a series of psalms. And inasmuch as I have mentioned these birds that keep vigil through the night, I do not want you to imitate the night owl: although it stays awake during the night it is nonetheless lazy and blind by day, and with its huge eyes it loves the gloom of darkness but shudders at the brightness of the sun. Marvelous to say, it is given sight in darkness and blinded by light. This creature is an image of the heretics and pagans. They embrace the darkness of the devil and shudder at the light of the Savior, and with the huge eyes of disputation

they look at vain things but do not observe what is everlasting. Of these the Lord says, "They have eyes and do not see; they walk in darkness."[12] For they are acute as far as superstitions are concerned but dull with respect to divine matters. While thinking that they are flying about with subtle words, they are confused, like the night owl, by the brightness of the true light. SERMON 73.5.[13]

---

[12]See also Ps 82:5 (81:5 LXX, Vg.). [13]ACW 50:180*.

136:1-26 PRAISE FOR OUR CREATOR AND REDEEMER

[1]O give thanks to the LORD, for he is good,
  for his steadfast love endures for ever.
[2]O give thanks to the God of gods,
  for his steadfast love endures for ever.
[3]O give thanks to the Lord of lords,
  for his steadfast love endures for ever;

[4]to him who alone does great wonders,
  for his steadfast love endures for ever;
[5]to him who by understanding made the
    heavens,
  for his steadfast love endures for ever;
[6]to him who spread out the earth upon the
    waters,
  for his steadfast love endures for ever;
[7]to him who made the great lights,
  for his steadfast love endures for ever;
[8]the sun to rule over the day,
  for his steadfast love endures for ever;
[9]the moon and stars to rule over the night,

  for his steadfast love endures for ever;

[10]to him who smote the first-born of Egypt,
  for his steadfast love endures for ever;
[11]and brought Israel out from among them,
  for his steadfast love endures for ever;
[12]with a strong hand and an outstretched arm,
  for his steadfast love endures for ever;
[13]to him who divided the Red Sea in sunder,
  for his steadfast love endures for ever;
[14]and made Israel pass through the midst of it,
  for his steadfast love endures for ever;
[15]but overthrew Pharaoh and his host in the
    Red Sea,
  for his steadfast love endures for ever;
[16]to him who led his people through the
    wilderness,
  for his steadfast love endures for ever;
[17]to him who smote great kings,
  for his steadfast love endures for ever;

[18]and slew famous kings,
for his steadfast love endures for ever;
[19]Sihon, king of the Amorites,
for his steadfast love endures for ever;
[20]and Og, king of Bashan,
for his steadfast love endures for ever;
[21]and gave their land as a heritage,
for his steadfast love endures for ever;
[22]a heritage to Israel his servant,
for his steadfast love endures for ever.

[23]It is he who remembered us in our low estate,
for his steadfast love endures for ever;
[24]and rescued us from our foes,
for his steadfast love endures for ever;
[25]he who gives food to all flesh,
for his steadfast love endures for ever.

[26]O give thanks to the God of heaven,
for his steadfast love endures for ever.

OVERVIEW: To refer to the true God as "God of gods" means that he is superior to the demons, which the pagans consider gods (AUGUSTINE). God is described anthropomorphically in Scripture so that people will be able to understand him, at least to some degree (NOVATIAN).

136:2 Give Thanks to God for His Steadfast Love

THE TRUE GOD IS ABOVE ALL GODS AND DEMONS. AUGUSTINE: That this is the opinion of the Platonists,[1] or at least of the better Platonists, can be proved from their writings. As for the actual title, the fact that they give the name "gods" to creatures who are immortal and blessed in the above sense, there is here no dispute between us, simply because one can find in our sacred Scriptures such quotations as "The Lord, the lord of gods, has spoken,"[2] and, in another place, "Give thanks to the God of gods,"[3] and "a great king above all gods."[4] The passage where it says, "He is terrible above all gods,"[5] is explained by what immediately follows, "Since all the gods of the nations are demons; but the Lord made the heavens."[6] The psalmist says "above all gods"; but he adds "of the nations," meaning those whom the nations regard as gods, who are really "demons": "terrible" refers to the terror that made the demons say to the Lord, "Have you come to destroy us?"[7] But "god of gods" cannot be understood as meaning "God of demons." It is unthink-

able that "a great king above all gods" should mean "a great king above all demons." CITY OF GOD 9.23.[8]

136:12 A Strong Hand and an Outstretched Arm

GOD'S MIGHTY HAND AND UPLIFTED ARM. NOVATIAN: Although heavenly Scripture frequently changes the divine countenance to human form when it says "the eyes of the Lord are on the just";[9] or "the Lord God smelled the scent of a good fragrance"[10] or "tables written with the finger of God"[11] are given to Moses; or the children of Israel are delivered from the land of Egypt "with a mighty hand and uplifted arm." Again Scripture asserts, "The mouth of the Lord has spoken these things";[12] or when the earth is considered "the footstool of God";[13] or when it says, "Incline your ear, and hear."[14] We who say "that the law is spiritual" do not confine the measure or form of the divine Majesty within these outlines of our own bodily frame. On the contrary, we extend it infinitely over the field, if I may use the expression, of its own illimitable greatness. For it is written, "If I ascend into

---

[1]The Platonists called good angels "gods" rather than "demons" and included them among the beings created by the supreme God (see Plato *Timaeus* 50). [2]Ps 50:1 (49:1 LXX, Vg.). [3]Ps 136:2 (135:5 LXX, Vg.). [4]Ps 95:3 (94:3 LXX, Vg.). [5]Ps 96:4 (95:4 LXX, Vg.). [6]Ps 96:5 (95:5 LXX, Vg.). [7]Mk 1:24. [8]CG 368-69. [9]Ps 34:15 (33:16 LXX). [10]Gen 8:21. [11]Ex 31:18. [12]Is 1:20. [13]Is 66:1. [14]2 Kings 19:16.

heaven, you are there; if I descend into hell, you are present; and if I take my wings and depart across the sea, there shall your hand take hold of me and your right hand hold me fast."[15] We know the meaning of holy Scripture from the unfolding of the divine dispensation. The prophet, at that time, was still speaking about God in parables according to the faith of the times, not as God really was but as the people were able to comprehend him. The use of such language to describe God must be attributed to the people, not to God. Thus the people were permitted to erect the tabernacle, although God cannot be contained within a tabernacle. The temple was constructed, although God cannot possibly be enclosed within the narrow limits of a temple. God is not finite, but the people's faculty of perceiving is finite. God is not restricted, but rather the understanding of people's minds is limited. Accordingly, our Lord said in the Gospel, "The hour shall come when neither on this mountain nor in Jerusalem will you worship the Father," and he gave the reason: "God is spirit, and therefore they who worship him must worship in spirit and in truth."[16] Thus it is the divine powers that are represented there by means of bodily members, and neither any external appearance nor bodily features of God are set before us. ON THE TRINITY 6.1-5.[17]

---

[15]Ps 139:8-10 (138:8-10 LXX). [16]Jn 4:21, 24. [17]FC 67:34-36*.

137:1-9 A PLAINTIVE SONG OF EXILES

[1]*By the waters[o] of Babylon,*
there we sat down and wept,
when we remembered Zion.
[2]*On the willows[p] there*
we hung up our lyres.
[3]*For there our captors*
required of us songs,
and our tormentors, mirth, saying,
"Sing us one of the songs of Zion!"

[4]*How shall we sing the LORD's song*
in a foreign land?
[5]*If I forget you, O Jerusalem,*
let my right hand wither!

[6]*Let my tongue cleave to the roof of my mouth,*
if I do not remember you,
if I do not set Jerusalem
above my highest joy!

[7]*Remember, O LORD, against the Edomites*
the day of Jerusalem,
how they said, "Raze it, raze it!
Down to its foundations!"
[8]*O daughter of Babylon, you devastator![q]*
Happy shall he be who requites you
with what you have done to us!
[9]*Happy shall he be who takes your little ones*
and dashes them against the rock!

o Heb *streams*   p Or *poplars*   q Or *you who are devastated*

OVERVIEW: By way of allegory, Babylon refers to the disturbances of life and the harps are people's bodies that must be restrained and disciplined so that they overcome or resist the temptations of the world (METHODIUS).

Christians should not air their internal differences and disputes publicly but deal with them internally (GREGORY OF NAZIANZUS).

Fleshly lusts must be removed from one's life by allowing the sun of God's righteousness to shine into one's soul (ORIGEN). Blessed is the person who rids himself of all sinful thoughts, adulterous passions and everything that is contrary to Christ; only then will he be saved (AMBROSE).

137:1-2 The Waters of Babylon

SURROUNDED BY RIVERS OF EVIL. METHOD-IUS: To continue with our subject,[1] let us take in our hands and examine this psalm, which the pure and stainless souls sing to God, saying, "By the rivers of Babylon, there we sat down; we wept, when we remembered Zion. We hanged our harps on the willows in the midst thereof," clearly giving the name of harps to their bodies, which they hung on the branches of chastity, fastening them to the wood that they might not be snatched away and dragged along again by the stream of incontinence. For Babylon, which is interpreted "disturbance" or "confusion," signifies this life around which the water flows, while we sit in the midst of the water that flows round us, as long as we are in the world, the rivers of evil always beating on us. Wherefore, also, we are always fearful, and we groan and cry with weeping to God, that our harps may not be snatched off by the waves of pleasure and slip down from the tree of chastity. SYMPOSIUM OR THE BAN-QUET OF THE TEN VIRGINS 4.3.[2]

137:4 Sing Praise to God in Exile

THE RESTRAINTS OF REASON AND DISCRE-TION. GREGORY OF NAZIANZUS: Certainly not, friends and brethren—I still call you "brethren," though your attitude is not brotherly—do not let us accept such a view. We must not be like fiery, unruly horses, throwing reason our rider and spitting out the bit of discretion that so usefully restrains us, and running wide of the turning post. Let us conduct our debates within our fron-

tiers and not be carried away to Egypt or dragged off to Assyria. Let us not "sing the song of the Lord in a foreign land," by which I mean before any and every audience, heathen or Christian, friend or foe, sympathetic or hostile: these keep all too close a watch on us, and they would wish that the spark of our dissensions might become a conflagration; they kindle it, they fan it, by means of its own draught they raise it to the skies, and without our knowing what they are up to, they make it higher than the flames of Babylon that blazed all around. Having no strength in their own teaching, they hunt for it in our weakness, and for this reason like flies settling on wounds, they settle on our misfortune—or should I say our mistakes? Let us be blind to our doings no longer, and let us not neglect the proprieties in these matters. If we cannot resolve our disputes outright, let us at least make this mutual concession, to utter spiritual truths with the restraint due to them, to discuss holy things in a holy manner and not be broadcast to profane hearing what is not to be divulged. AGAINST THE EUNOMIANS, THEOLOGICAL ORATION 1[27].5.[3]

137:8-9 Cleanse Your Soul of All Bad Thoughts

DESTROY ALL YOUR VICES. ORIGEN: And in this way also the just give up to destruction all their enemies, which are their vices, so that they do not spare even the children, that is, the early beginnings and promptings of evil. In this sense also we understand the language of Psalm 137: "O daughter of Babylon, who is to be destroyed; happy shall he be that rewards you as you have served us; happy shall he be that takes and dashes your little ones against the stones." For "the little ones" of Babylon (which signifies confusion) are those troublesome sinful thoughts that arise in the soul, and one who subdues them by striking, as it were, their heads against the firm and solid strength of reason and truth, is the person who

---

[1]The virtue of charity. [2]ANF 6:323-24**. [3]FGFR 219-20.

"dashes the little ones against the stones"; and he is therefore truly blessed. God may therefore have commanded people to destroy all their vices utterly, even at their birth, without having enjoined anything contrary to the teaching of Christ. And he may himself have destroyed before the eyes of those who were "Jews inwardly" all the offspring of evil as his enemies. And, in like manner, those who disobey the law and word of God may well be compared with his enemies led astray by sin; and they may well be said to suffer the same fate as they deserve who have proved traitors to the truth of God. AGAINST CELSUS 7.22.[4]

RID YOURSELF OF BAD THOUGHTS. AMBROSE: And David, pitying her, says, "O wretched

daughter of Babylon." Wretched indeed, as being the daughter of Babylon, when she ceased to be the daughter of Jerusalem. And yet he calls for a healer for her and says, "Blessed is he who shall take your little ones and dash them against the rock." That is to say, shall dash all corrupt and filthy thoughts against Christ, who by his fear and his rebuke will break down all actions against reason, so as, if any one is seized by an adulterous love, to extinguish the fire, that he may by his zeal put away the love of a harlot and deny himself that he may gain Christ. CONCERNING REPENTANCE 2.11.106.[5]

---

[4]ANF 4:619-20*. [5]NPNF 2 10:358*.

138:1-8 A ROYAL SONG OF PRAISE FOR GOD'S HELP AGAINST ENEMIES

A Psalm of David.

[1]*I give thee thanks, O LORD with my whole heart;*
before the gods I sing thy praise;
[2]*I bow down toward thy holy temple*
and give thanks to thy name for thy steadfast love and thy faithfulness;
for thou hast exalted above everything thy name and thy word.[r]
[3]*On the day I called, thou didst answer me, my strength of soul thou didst increase.[s]*

[4]*All the kings of the earth shall praise thee, O LORD,*
for they have heard the words of thy mouth;

[5]*and they shall sing of the ways of the LORD, for great is the glory of the LORD.*
[6]*For though the LORD is high, he regards the lowly;*
but the haughty he knows from afar.

[7]*Though I walk in the midst of trouble, thou dost preserve my life;*
thou dost stretch out thy hand against the wrath of my enemies,
and thy right hand delivers me.
[8]*The LORD will fulfil his purpose for me; thy steadfast love, O LORD, endures for ever.*
Do not forsake the work of thy hands.

---

r Cn: Heb *thou hast exalted thy word above all thy name*   **s** Syr Compare Gk Tg: Heb *thou didst make me arrogant in my soul with strength*

OVERVIEW: A sincere confession of sins means confession of all sins, not just a particular sin or one category of sin (JEROME). God-pleasing worship includes, among other things, an awareness that we are praising God in the presence of angels (BEDE). God directs his attention to those who are humble and lowly; the proud and mighty he knows only from a distance (AUGUSTINE). We must lift up our hearts only to God; to lift them up to anyone else is pride (CAESARIUS).

138:1 Thank God with a Whole Heart

CONFESS WITH ALL YOUR HEART. JEROME: "I will confess to you, Lord, with all my heart." The nature of a wound determines the medication to be applied. Just as the body has wounds of various kinds, so also the soul has its passions and its wounds, and we must do penance in proportion to the nature of our sin. If a person makes confession of all his sins, he is acknowledging his sins to the Lord wholeheartedly. If, for example, someone has committed fornication and he confesses only that and is greedy, or quick-tempered, or a slanderer or blasphemer and is full of faults and vices, his confession is not sincere. The person who repents for all the sins and passions of his soul is the person who is able to say, I confess and give thanks to you, O Lord, with all my heart. "For you have heard the words of my mouth."[1] This verse is not found in the Hebrew text. Nonetheless, what it means is, In my confession I have poured out my whole heart, O Lord; I have confessed all my sins and faults, for I have not admitted merely one sin to you, and you have listened to me graciously. HOMILIES ON THE PSALMS 49.[2]

IN THE PRESENCE OF ANGELS. BEDE: It is no secret that angels are frequently present, invisibly, at the side of the elect, in order to defend them from the snares of the cunning enemy and uphold them by the great gift of heavenly desire. The apostle attests to this when he says, "Are they not all ministering spirits sent to serve on account of

those who receive an inheritance of salvation?"[3] Nevertheless, we should believe that the angelic spirits are especially present to us when we give ourselves in a special way to divine services, that is, when we enter a church and open our ears to sacred reading, or give our attention to psalm singing, or apply ourselves to prayer or celebrate the solemnity of the mass. Hence the apostle advises women to have a veil over their heads in church on account of the angels. And a prophet says, "I will sing psalms to you in the sight of the angels." We are not permitted to doubt that where the mysteries of the Lord's body and blood are being enacted, a gathering of the citizens from on high is present—those who were keeping such careful watch at the tomb where [Christ's] venerable body had been placed and from which he had departed by rising. Hence we must strive meticulously my brothers, when we come into the church to pay the due service of divine praise or to perform the solemnity of the mass, to be always mindful of the angelic presence and to fulfill our heavenly duty with fear and fitting veneration, following the example of the women devoted to God who were afraid when the angels appeared to them at the tomb, and who, we are told, bowed their faces to the earth. HOMILIES ON THE GOSPELS 2.10.[4]

138:6 God Watches over the Humble

THE LORD OBSERVES THE LOWLY. AUGUSTINE: Perhaps because [the psalm] said, "The Lord is sublime and observes lowly things," you say to yourself, "Then he does not observe me." What could be more unfortunate than you, if he does not observe you but ignores you? Observing indicates compassion; ignoring indicates contempt. But no doubt, because the Lord observes lowly things, you imagine you escape his notice, because you are not humble or lowly, you are high and mighty, you are proud. That is not the way to

---

[1]Ps 138:3 (137:3 LXX, Vg.). [2]FC 48:361*. [3]Heb 1:14. [4]CS 111:91-92.

be missed by the eyes of God. I mean, just see what it says there: "The Lord is sublime." Sublime indeed. How are you going to get to him? Will you look for a ladder? Look for the wood of humility,[5] and you have already gotten to him. "The Lord is sublime, he observes lowly things, but high and mighty things" (do not imagine you escape notice, you that are so proud) "but high and mighty things he knows from afar." He knows them, all right, but from afar. "Salvation is far from sinners."[6] SERMON 70A.2.[7]

GOD SEES THE PROUD FROM AFAR. AUGUSTINE: We have heard, and it is clear; we had gone outside, we have been sent within. "O would that I had found," you said, "some high and lonely mountain! For, I believe, because God is on high, he hears me from a high place." Because you are on a mountain, do you think that you are near God and that you are heard quickly, as if shouting from nearby? He dwells on high, but "he looks on the lowly." "The Lord is near." To whom? Perhaps to the high? "To those who are contrite of heart." It is a wondrous thing: he both lives on high and draws near to the lowly. "He looks on the lowly, but the high he knows from afar." He sees the proud from afar; the higher they seem to themselves, so much of the less does he approach them. TRACTATES ON THE GOSPEL OF JOHN 15.25.1.[8]

LIFT UP YOUR HEARTS TO THE LORD. CAESARIUS OF ARLES: Today we are keeping the solemn festival of the ascension. If, therefore, we celebrate the Lord's ascension in a manner that is right, holy, faithful, devout and pious, we must ascend with him and lift up our hearts. Now as we ascend, let us not be lifted up with pride or presume on our merits as if they were our own. For we ought indeed to lift up our hearts, but to the Lord alone. A heart lifted up but not to the Lord is called pride; a heart lifted up to the Lord is called a refuge. See, brethren, the great miracle. God is on high. You exalt yourself, and he flees from you; you humble yourself, and he descends to you. Why is this? Because "the Lord is exalted, yet the lowly he sees, and the proud he knows from afar." He recognizes what is lowly from close at hand in order that he may raise it up; what is high, that is, what is proud, he knows from afar in order that he may bring it down. Christ truly arose from the dead in order to give us hope, because the person who dies rises again. He gave us assurance, so that we might not despair in dying and think our whole life ended in death. We were troubled about our very soul, but by rising from the dead he also gave us confidence in the resurrection of the body. SERMON 210.2.[9]

---

[5]The cross. [6]Ps 119:155 (118:155 LXX, Vg.). [7]WSA 3 3:244. [8]FC 79:94*. [9]FC 66:94.

139:1-24 A PRAYER FOR GOD TO EXAMINE THE HEART

To the choirmaster. A Psalm of David.

[1]*O LORD, thou hast searched me and known me!*
[2]*Thou knowest when I sit down and when I rise up;*
thou discernest my thoughts from afar.
[3]*Thou searchest out my path and my lying down,*
and art acquainted with all my ways.

⁴*Even before a word is on my tongue,*
  lo, O LORD, thou knowest it altogether.
⁵*Thou dost beset me behind and before,*
  and layest thy hand upon me.
⁶*Such knowledge is too wonderful for me;*
  it is high, I cannot attain it.

⁷*Whither shall I go from thy Spirit?*
  Or whither shall I flee from thy presence?
⁸*If I ascend to heaven, thou art there!*
  If I make my bed in Sheol, thou art there!
⁹*If I take the wings of the morning*
  and dwell in the uttermost parts of the sea,
¹⁰*even there thy hand shall lead me,*
  and thy right hand shall hold me.
¹¹*If I say, "Let only darkness cover me,*
  and the light about me be night,"
¹²*even the darkness is not dark to thee,*
  the night is bright as the day;
  for darkness is as light with thee.

¹³*For thou didst form my inward parts,*
  thou didst knit me together in my mother's
  womb.
¹⁴*I praise thee, for thou art fearful and*
  wonderful.ᵗ
  Wonderful are thy works!
Thou knowest me right well;

¹⁵*my frame was not hidden from thee,*
when I was being made in secret,
  intricately wrought in the depths of the earth.
¹⁶*Thy eyes beheld my unformed substance;*
  in thy book were written, every one of them,
the days that were formed for me,
  when as yet there was none of them.
¹⁷*How precious to me are thy thoughts, O God!*
  How vast is the sum of them!
¹⁸*If I would count them, they are more than the*
  sand.
  When I awake, I am still with thee.ᵘ

¹⁹*O that thou wouldst slay the wicked, O God,*
  and that men of blood would depart from
  me,
²⁰*men who maliciously defy thee,*
  who lift themselves up against thee for evil!ᵛ
²¹*Do I not hate them that hate thee, O LORD?*
  And do I not loathe them that rise up
  against thee?
²²*I hate them with perfect hatred;*
  I count them my enemies.
²³*Search me, O God, and know my heart!*
  Try me and know my thoughts!
²⁴*And see if there be any wickedʷ way in me,*
  and lead me in the way everlasting!ˣ

t Cn Compare Gk Syr Jerome: Heb *fearful things I am wonderful* u Or *were I to come to the end I would still be with thee* v Cn: Heb uncertain w Heb *hurtful* x Or *the ancient way.* Compare Jer 6.16

OVERVIEW: We can better understand the depth of God's wisdom by observing the marvelous nature and functions of our physical constitution (BASIL). Although it is more difficult for people to know themselves than the world around them, yet there is no better resource for understanding the greatness of God than the constitution of our nature (BASIL, AUGUSTINE). Divine providence is marvelous, provides wonderful and magnificent resources to humanity and motivates us to praise our divine Benefactor. No matter what language a people speaks, they receive the proclamation of God and praise his wonderful knowledge (THEODORET). Not only is humanity unable to understand the nature of God's being, but also how he can be present everywhere simultaneously (CHRYSOSTOM).

Since God is present everywhere, it is impossible for people to flee from him (CLEMENT OF ROME). Since we cannot flee from God and his judgment on our sins, we should flee to him and confess our sins (AUGUSTINE). Every living creature is surrounded by the power and presence of God (FULGENTIUS). God is truly infinite, incomprehensible and omnipresent (HILARY). Since God is omnipresent, we cannot hide our sins from him and therefore should be ashamed to sin in his sight (PETER CHRYSOLOGUS). The omnipresence of Father and Son supports their personal equality in the godhead (BASIL). If God is present everywhere, then his wisdom and Spirit are also omnipresent. While everyone is in the presence of God, only the blessed are truly with him (AUGUSTINE).

God supports us as our creator and as the one who protects us once he has given us life (AMBROSE). If we obey human authority instead of God, the disobedience will be known by God (CYPRIAN). God promises to be with us; that is an important incentive not to lapse into sleep and spiritual sluggishness (EPHREM).

God has given people the ability to love and to hate so that they may love what is good and hate what is evil (BASIL). Why some people believe and others do not is an imponderable question, but Scripture clearly teaches that only believers in Christ will be saved (AUGUSTINE).

139:6 God's Omniscience

BODILY FUNCTIONS WITNESS THE WISDOM OF GOD. BASIL THE GREAT: And so, when you have gone over all these points[1] with suitable reflections on each, when you have, in addition, studied the process of breathing, the manner in which the heart conserves its warmth, the organs of digestion and the veins, you will discern in all of these wonders the inscrutable wisdom of the Creator; so that you will be able to say with the prophet: "Your knowledge is become wonderful" from the study of myself. "Give heed, therefore, to yourself," that you may give heed to God, to whom be glory and power forever and ever.

Amen. HOMILY ON THE WORDS "GIVE HEED TO THYSELF."[2]

THE CONSTITUTION OF THE HUMAN BODY REVEALS THE WISDOM OF GOD. BASIL THE GREAT: In truth, to know oneself seems to be the hardest of all things. Not only our eye, which observes external objects, does not use the sense of sight on itself, but even our mind, which contemplates intently another's sin, is slow in the recognition of its own defects. Therefore, even at present our speech, after eagerly investigating matters pertaining to others, is slow and hesitant in the examination of our own nature. Yet, it is not possible for one, intelligently examining himself, to learn to know God better from the heavens and earth than from our own constitution, as the prophet says, "Your knowledge is become wonderful from myself"; that is, having carefully observed myself, I have understood the superabundance of wisdom in you. HOMILIES ON THE HEXAEMERON 9.6.[3]

GOD'S KNOWLEDGE IS SUBLIME. AUGUSTINE: Do we, whose minds are so feeble, believe that we can comprehend whether God's foresight is the same as his memory and understanding, who do not behold individual things by thought but embraces all that he knows in one eternal, unchangeable and ineffable vision? In this difficulty and distress, therefore, we may indeed cry aloud to the living God, "Your knowledge is become wonderful to me; it is sublime, and I cannot reach it." For I understand from myself how wonderful and how incomprehensible your knowledge is, by which you have made me, when I consider that I cannot even comprehend myself whom you have made; and yet in my meditation a fire flames out,[4] "so that I seek your face evermore."[5] ON THE TRINITY 15.7.13.[6]

---

[1]The magnificence of the various parts of the human body. [2]FC 9:445-46*. [3]FC 46:147*. [4]See Ps 39:3 (38:4 LXX, Vg.). [5]See Ps 105:4 (104:4 LXX, Vg.). [6]FC 45:468-69**.

THE MARVEL OF DIVINE PROVIDENCE. THE-ODORET OF CYR: Since water does not support horses, donkeys, mules, the tracks of wheels and the marks of wagons and chariots, which are all unmistakable guides to travelers by land, the Maker of the universe has given to the broad seas the disposition of the stars like road tracks on land.

Praise the wonders of divine providence!
Oh! Ineffable love! Oh! unspeakable wisdom!

Who could marvel enough at the goodness of divine providence, at its power, its nobility in difficulties, its ease in managing awkward situations, its magnificence, its resourcefulness? Truly your knowledge was wonderful to me: "I was overwhelmed and could not reach to it." That is my exclamation, too. If you listen to me, you too will recite these words with me, praise the Benefactor with all your might and render grateful words of thanks for his countless blessings. DISCOURSE 1.39.[7]

GOD'S KNOWLEDGE IS WONDERFUL. THE-ODORET OF CYR: And so loud is their proclamation that the whole human race hears their voice, "There are no speeches or utterances where their voices are not heard."[8] For every race and every tongue hears the proclamations of day and night. Tongue differs from tongue, but nature is one and derives the same lesson from day and night. Thus the same author, singing the praises of the Creator in another psalm, says, "Your knowledge was wonderful to me; I was overwhelmed, and I could not reach to it." DISCOURSE 4.4.[9]

GOD'S OMNIPRESENCE IS INCOMPREHENSIBLE. CHRYSOSTOM: Therefore, let us listen to what the prophet says about this: "Your knowledge is too wonderful for me." But let us see what he says further on: "I will give you thanks, for you are fearful and wonderful." Why "fearful"? We wonder at the beauty of columns, mural art, the physical bloom of youth. Again, we wonder at the open sea and its limitless depth, but we wonder

fearfully when we stoop down and see how deep it is. It was in this way that the prophet stooped down and looked at the limitless and yawning sea of God's wisdom. And he was struck with shuddering. He was deeply frightened, he drew back, and he said in a loud voice, "I will give you thanks for you are fearfully wondrous; wondrous are your works."[10] And again, "Your knowledge is too wondrous for me; it is too lofty and I cannot attain to it."

Do you see how prudent the servant is and how grateful is his heart? What he is saying is this: "I thank you that I have a Master whom I cannot comprehend." And he is not now speaking of God's essence. He passes over the incomprehensibility of his essence as if it is something on which everybody is agreed. What he is speaking of here is God's omnipresence; and he is showing that this is the very thing that he does not understand, namely, how God is present everywhere. To prove to you that he is speaking of God's omnipresence, listen to what follows: "If I go up to heaven, you are there; if I go down to hell, you are present."[11] Do you see how God is everywhere present? The prophet did not know how this was true but he shudders, he is upset, he is at a loss when he so much as thinks about it. AGAINST THE ANOMOEANS 1.24-25.[12]

139:7-10 God's Omnipresence

WE CANNOT ESCAPE FROM GOD. CLEMENT OF ROME: Since, therefore, all things are seen and heard, let us fear him and abandon the abominable lusts that spawn evil works, in order that we may be shielded by his mercy from the coming judgments. For where can any of us escape from his mighty hand? For the Scripture says somewhere, "Where shall I go, and where shall I be hidden from your presence? If I ascend to heaven, you are there; if I depart to the ends of the earth, there is your right hand; if I take my bed in the

---

[7]ACW 49:22-23. [8]Ps 19:4 (18:4 LXX). [9]ACW 49:48. [10]Ps 139:14 (138:14 LXX). [11]Ps 139:8 (138:8 LXX). [12]FC 72:60-61*.

depths, there is your Spirit." Where, then, can one go, or where can one flee from him who embraces the universe? 1 CLEMENT 28.[13]

NO ONE CAN ESCAPE GOD'S JUDGMENT. AUGUSTINE: "For if our heart should have a bad opinion [of us]," that is, should accuse us within, because we do not do with that intention with which it ought to be done, "God is greater than our heart and knows all things." You conceal your heart from people; conceal it from God if you can. How will you conceal it from him to whom it was said by a certain sinner, "Where shall I go from your spirit, and from your face where shall I flee?" He was asking where he might flee to escape the judgment of God and did not find [an answer]. For where is God not? "If I ascend into heaven," he says, "you are there. If I descend into hell, you are present." Where will you go? Where will you flee? Do you wish to listen to advice? If you wish to flee from him, flee to him! Flee to him by confessing, not by hiding from him. For you cannot hide, but you can confess. Say to him, "You are my refuge,"[14] and let love be nurtured in you, which alone leads to life. Let your conscience bear testimony to you because it is of God. If it is of God, do not wish to boast of it before people because neither the praises of people lift you into heaven nor do their censurings put you down from there. Let him who gives the crown see; let him be witness by whom as Judge you are crowned. God is greater than our heart and knows all things. HOMILIES ON 1 JOHN 6.3.2.[15]

THE HOLY SPIRIT FILLS THE WORLD. FULGENTIUS OF RUSPE: Hold most firmly and never doubt that God the Trinity is unbounded in power, not in mass; and that every creature, spiritual and bodily, is bound by his power and his presence. For God the Father says, "I fill the heavens and the earth."[16] For it is said of the Wisdom of God, which his Son is, that "it reaches mightily from one end of the earth to the other and orders all things well."[17] Concerning the Holy Spirit we read that "the Spirit of the Lord has

filled the whole world."[18] And David the prophet says, "Where can I go from your Spirit? Or where can I flee from your presence? If I ascend to heaven, you are there; if I make my bed in Sheol, you are there." TO PETER ON THE FAITH 12.55.[19]

GOD IS BEYOND HUMAN COMPREHENSION. HILARY OF POITIERS: My mind, intent on the study of truth, took delight in these most pious teachings about God. For it did not consider any other thing worthy of God than that he is so far beyond the power of comprehension that the more the infinite spirit would endeavor to encompass him to any degree, even though it be by an arbitrary assumption, the more the infinity of a measureless eternity would surpass the entire infinity of the nature that pursues it. Although we understood this teaching in a reverent manner, it was clearly confirmed by these words of the prophet: "Whither shall I go from your spirit? Or whither shall I flee from your face? If I ascend into heaven, you are there; if I descend into hell, you are present. If I take my wings early in the morning and dwell in the uttermost parts of the sea, even there also shall your hand lead me and your right hand shall hold me." There is no place without God, nor is there any place which is not in God. He is in heaven, in hell and beyond the seas. He is within all things; he comes forth and is outside all things. While he thus possesses and is possessed, he is not included in anything nor is he not in all things. ON THE TRINITY 1.6.[20]

SIN CANNOT BE HIDDEN FROM GOD. PETER CHRYSOLOGUS: "I have sinned against heaven and before you. I am no longer worthy to be called your son."[21] The son set out abroad and fled into a far country; but he did not escape from those accusing witnesses, the eyes of the heavenly Father. David explains this more clearly by his words: "Whither shall I go from your spirit? or whither shall I flee from your face? If I ascend

---

[13]AF 61. [14]Ps 32:7 (31:7 LXX, Vg.). [15]FC 92:201-2. [16]Jer 23:24. [17]Wis 8:1. [18]Wis 1:7. [19]FC 95:94. [20]FC 25:7-8. [21]Lk 15:21.

into heaven, you are there; if I descend into hell, you are present. If I take my wings early in the morning and dwell in the uttermost parts of the sea, even there shall your hand lead me, and your right hand shall hold me." David sees that throughout the world all transgressions stand exposed to the eyes of God. Neither the sky, nor the earth, nor the seas, nor a deep cavern nor night itself can hide sins from him. The psalmist perceives how lawless and evil it is to sin in the sight of God. Therefore, he cries out, "To you only have I sinned and have done evil before you."[22] SERMON 2.[23]

EQUALITY AMONG THE PERSONS OF THE TRINITY. BASIL THE GREAT: If they[24] really conceive of a kind of subordination of the Son in relation to the Father, as though he were in a lower place, so that the Father sits above and the Son is thrust off to the next seat below, let them confess what they mean. We shall have no more to say. A plain statement of the view will at once expose its absurdity. They who refuse to allow that the Father pervades all things do not so much as maintain the logical sequence of thought in their argument. The faith of the orthodox is that God fills all things; but they who divide their up and down between the Father and the Son do not remember even the word of the prophet: "If I climb up into heaven, you are there; if I go down to hell, you are there also." Now, to omit all proof of the ignorance of those who predicate place of incorporeal things, what excuse can be found for their attack upon Scripture, shameless as their antagonism is, in the passages "Sit on my right hand"[25] and "Sat down on the right hand of the majesty of God"?[26] The expression "right hand" does not, as they contend, indicate the lower place, but equality of relation; it is not understood physically, in which case there might be something sinister about God, but Scripture puts before us the magnificence of the dignity of the Son by the use of dignified language indicating the seat of honor. It is left then for our opponents to allege that this expression signifies inferiority

of rank. Let them learn that "Christ is the power of God and wisdom of God,"[27] and that "he is the image of the invisible God"[28] and "brightness of his glory"[29] and that "him has God the Father sealed,"[30] by engraving himself on him. ON THE SPIRIT 6.15.[31]

THE HOLY SPIRIT IS EVERYWHERE. AUGUSTINE: For God was everywhere who said, "I fill heaven and earth."[32] But if this was said of the Father, where could he be without his Word and his Wisdom, "which teaches from end to end mightily, and orders all things sweetly"?[33] But neither could he be anywhere without his Spirit. If, therefore, God is everywhere, then his Spirit is also everywhere. Consequently, the Holy Spirit was also sent to that place where he already was. For he, too, who finds no place to which he could go from the face of God, says, "If I shall ascend into heaven, you are there; if I shall descend into hell, you are present," wishing it to be understood that God is present everywhere, referred to his Spirit in the preceding verse. For there he spoke as follows: "Where shall I go from your Spirit? And where shall I flee from your face?" ON THE TRINITY 2.5.7.[34]

TO BE WITH GOD IS A GREAT GOOD. AUGUSTINE: For this reason, of course, it was not enough for Jesus to say, "I will that where I am they also may be," but he added, "with me."[35] For to be with him is a great good. For even the wretched can be where he is because wherever anybody at all may be [there] he also is; but the blessed alone are with him, because they will be unable to be blessed except by his action. Or has it not been truly said to God, "If I ascend into heaven, you are there; and if I descend into hell, you are present"? Or on the other hand is Christ not God's Wisdom, which "reaches everywhere

[22]Ps 51:4 (50:6 LXX, Vg.). [23]FC 17:32*. [24]Arian heretics, who taught that the Son was subordinate to the Father and not co-eternal with him. [25]Ps 110:1 (109:1 LXX). [26]Heb 1:3, with the variation of "of God" for "on high." [27]1 Cor 1:24. [28]Col 1:15. [29]Heb 1:3. [30]Jn 6:27. [31]NPNF 2 8:9*. [32]Jer 23:24. [33]Wis 8:1. [34]FC 45:59*. [35]Jn 17:24.

by reason of its purity"?[36] TRACTATES ON THE GOSPEL OF JOHN III.2.3.[37]

139:11-12 With God Darkness Is Light

VALIANT IN WAKEFULNESS. SAHDONA: Likewise we Christians who are Christ's servants should truly stand valiantly in wakefulness like "good and faithful servants"[38] who are eager to do honor to their master. Let us gird ourselves in asceticism, inwardly strengthened by austerity, having the lamps of our hearts filled with the oil of grace[39] from the Spirit and illumined by prayer; in this way we shall valiantly do battle with the powerful incitement provided by the sweetness of sleep. In this way "the dark will be light for us," just as the prophet said, "and night will be illumined by our faces": the darkness will not make our minds dark, so let us spend the dark night awake as if it were bright daylight. BOOK OF PERFECTION 69.[40]

139:13-18 God's Works Are Wonderful

GOD IS OUR SUPPORTER. AMBROSE: Therefore the Lord supported us when he fashioned us; he supports us also when he bids us to be born. Consequently, the just person says, "You have supported me from my mother's womb." Whose mother's? "Before I formed you in the womb, I knew you."[41] Those, whom the Lord forms, he also supports; he supports them even in their coming forth: "And before you came forth from your mother's womb, I sanctified you."[42] He is our supporter, for he has supported us with his hands. He is called a supporter as the Creator of the human race. And he is our supporter, for he has supported us by his visitation, that he may protect us. In view of this, the psalmist himself says in another passage, "He that dwells in the aid of the most High shall say to the Lord, 'You are my supporter and my refuge.'"[43] The first support is that of God's working in us, the second in that of his protection of us. Indeed, listen to Moses saying, "Spreading his wings he received

them and supported them upon his shoulders."[44] He supported them like the eagle, which was accustomed to examine its progeny, so as to keep and to bring up those whom it observed to possess the qualities of a true offspring and the gift of an undamaged constitution and to reject those in whom it detected weakness of a degenerate origin even at that tender age. THE PRAYER OF JOB AND DAVID 4.5.21.[45]

WE CANNOT ESCAPE THE JUDGMENT OF GOD. CYPRIAN: Let them not persuade themselves that they should not do penance, who, although they have not contaminated their hands by impious sacrifices, yet have defiled their consciences with certificates.[46] That profession is of one who denies; the testimony is of a Christian who rejects what he had been. He said that he had done what another actually did, and, although it is written, "You cannot serve two masters,"[47] he served a secular master, he submitted to his edict, he obeyed human authority rather than God. He should have seen whether he published what he committed with less scandal or less guilt among people; however, he will not be able to escape and avoid God as his judge, for the Holy Spirit says in the Psalms, "Your eyes have seen my imperfection, and all will be written in your book," and again, "People look on the face, but God [looks] on the heart. Let the Lord himself also forewarn and instruct you with these words: "And all the churches shall know that I am he who searches the desires and hearts."[48] He perceives the concealed and the secret and considers the hidden, nor can anyone evade the eyes of God who says, "Am I a God at hand, and not a God afar off? Shall a person be hid in secret places and I not see him?"[49] He sees the hearts and breasts of each

---

[36]See Wis 7:24; the word for wisdom is feminine in Latin. [37]FC 90:302-3*. [38]Mt 25:23. [39]See Lk 12:35; Mt 25:4. [40]CS 101:230. [41]Jer 1:5. [42]Jer 1:5. [43]Ps 91:1-2 (90:1-2 LXX, Vg.). [44]Deut 32:11 (LXX). [45]FC 65:405*. [46]The reference is to the certificates or *libelli* that Christians received from Roman officials during the Decian persecution (250-251) as proof that they had renounced their Christian faith. [47]Mt 6:24. [48]See 1 Sam 16:7. [49]Jer 23:23-24.

one, and, when about to pass judgment not only on our deeds but also on our words and thoughts, he looks into the minds and the wills conceived in the very recess of a still closed heart. THE LAPSED 27.[50]

VIGILANCE OF BODY AND SOUL. EPHREM THE SYRIAN: Watch, for when the body is sleeping it is nature that holds sway over us, and our activity is directed not by our wills but by the impulse of nature. When a heavy torpor of weakness and sadness rules over the soul, it is the enemy who holds sway over it and leads it against its own desire. It is force that holds sway over nature and the enemy who holds sway over the soul. That is why our Lord spoke of vigilance of soul and of body lest the body sink into a heavy sleep and the soul into a sluggishness born of timidity; just as [Scripture] says, "Let justice awaken you,"[51] and, "When I awake I am still with you," and, "Do not lose heart."[52] This is why "we do not lose heart"[53] in the ministry confided to us. COMMENTARY ON TATIAN'S DIATESSARON 18.17.[54]

139:21-22 Hatred of Those Who Hate God

LOVE VIRTUE AND HATE VICE. BASIL THE GREAT: Yet, it is not hard for us, if we wish it, to take up a love for justice and a hatred for iniquity. God has advantageously given all power to the rational soul, as that of loving, so also that of hating, in order that, guided by reason, we may love virtue but hate vice. It is possible at times to use hatred even praiseworthily. "Have I not hated them, O Lord, that hated you and pined away because of your enemies? I have hated them with a perfect hatred."[55] HOMILIES ON THE PSALMS 17.8.[56]

ENEMIES OF GOD. PAULINUS OF NOLA: I also ask and beg of you to expound for me what [Paul] says to the Romans, for I admit I have very poor sight for this opinion of the apostle about the Jews, where he says, "As concerning the gospel,

indeed they are enemies for your sake, but as touching the election they are most dear for the sake of the ancestors."[57] How can these same ones be enemies for our sake, now that we former Gentiles have become believers, as if Gentiles could only believe if the Jews had refused to believe? Is not God the one Creator of all, "who will have all people to be saved and to come to the knowledge of the truth,"[58] and was he not able to gain both without dispossessing one for the other? Second, "most dear for the sake of the ancestors": how or why this "most dear," if they do not believe and if they continue to be enemies of God? "O God," he says, "have I not hated them that hated you and pined away because of your enemies? I have hated them with a perfect hatred."[59] Certainly, I think the Father's voice speaks to his Son by the prophet in the same psalm where he spoke on behalf of believers: "But to me your friends, O God, are made exceedingly honorable; their dominions are exceedingly strengthened." How can it be profitable for their salvation to be "most dear to God for the sake of the ancestors" when salvation is acquired only through the faith and grace of Christ? What good does it do them to be loved, when they are inevitably to be damned because of their unbelief, because they have fallen away from the faith of the prophets and of the patriarchs, their ancestors, and have become enemies of the gospel of Christ? If they are most dear to God, how shall they be lost? And if they do not believe, how can they fail to be lost? If they are loved for the sake of the ancestors, without any merit of their own, why will they not be saved for the sake of the ancestors, too? "And if, Noah, Daniel and Job shall be in the midst thereof, they shall not deliver the wicked children: they shall be delivered."[60] LETTER 121.[61]

---

[50]FC 36:80-81. [51]See 1 Cor 15:34. [52]Eph 3:13. [53]See 2 Cor 4:1. [54]ECTD 280. [55]Ps 139:21-22 (138:21-22 LXX). [56]FC 46:289. [57]Rom 11:28. [58]1 Tim 2:4. [59]Ps 139:21-22 (138:21-22 LXX, Vg.). [60]Ezek 14:14. [61]FC 18:324-26*. This letter was written by Paulinus of Nola to Augustine. Augustine's response is contained in Letter 149.

140:1-13 A PRAYER FOR DELIVERANCE

To the choirmaster. A Psalm of David.

¹*Deliver me, O* LORD, *from evil men;*
  preserve me from violent men,
²*who plan evil things in their heart,*
  and stir up wars continually.
³*They make their tongue sharp as a serpent's,*
  and under their lips is the poison of vipers.
                                      Selah
⁴*Guard me, O* LORD, *from the hands of the*
    wicked;
  preserve me from violent men,
  who have planned to trip up my feet.
⁵*Arrogant men have hidden a trap for me,*
  and with cords they have spread a net,ʸ
  by the wayside they have set snares for me.
                                      Selah

⁶*I say to the* LORD, *Thou art my God;*
  give ear to the voice of my supplications,
    O LORD!

⁷*O* LORD, *my Lord, my strong deliverer,*
  thou hast covered my head in the day of
    battle.
⁸*Grant not, O* LORD, *the desires of the wicked;*
  do not further his evil plot!   Selah

⁹*Those who surround me lift up their head,ᶻ*
  let the mischief of their lips overwhelm
    them!
¹⁰*Let burning coals fall upon them!*
  Let them be cast into pits, no more to rise!
¹¹*Let not the slanderer be established in the*
    land;
  let evil hunt down the violent man speedily!

¹²*I know that the* LORD *maintains the cause of*
    the afflicted,
  and executes justice for the needy.
¹³*Surely the righteous shall give thanks to thy*
    name;
  the upright shall dwell in thy presence.

y Or *they have spread cords as a net*   z Cn Compare Gk: Heb *those who surround me are uplifted in head*

OVERVIEW: The vast majority of evil that people suffer is caused by other human beings; evils that do not have their origin in other people are extremely few (AUGUSTINE). Scripture calls people "human" who live lives of virtue, but those who lapse into evil and irrational passions are referred to as animals of various species (CHRYSOSTOM).

Demons, desiring to corrupt saintly people, relentlessly lay snares to cause them to sin (ATHANASIUS). We are safe from the snare of Satan if we travel on the way that is Christ, but if we travel along the wayside we will encounter the snares laid by Satan to entrap us. When we pray that God will not give us up to our wickedness, we are imploring his mercy, because God allows people to pursue wickedness as a punishment for their sins, not just to manifest his goodness (AUGUSTINE).

140:1-3 Deliver Me, O Lord, from Evil People

PEOPLE ARE THE MAJOR SOURCE OF EVIL TO PEOPLE. AUGUSTINE: Where, after all, does evil come to a human being from, but from a human being? Count how many evils people suffer from outwardly. Those that are not evidently caused by other people are extremely few. Of evils coming to a human being from a human being there are plenty. Thefts come from a human being, adultery with his wife he suffers from a man, his slave is induced to do something unlawful by a human being, he is hoodwinked by a human being, he is outlawed by a human being, he is overthrown by a human being, he is taken prisoner by a human being. "Deliver me, Lord, from the evil person." SERMON 297.9.[1]

HUMAN BEINGS ARE PEOPLE OF VIRTUE.
CHRYSOSTOM: Do you see how holy Scripture knows how to call human only the person practicing virtue and does not think the others are human, calling them instead flesh at one time and earth at another? Hence at this place, too, in promising to list the genealogy of the good person it says, "Noah was a human being." You see, he alone was a human being, whereas the others were not human beings; instead, while having the appearance of human beings they had forfeited the nobility of their kind by the evil of their intention, and instead of being human they reverted to the irrationality of wild animals. Sacred Scripture assigns the names of wild beasts to human beings, rational creatures that they should be, in the event of their lapsing into evil and falling prey to irrational passions. Listen, for example, to its words, "They turned into rutting horses."[2] See how it gives them the animal's name on account of their unbridled lust. Elsewhere, on the other hand, it says, "Poison of serpents on their lips"; here it highlights their resemblance to the animal's trickery and duplicity. Again, it calls them "dumb dogs."[3] And again, "Like a deaf adder that blocks its ears,"[4] referring to their stopping their ears against instruction in virtue. You would find many other names imposed by sacred Scripture on people seduced by their indifference into bestial passions. HOMILIES ON GENESIS 23.11.[5]

140:5 Snares and Traps Set for the Righteous

BEWARE THE WICKEDNESS OF DEMONS.

ATHANASIUS: Now these demons, if they see all Christians—and especially monks—joyfully laboring and making progress, first attack by attempting to place stumbling blocks in their way. Their "stumbling blocks" are filthy thoughts.[6] But there is no need for us to fear the things they throw at us; through prayer and fasting and faith in the Lord the demons immediately fall. Having fallen, however, they do not stop but advance once more with deceit and cunning. Since they have been unable to deceive the heart openly through filthy pleasure, they renew their attacks on it by other means. From this point on, fabricating apparitions, they pretend to frighten us by changing their shapes and taking on the appearance of women, wild beasts, reptiles and huge bodies and legions of soldiers.

Nevertheless, we need have no fear at all of their apparitions, for they are nothing, and they disappear in a hurry, especially if each person protects himself with faith and the sign of the cross. But they are brazen and completely shameless, for even if they are defeated by these means they attack again by some other method. They act like soothsayers, saying they can predict the future, and they make themselves as tall as the roof and as wide as a house so that by illusions of this sort they can carry away those whom they have been unable to deceive by thoughts. But if they find that the soul has been secured with faith and hopeful resolve, then they bring in their leader. LIFE OF ST. ANTHONY 23.1-6.[7]

SNARES ALONG THE WAYSIDE. AUGUSTINE: So let us walk serenely along this highway without a care in the world, but let us have a healthy fear of the traps set beside the road. The enemy does not dare lay his traps on the highway, because Christ is the way; but next to the road, on the wayside, he certainly never stops doing so. That is why it

---

[1]WSA 3 8:221**. [2]Jer 5:8. [3]Is 56:10. [4]Ps 58:4 (57:5 LXX). [5]FC 82:96*. [6]"Their" is ambiguous; it could refer to the thoughts of the Christians or the impediments of the demons. [7]CS 202:111, 113.

says in the psalm, "They set trip wires[8] for me next to the path." Another text of Scripture also says, "Remember that you are treading in the midst of snares."[9] These snares we are treading among are not on the highway, but they are by the wayside. Why be in dread, why feel frightened, if you are walking along the way? If you abandon the way, that is the time to be afraid. I mean, the reason the enemy is even permitted to set his snares beside the way is to make sure that in a mood of happy-go-lucky carelessness you do not abandon the way and fall into his traps. SERMON 142.1.[10]

140:8 *Hinder the Desires of the Wicked*

AN APPEAL TO GOD'S MERCY. AUGUSTINE: Who is so foolish that, when he hears what is sung in the psalm, "Do not give me up, O Lord, from my desire to the wicked," he says this person was praying that God should not be patient with

him, as though, as you say, "God does not give a man up so that evils are done except to show his patient goodness"? Do we not ask daily, "Lead us not into temptation,"[11] lest we be given up to our lusts? "For everyone is tempted by being drawn away and enticed by his own concupiscence."[12] Therefore, should we not ask for God's mercy instead of asking him to show us his patient goodness? What sane person understands this; indeed, what maniac says this? Therefore, God gives people up to shameful lusts that they may do what is not fitting; but he gives them up fittingly, and these acts not only are sins, as well as punishments for past sins, but also they demand future punishments, just as he gave Ahab up to the lie of the false prophets and gave Rehoboam up to false advice.[13] AGAINST JULIAN 5.4.15.[14]

---

[8]*Scandala* (scandal). [9]Sir 9:13. [10]*WSA* 3 4:413. [11]Mt 6:13. [12]Jas 1:14. [13]See 1 Kings 12. [14]FC 35:259.

141:1-10 A PRAYER FOR DELIVERANCE FROM THE WICKED

A Psalm of David.

[1]*I call upon thee, O LORD; make haste to me!*
   Give ear to my voice, when I call to thee!
[2]*Let my prayer be counted as incense before thee,*
   and the lifting up of my hands as an evening sacrifice!

[3]*Set a guard over my mouth, O LORD,*
   keep watch over the door of my lips!
[4]*Incline not my heart to any evil,*

to busy myself with wicked deeds
in company with men who work iniquity;
   and let me not eat of their dainties!

[5]*Let a good man strike or rebuke me in kindness,*
   but let the oil of the wicked never anoint my head;[a]
   for my prayer is continually[b] against their wicked deeds.
[6]*When they are given over to those who shall condemn them,*

then they shall learn that the word of the
　　Lord *is true.*
[7]*As a rock which one cleaves and shatters on*
　　the land,
　　so shall their bones be strewn at the mouth
　　of Sheol.[c]

[8]*But my eyes are toward thee, O* Lord *God;*

in thee I seek refuge; leave me not
　　defenseless!
[9]*Keep me from the trap which they have laid*
　　for me,
　　and from the snares of evildoers!
[10]*Let the wicked together fall into their own*
　　nets,
　　while I escape.

a Gk: Heb obscure   b Cn: Heb *for continually and my prayer*   c The Hebrew of verses 5-7 is obscure

OVERVIEW: While the life of a saint is considered a great single prayer, ordinarily a believer should pray three times a day—morning, evening as the psalmist here says, and at midnight (ORIGEN). It is appropriate to celebrate the sacrament of the altar in the evening since evening is a reminder of the end of the world (CYPRIAN). Hands elevated in prayer reminds us of the cross on which Christ sacrificed himself for the world (AUGUSTINE). "The lifting up of hands in an evening sacrifice" is a prophecy of the sacrifice of Christ on the cross, the benefits of which were given to the apostles on Maundy Thursday in the sacrament of the Lord's Supper for their eternal salvation (CASSIAN).

Restraint on what we say is necessary so that the mouth, which can rightly confess sins, will not be used to make excuses for sins. Continence of the lips requires a continence of the heart where all thoughts, whether spoken or unspoken, originate. We should have a great determination not to sin because sin is as deadly as the venom of a serpent; we should pray for God's help in avoiding it (AUGUSTINE). Care in what we say is especially important in light of the enormous and irretrievable evil that the tongue can cause (VALERIAN). We cannot excuse our sins by blaming someone else for them; each person will be judged according to what he has done or not done. If we are enticed to sin by wicked people, the sins that we commit may come back to hurt us (JEROME).

The mark of a true friend is positive criticism; the mark of a false friend is flattery. The dangers of self-criticism is that we tend to be either too strict or too lenient on ourselves rather than fair (AUGUSTINE). It is best for us, if a just person reproves us for sin, to keep silent (CAESARIUS). It is better to be advised by a just person than be praised by a flatterer, since duplicity of heart and mouth is the greater and most detestable sin (MARTIN). When heretics, who are offended by the simplicity of the Christian message, turn to Scripture, they encounter Christ and are converted to the orthodox faith (JEROME).

141:2 Prayer and Lifting Up of Hands

THE LIFE OF A SAINTLY PERSON IS A SINGLE GREAT PRAYER. ORIGEN: And he prays "constantly" (deeds of virtue or fulfilling the commandments are included as part of prayer) who unites prayer with the deeds required and right deeds with prayer. For the only way we can accept the command to "pray constantly"[1] as referring to a real possibility is by saying that the entire life of the saint taken as a whole is a single great prayer. What is customarily called prayer is, then, a part of this prayer. Now prayer in the ordinary sense ought to be made no less than three times each day. This is evident from the story of Daniel, who prayed three times a day when such great peril had been devised for him.[2] And Peter went up to

[1]1 Thess 5:17. [2]Dan 6:13.

the housetop about the sixth hour to pray; that is when he saw the sheet descending from heaven let down by four corners.[3] He was offering the middle prayer of the three, the one referred to before him by David, "In the morning may you hear my prayer, in the morning I will offer to you and I will watch."[4] And the last time of prayer is indicated by "the lifting up of my hands is an evening sacrifice." Indeed, we do not even complete the nighttime properly without that prayer of which David speaks when he says, "At midnight I rise to praise you because of your righteous ordinances."[5] And Paul, as it says in the Acts of the Apostles, prayed "about midnight" with Silas in Philippi and sang a hymn to God so that even the prisoners heard them.[6] ON PRAYER 12.2.[7]

SACRIFICE IN EVENING SUGGESTS THE EVENING OF THE WORLD. CYPRIAN: Or is anyone enticed by this contemplation[8] that, although water alone seems to be offered in the morning, yet, when we come to dinner, we offer a mixed chalice? But when we dine, we cannot call the people to our banquet that we may celebrate the truth of the sacrament with all of the brotherhood present. But, in fact, the Lord offered the mixed chalice not in the morning but after dinner. Ought we then to celebrate the sacrifice of the Lord after dinner so that by repeated sacrifices we may offer the mixed chalice? It was fitting for Christ to offer the sacrifice about evening of the day that the very hour might show the setting and evening of the world as it is written in Exodus: "And the whole multitude of the children of Israel shall slaughter it in the evening."[9] And again in the Psalms: "The lifting up of my hands as evening sacrifice." But we celebrate the resurrection of the Lord in the morning. LETTER 63.16.[10]

THE CROSS IS EVIDENT IN HANDS RAISED IN PRAYER. AUGUSTINE: A sermon has to be preached about the evening sacrifice. We prayed after all as we sang, and we sang as we prayed,

"May my prayer rise straight up like incense in your presence; the lifting up of my hands an evening sacrifice." In the prayer we observe the person, in the extension of the hands we recognize the cross. So this is the sign that we carry on our foreheads, the sign by which we have been saved. A sign that was mocked, in order to be honored; despised in order to be glorified. God appears in visible form, so that as man he may intercede; he remains hidden so that as man he may die. "For if they had known, they would never have crucified the Lord of glory."[11] So this sacrifice, in which the priest is also the victim, has redeemed us by the shedding of the Creator's blood. SERMON 342.1.[12]

A PROPHECY OF THE LORD'S SUPPER AND CHRIST'S DEATH ON THE CROSS. JOHN CASSIAN: But what should be said concerning the evening sacrifices, which even in the Old Testament were appointed by the Mosaic law to be offered continually?[13] We can prove that morning burnt offerings and evening sacrifices were unceasingly offered every day in the temple, although with figurative victims, from the fact that David sings, "Let my prayer come like incense in your presence, the raising of my hands like an evening sacrifice." Here the true evening sacrifice can be understood in a more spiritual way as either that which the Lord, the Savior, delivered to his apostles as they supped in the evening, when he initiated the sacred mysteries of the church,[14] or as that evening sacrifice that he offered to the Father on the last day—namely, at the end of the ages[15]—by the raising of his hands for the salvation of the whole world. This stretching out of his hands on the gallows is appropriately called a raising, for all of us who were sunk in hell he raised to the heavens in accordance

---

[3]Acts 10:9-11. [4]Ps 5:3 (5:4 LXX). [5]Ps 119:62 (118:62 LXX). [6]Acts 16:25. [7]OSW 104-5. [8]Cyprian is referring to the erroneous practice of some clergy in the church at the time who were using only water instead of wine or a water and wine mixture in the celebration of the Lord's Supper. [9]Ex 12:6. [10]FC 51:213. [11]1 Cor 2:8. [12]WSA 3 10:34. [13]See Num 28:4. [14]See Mt 26:26-29. [15]See Heb 9:26.

with his promise, which says, "When I have been lifted up from the earth, I will draw all things to myself."[16] INSTITUTES 3.3.8-10.[17]

141:3-4 Keep from Doing Evil

THE MOUTH CAN BE USED FOR CONFESSION OF SINS. AUGUSTINE: But of course it is also true that the confession of sins is equally salutary. That is why we heard in the psalm that was read first, "Set a guard, Lord, on my mouth, and a door of restraint around my lips, and do not incline my heart to words of malice, to excusing my sins with excuses." He asks God to put a guard on his mouth. And he goes on to explain what it is a guard against. There are people, you see, and plenty of them, who as soon as they are blamed for anything rush to make excuses. Now to make excuses is to look for reasons and to adduce pretexts why a sin should not be regarded as belonging to you. One says, "The devil did it for me"; another says, "My luck did it for me"; another, "I was forced to it by fate"; no one blames himself. SERMON 29.3.[18]

THE MOUTH IS A GIFT OF GOD. AUGUSTINE: Unless one thinks that God requires only self-restraint in terms of the desires of the inferior parts of one's flesh, the following is also sung in the psalm: "Set a watch, O Lord, before my mouth and a door of continence round about my lips." Now, in this testimony of divine eloquence if we understand "mouth" as we ought to understand it, the watch placed there is continence, inasmuch as we understand it as a gift of God. Surely, it is a slight matter to restrain the mouth of the body lest something that is not expedient come forth from it through the sound of the voice. Within is the mouth of the heart where he who said those words and directed us to say them desired that a guard and gate of continence be set for him by God. There are many things that we do not speak from the mouth of the body but shout from the heart. Yet, no word of any thing proceeds from the mouth of that body in whose heart there is silence. Thus, whatever does not emanate from there does not sound outside, but what does emanate from there, if it is evil—even though it does not move the tongue—defiles the soul. Continence, therefore, must be placed there where the conscience, even of those who are outwardly silent, speaks.

And so that he might more clearly indicate the interior mouth that he signified by those words when he said, "Set a watch, O Lord, before my mouth, and a door of continence round about my lips," he immediately added, "Incline not my heart to evil words." This inclination of the heart, what is it if not consent? For, he has not yet spoken who has not yet consented by an inclination of the heart to the onrushing suggestions in his heart of any act whatsoever. If, however, he consented, he has already spoken in his heart even though he has not made a sound with his mouth. Even though he has not done the deed with his hand or any other part of his body, he has committed it because he has determined in his mind to do it, and he is guilty of the act, by the laws of God even though it remains concealed from the sight of people—the word being spoken in the heart though no act be committed in the body. ON CONTINENCE 1.2-2.3.[19]

THE DEADLY NATURE OF SIN. AUGUSTINE: Of course, what we have to set our minds on first and foremost is not to sin, in case we get on fairly familiar and friendly terms with sin, as a serpent. In fact, of course, it slays the sinner with its poisonous fangs and is not at all the sort of thing to make friends with. But if it should happen to catch you in its coils when you are weak, or creep up on you when you are getting careless, or grab you when you have lost your way or trick you into losing it again, then you must not let it irk you to confess and to accuse yourself instead of looking for excuses. That is what he prayed about in some psalm or other when he said, "Lord, set a guard on my mouth and a door of self-restraint around

---

[16]Jn 12:32. [17]ACW 58:62*. [18]WSA 3 2:117*. [19]FC 16:190-91**.

my lips, and do not turn aside my thoughts to ill-natured words, to excuse on excuse for sins." SERMON 20.2.[20]

THE SINS OF THE TONGUE. VALERIAN OF CIM-IEZ: But the blow inflicted by the tongue is incurable. The tongue strikes lightly, but it always stirs up deep sighs in the chest through the sorrow it causes. The prophet no doubt knew how great was the evil of the tongue when he cried out, "Set a watch, O Lord, before my mouth, and a door about my lips, that my heart may not turn to evil words." Therefore, if anyone is wise, let him set a guard before his mouth, and let him put the bond of silence on his lips. HOMILY 5.2.[21]

DO NOT MAKE EXCUSE FOR SIN. JEROME: "Let not my heart incline to evil words, to make excuses in sins." O unhappy race of human beings! We seek excuse for sin by saying, "Nature got the better of me," and all the while it has been in our power to sin or not to sin. We are always justifying ourselves and saying, I did not want to sin, but lust overwhelmed me; that woman came to me; she made the advances; she touched me; she said this or that to me; she called me; and while we ought to be doing penance and crying, "Lord, I have sinned," we excuse ourselves instead, and yoke sins to sin. We all have the same kind of body, but with our own particular difficulties. "God is not a respecter of persons."[22] Would you know that we have the same bodies as the saints? Paul the apostle says, "I see another law in my members, warring against the law of my mind and making me prisoner to the law of sin that is in my members";[23] and again, "But I chastise my body and bring it into subjection, lest perhaps after preaching to others I myself should be rejected."[24] Later, he says, "Unhappy man that I am! Who will deliver me from the body of this death?"[25] We all have our own struggles, therefore, and it is in proportion to his struggles that each one receives his reward. HOMILIES ON THE PSALMS 51.[26]

TURN ASIDE FROM WORDS OF EVIL. JEROME: When a person is advanced in years, you must not be too ready to believe evil of him; his past life is itself a defense, and so also is his rank as an elder. Still, since we are but human and sometimes in spite of the ripeness of our years fall into the sins of youth, if I do wrong and you wish to correct me, accuse me openly of my fault: do not backbite me secretly. "Let the righteous smite me, it shall be a kindness, and let him reprove me; but let not the oil of the sinner enrich my head."[27] For what does the apostle say? "Whom the Lord loves, he chastens, and scourges every son whom he receives."[28] By the mouth of Isaiah the Lord speaks thus: "O my people, they who call you happy cause you to err and destroy the way of your paths."[29] How do you help me by telling my misdeeds to others? You may, without my knowing of it, wound some one else by the narration of my sins or rather of those which you slanderously attribute to me; and while you are eager to spread the news in all quarters, you may pretend to confide in each individual as though you had spoken to no one else. Such a course has for its object not my correction but the indulgence of your own failing. The Lord commands that those who sin against us are to be arraigned privately or else in the presence of a witness and that if they refuse to hear reason the matter is to be laid before the church, and those who persist in their wickedness are to be regarded as heathens and publicans.[30] LETTER 125.19.[31]

141:5-7 The Value of Positive Reprimand

THE BEST KIND OF CRITICISM. AUGUSTINE: This is the oil of the sinner with which the prophet does not want his head to be anointed, as he says: "The just person shall correct me in mercy and shall reprove me, but let not the oil of

---

[20]WSA 3 2:15-16. [21]FC 17:330-31*. [22]Acts 10:34. [23]Rom 7:23. [24]1 Cor 9:27. [25]Rom 7:24. [26]FC 48:367-68*. [27]Ps 141:5 (140:5 LXX, Vg.). [28]Heb 12:6. [29]Is 3:12 (LXX). [30]Mt 18:15-17. [31]NPNF 2 6:251*.

the sinner fatten my head." Thus, he prefers to be corrected by the severe mercy of the just rather than to be praised by the soothing ointment of flattery. Whence, the prophet said, "They that call you blessed, the same deceive you."[32] Therefore, regarding a person whom false flattery has made arrogant, the popular saying states it correctly: "He has a swelled head"; that is, his head has been fattened by the oil of the sinner, and this is not the effect of the harsh truth of correction but of the soothing deceit of praise. LETTER 33.[33]

THE SHARP CORRECTION OF THE RIGHTEOUS. AUGUSTINE: And again, he[34] quotes as words of David, "Let not the oil of the sinner anoint my head," when David has been speaking of the flattery of the smooth speaker deceiving with false praise, so as to cause the head of the person praised to become great with pride. And this meaning is made manifest by the words immediately preceding in the same psalm. For he says, "Let the righteous smite me. It shall be a kindness, and let him reprove me; but the oil of the sinner shall not break my head." What can be clearer than this sentence? What more manifest? For he declares that he would rather be reproved in kindness with the sharp correction of the righteous, so that he may be healed, than anointed with the soft speaking of the flatterer, so as to be puffed up with pride. LETTERS OF PETILIAN THE DONATIST 3.33-38.[35]

THE DIFFICULTY OF SELF-CRITICISM. AUGUSTINE: This brother[36] will bring you[37] some things I have written. If you have the time to read them, please be completely candid and merciless in your criticism. The Bible reminds us, "The righteous shall correct me in compassion and reprove me, but the oil of the sinner shall not anoint my head." This means that the real friend heals me by his criticism, but the false friend merely flatters me. I cannot be a fair critic of my own work because I am either too strict or not strict enough. For I sometimes see my own faults, but I would rather hear a better judge, just in case I

begin to flatter myself after a harsh bit of self-criticism, because I decide I am too hard on myself. LETTER 28.6.[38]

WHEN WE SIN, WE NEED TO BE CORRECTED. CAESARIUS OF ARLES: "The just person shall correct me in mercy and shall reprove me—but let not the oil of the sinner fatten my head."[39] What does this mean? It would be better for me if the just person who sees my sin would correct me, not spare me, tell me that I have done wrong, be furious over my sin, in order to free me from it. He would seem to speak harshly, but inside he would be gentle in mercy, according to the words "The just person shall correct me in mercy and shall reprove me." When the just person thus reproves and shouts and rages, he shows mercy, for it all arises from his paternal pity and not hostile cruelty. Moreover, since he does not want you to die in sin, he loves you all the more when he cuts; he is unwilling to allow your other members to decay from the rottenness of sin. SERMON 59.6.[40]

FLATTERY IS THE MOST DETESTABLE CRIME. MARTIN OF BRAGA: Therefore in all matters where great flattery has even exceeded the limits proper to humanity, you must recall that well-known lesson of David, in which he shunned the poison of flatterers with these words: "The just person shall correct me in kindness and shall reprove me, but let not the oil of the sinner fatten my head."[41] The "oil of the sinner" is flattery, which uses a smooth, suave unction to brighten up, as though with cosmetics, the head of the inner person, that is, the heart. Therefore, the prophet David said that it was better for him to be corrected or advised by a just person than to be praised by any flatterer. It was right that he

---

[32]See Is 5:12. [33]FC 12:128**. [34]Petilian, a Donatist bishop in Cirta, North Africa. [35]NPNF 1 4:612*. [36]Profuturus, who was the intended courier of this letter to Jerome and who later was consecrated bishop of Cirta. [37]Jerome, to whom the letter is written. [38]MFC 9:262. [39]Ps 141:5 (140:5 LXX, Vg.). [40]FC 31:293-94*. [41]Ps 141:5 (140:5 LXX, Vg.).

should denote the flatterer with the name of "sinner," since his is the greatest and most detestable crime in the sight of God—to hold one thing in his heart, to speak another with his lips. Of such he also says in another psalm: "His words are smoother than oil, but they are drawn swords."[42] Of the just person he says, "He speaks the truth in his heart and works not deceit with his tongue."[43] Although in these ways any subtle remarks of people, even without the pleasing sensations of praise, may draw your credulous mind to agreement, turn rather to the deeds of our Lord Jesus Christ in the Gospels, and you will find that the "Lord of lords"[44] left us a great example of sacred humility amid the praises of people. Practice humility, then, take it for your mistress, set it as your guide when flatterers entice. Humility will tell you just how much of the things that people ascribe to you in praise is really yours and how long it will last. Humility does not let you be attentive to lies. EXHORTA-TION TO HUMILITY 3.[45]

DRIVEN AGAINST THE ROCK, WHICH IS CHRIST JEROME: "Their judges driven against the rock were swallowed up," just as another passage in Scripture says: "Happy the one who shall seize and smash your little ones against the rock!"[46] "But the rock was Christ."[47] "The little ones" are trifling thoughts before they grow into ones of serious consequences. Even heretics, although they seem to despise the simplicity of the church, as compared with Aristotle and Plato; when they turn to the Scriptures, are swallowed up immediately by the Rock, that is, by Christ, and are converted to him. HOMILIES ON THE PSALMS 51.[48]

---

[42]Ps 55:21 (54:22 LXX, Vg.). [43]Ps 15:2 (14:2 LXX, Vg.). [44]Rev 19:16. [45]FC 62:52-53*. [46]Ps 137:9 (136:9 LXX, Vg.). [47]1 Cor 10:4. [48]FC 48:370*.

142:1-7 A PLAINTIVE PRAYER FOR FORGIVENESS

A Maskil of David, when he was in the cave. A Prayer.

[1]*I cry with my voice to the LORD,*
with my voice I make supplication to the LORD,
[2]*I pour out my complaint before him,*
I tell my trouble before him.
[3]*When my spirit is faint,*
thou knowest my way!

In the path where I walk
they have hidden a trap for me.

[4]*I look to the right and watch,[d]*
but there is none who takes notice of me;
no refuge remains to me,
no man cares for me.

[5]*I cry to thee, O LORD;*
I say, Thou art my refuge,
my portion in the land of the living.
[6]*Give heed to my cry;*
for I am brought very low!

Deliver me from my persecutors;
for they are too strong for me!

⁷Bring me out of prison,
that I may give thanks to thy name!

The righteous will surround me;
for thou wilt deal bountifully with me.

d Or *Look to the right and watch*

Overview: Satan cunningly places extra temptations before those who successfully pursue spiritual excellence (Palladius). Some people seek Christ to destroy him, others that they may have and hold onto him for the right reason. When God promised in the Old Testament to give his people a promised land, he was also making a promise to Christians, whose promised land is heaven (Augustine).

142:3 God Knows Our Life's Course

Hidden Snares. Palladius of Helenopolis: There was a certain old man who used to live in the desert that is called Scete, and he had a disciple who lived with him; now this [latter] brother was adorned with the spiritual excellences of every kind that befit those who are in subjection to old men, and he was exceedingly conspicuous for his obedience, which was the greatest of all his virtues. And he was sent to the village continually by the old man to sell their work and to bring back whatsoever was needed for their habitation, and that brother, without any compulsion whatsoever, performed every command that the old man gave him with zeal and diligence. Now when the enemy of righteousness, the foe of the human race, and especially of the orders of the monks, that is to say, Satan, the opponent of all virtues and the hater of the upright life of the children of humankind, saw that this brother was overcoming and bringing to naught all his crafty designs by the might of his simple obedience, which was full of discretion, he made a plan to lay two snares for him in the path of his spiritual excellence, even as it is said concerning him in the psalm, as it were by the mouth of those who cultivate spiritual excellence and who walk in the way of righteousness, "In the way of my steps have they hidden snares for me." Now the two snares were these: The first consisted in making that brother to pursue fornication, and the second was in making him to fall into disobedience; and the enemy, in his cunning, expected that the brother would not only be caught by one of these, and so become involved in both, but also that deliverance from the one would be found to be the occasion for his falling into the other, for he saw that he was being sent continually to Egypt by his master [on the business] of the work of their hands and of the matter of their need. Lausiac History 2.4.[1]

142:4 There Is No Refuge

Seek Christ for the Right Reason. Augustine: "And they[2] were seeking Jesus," but in an evil way. For blessed are they who are seeking Jesus, but in a good way. Those people were seeking Jesus that neither they nor we might have him; but we have received him who withdrew from them. They who are seeking are reproached, they who are seeking are praised; for it is the disposition of the seeker that finds either praise or condemnation. For you have this also in the Psalms: "Let them be confounded and covered with shame who seek my life."[3] These are the ones who seek in an evil way. In another place, however, it says, "Flight has perished from me; and there is no one who seeks after my life." They who seek are blamed; they who do not seek are blamed. Therefore let us seek Christ that we may have him; let us seek him that we may hold him but not that we may kill him. For these people, too, were seeking him precisely in order that they might hold him but that soon they might not have him. "They were seeking, therefore, and

---

[1]*PHF* 1:209*. [2]Jesus' enemies who were seeking to put him to death. [3]Ps 40:14 (39:15 LXX, Vg.).

they were saying to one another, 'What do you think, that he is not coming to the feast day?'" TRACTATES ON THE GOSPEL OF JOHN 50.3.[4]

142:5-7 A Cry for Refuge

THE PROMISED LAND FOR CHRISTIANS IS HEAVEN. AUGUSTINE: What does it mean, then, that the younger was blessed in the guise of the elder, but that under the symbols of the Old Testament and its promise to the people of the Jews a spiritual blessing has lighted on the people of the Christians? Pay attention, brothers! They hear about the promised land, and so do we. Scripture seems to be speaking to the Jews about the promised land, and it is we who are blessed with the true understanding of the promised land, we who can say to God, "You are my hope, my portion in the land of the living." But it is our mother who taught us to say this that is to say the church teaches us in the holy prophets how to understand spiritually these material promises. SERMON 4.13.[5]

---

[4]FC 88:261-62. [5]WSA 3 1:193.

143:1-12 A PRAYER FOR DELIVERANCE FROM ENEMIES

A Psalm of David.

[1]*Hear my prayer, O LORD;*
give ear to my supplications!
In thy faithfulness answer me, in thy
righteousness!
[2]*Enter not into judgment with thy servant;*
for no man living is righteous before thee.

[3]*For the enemy has pursued me;*
he has crushed my life to the ground;
he has made me sit in darkness like those
long dead.
[4]*Therefore my spirit faints within me;*
my heart within me is appalled.

[5]*I remember the days of old,*
I meditate on all that thou hast done;
I muse on what thy hands have wrought.

[6]*I stretch out my hands to thee;*
my soul thirsts for thee like a parched land.
                                             Selah
[7]*Make haste to answer me, O LORD!*
My spirit fails!
Hide not thy face from me,
lest I be like those who go down to the Pit.
[8]*Let me hear in the morning of thy steadfast*
love,
for in thee I put my trust.
Teach me the way I should go,
for to thee I lift up my soul.

[9]*Deliver me, O LORD, from my enemies!*
I have fled to thee for refuge![e]
[10]*Teach me to do thy will,*
for thou art my God!
Let thy good spirit lead me
on a level path!

^{11}*For thy name's sake, O* LORD, *preserve my life!*
    In thy righteousness bring me out of trouble!

^{12}*And in thy steadfast love cut off my enemies,*
    and destroy all my adversaries,
    for I am thy servant.

e One Heb Ms Gk: Heb *to thee I have hidden*

OVERVIEW: There are two kinds of perfections, two kinds of justices and two kinds of fear—the first kind belongs to God and cannot change, the second belongs to creatures according to the knowledge of God and can change. People can fall from grace but can also reach it again—they live in constant tension between virtue and vice (JEROME). Sins need to be forgiven by God through the work of Christ on the cross. No matter how much virtue a person possesses, there is still room for an increase; therefore, people must seek perfection elsewhere, namely, from a forgiving and merciful God. No one can attain absolute perfection on his own; it is possible only through the work of the crucified Christ and the work of the Holy Spirit (AUGUSTINE). Prayers for deliverance from God's judgment are sometimes motivated by fear of hell and final condemnation (CASSIAN). God promised his saints justification and glorification because they will be of great benefit to his saints and since people cannot achieve them on their own (FULGENTIUS).

Do not return hurtful words, but tolerate them and use them as a means of disciplining oneself (BASIL). Some people desire God while others desire the world; since the soul of the believer is like a parched land that needs water, it longs for God (AUGUSTINE). Goodness is attributed to the Father and to the Son; so David attributes the same quality to the Holy Spirit (NICETAS). Believers should ask God for the Holy Spirit so that he may enlighten their minds, give them joy and promises and entrust them to Jesus Christ (BEDE).

143:2 No One Is Righteous Before God

MEASURED AGAINST THE PERFECT JUSTICE OF GOD. JEROME: It is clear from all this[1] that

there are two kinds of perfections in holy Scripture, and two kinds of justices and two kinds of fears. The first kind of perfection, and its comparable truth, and perfect justice and fear, which is the beginning of wisdom, are compatible with the virtues of God; but the second kind of perfection, which befits not only human beings but also every living creature, and our weakness, according to what is said in the Psalms: "In your sight no one living shall be justified," is the kind of justice that is called perfect, not in comparison with God but according to the knowledge of God. Job, Zachariah and Elizabeth are called just, according to this latter type of perfection, which can change on occasions into injustice, and not according to the former type, which can never change, of which it is said, "I am God, and I change not."[2] AGAINST THE PELAGIANS 1.15.[3]

PEOPLE MAY FALL FROM GRACE. JEROME: Atticus:[4] From this[5] it is clear that people are called righteous and said to be without fault; but that, if negligence comes over them, they may fall. [It is also clear] that a person always occupies a middle place, so that he may slip from the height of virtue into vice or may rise from vice to virtue. He is never safe but must dread shipwreck even in fair weather. Therefore, a person cannot be without sin. Solomon says, "There is not a righteous person on earth that does good and sins not."[6] Like-

---

[1]On the basis of Philippians 3:12-16, Jerome had just been arguing that there are two kinds of righteousness, namely, the righteousness that Paul was striving for but could not achieve, and the true righteousness that comes through Christ. On the basis of Proverbs 1:3 (LXX), he argues that if there is a true righteousness, there must also be a false righteousness. [2]Mal 3:6. [3]FC 53:253*. [4]Atticus was an orthodox Christian who was in a dialogue with a Pelagian heretic named Critobulus. [5]Jerome had just been quoting Job 16:21 (Vulg.); 31:35; 9:20, 30-31; Lk 1:18, 20. [6]Eccles 7:20.

wise in the book of Kings [2 Chronicles]: "There is no one that sins not."[7] So, also, the blessed David says, "Who can understand his errors? Cleanse me from hidden faults, and keep back your servant from presumptuous sins."[8] And again, "Enter not into judgment with your servant, for in your sight shall no one living be justified." Holy Scripture is full of passages to the same effect. AGAINST THE PELAGIANS 1.12.[9]

ENTER NOT INTO JUDGMENT WITH SINNERS.

AUGUSTINE: And so, my glory and my life, God of my heart, I will lay aside for a while all the good deeds that my mother did. For them I thank you, but now I pray to you for her sins. Hear me through your Son, who hung on the cross and now "sits at your right hand and pleads for us,"[10] for he is the true medicine of our wounds. I know that my mother always acted with mercy and that she forgave others with all her heart when they trespassed against her. Forgive her too, O Lord, if ever she trespassed against you in all the long years of her life after baptism. Forgive her, I beseech you; "do not call her to account."[11] "Let your mercy give your judgment an honorable welcome,"[12] for your words are true and you have promised mercy to the merciful. If they are merciful, it is by your gift; and "you will show pity on those whom you pity; you will show mercy where you are merciful."[13] CONFESSIONS 9.13.[14]

THERE IS NO JUST PERSON ON EARTH.

AUGUSTINE: And now, to summarize briefly and comprehensively the idea I have of the virtue that belongs to right living: that virtue is charity by means of which we love what we should love. This is greater in some, less in others, lacking in still others; its fullest measure, beyond which there is no increase, is found in no one as long as he lives the life of a human being. As long as it is subject to increase, the defect by which it is less than it ought to be is accounted as vice; by reason of this vice "there is no just person on earth who will do good and sin not";[15] because of this vice, "no one living shall be justified in the sight

of God"; because of this vice, "If we say that we have no sin, we deceive ourselves and the truth is not in us";[16] because of it, also, however much progress we have made, we still have to say, "Forgive us our debts,"[17] even though in baptism all our words, deeds, thoughts have been forgiven. Therefore, he who sees rightly sees where and when and whence that perfection is to be hoped for, to which no addition is possible. But, if there were no commandments, there would certainly be no norm by which a person might look into himself and see what he should avoid, what he should strive after, what he should rejoice in, what he should pray for. Commandments, then, are highly useful, if only because free will is thereby given the opportunity of doing greater honor to the grace of God. LETTER 167.15.[18]

THERE IS NO JUSTIFICATION APART FROM

CHRIST. AUGUSTINE: Whether in this world there has ever been or could be anyone living so just a life as to be entirely without sin can be a subject of some discussion among true and pious Christians. Nevertheless, if anyone doubts that such a person surely can exist after this life, he lacks good sense. But, for my part, I do not wish to argue the point even as it concerns this life. For although it appears to me that one cannot understand otherwise the passage of Scripture that reads, "In your sight no one living shall be justified," and other similar passages, still I would that it were possible to show either that such testimonies could be understood more favorably or that a complete and perfect justice, to which it would be impossible to add anything, had in the past been realized in someone while he lived in this body, is presently being realized and will be realized in the future. But even so, there are far more who, while not doubting it is necessary for them up to

---

[7]2 Chron 6:36. [8]Ps 19:12-13 (18:13-14 LXX, Vg.). [9]NPNF 2 6:453-54**. [10]Rom 8:34. [11]Ps 143:2 (142:2 LXX, Vg.) [12]Jas 2:13. [13]Rom 9:15. [14]AC 203-4. [15]1 Kings 8:46. [16]1 Jn 1:8. [17]Mt 6:12; Lk 11:4. [18]FC 30:44-45.

the last day of their life to say, "Forgive us our debts, as we also forgive our debtors,"[19] still confess that in Christ and his promises they have a true, certain and firm hope. At all events, there is no other way than the helping grace of the Savior, Christ crucified, and the gift of his Spirit, by which any persons, whoever they be, can arrive at absolute perfection or by which anyone can attain the slightest progress to true and holy justice—whoever denies this, I question whether he can be counted in the number of true Christians of any sort. ON NATURE AND GRACE 60.70.[20]

REAL FEAR. JOHN CASSIAN: There is another way that tears flow, proceeding not, indeed, from any consciousness of deadly crimes but nonetheless from a fear of Gehenna and from an awareness of that terrible judgment. The prophet smitten with this terror, prays to God and says, "Do not enter into judgment with your servant, for in your sight no one living shall be justified." CONFERENCES 9.29.3.[21]

GOD'S MERCY SURPASSES HIS JUDGMENT. FULGENTIUS OF RUSPE: But if someone asks why God predicted all the things predestined and still did not promise all the predestined things, we answer that it cannot be called a promise unless when it is predicted that something is going to be done, what is done can be of use to the one to whom it is promised. What is promised is always something of a gift but not always something of a judgment, since the gift of what is promised always brings happiness while the severity of a judgment sometimes saddens.

As the prophet, fearing something of this sort, pours out his prayer to God: "Do not enter into judgment with your servant, for no one living is righteous before you." For he knew that all would have to be restrained by the equal chain of punishment unless God, in those whom he willed, made mercy surpass judgment. Justification and glorification that do not exist in a human being from a human being, but from God, have been both predicted and promised because they were to be of

great benefit to the saints. LETTER TO MONIMUS 1.25.1-2.[22]

143:4 My Spirit Faints Within Me

DO NOT MAKE PUBLIC YOUR INNER TROUBLES. BASIL THE GREAT: Let that foe[23] of yours upbraid you,[24] but do you not upbraid him. Regard his words as a training ground in which to exercise philosophy. If you have not been pierced, you are still unwounded, and, if your spirit suffers some injury, confine the hurt within yourself; for the psalmist says, "my heart within me is troubled," that is, he gave no outward expression of his feelings but repressed them, as a wave that breaks against the shore and subsides. Quiet your heart, I beg you, when it howls and rages. Make your passions honor your reason, as an unruly boy respects the presence of a venerable man. HOMILY 10.[25]

143:6 My Soul Thirsts for God

THE SOUL IS LIKE LAND WITHOUT WATER. AUGUSTINE: Put two people together; one wants to go to the show, the other to church. They are joined in body, separated by their desires. The first is like the salt water, the second appears as dry land. How can we prove that this land is dry, which signifies people desiring good things? The psalmist says to God, "My soul is like land without water to you." My soul has thirsted for you; it is thirsty, it is dry, it is segregated from the waters of the sea. It must not bother about not yet being segregated in the body; its desire has already made the separation. Some desire God, others desire the world. SERMON 229s.[26]

143:10 Teach Me to Do God's Will

THE GOODNESS OF THE HOLY SPIRIT. NICETAS OF REMESIANA: It can be proved, too, that

---

[19]Mt 6:12. [20]FC 86:76-77. [21]ACW 57:348. [22]FC 95:220. [23]An ungrateful person who abuses and berates other people. [24]The audience to whom the sermon is addressed. [25]FC 9:456**. [26]WSA 3 6:333*.

just as the Father is good and the Son is good, so the Holy Spirit is good. Of the Father, the Only-Begotten speaks in the Gospel: "One there is who is good, that is God."[27] Of himself he says, "I am the good Shepherd."[28] So, too, of the Holy Spirit, David in his psalms says to the Lord, "Your good spirit shall lead me into the right land." Just as it is said of the Son, "The word of the Lord is right,"[29] so of the Holy Spirit it is said, "Renew a right spirit within [me]."[30] THE POWER OF THE HOLY SPIRIT 14.[31]

PRAY FOR THE GIFT OF THE HOLY SPIRIT.
BEDE: Let us entreat the help of the grace of this Spirit in all our actions, dearly beloved. Let us all,

individually and collectively, say to the Lord, "Let your good Spirit lead me in the right way." And so it will come to pass that the one who came down on the apostles and declared to them the things that were to come may disclose also to our minds the joys of the life to come. May he kindly set us on fire to seek these joys, with the cooperation of the one who is accustomed both to promise and to give him to his faithful, Jesus Christ our Lord, who lives and reigns with the Father in the unity of the Holy Spirit, God forever and ever. Amen. HOMILIES ON THE GOSPELS 2.11.[32]

---

[27]Mt 19:17. [28]Jn 10:11. [29]Ps 33:4 (32:4 LXX). [30]Ps 51:12 (50:14 LXX). [31]FC 7:35*. [32]CS 111:107.

144:1-15 A PRAYER FOR VICTORY OVER TREACHEROUS ENEMIES

A Psalm of David.

[1]*Blessed be the* LORD, *my rock,*
who trains my hands for war,
and my fingers for battle;
[2]*my rock[j] and my fortress,*
my stronghold and my deliverer,
my shield and he in whom I take refuge,
who subdues the peoples under him.[g]

[3]*O* LORD, *what is man that thou dost regard him,*
or the son of man that thou dost think of him?
[4]*Man is like a breath,*
his days are like a passing shadow.

[5]*Bow thy heavens, O* LORD, *and come down!*
Touch the mountains that they smoke!
[6]*Flash forth the lightning and scatter them,*
send out thy arrows and rout them!
[7]*Stretch forth thy hand from on high,*
rescue me and deliver me from the many waters,
from the hand of aliens,
[8]*whose mouths speak lies,*
and whose right hand is a right hand of falsehood.

[9]*I will sing a new song to thee, O God;*
upon a ten-stringed harp I will play to thee,
[10]*who givest victory to kings,*
who rescuest David thy[b] servant.

¹¹*Rescue me from the cruel sword,*
 and deliver me from the hand of aliens,
whose mouths speak lies,
 and whose right hand is a right hand
  of falsehood.

¹²*May our sons in their youth*
 be like plants full grown,
our daughters like corner pillars
 cut for the structure of a palace;

¹³*may our garners be full,*
 providing all manner of store;
may our sheep bring forth thousands
 and ten thousands in our fields;
¹⁴*may our cattle be heavy with young,*
 suffering no mischance or failure in bearing;
may there be no cry of distress in our
  streets!
¹⁵*Happy the people to whom such blessings fall!*
 Happy the people whose God is the LORD!

f With Ps 18.2, 2 Sam 22.2: Heb *my steadfast love*   g Another reading is *my people under me*   h Heb *his*

OVERVIEW: The believer wages his battle against the temptations of evil desires, greed, pride and lust internally or secretly; the victor's prize is eternal life. Good people do not always suffer and the wicked do not always prosper in this life; sometimes bad luck befalls bad people and good luck befalls good people—this is further evidence that God's ways are inscrutable to us (AUGUSTINE). Goodness is attributed to the Father and to the Son; so David attributes the same quality to the Holy Spirit (NICETAS). Believers should ask God for the Holy Spirit so that he may enlighten their minds, give them joy and promises, and entrust them to Jesus Christ (BEDE).

The ten strings of a harp represent the Ten Commandments—in the old dispensation they were a source of fear, in the new a source of love.

The expression "right hand of iniquity" means temporal, not eternal prosperity; when good people have temporal prosperity, they hold it in the left hand. The accumulation of earthly fortune is considered a blessing by unregenerate people. True happiness is knowing God and being assured of eternal life (AUGUSTINE). Blessedness is not derived ultimately from worldly abundance, joy and security but from being immoveable in faith (CASSIODORUS).

144:1 God Trains Us for Spiritual Warfare

THE INNER BATTLE WITH SIN. AUGUSTINE: But because you turn a blind eye to the interior battle and take pleasure in exterior battles, it means you do not want to belong to the new song, in which it says "who trains my hands for battle and my fingers for war." There is a war a person wages with himself, engaging evil desire, curbing greed, crushing pride, stifling ambition, slaughtering lust. You fight these battles in secret, and you do not lose them in public! It is for this that your hands are trained for battle and your fingers for war. You do not get this in your amphitheater show. In those shows the hunter is not the same as the guitarist; the hunter does one thing, the guitarist another. In God's circus show they are one and the same. Touch these same ten strings, and you will be killing wild beasts. You do each simultaneously. You touch the first string by which the one God is worshiped, and the beast of superstition falls dead. You touch the second by which you do not take the name of the Lord your God in vain, and at your feet is fallen the beast of the error of impious heresies that thought to do just that. You touch the third string, where whatever you do, you do in hope of resting in peace in the age to come, and something more cruel than the other beasts is slain, love of this world. It is for love of this world, after all, that people slave away at all their affairs. But as for you, make sure you slave away at all your good works, not for love of this world but for the sake of the eternal rest that God promises you. Notice how you do each thing simultaneously. You touch the strings, and you kill the beasts. That is, you are both a guitarist and a hunter. Are you not delighted with such performances, where it is not the attention of the presidential box we attract but the attention and favor of the redeemer? Sermon 9.13.[1]

144:4 Our Days Are Like a Passing Shadow

God's Inscrutable Judgments in Light of Human Vanity. Augustine: Now if such cases[2] exhibited some consistency in their very irrationality, as we may call it, if, that is, in this life (in which as the sacred psalm says, "[a] man is like a mere nothing, and his days pass by like a shadow") only the wicked obtain the transitory goods of this world, and only the good suffered the transitory ills, this situation could be ascribed to the just, or even the benevolent, judgment of God. Thus those who were not to attain the eternal blessings that bring true happiness would be either deluded by temporal benefits in return for their wickedness or else, by God's mercy, would be consoled by them, while those who were not to suffer eternal torments would be either afflicted by temporal ills in retribution for whatever sins, however small, they had committed or would be trained by them to bring their virtue to perfection. But in fact, though there are good people in adversity and bad people in prosperity, which seems unjust, it remains true that, in general, bad people come to a bad end, and good people enjoy eventual success. And so the judgments of God become the more inscrutable and his ways the more untraceable.[3] City of God 20.2.[4]

144:5-7 O Lord, Rescue Me

God's Descent for Human Salvation. Eusebius of Caesarea: I consider this to be connected with my present subject.[5] For in his wonder at the knowledge of God the Word coming to people, the psalmist is astonished beyond measure at the love by which he descends from his divinity,

and lessens his natural majesty and reckons the human race worthy of bearing him. So here he prays, saying, "Lord, bow the heavens and descend." While in the seventeenth psalm [LXX] it is written, "And he bowed the heavens and descended, and it was dark under his feet. And he rode on cherubim and flew, he flew on the wings of the winds,"[6] wherein there is a prophecy of his ascension from earth to heaven. And when there is a fit opportunity I will show that we must understand the descent and ascension of God the Word not as of one moving locally, but in the metaphorical sense that Scripture intends in the use of such conventional terms. Proof of the Gospel 6.9.[7]

Christ Did Not Change His Nature Or Lessen His Divinity. Leo the Great: The psalmist is a witness of this matter[8] when he says, "All have gone astray together; they have become worthless."[9] And Christ's prophets, praying for help, said, "Lord, bow down your heavens and descend"; not that he might change the places in which all things are now located but that he might take on the flesh of human weakness for our salvation. Paul says the same thing: "How, being rich, he became poor for our sakes, that by his poverty we might become rich."[10] And he came to the earth and proceeded as a man from the virgin's womb, which he sanctified. Confirming by this process the interpretation of his name, Emmanuel, that is, "God with us," he began in a marvelous way to be what we are and did not cease to be what he was. He assumed our nature in such a way as not to lose what he himself was. Testimonia 19.[11]

God Reaches Down to Us in Mercy. Augustine: "But you sent down your help from above" and rescued my soul from the depths of this darkness because my mother, your faithful

---

[1]WSA 3 1:270-71*. [2]Augustine is discussing the diversity of human fortunes, that is, why the good seem to suffer and the wicked seem to prosper. [3]See Rom 11:33. [4]CG 897*. [5]Christ's incarnation. [6]Ps 18:9-10 (17:10-11 LXX). [7]POG 2:9*. [8]Christ's incarnation. [9]Rom 3:12; cf. Ps 14:3 (13:3 LXX, Vg.). [10]2 Cor 8:9. [11]FC 34:282-83**. Theophilus of Alexandria, in Jerome, *Epistola* 98.4 (CSEL 55:188).

servant, wept to you for me, shedding more tears for my spiritual death than other mothers shed for the bodily death of a son. For in her faith and in the spirit that she had from you she looked on me as dead. You heard her and did not despise the tears that streamed down and watered the earth in every place where she bowed her head in prayer. CONFESSIONS 3.11.[12]

144:9 *Singing a New Song to the Lord*

A HARP'S TEN STRINGS ARE THE TEN COM-MANDMENTS. AUGUSTINE: As it is written, "O God, I will sing you a new song, on a harp of ten strings I will play to you," we take the harp of ten strings to be the Ten Commandments of the law. Now to sing and play is usually the occupation of lovers. The old person, you see, is in fear; the young is in love. In this way also we distinguish the two testaments or covenants, the old and the new, that the apostle says are allegorically represented by the sons of Abraham, one born of the slave woman, the other of the free; "which," he says, "are two covenants."[13] Slavery, surely, goes with fear, freedom with love, seeing that the apostle says, "You have not received the spirit of slavery again in fear, but you have received the spirit of sonship by adoption, in which we cry out, Abba, Father."[14] And John says, "There is no fear in charity, but perfect charity throws out fear."[15] So it is charity that sings the new song.

True, that slavish fear embodied in the old person can indeed have the harp of ten strings, because that law of the Ten Commandments was also given to the Jews according to the flesh, but it cannot sing to its accompaniment the new song. It is under the law and cannot fulfill the law. It carries the instrument but does not manage to play it; it is burdened, not embellished, with the harp. But any under grace, not under law, they are the ones who fulfill the law, because for them it is not a weight to shoulder but an honor to wear; it is not a rack for their fears but a frame for their love. Fired by the spirit of love, they are already

singing the new song on the harp of ten strings. SERMON 33.1.[16]

144:11-15 *A Prayer for Temporal Blessings*

THE DUTIES OF THE RIGHT AND THE LEFT HANDS. AUGUSTINE: "Lord, deliver me from the hand of the sons of foreigners, whose mouth has spoken vanity, and their right hand is a right hand of iniquity." And he explains what kind of vanity he means, and what kind of right hand. What he calls the right hand of iniquity is the prosperity of this world. Not because it is never to be found with good people, but because when good people have it they hold it in the left hand, not in the right. They hold everlasting felicity in their right hand, temporal happiness they hold in their left. Greed for eternal things and eternal felicity ought not to be mixed with greed for temporal things, that is to say, for present and temporal felicity. And that is the meaning of "Do not let your left hand know what your right hand is doing."[17] So then, "their right hand is a right hand of iniquity." SERMON 32.22.[18]

A RIGHT RELATIONSHIP WITH GOD PRODUCES TRUE HAPPINESS. AUGUSTINE: Since we know that you are devoted to the public welfare, you must see how plainly the sacred writings show that the happiness of the state has no other source than the happiness of humankind. One of the sacred writers, filled with the Holy Spirit, speaks thus as he prays: "Rescue me out of the hand of strange children, whose mouth has spoken vanity, and their right hand is the right hand of iniquity; whose sons are as new plants in their youth; their daughters decked out, adorned round about after the similitude of a temple; their storehouse full, flowing out of this into that; their sheep fruitful in young, abounding in their goings forth; their oxen fat. There is no breach of wall nor passage nor crying out in their streets. They

---

[12]AC 68. [13]Gal 4:22-23. [14]Rom 8:15. [15]1 Jn 4:18. [16]*WSA* 3 2:154*. [17]Mt 6:3. [18]*WSA* 3 2:147*.

have called the people happy that have these things, but happy is the people whose God is the Lord."

You[19] see that a people is not called happy because of an accumulation of earthly good fortune, except by the "strange children," that is, by those who do not belong to the regeneration by which we become children of God. The psalmist prays to be rescued out of their hand, lest he be drawn by them into that false opinion and into their impious sins. Truly they speak vanity when they "have called the people happy that have these things"—the things that he had listed above, in which that good fortune consisted, the only good fortune that the lovers of this world seek. Therefore, "their right hand is the right hand of iniquity" because they have preferred those things that should have been set aside, as the right hand is preferred to the left. Happiness in life is not to be attributed to the possession of those things; they should be subordinate, not preeminent; they are intended to follow, not to lead. If, then, we were to speak to him who prayed thus and desired to be rescued from the "strange children" who "called that people happy that have these things," and if we said, "What is your own opinion? What people do you call happy?" he would not say, "Happy is the people whose strength is in their own mind." If he had said this, he would, it is true, distinguish that people from the former, which made happiness consist in that visible and corporeal good fortune, but he would not yet have passed beyond all the vanities and lying follies, for, as the same writings teach elsewhere, "Cursed be everyone that places his hope in humankind."[20] Therefore, he ought not to place it in himself, because he himself is a human being. Thus, in order to pass beyond the boundaries of all vanities and lying follies and to place happiness where it truly exists, he says: "Happy is the people whose God is the Lord." LETTER 155.[21]

THE NATURE OF TRUE HAPPINESS. AUGUSTINE: Now, you[22] know, I think, not only the

nature of your prayer but its object, and you have learned this not from me but from him who has deigned to teach us all. Happiness is what we must seek and what we must ask of the Lord God. Many arguments have been fashioned by many people about the nature of happiness, but why should we turn to the many people or the many arguments? Brief and true is the word in the Scripture of God: "Happy is the people whose God is the Lord." That we may belong to that people and that we may be able to attain to contemplation of him and to eternal life with him, "the end of the commandment is charity from a pure heart and a good conscience, and an unfeigned faith."[23] Among those same three, hope is put for a good conscience. "Faith therefore, and hope and charity,"[24] lead the praying soul to God, that is, the believing and hoping and desiring soul who attends to what he asks of the Lord in the Lord's Prayer. Fasting and abstinence from other pleasures of carnal desire—with due regard for our health—and especially almsgiving are great helps to prayer, so that we may be able to say: "In the day of my trouble I sought God with my hands lifted up to him in the night, and I was not deceived."[25] How is it possible to seek an incorporeal God who cannot be felt with the hands, unless he is sought by good works? LETTER 130.[26]

TRUE BLESSEDNESS COMES FROM FAITH IN GOD. CASSIODORUS: "Blessed is the one."[27] This is a most beautiful and apt beginning; since the Holy Spirit was to warn us of the weakness of the human race, he seems to have begun with blessedness so as to entice the minds of the fearful with this hope, so that mortals' frail hearts should not withdraw, for who is not fired to perform difficult tasks when contented blessedness is predicted? So he is called a blessed person, as our forebears' authority tells us, as being well-

---

[19]Macedonius, vicar of Africa, entrusted with the duty of enforcing imperial decrees against the Donatists. [20]Jer 17:5. [21]FC 20:310-11*. [22]Proba, a noble Roman lady and wife of Probus, praetorian prefect and former consul. [23]1 Tim 1:5. [24]1 Cor 13:13. [25]Ps 77:2 (76:3 LXX, Vg.). [26]FC 18:394-95*. [27]Ps 1:1.

suited to obtain all that he desires. But in Psalm 143 [LXX] the prophet reminds us that the adjective has two senses: "They have called the people blessed that have these things, but blessed is that people whose god is the Lord." So in the worldly sense the blessed person is one who thinks that he is supported by the greatest security and who continues in abiding joy and worldly abundance. But the psalmist splendidly appended *man* to the second sense of *blessed*, which is deterred from its

purpose by no opposition. *Vir* (man) derives from *vires*, (strength). In his endurance he admits of no failure, and in his prosperity of no proud self-inflation. Rather, he is immovable and steadfast in mind, strengthened by contemplation of heavenly things and abidingly fearless. EXPOSITIONS OF THE PSALMS 1.1.[28]

---

[28]ACW 51:47-48.

145:1-21 A HYMN OF PRAISE TO GOD

A Song of Praise. Of David.

[1]*I will extol thee, my God and King,*
and bless thy name for ever and ever.
[2]*Every day I will bless thee,*
and praise thy name for ever and ever.
[3]*Great is the LORD, and greatly to be praised,*
and his greatness is unsearchable.

[4]*One generation shall laud thy works to another,*
and shall declare thy mighty acts.
[5]*On the glorious splendor of thy majesty,*
and on thy wondrous works, I will meditate.
[6]*Men shall proclaim the might of thy terrible*
acts,
and I will declare thy greatness.
[7]*They shall pour forth the fame of thy*
abundant goodness,
and shall sing aloud of thy righteousness.

[8]*The LORD is gracious and merciful,*
slow to anger and abounding in steadfast
love.

[9]*The LORD is good to all,*
and his compassion is over all that he has
made.

[10]*All thy works shall give thanks to thee,*
O LORD,
and all thy saints shall bless thee!
[11]*They shall speak of the glory of thy kingdom,*
and tell of thy power,
[12]*to make known to the sons of men thy[b]*
mighty deeds,
and the glorious splendor of thy[b] kingdom.
[13]*Thy kingdom is an everlasting kingdom,*
and thy dominion endures throughout all
generations.

The LORD is faithful in all his words,
and gracious in all his deeds.[i]
[14]*The LORD upholds all who are falling,*
and raises up all who are bowed down.
[15]*The eyes of all look to thee,*
and thou givest them their food in due
season.

^{16}Thou openest thy hand,
   thou satisfiest the desire of every living
      thing.
^{17}The LORD is just in all his ways,
   and kind in all his doings.
^{18}The LORD is near to all who call upon him,
   to all who call upon him in truth.
^{19}He fulfils the desire of all who fear him,

   he also hears their cry, and saves them.
^{20}The LORD preserves all who love him;
   but all the wicked he will destroy.

^{21}My mouth will speak the praise of the LORD
   and let all flesh bless his holy name for ever
      and ever.

h Heb *his*   i These two lines are supplied by one Hebrew Ms, Gk and Syr

---

OVERVIEW: It is impossible for people to know and understand the essence and nature of God since God is incomprehensible and without any limitations (GREGORY OF NYSSA). Since God is beyond human comprehension, to use human generation as a pattern for understanding divine generation only leads to heresy (AMBROSE). Since people cannot praise God without first knowing him or they run the risk of praising a false god, God prompts people, who are part of creation, so that they can praise him (AUGUSTINE).

In difficult times we should take our concerns to God, who will answer them, since he inspired us to make the request (LEO). God instilled in all creatures a natural longing and love for him (AMBROSE). If a person claims to have been spiritually transformed in baptism, his person and life must bear the marks of a child of God (GREGORY OF NYSSA). Church membership is inconsistent with an evil life and is not sufficient for salvation if it is membership in name only (FULGENTIUS). People who pray to God in truth are those who believe in him, fear him and live lives consistent with their prayers (BEDE).

When we confess that Christ assumed a human body, we implicitly acknowledge that he also took a human soul (THEODORET).

145:3 God's Greatness Is Unsearchable

HUMBLED BY THE TRANSCENDENCE OF GOD.
GREGORY OF NYSSA: Now if any one should ask for some interpretation, description and expla-

nation of the divine essence, we are not going to deny that we are unlearned in this kind of wisdom, acknowledging only so much as this, that it is not possible that which is by nature infinite should be comprehended in any conception expressed by words. The fact that the divine greatness has no limit is proclaimed by prophecy, which declares expressly that of his splendor, his glory and his holiness, "there is no end." If his surroundings have no limit, much more is he himself in his essence, whatever it may be, comprehended by no limitation in any way. If then interpretation by way of words and names implies by its meaning some sort of comprehension of the subject, and if, on the other hand, that which is unlimited cannot be comprehended, no one could reasonably blame us for ignorance, if we are not bold in respect of what none should venture on. For by what name can I describe the incomprehensible? By what speech can I declare the unspeakable? Accordingly, since the Deity is too excellent and lofty to be expressed in words, we have learned to honor in silence what transcends speech and thought. If he who "thinks more highly than he ought to think"[1] tramples on this cautious speech of ours making a jest of our ignorance of things incomprehensible, and recognizes a difference of unlikeness in that which is without figure, or limit, or size or quantity (I mean in the Father, the Son and the Holy Spirit) and brings forward

---

[1]Rom 12:3.

to reproach our ignorance that phrase that is continually alleged by the disciples of deceit, " 'You worship you know not what,'[2] if you know not the essence of that which you worship," we shall follow the advice of the prophet. We shall not fear the reproach of fools[3] or be led by their reviling to talk boldly of things unspeakable. That unpracticed speaker Paul we make our teacher in the mysteries that transcend knowledge. He is so far from thinking that the divine nature is within the reach of human perception that he calls even the judgments of God "unsearchable" and his ways "past finding out."[4] He affirms that the things promised to them that love him, for their good deeds done in this life, are above comprehension so that it is not possible to behold them with the eye, or to receive them by hearing or to contain them in the heart.[5] AGAINST EUNOMIUS 3.5.[6]

THE INFINITE NATURE OF GOD IS INCOMPREHENSIBLE. GREGORY OF NYSSA: Instead of speaking of him [God the Father] as "ungenerated," it is permissible to call him the "First Cause" or "Father of the Only-Begotten," or to speak of him as "existing without cause," and many such expressions that lead to the same thought. In that case Eunomius[7] confirms our doctrines by the very arguments in which he brings charges that we do not know any name indicative of the divine nature. We are taught the fact of its existence, while we assert that a name of such breath as to include the unspeakable and infinite nature either does not exist at all or at any rate is unknown to us. Let him then abandon his usual fictive language, and show us the names that signify the real meanings and then proceed further to divide the subject by the divergence of their names. But as long as the statement of the Scripture is correct that Abraham and Moses were not capable of the knowledge of the name, and that "no one has seen God at any time,"[8] and that "no one has seen him, nor can see,"[9] and that the light around him is unapproachable and "there is no end of his great-

ness," so long can we say and believe these things. This is similar to an argument that promises any comprehension and expression of the infinite nature by means of the meaning of names to one who thinks that he can enclose the whole sea in his own hand! Just as the hollow of one's hand is comparable to the entire depth of the sea, so is all the power of language comparable to that nature that is unspeakable and incomprehensible. AGAINST EUNOMIUS 7.4.[10]

DIVINE GENERATION AND HUMAN GENERATION ARE TOTALLY DIFFERENT. AMBROSE: You cannot, then, heretic [Arian], build up a false doctrine on the basis of an analogy of human procreation.[11] Nor can you gather the means for such a purpose from our discussion, for we cannot embrace the greatness of infinite godhead, "of whose greatness there is no end,"[12] in our limited speech. If you should seek to give an account of a human's birth, you must certainly point to a time. But the divine generation is above all things. It reaches far and wide, and it rises high above all thought and feeling. For it is written, "No one comes to the Father, except by me."[13] Whatever, therefore, you conceive concerning the Father—yes, even his eternity—you cannot conceive anything concerning him except with the Son's aid nor can any understanding ascend to the Father except through the Son. "This is my dearly beloved Son,"[14] the Father said. "Is," please note, means that who he is, and what he is, is [true] forever. Hence David is also moved to say, "O Lord, your Word abides forever in heaven,"[15] for what abides fails neither in time nor in eternity. ON THE CHRISTIAN FAITH 1.10.63.[16]

---

[2]Jn 4:22. [3]See Is 51:7. [4]Rom 11:33. [5]See 1 Cor 2:9. [6]NPNF 2 5:146-47**. [7]A supporter of an extreme form of Arian subordinationism. [8]Jn 1:18. [9]1 Tim 6:16. [10]NPNF 2 5:198**. [11]The Arian heretics tried to explain the incarnation of Christ by comparing it with human generation and reasoned that if the Son was begotten of the Father, the Father had to exist prior to the Son and, therefore, the Son could not be eternal. [12]Ps 145:3 (144:3 LXX, Vg.). [13]Jn 14:6. [14]Mt 17:5; Mk 9:7; Lk 9:35. [15]Ps 119:89 (118:89 LXX, Vg.). [16]NPNF 2 10:211-12**.

PRAISE PRECEDES PETITION. AUGUSTINE:
"Can any praise be worthy of the Lord's majesty?"
"How magnificent his strength! How inscrutable
his wisdom!"[17] Humankind is one of your creatures, Lord, and his instinct is to praise you. He
bears about him the mark of death, the sign of his
own sin, to remind him that you "thwart the
proud."[18] But still, since he is a part of your creation, he wishes to praise you. The thought of
you stirs him so deeply that he cannot be content
unless he praises you, because you made us for
yourself and our hearts find no peace until they
rest in you.

Grant me, Lord, to know and understand
whether a person is first to pray to you for help or
to praise you and whether he must know you
before he can call you to his aid. If he does not
know you, how can he pray to you? For he may
call for some other help, mistaking it for yours.

Or are people to pray to you and learn to know
you through their prayers? "Only, how are they to
call on the Lord until they have learned to believe
in him? And how are they to believe in him without a preacher to listen to?"[19]

"Those who look for the Lord will cry out in
praise of him,"[20] because all who look for him
shall find him, and when they find him they will
praise him. I shall look for you, Lord, by praying
to you, and as I pray I shall believe in you,
because we have had preachers to tell us about
you. It is my faith that calls to you, Lord, the faith
that you gave me and made to live in me through
the merits of your Son, who became man, and
through the ministry of your preacher. CONFES-
SIONS 1.1.[21]

145:14-16 God Provides for His Creatures

LET THE CHAINS OF EVIL HABIT BE BROKEN.
LEO THE GREAT: Whoever finds the healing of
correction to be difficult should flee to the mercy
of God for help and beg that the chains of evil
habit be broken away from them, for "the Lord
lifts up all who collapse and raises up all who
have been broken down." No, the prayer of a

believer will not be empty, since our merciful
God "will accomplish the intentions of those who
fear him."[22] He will give what has been asked for,
since he provided the inspiration to ask it.
Through our Lord Jesus Christ, living and reign-
ing with the Father and the Holy Spirit forever
and ever. Amen. SERMON 36.4.2.[23]

ALL CREATURES TURN TO GOD BY NATURE.
AMBROSE: And the apostle [Paul] added, "For of
him, and through him and in him are all things."[24]
What does "of him" mean? It means that the
nature of everything exists according to his will
and that he is the creator of everything that has
come into existence. What does "through him"
mean? It means that the creation and preservation of all things is his gift. What does "in him"
mean? It means that all things by a wonderful
kind of longing and unspeakable love look on the
author of their life and the giver of their abilities
and functions according to that which is written: "The eyes of all look to you," and "You open
your hand and fill every living creature with your
good pleasure." ON THE HOLY SPIRIT 2.9.91.[25]

**THE CHILDREN OF GOD MANIFEST THEIR
RELATION TO GOD.** GREGORY OF NYSSA: A person, then, who remains the same and yet babbles
to himself about the change for the better he has
undergone in baptism should attend to what
Paul says: "If anyone thinks he is something
when he is nothing, he deceives himself."[26] For
you are not what you have not become; whereas
the gospel says of the regenerate that "he gave
all those who received him the power to become
God's children."[27] Now the child born of someone certainly shares his parent's nature. If, then,
you have received God and become his child, let
your way of life testify to the God within you;
make it clear who your Father is! The marks by
which we recognize God are the very ones by

---

[17]Ps 147:5 (146:5 LXX, Vg.). [18]1 Pet 5:5. [19]Rom 10:14. [20]Ps 22:26
(21:27 LXX, Vg.). [21]AC 21*. [22]Ps 145:19 (144:19 LXX, Vg.). [23]FC
93:158-59. [24]Rom 11:36. [25]NPNF 2 10:126**. [26]Gal 6:3. [27]Jn 1:12.

which a son of his must show his relation to him: "he opens his hand and fills everything living with joy"; "he overlooks iniquity";[28] "he relents of his evil purpose";[29] "the Lord is kind to all and is not angry with us every day";[30] "God is straightforward, and there is no unrighteousness in him"[31]—and the similar sayings scattered through Scripture for our instruction. If you are like this, you have genuinely become a child of God. But if you persist in displaying the marks of evil, it is useless to babble to yourself about the birth from above. Prophecy will tell you, "You are a son of humankind, not a son of the most High. You love vanity and seek lies. You fail to realize that the only way one is magnified is by becoming holy." ADDRESS ON RELIGIOUS INSTRUCTION 40.[32]

145:18-19 God Is Near to Those Who Call on Him in Truth

THOSE WHO BELIEVE IN GOD DO HIS WILL. FULGENTIUS OF RUSPE: If there are any who are even in the catholic church and live evil lives, before they finish this life, let them hasten to give up the evil life, and let them not think that the catholic [Christian] name is enough for salvation, if they do not do the will of God. For our Savior says, "not everyone who says to me, 'Lord, Lord' will enter the kingdom of heaven, but only the one who does the will of my Father in heaven."[33] In the book of Psalms as well, it is written that "the Lord is near to all who call on him, to all who call on him in truth. He fulfills the desire of all who fear him; he also hears their cry and saves them." Wherefore also in Proverbs each one of us is commanded both to fear the Lord and to depart from evil. There it is said, "fear the Lord and turn away from evil. It will be a healing for your flesh and a refreshment for your body."[34] ON THE FORGIVENESS OF SINS 1.26.2.[35]

GOD ANSWERS PRAYERS SPOKEN IN FAITH. BEDE: But we must look attentively at this—that

not everyone who seems to pray before other people is proven to ask or to seek or to knock at the entrance of the heavenly kingdom in the sight of the searcher of hearts. The prophet would not have said, "The Lord is near to all who call on him in truth," unless he recognized that there are some who call on the Lord, but not in truth. They do indeed call upon the Lord in truth who do not contradict in their lives what they say in their prayers. They call on the Lord in truth who, as they are about to offer their petitions, first busy themselves with carrying out his orders. Those who, as they are about to say to him in prayer, "And forgive us our debts, as we also forgive our debtors,"[36] have fulfilled that mandate of his that says, "And whenever you stand to pray, grant pardon if you have anything against anyone, so that your Father too, who is in heaven, may forgive you your sins."[37] Hence about such persons the prophet appropriately adds, "He will fulfill the will of those who fear him, and will hearken to their prayers and will save them." Accordingly, they call on the Lord in truth who are acknowledged to fear him. He listens to their prayers when they cry out [to him]; he grants their pious desires when they long for him; he raises them up to eternal salvation when they have passed from this life. HOMILIES ON THE GOSPELS 2.14.[38]

145:21 Let Everyone Bless God's Holy Name

WE PRAISE GOD WITH BODY AND SOUL. THEODORET OF CYR: We have confessed that God the Word took not a body only but also a soul. Why then did the divine Evangelist omit in this place[39] mention of the soul and mention the flesh only? Is it not clear that he mentioned the visible nature and intended to include the nature united to it? For the mention of the soul is understood of course in that of the flesh. For when we hear the

---

[28]Mic 7:18 (LXX). [29]Joel 2:14. [30]Ps 145:9 (144:9 LXX). [31]Ps 92:15 (91:16 LXX). [32]LCC 3:324-25*. [33]Mt 7:21. [34]Prov 3:7-8. [35]FC 95:143. [36]Mt 6:12. [37]Mk 11:25. [38]CS 111:126-27*. [39]Jn 1:14.

prophet saying, "Let all flesh bless his holy name," we do not understand the prophet to be exhorting bodies of flesh without souls but believe the whole to be summoned to give praise

in the summoning of a part. DIALOGUE 9.[40]

[40]NPNF 2 3:246**.

146:1-10 AN EXHORTATION TO TRUST IN THE LORD

[1]Praise the LORD!
Praise the LORD, O my soul!
[2]I will praise the LORD as long as I live;
  I will sing praises to my God while I have
    being.

[3]Put not your trust in princes,
  in a son of man, in whom there is no help.
[4]When his breath departs he returns to his
    earth;
  on that very day his plans perish.

[5]Happy is he whose help is the God of Jacob,
  whose hope is in the LORD his God,
[6]who made heaven and earth,
  the sea, and all that is in them;

who keeps faith for ever;
  [7]who executes justice for the oppressed;
  who gives food to the hungry.

The LORD sets the prisoners free;
  [8]the LORD opens the eyes of the blind.
The LORD lifts up those who are bowed down;
  the LORD loves the righteous.
[9]The LORD watches over the sojourners,
  he upholds the widow and the fatherless;
  but the way of the wicked he brings to ruin.

[10]The LORD will reign for ever,
  thy God, O Zion, to all generations.
Praise the LORD!

OVERVIEW: Praising God will not cease when we die; rather the next life will be characterized by our seeing, loving and praising God forever and ever (AUGUSTINE).

God brought to justice the enemies and persecutors of Christians and then brought about a reversal of fortune for Christians in the famous Edict of Milan (EUSEBIUS). When a Christian compares his lot with that of successful pagans, he wonders what the benefit of his faith is. The benefit is that he will live eternally, while the unbeliever will die eternally. Like Lazarus in the New Testament parable, whose name means "helped," God-fearing people will be helped by the true Savior to receive eternal life (AUGUSTINE). Although the word *spirit* has many uses, which must be correctly distinguished, the "spirit" that departs at death is the soul of a person (CYRIL OF JERUSALEM). No one should be so foolish and negligent of his soul's well-being as to believe that his existence ends at the time of his temporal death (AUGUSTINE). It is imperative that we never doubt that the triune God created all things (FULGENTIUS).

The church never stops praying for and having compassion on those who have lapsed from faith because, as long as they are alive, there is hope for their conversion (LEO). God promises kindness and help to those suffering calamity, and there are many examples that he keeps his promises when people often lose hope (GREGORY OF NAZIANZUS). All spiritual blessings come from God and are not the result of human effort (CASSIAN). God has promised to provide for children and wives when their father and husband has been taken from them (CHRYSOSTOM). Although it is natural to be saddened by the death of a loved one or the unfortunate condition of orphans and widows, we must trust in the unfailing providence of God, especially in the knowledge that eternal life awaits the faithful (THEODORET).

146:2 I Will Praise God As Long As I Live

WE WILL PRAISE GOD ALSO IN ETERNITY. AUGUSTINE: May the Lord grant me the ability to say something worthwhile to you about the words of this psalm that we have sung just now. What we said was, "I will praise the Lord all my life, I will play music to my God as long as I live." The first thing I would do regarding these words is warn you, dear friends, against assuming, when you hear or say "as long as I live I will play music to my God," that when this life comes to an end that is the end for us of God's praises. Not at all; we shall praise him then much more, when we are living without end. If we praise him during the exile we are passing through, how, do you think, shall we praise him at the home we are never going to leave? As it is said, read and sung in another psalm, "Blessed are those who dwell in your home; they shall praise you forever and ever."[1] Where you hear "forever and ever," there is no end. And living the blessed life in which God is to be perceived without any uncertainty, to be loved without any weariness, to be praised without end, why, yes indeed, that will be what our

being alive consists in—seeing, loving, praising God. SERMON 33A.1.[2]

146:3-6 Happy Is the Person Who Hopes in God

DO NOT PUT YOUR TRUST IN PEOPLE. EUSEBIUS OF CAESAREA: To these[3] were added the sons of Maximin,[4] with whom he had already shared imperial honors and whose features he had displayed publicly in portraits. Those who previously had boasted that they were related to the tyrant and tried to lord it over others endured the same sufferings and disgrace, for they did not accept correction or understand the precept in the sacred books:

> Put not your trust in princes,
> In the sons of men who cannot save.
> His breath shall depart and he shall return to
>   his earth.
> In that day all his thoughts shall perish.

When the impious were thus removed, the rule that belonged to them was preserved secure and undisputed for Constantine and Licinius[5] alone. They had made it their priority to purge the world of hostility to God, and, acknowledging the blessings he had conferred on them, they showed their love of virtue and of God, their devotion and gratitude to the Deity, through their edict[6] in behalf of the Christians. ECCLESIASTICAL HISTORY 9.11.[7]

DO NOT PUT YOUR TRUST IN PRINCES. AUGUSTINE: A Christian sees this, poor, proletarian, moaning and groaning at his daily drudgery,

---

[1] Ps 84:4 (83:5 LXX, Vg.). [2] WSA 3 2:160*. [3] Enemies of the Christian faith, such as Maximin and Theotecnus, who are mentioned in the previous paragraphs. [4] The Roman emperor in the East who died in 310. [5] Co-emperors in the western and eastern halves of the Roman empire, respectively, from 311 to 324. [6] The reference is to the famous Edict of Milan issued in 313 by co-emperors Constantine and Licinius, granting absolute religious freedom to people of all religious persuasions. [7] ECH 336-37.

and perhaps he says to himself, "What's the good of my having become a Christian? Has it made me any better off than that fellow who isn't, than that guy who doesn't believe in Christ, than that so-and-so who blasphemes my God?" That psalm warns him, "Do not put your trust in princes." Why do you take pleasure in the flower of the field? "All flesh is grass," says the prophet. He does not merely say it, he shouts it. The Lord shouts to him: "Shout," he says. And he answers, "What shall I shout? All flesh is grass, and all the honor of the flesh as the flower of the field. The grass has withered, the flower fallen." So has everything perished then? Heaven forbid! "But the word of the Lord abides forever."[8] Why take pleasure in grass? Look, the grass has perished. Do you want to avoid perishing? Hold fast to the Word.

So too in this psalm. Perhaps a poor, lowly Christian had his eyes fixed on a pagan, rich and powerful perhaps, had his eyes fixed on the flower of the field, and was perhaps halfway to choosing him for a patron rather than God. The psalm has a word for this person: "Do not put your trust in princes and in the sons of people, in whom there is no help." He immediately replies, "It cannot be speaking of this person, can it? He was very well off. Look how healthy he is. This very day I see him flourishing. It is me, rather, who am constantly and miserably ill." Why are you obsessed with these things as the only means of pleasure and satisfaction? That is not well-being. "His spirit will go out, and he will return to his earth." Sermon 33a.3.[9]

God Is Our Helper. Augustine: There can be no doubt, of course, that the poor man[10] being God-fearing, while trapped in his temporal miseries, was thinking how this life must end sometime and how eternal rest is to be gained. They both died, but that poor man's thoughts did not perish on that day. You see, it happened that the beggar died and was taken away by the angels to Abraham's bosom. On that day all his thoughts were healed. And because Lazarus translated into English[11] means "Helped"—if you are called Laz-

arus in Hebrew, you are called "Helped" in English[12]—this psalm has rightly advised us, "Blessed is he whose helper is the God of Jacob." When his spirit goes out and his flesh returns to its earth, his thoughts will not perish, because "his hope is in the Lord his God." This is the lesson learned in the school of Christ the teacher, this is what is hoped for by the heart of the faithful hearer, this is the reward of the only true savior."[13] Sermon 33a.4.[14]

Understanding the Word Spirit. Cyril of Jerusalem: There are many uses of the word *spirit* in general in the sacred Scriptures, and a person could easily become confused from ignorance, if he did not know to what sort of spirit the particular text refers. Therefore, we must be sure of the nature of the Holy Spirit according to Scripture. For example Aaron is called Christ (anointed), and David also, and Saul and others are called Christs, yet there is only one true Christ; similarly since the name of spirit has been given to many things, we must determine what in particular is called the Holy Spirit. Many things are called spirits; our soul is called spirit; this wind that is blowing is called spirit; great valor is called spirit; impure action is called spirit; and a hostile devil is called spirit. Take care, therefore, when you hear such things, not to mistake one for another because of the similarity of name. Scripture says of the soul, "When his spirit departs he returns to the earth"; and again of the soul, "Who forms the spirit of a person within him."[15] It says in the Psalms of the angels, "Who make your angels spirits";[16] it says of the wind: "With a vehement spirit you shall break in pieces the ships of Tharsis";[17] and "As the trees of the woods are moved with the spirit";[18] and "Fire, hail, snow, ice, spirit of storm."[19] Our Lord says of his blessed teaching: "The words that I

---

[8]Is 40:6-8. [9]*WSA* 3 2:162**. [10]See the parable of the rich man and Lazarus (Lk 16:19-31). [11]Augustine, of course, spoke in Latin. [12]Ibid. [13]Augustine's argument is that God/Christ is the true savior in whom we should put our trust, rather than in "princes" and wealthy pagan patrons. [14]*WSA* 3 2:164. [15]Zech 12:1. [16]Ps 104:4 (103:4 LXX). [17]Ps 48:7 (47:8 LXX). [18]Is 7:2. [19]Cf. Ps 148:8.

have spoken to you are spirit and life,"[20] that is, they are spiritual. The Holy Spirit is not an utterance of the tongue; he is living, granting wise speech, speaking and discoursing himself. CATECHETICAL LECTURES 16.13.[21]

BE CONCERNED ABOUT THE FUTURE OF YOUR SOUL. AUGUSTINE: "I am afraid," says the apostle, "that just as the serpent led Eve astray by his cunning, in the same way your minds too may be corrupted from the chastity that is in Christ."[22] Now the minds of these people are corrupted by that sort of conversation, "Let us eat and drink; for tomorrow we die."[23] Those who love these things, who pursue these things, who assume this is the only life there is, who hope for nothing further, who either do not pray to God or pray to him for this life alone, who find any talk of diligence very tedious, will be very downcast when they hear me saying all this. They want to eat and drink, for tomorrow they die. If only they would give genuine thought to the fact that they are going to die tomorrow! Can there be any, after all, so mindless, so perverse, so hostile to their own souls, that they do not reflect, when they are about to die the next day, on how everything they have worked for has come to an end? That, you see, is what is written: "On that day shall all his schemes come to nothing." SERMON 361.5.[24]

THE TRIUNE GOD CREATED HEAVEN AND EARTH. FULGENTIUS OF RUSPE: Hold most firmly and never doubt that the holy Trinity, the only true God, is the Creator of all things, visible and invisible—concerning which it is said in the psalms, "Happy are those whose help is the God of Jacob, whose hope is in the Lord their God who made heaven and earth, the sea and all that is in them." Concerning this the apostle too says, "For from him and through him and in him are all things. To him be glory forever."[25] To PETER ON THE FAITH 4.51.[26]

146:7-9 The Lord Helps Those Who Need Him

WE SHOULD NEVER DESPAIR OF ANYONE'S SALVATION WHILE THEY ARE ALIVE. LEO THE GREAT: We not only do not hold back, but even encourage, compassion, wisely and divinely set up by the church, that even for such people you should pray to the Lord with us. We also, with tears of sorrow, have pity on the downfall of misled souls. Following the example of the apostle's compassion, "we are made weak with the weak,"[27] and "we weep with those who weep."[28] We hope that the mercy of God may be gained with many tears and requisite satisfaction on the part of those who have lapsed. While we live in this body, no one's rehabilitation is to be despaired of. We should desire the amendment of all, with the Lord helping us, who "raises up those who have been broken down, sets captives free, gives sight to the blind," to whom is honor and glory "with the Father and with the Holy Spirit" forever and ever. Amen. SERMON 34.5.2.[29]

UNHOPED FOR RECOVERY FROM MISFORTUNE. GREGORY OF NAZIANZUS: She[30] owed her recovery to none other than to [God] with the result that people were no less impressed by her unexpected recovery than by her misfortune. They concluded that the tragedy had happened for her glorification through sufferings—the suffering being human, the recovery superhuman. This will provide a lesson for people in the future who exhibit a high degree of faith in the midst of suffering and patience in calamity, but in a still higher degree experience the kindness of God that she received. To God's beautiful promise to the righteous "though he fall, he shall not be utterly broken,"[31] has been added a more recent one, "though he be utterly broken, he shall speedily be raised up and glorified." For if her misfortune was unreasonable, her recovery was extraordinary, so that health soon replaced the

[20]Jn 6:63. [21]FC 64:83-84*. [22]2 Cor 11:3. [23]1 Cor 15:32. [24]*WSA* 3 10:227. [25]Rom 11:36. [26]FC 95:92. [27]See 2 Cor 11:29. [28]Rom 12:15. [29]FC 93:149. [30]His sister, Gorgonia. [31]Ps 37:24 (36:24 LXX).

injury, and the cure became more celebrated than the illness. ON HIS SISTER ST. GORGIANA, ORATION 8.15.[32]

GOD ALONE IS THE SOURCE OF ALL BLESSINGS. JOHN CASSIAN: For it is not free will but the Lord who "looses those who are bound." It is not our power but the Lord who "raises up the fallen." It is not the effort of our reading but the Lord who "enlightens the blind," since in Greek it is said: *kyrios sophoi typhlous*, which means that the Lord makes blind the wise. It is not our concern but the Lord who "cares for the stranger." It is not our strength but the Lord who "lifts up"—or "supports"—"all those who are falling."[33] CONFERENCES 3.15.3.[34]

CARE FOR THE FATHERLESS AND WIDOWS. CHRYSOSTOM: For as long as your blessed husband was with you,[35] you enjoyed honor and care and zealous attention. In fact you enjoyed such as you might expect to enjoy from a husband; but, since God took him to himself, [God] has taken his place with you. And this is not my saying but that of the blessed prophet David, for he says, "He will take up the fatherless and the widow,"[36] and elsewhere he calls him "father of the fatherless and judge of the widow." Thus in many passages you will see that he is earnestly concerned about the cause of this class of people. LETTER TO A YOUNG WIDOW 1.[37]

GOD IS THE GUARDIAN OF ORPHANS AND WIDOWS. THEODORET OF CYR: But what excuse for despondency will we have left if we take to heart God's own promises and the hopes of Christians: the resurrection, I mean, eternal life, continuance in the kingdom, and all that "eye has not seen, nor ear heard, neither have entered into the heart of people, the things that God has prepared for them that love him"?[38] Does not the apostle say emphatically, "I would not have you to be ignorant, brethren, concerning them which are asleep, that you sorrow not even as others which have no hope"?[39] I have known many people who even without hope have got the better of their grief by the strength of reason alone, and it would indeed be extraordinary if they who are supported by such a hope should prove weaker than they who have no hope at all. Let us then, I implore you,[40] look at the end as a long journey. When he went on a journey, we used indeed to be sorry, but we waited for his return. Now let the separation sadden us indeed in some degree, for I am not exhorting what is contrary to human nature, but do not let us wail as over a corpse; let us rather congratulate him on his setting forth and his departure hence, because he is now free from a world of uncertainties and fears no further change of soul or body or of corporeal conditions. The strife now ended, he waits for his reward. Do not grieve too much for orphans and widows. We have a greater Guardian whose law it is that all should take good care of orphans and widows and about whom the divine David says, "The Lord relieves the fatherless and widow, but the way of the wicked he turns upside down." Only let us put the rudders of our lives in his hands, and we shall meet with an unfailing providence. His guardianship will be surer than can be that of any man, for his are the words "Can a woman forget her sucking child that she should not have compassion on the son of her womb? Yet will I not forget you."[41] He is nearer to us than father and mother for he is our Maker and Creator. It is not marriage that makes fathers, but fathers are made fathers at his will. LETTER 14.[42]

---

[32]NPNF 2 7:242-43**. [33]Ps 145:14 (144:14 LXX). [34]ACW 57:134. [35]An unnamed widow. [36]Ps 146:9 (145:9 LXX). [37]NPNF 1 9:121-22**. [38]1 Cor 2:9. [39]1 Thess 4:13. [40]Alexandra, to whom the letter is addressed. [41]Is 49:15. [42]NPNF 2 3:254-55*.

147:1-20 PRAISE OF GOD, THE CREATOR

¹Praise the LORD!
For it is good to sing praises to our God;
   for he is gracious, and a song of praise is
    seemly.
²The LORD builds up Jerusalem;
   he gathers the outcasts of Israel.
³He heals the brokenhearted,
   and binds up their wounds.
⁴He determines the number of the stars,
   he gives to all of them their names.
⁵Great is our LORD, and abundant in power;
   his understanding is beyond measure.
⁶The LORD lifts up the downtrodden,
   he casts the wicked to the ground.

⁷Sing to the LORD with thanksgiving;
   make melody to our God upon the lyre!
⁸He covers the heavens with clouds,
   he prepares rain for the earth,
   he makes grass grow upon the hills.
⁹He gives to the beasts their food,
   and to the young ravens which cry.
¹⁰His delight is not in the strength of the horse,
   nor his pleasure in the legs of a man;

¹¹but the LORD takes pleasure in those who
   fear him,
   in those who hope in his steadfast love.

¹²Praise the LORD, O Jerusalem!
   Praise your God, O Zion!
¹³For he strengthens the bars of your gates;
   he blesses your sons within you.
¹⁴He makes peace in your borders;
   he fills you with the finest of the wheat.
¹⁵He sends forth his command to the earth;
   his word runs swiftly.
¹⁶He gives snow like wool;
   he scatters hoarfrost like ashes.
¹⁷He casts forth his ice like morsels;
   who can stand before his cold?
¹⁸He sends forth his word, and melts them;
   he makes his wind blow, and the waters
    flow.
¹⁹He declares his word to Jacob,
   his statutes and ordinances to Israel.
²⁰He has not dealt thus with any other nation;
   they do not know his ordinances.
Praise the LORD!

OVERVIEW: Much like a medical doctor, God binds up the battered hearts of the penitent with the bandages of his love in order to restore them to their original condition (CASSIODORUS). People can learn about the power of God from the numberless stars and raindrops, as well as other celestial bodies that God made (CYRIL OF JERUSALEM).

Scripture frequently uses synecdoche, a figure of speech in which reference to a part is understood as reference to the whole—thus a reference to a raven implies the entire avian kingdom (GREGORY OF NAZIANZUS). Not only did God work six days in creating the world, but he works continuously, even on the sabbath, in the providential care of his creation (BEDE).

All the pains and problems of this world will come to an end; then the gates of heaven will be closed, and not one will be able to enter or leave (AUGUSTINE). The phenomenal spread of Christianity throughout the world was predicted in the Psalms (EUSEBIUS).

147:2-3 God Heals the Brokenhearted

THE HEAVENLY PHYSICIAN HEALS CONTRITE HEARTS. CASSIODORUS: "Who heals the contrite of heart, who binds up their wounds." A wonderful mode of healing is announced, so that if we wish to be restored we must make ourselves contrite in a most vigorous way. This contrition, however, is aimed at renewal and leads to full recovery; what transcends every blessing, it admits the Physician who grants eternal health. Next comes, "Who binds up their bruises." The metaphor is adopted from those skilled in techniques of healing, who bind broken and bruised bones with linen bandages when they wish to restore them, so that limbs can return to their original positions and fuse into their previous solidity. In the same way the heavenly Physician treats the hearts of penitents when they are battered with heavy affliction. He binds and strengthens them by wrapping them, so to say, with the bandage of his devoted love and impels them to the strongest hope of recovery. As was said in Psalm 50 (LXX): "A contrite and humble heart God does not despise."[1] The tax collector who smote his breast with continual beating was seen to have imposed on himself the contrition that he unceasingly inflicted on his guilty breast. EXPOSITIONS OF THE PSALMS 146.3.[2]

147:4-5 God's Infinite Power and Wisdom

THE POWER OF GOD IS BEYOND HUMAN RECOGNITION. CYRIL OF JERUSALEM: If anyone undertakes to speak of the attributes of God, let him first describe the bounds of the earth. Though you dwell on the earth, you do not know the limit of your dwelling place; how then will you be able to form a worthy concept of its Creator? You see the stars, but their Maker you do not see; first, number the stars, which are seen, and then set forth him who is not seen; "He tells the number of the stars; he calls each by name."[3] The recent violent rains all but destroyed us;

number the drops of rain in this city alone; rather, not in the city, but number the drops that fell on your own house in a single hour, if you can. But since you cannot, you acknowledge your own weakness. From this learn the power of God. For "he has numbered the raindrops"[4] poured down on the whole earth, not only now but through all time. The sun is a work of God, great indeed, but very small compared with the whole heavens. Fix your attention on the sun first, and then inquire assiduously about its Lord. "What is too sublime for you seek not; into things beyond your strength search not. What is committed to you, O attend to."[5] CATECHETICAL LECTURES 6.4.[6]

147:8 God Provides for His Creation

RAVENS REPRESENT ALL BIRDS. GREGORY OF NAZIANZUS: They[7] must suppose that our ancestors went down into Egypt without bodies and invisible and that only the soul of Joseph was imprisoned by Pharaoh, because it is written, "They went down into Egypt with threescore and fifteen souls,"[8] and "The iron entered into his soul,"[9] a thing that could not be bound. They who argue thus do not know that such expressions are used by synecdoche, declaring the whole by the part, as when Scripture says that the young ravens call on God,[10] to indicate the whole feathered race; or Pleiades, Hesperus and Arcturus[11] are mentioned, instead of all the stars and his providence over them. LETTER 101.[12]

GOD'S PROVIDENCE IS DAILY AND CONTINUOUS. BEDE: That you may be aware that God the Father worked not only on those first six days but "even until now," read the [saying] of the prophet, "Before I formed you in the womb, I knew you";[13] and in the psalm, "He who shaped the hearts of

---

[1]Ps 51:17 (50:19 LXX, Vg.). [2]ACW 53: 439-40*. [3]Ps 147:4 (146:4 LXX). [4]Job 36:27 (LXX). [5]Sir 3:20-21. [6]FC 61:150. [7]People who held the view of Apollinarius, who taught that the incarnate Christ did not have a rational human soul. [8]Acts 7:14. [9]Ps 105:18 (104:18 LXX). [10]Ps 147:9 (146:9 LXX). [11]Job 9:9. [12]NPNF 2 7:442*. [13]Jer 1:5.

every one of them";[14] and elsewhere, "Who covers the heavens with clouds and prepares rain for the earth, who produces hay on the mountains,"[15] and other things of this sort. We must indeed note that [the psalmist] did not put the verb in the past tense, saying, "who covered and prepared and produced," but in the present, "he covers, prepares, produces" in order to demonstrate that the Father works every day, no less on the sabbath than on other days. So that you may not doubt that the Son works all things equally, recall that [saying] of the psalmist: "He spoke, and flies and gnats came; he spoke, and the locust and the grasshopper came; he spoke, and there stood forth the wind of a storm."[16] HOMILIES ON THE GOSPELS 1.23.[17]

147:12-15 God Provides Safety and Peace for His People

OUR REAL SECURITY WILL BE WITH GOD IN HEAVEN. AUGUSTINE: Because whatever pains and difficulties we may have endured in this world, everything that comes to an end is in fact nothing. Good things are coming that will not come to an end; it is through toils and troubles that we come to them. But when we get there, no one can tear us away from them. The gates of

Jerusalem are closed, their bars are also put in place, so that it may be said to that city, "Praise the Lord, Jerusalem; Zion, praise your God, because he has strengthened the bars of your gates, he has blessed your children within you, he has made peace in your borders." The gates being shut, the bars bolted home, no friend can go out, no enemy come in. There we are to enjoy true and real security, if here we have not let go of true reality. SERMON 130.5.[18]

GOD SENDS HIS WORD TO EARTH. EUSEBIUS OF CAESAREA: "He that sends his word on earth, until his word runs swiftly." He that sends is evidently distinct from him that is sent. You have then, here, both the Sender, the almighty God, and also the Word that was sent, who having many names is called by the holy oracles now Wisdom, now Word, now God, and also Lord. And as you know how in a very short time the word of his teaching has filled the whole world, I am sure you will wonder at the fulfillment of the prophecy, "Till his word runs swiftly." PROOF OF THE GOSPEL 6.10.[19]

---

[14]Ps 33:15 (32:15 LXX, Vg.). [15]Ps 147:8 (146:8 LXX, Vg.). [16]Ps 105:31, 34 (104:31, 34 LXX, Vg.). [17]CS 110:231. [18]WSA 3 4:314. [19]POG 2:10*.

148:1-14 A CALL TO PRAISE GOD

[1]Praise the LORD!
Praise the LORD from the heavens,
　praise him in the heights!
[2]Praise him, all his angels,
　praise him, all his host!

[3]Praise him, sun and moon,

　praise him, all you shining stars!
[4]Praise him, you highest heavens,
　and you waters above the heavens!

[5]Let them praise the name of the LORD!
　For he commanded and they were created.
[6]And he established them for ever and ever;

he fixed their bounds which cannot be
  passed.[j]

[7]Praise the LORD from the earth,
  you sea monsters and all deeps,
[8]fire and hail, snow and frost,
  stormy wind fulfilling his command!

[9]Mountains and all hills,
  fruit trees and all cedars!
[10]Beasts and all cattle,
  creeping things and flying birds!

[11]Kings of the earth and all peoples,
  princes and all rulers of the earth!
[12]Young men and maidens together,
  old men and children!

[13]Let them praise the name of the LORD,
  for his name alone is exalted;
  his glory is above earth and heaven.
[14]He has raised up a horn for his people,
  praise for all his saints,
  for the people of Israel who are near to him.
Praise the LORD!

---

j Or he set a law which cannot pass away

OVERVIEW: The creation of the angels is amply attested in Scripture, although not explicitly mentioned in the Genesis account of creation; the psalmist attests to their existence by referring to their praise of God (AUGUSTINE). We cannot learn anything about God's substance or nature, but the Scriptures do teach us the necessity of praising God (CHRYSOSTOM). All God's creatures, angels and human beings, must sing hymns of praise to God (PRUDENTIUS). Scripture teaches us that there are ranks among the angels but says nothing more specific on the subject. Scripture, in different places, testifies to the two societies of angels, the good and evil, and informs us of some of the differences in their character (AUGUSTINE). Between God and the physical world there exists a category of beings whom Scripture describes as "heaven of heavens" and "waters above the heavens"—these are known as angels.

God the Father, who is the uncreated God, commanded his Son, the firstborn of all creation, to create the world (ORIGEN). Since the divine mysteries are beyond human comprehension, the Holy Spirit describes creation and the generation of the Son in language that is familiar to us (GREGORY OF NYSSA). God, who created the material universe in an instant with a word, can just as easily bring the dead to life again. God, who created the universe with a word, did not need any human assistance (AMBROSE). People who claim that the Father is greater than the Son on the basis of the Genesis account of creation are wrong (JEROME). God definitely created the angels, but they were not created first. If God can make a universe, he can just as easily perform lesser tasks, such as, enabling old people to have a child. God did not beget the world or compose it out of things already in existence, but he made it by his Word, out of nothing (AUGUSTINE).

148:1-2 Let the Heavenly Hosts Praise God

THE ANGELS TOO PRAISE GOD. AUGUSTINE: Now although the fact that angels are a work of God is not passed over in this narrative,[1] it is not explicitly stated, but in other places the holy Scripture testifies to the fact with the utmost clarity. For the hymn of the three men in the furnace starts with the words, "Bless the Lord, all you works of the Lord";[2] and in the enumeration

---

[1]Gen 1. [2]Dan 3:57 (LXX, Vg.) = Prayer of Azariah 1:35.

of his works the angels are included. And in one of the psalms there are these verses: "Praise the Lord from the heavens, praise him in the heights. Praise him, all his angels: praise him, all his powers. Praise him, sun and moon: praise him, all stars and light. Praise him heaven of heavens; and the waters that are above the heavens, let them praise the Lord. For he spoke, and things were made; he gave the command, and they were created."[3] CITY OF GOD 11.9.[4]

THE ROLE OF THE ANGELS IS TO PRAISE GOD. CHRYSOSTOM: However, what God actually is, not only have the prophets not seen, but not even angels or archangels. If you ask them, you will not hear them reply anything about his substance, but only singing, "Glory to God in the highest and peace on earth among people of good will."[5] If you desire to learn something even from the cherubim or seraphim, you will hear the mystical melody of his holiness and that "heaven and earth are full of his glory."[6] If you inquire of the higher powers, you will discover nothing else than that their one work is to praise God, for, "Praise him, all his powers," the psalmist said. HOMILIES ON THE GOSPEL OF JOHN 15.[7]

LET THE ANGELS PRAISE GOD. PRUDENTIUS:
Sing his praises heights of heaven,
    all you angels sing his praise,
Let the mighty hosts of heaven sing in
    joyous praise of God;
Let no tongue of humanity be silent,
    let all voices join the hymn.
HYMNS FOR EVERY DAY 22-24.[8]

IGNORANCE REGARDING DISTINCTION IN THE RANKS OF ANGELS. AUGUSTINE: Now, how that celestial and most blessed company[9] is constituted, how the various ranks differ one from the other, so that, while all the citizens share the general name of angel (as we read in the epistle to the Hebrews: "Now to which of the angels has he ever said:, 'Sit at my right hand'?,"[10] which shows that all are together called angels), still, there are

archangels among them; and whether it is these same archangels who are called hosts, and the passage, "Praise him, all you his angels: praise him, all you his hosts" is to mean "Praise him, all you his angels: praise him, all you his archangels"; and what distinction there is among the four names under which the apostle seems to embrace the whole celestial company: "Whether thrones, or dominations, or principalities or powers"—to these questions let those reply who can, if, that is, they can prove their answers true. I acknowledge my own ignorance of these things. I am not even certain on this point, whether the sun and the moon and the other stars belong to this same company, though some believe these to be merely luminous bodies, without either sensation or intelligence. ENCHIRIDION 15.58.[11]

THE DIFFERENCE BETWEEN GOOD AND EVIL ANGELS. AUGUSTINE: But for the reasons stated, we think that the two companies of angels are also meant by the terms "Light" and "Darkness." One of these companies enjoys God, the other swells with pride; to one is said, "Adore him, all you angels of his"; while the chief of the other company says, "I will give you all these things, if you bow down and worship me."[12] The one company burns with holy love of God; the other smolders with the foul desire for its own exaltation; and since "God resists the proud, while he gives his favor to the humble,"[13] the one dwells in the heaven of heavens, the other is cast down in confusion to inhabit this air, the lowest region of the sky. The one enjoys tranquility in the bright radiance of devotion; the other rages in the dark shows of desire. The one brings merciful aid, or just punishment, in obedience to God's bidding; the other seethes with the lust to subdue and to injure, at the behest of its own arrogance. The one serves the good purposes of God, striving to give full effect to the desire to help; the other is

---

[3]Ps 148:1-5. [4]CG 439. [5]Lk 2:14. [6]Is 6:3. [7]FC 33:143*. [8]FC 43:61. [9]The church universal in heaven and on earth. [10]Heb 1:13. [11]FC 2:418-19*. [12]Mt 4:9. [13]Jas 4:6; 1 Pet 5:5.

restrained by God's power, to prevent their fulfilling the desire to harm. The good angels hold the others in derision, because by their persecutions they unwillingly benefit the faithful; the evil angels envy the good, as they gather the pilgrims into their fellowship. CITY OF GOD 11.33.[14]

148:4 The Highest Heaven

ANGELS ARE INTERMEDIATE SPIRITUAL BEINGS. ORIGEN: The Persians therefore may call the "whole circle of heaven" Jupiter; but we maintain that "the heaven" is neither Jupiter nor God, as we indeed know that certain beings of a class inferior to God have ascended above the heavens and all visible nature: and in this sense we understand the words, "Praise God, you heaven of heavens, and you waters that are above the heavens; let them praise the name of the Lord."[15] AGAINST CELSUS 5.44.[16]

148:5 God Creates the World by a Mere Command

THE UNCREATED GOD AND THE FIRSTBORN OF ALL CREATION. ORIGEN: This is not the time to prove that the Creator did not become the servant of the Word and make the world and to show that the Word became the servant of the creator and prepared the world. For according to the prophet David, "God spoke, and they were made; he commanded, and they were created."[17] For the uncreated God "commanded" the firstborn of all creation,[18] and "they were created." This includes not only the cosmos and the things in it, but also all that remains, "whether thrones, or dominations, or principalities or powers; for all things have been created through him and for him, and he is before all things."[19] COMMENTARY ON THE GOSPEL OF JOHN 2.104.[20]

GOD REVEALS DIVINE MYSTERIES IN HUMAN TERMS. GREGORY OF NYSSA: And now that we have thus distinguished the various modes of generation, it will be time to observe how the benevolent provision of the Holy Spirit, in delivering to us the divine mysteries, imparts that instruction that transcends reason by such methods as we can receive. For the inspired teaching adopts, in order to set forth the unspeakable power of God, all the forms of generation that human intelligence recognizes, yet without including the bodily senses attaching to the words. For when it speaks of the creative power, it gives to such an energy the name of generation, because its expression must stoop to our level of understanding. It does not, however, convey thereby all that we include in creative generation, as time, place, the furnishing of matter, the fitness of instruments, the design in the things that come into being. It leaves these and asserts of God in lofty and magnificent language the creation of all existent things, when it says, "He spoke the word, and they were made, He commanded, and they were created." Again when it interprets to us the unspeakable and transcendent existence of the Only-Begotten from the Father, as the poverty of human intellect is incapable of receiving doctrines that surpass all power of speech and thought, there too it borrows our language and terms him "Son," a name that our usage assigns to those who are born of matter and nature. AGAINST EUNOMIUS 2.9.[21]

THE POWER TO RECREATE THE WORLD. AMBROSE: The causes of the beginnings of all things are seeds. And the apostle of the Gentiles has said that the human body is a seed.[22] And so in succession after sowing there is the substance that is needed for the resurrection. But even if there were no substance and no cause, who could think it difficult for God to create people anew whence he will and as he wills. Who commanded the world to come into being out of no matter and no substance? Look at the heaven, behold the earth. Whence are the fires of the stars? Whence the orb and rays of the sun? Whence the globe of

---

[14]CG 468-69. [15]Ps 148:4-5. [16]ANCL 23:314-15. [17]Ps 148:5. [18]Col 1:15. [19]Col 1:16-17. [20]FC 80:121. [21]NPNF 2 5:114*. [22]1 Cor 15:43.

the moon? Whence the mountain heights, the hard rocks, the woody groves? Whence are the air diffused around, and the waters, whether enclosed or poured abroad? But if God made all these things out of nothing (for "he spoke, and they were made; he commanded, and they were created"), why should we wonder that which has been should be brought to life again, since we see produced that which had not been? ON HIS BROTHER SATYRUS 2.64.[23]

GOD CREATED THE WORLD EASILY AND QUICKLY WITH WORDS. AMBROSE: God has no need of human assistance. God commanded the heavens to come into existence, and it was done. He decided to create the earth, and it was created.[24] Who carried the stones on his shoulders? Who paid the cost? Who helped him with the work? These things were done in a moment. Do you want to know how quickly? "He spoke, and they were made." If the material universe sprang into being at a word, why should not the dead also rise again at a word? ON HIS BROTHER SATYRUS 2.85.[25]

THE FALSE REASONING OF HERETICS. JEROME: "For he spoke, and they were made." For God to have commanded is to have created; the command is creation. He spoke, and they were made, according to that which is written in Genesis: God said, and God created; that is, God the Father gave the command; God the Son created. Someone may say, He is the greater who gives the command, and he is the less to whom it is given. That is what the Arians,[26] the Eunomians[27] and the Macedonians[28] maintain. I answer you, O heretics, in accordance with your own reasoning. You say, the Father is greater because he gives the command, and the Son is less because he is commanded by the Father. If this is in accord with human understanding, answer me: Is it greater to command or to create? I say, "Let a house be made," and another builds the house. There is nothing great in uttering the words; it is difficult to build the house. He is greater, therefore, who

creates than he who gives the command. But that is impious irreverence, for the Son is not greater than the Father. It is just as blasphemous to believe this of the Son against the Father as it is to believe it of the Father against the Son. "For he spoke, and they were made; he commanded, and they were created." One nature both commands and creates; God gives the order, God fulfills it. A painter bids a painter paint, and the painter paints what he has bid be painted. HOMILIES ON THE PSALMS 58.[29]

THE CREATION OF ANGELS. AUGUSTINE: Did it [Gen 1:1] say, "In the beginning," because it was made first? Or was it impossible for heaven and earth to have been made first among the creatures, if the angels and all the intellectual powers were made first? We must believe that the angels are the creation of God and were made by him. For the prophet included the angels in Psalm 148, when he said, "He commanded, and they were made; he gave the order, and they were created." But if the angels were made first, we can ask whether they were made in time or before all time or at the start of time. If [they were made] in time, there already was time before the angels were made, and since time itself is also a creature, it turns out that we have to admit that something was made before the angels. But if we say that they were made at the start of time, so that time began with them, we have to say that it is false that time began with heaven and earth, as some claim.[30] ON THE LITERAL INTERPRETATION OF GENESIS 3.7.[31]

GOD IS CAPABLE OF BOTH DIFFICULT AND EASY TASKS. AUGUSTINE: After all, what is beyond hoping for from God, to whom nothing is difficult? He does great things just as he does

---

[23]NPNF 2 10:184. [24]See Gen 1:6-8. [25]FC 22:234. [26]Heretics who taught the subordination of the Son to the Father. [27]Extreme Arian heretics. [28]Heretics who applied the Arian subordination also to the Holy Spirit. [29]FC 48:418-19*. [30]Augustine does not identify the exegete to whom he refers, but his position seems similar to that of Origen. [31]FC 84:148-49.

small ones; he raises the dead, just as he creates the living. If a painter can make a mouse with the same art as he makes an elephant—different subjects, one and the same art—how much more God, who "spoke and they were made, commanded and they were created"? What can be difficult for him to make who makes with a word? He created the angels above the heavens with ease, with equal ease the luminaries in the heavens, with equal ease the fishes in the sea, with equal ease the trees and animals on the earth, great things with the same ease as small. It was supremely easy for him to make everything out of nothing—is it astonishing that he gave some old people a son?[32] SERMON 2.7.[33]

GOD CREATED ALL THINGS OUT OF NOTH-ING. AUGUSTINE: All things that God did not beget of himself but made through his Word, he made not out of things that already existed but out of what did not exist at all, that is, out of nothing. Thus the apostle says, "Who calls those things that are not as though they were."[34] But it is written more clearly in the book of the Maccabees. "I beseech you, my child, lift your eyes to the heaven and the earth and all that are therein. See and know that God did not make those things out of anything that already existed."[35] There is also what is written in the Psalms. "He spoke, and they were made." Clearly he did not beget these things of himself but made them by his Word and command. What he did not beget he made of nothing; for there was nothing else out of which he might have made them. Of him the apostle says most openly, "Since of him and through him and in him are all things."[36] ON THE NATURE OF THE GOOD 26.[37]

148:7-12 Let All the Elements of Creation Praise the Lord

THE HEAVENS ARE NOT ANIMATE, EVEN THOUGH THEY PRAISE GOD. BASIL THE GREAT: And, even if the waters above the heavens are sometimes invited to praise the common Mas-

ter of the universe, yet we do not for this reason consider them to be an intellectual nature. The heavens are not endowed with life because they "show forth the glory of God,"[38] nor is the firmament a perceptive being because it "declares the work of his hands." And, if someone says that the heavens are speculative powers, and the firmament, active powers productive of the good, we accept the expression as neatly said, but we will not concede that it is altogether true. For, in that case, dew, hoarfrost, cold and heat, since they were ordered by Daniel[39] to praise in hymns the Creator of the universe, will be intelligent and invisible natures. The meaning in these words, however, accepted by speculative minds, is a fulfillment of the praise of the Creator. Not only the water that is above the heavens, as if holding the first place in honor because of the preeminence added to it from its excellence, fulfills the praise of God, but, "Praise him," the psalmist says, "from the earth, you dragons and all you deeps." So that even the deep, which those who speak allegories relegated to the inferior portion, was not itself judged deserving of rejection by the psalmist, since it was admitted to the general chorus of creation; but even it harmoniously sings a hymn of praise to the Creator through the language assigned to it. HOMILIES ON THE HEXAEMERON 3.9.[40]

EVERYTHING HAPPENS BY DIVINE PROVIDENCE. AUGUSTINE: There follows the seventh commandment: "You shall not steal,"[41] and the seventh plague: hail on the crops. What you steal from the commandment, you lose from your account in heaven. No one makes an unjust gain without suffering a just loss. For example, someone steals and acquires a suit, but by the judgment of heaven he forfeits trust. Where there is gain, there is loss; visible gain, invisible loss; gain from his own blindness, loss from the Lord's

---

[32]Such as Abraham and Sarah in the Old Testament and Zechariah and Elizabeth in the New Testament. [33]WSA 3 1:179-80. [34]Rom. 4:17. [35]2 Macc 7:28. [36]Rom 11:36. [37]LCC 6:334-35*. [38]See Ps 18:2 (17:3 LXX). [39]See Dan 3:64-70 (LXX) = Prayer of Azariah 1:42-46. [40]FC 46:52-53*. [41]Ex 20:15.

cloud. You see, dearly beloved, there is nothing that escapes providence. Or do you really think that what people suffer, they suffer while God is asleep? We see these things happening all the time and all around; clouds gather, rain comes down in buckets, hail is hurled down, the earth shaken by thunder, scared out of its wits by lightning. Everywhere these things are thought to happen as though they had nothing to do with divine providence. Against such ideas that psalm is on its guard: "Praise the Lord from the earth"—his praises had already been told from the heavens—"dragons and all deeps, fire, hail, snow, ice, stormy winds, which all carry out his word." So those who for their own evil desire steal outwardly are hailed on inwardly by the judgment of God. SERMON 8.10.[42]

WE SHOULD PRAISE GOD FOR ALL THINGS AND OCCURRENCES IN NATURE. AUGUSTINE:

For you [God] evil does not exist, and not only for you but for the whole of your creation as well, because there is nothing outside it that could invade it and break down the order that you have imposed on it. Yet in the separate parts of your creation there are some things that we think of as evil because they are at variance with other things. But there are other things again with which they are in accord, and then they are good. In themselves, too, they are good. And all these things that are at variance with one another are in accord with the lower part of creation that we call the earth. The sky, which is cloudy and windy, suits the earth to which it belongs. So it would be wrong for me to wish that these earthly things did not exist, for even if I saw nothing but them, I might wish for something better, but still I ought to praise you for them alone. For all things "give praise to the Lord on earth, monsters of the sea and all its depths; fire and hail, snow and mist, and the storm-wind that executes his decree; all you mountains and hills, all you fruit trees and cedars; all you wild beasts and cattle, creeping things and birds that fly in air; all you kings and peoples of the world, all you that are princes and judges on earth; young men and maids, old men and boys together; let them all give praise to the Lord's name." The heavens, too, ring with your praises, O God, for you are the God of us all. "Give praise to the Lord in heaven; praise him, all that dwells on high. Praise him, all you angels of his, praise him, all his armies. Praise him, sun and moon; praise him, every star that shines. Praise him, you highest heavens, you waters beyond the heavens. Let all these praise the Lord."[43] And since this is so, I no longer wished for a better world, because I was thinking of the whole of creation, and in the light of this clearer discernment I had come to see that though the higher things are better than the lower, the sum of all creation is better than the higher things alone. CONFESSIONS 7.13.[44]

NOTHING HAPPENS SOLELY BY CHANCE OR NATURAL CAUSATION. AUGUSTINE: I am, there-

fore, leaving out those things that are done corporeally in a quite ordinary period of time, such as the rising and the setting of the stars, the births and the deaths of animals, the innumerable diversities of seeds and buds, the mists and the clouds, the snows and the rain, the lightnings and the thunders, the thunderbolts and the hails, the winds and the fires, the cold and the heat, and all such things. Nor am I taking into account the things that rarely happen in the same order, such as the eclipses of the heavenly bodies, the appearances of unusual stars, monsters, earthquakes, and similar things. I am considering none of these things, for their first and highest cause is nothing else than the will of God. Hence, when certain things of this kind are also mentioned in the psalm, such as "fire, hail, snow, mists," it immediately adds "that fulfill his words," lest anyone might believe that they were done by chance or by corporeal causes only, or even by spiritual causes that exist outside the will of God. ON THE TRINITY 3.10.19.[45]

---

[42]WSA 3 1:246*. [43]Ps 148:1-5. [44]AC 148-49. [45]FC 45:114.

149:1-9 PRAISE FOR THE HIGH HONOR
GIVEN HIS PEOPLE

¹*Praise the Lord!*
Sing to the Lord a new song,
  his praise in the assembly of the faithful!
²*Let Israel be glad in his Maker,*
  let the sons of Zion rejoice in their King!
³*Let them praise his name with dancing,*
  making melody to him with timbrel
    and lyre!
⁴*For the Lord takes pleasure in his people;*
  he adorns the humble with victory.
⁵*Let the faithful exult in glory;*

  let them sing for joy on their couches.
⁶*Let the high praises of God be in their throats*
  and two-edged swords in their hands,
⁷*to wreak vengeance on the nations*
  and chastisement on the peoples,
⁸*to bind their kings with chains*
  and their nobles with fetters of iron,
⁹*to execute on them the judgment written!*
  This is glory for all his faithful ones.
Praise the Lord!

OVERVIEW: God is praised in the church when believers glorify him not just with their tongues but with their lives and in everything they do (AUGUSTINE). All the saints in heaven will compose a chorus that will abide in loving unity, without dispersal, weariness or scandal (CASSIODORUS). Righteous people glorify God in their beds where they find some rest and quiet in the recesses of their mind, away from the external struggles with the flesh (GREGORY THE GREAT).

149:1-3 *Sing to the Lord a New Song*

SING PRAISE TO GOD. AUGUSTINE: My brothers and sisters, my children, O seedlings of the catholic church, O holy and heavenly seed, O you that have been born again in Christ and been born from above, listen to me—or rather, listen to God through me: "Sing to the Lord a new song." "Well, I am singing," you say. Yes, you are singing, of course you are singing, I can hear you. But do not let your life give evidence against your tongue. Sing with your voices, sing also with your hearts; sing with your mouths, sing also with your conduct. "Sing to the Lord a new song." You

ask what you should sing about the one you love? For of course you do want to sing about the one you love. You are asking for praises of his to sing. You have been told, "Sing to the Lord a new song." You are looking for songs of praise, are you? "His praise is in the church of the saints." The praise of the one to be sung about is the singer himself. Do you want to sing God his praises? Be yourselves what you sing. You are his praise if you lead good lives.

His praise, you see, is not to be found in the synagogues of the Jews, or in the madness of the pagans, or in the errors of the heretics or in the applause of the theaters. You ask, "Where it is to be found?" Look at yourselves: you are it. "His praise is in the church of the saints." You ask what to rejoice about when you are singing? "Let Israel rejoice in the one who made him," and all he can find to rejoice about is God. SERMON 34.6.[1]

THE HEAVENLY CHORUS. CASSIODORUS: "Let them praise his name in chorus; let them ring to him with the timbrel and the lyre." In the previ-

---

[1]WSA 3 2:168*.

ous verse he said that we must rejoice in the Lord Christ, and now he says that the Lord's name is to be praised in chorus. This is the chorus that by then allows no dispersal or weariness or scandal but is gathered on the worth of its merits and ever abides in the most loving unity. Another psalm explains the nature and scope of this chorus in the words "From the rising of the sun to its going down, praise the name of the Lord."[2] The chorus is that gathered from the world's beginning from the aggregate of nations; it can be fully mustered only in the homeland to come. EXPOSITIONS OF THE PSALMS 149.3.[3]

149:5 Let the Faithful Exult God in Glory

REJOICE IN YOUR BED. GREGORY THE GREAT: It is said in the psalm regarding just individuals: "The saints will rejoice exceedingly in glory; they will rejoice in their beds"; because when they flee evils from the outside, they glory secure within the secret recesses of their minds. Then the joys of their hearts will have been fulfilled when there will have been no external struggles with the flesh. For until the flesh is subdued, one's bed is disturbed just as the wall of our house shakes. MORALS ON THE BOOK OF JOB 8.24.41.[4]

[2]Ps 113:3 (112:3 LXX, Vg.). [3]ACW 53:458*. [4]CCL 143:412.

150:1-6 THE FINAL GREAT HALLELUJAH

[1]*Praise the LORD!*
Praise God in his sanctuary;
    praise him in his mighty firmament!
[2]*Praise him for his mighty deeds;*
    praise him according to his exceeding
        greatness!

[3]*Praise him with trumpet sound;*

    praise him with lute and harp!
[4]*Praise him with timbrel and dance;*
    praise him with strings and pipe!
[5]*Praise him with sounding cymbals;*
    praise him with loud clashing cymbals!
[6]*Let everything that breathes praise*
    the LORD!
Praise the LORD!

OVERVIEW: Various musical instruments, when used in praising God, reflect different aspects of Christian life, such as obedience to God's commands, suppression of sinful physical desires, unity of belief, moral excellence and desire for Christ and his salvation (ORIGEN). God is properly praised by people who are united in faith and cleansed of the blight of sin (ARNOBIUS). Although God is incomprehensible, we need to understand him as best we can, and although we

cannot praise him as fully and worthily as he deserves, still we must strive to praise him as best we can (CYRIL OF JERUSALEM).

150:3-5 Praise the Lord with Instruments

THE SYMBOLIC SIGNIFICANCE OF DIFFERENT MUSICAL INSTRUMENTS. ORIGEN: The trumpet is the contemplative mind or the mind by which the teaching of the spirit is embraced. The harp is the busy mind that is quickened by the commands of Christ. The timbrel represents the death of fleshly desire because of honesty itself. Dancing is the agreement of reasonable spirits all saying the same thing and in which there are no divisions. The stringed instruments suggest the unison of the voices of moral excellence and the unity of the organ which is the church of God resting on reflective and active minds. The melodious cymbal reflects the active mind affixed on its desire for Christ; the joyous cymbal the purified mind inspired by the salvation of Christ. COMMENTARY ON THE PSALMS 150.3-5.[1]

PRAISE GOD BY MEANS OF MUSICAL INSTRUMENTS. ARNOBIUS THE YOUNGER: Let us praise him on the psaltery and on the harp, supposing that on the harp we may embrace the wood of the cross and on the psaltery we may maintain the universal confession. The sound is harsh because the confession is not held in unity. Let us praise on timbrel and with dance, when we, firmly set upon a restored way of life, adorn the timbrel of our body with the models of best behavior. Let us praise him on stringed instruments and on the organ as we play the fresh strings that are on our harp, let us also, as with the narrow needs of modesty make melodious sounds to God, cleansing ourselves from all the blight of sin. SELECTIONS FROM THE PSALMS 150.[2]

150:6 Let Every Living Thing Praise God

PRAISE GOD AS BEST YOU CAN. CYRIL OF JERUSALEM: But someone will say: if the divine nature is incomprehensible, then why do you discourse about these things? Well then, because I cannot drink up the whole stream, am I not even to take in proportion to my need? Or because I cannot take in all the sunlight owing to the constitution of my eyes, am I not even to gaze on what is sufficient for my wants? On entering a vast orchard, because I cannot eat all the fruit therein, would you have me go away completely hungry? I praise and glorify him who made us; for it is a divine command that says, "Let everything that has breath praise the Lord!" I am endeavoring now to glorify the Lord, not to describe him, though I know that I shall fall short of glorifying him worthily; still I consider it a godly work to try all the same. For the Lord Jesus encourages my weakness when he says, "No one has at any time seen God."[3] CATECHETICAL LECTURES 6.5.[4]

---

[1]PG 12:1684. [2]CCL 25 1:257-58. [3]Jn 1:15. [4]FC 61:150-51.

APPENDIX

Early Christian Writers and the Documents Cited

The following table lists all the early Christian documents cited in this volume by author, if known, or by the title of the work. The English title used in this commentary is followed in parentheses with the Latin designation and, where available, the Thesaurus Linguae Graecae (=TLG) digital references or Cetedoc Clavis numbers. Printed sources of original language versions may be found in the bibliography of works in original languages.

Acts of the Holy Apostles Peter and Paul

Alexander of Alexandria
Epistles on the Arian Heresy

Ambrose
Cain and Abel (De Cain et Abel)	Cetedoc 0125
Concerning Repentance (De paenitentia)	Cetedoc 0156
Concerning Virgins (De virginibus)	Cetedoc 0145
Death as a Good (De bono mortis)	Cetedoc 0129
Duties of the Clergy (De officiis ministrorum)	Cetedoc 0144
Flight from the World (De fuga saeculi)	Cetedoc 0133
Jacob and the Happy Life (De Jacob et vita beata)	Cetedoc 0130
Letters (Epistulae)	Cetedoc 0160
On His Brother Satyrus (De excessu fratris Satyri)	Cetedoc 0157
On Paradise (De paradiso)	Cetedoc 0124
On the Christian Faith (De fide)	Cetedoc 0150
On the Death of Theodosius (De obitu Theodosii)	Cetedoc 0159
On the Holy Spirit (De Spiritu Sancto)	Cetedoc 0151
On the Mysteries (De mysteriis)	Cetedoc 0155
On Virginity (De virginitate)	Cetedoc 0147
Six Days of Creation (Hexaemeron)	Cetedoc 0123
The Prayer of Job and David (De interpellatione Job et David)	Cetedoc 0134

Ammon
Letter of Bishop Ammon

Aphrahat
Demonstrations (Demonstrationes)

Apocryphal Revelation of John the Theologian

Archelaus
The Acts of the Disputation with the Heresiarch Manes

Arnobius the Younger
Commentary on the Psalms (*Commentarii in Psalmos*)   Cetedoc 0242

Ascetic Monks of Egypt
Sayings of the Egyptian Fathers (*Sententiae Patrum Aegyptiorum*)

Athanasius
Against the Heathen (*Contra gentes*)   TLG 2035.001
Defense Before Constantius (*Apologia ad Constantium imperatorem*)   TLG 2035.011
Defense of His Flight (*Apologia de fuga sua*)   TLG 2035.012
Defense of the Nicene Definition (*De decretis Nicaenae synodi*)   TLG 2035.003
Discourses Against the Arians (*Orationes tres contra Arianos*)   TLG 2035.042
Festal Letters (*Epistulae festalis*)
Life of St. Anthony (*Vita sancti Antonii*)   TLG 2035.047
On the Incarnation (*De incarnatione verbi*)   TLG 2035.002
Second Letter to Orsisius (*Secunda Epistola ad Orsisium*)

Augustine
Admonition and Grace (*De corruptione et gratia*)   Cetedoc 0353
Against Faustus, a Manichean (*Contra Faustum*)   Cetedoc 0321
Against Julian (*Contra Julianum*)   Cetedoc 0351
Against Lying (*Contra mendacium*)   Cetedoc 0304
The Catholic and Manichaean Ways of Life
    (*De moribus ecclesiae catholicae et de moribus Manichaeorum*)   Cetedoc 0261
Christian Combat (*De agone christiano*)   Cetedoc 0296
City of God (*De civitate Dei*)   Cetedoc 0313
Confessions (*Confessionum libri tredecim*)   Cetedoc 0251
The Correction of the Donatists (In *Epistulae*)   Cetedoc 0262
Eight Questions of Dulcitius (*De octo Dulcitii quaestionibus*)   Cetedoc 0291
Enchiridion (*Enchiridion de fide, spe et caritate*)   Cetedoc 0295
Explanations of the Psalms (*Enarrationes in Psalmos*)   Cetedoc 0283
Holy Virginity (*De sancta virginitate*)   Cetedoc 0300
Homilies on 1 John (*In Johannis epistulam ad Parthos tractatus*)   Cetedoc 0279
In Answer to the Jews (*Adversus Judaeos*)   Cetedoc 0315
Letters (*Epistulae*)   Cetedoc 0262
Letters of Petilian the Donatist (*Contra litteras Petiliani*)   Cetedoc 0333
On Continence (*De continentia*)   Cetedoc 0298
On Eighty-three Varied Questions (*De diversis quaestionibus octoginta tribus*)   Cetedoc 0289
On Faith in Things Unseen (*De fide rerum invisibilium*)   Cetedoc 0292
On Nature and Grace (*De natura et gratia*)   Cetedoc 0344

On Patience (*De patientia*)   Cetedoc 0308
On the Christian Life (*De vita christiana, [sp.]*)   Cetedoc 0730
On the Gift of Perseverance (*De dono perseverantiae*)   Cetedoc 0355
On the Literal Interpretation of Genesis (*De Genesi ad litteram imperfectus liber*)   Cetedoc 0268
On the Nature of the Good (*De natura boni*)   Cetedoc 0323
On the Trinity (*De trinitate*)   Cetedoc 0329
On Various Questions to Simplician (*De diversis quaestionibus ad Simplicianum*)   Cetedoc 0290
Predestination of the Saints (*De praedestinatione sanctorum*)   Cetedoc 0354
Proceedings of Pelagians (*De gestis Pelagii*)   Cetedoc 0348
Sermon on the Mount (*De sermone Domini in monte*)   Cetedoc 0274
Sermons (*Sermones*)   Cetedoc 0284
Tractates on the Gospel of John (*In Johannis evangelium tractatus*)   Cetedoc 0278

Basil the Great
Concerning Baptism (*De baptismo libri duo*)   TLG 2040.052
Homilies on the Hexaemeron (*Homiliae in hexaemeron*)   TLG 2040.001
Homilies on the Psalms (*Homiliae super Psalmos*)   TLG 2040.018
Homily Against Those Who Are Prone to Anger (*Homilia adversus eos qui irascuntur*)   TLG 2040.026
Homily on Detachment (*Quod rebus mundanis abhaerendum non sit*)   TLG 2040.037
Homily on the Words "Give Heed to Thyself" (*Homilia in illud: Attende tibi ipsi*)   TLG 2040.006
Letters (*Epistulae*)   TLG 2040.004
The Long Rules (*Asceticon magnum sive Quaestiones [regulae fusius tractatae]*)   TLG 2040.048
The Long Rules, Preface (*Prologus 4 [prooemium in asceticum magnum]*)   TLG 2040.047
On the Holy Spirit (*De spiritu sancto*)   TLG 2040.003

Bede
Commentary on the Acts of the Apostles (*Expositio actuum apostolorum*)   Cetedoc 1357
Homilies on the Gospels (*Homiliarum evangelii libri ii*)   Cetedoc 1367
On the Tabernacle (*De tabernaculo et vasis eius ac vestibus sacerdotum libri iii*)   Cetedoc 1345

Braulio of Saragossa
Letters (*Epistulae*)
Life of St. Emilian (*Vita sancti Aemiliani*)

Caesarius of Arles
Additional Sermon (*See Augustine Sermones*)   Cetedoc 0284
Sermons (*Sermones*)   Cetedoc 1008

Callistus of Rome
Epistles (*Epistola Papae Calixti ad omnes Galliae episcopos*)

Cassian, John
Conferences (*Collationes*)   Cetedoc 0512
Institutes (*De institutis coenobiorum et de octo principalium vitiorum remedies*)   Cetedoc 0513

Cassiodorus
Expositions of the Psalms (*Expositio psalmorum*) — Cetedoc 0900

Clement of Alexandria
Christ the Educator (*Paedagogus*) — TLG 0555.002
Stromateis (*Stromata*) — TLG 0555.004

Clement of Rome
1 Clement (*Epistula i ad Corinthios*) — TLG 1271.001

Constitutions of the Holy Apostles (*Constitutiones apostolorum*) — TLG 2894.001

Cyprian
Exhortation to Martyrdom (*Ad Fortunatum [De exhortatione martyrii]*) — Cetedoc 0045
The Lapsed (*De lapsis*) — Cetedoc 0042
Letters (*Epistulae*) — Cetedoc 0050
The Lord's Prayer (*De dominica oratione*) — Cetedoc 0043
The Unity of the Church (*De ecclesiae catholicae unitate*) — Cetedoc 0041

Cyril of Alexandria
Letters (*Epistulae in Concilium universale Ephesenum anno*) — TLG 5000.001
On the Unity of Christ (*Quod unus sit Christus*) — TLG 4090.027

Cyril of Jerusalem
Catechetical Lectures (*Catecheses ad illuminandos*) — TLG 2110.003
Catechetical Lectures, Procatechesis (*Procatechesis*) — TLG 2110.001
Mystagogical Lectures (*Mystagogiae [sp.]*) — TLG 2110.002

Desert Fathers
Sayings of the Fathers (*Sententiae Patrum*)

Didache (*Didache xii apostolorum*) — TLG 1311.001

Dionysius of Alexandria
Fragments (*Fragmenta*)

Ephrem the Syrian
Commentary on Tatian's Diatessaron (*In Tatiani Diatessaron*)

Epiphanius of Salamis
Panarion (*Panarion [Adversus haereses]*) — TLG 2021.002

Epistle of Barnabas (*Barnabae epistula*) — TLG 1216.001

Eugippius
The Life of Saint Severin *(Vita sancti Severini)*

Eusebius of Caesarea
Ecclesiastical History *(Historia ecclesiastica)* — TLG 2018.002
Proof of the Gospel *(Demonstratio evangelica)* — TLG 2018.005

Evagrius of Pontus
Praktikos *(Practicus)* — TLG 4110.001

Fulgentius of Ruspe
Book to Victor Against the Sermon of Fastidiosus the Arian
   (Liber ad Victorem contra sermonem Fastidiosi Ariani) — Cetedoc 0820
Letters *(Epistulae)* — Cetedoc 0817
Letter to Monimus *(Ad Monimus libri III)* — Cetedoc 0814
On the Forgiveness of Sins *(Ad Euthymium de remissione peccatorum libri II)* — Cetedoc 0821
To Peter on the Faith *(De fide ad Petrum seu de regula fidei)* — Cetedoc 0826

Gregory of Nazianzus
Against the Eunomians, Theological Oration 1(27) *(Adversus Eunomianos)* — TLG 2022.007
In Defense of His Flight to Pontus, Oration 2 *(Apologetica)* — TLG 2022.016
Letters *(Epistulae)* — TLG 2022.001
On His Brother St. Caesarius, Oration 7 *(Funebris in laudem Caesarii fratris oratio)* — TLG 2022.005
On His Father's Silence, Oration 16 *(In patrem tacentem)* — TLG 2022.029
On His Sister St. Gorgiana, Oration 8 *(In laudem sororis Gorgoniae)* — TLG 2022.021
On Holy Baptism, Oration 40 *(In sanctum baptisma)* — TLG 2022.048
On Pentecost, Oration 41 *(In pentecosten)* — TLG 2022.049
On the Great Athanasius, Oration 21 *(In laudem Athanasii)* — TLG 2022.034
On the Holy Spirit, Theological Oration 5(31) *(De spiritu sancto)* — TLG 2022.011
On the Son, Theological Oration 4(30) *(De filio)* — TLG 2022.010

Gregory of Nyssa
Address on Religious Instruction *(Oratio catechetica magna)* — TLG 2017.046
Against Eunomius
   (Contra Eunomium) — TLG 2017.030
   (Refutatio confessionis Eunomii) — TLG 2017.031
Answer to Eunomius' Second Book *(Contra Eunomium)* — TLG 2017.030
Life of Moses *(De vita Mosis)* — TLG 2017.042
On the Soul and the Resurrection *(Dialogus de anima et resurrectione)* — TLG 2017.056
On Virginity *(De virginitate)* — TLG 2017.043

Gregory the Great
Letters *(Registrum epistularum)* — Cetedoc 1714
Morals on the Book of Job *(Moralia in Job)* — Cetedoc 1708

Hilary of Poitiers
Homilies on the Psalms (*Tractatus super psalmos I-XCI*)   Cetedoc 0428
On the Trinity (*De trinitate*)   Cetedoc 0433

Hippolytus
On the Theophany (*De theophania [dubious]*)   TLG 2115.026

Horsiesi
The Testament of Horsiesi

Isaac of Nineveh
Ascetical Homilies

Jacob of Sarug
On the Establishment of Creation (*Hexaemeron*)

Jerome
Against Jovinianus (*Adversus Jovinianum*)   Cetedoc 0610
Against Rufinus (*Apologia adversus libros Rufini*)   Cetedoc 0613
Against the Pelagians (*Dialogi contra Pelagianos libri iii*)   Cetedoc 0615
Commentary on Ecclesiastes (*Commentarius in Ecclesiasten*)   Cetedoc 0583
The Histories of the Monks
Homilies on the Psalms (*Tractatus lix in psalmos*)   Cetedoc 0592
Letters (*Epistulae*)   Cetedoc 0620
The Perpetual Virginity of Mary
   (*Adversus Helvidium de Mariae virginitate perpetua*)   Cetedoc 0609

John Chrysostom
Against the Anomoeans
   1-5 (*Contra Anomoeos homiliae 1-5 = De incomprehensibili dei natura*)   TLG 2062.012
   7 (*De consubstantiali*)   TLG 2062.015
Baptismal Instructions (*Catecheses ad illuminandos [series tertia]*)   TLG 2062.382
Demonstration Against the Pagans (*Contra Judaeos et Gentiles, Quod Christus sit Deus*)   TLG 2062.372
Discourses Against Judaizing Christians (*Adversus Judaeos [orationes 1-8]*)   TLG 2062.021
Homilies Concerning the Statues (*Ad populam Antiochenum homiliae [de statuis]*)   TLG 2062.024
Homilies on 1 Corinthians (*In epistulam i ad Corinthios [homiliae 1-44]*)   TLG 2062.156
Homilies on Genesis (*In Genesim [homiliae 1-67]*)   TLG 2062.112
Homilies on Philemon (*In epistulam ad Philemonem*)   TLG 2062.167
Homilies on Repentance and Almsgiving (*De paenitentia [homiliae 1-9]*)   TLG 2062.027
Homilies on 2 Timothy (*In epistulam ii ad Timotheum*)   TLG 2062.165
Homilies on the Gospel of John (*In Joannem [homiliae 1-88]*)   TLG 2062.153
Letter to a Young Widow (*Ad viduam juniorem*)   TLG 2062.010
On the Epistle to the Hebrews (*In epistulam ad Hebraeos*)   TLG 2062.168

John of Damascus

Barlaam and Joseph (*Vita Barlaam et Joasaph [Sp.]*) TLG 2934.066
Orthodox Faith (*Expositio fidei*) TLG 2934.004

Justin Martyr

Dialogue with Trypho (*Dialogus cum Tryphone*) TLG 0645.003
First Apology (*Apologia*) TLG 0645.001

Leo the Great

Letters (*Epistulae*) Cetedoc 1657
Sermons (*Tractatus septem et nonaginta*) Cetedoc 1657
Testimonia (*Testimonia*)

Marius Victorinus

Against Arius (*Adversus Arium*) Cetedoc 0095

Martin of Braga

Driving Away Vanity (*Pro repellenda jactantia*)
Exhortation to Humility (*Exhortatio humilitatis*)

Maximus of Turin

Sermons (*Collectio sermonum antiqua*) Cetedoc 0219a

Methodius

On the Resurrection (*De resurrectione*) TLG 2959.003
Symposium *or* Banquet of the Ten Virgins (*Symposium sive Convivium decem virginum*) TLG 2959.001

Nicetas of Remesiana

Explanation of the Creed (*Explanatio symboli habita ad competentes*)
Liturgical Singing (*De utilitate hymnorum*)
The Power of the Holy Spirit (*De spiritus sancti potentia*)
Vigils of the Saints (*De Vigiliis servorum Dei*)

Novatian

On the Trinity (*De trinitate*) Ceteodc 0071

Origen

Against Celsus (*Contra Celsum*) TLG 2042.001
Commentary on Matthew (*Commentarium in evangelium Matthaei [lib.12-17]*) TLG 2042.030
Commentary on the Gospel of John
  (*Commentarii in evangelium Joannis [lib. 1, 2, 4, 5, 6, 10, 13]*) TLG 2042.005
  (*Commentarii in evangelium Joannis [lib. 19, 20, 28, 32]*) TLG 2042.079
Homilies on Exodus (*Homiliae in Exodum*) TLG 2042.023
Homilies on Genesis (*Homiliae in Genesim*) TLG 2042.022
Homilies on Leviticus (*Homiliae in Leviticum*) TLG 2042.024

On Prayer (De oratione)   TLG 2042.008
Selections from the Psalms (Selecta in Psalmos [dub.])   TLG 2042.058

Pachomius
Instructions (Catecheses)
Letters (In Catecheses)
Life of Pachomius (Bohairic) (Vita Pachomii)
Life of Pachomius (First Greek)
Paralipomena

Palladius of Helenopolis
Lausiac History

Paschasius of Dumium
Questions and Answers of the Greek Fathers (De vitis patrum liber septimus, sive verba
    seniorum auctore graeco incerto, interprete Paschasio S. R. E. Diacono)

Paulinus of Milan
The Life of St. Ambrose (Vita S. Ambrosii)

Paulinus of Nola
Letters (Epistulae)   Cetedoc 0202

Peter Chrysologus
Sermons (Collectio sermonum)   Cetedoc 0227+

Philoxenus of Mabbug
Excerpt on Prayer

Poemen
Sayings of the Fathers (Sententiae Patrum)

Prudentius
Book of the Martyrs' Crowns (Liber Peristephanon)   Cetedoc 1443
The Divinity of Christ (Liber apotheosis)   Cetedoc 1439
Hymns for Every Day (Liber Cathemerinon)   Cetedoc 1438

Pseudo-Dionysius
Celestial Hierarchy (De caelesti hierarchia)   TLG 2798.001
Divine Names (De divinis nominibus)   TLG 2798.004

Rufinus of Aquileia
Apology (Apologia [contra Hieronymum])   Cetedoc 0197
Commentary on the Apostles' Creed (Expositio symboli)   Cetedoc 0196

Sahdona (Martyrius)
Book of Perfection

Salvian the Presbyter
The Governance of God (*De gubernatione Dei*) Cetedoc 0485

Sayings of the Fathers (*Sententiae Patrum*)

Syncletica
Sayings of the Fathers (*Sententiae Patrum*)

Tertullian
Against Hermogenes (*Adversus Hermogenem*) Cetedoc 0013
Against Marcion (*Adversus Marcionem*) Cetedoc 0014
Against Praxeas (*Adversus Praxean*) Cetedoc 0026
An Answer to the Jews (*Adversus Judaeos*) Cetedoc 0033
On Idolatry (*De idololatria*) Cetedoc 0023
On the Resurrection of the Flesh (*De resurrectione mortuorum*) Cetedoc 0019
Prescriptions Against Heretics (*De praescriptione haereticorum*) Cetedoc 0005
Scorpiace (*Scorpiace*) Cetedoc 0022

Theodore of Mopsuestia
Commentary on the Minor Prophets (on Zechariah)

Theodoret of Cyr
Commentary on the Psalms (*Interpretatio in Psalmos*) TLG 4089.024
Dialogues (*Eranistes*) TLG 4089.002
Discourses (*De providentia orationes decem*) TLG 4089.032
Ecclesiastical History (*Historia ecclesiastica*) TLG 4089.003
Letters
   (*Epistulae: Collectio Sirmondiana [1-95]*) TLG 4089.006
   (*Epistulae: Collectio Sirmondiana [96-147]*) TLG 4089.007
   (*Ad eos qui in Euphratesia et Osrhoena regione, Syria, Phoeni*) TLG 4089.034
On Divine Providence (*De providentia orationes decem*) TLG 4089.032

Valerian of Cimiez
Homilies (*Homiliae*)

Zephyrinus
Epistles of Zephyrinus (*Epistola Zephirini papae*)

Biographical Sketches & Short Descriptions of Select Anonymous Works

This listing is cumulative, including all the authors and works cited in this series to date.

Abraham of Nathpar (fl. sixth-seventh century). Monk of the Eastern Church who flourished during the monastic revival of the sixth to seventh century. Among his works is a treatise on prayer and silence that speaks of the importance of prayer becoming embodied through action in the one who prays. His work has also been associated with John of Apamea or Philoxenus of Mabbug.

Acacius of Beroea (c. 340-c. 436). Syrian monk known for his ascetic life. He became bishop of Beroea in 378, participated in the council of Constantinople in 381, and played an important role in mediating between Cyril of Alexandria and John of Antioch; however, he did not take part in the clash between Cyril and Nestorius.

Acacius of Caesarea (d. c. 365). Pro-Arian bishop of Caesarea in Palestine, disciple and biographer of Eusebius of Caesarea, the historian. He was a man of great learning and authored a treatise on Ecclesiastes.

Adamantius (early fourth century). Surname of Origen of Alexandria and the main character in the dialogue contained in *Concerning Right Faith in God*. Rufinus attributes this work to Origen. However, Trinitarian terminology, coupled with references to Methodius and allusions to the fourth-century Constantinian era bring this attri-

bution into question.

Adamnan (c. 624-704). Abbot of Iona, Ireland, and author of the life of St. Columba. He was influential in the process of assimilating the Celtic church into Roman liturgy and church order. He also wrote *On the Holy Sites*, which influenced Bede.

Alexander of Alexandria (fl. 312-328). Bishop of Alexandria and predecessor of Athanasius, on whom he exerted considerable theological influence during the rise of Arianism. Alexander excommunicated Arius, whom he had appointed to the parish of Baucalis, in 319. His teaching regarding the eternal generation and divine substantial union of the Son with the Father was eventually confirmed at the Council of Nicaea (325).

Ambrose of Milan (c. 333-397; fl. 374-397). Bishop of Milan and teacher of Augustine who defended the divinity of the Holy Spirit and the perpetual virginity of Mary.

Ambrosiaster (fl. c. 366-384). Name given by Erasmus to the author of a work once thought to have been composed by Ambrose.

Ammonius (c. fifth century). An Aristotelian commentator and teacher in Alexandria, where he was born and of whose school he became head. Also an exegete of Plato, he enjoyed fame among his contemporaries and successors, although modern critics accuse him of pedantry and banality.

Amphilochius of Iconium (b. c. 340-345, d.c. 398-404). An orator at Constantinople before becoming bishop of Iconium in 373. He was a cousin of Gregory of Nazianzus and active in debates against the Macedonians and Messalians.

Andreas (c. seventh century). Monk who collected commentary from earlier writers to form a catena on various biblical books.

Andrew of Caesarea (early sixth century). Bishop of Caesarea in Cappadocia. He produced one of the earliest Greek commentaries on Revelation and defended the divine inspiration of its author.

Andrew of Crete (c. 660-740). Bishop of Crete, known for his hymns, especially for his "canons," a genre which supplanted the *kontakia* and is believed to have originated with him. A significant number of his canons and sermons have survived and some are still in use in the Eastern Church. In the early Iconoclastic controversy he is also known for his defense of the veneration of icons.

Antony (or Anthony) the Great (c. 251-c. 356). An anchorite of the Egyptian desert and founder of Egyptian monasticism. Athanasius regarded him as the ideal of monastic life, and he has become a model for Christian hagiography.

Aphrahat (c. 270-350; fl. 337-345). "The Persian Sage" and first major Syriac writer whose work survives. He is also known by his Greek name Aphraates.

Apollinaris of Laodicea (310-c. 392). Bishop of Laodicea who was attacked by Gregory of Nazianzus, Gregory of Nyssa and Theodore for denying that Christ had a human mind.

Aponius/Apponius (fourth–fifth century). Author of a remarkable commentary on Song of Solomon (c. 405-415), an important work in the history of exegesis. The work, which was influenced by the commentaries of Origen and Pseudo-Hippolytus, is of theological significance, especially in the area of Christology.

Apostolic Constitutions (c. 381-394). Also known as *Constitutions of the Holy Apostles* and thought to be redacted by Julian of Neapolis. The work is divided into eight books, and is primarily a collection of and expansion on previous works such as the *Didache* (c. 140) and the *Apostolic Traditions*. Book 8 ends with eighty-five canons from various sources and is elsewhere known as the *Apostolic Canons*.

Apringius of Beja (middle sixth century). Iberian bishop and exegete. Heavily influenced by Tyconius, he wrote a commentary on Revelation in Latin, of which two large fragments survive.

Arethas of Caesarea (c. 860-940) Byzantine scholar and disciple of Photius. He was a deacon in Constantinople, then archbishop of Caesarea from 901.

Arius (fl. c. 320). Heretic condemned at the Council of Nicaea (325) for refusing to accept that the Son was not a creature but was God by nature like the Father.

Arnobius the Younger (fifth century). A participant in christological controversies of the fifth century. He composed *Conflictus cum Serapione*, an account of a debate with a monophysite monk in which he attempts to demonstrate harmony between Roman and Alexandrian theology. Some scholars attribute to him a few more works, such as *Commentaries on Psalms*.

Athanasius of Alexandria (c. 295-373; fl. 325-373). Bishop of Alexandria from 328, though often in exile. He wrote his classic polemics against the Arians while most of the eastern bishops were against him.

Athenagoras (fl. 176-180). Early Christian philosopher and apologist from Athens, whose only authenticated writing, *A Plea Regarding Christians*, is addressed to the emperors Marcus Aurelius and Commodius, and defends Christians from the common accusations of atheism, incest and cannibalism.

Augustine of Hippo (354-430). Bishop of Hippo and a voluminous writer on philosophical, exegetical, theological and ecclesiological topics. He formulated the Western doctrines of predestination and original sin in his writings against the Pelagians.

Babai (c. early sixth century). Author of the Letter to Cyriacus. He should not be confused with either Babai of Nisibis (d. 484), or Babai the Great (d. 628).

Babai the Great (d. 628). Syriac monk who founded a monastery and school in his region of Beth Zabday and later served as third superior at the Great Convent of Mount Izla during a period of crisis in the Nestorian church.

Basil of Seleucia (fl. 444-468). Bishop of Seleucia in Isauria and ecclesiastical writer. He took part in the Synod of Constantinople in 448 for the condemnation of the Eutychian errors and the deposition of their great champion, Dioscurus of Alexandria.

Basil the Great (b. c. 330; fl. 357-379). One of the Cappadocian fathers, bishop of Caesarea and champion of the teaching on the Trinity propounded at Nicaea in 325. He was a great administrator and founded a monastic rule.

Basilides (fl. second century). Alexandrian heretic of the early second century who is said to have believed that souls migrate from body to body and that we do not sin if we lie to protect the body from martyrdom.

Bede the Venerable (c. 672/673-735). Born in Northumbria, at the age of seven, he was put under the care of the Benedictine monks of Saints Peter and Paul at Jarrow and given a broad classical education in the monastic tradition. Considered one of the most learned men of his age, he is the author of *An Ecclesiastical History of the English People*.

Benedict of Nursia (c. 480-547). Considered the most important figure in the history of Western monasticism. Benedict founded many monasteries, the most notable found at Montecassino, but his lasting influence lay in his famous Rule. The Rule outlines the theological and inspirational foundation of the monastic ideal while also legislating the shape and organization of the cenobitic life.

Besa the Copt (5th century). Coptic monk, disciple of Shenoute, whom he succeeded as head of the monastery. He wrote numerous letters, monastic catecheses and a biography of Shenoute.

Book of Steps (c. 400). Written by an anonymous Syriac author, this work consists of thirty homilies or discourses which specifically deal with the more advanced stages of growth in the spiritual life.

Braulio of Saragossa (c. 585-651). Bishop of Saragossa (631-651) and noted writer of the Visigothic renaissance. His *Life* of St. Aemilianus is his crowning literary achievement.

Caesarius of Arles (c. 470-543). Bishop of Arles renowned for his attention to his pastoral duties. Among his surviving works the most important is a collection of some 238 sermons that display an ability to preach Christian doctrine to a variety of audiences.

Callistus of Rome (d. 222). Pope (217-222) who excommunicated Sabellius for heresy. It is very probable that he suffered martyrdom.

Cassia (b. c. 805, d. between 848 and 867). Nun, poet and hymnographer who founded a convent in Constantinople.

Cassian, John (360-432). Author of the *Institutes* and the *Conferences*, works purporting to relay the teachings of the Egyptian monastic fathers on the nature of the spiritual life which were highly influential in the development of Western monasticism.

Cassiodorus (c. 485-c. 580). Founder of the monastery of Vivarium, Calabria, where monks transcribed classic sacred and profane texts, Greek and Latin, preserving them for the Western tradition.

Chromatius (fl. 400). Bishop of Aquileia, friend of Rufinus and Jerome and author of tracts and sermons.

Clement of Alexandria (c. 150-215). A highly educated Christian convert from paganism, head of the catechetical school in Alexandria and pioneer of Christian scholarship. His major works, *Protrepticus*, *Paedagogus* and the *Stromata*, bring Christian doctrine face to face with the ideas and achievements of his time.

Clement of Rome (fl. c. 92-101). Pope whose *Epistle to the Corinthians* is one of the most important documents of subapostolic times.

Commodian (probably third or possibly fifth

written some works attributed to Pelagius.

Faustinus (fl. 380). A priest in Rome and supporter of Lucifer and author of a treatise on the Trinity.

Faustus of Riez (c. 400-490). A prestigious British monk at Lérins; abbot, then bishop of Riez from 457 to his death. His works include *On the Holy Spirit*, in which he argued against the Macedonians for the divinity of the Holy Spirit, and *On Grace*, in which he argued for a position on salvation that lay between more categorical views of free-will and predestination. Various letters and (pseudonymous) sermons are extant.

The Festal Menaion. Orthodox liturgical text containing the variable parts of the service, including hymns, for fixed days of celebration of the life of Jesus and Mary.

Filastrius (fl. 380). Bishop of Brescia and author of a compilation against all heresies.

Firmicus Maternus (fourth century). An anti-Pagan apologist. Before his conversion to Christianity he wrote a work on astrology (334-337). After his conversion, however, he criticized paganism in *On the Errors of the Profane Religion*.

Flavian of Chalon-sur-Saône (d. end of sixth century). Bishop of Chalon-sur-Saône in Burgundy, France. His hymn *Verses on the Mandate in the Lord's Supper* was recited in a number of French monasteries after the washing of the feet on Maundy Thursday.

Fructuosus of Braga (d. c. 665). Son of a Gothic general and member of a noble military family. He became a monk at an early age, then abbot-bishop of Dumium before 650 and metropolitan of Braga in 656. He was influential in setting up monastic communities in Lusitania, Asturia, Galicia and the island of Gades.

Fulgentius of Ruspe (c. 467-532). Bishop of Ruspe and author of many orthodox sermons and tracts under the influence of Augustine.

Gaudentius of Brescia (fl. 395). Successor of Filastrius as bishop of Brescia and author of twenty-one Eucharistic sermons.

Gennadius of Constantinople (d. 471). Patriarch of Constantinople, author of numerous commentaries and an opponent of the Christology of Cyril of Alexandria.

Gerontius (c. 395-c.480). Palestinian monk, later archimandrite of the cenobites of Palestine. He led the resistance to the council of Chalcedon.

Gnostics. Name now given generally to followers of Basilides, Marcion, Valentinus, Mani and others. The characteristic belief is that matter is a prison made for the spirit by an evil or ignorant creator, and that redemption depends on fate, not on free will.

Gregory of Elvira (fl. 359-385). Bishop of Elvira who wrote allegorical treatises in the style of Origen and defended the Nicene faith against the Arians.

Gregory of Nazianzus (b. 329/330; fl. 372-389). Cappadocian father, bishop of Constantinople, friend of Basil the Great and Gregory of Nyssa, and author of theological orations, sermons and poetry.

Gregory of Nyssa (c. 335-394). Bishop of Nyssa and brother of Basil the Great. A Cappadocian father and author of catechetical orations, he was a philosophical theologian of great originality.

Gregory Thaumaturgus (fl. c. 248-264). Bishop of Neocaesarea and a disciple of Origen. There are at least five legendary *Lives* that recount the events and miracles which led to his being called "the wonder worker." His most important work was the *Address of Thanks to Origen*, which is a rhetorically structured panegyric to Origen and an outline of his teaching.

Gregory the Great (c. 540-604). Pope from 590, the fourth and last of the Latin "Doctors of the Church." He was a prolific author and a powerful unifying force within the Latin Church, initiating the liturgical reform that brought about the Gregorian Sacramentary and Gregorian chant.

Heracleon (fl. c.145-180). Gnostic teacher and disciple of Valentinus. His commentary on John, which was perhaps the first commentary to exist on this or any Gospel, was so popular that Ambrose commissioned Origen to write his own commentary in response, providing a more orthodox approach to the Fourth Gospel.

Hesychius of Jerusalem (fl. 412-450). Presbyter and exegete, thought to have commented on the whole of Scripture.

Hilary of Arles (c. 401-449). Archbishop of Arles and leader of the Semi-Pelagian party. Hilary incurred the wrath of Pope Leo I when he removed a bishop from his see and appointed a new bishop. Leo demoted Arles from a metropolitan see to a bishopric to assert papal power over the church in Gaul.

Hilary of Poitiers (c. 315-367). Bishop of Poitiers and called the "Athanasius of the West" because of his defense (against the Arians) of the common nature of Father and Son.

Hippolytus (fl. 222-245). Recent scholarship places Hippolytus in a Palestinian context, personally familiar with Origen. Though he is known chiefly for *The Refutation of All Heresies*, he was primarily a commentator on Scripture (especially the Old Testament) employing typological exegesis.

Horsiesi (c. 305-c. 390). Pachomius's second successor, after Petronius, as a leader of cenobitic monasticism in Southern Egypt.

Ignatius of Antioch (c. 35-107/112). Bishop of Antioch who wrote several letters to local churches while being taken from Antioch to Rome to be martyred. In the letters, which warn against heresy, he stresses orthodox Christology, the centrality of the Eucharist and unique role of the bishop in preserving the unity of the church.

Irenaeus of Lyons (c. 135-c. 202). Bishop of Lyons who published the most famous and influential refutation of Gnostic thought.

Isaac of Nineveh (d. c. 700). Also known as Isaac the Syrian or Isaac Syrus, this monastic writer served for a short while as bishop of Nineveh before retiring to live a secluded monastic life. His writings on ascetic subjects survive in the form of numerous homilies.

Isaiah of Scete (late fourth century). Author of ascetical texts, collected after his death under the title of the *Ascetic Discourses*. This work was influential in the development of Eastern Christian asceticism and spirituality.

Isho'dad of Merv (fl. c. 850). Nestorian bishop of Hedatta. He wrote commentaries on parts of the Old Testament and all of the New Testament, frequently quoting Syriac fathers.

Isidore of Seville (c. 560-636). Youngest of a family of monks and clerics, including sister Florentina and brothers Leander and Fulgentius. He was an erudite author of comprehensive scale in matters both religious and sacred, including his encyclopedic *Etymologies*.

Jacob of Nisibis (d. 338). Bishop of Nisibis. He was present at the council of Nicaea in 325 and took an active part in the opposition to Arius.

Jacob of Sarug (c. 450-c. 520). Syriac ecclesiastical writer. Jacob received his education at Edessa. At the end of his life he was ordained bishop of Sarug. His principal writing was a long series of metrical homilies, earning him the title "The Flute of the Holy Spirit."

Jerome (c. 347-420). Gifted exegete and exponent of a classical Latin style, now best known as the translator of the Latin Vulgate. He defended the perpetual virginity of Mary, attacked Origen and Pelagius and supported extreme ascetic practices.

John Chrysostom (344/354-407; fl. 386-407). Bishop of Constantinople who was noted for his orthodoxy, his eloquence and his attacks on Christian laxity in high places.

John of Antioch (d. 441/42). Bishop of Antioch, commencing in 428. He received his education together with Nestorius and Theodore of Mopsuestia in a monastery near Antioch. A supporter of Nestorius, he condemned Cyril of Alexandria, but later reached a compromise with him.

John of Apamea (fifth century). Syriac author of the early church who wrote on various aspects of the spiritual life, also known as John the Solitary. Some of his writings are in the form of dialogues. Other writings include letters, a treatise on baptism, and shorter works on prayer and silence.

John of Carpathus (c. seventh/eighth century). Perhaps John the bishop from the island of Carpathus, situated between Crete and Rhodes, who attended the Synod of 680/81. He wrote two "centuries" (a literary genre in Eastern spirituality consisting of 100 short sections, or chapters).

These were entitled *Chapters of Encouragement to the Monks of India* and *Chapters on Theology and Knowledge* which are included in the *Philokalia*.

John of Damascus (c. 650-750). Arab monastic and theologian whose writings enjoyed great influence in both the Eastern and Western Churches. His most influential writing was the *Orthodox Faith*.

John the Elder (c. eighth century). A Syriac author also known as John of Dalyatha or John Saba ("the elder") who belonged to monastic circles of the Church of the East and lived in the region of Mount Qardu (northern Iraq). His most important writings are twenty-two homilies and a collection of fifty-one short letters in which he describes the mystical life as an anticipatory experience of the resurrection life, the fruit of the sacraments of baptism and the Eucharist.

John the Monk. Traditional name found in *The Festal Menaion*, believed to refer to John of Damascus. *See* John of Damascus.

Josephus, Flavius (c. 37-c. 101). Jewish historian from a distinguished priestly family. Acquainted with the Essenes and Sadducees, he himself became a Pharisee. He joined the great Jewish revolt that broke out in 66 and was chosen by the Sanhedrin at Jerusalem to be commander-in-chief in Galilee. Showing great shrewdness to ingratiate himself with Vespasian by foretelling his elevation and that of his son Titus to the imperial dignity, Josephus was restored his liberty after 69 when Vespasian became emperor.

Julian of Eclanum (c. 385-450). Bishop of Eclanum in 416/417 who was removed from office and exiled in 419 for not officially opposing Pelagianism. In exile, he was accepted by Theodore of Mopsuestia, whose Antiochene exegetical style he followed. Although he was never able to regain his ecclesiastical position, Julian taught in Sicily until his death. His works include commentaries on Job and parts of the Minor Prophets, a translation of Theodore of Mopsuestia's commentary on the Psalms, and various letters. Sympathetic to Pelagius, Julian applied his intellectual acumen and rhetorical training to argue against Augustine on matters such as free will, desire and the locus of evil.

Julian the Arian (c. fourth century) Antiochene, Arian author of *Commentary on Job*, and probably a follower of Aetius and Eunomius. The *85 Apostolic Canons*, once part of the *Apostolic Constitutions*, and the Pseudo-Ignatian writings are also attributed to him.

Justin Martyr (c. 100/110-165; fl. c. 148-161). Palestinian philosopher who was converted to Christianity, "the only sure and worthy philosophy." He traveled to Rome where he wrote several apologies against both pagans and Jews, combining Greek philosophy and Christian theology; he was eventually martyred.

Lactantius (c. 260-c. 330). Christian apologist removed from his post as teacher of rhetoric at Nicomedia upon his conversion to Christianity. He was tutor to the son of Constantine and author of *The Divine Institutes*.

Leander (c. 545-c. 600). Latin ecclesiastical writer, of whose works only two survive. He was instrumental in spreading Christianity among the Visigoths, gaining significant historical influence in Spain in his time.

Leo the Great (regn. 440-461). Bishop of Rome whose *Tome to Flavian* helped to strike a balance between Nestorian and Cyrilline positions at the Council of Chalcedon in 451.

Letter of Barnabas (c. 130). An allegorical and typological interpretation of the Old Testament with a decidedly anti-Jewish tone. It was included with other New Testament works as a "Catholic epistle" at least until Eusebius of Caesarea (c. 260/263-340) questioned its authenticity.

Letter to Diognetus (c. third century). A refutation of paganism and an exposition of the Christian life and faith. The author of this letter is unknown, and the exact identity of its recipient, Diognetus, continues to elude patristic scholars.

Lucifer (d. 370/371). Bishop of Cagliari and vigorous supporter of Athanasius and the Nicene Creed. In conflict with the emperor Constantius, he was banished to Palestine and later to Thebaid (Egypt).

Luculentius (fifth century). Unknown author of a group of short commentaries on the New Testament, especially Pauline passages. His exegesis is mainly literal and relies mostly on earlier authors such as Jerome and Augustine. The content of his writing may place it in the fifth century.

Macarius of Egypt (c. 300-c. 390). One of the Desert Fathers. Accused of supporting Athanasius, Macarius was exiled c. 374 to an island in the Nile by Lucius, the Arian successor of Athanasius. Macarius continued his teaching of monastic theology at Wadi Natrun.

Macrina the Younger (c. 327-379). The elder sister of Basil the Great and Gregory of Nyssa, she is known as "the Younger" to distinguish her from her paternal grandmother. She had a powerful influence on her younger brothers, especially on Gregory, who called her his teacher and relates her teaching in *On the Soul and the Resurrection*.

Manichaeans. A religious movement that originated circa 241 in Persia under the leadership of Mani but was apparently of complex Christian origin. It is said to have denied free will and the universal sovereignty of God, teaching that kingdoms of light and darkness are coeternal and that the redeemed are particles of a spiritual man of light held captive in the darkness of matter (*see* Gnostics).

Marcellus of Ancyra (d. c. 375). Wrote a refutation of Arianism. Later, he was accused of Sabellianism, especially by Eusebius of Caesarea. While the Western church declared him orthodox, the Eastern church excommunicated him. Some scholars have attributed to him certain works of Athanasius.

Marcion (fl. 144). Heretic of the mid-second century who rejected the Old Testament and much of the New Testament, claiming that the Father of Jesus Christ was other than the Old Testament God (*see* Gnostics).

Marius Victorinus (b. c. 280/285; fl. c. 355-363). Grammarian of African origin who taught rhetoric at Rome and translated works of Platonists. After his conversion (c. 355), he wrote against the Arians and commentaries on Paul's letters.

Mark the Hermit (c. sixth century). Monk who lived near Tarsus and produced works on ascetic practices as well as christological issues.

Martin of Braga (fl. c. 568-579). Anti-Arian metropolitan of Braga on the Iberian peninsula. He was highly educated and presided over the provincial council of Braga in 572.

Martyrius. *See* Sahdona.

Maximinus (the Arian) (b. c. 360-65). Bishop of an Arian community, perhaps in Illyricum. Of Roman descent, he debated publicly with Augustine at Hippo (427 or 428), ardently defending Arian doctrine. Besides the polemical works he wrote against the orthodox, such as his *Against the Heretics, Jews and Pagans,* he also wrote fifteen sermons that are considered much less polemical, having been previously attributed to Maximus of Turin. He is also known for his twenty-four *Explanations of Chapters of the Gospels.*

Maximus of Turin (d. 408/423). Bishop of Turin. Over one hundred of his sermons survive on Christian festivals, saints and martyrs.

Maximus the Confessor (c. 580-662). Palestinian-born theologian and ascetic writer. Fleeing the Arab invasion of Jerusalem in 614, he took refuge in Constantinople and later Africa. He died near the Black Sea after imprisonment and severe suffering, having his tongue cut off and his right hand mutilated. He taught total preference for God and detachment from all things.

Melito of Sardis (d. c. 190). Bishop of Sardis. According to Polycrates, he may have been Jewish by birth. Among his numerous works is a liturgical document known as *On Pascha* (ca. 160-177). As a Quartodeciman, and one involved intimately involved in that controversy, Melito celebrated Pascha on the fourteenth of Nisan in line with the custom handed down from Judaism.

Methodius of Olympus (d. 311). Bishop of Olympus who celebrated virginity in a *Symposium* partly modeled on Plato's dialogue of that name.

Minucius Felix (second or third century). Christian apologist who was an advocate in Rome. His *Octavius* agrees at numerous points with the *Apologeticum* of Tertullian. His birthplace is believed to be in Africa.

Montanist Oracles. Montanism was an apocalyptic and strictly ascetic movement begun in the latter half of the second century by a certain Montanus in Phrygia, who, along with certain of his followers, uttered oracles they claimed were inspired by the Holy Spirit. Little of the authentic oracles remains and most of what is known of Montanism comes from the authors who wrote against the movement. Montanism was formally condemned as a heresy before by Asiatic synods.

Nemesius of Emesa (fl. late fourth century). Bishop of Emesa in Syria whose most important work, *Of the Nature of Man*, draws on several theological and philosophical sources and is the first exposition of a Christian anthropology.

Nestorius (c. 381-c. 451). Patriarch of Constantinople (428-431) who founded the heresy which says that there are two persons, divine and human, rather than one person truly united in the incarnate Christ. He resisted the teaching of *theotokos*, causing Nestorian churches to separate from Constantinople.

Nicetas of Remesiana (fl. second half of fourth century). Bishop of Remesiana in Serbia, whose works affirm the consubstantiality of the Son and the deity of the Holy Spirit.

Nilus of Ancyra (d. c. 430). Prolific ascetic writer and disciple of John Chrysostom. Sometimes erroneously known as Nilus of Sinai, he was a native of Ancyra and studied at Constantinople.

Novatian of Rome (fl. 235-258). Roman theologian, otherwise orthodox, who formed a schismatic church after failing to become pope. His treatise on the Trinity states the classic western doctrine.

Oecumenius (sixth century). Called the Rhetor or the Philosopher, Oecumenius wrote the earliest extant Greek commentary on Revelation. Scholia by Oecumenius on some of John Chrysostom's commentaries on the Pauline Epistles are still extant.

Olympiodorus (early sixth century). Exegete and deacon of Alexandria, known for his commentaries that come to us mostly in catenae.

Origen of Alexandria (b. 185; fl. c. 200-254). Influential exegete and systematic theologian. He was condemned (perhaps unfairly) for maintaining the preexistence of souls while purportedly denying the resurrection of the body. His extensive works of exegesis focus on the spiritual meaning of the text.

Pachomius (c. 292-347). Founder of cenobitic monasticism. A gifted group leader and author of a set of rules, he was defended after his death by Athanasius of Alexandria.

Pacian of Barcelona (c. fourth century). Bishop of Barcelona whose writings polemicize against popular pagan festivals as well as Novatian schismatics.

Palladius of Helenopolis (c. 363/364-c. 431). Bishop of Helenopolis in Bithynia (400-417) and then Aspuna in Galatia. A disciple of Evagrius of Pontus and admirer of Origen, Palladius became a zealous adherent of John Chrysostom and shared his troubles in 403. His *Lausaic History* is the leading source for the history of early monasticism, stressing the spiritual value of the life of the desert.

Paschasius of Dumium (c. 515-c. 580). Translator of sentences of the Desert Fathers from Greek into Latin while a monk in Dumium.

Paterius (c. sixth-seventh century). Disciple of Gregory the Great who is primarily responsible for the transmission of Gregory's works to many later medieval authors.

Paulinus of Milan (late 4th-early 5th century). Personal secretary and biographer of Ambrose of Milan. He took part in the Pelagian controversy.

Paulinus of Nola (355-431). Roman senator and distinguished Latin poet whose frequent encounters with Ambrose of Milan (c. 333-397) led to his eventual conversion and baptism in 389. He eventually renounced his wealth and influential position and took up his pen to write poetry in service of Christ. He also wrote many letters to, among others, Augustine, Jerome and Rufinus.

Paulus Orosius (b. c. 380). An outspoken critic of Pelagius, mentored by Augustine. His *Seven Books of History Against the Pagans* was perhaps the first history of Christianity.

Pelagius (c. 354-c. 420). Contemporary of Augustine whose followers were condemned in 418 and 431 for maintaining that even before Christ there were people who lived wholly without sin and that salvation depended on free will.

Peter Chrysologus (c. 380-450). Latin archbishop of Ravenna whose teachings included arguments for adherence in matters of faith to the Roman see, and the relationship between grace and Christian living.

Peter of Alexandria (d. c. 311). Bishop of Alexandria. He marked (and very probably initiated) the reaction at Alexandria against extreme doctrines of Origen. During the persecution of Christians in Alexandria, Peter was arrested and beheaded by Roman officials. Eusebius of Caesarea described him as "a model bishop, remarkable for his virtuous life and his ardent study of the Scriptures."

Philip the Priest (d. 455/56) Acknowledged by Gennadius as a disciple of Jerome. In his *Commentary on the Book of Job*, Philip utilizes Jerome's Vulgate, providing an important witness to the transmission of that translation. A few of his letters are extant.

Philo of Alexandria (c. 20 B.C.-c. A.D. 50). Jewish-born exegete who greatly influenced Christian patristic interpretation of the Old Testament. Born to a rich family in Alexandria, Philo was a contemporary of Jesus and lived an ascetic and contemplative life that makes some believe he was a rabbi. His interpretation of Scripture based the spiritual sense on the literal. Although influenced by Hellenism, Philo's theology remains thoroughly Jewish.

Philoxenus of Mabbug (c. 440-523). Bishop of Mabbug (Hierapolis) and a leading thinker in the early Syrian Orthodox Church. His extensive writings in Syriac include a set of thirteen *Discourses on the Christian Life*, several works on the incarnation and a number of exegetical works.

Photius (c. 820-891). An important Byzantine churchman and university professor of philosophy, mathematics and theology. He was twice the patriarch of Constantinople. First he succeeded Ignatius in 858, but was deposed in 863 when Ignatius

was reinstated. Again he followed Ignatius in 878 and remained the patriarch until 886, at which time he was removed by Leo VI. His most important theological work is *Address on the Mystagogy of the Holy Spirit*, in which he articulates his opposition to the Western filioque, i.e., the procession of the Holy Spirit from the Father and the Son. He is also known for his Amphilochia and Library (Bibliotheca).

Poemen (c. fifth century). One-seventh of the sayings in the *Sayings of the Desert Fathers* are attributed to Poemen, which is Greek for shepherd. Poemen was a common title among early Egyptian desert ascetics, and it is unknown whether all of the sayings come from one person.

Polycarp of Smyrna (c. 69-155). Bishop of Smyrna who vigorously fought heretics such as the Marcionites and Valentinians. He was the leading Christian figure in Roman Asia in the middle of the second century.

Potamius of Lisbon (fl. c. 350-360). Bishop of Lisbon who joined the Arian party in 357, but later returned to the Catholic faith (c. 359?). His works from both periods are concerned with the larger Trinitarian debates of his time.

Primasius (fl. 550-560). Bishop of Hadrumetum in North Africa (modern Tunisia) and one of the few Africans to support the condemnation of the Three Chapters. Drawing on Augustine and Tyconius, he wrote a commentary on the Apocalypse, which in allegorizing fashion views the work as referring to the history of the church.

Proclus of Constantinople (c. 390-446). Patriarch of Constantinople (434-446). His patriarchate dealt with the Nestorian controversy, rebutting, in his *Tome to the Armenian Bishops*, Theodore of Mopsuestia's Christology where Theodore was thought to have overly separated the two natures of Christ. Proclus stressed the unity of Christ in his formula "One of the Trinity suffered," which was later taken up and spread by the Scythian monks of the sixth century, resulting in the theopaschite controversy. Proclus was known as a gifted preacher and church politician, extending and expanding Constantinople's influence while avoiding conflict with Antioch, Rome and Alexandria.

Procopius of Gaza (c. 465-c. 530). A Christian exegete educated in Alexandria. He wrote numerous theological works and commentaries on Scripture (particularly the Hebrew Bible), the latter marked by the allegorical exegesis for which the Alexandrian school was known.

Prosper of Aquitaine (c. 390-c. 463). Probably a lay monk and supporter of the theology of Augustine on grace and predestination. He collaborated closely with Pope Leo I in his doctrinal statements.

Prudentius (c. 348-c. 410). Latin poet and hymn-writer who devoted his later life to Christian writing. He wrote didactic poems on the theology of the incarnation, against the heretic Marcion and against the resurgence of paganism.

Pseudo-Clementines (third-fourth century). A series of apocryphal writings pertaining to a conjured life of Clement of Rome. Written in a form of popular legend, the stories from Clement's life, including his opposition to Simon Magus, illustrate and promote articles of Christian teaching. It is likely that the corpus is a derivative of a number of Gnostic and Judeo-Christian writings. Dating the corpus is a complicated issue.

Pseudo-Dionysius the Areopagite (fl. c. 500). Author who assumed the name of Dionysius the Areopagite mentioned in Acts 17:34, and who composed the works known as the *Corpus Areopagiticum* (or *Dionysiacum*). These writings were the foundation of the apophatic school of mysticism in their denial that anything can be truly predicated of God.

Pseudo-Macarius (fl. c. 390). An anonymous writer and ascetic (from Mesopotamia?) active in Antioch whose badly edited works were attributed to Macarius of Egypt. He had keen insight into human nature, prayer and the inner life. His work includes some one hundred discourses and homilies.

Quodvultdeus (fl. 430). Carthaginian bishop and friend of Augustine who endeavored to show at length how the New Testament fulfilled the Old Testament.

Romanus Melodus (fl. c. 536-556). Born as a Jew in Emesa not far from Beirut where after his baptism later he later became deacon of the Church of the Resurrection. He later moved to Constantinople and may have seen the destruction of the Hagia Sophia and its rebuilding during the time he flourished there. As many as eighty metrical sermons (*kontakia*, sg. *kontakion*) that utilize dialogical poetry have come down to us under his name. These sermons were sung rather than preached during the liturgy, and frequently provide theological insights and Scriptural connections often unique to Romanus. His Christology, closely associated with Justinian, reflects the struggles against the Monophysites of his day.

Rufinus of Aquileia (c. 345-411). Orthodox Christian thinker and historian who nonetheless translated and preserved the works of Origen, and defended him against the strictures of Jerome and Epiphanius. He lived the ascetic life in Rome, Egypt and Jerusalem (the Mount of Olives).

Sabellius (fl. 200). Allegedly the author of the heresy which maintains that the Father and Son are a single person. The patripassian variant of this heresy states that the Father suffered on the cross.

Sahdona (fl. 635-640). Known in Greek as Martyrius, this Syriac author was bishop of Beth Garmai. He studied in Nisibis and was exiled for his christological ideas. His most important work is the deeply scriptural *Book of Perfection* which ranks as one of the masterpieces of Syriac monastic literature.

Salvian the Presbyter of Marseilles (c. 400-c. 480). An important author for the history of his own time. He saw the fall of Roman civilization to the barbarians as a consequence of the reprehensible conduct of Roman Christians. In *The Governance of God* he developed the theme of divine providence.

Second Letter of Clement (c. 150). The so-called *Second Letter of Clement* is an early Christian sermon probably written by a Corinthian author, though some scholars have assigned it to a Roman or Alexandrian author.

Severian of Gabala (fl. c. 400). A contemporary of John Chrysostom, he was a highly regarded preacher in Constantinople, particularly at the imperial court, and ultimately sided with Chrysostom's accusers. He wrote homilies on Genesis.

Severus of Antioch (fl. 488-538). A monophysite theologian, consecrated bishop of Antioch in 522. Born in Pisidia, he studied in Alexandria and Beirut, taught in Constantinople and was exiled to Egypt.

Shenoute (c. 350-466). Abbot of Athribis in Egypt. His large monastic community was known for very strict rules. He accompanied Cyril of Alexandria to the Council of Ephesus in 431, where he played an important role in deposing Nestorius. He knew Greek but wrote in Coptic, and his literary activity includes homilies, catecheses on monastic subjects, letters, and a couple of theological treatises.

Shepherd of Hermas (second century). Divided into five *Visions*, twelve *Mandates* and ten *Similitudes*, this Christian apocalypse was written by a former slave and named for the form of the second angel said to have granted him his visions. This work was highly esteemed for its moral value and was used as a textbook for catechumens in the early church.

Sulpicius Severus (c. 360-c. 420). An ecclesiastical writer from Bordeaux born of noble parents. Devoting himself to monastic retirement, he became a personal friend and enthusiastic disciple of St. Martin of Tours.

Symeon the New Theologian (c. 949-1022). Compassionate spiritual leader known for his strict rule. He believed that the divine light could be perceived and received through the practice of mental prayer.

Tertullian of Carthage (c. 155/160-225/250; fl. c. 197-222). Brilliant Carthaginian apologist and polemicist who laid the foundations of Christology and trinitarian orthodoxy in the West, though he himself was later estranged from the catholic tradition due to its laxity.

Theodore of Heraclea (d. c. 355). An anti-Nicene bishop of Thrace. He was part of a team seeking reconciliation between Eastern and Western Christianity. In 343 he was excommunicated at the council of Sardica. His writings focus on a literal interpretation of Scripture.

Theodore of Mopsuestia (c. 350-428). Bishop of Mopsuestia, founder of the Antiochene, or literalistic, school of exegesis. A great man in his day, he was later condemned as a precursor of Nestorius.

Theodore of Tabennesi (d. 368) Vice general of the Pachomian monasteries (c. 350-368) under Horsiesi. Several of his letters are known.

Theodoret of Cyr (c. 393-466). Bishop of Cyr (Cyrrhus), he was an opponent of Cyril who commented extensively on Old Testament texts as a lucid exponent of Antiochene exegesis.

Theodotus the Valentinian (second century). Likely a Montanist who may have been related to the Alexandrian school. Extracts of his work are known through writings of Clement of Alexandria.

Theophanes (775-845). Hymnographer and bishop of Nicaea (842-845). He was persecuted during the second iconoclastic period for his support of the Seventh Council (Second Council of Nicaea, 787). He wrote many hymns in the tradition of the monastery of Mar Sabbas that were used in the *Paraklitiki*.

Theophilus of Alexandria (d. 412). Patriarch of Alexandria (385-412) and the uncle of his successor, Cyril. His patriarchate was known for his opposition to paganism, having destroyed the Serapeion and its library in 391, but he also built many churches. He also was known for his political machinations against his theological enemies, especially John Chrysostom, whom he himself had previously consecrated as patriarch, ultimately getting John removed from his see and earning the intense dislike of Antioch Christians. He is, however, venerated among the Copts and Syrians, among whom many of his sermons have survived, although only a few are deemed authentically his. His *Homily on the Mystical Supper*, commenting on the Last Supper, is perhaps one of his most well known.

Theophilus of Antioch (late second century). Bishop of Antioch. His only surviving work is *Ad*

Autholycum, where we find the first Christian commentary on Genesis and the first use of the term *Trinity.* Theophilus's apologetic literary heritage had influence on Irenaeus and possibly Tertullian.

Theophylact of Ohrid (c. 1050-c. 1108). Byzantine archbishop of Ohrid (or Achrida) in what is now Bulgaria. Drawing on earlier works, he wrote commentaries on several Old Testament books and all of the New Testament except for Revelation.

Tyconius (c. 330-390). A lay theologian and exegete of the Donatist church in North Africa who influenced Augustine. His *Book of Rules* is the first manual of scriptural interpretation in the Latin West. In 380 he was excommunicated by the Donatist council at Carthage.

Valentinus (fl. c. 140). Alexandrian heretic of the mid-second century who taught that the material world was created by the transgression of God's Wisdom, or Sophia (*see* Gnostics).

Valerian of Cimiez (fl. c. 422-439). Bishop of Cimiez. He participated in the councils of Riez (439) and Vaison (422) with a view to strengthening church discipline. He supported Hilary of Arles in quarrels with Pope Leo I.

Verecundus (d. 552). An African Christian writer, who took an active part in the christological controversies of the sixth century, especially in the debate on Three Chapters. He also wrote allegorical commentaries on the nine liturgical church canticles.

Victorinus of Petovium (d. c. 304). Latin biblical exegete. With multiple works attributed to him, his sole surviving work is the *Commentary on the Apocalypse* and perhaps some fragments from *Commentary on Matthew.* Victorinus expressed strong millenarianism in his writing, though his was less materialistic than the millenarianism of Papias or Irenaeus. In his allegorical approach he could be called a spiritual disciple of Origen. Victorinus died during the first year of Diocletian's persecution, probably in 304.

Vincent of Lérins (d. before 450). Monk who has exerted considerable influence through his writings on orthodox dogmatic theological method, as contrasted with the theological methodologies of the heresies.

Timeline of Writers of the Patristic Period

Location	British Isles	Gaul	Spain, Portugal	Rome* and Italy	Carthage and Northern Africa
Period					
2nd century				Clement of Rome, fl. c. 92-101 (Greek)	
				Shepherd of Hermas, c. 140 (Greek)	
				Justin Martyr (Ephesus, Rome), c. 100/110-165 (Greek)	
		Irenaeus of Lyons, c. 135-c. 202 (Greek)		Valentinus the Gnostic (Rome), fl. c. 140 (Greek)	
3rd century				Marcion (Rome), fl. 144 (Greek) Heracleon, 145-180 (Greek)	
				Callistus of Rome, regn. 217-222 (Latin)	Tertullian of Carthage, c. 155/160-c. 225 (Latin)
				Minucius Felix of Rome, fl. 218-235 (Latin)	
				Hippolytus (Rome, Palestine?), fl. 222-235/245 (Greek)	Cyprian of Carthage, fl. 248-258 (Latin)
				Novatian of Rome, fl. 235-258 (Latin)	
				Victorinus of Petovium, 230-304 (Latin)	

*One of the five ancient patriarchates

Alexandria* and Egypt	Constantinople* and Asia Minor, Greece	Antioch* and Syria	Mesopotamia, Persia	Jerusalem* and Palestine	Location Unknown
Philo of Alexandria, c. 20 B.C. – c. A.D. 50 (Greek)				Flavius Josephus (Rome), c. 37-c. 101 (Greek)	
Basilides (Alexandria), 2nd cent. (Greek)	Polycarp of Smyrna, c. 69-155 (Greek)	*Didache* (Egypt?), c. 100 (Greek)			
Letter of Barnabas (Syria?), c. 130 (Greek)		Ignatius of Antioch, c. 35–107/112 (Greek)			
Theodotus the Valentinian, 2nd cent. (Greek)	Athenagoras (Greece), fl. 176-180 (Greek)	Theophilus of Antioch, c. late 2nd cent. (Greek)			*Second Letter of Clement* (spurious; Corinth, Rome, Alexandria?) (Greek), c. 150
	Melito of Sardis, d.c. 190 (Greek)	*Didascalia Apostolorum*, early 3rd cent. (Syriac)			
Clement of Alexandria, c. 150-215 (Greek)	*Montanist Oracles*, late 2nd cent. (Greek)				
Sabellius (Egypt), 2nd–3rd cent. (Greek)					Pseudo-Clementines 3rd cent. (Greek)
			Mani (Manichaeans), c. 216-276		
Letter to Diognetus, 3rd cent. (Greek)	Gregory Thaumaturgus (Neocaesarea), fl. c. 248-264 (Greek)				
Origen (Alexandria, Caesarea of Palestine), 185-254 (Greek)					
Dionysius of Alexandria, d. 264/5 (Greek)					
	Methodius of Olympus (Lycia), d. c. 311 (Greek)				

Timeline of Writers of the Patristic Period

Location	British Isles	Gaul	Spain, Portugal	Rome* and Italy	Carthage and Northern Africa
Period					
4th century				Firmicus Maternus (Sicily), fl. c. 335 (Latin)	Isaiah of Scete, late 4th cent. (Greek)
		Lactantius, c. 260-330 (Latin)		Marius Victorinus (Rome), fl. 355-363 (Latin)	
				Eusebius of Vercelli, fl. c. 360 (Latin)	
			Hosius of Cordova, d. 357 (Latin)	Lucifer of Cagliari (Sardinia), d. 370/371 (Latin)	
		Hilary of Poitiers, c. 315-367 (Latin)	Potamius of Lisbon, fl. c. 350-360 (Latin)	Faustinus (Rome), fl. 380 (Latin)	
				Filastrius of Brescia, fl. 380 (Latin)	
			Gregory of Elvira, fl. 359-385 (Latin)	Ambrosiaster (Italy?), fl. c. 366-384 (Latin)	
			Prudentius, c. 348-c. 410 (Latin)	Faustus of Riez, fl. c. 380 (Latin)	
			Pacian of Barcelona, 4th cent. (Latin)	Gaudentius of Brescia, fl. 395 (Latin)	Paulus Orosius, b. c. 380 (Latin)
				Ambrose of Milan, c. 333-397; fl. 374-397 (Latin)	
				Paulinus of Milan, late 4th-early 5th cent. (Latin)	
5th century				Rufinus (Aquileia, Rome), c. 345-411 (Latin)	
	Fastidius (Britain), c. 4th-5th cent. (Latin)	Sulpicius Severus (Bordeaux), c. 360-c. 420/425 (Latin)		Aponius, fl. 405-415 (Latin)	Quodvultdeus (Carthage), fl. 430 (Latin)
		John Cassian (Palestine, Egypt, Constantinople, Rome, Marseilles), 360-432 (Latin)		Chromatius (Aquileia), fl. 400 (Latin)	
				Pelagius (Britain, Rome), c. 354-c. 420 (Greek)	Augustine of Hippo, 354-430 (Latin)
				Maximus of Turin, d. 408/423 (Latin)	Luculentius, 5th cent. (Latin)
		Vincent of Lérins, d. 435 (Latin)		Paulinus of Nola, 355-431 (Latin)	
		Valerian of Cimiez, fl. c. 422-449 (Latin)		Peter Chrysologus (Ravenna), c. 380-450 (Latin)	
		Eucherius of Lyons, fl. 420-449 (Latin)		Julian of Eclanum, 386-454 (Latin)	

*One of the five ancient patriarchates

Alexandria* and Egypt	Constantinople* and Asia Minor, Greece	Antioch* and Syria	Mesopotamia, Persia	Jerusalem* and Palestine	Location Unknown
Antony, c. 251-355 (Coptic /Greek)	Theodore of Heraclea (Thrace), fl. c. 330-355 (Greek)	Eustathius of Antioch, fl. 325 (Greek)	Aphrahat (Persia) c. 270-350; fl. 337-345 (Syriac)	Eusebius of Caesarea (Palestine), c. 260/ 263-340 (Greek)	Commodius, c. 3rd or 5th cent. (Latin)
Peter of Alexandria, d.c. 311 (Greek)	Marcellus of Ancyra, d.c. 375 (Greek)	Eusebius of Emesa, c. 300-c. 359 (Greek)			
Arius (Alexandria), fl. c. 320 (Greek)	Epiphanius of Salamis (Cyprus), c. 315-403 (Greek)	Ephrem the Syrian, c. 306-373 (Syriac)	Jacob of Nisibis, fl. 308-325 (Syriac)		
Alexander of Alexandria, fl. 312-328 (Greek)	Basil (the Great) of Caesarea, b. c. 330; fl. 357-379 (Greek)	Julian the Arian (c. fourth century)			
Pachomius, c. 292-347 (Coptic/Greek?)	Macrina the Younger, c. 327-379 (Greek)				
Theodore of Tabennesi, d. 368 (Coptic/Greek)	Apollinaris of Laodicea, 310-c. 392 (Greek)				
Horsiesi, c. 305-390 (Coptic/Greek)	Gregory of Nazianzus, b. 329/330; fl. 372-389 (Greek)	Nemesius of Emesa (Syria), fl. late 4th cent. (Greek)			Maximinus, b.c. 360-365 (Latin)
Athanasius of Alexandria, c. 295-373; fl. 325-373 (Greek)	Gregory of Nyssa, c. 335-394 (Greek)	Diodore of Tarsus, d. c. 394 (Greek)		Acacius of Caesarea (Palestine), d. c. 365 (Greek)	
Macarius of Egypt, c. 300-c. 390 (Greek)	Amphilochius of Iconium, c. 340/ 345- c. 398/404 (Greek)	John Chrysostom (Constantinople), 344/354-407 (Greek)		Cyril of Jerusalem, c. 315-386 (Greek)	
Didymus (the Blind) of Alexandria, 313-398 (Greek)	Evagrius of Pontus, 345-399 (Greek)	Apostolic Constitutions, c. 375-400 (Greek)			
		Didascalia, 4th cent. (Syriac)			
Tyconius, c. 330-390 (Latin)	Eunomius of Cyzicus, fl. 360-394 (Greek)	Theodore of Mopsuestia, c. 350-428 (Greek)		Diodore of Tarsus, d. c. 394 (Greek)	
	Pseudo-Macarius (Mesopotamia?), late 4th cent. (Greek)	Acacius of Beroea, c. 340-c. 436 (Greek)			
Theophilus of Alexandria, d. 412 (Greek)	Nicetas of Remesiana, d. c. 414 (Latin)			Jerome (Rome, Antioch, Bethlehem), c. 347-420 (Latin)	
Palladius of Helenopolis (Egypt), c. 365-425 (Greek)	Proclus of Constantinople, c. 390-446 (Greek)	Book of Steps, c. 400 (Syriac)	Eznik of Kolb, fl. 430-450 (Armenian)		
	Nestorius (Constantinople), c. 381-c. 451 (Greek)	Severian of Gabala, fl. c. 400 (Greek)			
Cyril of Alexandria, 375-444 (Greek)				Philip the Priest (d. 455/56)	
	Basil of Seleucia, fl. 440-468 (Greek)	Nilus of Ancyra, d.c. 430 (Greek)		Hesychius of Jerusalem, fl. 412-450 (Greek)	
	Diadochus of Photice (Macedonia), 400-474 (Greek)				
				Euthymius (Palestine), 377-473 (Greek)	

Timeline of Writers of the Patristic Period

Location / Period	British Isles	Gaul	Spain, Portugal	Rome* and Italy	Carthage and Northern Africa
5th century (cont.)		Hilary of Arles, c. 401-449 (Latin)			
		Eusebius of Gaul, 5th cent. (Latin)		Leo the Great (Rome), regn. 440-461 (Latin)	
		Prosper of Aquitaine, c. 390-c. 463 (Latin)		Arnobius the Younger (Rome), fl. c. 450 (Latin)	
		Salvian the Presbyter of Marseilles, c. 400-c. 480 (Latin)		Ennodius (Arles, Milan, Pavia) c. 473-521 (Latin)	
		Gennadius of Marseilles, d. after 496 (Latin)		Epiphanius the Latin, late 5th–early 6th cent. (Latin)	
6th century		Caesarius of Arles, c. 470-543 (Latin)	Paschasius of Dumium (Portugal), c. 515-c. 580 (Latin)	Eugippius, c. 460- c. 533 (Latin)	Fulgentius of Ruspe, c. 467-532 (Latin)
			Apringius of Beja, mid-6th cent. (Latin)	Benedict of Nursia, c. 480-547 (Latin)	
			Leander of Seville, c. 545-c. 600 (Latin)	Cassiodorus (Calabria), c. 485-c. 540 (Latin)	Verecundus, d. 552 (Latin)
					Primasius, fl. 550-560 (Latin)
		Flavian of Chalon-sur-Saône, fl. 580-600 (Latin)	Martin of Braga, fl. 568-579 (Latin)	Gregory the Great (Rome), c. 540-604 (Latin)	Facundus of Hermiane, fl. 546-568 (Latin)
				Gregory of Agrigentium, d. 592 (Greek)	
7th century			Isidore of Seville, c. 560-636 (Latin)	Paterius, 6th/7th cent. (Latin)	
			Braulio of Saragossa, c. 585-651 (Latin)		
	Adamnan, c. 624-704 (Latin)		Fructuosus of Braga, d.c. 665 (Latin)		
8th-12th century	Bede the Venerable, c. 672/673-735 (Latin)				

*One of the five ancient patriarchates

Alexandria* and Egypt	Constantinople* and Asia Minor, Greece	Antioch* and Syria	Mesopotamia, Persia	Jerusalem* and Palestine	Location Unknown
Ammonius of Alexandria, c. 460 (Greek)	Gennadius of Constantinople, d. 471 (Greek)	John of Antioch, d. 441/2 (Greek)		Gerontius of Petra c. 395-c. 480 (Syriac)	
Poemen, 5th cent. (Greek)		Theodoret of Cyr, c. 393-466 (Greek)			
		Pseudo-Victor of Antioch, 5th cent. (Greek)			
Besa the Copt, 5th cent.		John of Apamea, 5th cent. (Syriac)			
Shenoute, c. 350-466 (Coptic)					
	Andrew of Caesarea (Cappadocia), early 6th cent. (Greek)				
Olympiodorus, early 6th cent.	Oecumenius (Isauria), 6th cent. (Greek)	Philoxenus of Mabbug (Syria), c. 440-523 (Syriac)	Jacob of Sarug, c. 450-520 (Syriac)	Procopius of Gaza (Palestine), c. 465-530 (Greek)	Pseudo-Dionysius the Areopagite, fl. c. 500 (Greek)
	Romanus Melodus, fl. c. 536-556 (Greek)	Severus of Antioch, c. 465-538 (Greek)	Abraham of Nathpar, fl. 6th-7th cent. (Syriac)	Dorotheus of Gaza, fl. 525-540 (Greek)	
		Mark the Hermit (Tarsus), c. 6th cent. (4th cent.?) (Greek)	Babai the Great, c. 550-628 (Syriac)	Cyril of Scythopolis, b. c. 525; d. after 557 (Greek)	
			Babai, early 6th cent. (Syriac)		
	Maximus the Confessor (Constantinople), c. 580-662 (Greek)	Sahdona/Martyrius, fl. 635-640 (Syriac)	Isaac of Nineveh, d. c. 700 (Syriac)		(Pseudo-) Constantius, before 7th cent.? (Greek)
	Andrew of Crete, c. 660-740 (Greek)			Cosmas Melodus, c. 675-751 (Greek)	Andreas, c. 7th cent. (Greek)
	John of Carpathus, 7th-8th cent. (Greek)	John of Damascus (John the Monk), c. 650-750 (Greek)	John the Elder of Qardu (north Iraq), 8th cent. (Syriac)		
	Theophanes (Nicaea), 775-845 (Greek)				
	Cassia (Constantinople), c. 805-c. 848/867 (Greek)		Isho'dad of Merv, d. after 852 (Syriac)		
	Arethas of Caesarea (Constantinople/Caesarea), c. 860-940 (Greek)				
	Photius (Constantinople), c. 820-891 (Greek)				
	Symeon the New Theologian (Constantinople), 949-1022 (Greek)				
	Theophylact of Ohrid (Bulgaria), 1050-1126 (Greek)				

Bibliography of Works in Original Languages

This bibliography refers readers to original language sources and supplies Thesaurus Linguae Graecae (=TLG) or Cetedoc Clavis (=Cl.) numbers where available. The edition listed in this bibliography may in some cases differ from the edition found in TLG or Cetedoc databases.

Alexander of Alexandria. *See* Theodoret of Cyr. "Historia ecclesiastica." In *Theodoret: Kirchengeschichte.* 2nd ed. Edited by L. Parmentier and F. Scheidweiler. GCS 44, pp. 1-349. Berlin: Akademie-Verlag, 1954. TLG 4089.003.

Ambrose. "De bono mortis." In *Sancti Ambrosii opera.* Edited by Karl Schenkl. CSEL 32, pt. 1, pp. 701-53. Vienna, Austria: F. Tempsky; Leipzig, Germany: G. Freytag, 1897. Cl. 0129.

———. "De Cain et Abel." In *Sancti Ambrosii opera.* Edited by Karl Schenkl. CSEL 32, pt. 1, pp. 339-409. Vienna, Austria: F. Tempsky; Leipzig, Germany: G. Freytag, 1897. Cl. 0123.

———. "De excessu fratris Satyri." In *Sancti Ambrosii opera.* Edited by Otto Faller. CSEL 73, pp. 207-325. Vienna, Austria: Hoelder-Pichler-Tempsky, 1895. Cl. 0157.

———. "De fide libri v." In *Sancti Ambrosii opera.* Edited by Otto Faller. CSEL 78. Vienna, Austria: Hoelder-Pichler-Tempsky, 1962. Cl. 0150.

———. "De fuga saeculi." In *Sancti Ambrosii opera.* Edited by Karl Schenkl. CSEL 32, pt. 2, pp. 163-207. Vienna, Austria: F. Tempsky; Leipzig: G. Freytag, 1897. Cl. 0133.

———. "De Iacob et vita beata." In *Sancti Ambrosii opera.* Edited by Karl Schenkl. CSEL 32, pt. 2, pp. 3-10. Vienna, Austria: F. Tempsky; Leipzig: G. Freytag, 1897. Cl. 0130.

———. "De Interpellatione Iob et David." In *Sancti Ambrosii opera.* Edited by Karl Schenkl. CSEL 32, pt. 2, pp. 211-96. Vienna, Austria: F. Tempsky; Leipzig: G. Freytag, 1897. Cl. 0134.

———. "De mysteriis." In *Sancti Ambrosii opera.* Edited by Otto Faller. CSEL 73, pp. 87-116. Vienna, Austria: Hoelder-Pichler-Tempsky, 1955. Cl. 0155.

———. "De obitu Theodosii." In *Sancti Ambrosii opera.* Edited by Otto Faller. CSEL 73, pp. 371-401. Vienna, Austria: Hoelder-Pichler-Tempsky, 1955. Cl. 0159.

———. De officiis ministrorum. Edited by Maurice Testard. CCL 15. Turnhout, Belgium: Brepols, 2000. Cl. 0144.

———. De Paenitentia. Edited by Roger Gryson. SC 179. Paris: Éditions du Cerf, 1971. Cl. 0156.

———. "De Paradiso." In *Sancti Ambrosii opera.* Edited by Karl Schenkl. CSEL 32, pt. 1, pp. 263-336. Vienna, Austria: F. Tempsky; Leipzig, Germany: G. Freytag, 1897. Cl. 0123.

———. "De spiritu sancto." In *Sancti Ambrosii opera.* Edited by Otto Faller. CSEL 79, pp. 5-222. Vienna, Austria: Hoelder-Pichler-Tempsky, 1964. Cl. 0151.

———. "De virginibus." In *Opere II/2: Verginità e vedovanza.* Edited by F. Gori. Opera omnia di Sant'Ambrogio 14.1, pp. 100-240. Milan: Biblioteca Ambrosiana; Rome: Città nuova, 1989. Cl. 0145.

———. "De virginitate." In *Opere II/2: Verginità e vedovanza.* Edited by F. Gori. Opera omnia di Sant'Ambrogio 14.2, pp. 16-106. Milan: Biblioteca Ambrosiana; Rome: Città nuova, 1989. Cl. 0147.

———. "Epistulae extra collectionem traditae." In *Sancti Ambrosii opera.* Edited by Otto Faller and

Michaela Zelzer. CSEL 82. 4 vols. Vienna, Austria: F. Tempsky; Leipzig, Germany: G. Freytag, 1968-1990. Cl. 0160.

———."Exameron." In *Sancti Ambrosii opera*. Edited by Karl Schenkl. CSEL 32, pt. 1, pp. 1-261. Vienna, Austria: F. Tempsky; Leipzig, Germany: G. Freytag, 1897. Cl. 0123.

Ammon."Letter of Bishop Ammon." In *Sancti Pachomii vitae Graecae*. Subsidia hagiographica 19, pp. 97-121. Edited by F. Halkin. Brussels, 1932.

"Apocalypsis Iohannis." In *Apocalypses Apocryphae*, pp. 70-94. Edited by Konstantin von Tischendorf. Hildesheim: Georg Olms, 1966.

"Apophthegmata patrum (collectio alphabetica)." In *S. P. N. Procli Archiepiscopi Constantinopolitani opera omnia*. Edited by J.-P. Migne. PG 65, cols. 72-440. Paris: Migne, 1864. TLG 2742.001.

Aphrahat."Demonstrationes." In *Aphraatis sapientis Persae Demonstrationes*. Edited by J. Parisot. *Patrologia Syriaca* vol. 1, pt. 1, pp. 5-1050. Paris: Instituti Francici, 1894.

———."Demonstrationes (IV)." In *Opera omnia*. Edited by R. Graffin. Patrologia Syriaca 1, cols. 137-82. Paris: Firmin-Didor, 1910.

Archelaus."Acta disputationis cum Manete (versio Latine)." In *S. P. N. Gregorii, cognomento Thaumaturgi, opera quae reperiri potuerunt omnia*. Edited by J.-P. Migne. PG 10, cols. 1429-1528. Paris: Migne, 1857.

Arnobius Iunior. *Commentarii in Psalmos*. Edited by K.-D Daur. CCL 25.1. Turnhout, Belgium: Brepols, 1990.

Athanasius. "Apologia ad Constantium imperatorem." In Athanase d'Alexandrie, *Apologie à l'empereur Constance: Apologie pour sa fuite*. Edited by J.-M. Szymusiak. SC 56, pp. 88-132. Paris: Éditions du Cerf, 1958. TLG 2035.011.

———."Apologia de fuga sua." In Athanase d'Alexandrie. *Apologie à l'empereur Constance: Apologie pour sa fuite*. SC 56, pp. 133-167. Paris: Éditions du Cerf, 1958. TLG 2035.012.

———."Contra gentes." In *Contra gentes, and De incarnatione*, pp. 2-132. Edited by Robert W. Thompson. Oxford: Clarendon Press, 1971. TLG 2035.001.

———. "De decretis Nicaenae synodi." In *Athanasius Werke*. Vol. 2.1, pp, 1-45. Edited by Hans-Georg Opitz. Berlin: de Gruyter, 1940. TLG 2035.003.

———. "De incarnatione verbi." In *Sur l'incarnation du verbe*. Edited by C. Kannengiesser. SC 199, pp. 258-468. Paris: Éditions du Cerf, 1973. TLG 2035.002.

———. "Orationes tres contra Arianos." In *Opera omnia*. Edited by J.-P. Migne. PG 26, cols. 813-920. Paris: Migne, 1887. TLG 2035.042.

———."Oratio quarta contra Arianos [Sp.]." In *Die pseudoathanasianische "IVte Rede gegen die Arianer" als "κατὰ Ἀρειανῶν λόγος" ein Apollinarisgut*, pp. 43-87. Edited by A. Stegmann. Rottenburg: Bader, 1917. TLG 2035.117.

———."Vita sancti Antonii." In *Opera omnia*. Edited by J.-P. Migne. PG 26, cols. 835-976. Paris: Migne, 1887. TLG 2035.047.

Augustine."Adversus Judaeos." In *Opera omnia*. Edited by J.-P. Migne. PL 42, cols. 51-64. Paris: Migne, 1861. Cl. 0315.

———. *Confessionum libri tredecim*. Edited by L. Verheijen. CCL 27. Turnhout, Belgium: Brepols, 1981. Cl. 0251.

———."Contra Faustum." In *Sancti Aurelii Augustini opera*. Edited by Joseph Zycha. CSEL 25, pp. 249-797. Vienna, Austria: F. Tempsky; Leipzig, Germany: G. Freytag, 1891. Cl. 0321.

———."Contra litteras Petiliani." In *Sancti Aureli Augustini opera*. Edited by M. Petschenig. CSEL 52, pp. 3-227. Vienna, Austria: F. Tempsky, 1909. Cl. 0333.

———. "Contra Julianum." In *Opera omnia*. Edited by J.-P. Migne. PL 44, cols. 641-874. Paris: Migne, 1861. Cl. 0351.

————."Contra mendacium." In *Sancti Aureli Augustini opera*. Edited by Joseph Zycha. CSEL 41, pp. 469-528. Vienna, Austria: F. Tempsky, 1900. Cl. 0304.

————. "De agone christiano." In *Sancti Aureli Augustini opera*. Edited by Joseph Zycha. CSEL 41, pp. 101-38. Vienna, Austria: F. Tempsky, 1900. Cl. 0296.

————. *De civitate Dei*. In *Aurelii Augustini opera*. Edited by Bernhard Dombart and Alphons Kalb. CCL 47 and 48. Turnhout, Belgium: Brepols, 1955. Cl. 0313.

————. "De continentia." In *Sancti Aurelii Augustini opera*. Edited by Joseph Zycha. CSEL 41, pp. 141-183. Vienna, Austria: F. Tempsky, 1900. Cl. 0298.

————. "De correptione et gratia." In *Opera omnia*. Edited by J.-P. Migne. PL 44, cols. 915-46. Paris: Migne, 1845. Cl. 0353.

————. "De diversis quaestionibus ad Simplicianum." In *Aurelii Augustini opera*. Edited by Almut Mutzenbecher. CCL 44. Turnhout, Belgium: Brepols, 1970. Cl. 0290.

————. "De diuersis quaestionibus octoginta tribus." In *Opera*. Edited by A. Mutzenbecher. CCL, vol. 44A, pp. 11-249. Turnhout, Belgium: Brepols, 1975. Cl. 0289.

————. "De dono perseverantiae." In *Opera omnia*. Edited by J.-P. Migne. PL 45, cols. 993-1034. Paris: Migne, 1845. Cl. 0355.

————. "De fide rerum invisibilium." In *Aurelii Augustini opera*. Edited by M. P. J. van den Hout. CCL 46, pp. 1-19. Turnhout, Belgium: Brepols, 1969. Cl. 0292.

————. "De Genesi ad litteram imperfectus liber." In *Sancti Aurelii Augustini opera*. Edited by Joseph Zycha. CSEL 28.1, pp. 459-503. Vienna, Austria: F. Tempsky, 1894. Cl. 0268.

————. "De gestis Pelagii." In *Sancti Aureli Augustini opera*. Edited by Karl Franze Urba and Joseph Zycha. CSEL 42, pp. 51-122. Vienna, Austria: F. Tempsky; Leipzig, Germany: G. Freytag, 1902. Cl. 0348.

————. "De moribus ecclesiae catholicae et de moribus Manichaeorum." In *Opera omnia*. Edited by J.-P. Migne. PL 32, cols. 1309-78. Paris: Migne, 1861. Cl. 0261.

————. "De natura boni." In *Sancti Aurelii Augustini opera*. Edited by Joseph Zycha. CSEL 25, pp. 855-889. Vienna, Austria: F. Tempsky; Leipzig, Germany: G. Freytag, 1891. Cl. 0323.

————. "De natura et gratia." In *Sancti Aurelii Augustini opera*. Edited by Karl Franze Urba and Joseph Zycha. CSEL 60, pp. 233-99. Vienna, Austria: F. Tempsky; Leipzig, Germany: G. Freytag, 1913. Cl. 0344.

————. "De octo Dulcitii quaestionibus." In *Aurelii Augustini opera*. Edited by Almut Mutzenbecher. CCL 44A, 253-97. Turnhout, Belgium: Brepols, 1975. Cl. 0291.

————. "De patientia." In *Sancti Aureli Augustini opera*. Edited by Joseph Zycha. CSEL 41, pp. 663-91. Vienna, Austria: F. Tempsky, 1900. Cl. 0308.

————. "De praedestinatione sanctorum." In *Opera omnia*. Edited by J.-P. Migne. PL 44, cols. 959-92. Paris: Migne, 1861. Cl. 0354.

————. "De sancta virginitate." In *Sancti Aureli Augustini opera*. Edited by Joseph Zycha. CSEL 41, pp. 235-301. Vienna, Austria: F. Tempsky, 1900. Cl. 0300.

————. "De sermone Domini in monte." In *Aurelii Augustini opera*. Edited by Almut Mutzenbecher. CCL 35. Turnhout, Belgium: Brepols, 1967. Cl. 0274.

————. "De trinitate." In *Opera*. Edited by W. J. Mountain. CCL 50-50A. Turnhout, Belgium: Brepols, 1968. Cl. 0329.

————. "De vita Christiana [Sp.]." In *Opera omnia*. Edited by J.-P. Migne. PL 40, cols. 1031-46. Paris: Migne, 1841.

————. "Enarrationes in Psalmos." In *Aurelii Augustini opera*. Edited by Eligius Dekkers and John Fraipont. CCL 38, 39 and 40. Turnhout, Belgium: Brepols, 1956. Cl. 0283.

————. "Enchiridion de fide, spe et caritate." In *Aurelii Augustini opera*. Edited by E. Evans. CCL 46, pp. 49-114. Turnhout, Belgium: Brepols, 1969. Cl. 0295.

————. "In Iohannis epistulam ad Parthos tractatus." In *Opera omnia*. Edited by J.-P. Migne. PL 35, cols. 1977-2062. Paris: Migne, 1845. Cl. 0279.

————. "Epistulae." In *Sancti Aureli Augustini opera*. Edited by A. Goldbacher. CSEL 34 pts.1, 2; 44; 57; and 58. Vienna, Austria: F. Tempsky, 1895-1898. Cl. 0262.

————. "Epistulae." In *Sancti Aureli Augustini opera*. Edited by G. Hartel. CSEL 29. Edited by A. Goldbacher. CSEL 34 pts.1, 2. Vienna, Austria: F. Tempsky, 1894, 1895-1898. Cl. 0202.

————. "Epistulae ad Augustinum Hipponensem et alios." In *Sancti Aureli Augustini opera*. Edited by A. Goldbacher. CSEL 34.1,2; 44; and 57. Edited by J. Divjak. CSEL 88. Vienna, Austria: F. Tempsky, 1895-1898; 1981. Cl. 0262 °.

————. "In Johannis evangelium tractatus." In *Aurelii Augustini opera*. Edited by R. Willems. CCL 36. Turnhout, Belgium: Brepols, 1954. Cl. 0278.

————. "Sermones." In *Augustini opera omnia*. PL 38 and 39. Edited by J.-P. Migne. Paris: Migne, 1844-1865 and other editions. Cl. 0284.

————. "Sermones novissimi." In *Augustin d'Hippone, Vingt-six sermons au peuple d'Afrique*. Collection des études augustiniennes, Série Antiquité 147. Edited by F. Dolbeau. Paris: Institut des études augustiniennes, 1996. Cl. 0288.

————. "Sermones dubii." In *Augustini opera omnia*. Edited by J.-P. Migne. PL 39, cols. 1639-1718. Paris: Migne, 1865.

————. *Sermones Caesarii Arelatensis*. 2 vols. Edited by Germain Morin. CCL 103-104. Turnhout, Belgium: Brepols, 1953. Cl. 1008.

Barnabae epistula. In *Épître de Barnabé*. Edited by Pierre Prigent and Robert A. Kraft. SC 172, pp. 72-218. Paris: Éditions du Cerf, 1971. TLG 1216.001.

Basil the Great. "Asceticon magnum sive Quaestiones (regulae fusius tractatae)." In *Opera omnia*. Edited by J.-P. Migne. PG 31, cols. 901-1052. Paris: Migne, 1885. TLG 2040.048.

————. "De baptismo libri duo." In *Opera omnia*. Edited by J.-P. Migne. PG 31, cols. 1513-1628. Paris: Migne, 1885. TLG 2040.052.

————. *De spiritu sancto*. In *Basile de Césarée: Sur le Saint-Esprit*. 2nd ed. Edited by Benoit Pruche. SC 17, pp. 250-530. Paris: Éditions du Cerf, 1968. TLG 2040.003.

————. "Epistulae." In *Saint Basil: Lettres*, 3 vols. Edited by Yves Courtonne. Paris: Les Belles Lettres, 1957-1966. TLG 2040.004.

————. "Homilia adversus eos qui irascuntur." In *Opera omnia*. Edited by J.-P. Migne PG 31, cols. 353-72. Paris: Migne, 1885. TLG 2040.026.

————. "Homiliae in hexaemeron." In *Basile de Césarée. Homélies sur l'hexaéméron*. 2nd ed. Edited by S. Giet. SC 26, pp. 86-522. Paris: Éditions du Cerf, 1968. TLG 2040.001.

————. "Homilia in illud: Attende tibi ipsi." In *L'homélie de Basile de Césarée sur le mot 'observe-toi toi-même,'* pp. 23-37. Edited by S. Y. Rudberg. Stockholm: Almqvist & Wiksell, 1962. TLG 2040 006.

————. "Homiliae super Psalmos." In *Opera omnia*. Edited by J.-P. Migne. PG 29, cols. 209-494. Paris: Migne, 1857. TLG 2040.018.

————. "Prologus 4 (prooemium in asceticum magnum)." In *Opera omnia*. Edited by J.-P. Migne. PG 31, cols. 889-901. Paris: Migne, 1885. TLG 2040.048.

————. "Quod rebus mundannis adhaerendum non sit." In *Opera omnia*. Edited by J.-P. Migne. PG 31, cols. 540-64. Paris: Migne, 1885. TLG 2040.037.

Bede. "Expositio actuum apostolorum." In *Bedae opera*. Edited by M. L. W. Laistner. CCL 121, pp. 3-99. Turnhout, Belgium: Brepols, 1983. Cl. 1357.

———. "Homiliarum evangelii libri ii." In *Bedae opera.* Edited by David Hurst. CCL 122, pp. 1-378. Turnhout, Belgium: Brepols, 1956. Cl. 1367.

———. "De tabernaculo et vasis eius ac vestibus sacerdotum libri iii." In *Bedae opera.* Edited by David Hurst. CCL 119A, pp. 5-139. Turnhout, Belgium: Brepols, 1969. Cl. 1345.

Braulio of Saragossa. "Epistolae." In *Opera omnia.* Edited by J.-P. Migne. PL 80, cols. 655-700. Paris: Migne, 1850.

———. "Vita S. Aemiliani Confessoris." In *Opera omnia.* Edited by J.-P. Migne. PL 80, cols. 699-714. Paris: Migne, 1850.

Caesarius of Arles. "Sermones." In *Augustini opera omnia.* Edited by J.-P. Migne. PL 38 and 39. Paris: Migne, 1844-1865 and other editions. Cl. 0284.

———. *Sermones Caesarii Arelatensis.* 2 vols. Edited by Germain Morin. CCL 103-104. Turnhout, Belgium: Brepols, 1953. Cl. 1008.

Callistus of Rome. "Epistola Papae Calixti ad omnes Galliae episcopos." In *Decretalium Collectio.* Edited by J.-P. Migne. PL 130, cols. 131-38. Paris: Migne, 1853.

Cassian, John. *Collationes xxiv.* Edited by Michael Petschenig. CSEL 13. Vienna, Austria: F. Tempsky; Leipzig, Germany: G. Freytag, 1886. Cl. 0512.

———. "De institutis coenobiorum et de octo principalium vitiorum remediis." In *Johannis Cassiani.* Edited by Michael Petschenig. CSEL 17, pp. 1-231. Vienna, Austria: F. Tempsky; Leipzig, Germany: G. Freytag, 1888. Cl. 0513.

Cassiodorus. *Expositio psalmorum.* Edited by Mark Adriaen. CCL 97 and 98. Turnhout, Belgium: Brepols, 1958. Cl. 0900.

Clement of Alexandria. "Paedagogus." In *Le pédagogue [par] Clement d'Alexandrie.* 3 vols. Translated by Mauguerite Harl, Chantel Matray and Claude Mondésert. Introduction and notes by Henri-Irénée Marrou. SC 70, 108 and 158. Paris: Éditions du Cerf, 1960-1970. TLG 0555.002.

———. "Stromata." In *Clemens Alexandrinus.* Vol. 2, 3rd ed., and vol. 3, 2nd ed. Edited by Otto Stählin, Ludwig Früchtel and Ursula Treu. GCS 15, pp. 3-518 and GCS 17, pp. 1-102. Berlin: Akademie-Verlag, 1960-1970. TLG 0555.004.

Clement of Rome. "Epistula i ad Corinthios." In *Clément de Rome: Épitre aux Corinthiens.* Edited by Annie Jaubert. SC 167. Paris: Éditions du Cerf, 1971. TLG 1271.001.

Constitutiones apostolorum. In *Les constitutions apostoliques.* 3 vols. Edited by Marcel Metzger. SC 320, 329 and 336. Paris: Éditions du Cerf, 1985-1987. TLG 2894.001.

Cyprian. "Ad Fortunatum." In *Sancti Cypriani episcopi opera.* Edited by R. Weber. CCL 3A, pp. 183-216. Turnhout, Belgium: Brepols, 1972. Cl. 0045.

———. "De dominica oratione." In *Sancti Cypriani episcopi opera.* CCL 3A, pp. 87-113. Edited by Claudio Moreschini. Turnhout, Belgium: Brepols, 1976. Cl. 0043.

———. "De ecclesiae catholicae unitate." In *Sancti Cypriani episcopi opera.* CCL 3, pp. 249-68. Edited by M. Bévenot. Turnhout, Belgium: Brepols, 1972. Cl. 0041.

———. "De lapsis." In *Sancti Cypriani episcopi opera.* Edited by R. Weber. CCL 3, pp. 221-42. Turnhout, Belgium: Brepols, 1972. Cl. 0042.

———. *Epistulae.* Edited by Gerardus Frederik Diercks. CCL 3B and 3C. Turnhout, Belgium: Brepols, 1994-1996. Cl. 0050.

Cyril of Alexandria. "Concilium universale Ephesenum anno 431." In *Acta conciliorum oecumenicorum.* Vols 1.1.1-1.1.7. Edited by E. Schwartz. Berlin: De Gruyter, 1927-29 (repr.1960-65). TLG 5000.001.

———. "Quod unus sit Christus." In *Cyrille d'Alexandrie: Deux dialogues christologiques.* SC 97. Paris: Éditions du Cerf, 1964. TLG 4090.027.

Cyril of Jeruslaem. "Catecheses ad illuminandos 1-18." In *Cyrilli Hierosolymorum archiepiscopi opera quae su-*

persunt omnia. Vol. 1, pp. 28-320; vol. 2, pp. 2-342. Edited by Wilhelm Karl Reischl and Joseph Rupp. Munich: Lentner, 1860 (repr. Hildesheim: Olms, 1967). TLG 2110.003.

———. "Mystagogiae 1-5 (Sp.)." In *Cyrille de Jérusalem: Catéchèses, mystagogigues.* 2nd ed. SC 126, pp. 82-174. Edited by Auguste Piédagnel. Paris: Éditions du Cerf, 1988. TLG 2110.002.

———. "Procatechesis." In *Cyrilli Hierosolymorum archiepiscopi opera quae supersunt omnia.* Vol. 1. Edited by W. C. Reischl and J. Rupp. Munich: Lentner, 1860. Reprint. Hildesheim: Olms, 1967. TLG 2110.001.

Didache xii apostolorum. In *La Didachè. Instructions des Apôtres,* pp. 226-42. Edited by Jean Paul Audet. Paris: Lecoffre, 1958. TLG 1311.001.

Dionysius of Alexandria. "Fragments." In *The Letters and Other Remains of Dionysius of Alexandria.* Edited by Charles L. Feltoe. Cambridge Patristic Texts. Cambridge: Cambridge University Press, 1904.

Ephrem the Syrian. "In Tatiani Diatessaron." In *Saint Ephrem, Commentaire de l'evangile concordant: texte syriaque (Manuscrit Chester Beatty 709).* Edited by Louis Leloir. Dublin: Hodges Figgis, 1963.

Epiphanius of Salamis. "Panarion († Adversus haereses)." *Epiphanius, Bände 1-3: Ancoratus und Panarion.* 3 vols. Edited by K. Holl. GCS 25, 31 and 37. Leipzig: Hinrichs, 1915, 1922, 1933. TLG 2021.002.

Eugippius. *Vita Sancti Severini.* Edited by Pius Knoell. CSEL 9.2. Vienna, Austria: F. Tempsky, 1886.

Eusebius of Caesarea. "Demonstratio evangelica." In *Eusebius Werke, Band 6: Die Demonstratio evangelica.* Edited by Ivar A. Heikel. GCS 23. Leipzig: Hinrichs, 1913. TLG 2018.005.

———. "Historia ecclesiastica." In *Eusèbe de Césarée. Histoire ecclésiastique.* 3 vols. Edited by Gustave Bardy. SC 31, 41 and 55, pp. (1:)3-215, (2:)4-231, (3:)3-120. Paris: Éditions du Cerf, 1952, 1955, 1958. TLG 2018.002.

Evagrius of Pontus. "Practicus (capita centum)." In *Évagre le Pontique. Traité pratique ou le moine,* vol. 2. SC 171. Edited by A. Guillaumont and C. Guillaumont. Paris: Éditions du Cerf, 1971. TLG 4110.001.

Fulgentius of Ruspe. "Ad Euthymium de remissione peccatorum libri II." In *Opera.* Edited by John Fraipont. CCL 91A, pp. 649-707. Turnhout, Belgium: Brepols, 1968. Cl. 0821.

———. "Ad Monimum libri III." In *Opera.* Edited by John Fraipont. CCL 91, pp. 1-64. Turnhout, Belgium: Brepols, 1968. Cl. 0814.

———. *Epistulae XVIII.* In *Opera.* Edited by John Fraipont. CCL 91, pp. 189-280, 311-12, 359-44; and CCL 91A, pp. 447-57, 551-629. Turnhout, Belgium: Brepols, 1968. Cl. 0817.

———. "Liber ad Scarilam de incarnatione filii dei et vilium animalium auctore." In *Opera.* Edited by John Fraipont. CCL 91, pp. 312-56. Turnhout, Belgium: Brepols, 1968. Cl. 0822.

———. "Liber ad Victorem contra sermonem Fastidiosi Ariani." In *Opera.* Edited by John Fraipont. CCL 91, pp. 283-308. Turnhout, Belgium: Brepols, 1968. Cl. 0820.

Gregory of Nazianzus. "Adversus Eunomianos (orat. 27)." In *Gregor von Nazianz. Die fünf theologischen Reden,* pp. 38-60. Edited by J. Barbel. Düsseldorf: Patmos-Verlag, 1963. TLG 2022.007.

———. "Apologetica (orat. 2)." In *Opera omnia.* Edited by J.-P. Migne. PG 35, cols. 408-513. Paris: Migne, 1857. TLG 2022.016.

———. "De filio (orat. 30)." In *Gregor von Nazianz. Die fünf theologischen Reden,* pp. 170-216. Edited by Joseph Barbel. Düsseldorf, Germany: Patmos-Verlag, 1963. TLG 2022.010.

———. "De spiritu sancto (orat. 31)." In *Gregor von Nazianz. Die fünf theologischen Reden,* pp. 218-76. Edited by Joseph Barbel. Düsseldorf, Germany: Patmos-Verlag, 1963. TLG 2022.011.

———. "Funebris in laudem Caesarii fratris oratio (orat. 7)." In *Grégoire de Nazianze. Discours funèbres en l'honneur de son frère Césaire et de Basile de Césarée,* pp. 2-56. Edited by F. Boulenger. Paris: Picard, 1908. TLG 2022.005.

———. "Epistulae theologicae." In *Grégoire de Nazianze: Lettres théologiques.* Edited by P. Gallay. SC 208, pp. 36-94. Paris: Éditions du Cerf, 1974. TLG 2022.002.

———. "In laudem Athanasii (orat. 21)." In *Opera omnia*. Edited by J.-P. Migne. PG 35, cols. 1081-1128. Paris: Migne, 1857. TLG 2022.034.

———. "In laudem sororis Gorgoniae (orat.8)." In *Opera omnia*. Edited by J.-P. Migne. PG 35, cols. 789-817. Paris: Migne, 1857. TLG 2022.021.

———. "In patrem tacentem (orat. 16)." In *Opera omnia*. Edited by J.-P. Migne. PG 35, cols. 933-64. Paris: Migne, 1857. TLG 2022.029.

———. "In sanctum baptisma (orat. 40)." In *Opera omnia*. Edited by J.-P. Migne. PG 36, cols. 360-425. Paris: Migne, 1858. TLG 2022.048.

———. "In pentecosten (orat. 41)." In *Opera omnia*. Edited by J.-P. Migne. PG 36, cols. 428-52. Paris: Migne, 1858. TLG 2022.049.

Gregory of Nyssa. "Oratio catechetica magna." In *The Catechetical Oration of Gregory of Nyssa*, pp. 1-164. Edited by J. Srawley. Cambridge: Cambridge University Press, 1903. Reprinted 1956. TLG 2017.046.

———. "Contra Eunomium." In *Gregorii Nysseni opera*. 2 vols. Vol. 1.1, pp. 3-409; vol. 2.2, pp. 3-311. Edited by Werner William Jaeger. Leiden: Brill, 1960. TLG 2017.030.

———. "De virginitate." In *Grégoire de Nysse. Traité de la virginité*. Edited by Michel Aubineau. SC 119, pp. 246-560. Paris: Éditions du Cerf, 1966. TLG 2017.043.

———. "De vita Mosis." In *Grégoire de Nysse. La vie de Moïse*. Edited by J. Danielou. 3rd ed. SC 1, pp. 44-326. Paris: Éditions du Cerf, 1968. TLG 2017.042.

———. "Dialogus de anima et resurrectione." In *S. P. N. Gregorii Episcopi Nysseni opera*. Edited by J.-P. Migne. PG 46, cols. 12-160. Paris: Migne, 1863. TLG 2017.056.

———. "Refutatio confessionis Eunomii." In *Gregorii Nysseni opera*, vol. 2.2, pp. 312-410. Edited by W. Jaeger. Leiden: Brill, 1960. TLG 2017.031.

Gregory the Great. *Registrum epistularum*. 2 vols. Edited by Dag Norberg. CCL 140 and 140A. Turnhout, Belgium: Brepols, 1982. Cl. 1714.

———. *Moralia in Iob*. Edited by Mark Adriaen. CCL143, 143A and 143B. Turnhout, Belgium: Brepols, 1979-81. Cl. 1708.

Hilary of Poitiers. *De trinitate*. Edited by Pieter F. Smulders. CCL 62 and 62A. Turnhout, Belgium: Brepols, 1979-80. Cl. 0433.

———. *Tractatus super psalmos I-IXI*. Edited by Jean Doignon. CCL 61-61A. Turnhout, Belgium: Brepols, 1997-2002. Cl. 0428.

Hippolytus. "De theophania." In *Hippolyt's kleinere exegetische und homiletische Schriften*, pp. 257-63. Edited by H. Achelis. GCS 1.2. Leipzig: Teubner, 1897. TLG 2115.026.

Horsiesi. "Liber Orsiesii." In *Pachomiana Latina. Règle et épîtres de s. Pachôme, épître de s. Théodore et "Liber" de s. Orsiesius. Texte latin de s. Jérome*. Edited by Amand Boon. Bibliothèque de la Revue d'histoire ecclésiastique 7. Louvain, Belgium: Bureaux de la Revue, 1932.

Isaac of Nineveh. *De perfectione religiosa*. Edited by Paul Bedjan. Paris: Otto Harrassowitz, 1909.

Jacob of Sarug. *Homiliae Selectae Mar Jacobi Sarugensis*. Edited by Paul Bedjan. Paris: Otto Harrassowitz, 1905-10.

Jerome. "Adversus Helvidium de Mariae virginitate perpetua." In *Opera omnia*. Edited by J.-P. Migne. PL 23, cols. 193-216. Paris: Migne, 1865. Cl. 0609.

———. "Adversus Jovinianum." In *Opera omnia*. Edited by J.-P. Migne. PL 23, cols. 211-338. Paris: Migne, 1865. Cl. 0610.

———. "Apologia adversus libros Rufini." In *S. Hieronymi presbyteri opera*. Edited by P. Lardet. CCL 79, pp. 1-72. Turnhout, Belgium: Brepols, 1982. Cl. 0613.

———. "Commentarius in Ecclesiasten." In *Hebraicae quaestiones in libro Geneseos*. Edited by Mark Adriaen. CCL 72, pp. 249-361. Turnhout, Belgium: Brepols, 1959. Cl. 0583.

————. *Dialogus adversus Pelagianos.* Edited by Claudio Moreschini. CCL 80. Turnhout, Belgium: Brepols, 1990. Cl. 0615.

————. *Epistulae.* Edited by I. Hilberg. CSEL 54, 55 and 56. Vienna, Austria: F. Tempsky; Leipzig, Germany: G. F. Freytag, 1910-1918. Cl. 0620.

————. "Liber tertius adversus libros Rufini." In *S. Hieronymi presbyteri opera.* Edited by P. Lardet. CCL 79, pp. 73-116. Turnhout, Belgium: Brepols, 1982. Cl. 0614.

————. "Tractatus lix in psalmos." In *S. Hieronymi presbyteri opera.* Edited by Germain Morin. CCL 78, pp. 3-352. Turnhout, Belgium: Brepols, 1958. Cl. 0592.

John Chrysostom. "Ad populam Antiochenum homiliae (de statuis)." In *Opera omnia.* Edited by J.-P. Migne. PG 49, cols. 15-222. Paris: Migne, 1862. TLG 2062.024.

————. "Adversus Judaeos (orationes 1-8)." In *Opera omnia.* Edited by J.-P. Migne. PG 48, cols. 843-942. Paris: Migne, 1862. TLG 2062.021.

————. "Ad viduam juniorem." In *Jean Chrysostome. A une jeune veuve. Sur le mariage unique.* Edited by G. H. Ettlinger and B. Grillet. SC 138, pp. 112-59. Paris: Éditions du Cerf, 1968. TLG 2062.010.

————. "De consubstantiali (Contra Anomoeos, homilia 7)." In *Opera omnia.* Edited by J.-P. Migne. PG 48, cols. 755-68. Paris: Migne, 1862. TLG 2062.015.

————. "Catecheses ad illuminandos 1-8 (series tertia)." In *Jean Chrysostome. Huit catéchèses baptismales.* 2nd ed. Edited by A. Wenger. SC 50, pp. 108-260. Paris: Éditions du Cerf, 1970. TLG 2062.382.

————. "Contra Judaeos et Gentiles, Quod Christus sit Deus." In *Opera omnia.* Edited by J.-P. Migne. PG 48, cols. 811-38. Paris: Migne, 1862. TLG 2062.372.

————. "De incomprehensibili dei natura (& Contra Anomoeos, homiliae 1-5)." In *Jean Chrysostome. Sur l'incompréhensibilité de Dieu.* Edited by A.-M. Malingrey. SC 28. Paris: Éditions du Cerf, 1970. TLG 2062.012.

————. "De paenitentia (homiliae 1-9)." In *Opera omnia.* Edited by J.-P. Migne. PG 49, cols. 277-348. Paris: Migne, 1862. TLG 2062.027.

————. "In epistulam ad Galatas commentarius." In *Opera omnia.* Edited by J.-P. Migne. PG 61, cols. 611-82. Paris: Migne, 1862. TLG 2062.158.

————. "In epistulam ad Hebraeos (homilae 1-34)." In *Opera omnia.* Edited by J.-P. Migne. PG 63, cols. 9-236. Paris: Migne, 1862. TLG 2062.168.

————. "In epistulam ad Philemon (homiliae 1-3)." In *Opera omnia.* Edited by J.-P. Migne. PG 62, cols. 701-20. Paris: Migne, 1862. TLG 2062.167.

————. "In epistulam i ad Corinthios (homiliae 1-44)." In *Opera omnia.* Edited by J.-P. Migne. PG 61, cols. 9-382. Paris: Migne, 1862. TLG 2062.156.

————. "In epistulam ii ad Timotheum (homiliae 1-10)." In *Opera omnia.* Edited by J.-P. Migne. PG 62, cols. 599-662. Paris: Migne, 1862. TLG 2062.165.

————. "In Genesim (homiliae 1-67)." In *Opera omnia.* Edited by J.-P. Migne. PG 53, cols. 21-385 and PG 54, cols. 385-580. Paris: Migne, 1859-1862. TLG 2062.112.

————. "In Joannem (homiliae 1-88)." In *Opera omnia.* Edited by J.-P. Migne. PG 59, cols. 23-482. Paris: Migne, 1862. TLG 2062.153.

John of Damascus. "Expositio fidei." In *Die Schriften des Johannes von Damaskos,* vol. 2, pp. 3-239. Edited by Bonifatius Kotter. Patristische Texte und Studien 12. Berlin: De Gruyter, 1973. TLG 2934.004.

————. *Vita Barlaam et Joasaph* [Sp.]. Edited by G. R. Woodward and H. Mattingly. Cambridge, Mass.: Harvard University Press, 1914. Reprinted 1983. TLG 2934.66.

Justin Martyr. "Apologia." In *Die ältesten Apologeten,* pp. 26-77. Edited by E. J. Goodspeed. Göttingen, Germany: Vandenhoeck & Ruprecht, 1915. TLG 0645.001.

———. "Dialogus cum Tryphone." In *Die ältesten Apologeten*, pp. 90-265. Edited by E. J. Goodspeed. Göttingen, Germany: Vandenhoeck & Ruprecht, 1915. TLG 0645.003.

Leo the Great. "Epistulae." In *Opera omnia Leonis Magni*. Edited by J.-P. Migne. PL 54, cols. 581-1218. Paris: Migne, 1846.

———. "Testimonia (Ep. 165)." In *Opera omnia Leonis Magni*. Edited by J.-P. Migne. PL 54, cols. 1173-90. Paris: Migne, 1846.

———. *Tractatus septem et nonaginta*. Edited by Antonio Chavasse. CCL 138 and 138A. Turnhout, Belgium: Brepols, 1973. Cl. 1657.

Marius Victorinus. "Adversus Arium." In *Marii Victorini opera*. Edited by Paul Henry and Pierre Hadot. CSEL 83.1, pp. 54-277. Vienna, Austria: Hoelder-Pichler-Tempsky, 1971. Cl. 0095.

Martin of Braga. "Exhortatio humilitatis." In *Opera omnia*, pp. 74-79. Edited by Claude W. Barlow. New Haven: Yale University Press, 1950.

———. "Pro repellenda iactania." In *Opera omnia*, pp. 65-69. Edited by Claude W. Barlow. New Haven: Yale University Press, 1950.

———. "Sententiae patrum Aegyptiorum." In *Opera omnia*, pp. 11-51. Edited by Claude W. Barlow. New Haven: Yale University Press, 1950.

Martyrius. *See* Sahdona.

Maximus of Turin. *Collectio sermonum antiqua*. Edited by A. Mutzenbecher. CCL 23. Turnhout, Belgium: Brepols, 1962. Cl. 0219 a.

Methodius. "De Resurrectione." In *Methodius*. Edited by G. Nathanael Bonwetsch. GCS 27, pp. 226-420 *passim*. Leipzig: Hinrichs, 1917. TLG 2959.003.

———. "Symposium *sive* Convivium decem virginum." In *Opera omnia*. Edited by J.-P. Migne. PG 18, cols. 27-220. Paris: Migne, 1857. TLG 2959.001.

Nicetas of Remesiana. "De psalmodiae bono." In *Niceta of Remesiana: His Life and Works*, pp. 67-82. Edited by A. E. Burn. Cambridge: Cambridge University Press, 1905.

———. "De Spiritus sancti potentia." In *Niceta of Remesiana: His Life and Works*, pp. 18-38. Edited by A. E. Burn. Cambridge: Cambridge University Press, 1905.

———. "De Vigiliis servorum Dei." In *Niceta of Remesiana: His Life and Works*, pp. 55-67. Edited by A. E. Burn. Cambridge: Cambridge University Press, 1905.

———. "Libellus quintus de symbolo." In *Niceta of Remesiana: His Life and Works*, pp. 38-54. Edited by A. E. Burn. Cambridge: Cambridge University Press, 1905.

Novatian. "De Trinitate." In *Opera*. Edited by Gerardus Frederik Diercks. CCL 4, pp. 11-78. Turnhout, Belgium: Brepols, 1972. Cl. 0071.

Origen. "Commentarii in evangelium Joannis" (lib. 1, 2, 4, 5, 6, 10, 13). In *Commentaire sur saint Jean*. 3 vols. Edited by Cécil Blanc. SC 120, 157 and 222. Paris: Éditions du Cerf, 1966-1975. TLG 2042.005.

———. "Commentarii in evangelium Joannis" (lib. 19, 20, 28, 32). In *Origenes Werke*, vol. 4. Edited by E. Preuschen. GCS 10, pp. 298-480. Leipzig: Hinrichs, 1903. TLG 2042.079.

———. "Commentariorum series in evangelium Matthaei (Mt. 22.34-27.63)." In *Origenes Werke*, vol. 11. Edited by E. Klostermann. GCS 38.2. Leipzig: Teubner, 1933.

———. "Commentarium in evangelium Matthaei" (lib. 10-11). In *Commentaire sur l'Evangile selon Matthieu*, vol. 1. Edited by R. Girod. SC 162. Paris: Éditions du Cerf, 1970. TLG 2042.029.

———. "Commentarium in evangelium Matthaei" (lib. 12-17). In *Origenes Werke*, vol. 10.1-2. Edited by E. Klostermann. GCS 40.1-2. Leipzig: Teubner, 1935, 1937. TLG 2042.030.

———. "Contra Celsum." In *Origène Contre Celse*. Edited by Marcel Borret. SC 132, 136, 147 and 150. Paris: Éditions du Cerf, 1967-1969. TLG 2042.001.

———. "De oratione." In *Origenes Werke*, vol. 2. Edited by P. Koetschau. GCS 3, pp. 297-403. Leipzig: Hinrichs 1899. TLG 2042.008.

———. "In Exodum homiliae." In *Origenes secundum translationem quam fecit Rufinus*. Edited by W. A. Baehrens. GCS (CB) 29, pp. 145-279. Leipzig: Teubner, 1920. Cl. 0198 5 (A).

———. "In Genesim homiliae." In *Origenes secundum translationem quam fecit Rufinus*. Edited by W. A. Baehrens. GCS (CB) 29, pp. 1-144. Leipzig: Teubner, 1920. Cl. 0198 6.

———. "In Leuiticum homiliae." In *Origenes secundum translationem quam fecit Rufinus*. Edited by W. A. Baehrens. GCS (CB) 29, pp. 280-507. Leipzig: Teubner, 1920. Cl. 0198 3.

Pachomius. *Die Briefe Pachoms: Griechischer Text der Handschrift W. 145 of the Chester Beatty Library*. Edited by Hans Quecke. Textus patristici et liturgici 11, pp. 99-110. Regensburg: Pustet [in Komm.], 1975.

———. "Instructions." In *Oeuvres de S. Pachôme et de ses disciples*. Edited by L. T. Lefort. CSCO 159, pp. 1-26. Louvain, Belgium: Durbecq, 1956.

———. *Paralipomena*. In *Sancti Pachomii vitae Graecae*. Edited by F. Halkin. Subsidia hagiographica 19, pp. 122-165. Brussels, Belgium: Société des Bollandistes, 1932.

———. *Sancti Pachomii vitae Graecae*. Edited by F. Halkin. Subsidia hagiographica 19. Brussels, Belgium: Société des Bollandistes, 1932.

Palladius. "Historia Lausiaca (recensio G)." In *Palladio. "La storia Lausiaca."* Edited by G. J. M. Bartelink. Verona: Fondazione Lorenzo Valla, 1974. TLG 2111.001.

Paschasius of Dumium. "Verba Seniorum auctore Graeco incerto." In *Opera omnia*. Edited by J.-P. Migne. PL 73, cols. 1025-62. Paris: Migne, 1879.

Paulinus of Milan. "Vita Sancti Ambrosii." In *Opera omnia*. Edited by J.-P. Migne. PL 14, cols. 27-46. Paris: Migne, 1845.

Paulinus of Nola. "Epistulae." In *Sancti Paulinus Nolianii opera*. Edited by G. Hartel. CSEL 29. Edited by A. Goldbacher. CSEL 34, pts. 1 and 2. Vienna, Austria: F. Tempsky, 1894, 1895-1898. Cl. 0202.

———. "Epistulae ad Augustinum Hipponensem et alios." In *Sancti Aureli Augustini opera*. Edited by A. Goldbacher. CSEL 34.1,2; 44; 57. Edited by J. Divjak. CSEL 88. Vienna, Austria: F. Tempsky, 1895-1898; 1981. Cl. 0262 °.

Peter Chrysologus. "Collectio Sermonum." In *Opera*. Edited by A Olivar. CSEL 24, 24A and 24B. Turnhout, Belgium: Brepols, 1975. Cl. 0227 +.

Philoxenus of Mabbug. "Sulla Preghiera. Filosseno O Giovanni?" In *Le Muséon* 94, pp. 76-77. Edited by Paolo Bettiolo. Louvain, Belgium: Peeters, 1981.

Prudentius. "Liber Cathemerinon." In *Opera*. Edited by M. P. Cunningham. CSEL 126, 3-72. Turnhout, Belgium: Brepols, 1966. Cl. 1438.

———. "Liber Peristefanon." In *Opera*. Edited by M. P. Cunningham. CSEL 126, pp. 251-389. Turnhout, Belgium: Brepols, 1966. Cl. 1443.

Pseudo-Dionysius. "De coelesti hierarchia." In *Corpus Dionysiacum ii: Pseudo-Dionysius Areopagita. De coelesti hierarchia, de ecclesiastica hierarchia, de mystica theologia, epistulae*. PTS 36, pp. 7-59. Edited by G. Heil and A. M. Ritter. Berlin: Walter de Gruyter, 1991. TLG 2798.001.

———. "De divinis nominibus." In *Corpus Dionysiacum i: Pseudo-Dionysius Areopagita. De divinis nominibus*. Edited by B. R. Suchla. PTS 33, pp.107-231. Berlin: Walter de Gruyter, 1990. TLG 2798.004.

Rufinus of Aquileia. "Expositio symboli." In *Opera*. Edited by Manlio Simonetti. CCL 20, pp. 125-82. Turnhout, Belgium: Brepols, 1961. Cl. 0196.

———. "Apologia (contra Hieronymum)." In *Opera*. Edited by Manlio Simonetti. CCL 20, pp. 37-123. Turnhout, Belgium: Brepols, 1961. Cl. 0197.

Sahdona. "Liber de perfectione." In *Martyrius [Sahdona]. Oeuvres spirituelles*, vol. 3. Edited by A. de Halleux. CSCO 252 (Scriptores Syri 110), pp. 1-27. Louvain, Belgium: Secrétariat du Corpus Scriptorum Christianorum Orientalium, 1965.

Salvian the Presbyter. "De gubernatione Dei." In *Ouvres*, vol. 2. Edited by G. Lagarrigue. SC 220, pp. 95-527. Paris: Éditions du Cerf, 1975. Cl. 0485.

Syncletica. "Apophthegmata patrum (collectio systematica) (cap. 1-9)." In *Les apophtegmes des pères. Collection systématique, chapitres i-ix*. Edited by J.-C. Guy. SC 387, pp. 92-448. Paris: Éditions du Cerf, 1993. TLG 2742.005.

Tertullian. "Adversus Hermogeñem." In *Opera*. Edited by E. Kroymann. CCL 1, pp. 397-435. Turnhout, Belgium: Brepols, 1954. Cl. 0013.

———. "Adversus Judaeos." In *Opera*. Edited by E. Kroymann. CCL 2, pp. 1339-96. Turnhout, Belgium: Brepols, 1954. Cl. 0033.

———. "Adversus Marcionem." In *Opera*. Edited by E. Kroymann. CCL 1, pp. 437-726. Turnhout, Belgium: Brepols, 1954. Cl. 0014.

———. "Adversus Praxean." In *Opera*. Edited by E. Kroymann and E. Evans. CCL 2, pp. 1159-205. Turnhout, Belgium: Brepols, 1954. Cl. 0026.

———. "De idololatria." In *Opera*, vol. 2. Edited by August Reifferscheid and George Wissowa. CCL 2, pp. 1101-24. Turnhout, Belgium: Brepols, 1954. Cl. 0023.

———. "De resurrectione mortuorum." In *Opera*. Edited by J. G. Ph. Borleffs. CCL 2, pp. 919-1012. Turnhout, Belgium: Brepols, 1954. Cl. 0019.

Theodore of Mopsuestia. "In Zachariam." In *Opera omnia*. Edited by J.-P. Migne. PG 66, cols. 493-596. Paris: Migne, 1869.

Theodoret of Cyr. "Ad eos qui in Euphratesia et Osrhoena regione, Syria, Phoenicia et Cilicia vitam monasticam degunt (ex epistula 151)." In *Opera omnia*. Edited by J.-P. Migne. PG 83, cols. 1416-33. Paris: Migne, 1864. TLG 4089.034.

———. "De providentia orationes decem." In *Opera omnia*. Edited by J.-P. Migne. PG 83, cols. 556-773. Paris: Migne, 1864. TLG 4089.032.

———. "Epistulae: Collectio Sirmondiana (1-95)." In *Théodoret de Cyr: Correspondance II*. Edited by Y. Azema. SC 98, pp. 20-248. Paris: Éditions du Cerf, 1964. TLG 4089.006.

———. "Epistulae: Collectio Sirmondiana (96-147)." In *Théodoret de Cyr: Correspondance III*. Edited by Y. Azema. SC 111, pp. 10-232. Paris: Éditions du Cerf, 1964. TLG 4089.007.

———. *Eranistes*, pp. 61-266. Edited by Gérard H. Ettlinger. Oxford: Clarendon Press, 1975. TLG 4089.002.

———. "Historia ecclesiastica." In *Theodoret. Kirchengeschichte*, 2nd ed. Edited by L. Parmentier and F. Scheidweiler. GCS 44, pp. 1-349. Berlin: Akademie-Verlag, 1954. TLG 4089.003.

———. "Interpretatio in Psalmos." In *Opera omnia*. Edited by J.-P. Migne. PG 80, cols. 857-1997. Paris: Migne, 1864. TLG 4089.024.

Valerian of Cimiez. "Homiliae xx." In *Sancti Petri Chrysologi opera omnia, Valeriani et Nicetae*. Edited by J.-P. Migne. PL 52, cols. 691-756. Paris: Migne, 1845.

Vitae Patrum. Edited by J.-P. Migne. PL 73, cols. 855-1022. Paris: Migne, 1849.

Zephyrinus. "Epistola Zephirini papae." In *Opera omnia*. Edited by J.-P. Migne. PL 130, cols. 127-30. Paris: Migne, 1853.

Bibliography of Works
in English Translation

"Acts of the Holy apostles Peter and Paul." See "Apocrypha of the New Testament." In *The Twelve Patriarchs, Excerpts and Epistles, The Clementia, Apocryphal Gospels and Acts, Syriac Documents, Remains of the First Ages*, pp. 361-598. Translated by B. P. Pratten. ANF 8. Edited by Alexander Roberts and James Donaldson. 10 vols. 1885-1887. Reprint, Peabody, Mass.: Hendrickson, 1994.

Alexander of Alexandria. "Epistles on the Arian Heresy." In *Gregory Thaumaturgus, Dionysius the Great, Julius Africanus, Anatolius and Minor Writers, Methodius, Arnobius.* Edited by James Donaldson. ANF 6. Edited by Alexander Roberts and James Donaldson. 10 vols. 1885-1887. Reprint, Peabody, Mass.: Hendrickson, 1994.

Ambrose. *Funeral Orations by Saint Gregory Nazianzen and Saint Ambrose.* Translated by Leo P. McCauley et al. FC 22. Washington, D.C.: The Catholic University of America Press, 1953.

———. *Hexaemeron, Paradise, and Cain and Abel.* Translated by John J. Savage. FC 42. Washington, D.C.: The Catholic University of America Press, 1961.

———. *Letters.* Translated by Mary Melchior Beyenka. FC 26. Washington, D.C.: The Catholic University of America Press, 1954.

———. *Select Works and Letters.* Translated by H. De Romestin. NPNF 10. Series 2. Edited by Philip Schaff and Henry Wace. 14 vols. 1886-1900. Reprint, Peabody, Mass.: Hendrickson, 1994.

———. *Seven Exegetical Works.* Translated by Michael P. McHugh. FC 65. Washington, D.C.: The Catholic University of America Press, 1972.

———. *On Virginity.* Translated by Daniel Callam. Toronto: Peregrina Publishing Co., 1996.

Ammon. "Letter of Bishop Ammon." In *Pachomian koinonia*, 2:71-109. Translated by Armand Veilleux. CS 46. Kalamazoo, Mich.: Cistercian Publications, 1981.

"Apocryphal Revelation of John the Theologian." See "Apocrypha of the New Testament." In *The Twelve Patriarchs, Excerpts and Epistles, The Clementia, Apocryphal Gospels and Acts, Syriac Documents, Remains of the First Ages*, pp. 361-598. Translated by B. P. Pratten. ANF 8. Edited by Alexander Roberts and James Donaldson. 10 vols. 1885-1887. Reprint, Peabody, Mass.: Hendrickson, 1994.

Aphrahat. "Demonstration IV, On Prayer." In *The Syriac Fathers on Prayer and the Spiritual Life*, pp. 5-25. Translated by Sebastian Brock. CS 101. Kalamazoo, Mich.: Cistercian Publications, 1987.

———. "Select Demonstrations." In *Gregory the Great, Ephraim Syrus, Aphrahat*, pp. 345-412. Translated by James Barmby. NPNF 13. Series 2. Edited by Philip Schaff and Henry Wace. 14 vols. 1886-1900. Reprint, Peabody, Mass.: Hendrickson, 1994.

Archelaus. "The Acts of the Disputation with the Heresiarch Manes." In *Gregory Thaumaturgus, Dionysius the Great, Julius Africanus, Anatolius and Minor Writers, Methodius, Arnobius*, pp. 179-235. Translated by S. D. F. Salmond. ANF 6. Edited by Alexander Roberts and James Donaldson. 10 vols. 1885-1887. Reprint, Peabody, Mass.: Hendrickson, 1994.

Ascetic Monks of Egypt. "Sayings of the Egyptian Fathers." In *Iberian Fathers*, 1:17-34. Translated by Claude W. Barlow. FC 62. Washington, D.C.: The Catholic University of America Press, 1969.

Athanasius. *The Resurrection Letters.* Paraphrased and introduced by Jack N. Sparks. Nashville: Thomas Nelson, 1979.

———. *Life of St. Antony.* Translated by Tim Vivian and Apostolos N. Athanassakis with Rowan A.

Greer. CS 202. Kalamazoo, Mich.: Cistercian Publications, 2003.

———. "On the Incarnation." In *Christology of the Later Fathers*, pp. 55-110. Translated by Archibald Robertson. Edited by Edward Rochie Hardy. LCC 3. Philadelphia: Westminster Press, 1954.

———. *Selected Works and Letters*. Translated by Archibald Robertson. NPNF 4. Series 2. Edited by Philip Schaff and Henry Wace. 14 vols. 1886-1900. Reprint, Peabody, Mass.: Hendrickson, 1994.

Augustine. *Against Julian*. Translated by Matthew A. Schumacher. FC 35. Washington, D.C.: The Catholic University of America Press, 1957.

———. *Augustine: Earlier Writings*. Translated by John H. S. Burleigh. LCC 6. London: SCM Press, 1953.

———. *Christian Instruction; Admonition and Grace; The Christian Combat; Faith, Hope and Charity*. Translated by John J. Gavigan et al. FC 2. Washington, D.C.: The Catholic University of America Press, 1947.

———. *The City of God*. Translated by Henry S. Bettenson with an introduction by David Knowles. 1972. Reprint, with an introduction by John O'Meara. Harmondsworth, Middlesex: Penguin Books, 1984.

———. *Commentary on the Lord's Sermon on the Mount with Seventeen Related Sermons*. Translated by Denis J. Kavanagh. FC 11. Washington, D.C.: The Catholic University of America Press, 1951.

———. *Confessions*. Translated by R. S. Pine-Coffin. Harmondsworth, Middlesex, England: Penguin, 1961. Reprint, New York: Penguin, 1986.

———. *Eighty-three Different Questions*. Translated by David L. Mosher. FC 70. Washington, D.C.: The Catholic University of America Press, 1982.

———. "Enchiridion." In *Confessions and Enchiridion*, pp. 335-412. Translated by Albert C. Outler. LCC 7. London: SCM Press, 1955.

———. *Expositions on the Book of Psalms*. Edited from the Oxford translation by A. Cleveland Coxe. NPNF 8. Series 1. Edited by Philip Schaff. 14 vols. 1886-1889. Reprint, Peabody, Mass.: Hendrickson, 1994.

———. *Four Anti-Pelagian Writings: On Nature and Grace, On the Proceedings of Pelagius, On the Predestination of the Saints, On the Gift of Perseverance*, pp. 218-70. Translated by John A. Mourant and William J. Collinge. FC 86. Washington, D.C.: The Catholic University of America Press, 1992.

———. "Homilies on 1 John." In *Tractates on the Gospel of John 112-24; Tractates on the First Epistle of John*, pp. 119-277. Translated by John W. Rettig. FC 92. Washington, D.C.: The Catholic University of America Press, 1995.

———. *Letters*. Translated by Wilfred Parsons. FC 12, 18, 20, 30 and 32. Washington, D.C.: The Catholic University of America Press, 1951-1956.

———. "Letters." See Augustine/Jerome Correspondence. In *Biblical Interpretation*, pp. 257-95. Translated by Paige Lindsey and F. Lewis Shaw. MFC 9. Edited by Joseph W. Trigg. Wilmington, Del.: Michael Glazier, 1988.

———. "On Faith in Things Unseen." In *The Immortality of the Soul, The Magnitude of the Soul, On Music, The Advantage of Believing, On Faith in Things Unseen*, pp. 451-69. Translated by Roy Joseph Deferrari and Mary Francis McDonald. FC 4. Washington, D.C.: The Catholic University of America Press, 1947.

———. "On the Literal Interpretation of Genesis." In *On Genesis*, pp. 145-88. Translated by Roland J. Teske. FC 84. Washington, D.C.: The Catholic University of America Press, 1991.

———. *Sermons*. Translated by Edmund Hill. WSA 1-11. Part 3. Edited by John E. Rotelle. New York: New City Press, 1990-1997.

———. *Sermons on the Liturgical Seasons*. Translated by Mary Sarah Muldowney. FC 38. Washington, D.C.: The Catholic University of America Press, 1959.

———. *Tractates on the Gospel of John, 1-124.* Translated by John W. Rettig. FC 78, 79, 88, 90 and 92. Washington, D.C.: The Catholic University of America Press, 1988-1995.

———. *Treatises on Marriage and Other Subjects.* Translated by Charles T. Huegelmeyer. FC 27. Washington, D.C.: The Catholic University of America Press, 1955.

———. *Treatises on Various Subjects.* Translated by Mary Sarah Muldowney et al. FC 16. Washington, D.C.: The Catholic University of America Press, 1952.

———. *The Trinity.* Translated by Edmund Hill. WSA 1 5. New York: New City Press, 1991.

———. *The Trinity.* Translated by Stephen McKenna. FC 45. Washington, D.C.: The Catholic University of America, 1963.

———. *The Writings Against the Manichaeans and Against the Donatists.* Translated by J. R. King. NPNF 4. Series 1. Edited by Philip Schaff. 14 vols. 1886-1889. Reprint, Peabody, Mass.: Hendrickson, 1994.

Basil the Great. *Ascetical Works.* Translated by M. Monica Wagner. FC 9. New York: Fathers of the Church, 1950.

———. *Exegetic Homilies.* Translated by Agnes Clare Way. FC 46. Washington, D.C.: The Catholic University of America Press, 1963.

———. *Letters 1-368.* Translated by Agnes Clare Way, with notes by Roy J. Deferrari. FC 13 and 28. Washington, D.C.: The Catholic University of America Press, 1951-1955.

———. *On the Holy Spirit.* Translated by David Anderson, Crestwood, N.Y.: St. Vladimir's Seminary Press, 1980.

———. "On the Holy Spirit." In *Letters and Select Works,* pp. 1-50. Translated by Blomfield Jackson. NPNF 8. Series 2. Edited by Philip Schaff. 14 vols. 1886-1889. Reprint, Peabody, Mass.: Hendrickson, 1994.

Bede. *Commentary on the Acts of the Apostles.* Translated by Lawrence T. Martin. CS 117. Kalamazoo, Mich.: Cistercian Publications, 1989.

———. *Homilies on the Gospels.* Translated by Lawrence T. Martin and David Hurst. 2 vols. CS 110 and 111. Kalamazoo, Mich.: Cistercian Publications, 1991.

———. *On the Tabernacle.* Translated by Arthur G. Holder. TTH 18. Liverpool: Liverpool University Press, 1994.

Braulio of Saragossa. "Writings of Braulio of Saragossa." In *Iberian Fathers,* 2:15-142. Translated by Claude W. Barlow. FC 63. Washington, D.C.: The Catholic University of America Press, 1969.

Caesarius of Arles. *Sermons.* 3 vols. Translated by Mary Magdeleine Mueller. FC 31, 47 and 66. Washington, D.C.: The Catholic University of America Press, 1956-64.

Callistus of Rome. "The Epistles of Callistus." In *The Twelve Patriarchs, Excerpts and Epistles, The Clementia, Apocryphal Gospels and Acts, Syriac Documents, Remains of the First Ages,* pp. 613-18. Translated by B. P. Pratten. ANF 8. Edited by Alexander Roberts and James Donaldson. 10 vols. 1885-1887. Reprint, Peabody, Mass.: Hendrickson, 1994.

Cassian, John. *The Conferences.* Translated and annotated by Boniface Ramsey. ACW 57. New York: Paulist Press, 1997.

———. *The Institutes.* Translated by Boniface Ramsey. ACW 58. New York: Newman Press, 2000.

Cassiodorus. *Explanation of the Psalms.* 3 vols. Translated by P. G. Walsh. ACW 51, 52 and 53. New York: Paulist Press, 1990-1991.

Clement of Alexandria. *Christ the Educator.* Translated by Simon P. Wood. FC 23. Washington, D.C.: The Catholic University of America Press, 1954.

———. *Stromateis: Books 1-3.* Translated by John Ferguson. FC 85. Washington, D.C.: The Catholic University of America Press, 1991.

———. "Stromateis." In *Fathers of the Second Century: Hermas, Tatian, Athenagoras, Theophilus, and Clement of Alexandria*, pp. 299-567. Translated by F. Crombie et al. ANF 2. Edited by Alexander Roberts and James Donaldson. 10 vols. 1885-1887. Reprint, Peabody, Mass.: Hendrickson, 1994.

Clement of Rome. "Clement's First Letter." In *Early Christian Fathers*, pp. 43-73. Translated by Cyril C. Richardson. LCC 1. Philadelphia: Westminster Press, 1953.

———. "1 Clement." See "The Letter to the Corinthians." In *The Apostolic Fathers*, pp. 1-64. Translated by Francis X. Grimm. FC 1. Washington, D.C.: The Catholic University of America Press, 1947.

———. "The Epistle of S. Clement to the Corinthians." In *The Apostolic Fathers*, pp. 13-41. Translated by J. B. Lightfoot. London: Macmillan and Company, 1891. Reprint, Grand Rapids, Mich.: Baker Book House, 1956.

"Constitutions of the Holy Apostles." In *Lactantius, Venantius, Asterius, Victorinus, Dionysius, Apostolic Teaching and Constitutions, 2 Clement, Early Liturgies*, pp. 385-508. Edited by James Donaldson. ANF 7. Edited by Alexander Roberts and James Donaldson. 10 vols. 1885-1887. Reprint, Peabody, Mass.: Hendrickson, 1994.

Cyprian. *Letters 1-81*. Translated by Rose Bernard Donna. FC 51. Washington, D.C.: The Catholic University of America Press, 1964.

———. "Letter 8." In *Divine Providence and Human Suffering*, pp. 126-30. Translated by James Walsh and P. G. Walsh. MFC 17. Wilmington, Del.: Michael Glazier, 1985.

———. *Treatises*. Translated by Roy J. Deferrari. FC 36. Washington, D.C.: The Catholic University of America Press, 1958.

Cyril of Alexandria. *Letters: 1-50*. Translated by John I. McEnerney. FC 76. Washington, D.C.: The Catholic University of America Press, 1987.

———. *On the Unity of Christ*. Translated by John A. McGuckin. Crestwood, N.Y.: St. Vladimir's Seminary Press, 1995.

Cyril of Jerusalem. "Catechetical Lectures." In *Cyril of Jerusalem and Nemesius of Emesa*, pp. 64-192. Translated by William Telfer. LCC 4. Philadelphia: Westminster Press, 1955.

———. "Cyril of Jerusalem." In *Cyril of Jerusalem and Nemesius of Emesa*, pp. 64-199. Edited by William Telfer. Philadelphia: Westminster Press, 1955.

———. *S. Cyril of Jerusalem, S. Gregory Nazianzen*. Translated by Edward Hamilton Gifford et al. NPNF 7. Series 2. Edited by Philip Schaff and Henry Wace. 14 vols. 1886-1900. Reprint, Peabody, Mass.: Hendrickson, 1994.

———. *The Works of Saint Cyril of Jerusalem*. Vols. 1-2. Translated by Leo P. McCauley. FC 61 and 64. Washington, D.C.: The Catholic University of America Press, 1969-70.

Desert Fathers. "Sayings of the Fathers." In *Western Asceticism*, pp. 33-189. Translated by Owen Chadwick. LCC 12. Philadelphia: Westminster Press, 1958.

Didache. See "The Letter of St. Clement of Rome to the Corinthians." In *The Apostolic Fathers*, pp. 9-58. Translated by Francis X. Glimm. FC 1. New York: Christian Heritage, 1947.

Dionysius of Alexandria. "Fragments." In *Gregory Thaumaturgus, Dionysius the Great, Julius Africanus, Anatolius and Minor Writers, Methodius, Arnobius*, pp. 81-120. Translated by S. D. F. Salmond. ANF 6. Edited by Alexander Roberts and James Donaldson. 10 vols. 1885-1887. Reprint, Peabody, Mass.: Hendrickson, 1994.

Ephrem the Syrian. *Commentary on Tatian's Distessaron*. Translated and edited by C. McCarthy. *Journal of Semitic Studies* Supplement 2. Oxford: Oxford University Press, 1993.

Epiphanius of Salamis. *Panarion*. In *MOT*, pp. 26-51. Translated by Ronald E. Heine. Macon, Ga.: Mercer University Press, 1989.

Epistle of Barnabas. In *The Apostolic Fathers*. 2nd ed, pp. 133-56. Translated by J. B. Lightfoot and J. R. Harmer. Edited by M. W. Holmes. Grand Rapids, Mich.: Baker, 1989.

Eugippius. *The Life of Saint Severin.* Translated by Ludwig Bieler, with the collaboration of Ludmilla Krestan. FC 55. Washington D.C.: The Catholic University of America Press, 1965.

Eusebius of Caesarea. *Ecclesiastical History: Books 1-10.* 2 vols. Translated by Roy J. Deferrari. FC 19 and 29. Washington D.C.: The Catholic University of America Press, 1953-1955.

———. *Eusebius, the Church History: A New Translation with Commentary.* Translated by Paul L. Maier. Grand Rapids, Mich.: Kregel Publications, 1999.

———. *Proof of the Gospel.* 2 vols. Translated by W. J. Ferrar. London: SPCK, 1920. Reprint, Grand Rapids, Mich.: Baker, 1981.

Evagrius of Pontus. *Praktikos and the Chapters on Prayer.* Translated by John Eudes Bamberger. CS 4. Kalamazoo, Mich.: Cistercian Publications, 1981.

Fulgentius of Ruspe. *Selected Works.* Translated by Robert B. Eno. FC 95. Washington D.C.: The Catholic University of America Press, 1997.

Gregory of Nazianzus. *Cyril of Jerusalem, Gregory of Nazianzen.* Translated by Charles Gordon Browne and James Edward Swallow. NPNF 7. Series 2. Edited by Philip Schaff and Henry Wace. 14 vols. 1886-1900. Reprint, Peabody, Mass.: Hendrickson, 1994.

———. *Faith Gives Fullness to Reasoning: The Five Theological Orations of Gregory Nazianzen.* Translated by F. W. Norris. Leiden and New York: E. J. Brill, 1990.

———. *Funeral Orations.* Translated by Leo P. McCauley et al. FC 22. Washington D.C.: The Catholic University of America Press, 1953.

Gregory of Nyssa. "Address on Religious Instruction." In *Christology of the Later Fathers,* pp. 268-325. Translated by Archibald Robertson. Edited by Edward Rochie Hardy. LCC 3. Philadelphia: Westminster Press, 1954.

———. *Ascetical Works.* Translated by Virginia Woods Callahan. FC 58. Washington D.C.: The Catholic University of America Press, 1967.

———. *On the Soul and the Resurrection.* Translated by Catharine P. Roth. Crestwood, N.Y.: St. Vladimir's Seminary Press, 1993.

———. "Life of Moses." In *Biblical Interpretation,* pp. 152-60. Translated by Abraham Malherbe and Everett Ferguson. MFC 9. Edited by Joseph W. Trigg. Wilmington, Del.: Michael Glazier, 1988.

———. *Select Writings and Letters of Gregory, Bishop of Nyssa,* pp. 33-248. Translated by William Moore and Henry Austin Wilson. NPNF 5. Series 2. Edited by Philip Schaff and Henry Wace. 14 vols. 1886-1900. Reprint, Peabody, Mass.: Hendrickson, 1994.

Gregory the Great. "Letters." In *Leo the Great, Gregory the Great,* pp. 73-243. Translated by Charles Lett Feltoe. NPNF 12. Series 2. Edited by Philip Schaff and Henry Wace. 14 vols. 1886-1900. Reprint, Peabody, Mass.: Hendrickson, 1994.

———. "Letters." In *Part 11: Gregory the Great, Ephraim Syrus, Aphrahat,* pp. 1-111. Translated by James Barmby. NPNF 13. Series 2. Edited by Philip Schaff and Henry Wace. 14 vols. 1886-1900. Reprint, Peabody, Mass.: Hendrickson, 1994.

Hilary of Poitiers. "Homilies on the Psalms." In *Hilary of Poitiers, John of Damascus,* pp. 236-48. Translated by E. W. Watson et al. NPNF 9. Series 2. Edited by Philip Schaff and Henry Wace. 14 vols. 1886-1900. Reprint, Peabody, Mass.: Hendrickson, 1994.

———. "Homilies on the Psalms." In *Divine Providence and Human Suffering,* pp. 57-59, 167-69, 183-84. Translated by James Walsh and P. G. Walsh. MFC 17. Wilmington, Del.: Michael Glazier, 1985.

———. *The Trinity.* Translated by Stephen McKenna. FC 25. Washington, D.C.: The Catholic University of America Press, 1954.

Hippolytus. "On the Theophany." In *Hippolytus, Cyprian, Caius, Novatian, Appendix,* pp. 234-37. Arranged by A. Cleveland Coxe. ANF 5. Edited by Alexander Roberts and James Donaldson. 10 vols. 1885-

1887. Reprint, Peabody, Mass.: Hendrickson, 1994.

Horsiesi. "The Testament of Horsiesi." In *Pachomian koinonia*, 3:171-224. Translated by Armand Veilleux. CS 47. Kalamazoo, Mich.: Cistercian Publications, 1982.

Isaac of Nineveh. *The Ascetical Homilies of Saint Isaac the Syrian.* Edited by the Holy Transfiguration Monastery. Boston, Mass.: Holy Transfiguration Monastery, 1984.

Jacob of Sarug. "On the Establishment of Creation." In *Biblical Interpretation*, pp. 186-202. MFC 9. Edited by Joseph W. Trigg. Wilmington, Del.: Michael Glazier, 1988.

Jerome. "Against Rufinus." In *Dogmatic and Polemical Works*, pp. 59-220. Translated by John N. Hritzu. FC 53. Washington, D.C.: The Catholic University of America Press, 1965.

———. "Against Rufinus." In *Theodoret, Jerome, Gennadius, Rufinus: Historical Writings, etc.*, pp. 482-541. Translated by William Henry Fremantle. NPNF 3. Series 2. Edited by Philip Schaff and Henry Wace. 14 vols. 1886-1900. Reprint, Peabody, Mass.: Hendrickson, 1994.

———. "Commentary on Ecclesiastes." In *Divine Providence and Human Suffering*, pp. 185-86. Translated by James Walsh and P. G. Walsh. MFC 17. Wilmington, Del.: Michael Glazier, 1985.

———. "The Dialogue Against the Pelagians." In *Dogmatic and Polemical Works*, pp. 221-378. Translated by John N. Hritzu. FC 53. Washington, D.C.: The Catholic University of America Press, 1965.

———. *Homilies on the Psalms.* Translated by Marie Liguori Ewald. FC 48. Washington D.C.: The Catholic University of America Press, 1964.

———. "The Histories of the Monks." In *PHF* 1, 317-82. Edited by E. A. Wallis Budge. London: Chatto & Windus, 1907. Reprint, Seattle, Wash.: St. Nectarios Press, 1984.

———. "Letters." In *Early Latin Theology*, pp. 290-389. Translated by S. L. Greenslade. LCC 5. Philadelphia: Westminster Press, 1956.

———. *Letters and Select Works.* Translated by W. H. Fremantle. NPNF 6. Series 2. Edited by Philip Schaff and Henry Wace. 14 vols. 1886-1900. Reprint, Peabody, Mass.: Hendrickson, 1994.

John Chrysostom. "Against the Anomoeans." See *On the Incomprehensible Nature of God.* Translated by Paul W. Harkins. FC 72. Washington, D.C.: The Catholic University of America Press, 1984.

———. *Baptismal Instructions.* Translated by Paul W. Harkins. ACW 31. New York: Newman Press, 1963.

———. "Demonstrations Against the Pagans." In *Apologists*, 187-262. Translated by Paul W. Harkins. FC 73. Washington, D.C.: The Catholic University of America Press, 1985.

———. *Discourses Against Judaizing Christians.* Translated by Paul W. Harkins. FC 68. Washington, D.C.: The Catholic University of America Press, 1979.

———. *Homilies on 1 and 2 Corinthians.* Translated by Talbot W. Chambers. NPNF 12. Series 1. Edited by Philip Schaff. 14 vols. 1886-1889. Reprint, Peabody, Mass.: Hendrickson, 1994.

———. *Homilies on Galatians, Ephesians, Philippians, Colossians, Thessalonians, Timothy, Titus, and Philemon.* Translated by Gross Alexander et al. NPNF 13. Series 1. Edited by Philip Schaff. 14 vols. 1886-1889. Reprint, Peabody, Mass.: Hendrickson, 1994.

———. *Homilies on Genesis 18-45.* Translated by Robert C. Hill. FC 82. Washington, D.C.: The Catholic University of America Press, 1990.

———. *On Repentance and Almsgiving.* Translated by Gus George Christo. FC 96. Washington, D.C.: The Catholic University of America Press, 1998.

———. *Homilies on the Gospel of John 1-88.* Translated by Thomas Aquinas Goggin. FC 33 and 41. Washington, D.C.: The Catholic University of America Press, 1957-1959.

———. "On the Epistle to the Hebrews." In *Homilies on the Gospel of Saint John and the Epistle to the Hebrews*, pp. 363-522. The Oxford translation. NPNF 14. Series 1. Edited by Philip Schaff. 14 vols. 1886-1889. Reprint, Peabody, Mass.: Hendrickson, 1994.

———. *On the Priesthood, Ascetic Treatises, Select Homilies and Letters, Homilies on the Statues.* Translated by W. R. W. Stephens et al. NPNF 9. Series 1. Edited by Philip Schaff. 14 vols. 1886-1889. Reprint, Peabody, Mass.: Hendrickson, 1994.

John of Damascus. "An Exact Exposition of the Orthodox Faith." In *Writings,* pp. 165-406. Translated by Frederic H. Chase. FC 37. Washington, D.C.: The Catholic University of America Press, 1958.

Justin Martyr. *Writings of Saint Justin Martyr.* Translated by Thomas B. Falls. FC 6. New York: Christian Heritage, 1948.

Leo the Great. *Letters.* Translated by Edmund Hunt. FC 34. Washington, D.C.: The Catholic University of America Press, 1957.

———. *Sermons.* Translated by Jane Freeland et al. FC 93. Washington, D.C.: The Catholic University of America Press, 1996.

Marius Victorinus. "Against Arius." In *Theological Treatises on the Trinity,* pp. 89-303. Translated by Mary T. Clark. FC 69. Washington, D.C.: The Catholic University of America Press, 1981.

Martin of Braga. "Writings of Martin of Braga." In *Iberian Fathers,* 1:17-109. Translated by Claude W. Barlow. FC 62. Washington, D.C.: The Catholic University of America Press, 1969.

Maximus of Turin. *Sermons.* Translated by Boniface Ramsey. ACW 50. New York: Newman Press, 1989.

Methodius. "Extracts from the Work on Things Created." In *Gregory Thaumaturgus, Dionysius the Great, Julius Africanus, Anatolius and Minor Writers, Methodius, Arnobius,* pp. 379-81. Translated by William R. Clark. ANF 6. Edited by Alexander Roberts and James Donaldson. 10 vols. 1885-1887. Reprint, Peabody, Mass.: Hendrickson, 1994.

Nicetas of Remesiana. "Writings." In *Niceta of Remesiana, Sulpicius Severus, Vincent of Lerins, Prosper of Aquitaine,* pp. 9-76. Translated by Gerald G. Walsh. New York: Fathers of the Church, 1949.

Novatian. "On the Trinity." In *Novatian: The Trinity, The Spectacles, Jewish Foods, In Praise of Purity, Letters,* pp. 23-111. Translated by Russel J. DeSimone. FC 67. Washington, D.C.: The Catholic University of America Press, 1974.

Origen. "Against Celsus." In *Tertullian, Part Fourth; Miucius Felix; Commodian; Origen, Parts First and Second,* pp. 395-669. Translated by Frederick Crombie. ANF 4. Edited by Alexander Roberts and James Donaldson. 10 vols. 1885-1887. Reprint, Peabody, Mass.: Hendrickson, 1994.

———. "Against Celsus." Vol. 2 in *The Writings of Origen.* Translated by Frederick Crombie. ANCL 23. Edinburgh, Scotland: T & T Clark, 1894.

———. "Commentary on Matthew." In *The Gospel of Peter, The Diatessaron of Tatian, The Apocalypse of Peter, The Vision of Paul, The Apocalypses of the Virgin and Sedrach, The Testament of Abraham, The Acts of Xanthippe and Polyxena, The Narrative of Zosimus, The Apology of Aristides, The Epistles of Clement (Complete Text), Origen's Commentary on John, Books 1-10, and Commentary on Matthew, Books 1, 2, and 10-14,* pp. 409-512. Translated by John Patrick. ANF 9. Edited by Alexander Roberts and James Donaldson. 10 vols. 1885-1887. Reprint, Peabody, Mass.: Hendrickson, 1994.

———. *Commentary on the Gospel of John.* Translated by Ronald E. Heine. FC 80 and 89. Washington, D.C.: The Catholic University of America Press, 1989-1993.

———. *Homilies on Genesis and Exodus.* Translated by Ronald E. Heine. FC 71. Washington, D.C.: The Catholic University of America Press, 1982.

———. *Homilies on Leviticus: 1-16.* Translated by Gary Wayne Barkley. FC 83. Washington, D.C.: The Catholic University of America Press, 1990.

———. "On Prayer." In *Origen: An Exhortation to Martyrdom, Prayer and Selected Writings,* pp. 81-170. Translated by Rowan A. Greer with preface by Hans Urs von Balthasar. The Classics of Western Spirituality. New York: Paulist Press, 1979.

Pachomius. *Pachomian koinonia.* 3 vols. Translated by Armand Veilleux. CS 45, 46 and 47. Kalamazoo,

Mich.: Cistercian Publications, 1980-1982.

Palladius of Helenopolis. "Lausiac History." In *PHF* 1:89-281. Edited by E. A. Wallis Budge. London: Chatto & Windus, 1907. Reprint, Seattle, Wash.: St. Nectarios Press, 1984.

Paschasius of Dumium. "Questions and Answers of the Greek Fathers." In *Iberian Fathers*, 1:117-71. Translated by Claude W. Barlow. FC 62. Washington, D.C.: The Catholic University of America Press, 1969.

Paulinus of Milan. "The Life of St. Ambrose." In *Early Christian Biographies*, pp. 33-66. Translated by John A. Lacy. FC 15. Washington, D.C.: The Catholic University of America Press, 1952.

Paulinus of Nola. "Letter to Augustine." In *Letters*, pp. 317-33. Translated by Wilfrid Parsons. FC 18. Washington, D.C.: The Catholic University of America Press, 1953.

Peter Chrysologus. "Sermons." In *Saint Peter Chrysologus Selected Sermons and Saint Valerian Homilies*, pp. 25-282. Translated by George E. Ganss. FC 17. New York: Fathers of the Church, 1953.

Philoxenus of Mabbug. "Excerpt on Prayer." In *The Syriac Fathers on Prayer and the Spiritual Life*, pp. 128-31. Translated by Sebastian Brock. CS 101. Kalamazoo, Mich.: Cistercian Publications, 1987.

Poemen. "Sayings of the Fathers." In *PHF* 2. Edited by E. A. Wallis Budge. London: Chatto & Windus, 1907. Reprint, Seattle, Wash.: St. Nectarios Press, 1984.

Prudentius. *The Poems of Prudentius*. Translated by M. Clement Eagan. FC 43. Washington, D.C.: The Catholic University of America Press, 1962.

———. "The Divinity of Christ." In *The Poems of Prudentius*, 2:3-40. Translated by M. Clement Eagan. FC 52. Washington, D.C.: The Catholic University of America Press, 1965.

Pseudo-Dionysius. *Pseudo-Dionysius: The Complete Works*. Translated by Colm Luibheid. The Classics of Western Spirituality. New York: Paulist Press, 1987.

Rufinus of Aquileia. In *Theodoret, Jerome, Gennadius, Rufinus: Historical Writings, etc.* Translated by William Henry Fremantle. NPNF 3. Series 2. Edited by Philip Schaff and Henry Wace. 14 vols. 1886-1900. Reprint, Peabody, Mass.: Hendrickson, 1994.

Sahdona. "Book of Perfection." In *The Syriac Fathers on Prayer and the Spiritual Life*, pp. 202-37. Translated by Sebastian Brock. CS 101. Kalamazoo, Mich.: Cistercian Publications, 1987.

Salvian the Presbyter. "The Governance of God." In *The Writings of Salvian, the Presbyter*, pp. 21-232. Translated by Jeremiah F. O'Sullivan. FC 3. Washington, D.C.: The Catholic University of America Press, 1962.

"Sayings of the Fathers." In *PHF*, vol. 2. Edited by E. A. Wallis Budge. London: Chatto & Windus, 1907. Reprint. Seattle, Wash.: St. Nectarios Press, 1984.

Syncletica. "Sayings of the Fathers." In *Western Asceticism*, pp. 33-189. Translated by Owen Chadwick. LCC 12. Philadelphia: Westminster Press, 1958.

Tertullian. *Latin Christianity: Its Founder, Tertullian.* Arranged by A. Cleveland Coxe. ANF 3. Edited by Alexander Roberts and James Donaldson. 10 vols. 1885-1887. Reprint, Peabody, Mass.: Hendrickson, 1994.

———. "On Idolatry." In *Early Latin Theology*, pp. 83-110. Translated by S. L. Greenslade. LCC 5. Philadelphia: Westminster Press, 1956.

Theodore of Mopsuestia. "Commentary on Zechariah." In *Biblical Interpretation*, pp. 165-71. MFC 9. Edited by Joseph W. Trigg. Wilmington, Del.: Michael Glazier, 1988.

Theodoret of Cyr. *Commentary on the Psalms 1-150*. Translated by Robert C. Hill. FC 101 and 102. Washington, D.C.: The Catholic University of America Press, 2000-2001.

———. "Letters." In *Theodoret, Jerome, Gennadius, Rufinus: Historical Writings, Etc.*, pp. 250-348. Translated by Blomfield Jackson. NPNF 3. Series 2. Edited by Philip Schaff and Henry Wace. 14 vols. 1886-1900. Reprint, Peabody, Mass.: Hendrickson, 1994.

————. *Theodoret of Cyrus: On Divine Providence*. Translated by Thomas Halton. ACW 49. New York: Newman Press, 1988.

Valerian of Cimiez. "Homilies." In *Saint Peter Chrysologus Selected Sermons and Saint Valerian Homilies*, pp. 299-435. Translated by George E. Ganss. FC 17. New York: Fathers of the Church, 1953.

Zephyrinus. "Epistles of Zephyrinus." In *The Twelve Patriarchs, Excerpts and Epistles, The Clementia, Apocryphal Gospels and Acts, Syriac Documents, Remains of the First Ages*, pp. 609-12. Translated by S. D. F. Salmond. ANF 8. Edited by Alexander Roberts and James Donaldson. 10 vols. 1885-1887. Reprint, Peabody, Mass.: Hendrickson, 1994.

Authors/Writings Index

Subject Index

Scripture Index